Praise for: How to Live Your Dream of Volunteering Overseas

"Volunteering overseas can be a rewarding and enriching experience. But it requires sympathy, reciprocity, willingness to learn as well as to give, and an understanding of the problems and opportunities, which are many and complex. This book is a wonderful guide that addresses all of these issues and more—informed, sensitive, comprehensive. A most valuable contribution."—*Noam Chomsky, MIT, Political Analyst, author of* Manufacturing Consent

"This remarkably comprehensive handbook is what so many of us have long been waiting for: it truly tells it like it is. After six years research and many more years of immersion in their subject, the authors seem to know everything about volunteering overseas and are generous and direct in sharing their knowledge. Anyone who has even considered volunteering abroad—whatever his or her age, interests, or abilities—will read it with delight and appreciation."—*Clay Hubbs, Ph.D., Editor and Publisher,* Transitions Abroad Magazine.

"Realistic and practical advice on the opportunities and pitfalls of international volunteering, told through the voices of global volunteers and in-country activists, and synthesized by an authorial trio with first-hand experience and a savvy world view." —*L. Peat O'Neil,* Washington Post *news staff, author of "Travel Writing: See the World—Sell the Story,"* Writer's Digest Books, 2000.

"This comprehensive guide is an essential resource for anyone considering a volunteer experience overseas. I will definitely have a copy on my bookshelf and will continue to recommend it to people I know. It's hard to imagine why such a book hasn't been published before."—*Heather Gardner, Peace Corps Volunteer, Nicaragua*

"This is an exciting book. It will be useful to readers, not only because of the wealth of practical information about volunteering but also because of the concrete suggestions about how to get involved in organizing for social justice on a global level. The section on staying involved internationally after returning home will prove to be a much-used reference for anyone interested in working in global justice, fair trade, or human rights."—*Dennis Brutus, poet and activist, former political prisoner on Robben Island in South Africa*

"I truly wish I had read this book before I went overseas. I would have been able to get so much more out of my experiences. As I read the book, I kept thinking to myself 'If only I had known . . .' If only I had known the practical tips for cultural immersion, the no-nonsense ideas for effective volunteering, even the detailed suggestions about dealing with reverse culture shock when coming home—this information would have really enriched all of my volunteer experiences, in addition to my travels and studies overseas. The analysis of the pros and cons of the Peace Corps and the evaluations of other volunteer programs just aren't available anywhere else. For anyone considering volunteering or working abroad, this is a priceless resource. I know I will use it the next time I go overseas."—*Ilisa Gertner, volunteer in Guatemala and Israel, teacher in Korea*

Authors' Biographies

JOSEPH COLLINS'S teenage experiences volunteering in Latin America and the Philippines four decades ago led to a lifetime of researching, writing, and lecturing on the impact of U.S. policies and institutions on the lives of the world's impoverished majority. He is the co-founder of the Institute for Food and Development Policy (Food First); a Guggenheim Fellow recognized for his work on issues of inequitable development; and he has been a Distinguished Visiting Professor at the University of California. His books include *Food First*, *World Hunger: Twelve Myths*, *Chile's Free-Market Miracle: A Second Look,* and *Aid As Obstacle*. Collins is a consultant in Africa, Asia, and Latin America to the United Nations and international nongovernmental organizations. He currently co-directs the program on the Development Context of AIDS of the United Nations Research Institute in Social Development (UNRISD). Together with his boyfriends, he lives and surfs (big) waves in Santa Cruz, California.

STEFANO DEZEREGA teaches high school social studies in the San Francisco Bay area. He was the founding director of the LaFetra Operating Foundation and played a leading role in the creation of the International Volunteer Programs Association (IVPA) and the BRIDGES fellowship. He has fifteen years of experience promoting global education and student action on high school and college campuses across the country and has designed and facilitated workshops to help students create meaningful international experiences. As executive director of the Overseas Development Network (now known as Just Act), he edited the 1994 publication "A Handbook for Creating Your Own Internship in International Development." A native of Berkeley, California, DeZerega lives with his wife in San Francisco, California.

ZAHARA HECKSCHER'S career as a writer and social justice organizer is grounded in her work overseas: volunteering to plant fruit trees in rural Zambia and helping to build a medical clinic in Nicaragua. The founder of the Community Alliance for Youth Action and former director of the Washington office of Global Exchange, Heckscher currently lectures on "Peace Corps and Alternatives" at college campuses around the country. She is a contributing editor at *Transitions Abroad* magazine. Her articles have been published in *Community Jobs* magazine, on the Center for Economic Justice website, and in the book *Global Basklash: Citizen Initiatives for a Just World Economy* (Rowman and Littlefiefl, 2002). Heckscher resides in Washington, D. C., where she is completing her graduate studies in International Development at American University.

How to Live
Your Dream
of Volunteering
Overseas

Joseph Collins

Stefano DeZerega

Zahara Heckscher

Penguin Books

PENGUIN BOOKS
Published by the Penguin Group
Penguin Putnam Inc., 375 Hudson Street,
New York, New York 10014, U.S.A.
Penguin Books Ltd, 80 Strand,
London WC2R 0RL, England
Penguin Books Australia Ltd, Ringwood, 250 Camberwell Road,
Camberwell, Victoria 3124, Australia
Penguin Books Canada Ltd, 10 Alcorn Avenue,
Toronto, Ontario, Canada M4V 3B2
Penguin Books India (P) Ltd, 11 Community Centre, Panchsheel Park,
New Delhi — 110 017, India
Penguin Books (N.Z.) Ltd, Cnr Rosedale and Airborne Roads, Albany,
Auckland, New Zealand
Penguin Books (South Africa) (Pty) Ltd, 24 Sturdee Avenue
Rosebank, Johannesburg 2196, South Africa

Penguin Books Ltd, Registered Offices:
Harmondsworth, Middlesex, England

First published in Penguin Books 2002

10 9 8 7 6 5 4 3 2 1

Library of Congress Cataloging in Publication Data

Collins, Joseph, 1945–
    How to live your dream of volunteering overseas / Joseph Collins, Stefano DeZerega,
and Zahara Heckscher.
        p.   cm.
    Includes index.
    ISBN 0 14 20.0071 X (pbk.)
        1. Volunteerism—Handbooks, manuals, etc. 2. Volunteerism—Directories. I. DeZerega, Stefano.
II. Heckscher, Zahara. III. Title.

HN49.V64 C65   2002
361.3'7—dc21   2001053113

Printed in the United States of America
Set in Times Roman
Designed by Manuela Paul

Table of Contents

Foreword

How to Live Your Dream of Volunteering Abroad

Twenty-six years ago Joe Collins blew into our lives. My daughter, Anna, was still in diapers; I was just pushing thirty. Barely thirty, too, Joe had already lived and worked much of his life abroad; I was awestruck. I figured if I hung around this man I'd learn a lot. How right I was. Since then, Anna and I have been fortunate to have traveled and worked in countries around the world, many described in these pages. Now Joe and his insightful colleagues, Stefano DeZerega and Zahara Heckscher, are teaching us both again, having created this unique tool, distilling their collected eight decades of experience.

For Anna and me, their book is a powerful call to think about the meaning of choice and its consequences. "Volunteer" derives from the Latin *voluntas*, meaning "choice." It suggests no coercion, no shoulds, no musts. Ordinarily, choice involves knowns, or it's not truly a choice—this is the assumption. Yet, the experience of volunteering abroad is, fundamentally, about the *un*known. Why would one choose, freely, something that by its nature is so utterly unpredictable as volunteering to work overseas?

Maybe it is because we sense that the very act of entering the unknown will change us. We know that change is necessary for growth; but change is also frightening. Sometimes we simply have to put ourselves in new, unpredictable circumstances in order to change. We have to leap.

And leap we must. For we're pushing our planet nearer and nearer to the edge, to the point at which the realistic possibility of planetary healing is almost nil—*almost.* To build honest hope in such an era requires more courage and insight than perhaps has ever been demanded of our species. So how do we prepare ourselves, and push ourselves, to take on these challenges?

In writing *Hope's Edge: The Next Diet for a Small Planet,* Anna and I were struck that virtually all of the individuals we chronicled experienced a moment of dissonance, a moment when their view of themselves and of their world got turned upside down and they saw with new eyes.

For the people we met, from landless peasants in Brazil to entrepreneurial crafts people in Bangladesh to village women in Kenya, this jarring moment—this dissonance—led to a cascade of choices that ultimately enabled them to create dramatic changes in their lives and their communities.

I was changed by visiting such disparate cultures, by meeting people who had found the courage to listen to their hearts and create more life-serving communities. I now know that the world we have created thus far is not the end of the line.

And for Anna, too, such experiences were transformational. From Brazil to Kenya to India, she heard people expressing similar desires for co-operation and community. She saw ways that people on the grassroots level were creating a different type of economic development—creating markets that build stronger communities instead of tearing them down. Through these encounters she returned with greater insight into how she can make change here, and with greater faith that change is possible.

Now we both see more clearly that indeed we are *all* fish for whom water does not exist until, of course, we leap (or are tossed) out of our element. We cannot see what is our own culture unless we leave it.

Throughout history different cultures have created many diverse stories to explain what it means to them to be human. Today, though, one story dominates, and it is spreading around the world. It portrays us humans as narrow materialists, ego-encapsulated consumers, ultimately driven by our selfishness to endlessly accumulate.

We, all of us, must be willing to jump out of the water in order to see that this story is a shabby caricature of human nature. And when we do, we will also begin to see the truly diverse range that is human possibility. As we begin to create our own stories, we are no longer victims or simply products of stories created by others. Only then can we choose—hopefully—that which is truer and more life-serving. Leaving the knowns of our own culture—through proactive action such as volunteering overseas—can give us the tools to be helpful at the level our planet now needs.

So maybe volunteering overseas is really about choice at the most profound level. Making a choice is based not on *knowing* but on *not knowing* may give us the opening we need to break free of limiting ideas and assumptions. That can be true if we combine our choices with the discipline of self-awareness and ongoing reflection these perceptive authors call us to.

This is a book that forces us to ask ourselves the hard questions, ones we may never have thought to ask. And through such asking, and answering, we become part of that long—unfinished—conversation about what it means to be human, what it means to volunteer, what it means to choose.

So, read this book and get ready to choose, not from knowing what will unfold, but precisely because you cannot know.

Frances Moore Lappé and Anna Lappé
August 2001

Acknowledgments

This book was a team effort lasting many years. We would like to thank all of those who participated on the team. We could not have completed this long journey without their unwavering support.

Perhaps our most profound debt is to a group too large to list—the hundreds of volunteers and community members who took the time from their busy lives to share their stories with us and help us in countless other ways. Some of them are mentioned by name in the text; all of them contributed to the ideas presented in this book, and we thank them for letting us pass on the lessons they learned. Most of the organizations profiled were generous with their time and information; we thank their staff members for their patience in answering our questions and facilitating our site visits.

We wish especially to thank Luke Wendt for his steady and reliable research and editorial assistance over the final two years of this endeavor.

For certain areas of the world in which we ourselves did not carry out fieldwork, we found specially qualified researchers to dispatch in our stead. We appreciate both their dedication and insights: Debra Farkas in Israel and Palestine, Rachel Glickman in the Caribbean, Jodi Hullinger in Eastern Europe, and Viviana Rennella in East Africa.

We wish to express our gratitude to those whose contributions were so varied that it is impossible to detail: Shenid Bayroo, Lisa Charley, Karen Decker, Charles Deull, David Dube, Kathy Flincker, Megan Fowler, Martin Garbus, Jessica Gidall, Sam Hummel, Bob Katz, Sahar Khoury, Bruce Khumalo, John, Elizabeth, and Emilie-Joy Kistnasamy, Edward Kulu, Joe Macharia and family, the Mendoza family, John Lear, Peter Mann, Yusuke Matsuo, Caitlin McGrath, Bettina Mok, Donna Mpengula, Shadrick Musonda, Kathima Najjaar-Ebrahim, Eric Pape, Wendy Phillips, Francis Potter, Joan Powell, Pearson Shangala, Christine Victorino, Lori Waselchuk, and Andrew Wells.

Among those who reviewed drafts of various parts of the texts and made helpful comments are Barry Bem, Andrea DaSilva, Dann Fox, Heather Gardner, Sarah Havre, Helmut Heckscher, Rachel Heckscher, and Amelia Peltz.

Zahara lost the ability to type early on in this project due to an ergonomic accident. We wish to express our gratitude to the volunteer typists who helped make possible her ongoing participation: Christina Abizeid, David Bryden, Naomi Friedman, John Friedrich, Patrick Lemmon, Olivia Parry, Zakora Roman, Kathy Sawyer, Mitch Scoggins, Susanna Shapiro, Susan Toohey, Latrice Vincent, and many others. Kate Peters deserves special mention for her professional assistance every week for over a year. We also acknowledge the many laughs provided to us by Zahara's voice recognition software.

Among the U.S.-based organizations particularly helpful in our research were Food First, Just Act, and the International Volunteer Programs Association.

We are thankful to Tim Maher, Margaret Lloyd, and Stan and Betty Sheinbaum for their financial assistance when we were only starting on this long undertaking. We would also like to thank Suzanne LaFetra and her family for discerning the value of the project and funding much of the intensive research as part of start-up activities of the LaFetra Operating Foundation.

We thank George Greenfield of Lecture Literary Management for believing in us. We are grateful to Jennifer Ehmann at Penguin Putnam for her enthusiasm and supportive editorial contributions.

On a more personal note, Zahara thanks her friends, family, and housemates for their love, support, and tolerance of stacks of paper on the dining room table. Joe thanks Matt Watson for his affectionate support from the start of this project. Stefano would especially like to thank his mom and dad, and his extended family for their support, as well as his loving wife, Jessica Tomlinson, for her tireless patience, understanding, and encouragement. Stefano offers this book in the memory of his brother, Ben Ulrich, who always encouraged Stefano to live his own dreams.

Our Stories

Like everyone, the three of us have many stories that explain who we are and what we do. This book is grounded in these personal stories, beginning long before we started working together. We include our stories here because we thought you would get more out of the book if you knew something about each of us, and the way the book came to be.

Joseph

I grew up in Wyoming, Ohio, a suburb of Cincinnati. Like many other boys in America in the 1950s, I delivered newspapers after school. My route included the regional headquarters of the Maryknoll Fathers, U.S. priests who worked in countries in Latin America, Africa, and Asia. Some afternoons one of the priests would take the paper from me, and we'd talk a little. In social studies class in parochial school we sometimes read copies of the *Maryknoll Magazine,* a publication like *National Geographic* with an American-Catholics-help-the-poor spin. I'd flip through the articles with color photos of priests saying Mass in thatch-roofed chapels and baptizing babies of parents who looked like my idea of headhunters. What really caught my attention, however, were stories and photos of white-cassocked priests doing cool things: helping Indians on the shores of Lake Titicaca start their own credit unions, driving jeeps through vast herds of wild animals in Tanzania in order to bring new seed varieties to African farmers, or meeting with a group of Chinese women in Hong Kong who hoped to organize a neighborhood noodle factory.

It was with such pictures in mind that one afternoon in my sophomore year in St. Xavier High School I asked one of the Maryknoll priests, as I handed him the *Cincinnati Times-Star,* whether I could spend the next summer's vacation helping out on one of the Maryknoll missions. I thought this request was something of a long shot. To my surprise, in just a couple of weeks, Father Dan found a parish in Santiago, Chile, where I could help out. Wow! I was excited. I had no idea at the time that this was the beginning of a train of experiences that in many ways would shape the rest of my life.

The Maryknoll parish mostly served a *población,* or shantytown, on the outskirts of Santiago. Though I was there for three months, I can hardly recall what "work" I really did. After all, what could a sixteen year old from Cincinnati—who showed up not even knowing Spanish—contribute? I could help with some filing in the credit union. I could drive downtown for supplies. Throughout the day dignified looking people, but poorer than any I had ever before met in my life, came and rang the doorbell. A major earthquake had hit Chile the year before, making the lives of many poor people even worse and forcing them to live from handouts. What I had to hand out were cheese sandwiches, opening can after can of Wisconsin cheddar, part of the U.S. food aid program.

So all summer long—mind you, that's a damp dreary *winter* in Santiago!—I tried to be helpful in any way I could. And to a certain extent I was. But it was the beginning of the 1960s. All over Latin America millions of people were protesting U.S. intervention and domination. No matter how golden your intentions, volunteering from the United States in those days plunged you into a cauldron of demonstrations that at any moment might take on a "Yankee Go Home" edge. Only months before I was in Chile, vast, angry crowds hurled eggs, tomatoes, and what-have-you at Vice President Nixon's Cadillac limo at virtually every stop on his "goodwill" tour of Latin America. In Chile, I quickly learned that lots of people thought that the *yanqui* copper companies Kennecott and Anaconda were plundering billions of dollars worth of Chile's resources. I also heard over and over that my government and its CIA intervened in Chilean politics in order to shore up politicians who opposed efforts for fair ownership of farm land, and other desperately needed changes, solely because these politicians would let the copper companies continue to have their way.

At first, I protested and resisted what so many Chileans told me. The truth is, however, that for the first time I had started to see the United States, my country, as experienced by people, especially impoverished people, overseas. (Later, the anti-democratic role of the United States in Chile escalated and was eventually exposed during hearings in the U.S. Congress.)

The connection between my country and the impoverishment and hunger of millions of Chileans was dramatized for me in a single night. On one edge of the sprawling parish was a large farm—a *very* large farm, consisting of tens of thousands of acres. Like many of these humongous Chilean *latifundios,* held for generations as a symbol of prestige, most of the land was uncultivated, with barbwire fences around it and perhaps a few cattle on it just to keep people off the land. With the terrible earthquake in the south that year, hundreds of families had moved into the already cramped homes of their relatives and friends in our *población.* People were desperate for more land to build more rough-hewn pine-plank houses. Many people spoke in anger about all this land being fenced off with no one using it while so many families were lacking even the smallest plot of land to build a shacklike house. Growing up in Cincinnati, I never had thought of justice in such terms and certainly had been taught that private property was sacrosanct. But, to my initial surprise, Father Dan agreed with the people that they had a right to land and to housing. One evening right after sunset, toward the end of my three months volunteering in the parish, several hundred people carrying torches and candles and banners marched toward the fence at the one end of the *población.* They were also chanting. The banners and some of the chanting proclaimed that they were hungry and needed housing. Some of the banners proclaimed that the copper belonged to all Chileans and that the *yanqui* companies should go home so that the mines would belong to all Chileans. Many of the men and boys were carrying wooden planks, hammers, and nails. The first ones to get to the fence cut the barbwire and tore down the fence. They started putting up shacks, more or less finishing by dawn. Father Dan and I were the only *Norteamericanos* there. It was the most exciting experience of my first sixteen years, and I knew that they were doing the right thing—and that night I realized how much being in Chile was changing the way I saw the world.

Fast-forward fourteen years later (including four summers of volunteer work in different countries) to 1975, when Frances Lappé and I founded the Institute for Food and Development Policy, better known as Food First. Food First (www.foodfirst.org) is a member-supported, nonprofit think tank and education-for-action center. Today, more than a quarter of a century later, the work of Food First continues to highlight both the root causes of hunger and poverty around the world. It argues for values-based solutions, declaring food to be a fundamental right of every human being. Food First has become a leader amongst coalitions seeking to eradicate the truly needless suffering in our world.

In a very real way, I owe my founding of Food First to the early volunteer experiences I was privileged to have. My volunteer experiences during high school and college gave me new glasses with which to see the world. Now, when Chile or Guatemala or Mexico or Peru or the Philippines came up on the U.S. TV evening news, I had been there and I had experienced that things were fundamentally—even outrageously—different than what we in the United States were being told. When Walter Cronkite, the U.S. TV news icon, ended his broadcast each evening with "That's the way it is," I found myself more and more often screaming, "No, it isn't!"

In college and graduate school, and then at the Institute for Policy Studies in Washington, D.C., I built on those experiences with courses and research. More than anything else I was ultimately asking "Why?" Why are so many people poor and hungry in the face of the abundance I had witnessed as a volunteer in country after country? Yes, I had come into direct contact with many poor Chileans, but I also experienced what a wealthy country Chile is. Thus I founded Food First in pursuit of answers *and* to help more of my fellow citizens become aware of and outraged by what is being done elsewhere in the world by powerful institutions based in our society, so often in our name and with our tax dollars.

We were not long at Food First when all of us realized that whenever we spoke publicly about hunger and poverty, people asked us for our opinion of the Peace Corps. They also wanted to know whether we thought it was a good idea at all to volunteer overseas and which volunteer placement programs we would recommend. As a result, in 1985 we came up with the idea of a new publication, *Alternatives to the Peace Corps.* This modest book proved to be immensely popular, but we always felt much more was needed.

When in 1990 Frances and I thought it was time to step down from the staff of Food First, one of the things I wanted to do was the research and analysis that would more fully respond to the questions many people continue to ask about volunteering overseas and the alternatives to the Peace Corps. That is how the idea of this book came into being. Of course I shared my idea with Frances, and in 1994 she sent me an article by Zahara Heckscher on the subject. The rest, as they say, is history.

Zahara

The story that led to my participation in this book is the story of an idealistic but sheltered and inexperienced college graduate in 1986. I had just completed my B.A. at Wesleyan University, and moved to Washington, DC, to intern at the Washington Office on Africa (WOA, now Africa Action), a lobbying organization that promotes democracy and human rights in Africa. As an undergraduate, I had camped out overnight with friends in a "shanty" we constructed to symbolize the apartheid system of South Africa. Along with over 200 other students, I had been arrested protesting the university's investments in companies that operated in South Africa. Working at WOA was my way of staying involved in the anti-apartheid movement, trying to put my idealism into action.

At WOA, I learned the difference between the House of Representatives and the Senate, made photocopies for Congressional hearings about South Africa, and lobbied to cut off U.S. military support for UNITA, a ruthlessly violent guerrilla movement in Angola. I was passionate about my work. But I eventually came to understand that U.S. policies toward Africa would not change until more people here were aware of the effects of these policies. I decided to start by educating myself, and realized that in order to concretely understand the issues I was working on I needed firsthand experience in Africa. Surprisingly, even though I was working for an Africa-related organization, it was extremely difficult for me to find substantial and accurate information on volunteer opportunities. I asked co-workers, visited libraries, read books, and still was stumped about how to volunteer. I knew I wasn't interested in the Peace Corps because, after studying the U.S. role in southern Africa, I was skeptical of government programs. So I decided to volunteer with the first non-governmental volunteer program I found (through the brother of a friend from college), the Institute for International Cooperation and Development (IICD).

In September 1987, I arrived for the IICD training in Massachusetts with great expectations and a huge reserve of the idealism (despite my time in Washington!). I ended up working in Zambia on a fruit tree–planting project that was both exciting—because of the amazing people I met—and frustrating—because I feared that the project was not sustainable. The nine-month program was an almost constant struggle with the IICD staff over a variety of issues. We spent part of our preparation time in Massachusetts working at a horse race track to earn money for IICD. We studied Swahili for two months, but were sent to Zambia, where Swahili is not spoken. The project we worked on used pesticides, but did not train the workers to use them safely. Local people were not consulted in the planning of the project. My colleagues and I tried to create changes at the project by pressuring the European directors to set up systems for worker involvement in decision-making, but we were kicked out of Zambia by the government before we created any real reorganization. (We spent the next month traveling in Zimbabwe, Tanzania, and Kenya.) Eventually we started to question IICD's parent organization, known as Tvind, because it appeared to have some elements of a cult (and I later found out that many ex-members do consider it to be a cult). Due to these and other problems, I resolved that I would do all I could to help other people make better choices about volunteering overseas than I had. This book is, in part, an outcome of my own difficulty in finding an appropriate volunteer experience in Africa.

Despite all my frustrations with IICD, my time in Mkushi, Zambia, was truly one of the most valuable times in my life. I worked in Mkushi with a mixed team of Americans and Zambians, planting hundreds of fruit tree seedlings in a huge outdoor nursery. Together, we created a "model orchard," with rows of banana, papaya, mango, and eucalyptus trees, intercropped with passionfruit vines and vegetables. Every day, as we waited for the afternoon showers to pass so we could return to the field, my coworkers, including Shadreck Musonda, took it upon themselves to teach my American colleagues and I Christian songs in ChiBemba, a local language. I'm Jewish, and Shadreck liked to point out that we were therefore like cousins, because he belonged to the Seventh Day Adventist Church, which, as he told me, also proclaims Saturday as the day of rest. I will always remember the day that Shadreck and his friends invited a group of us to his church to sing the songs he had taught us. I had never felt so welcome in a house of worship. I left Zambia feeling that instead of Americans helping Zambians to develop, Zambia should send people to the United States to help us develop our humanity—a more polite and civilized way of relating to each other as individuals, a more evolved concept of the extended family, and a higher level of integration of spiritual beliefs with day-to-day action.

My second trip to Africa in 1998 was more bittersweet. Certainly the apex was my arrival in the town of Mkushi, along with my travel companion Lori Waselchuk, who had volunteered with me in 1987 through 1988. While Lori rested, I walked down the dirt road toward the project where I had worked. Imagine my surprise and delight when I saw Shadreck, who at that moment happened to be on his way to church. Although ten years had passed, it took us only an instant to recognize each other and we greeted each other with the joy of long-lost friends. He invited me to visit the church service. Several of the parishioners remembered me from my visit ten years earlier, and somehow I remembered the songs Shadreck had taught me. After church he invited Lori and me to his farm the next day.

During the walk to his village, we saw that Zambia's economic situation had deteriorated since our last visit instead of developing. Scraggly corn grew sparsely in fields where we remembered Iowa-style rows of lush corn. It turns out that due to "structural adjustment programs" imposed by the World Bank, small farmers like Shadreck could no longer get loans for fertilizer, and corn does not grow well without fertilizer. When we arrived at Shadreck's village, we were shocked to see a baby with orange hair—a sign of severe malnutrition. The baby's mother had malaria. Again, due to structural adjustment programs, the Zambian government had been forced to cut funds for health care, and as a result there was no clinic in which the baby or mother could afford to get treatment. The visit to Shadreck's village was, on the whole, wonderful, but it was sad to see how our friend was struggling to keep his family alive. On the way back to town, Shadreck showed us the IICD project where we had worked. The project had been virtually abandoned. The nursery and orchard were overgrown with elephant grass. *None of the trees we planted had survived.*

Based on my experiences in Zambia, and a shorter but powerful experience volunteering in Nicaragua, I started offering a workshop about volunteering overseas to college students around the country. I wanted people to be able to avoid problems like those I had with IICD and find organizations that really matched their skills and interests. I wanted to share hard-to-find information about specific volunteer placement groups, so people wouldn't just choose the first group they heard about, as I had done. I wanted people in the "developed" world to have the opportunity to learn from what the "underdeveloped" countries have to teach us. In addition, I wanted people here to learn firsthand about the international institutions that make life harder for people like Shadreck and his family, and what can be done to change them.

The next chapter in my story is the story of my collaboration with Joseph Collins and Stefano DeZerega. Joe had transformed my life long before I met him. As an undergraduate, two of Joe's books, *Food First* and *Aid As Obstacle,* had inspired me to change career paths from medical research to international development. Six years later, I got a job directing the Washington office of Global Exchange, a spin-off from Food First, the organization Joe founded with Frances Lappé. So it was a cosmic event in my life that Frances mailed Joe a copy of an article I had written for my workshops on volunteering overseas. When Joe invited me to join him in this project, he had no idea what an honor it was for me to work with him. It still is.

One of my biggest contributions to this book was suggesting that we invite Stefano DeZerega to join the two of us. I knew Stefano through his work to involve students in international issues, and I just had a feeling that he would be the perfect person to complete our team.

Stefano

Imagine the scene: a half dozen Berkeley teenagers crammed into an editing room, carefully pasting text and pictures on top of a lighted drafting table. Working the late shift in a donated graphic arts studio, we were aware of the seriousness of our work and were giddy with anticipation. It was 1984, years before the desktop publishing revolution transformed production, and each step of the process seemed to take hours. The time flew by, however, and by dawn we were ready to drop off the final proof of our eight-page pamphlet to a sympathetic printer. 3,700 copies of *People for an Independent Nicaragua*'s debut publication were distributed, one for each and every student and staff member at our high school. In this publication we sought to expose our government's covert operations in Nicaragua, condemn the killing by the U.S.-backed Contras, and challenge our community to do something about it. The response was encouraging. Many people asked us how they could get involved, and before we knew it we found ourselves immersed in an international movement for justice in a land far away.

Activism was not new to the members of our fledgling student organization. At the ripe ages of fifteen and sixteen many of us were already veterans of the anti-nuclear and peace movements. As we passed through junior high and into high school we formed political action groups with names such as "As the World Burns" and "The Young and the Restless." Many of us had been jailed for acts of conscience, most notably civil disobedience at Livermore National Laboratories, where we were trying to stop the design of more and more destabilizing nuclear weapons that threatened the existence of our species and the planet. This work was going on in our own backyard under the sponsorship of the University of California, and we were not willing to sit by passively and let it happen. Although we became politically savvy beyond our years (and idealistic as only the young and young at heart are capable) during our experience as anti-nuclear activists, something different developed out of our opposition to the war in Nicaragua.

In our efforts to stop U.S.-sponsored violence against the people of Nicaragua, we became increasingly interested, not only in the injustices of United States policy toward Nicaraguans, but also in the efforts of Nicaraguans themselves to fight these injustices. We slowly learned that they weren't waiting, that Nicaraguans were working to improve their lives and their country despite the war. We figured there was no good reason for us to wait either. We began to ask ourselves what we could do to be proactive and somewhere along the way we realized the power of citizen-to-citizen links.

Our group gathered school supplies to send to students in Nicaragua, and we started to correspond with young Nicaraguans. There were always people traveling back and forth, and we learned a lot about our peers in Nicaragua through hand-delivered letters. We rarely missed an opportunity to hear the latest news from returned volunteers who had seen Nicaragua with their own eyes and who had heard about the aspirations and struggles of young Nicaraguans our age. As we raised money for small-scale agricultural projects, we met *brigadistas,* or volunteers, headed south to help with the coffee harvest. They became our representatives, the bridge between our different worlds, and when they came back with words of inspiration and struggle, they deepened our resolve to continue to work to end the injustice of the war.

Meeting with the returned *brigadistas* affected me deeply. These volunteers gave me faith to continue caring about people I had never met and challenged me to look at my own life and how it connected to others' struggles. These volunteers exuded determination and pragmatic optimism. I could see that they had derived great strength from their experiences living in solidarity with Nicaraguans and activists from other countries. These encounters showed me that international volunteer experiences can give volunteers the inspiration to make long-term commitments to international activism, and I knew in my heart even then that this type of people-to-people international exchange was something worth working for. Little did I know that this exposure and realization would lead me to work for international solidarity and volunteerism for the next fifteen years and provide my first inspiration for writing this book.

Eight years later I became the Executive Director of JustAct: Youth Action for Global Justice (then known as the Overseas Development Network). As I traveled to visit student groups and encourage them to be active on international issues, I met throngs of young people struggling to find volunteer opportunities overseas. They sensed what I had sensed from the *brigadistas,* that volunteering overseas was a powerful and unique experience, a chance to do something meaningful, and an opportunity to gain firsthand knowledge of the lives of people overseas. Our office received daily calls and letters from people interested in volunteering abroad and, with minimal publicity, we began selling hundreds of self-published directories on international volunteer opportunities. Our workshops on volunteering overseas were by far the most popular of the workshops we offered. Yet JustAct did not provide the resources required to help students find the volunteer placement organization that was right for them. JustAct was like a fisherman that could reel in fish but did not know what to do with them once they were caught.

Spending time with activists from around the world and crashing on students' couches around the country, I spent endless hours talking about international volunteering and I discovered that not all international volunteer programs or exchanges had positive effects on the volunteers or the local communities abroad. I met many young people who had been inspired by their experiences overseas, but I also met those who felt ill-prepared, who questioned the motives or methods of the organizations with which they volunteered, and who felt isolated upon their return home. After listening to stories about the nuances of good and bad international exchanges, I became partial to the ideas so well expressed in Ivan Illich's article "To Hell with Good Intentions" (available on our website, www.volunteeroverseas.org). I remember very clearly a conversation with a community activist from Zimbabwe, Isaac Makanani, who implored me to caution volunteers about their expectations. He asked me to suggest to volunteers that they "approach their volunteering with less arrogance and more openness." Another one of my many teachers, a grassroots leader from Bolivia named Waskar Ari, explained that he welcomed volunteers but only if they came to "learn from local organizations and to work for change when they returned home."

So I came to see international volunteering in all its complexity, including its pitfalls. At the same time I repeatedly heard testimony about how experiences overseas were formative in the lives of so many people, especially the people whom I respected most deeply. So I worked in my position at JustAct and later at a small family foundation to help future volunteers learn from the experiences of past volunteers. I have tried to amplify the voices and highlight the feedback of overseas hosts, and I have worked to increase access to international volunteering by groups traditionally excluded from the experience. With my growing awareness I resolved to focus my energy on the training and preparation of volunteers as well as help them to work for change when they return home. Writing this book is an attempt to bring forth the lessons I have learned over the past fifteen years.

When I joined Zahara and Joe on this project, I had little idea what I was getting myself into. I was certain, however, that a "how-to" book on international volunteering, one that thoroughly examined the issues and the players, was a book waiting to be written.

Joseph, Zahara, and Stefano: The Team

Like most worthwhile projects, this book took much more time and effort than we imagined at the outset. We kept going despite the challenges because we had a common vision of what this book should be, based on the proposal Joe first drafted in 1994.

We all wanted to create a book that would encourage readers' idealism without being blindly optimistic or Pollyannaish. We wanted to share a critical perspective on volunteering, one that was mindful of the limitations of volunteering as a strategy for creating social change, as well as its potential. We agreed that the book must be based on careful research, not just our experiences or hearsay. We knew that we wouldn't be able to convey the true flavor of the different placement organizations unless we actually visited the volunteers overseas, in the field—saw what they saw, ate what they ate, and listened to what they said—rather than just finding out what headquarters had to say. We shared a commitment to helping volunteers with both preparation and reentry, rather than focusing exclusively on the volunteers' time in the field. And, finally, we wanted to include the voices of local people overseas, to make sure that volunteers could hear directly from some of the people they wanted to help.

Our common vision probably stems in part from the fact that all three of us have founded and directed organizations dedicated to involving North Americans in international issues. We all have studied international community development and have extensive overseas experience.

But we also brought some different skills and experiences to the table. Joe, as the author or co-author of two-dozen books, was knowledgeable about the mysterious world of agents, publishers, and editors. Joe also has the most international experience on our team, with a focus on work in Latin America, Africa, and Southeast Asia. Zahara was familiar with a wide range of East Coast volunteer placement organizations through her workshops on alternatives to the Peace Corps, as well as with some of the concerns of volunteers from diverse backgrounds. Her regional expertise is Africa. Stefano had already edited a book for people who wanted to create their own overseas internships. He had a strong network of contacts with West Coast volunteer organizations, and a deep understanding of the issues facing college students, the primary, but not exclusive, target group of this book. Stefano's international network is particularly strong among youth.

Even with our common vision and complementary skills, it still took us over a year to create a detailed plan for how to proceed. Another year was spent fundraising, perhaps the hardest part of this project. Eventually, Stefano made contact with the LaFetra family, who funded the bulk of our research.

The overseas research took us and our research assistants to twenty-five countries on a dozen separate trips. We visited countries in many regions of the world, including Central and South America, the Caribbean, Eastern and Southern Africa, Eastern Europe, the Middle East, and South and Southeast Asia. We interviewed hundreds of volunteers and dozens of partner organizations overseas, as well as a staff of volunteer placement organizations, community members, and intended beneficiaries.

We experienced a few bumps on the road: lost luggage (with research notes, never recovered), a bus crash, carpal tunnel syndrome, and malaria, but the research experience has also been joyful. We were inspired by the creative work of the amazing community organizations we visited: the Legal Resources Center in South Africa, Ubiquita in Tanzania, LICHADO in Cambodia, Parroquia San Lucas Toliman in Guatemala, and the Andean Information Network in Bolivia to mention only a few.

We were dazzled by the hospitality of our hosts overseas. Among many other people who opened their homes and hearts to us, we were hosted by a small business owner and his family in Kenya, the director of an indigenous people's organization in Bolivia, and a professor and volunteer coordinator in India.

We were encouraged by the dedication of some exceptional volunteers: a medical student in Kenya, a human rights advocate in Guatemala, a teacher in India, and many, many more. The amazing people we met overseas, the people here who encouraged us to finish the book, and the synergy of our team, all have made writing this book a positive experience.

Many stories make a journey. The journey of this book has been spiritual, as we have been moved by the faith of our friends overseas. The journey has been physical, as, along with our research assistants, we've logged over 50,000 miles in our research. It has been political, as we have viewed the impact of the rich on poor people around the world. And it has been emotional, as our lives have changed during and sometimes because of the research we have carried out together in the past six years.

We hope that this book helps you write your own stories and embark on your own journey toward creating a more just world.

How to Use This Book

We have written this book with the various needs of prospective volunteers in mind. Broadly speaking, this book has two sections:

- **Thematic chapters about volunteering that are relevant regardless of the volunteer program you choose.**
- **Profiles of specific organizations that place volunteers overseas.**

The thematic chapters include practical advice for anyone interested in volunteering. They'll help with everything from clarifying your motives to figuring out what to pack, and from understanding the historical context of volunteering to learning about international careers. These chapters will not only be relevant to newcomers to the field of international volunteering but to veterans and staff of volunteer placement organizations as well.

If you are trying to figure out whether or not volunteering is for you, start with Chapter 1, "International Volunteering: What Is It? Why Do It," and then read Chapter 2, "Is Volunteering Overseas Right for You?"

If you have just been accepted by the Peace Corps and want help deciding whether to join, start with Chapter 11, "The Peace Corps."

If you are not sure where to begin in selecting an organization, start with Chapter 4, "Choosing the Right Organization," which has several useful worksheets to help guide you. "Examining Your Motivations" in Chapter 2, "Is Volunteering Overseas Right for You?," has useful worksheets as well. Or, if you have a particular type of work in mind, you can begin by consulting the Index of Profiled Organizations, which can refer you to groupings of organizations such as, for example, those that focus on health care or education.

If you want to find out more about a particular volunteer placement organization, or compare two organizations, go directly to Chapter 12, "Organizational Profiles."

If you have already selected an organization and want to be the best volunteer you can be, read Chapter 3, "The Big Picture: International Volunteering in Context," Chapter 8, "What to Do before You Go," and Chapter 9, "How to Be an Effective International Volunteer." We encourage you to bring this book with you so you can read Chapter 9, "How to Be an Effective International Volunteer," and Chapter 10, "Staying Involved After You Get Back," while overseas.

As you read various chapters, we encourage you to visit the book's website, www.volunteeroverseas.org, which has a section where you can tell us what you found most helpful, and what you think we should modify. There is also a section where you can give us feedback about particular organizations for future editions. Or you can fill out the survey on page 467.

We also encourage you to get a notebook to write down your answers to the questionnaires throughout this book, your thoughts and questions about volunteering, and your own notes about various programs and options you are considering.

No matter where you start, we hope you'll take the time to browse through the rest of the book and pick up tips that can help make your volunteer experience as positive as possible.

How to Live
Your Dream
of Volunteering
Overseas

CHAPTER 1

INTERNATIONAL VOLUNTEERING: WHAT IS IT? WHY DO IT?

I remember coming home every night from the school community center, physically and mentally drained, with only $5 for food, living in a beat-up, run-down apartment, but feeling better than I ever felt before because I was actually doing something meaningful.
—Eric Lob, volunteer, Project Otzma, Israel

During our research for this book, we met hundreds of people who wanted to volunteer overseas—college students who hoped to begin an international career by volunteering, busy professionals who sought to use vacation time to make a difference, and retired people who wanted to give something back through serving overseas. Some had a very specific idea of what they wanted to do—teach high school in South Africa, for example, or collect beetles in the Costa Rican rain forest. Many others had a general desire to get involved but lacked a concrete understanding of what volunteering really entails.

We therefore thought it would be useful to start by defining what we mean by "international volunteering" and exploring the reasons why people volunteer.

What Is International Volunteering?

International volunteers are all ages, come with a wide range of backgrounds, and get involved in a myriad of types of work overseas. The volunteers we interviewed for this book included a high school student helping a rural community in Mexico build environmentally friendly latrines, a teacher assisting with the restoration of a monastery in Mongolia during a summer vacation, and a retired businessman advising a bakery in Slovakia about how to increase profits.

For the purposes of this book, an experience is considered international volunteering if:

1. **The work takes place in a country other than the volunteer's home country.**

    This criterion underlines the fact that international volunteering is fundamentally about cross-cultural interactions. International volunteering affects the volunteer as well as the people with whom the volunteer works. In addition, the experience affects both the country where the volunteer works and potentially his or her home country.

    While there are many opportunities for volunteering in Australia, Canada, Japan, New Zealand, the United States and Western Europe, we did not include them in our research. Some groups do have programs in these regions, as noted in the organizational profiles and the Index of Profiled Organizations, but we did not visit these sites during our research. We focused instead on Asia, Africa, the Caribbean, Latin America, the Middle East, and Eastern Europe.

2. **The work offers no pay or low pay.**

    One of the most obvious characteristics of being a volunteer is that a volunteer does not get paid a "regular" salary. In many cases, volunteers even pay in order to volunteer. Some programs provide a stipend for the volunteer, ranging from a meager sum ($25/month) to amounts many times what most local people earn in an entire year ($1,500/month and up). We did not use a fixed dollar amount to determine if someone's salary qualifies him or her as a volunteer. We excluded from our definition organizations that paid a salary comparable to what participants might make at home.

3. **The volunteer work seeks to improve people's lives.**

    We defined improving people's lives very broadly. We included providing services in areas such as health and education as well as promoting human rights, democratization, and social and economic development. We also included environmental efforts that prevent or repair environmental destruction, as well as programs that protect wildlife. For the purposes of this book, international volunteering does not include programs with an exclusive goal of winning religious converts. We also excluded internships that did not have a goal of benefiting anyone other than the intern.

    While being an international volunteer can mean different things to different people, one thing is clear: international volunteering is an incredibly rewarding and challenging life option that more and more people are choosing. As Dennis Epp, a medical doctor and volunteer, told us, "No travel experience or vacation at a resort can match the satisfaction, enjoyment, and sheer pleasure of an international volunteer experience." In exploring the reasons why people volunteer, we'll look at how volunteers benefit as well as how they can help.

The Rewards of International Volunteering

Volunteering overseas could be one of the most educational, inspiring, and exciting things you do in your lifetime. Despite all the challenges—language barriers, red tape, health problems, culture clashes, financial costs—the vast majority of volunteers we interviewed said that, if given the opportunity, they would be glad to do it again. Living and working in another culture while donating your time to a potentially worthwhile cause offers substantial rewards and could enrich your life long after you return home.

The consensus among volunteers is that they receive much more than they contribute. As Elvira Williams of AHEAD explained, "Even with my twenty-five years of volunteering in Africa, I still don't feel like I've given as much as I have gained from the experience."

The personal rewards of volunteering include learning, cultural awareness, spiritual development, reassessing priorities, career development, and friendship.

Learning

The most universal benefit of volunteering is the opportunity to learn. In some cases, the new knowledge is practical. You may learn a new language or a skill such as teaching, farming, or building. In other cases, the learning is a process of self-discovery that may be less tangible but equally important. You may come to recognize your own emotional strength, uncover a talent you didn't know you had, or even face your own limitations or prejudices.

You may learn things that profoundly change you—new ways of relating to other people and new ideas about what is possible in this world. Marlene Larocque told us, "Volunteering in Ecuador has given me the opportunity to redefine who I am, to expand the way I view things, and to see the world through other people's eyes."

Some volunteers gain new understandings of the root causes of poverty and other social problems. They encounter political views and perspectives on the global economy that are rarely portrayed in the media back home. Debra Farkas, who volunteered in Central America, was told by a Nicaraguan how the United States had invaded his country numerous times in the twentieth century; her professor at home had told her that the Marines were invited.

Many volunteers go abroad as students with the explicit goal of learning. Ellen Donaghue, a volunteer in India with Minnesota Studies in International Development, was clear on her role as a volunteer: "I am not here to help or educate. I am twenty years old and know so little. I am here to learn. I am a student." Even if you have more life experience than Ellen, we encourage you to enter this experience with the attitude of a student. Frustrations and challenges can become positive experiences if you approach them as learning opportunities.

Cultural Awareness

As a volunteer, you may discover cultures that value sharing more than having money, old people more than the young, and family above all else. You may live in a community where being fat is considered beautiful, where being quiet is a sign of wisdom, or where being easygoing is a cultural ideal. In the country where you work, it may be considered rude to express your personal opinion, to smile at a stranger, or to show up on time when invited to dinner.

For many volunteers, being overseas helps them to better understand their own cultural heritage. A Latina volunteering in Latin America may recognize for the first time the source of some of her family traditions. She also may come to understand the ways in which she is distinctly North American. Children of immigrants from Asia may understand their parents better after volunteering there. For Zekora Romain, an African-American volunteer in Ghana, just being in Africa was one of the "greatest highlights" of her volunteer experience. "After 500 years, I was the first in my family to go back, see Africa through my own eyes, and not rely on someone else's interpretation, but create my own."

Volunteers often learn to value diversity back home more highly. European Americans may have the opportunity to experience being a minority. Some volunteers find, as did Peace Corps volunteer Janet Line, that they "have a much greater empathy for newcomers to the United States who are struggling with a new language and culture." Many returned volunteers end up working with immigrant communities they had previously ignored.

Volunteers often find it impossible not to compare their host culture with the one back home. On one hand, volunteers may identify aspects of the host culture that are challenging or disagreeable to them, such as rigidly defined gender roles, lack of personal space and privacy, or homophobia. Discovering these challenges can give volunteers a new appreciation of home. On the other hand, volunteers may find themselves quite comfortable with certain cultural norms of their host culture and may be inspired to work to integrate them into their lives at home. Nicaragua volunteer Jenny Russell told us that she "learned to take great pleasure in a sense of community, living in the present, and in a culture where talking with others, dancing, playing with children, and teaching are highly valued and hoarding money is not." Sometimes volunteers discover similarities between their own culture and that of their hosts as well as behaviors and attitudes that seem to transcend any particular culture.

Spiritual Development

Abraham Joshua Heschel said, 'God is hiding in the world; it is our task to let the divine emerge from our deeds.'—Eric Stern, volunteer, American Jewish World Service, Kenya

Many volunteers are motivated by religious beliefs, and the volunteer experience can help to renew and broaden the horizons of their faith. Even if you volunteer with people of a different religious background, you may gain new appreciation of your own religious tradition. Atheists and agnostics may be moved and inspired by the strong faith of the people with whom they are volunteering. Lifelong believers may see human suffering that makes them question God and sets them on a path of spiritual seeking. No matter what your religious background (or lack thereof), your volunteer experience may open new spiritual paths.

Historically, the main religious motivation for going abroad was to convert people. In their drive for converts, missionaries sometimes inadvertently created more problems than they solved, bringing disease, dividing families, destroying ancient cultures, and paving the way for colonization even as they built schools and hospitals. Recently, more culturally sensitive missionaries have begun to redefine what it means to be a missionary. Instead of focusing on suppressing other religions or beliefs, some have focused on becoming examples of faith in action by working for social justice. For Rachel Cornwell, volunteering with the United Methodist Mission program changed her view about her role as a Christian. "Although I am still committed to going into the ordained ministry, this experience has broadened the ways that I think of ministry and the possibilities for me to work within the church."

Reassessing Priorities

In many parts of the world, people live happy and fulfilling lives at income levels that would be considered unimaginably low in North America. When volunteers have the opportunity to live with and learn from such people, they often return with greater clarity about their own priorities. You may come home with a desire to improve your relationships with family members. You may find that volunteering inspires you to simplify your life. James Mungovan, with the Capuchin Volunteer Corps, told us that he no longer sees money as an important part of life. In Papua New Guinea, he "found happiness on $35 a month." Material accumulation and comforts may seem less important after you have lived in a simpler environment.

Career Development and Exploration

A large number of volunteers, especially recent college graduates, view overseas work as an important step in career development. In today's global economy, many employers are impressed by international experience in an applicant's job history. If you are seeking a career in an international field, overseas experience is often a prerequisite for finding paid employment. Lisa Washington-Sow used her experiences with the Peace Corps and Operation Crossroads Africa to obtain employment with a U.N. project in Senegal.

Volunteering can also help you clarify your graduate school plans. Jaklen Tuyen, after volunteering in Brazil, realized that she "couldn't help with ideology alone," and enrolled in a school of public health with a concentration in international health. (See Chapter 10, "Staying Involved after You Get Back," for more tips on careers in international development.)

For mid-career professionals, volunteering can be a way of using well-developed skills in a new context. Volunteering can also be a chance to try something totally new, to take a break, or to explore a possible change in the direction of your career.

Retired people often find that volunteering lets them share a lifetime of experience while continuing to learn. Some retirees relish the opportunity to volunteer in the field of their expertise. Others delight in getting involved in something that they never before had an opportunity to try.

In the five years following his retirement, banker Robert Willett volunteered seven times in various countries including Romania, Poland, Russia, and Uganda. "Now," says Willett, "I sit and wait to hear the phone ring, wondering where the next project will take me."

Friendship

My best experience in the Peace Corps was stopping in the road one day with my counterpart and his son to knock mangos out from a tree. The three of us sat under the tree and ate mangos, and at that moment it wasn't an American and two Dominicans, but just three people covered with mangos enjoying what life had to offer.—Peace Corps volunteer, Dominican Republic

Volunteers often make lifelong friends through their service. Your cohort of volunteers may become as close to you as your college roommates. You may become long-term pen pals with friends from the host community. Some volunteers return to their volunteer sites years later to visit friends.

While we recommend extreme caution in sex, love, and dating overseas (See Chapter 9, "How to Be an Effective International Volunteer"), some long-term volunteers do meet life partners overseas, most frequently among their peer group of volunteers. Others have the opportunity to fall in love again with their partner. One volunteer in Uganda told us, "I loved being able to share all my volunteer experiences with my wife, who can laugh, cry, and rejoice in all aspects of an assignment."

These are just some of the various ways that volunteers benefit from their experiences. While it is clear that volunteers themselves are the profound beneficiaries of the international volunteer experience, in some cases volunteers also contribute to the well-being of the people and communities in which they volunteer.

How Volunteers Contribute

Almost all volunteers are motivated in part by the desire to help others. Indeed, none of the pressing problems of our times such as poverty, inequality, war, environmental destruction, or racism will be solved unless there are those who desire to help others and act on that desire. Moreover, as these problems become increasingly international in their origins, we will have to generate responses that involve people working with one another across national borders.

Though volunteers' desire to "do good" does not always translate into positive results, there are ways that volunteers can make contributions. Help comes in many different shapes and sizes. Contributions range from simply being available to lend a hand to providing advanced training for local people. Office work, teaching, promoting human rights, and even networking can help communities overseas in their efforts to develop. Furthermore, returned volunteers can help through solidarity activities and bringing home ideas learned overseas.

Lending a Hand

I spent ten days basically doing manual labor—clearing trails and doing ground repairs for an ecological research center.—Valerie Chang, volunteer, International Volunteer Expeditions, Dominica

Volunteers who have no specialized training or background contribute primarily through their labor. They work directly with people or help protect and restore the environment by getting their hands dirty. Often this work entails joining an ongoing project such as a community effort to build a school.

When volunteers lend a hand, their labor speeds the work along and allows local groups to accomplish important tasks that might have taken twice as long to complete without the volunteers. As Celia Moreno of the Programa de Desarrollo Agropecuario Integrado in Bolivia stated succinctly, "Without the volunteers we would have to reduce the amount of work that we do." Michael Burns, a volunteer who worked with medicinal plants at the Parroquia San Lucas Toliman in Guatemala, told us, "These projects don't really need me, but I think I help sometimes. After all, nobody can begrudge free labor."

Specialized Skills and Expertise

In many countries, there are shortages of people with certain specialized skills or specific knowledge. In particular, there may be a shortage of doctors, midwives, nurses, lawyers, appropriate technology experts, trained business professionals, and managers experienced in working with nonprofit organizations. Frequently, people from rural or impoverished communities who do get professional training want to live in the city or move to Europe or North America.

Some volunteer programs do a good job of placing skilled volunteers with projects and organizations eager to utilize their skills. When there is a good match, volunteers can make significant contributions to the communities where they work. John Kaiser, a volunteer with International Executive Service Corps, described how, "In Lithuania, by helping keep a key plant open, we were able to save 1,500 jobs." Matthew Howard Thompson, a Peace Corps volunteer in Bolivia, told us that his "project helped improve the quality of life by replacing light generated by candles, natural gas, and kerosene with light from photovoltaic transmission. This light fostered more reading and studying at night and created another incentive, however small, for young adults to remain in the *campo* [countryside] and work with their family instead of migrating to the city."

Writing and Office Work

Writing and office work may not seem like the most glamorous of volunteer placements, but this type of work can be invaluable to your overseas host organization. As one organization supervisor put it, "Volunteers who do office work free up staff to do other things." Volunteers with writing skills can help prepare reports for international and governmental aid institutions. IFESH volunteer Umi Howard, for example, spent the majority of his time in South Africa writing and editing grant proposals. To make a contribution, volunteers often have to do what is needed rather than what they want to do or would find most interesting.

Teaching and Training

Teaching is one of the most common volunteer assignments. We met many volunteers who were making significant contributions to young peoples' educations. Teaching English is one of the most common international volunteer teaching assignments. Teacher Sarah Lukie found that, "In Korea, English skills are necessary for people who want to continue their education, so I knew I was helping my students. I had one student who refused to say even one word of English when I first met her. By the time I left, she could carry on a conversation." Volunteers also contribute by teaching subjects such as math and science at the primary, secondary, or even university level.

There is a growing trend of placing volunteers with specific knowledge in positions as trainers. This type of placement can be an effective way to magnify the impact of a volunteer's time abroad. Doctors and nurses, for example, can train local medical personnel; experienced business owners can train members of cooperatives; naturalists can train local tour guides; and computer experts can train repair technicians or nonprofit staff. A Ugandan doctor who works with Health Volunteers Overseas (HVO) commented on the success of the HVO training program: "Treatment is just short term. Training people who live and work here is more long term. When HVO started here," he told us, "we had only two orthopedic surgeons. Now we have ten."

Resources and Networking

Some programs explicitly use volunteering as a way to generate funds for development projects. Short-term volunteers with Habitat for Humanity, for example, pay a program fee that helps support the costs of constructing houses. The local people, who help build and then live in the houses, pay a long-term mortgage that goes toward the construction of future homes. Julia de Costas, the Bolivian host for Amizade, told us that, "While it was a great experience for the community to see the *gringos* building adobe houses, the most helpful thing from the volunteers was the money they provided." Service Civil International (SCI) India uses program fees to finance microprojects that are unable to attract other funding because they are too small. So what might seem to you a modest program fee can be an important source of funding for local development efforts.

Some volunteers find that their contributions come more from whom they know than what they know or how much money they contribute personally. If you work for a grassroots organization, for example, you may be able to help the staff set up a meeting with your government's embassy, a development agency, or a larger organization that works on similar issues. Teachers may be able to use their connections with a school back home to get donations of textbooks or supplies.

Local organizations overseas are often eager for access to information on a wide range of topics relevant to their work. Whether through the Internet or by arranging newsletter exchanges, volunteers can play an important role in bringing new information to their hosts.

Some volunteers have succeeded in connecting their hosts with advocacy campaigns back home. For example, when a local community opposes aggressive logging by a multinational company, volunteers may be able to link them up with an organization or international campaign pressuring the company to stop clear cutting. Volunteers can help bridge the gap of geography and connect distant struggles that share common goals.

Human Rights and Civil Society

In countries with a track record of human rights abuses, the mere presence of international volunteers can afford a degree of protection to local people working for social justice. Potential human rights abusers are keenly aware that they are more likely to be held accountable for their actions if an international spotlight is focused on them. Local union organizers, democracy advocates, and other human rights activists, therefore, feel that the presence of international volunteers helps them continue their work. As Peace Brigades International volunteer Winnie Romeril commented, "Guatemalans have told us that Peace Brigades has kept them alive. Our presence makes them feel that they can carry on their work in situations where they would have otherwise stopped."

Volunteers also publicize human rights abuses internationally. International volunteers working as journalists and election monitors help expand the political space for local people to organize to improve their situation. Volunteers' documentation of human rights abuses is particularly useful when it includes an analysis of the ways in which the volunteers' own governments support the perpetrators of these abuses and the exploration of possible avenues for policy change.

Solidarity, Inspiration, and New Perspectives

The fact that a group of volunteers has traveled thousands of miles to help build homes or plant trees is sometimes enough to lift the morale of local people and elicit energy from local volunteers, encouraging them to help out as well. As Bela Singh, Cross-Cultural Solutions country director in India, told us, "The volunteers' mere presence is motivating." Sometimes the most important thing you can offer as a volunteer is the power of telling people with deeds and action that they are not alone in their struggles.

International volunteers can also dispel certain myths about their own culture, especially the seductive and simplistic images projected by the U.S. media. Some things local people learn about Western culture may horrify them, such as the neglect of the elderly or the prevalence of homelessness. On the other hand, certain cultural differences, such as progress toward gender equality, for example, may represent ideals they want to see in their own society (although, of course, not everyone will see gender equality as a good thing).

Volunteers' fresh perspective, tempered by cultural sensitivity, can sometimes offer a new way of doing things.

Involvement after Returning Home

As we will discuss in other chapters, many overseas volunteer projects address the symptoms of underdevelopment, not the root causes. Volunteers overseas, however, while they observe and participate in development work often are drawn into looking at the root causes of the problems they are trying to solve. Volunteers may acquire a critical perspective that they can use to work for institutional change, especially after they return home. Many returned volunteers have been inspired by their overseas experiences to get involved in promoting democracy, protecting human rights, reforming foreign policy and aid programs, and redirecting resources from militarism to basic human needs. Twin brothers Steve and Doug Hellinger volunteered with the Peace Corps in 1970. Although they served in different countries, they both became frustrated by the negative impact of U.S. foreign policy on poor people overseas. When they returned home, they founded the Development Group for Alternative Policies, a nonprofit organization dedicated to making sure that people from the developing world would have a voice in shaping the policies that affect them. According to Doug, "The most important thing about volunteering is the learning, the knowledge and the inspiration you bring back to fight for change in your own government's systems."

Volunteers can also be educators when they return home, providing friends, family, and other members of their community with insight into how people live thousands of miles away. By sharing their firsthand experiences, volunteers can break down stereotypes while reminding people at home about the sometimes forgotten struggles of people in other countries for dignity and justice. As a church member in Nicaragua advised a volunteer dentist, "It's not the number of teeth you pulled here that makes the difference, but your telling people back home about the realities here."

In addition, many volunteers find positive examples overseas that they can use in their own communities. Amy Vongthavady brought home AIDS education materials from Thailand after volunteering with Global Service Corps. She felt that these materials would be more relevant and useful to the Asian communities in the San Francisco Bay area than some of the materials produced in the United States. Curtis Ogden volunteered in Zimbabwe with Visions in Action, and when he returned home worked on The Learning Web, a youth program in New York. Curtis found that "many of the lessons I learned and applied to the development of The Learning Web derive from my experiences working with the youth living on the streets of Harare, Zimbabwe." In his book, *Service Learning for Youth Empowerment and Social Change* (with J. Claus, New York: Peter Lang Publishing, 1999), Curtis details how working in Zimbabwe gave him practical ideas for empowering youth in the United States. Chapter 10, "Staying Involved after You Get Back," details other ways volunteers can help after returning home.

Despite all the benefits and potential contributions, being an international volunteer is not easy, and it is not for everyone. Furthermore, as we said, good intentions do not ensure good outcomes. In later chapters, we will offer guidance in selecting a volunteer program and will provide tips on preparing to go abroad as a volunteer. We'll discuss how to overcome financial obstacles to volunteering and how to be an effective volunteer.

As personal as volunteering may be, remember that it takes place in a larger historical context. Before offering concrete suggestions on how to become an international volunteer, we will introduce you to the context of international volunteering and help you decide whether international volunteering is right for you.

When you go to another country, not only do you take a fresh look at that country, you take a fresh look at your own country, and your own experiences, and you never quite accept things the same way.—Paula Morris, volunteer and staff, Voluntary Service Overseas, Zimbabwe and Indonesia

I changed my entire lifestyle so I could do more of this type of community service that I love and find so rewarding.—Mary Ryan, volunteer, Global Service Corps, Costa Rica

I will continue in medicine, but I now realize that to make long-lasting changes you have to get into the community. I am searching for ways I can be more creative in my work. —Patricia Dougherty, volunteer, Concern America, Guatemala

Don't go over there thinking you are going to change the world. Sit back and reflect on what you can learn.—Jennifer Holt, volunteer, YMCA World Fellows Program, Sri Lanka

CHAPTER 2

Is Volunteering Overseas Right for You?

International Volunteering: Is It for You?

Now that you have a better understanding of what volunteering is, how do you determine if it's right for you?

International volunteering can be extremely rewarding, but it is not for everyone. We have heard many stories from both volunteers and community members about the ills of misguided volunteer attempts. In some cases, volunteers didn't think through the implications of being an international volunteer. In others, their motivations for volunteering were incongruous with the volunteer work itself. In addition, we found that some people just were not aware of the alternatives to volunteering that might have been a better fit for them. In this chapter, in order to determine if volunteering is right for you, we would like to ask you first to look inward to find out a little more about yourself.

Examining Your Motivations

Many people considering volunteering abroad begin by looking at the different volunteer programs before taking the time to look at themselves. This often leads them to feel confused or overwhelmed by all of the options. Reflecting on why you are interested in volunteering overseas can guide you in deciding if volunteering is really the right option for you, and can help you to select a program that meets your needs and matches your interests, a subject we explore further in Chapter 4, "Choosing the Right Organization."

Begin by reflecting on some basic questions about your interests in international volunteer work:

- *Why are you interested in becoming an international volunteer?*
- *What life events have sparked this interest?*
- *What do you hope to get out of being an international volunteer?*
- *What do you hope to contribute?*
- *Where are you heading in your life and how does being an overseas volunteer fit into the picture?*

Next, build on your initial reflections by completing the following worksheet about the things that motivate your interest in international volunteering. Be as honest as you can with yourself about what your underlying motivations are, and add your own personal motivations to the bottom of the list.

WORKSHEET I

THINGS THAT MOTIVATE YOU TO VOLUNTEER	STRONG MOTIVATION	MODEST MOTIVATION	NOT A MOTIVATION
To put your concern for others into action			
To learn more about yourself			
To escape a bad relationship or other personal problems			
To assuage your guilt			
To gain a better firsthand perspective on the impact of wealthy countries in the world			
To save poor people; to lift poor people out of poverty			
You're unable to hold a job			
Your partner is doing it			
To gain experience in a field in which you have studied			
You're unable to pass your classes			
To be inspired by the efforts of people in developing countries			
To have an adventure			

	STRONG MOTIVATION	MODEST MOTIVATION	NOT A MOTIVATION
To share your skills and expertise by responding to a specific request from a foreign organization			
To get to know another culture			
To just impress future employers			
To live out your faith or religious beliefs by working for justice			
Everybody's doing it			
To learn a foreign language			
To make religious converts			
You have an addiction and you think that a change in environment will help you quit			
To travel			
For a change, or fresh start			
To become a more effective advocate for changes at home that will help poor people overseas			
Other Motivations			

Did some of your answers surprise you? Reflection can uncover some unseen motivations. As we suggested in Chapter 1, "International Volunteering: What Is It? Why Do It?," there are many reasons why people become international volunteers, and most people considering volunteering abroad will be inspired to volunteer for a number of different reasons.

Take a look at the things that motivate you most strongly in considering an international volunteer experience. Think about whether volunteering is the best way to respond to these motivations. And if you have just one or two main motivations take the time to examine those factors closely.

For example, if your primary motivations are to travel and to have an adventure, *travel* may be a better choice than volunteering. In addition to solo travel, there are a variety of group options, from eco-tourism to adventure travel to political tours.

If your motivations center on learning, such as learning another language or getting to know another culture, you may want to consider a *study abroad* program. Study doesn't just mean junior year abroad; it could include a language school in the Guatemalan highlands, a historical seminar for seniors in Prague, or a sculpture course in Zimbabwe.

If your goals are focused on helping others, you might want to consider *doing good at home* instead of doing overseas work.

If you have a variety of motivations, but think you might not be able to afford volunteering, read Chapter 7, "Overcoming Financial Obstacles." If you still think you can't afford to volunteer, you might want to consider *working abroad.* This option is more realistic if you have concrete skills, but there are some jobs available even to those who have little experience.

If one of these four options (study abroad, travel abroad, work abroad, or doing good at home) sounds like it might be a better fit than volunteering, we encourage you to read Bonus Section A, "Alternatives to Volunteering Overseas." We've compiled a wide range of information, advice, and data including websites dedicated to different forms of international exchange worth considering.

Keep in mind that the line between study, travel, work, and volunteering gets fuzzier every day. Many study programs are adding volunteer options, and volunteer programs often include time to study and travel. Some work options have very low salaries and might almost be considered volunteering, and some volunteer programs pay a stipend. Even if you know you are primarily interested in study or travel, you may want to consider the volunteer options profiled in the book that incorporate travel and/or study into the volunteering experience, such as the International Partnership for Service Learning, or Global Routes, both profiled in Chapter 12.

In our research we found that the people who have the most successful volunteer experiences are inspired by a combination of altruistic and selfish motivations. Volunteers encountered the most problems when they were either focused on an exclusively self-enriching experience or when they had a very specific agenda for what they were going to do for (and to) people overseas.

While there is not just one "right" reason to volunteer abroad, there are certain people who should not volunteer. If you are volunteering primarily to "save the poor people of the world," we encourage you to pause. Too often this desire to "solve other people's problems" or "fix things" has negatively affected communities and disempowered local people. Try putting a bookmark here and reading Chapter 3, "The Big Picture," and consider if there is another factor that might motivate you.

If you have an eating disorder, an addiction, or a serious emotional problem, deal with it *before* going overseas. Join a support group, twelve-step program, or treatment center. The stress of being overseas could exacerbate your problem, creating a situation that is dangerous to you and others.

Remember that motivations that may seem self-focused can be perfectly healthy if they are balanced with other reasons for volunteering. Getting educated and inspired about another country can have an effect beyond you, especially if you put your inspiration and knowledge to work when you return home. Gaining work experience can help you develop skills through which you can make a difference in the future, at home or abroad.

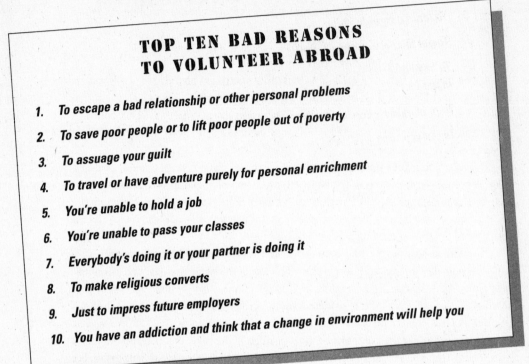

TOP TEN BAD REASONS TO VOLUNTEER ABROAD

1. To escape a bad relationship or other personal problems
2. To save poor people or to lift poor people out of poverty
3. To assuage your guilt
4. To travel or have adventure purely for personal enrichment
5. You're unable to hold a job
6. You're unable to pass your classes
7. Everybody's doing it or your partner is doing it
8. To make religious converts
9. Just to impress future employers
10. You have an addiction and think that a change in environment will help you

To Volunteer or Not to Volunteer

In Chapter 9, "How to Be an Effective International Volunteer," we discuss at length the five traits of a successful volunteer: *flexibility, patience, openness, humility, and dependability.* Think about these traits and ask yourself if you already have these qualities or are willing to develop them. If you can't stand things not going according to plan or if you think you have all the answers, then volunteering overseas is definitely not for you. If you have a tough time with responsibility at home or aren't really interested in learning anything new, then international volunteering is not for you either. If there is anything that we can stress it is that international volunteering is a learning experience!

Volunteering is not the only way to go overseas nor is it the only way to do good in the world. As you consider the different possibilities, remember that what is right for one person may not be right for you. Also, there is no perfect option. The key is to find an option that that will work for you. Even if you decide that volunteering overseas is not for you, there are hundreds of things you can do to be involved. And for those who decide that volunteering is right, it's never too soon to start preparing for what might just be the trip of a lifetime.

TOP TEN GOOD REASONS TO VOLUNTEER ABROAD

1. To learn a foreign language

2. To get to know another culture

3. To have a better firsthand perspective on the impact of wealthy countries in the world

4. To gain experience in a field in which you have studied

5. To put your concern for others into action

6. To learn more about yourself

7. To share your skills and expertise by responding to a specific request from a foreign organization

8. To be inspired by the efforts of people in developing countries

9. To become a more effective advocate for changes at home that will help poor people overseas

10. To live out your faith or religious beliefs through deeds and working for justice

Because preparing includes not only what you pack in your suitcase, but also what you pack in your mind, we encourage you to start preparing by reading about the context of international volunteering, an issue we explore in Chapter 3, "The Big Picture: International Volunteering in Context."

Action Steps for Deciding if Volunteering Overseas Is Right for You

1. *Consider Why You Want to Volunteer.* Ask yourself some basic questions about your interests in international volunteer work such as what you hope to get out of being an international volunteer and what you hope to contribute.

2. *List and Prioritize Your Motivations.* Fill out the questionnaire on "Things That Motivate You To Volunteer" at the beginning of this chapter.

3. *Reflect on Your Motivations.* Examine your motivations and compare them with the lists of ten good and bad reasons to volunteer.

4. *Explore Your Options.* If, after you read this chapter, you still are unsure if volunteering is for you, read more about the alternatives in Bonus Section A, "Alternatives to Volunteering Overseas," as well as Chapter 3, "The Big Picture: International Volunteering in Context."

5. *Make a Decision.* To volunteer or not to volunteer.

THE BIG PICTURE: INTERNATIONAL VOLUNTEERING IN CONTEXT

If we just go overseas and start doing things without understanding the complete picture, then even with our good intentions, we can err. Good intentions are not good enough.—Martin Jacks, Peace Corps volunteer, Ghana

People become international volunteers for many different reasons. As we suggested in Chapter 1, "International Volunteering: What Is It? Why Do It?," these reasons can be grouped into two general categories: benefits volunteers receive and contributions volunteers make. While we believe that volunteers invariably get more than they give, we also understand that most people interested in volunteering have altruistic intentions; they want to help the "less fortunate" and make a positive difference in the lives of people in other countries.

As you consider acting on these intentions, it is important that you take a moment to learn about the history of international exchange. Just as your attitudes and actions affect those around you when you volunteer, the context of volunteering affects you and your experience.

In 1968, Ivan Illich, a Catholic priest, spoke provocatively to a group of U.S. volunteers who had just arrived in Mexico. He told them: "Today the existence of organizations like yours is offensive to Mexico. I am here to entreat you to freely, consciously, and humbly give up the legal right you have to impose your benevolence on Mexico. I am here to entreat you to use your money, your status, and your education to travel in Latin America. Come to look, come to climb our mountains, to enjoy our flowers. Come to study. But do not come to help."

Why would he say such discouraging things to well-meaning volunteers? The answer lies in the context of international volunteering.

The most common images of international volunteers promote the idea that volunteering is a simple act of kindness. We may imagine, for example, a volunteer feeding a hungry baby in a refugee camp or helping a polio victim learn to walk. The reality, however, is that volunteering occurs within a broader context, and simple kindness is not usually all that simple.

When you arrive in another country, you will not be the first foreigner to set foot in that land. Soldiers who invaded and conquered or missionaries who persuaded and converted will have preceded you. Perhaps you will pass through customs days after a group of businessmen arrive to set up a new factory. You may arrive weeks after a delegation of policymakers from the International Monetary Fund negotiate the reduction of national spending on health and education as the conditions for a new loan to pay off an old loan, sending the country deeper into debt. You may follow in the footsteps of tourists who have come to simply wallow in the local fleshpots, or you might even arrive in the shadow of previous volunteers who enthusiastically implemented a project that raised expectations but failed unequivocally.

In this chapter, we will briefly examine the history of helping, the idea of development, and the reasons why good intentions sometimes have poor results. Although this background information is sometimes disheartening, we believe that knowing some of the potential pitfalls of volunteer work can help you avoid them and assist you in moving from good intentions to concrete contributions.

A Brief History of Helping

Altruism and cooperation predate recorded history. Our ancestors would never have survived if they had not helped each other to find food, create shelter, and raise children. We have evolved in societies of reciprocal interdependence, with the need and the desire to help each other. The Golden Rule is written deep within our hearts.

But altruism takes on radically different dimensions when it is applied cross-culturally, especially in a world that is full of injustice and inequalities that stretch back hundreds of years. The recipients of the "help" may experience what the "helper" considers to be a noble cause as a hostile act. Columbus and his followers, for example, may have thought of themselves as benevolent visionaries serving God and saving souls by bringing Christianity to pagans. From the Native American perspective, however, the Europeans were more likely seen as cruel conquerors and the perpetrators of genocide.

Unequal and often violent intercultural contact between native peoples and Europeans has been a frequent form of exchange during the past 500 years. Beginning in the fifteenth century, as European powers competed with one another to conquer lands around the world, explorers, merchants, soldiers, and bureaucrats set out for Africa, Asia, and Latin America, justifying their conquests with altruistic rhetoric. The conquerors claimed—and many of them believed—that they would reach "primitive" people, "civilize" them, and pacify brutal warrior tribes. In fact, in many places, the Europeans tore apart entire societies, destroyed the self-sufficiency of local communities, even turning some groups that had peacefully co-existed into mortal enemies. Whether unwittingly spreading disease or consciously mapping new territory for the colonial regimes, even missionaries participated in this devastation. Many of the colonized peoples would have gladly forgone their "help."

In the twentieth century, the former colonial powers found other ways of "assisting" nations with low per-capita incomes. The U.S. government, for example, based much of its foreign policy on supporting overseas regimes committed to fighting communism. In the process, however, the U.S. government overthrew democratically elected governments in Chile, Guatemala, and Zaire (Democratic Republic of the Congo), backed foreign-based military insurgencies in Nicaragua and Angola, and supported brutal dictators in the Philippines, Kenya, and the Dominican Republic, to name only a few. In many cases, the policies had more to do with supporting short-term U.S. political and business interests than assisting citizens of other countries, as documented in the book *Endless Enemies: The Making of an Unfriendly World* (Jonathon Kwitney, New York: St. Martins Press, 1984.). The people whose loved ones were killed by U.S.-backed wars and dictators surely did not appreciate this kind of aid.

Historically, then, the rhetoric of helping people in foreign countries has often been used to justify selfish behavior, and even those with a genuine desire to do good have inadvertently caused damage. Since the end of World War II, governments of the former colonial powers have worked along with private organizations and individuals to promote various "development" programs. These efforts marked a change in the rationale for international exchange and deserve examination as we attempt to untangle the context of international volunteering.

"Development" and the International Volunteer

When you work in international development, you're screwing around with someone else's life. If you make a mistake, you can go home. The people you work with already are home, and they probably can't just leave, so you better know what you are doing. The worst thing to do is just go in and do what you're told without thinking about it.
—Steve Arnold, International Development Program, School of International Service, American University

Most volunteer programs claim to address the problems of "underdevelopment" and promote some form of "development." At first glance, the meaning of these terms appears straightforward. We can understand *underdevelopment* to mean that the majority of people in low-income countries do not have adequate health care, clean water, food, education, housing, or jobs. It seems obvious that achieving *development* should mean creating societies in which people no longer lack these necessities.

In reality, however, there is much debate about the meaning of development, as well as the best strategies for promoting it. In every country and society there are national and international forces pushing the direction of development—defining goals, controlling resources, setting the pace, and advocating for specific outcomes. The process is often contentious, with vast inequalities in power among those involved.

To understand the challenges that volunteers face in understanding and contributing to development, we offer a scenario in which the tables are turned. Imagine that three groups of altruistic volunteers from other parts of the world come to Washington, DC, to help the city develop. Each of the groups has heard much about the problems in the U.S. capital through media reports about poverty, homelessness, and violence. Each of the three delegations are asked to assess the city's needs and then come up with a plan for a development project that donors in their home countries will be willing to support.

The first delegation is a group of elders from a rural village in Zambia, a country where most people are church-going Christians. The elders quickly identify the problem in Washington as a shortage of churches, and a lack of respect for elders. They plan a project that will involve the construction of twenty new churches throughout the city, and the establishment of a council of elders in each neighborhood, consisting of men aged seventy-five or older. The Zambians plan to work with a group of local citizens to promote the churches and councils, seeking to create a society in which all children have to work for their elders for at least three hours a day.

The second delegation is a group of indigenous women from the Amazon. In their initial study, conducted in the summer, they are horrified to see how much trash is produced by the city, the air pollution, and the lack of green space. Their solution is to tear down tall, ugly apartment buildings and build community gardens with simple but beautiful huts for people to live in.

The third delegation is a Rastafarian youth organization. Their analysis identifies the main problems of Washington to be too much focus on money and power and too little focus on spiritual connections. They decide to help Washington by promoting a reggae dance every evening and developing an educational program to train community leaders and politicians to grow ganja.

All of the visitors' assessments of needs may be based on elements of truth, and all of the visitors could probably find people in the community to support their projects. But, as you can imagine, the projects would also create problems. Non-Christians and young people might take offense at the Zambians' plan. The people who live in the apartment buildings that the South American women want to tear down would probably be very upset, to say the least, and not many people would like to live through the Washington winter in a hut. The Rastafarians and their local partners would most likely end up in jail.

In other words, people's ideas about development are closely connected to the cultural practices and values they bring from their own societies.

During our research for this book we talked to various community leaders in Asia, Africa, and Latin America who defined development as:

- *Living in a society that is free of war and violence.*
- *Gaining recognition for the collective rights of a community, not just individual rights.*
- *Being able to breathe clean air and drink clean water.*

- *Having access to jobs that pay a "living" wage.*
- *Achieving the right to protest government or corporate policies without fear of persecution, imprisonment, or death.*
- *Being able to have children play outside freely without the threat of land mines.*
- *Gaining the right to study in the local language.*
- *Enjoying the freedom to practice a traditional or minority religion.*
- *Living a lifestyle that allows people to spend time with their families and friends.*
- *Regaining the right for girls and boys to go to school without paying school fees.*
- *Having access to health care and affordable medicine.*
- *Living a life of dignity and respect.*

Some practitioners have recently coined the term "sustainable development" to describe development by the current generation in a way that does not jeopardize the potential development of future generations. Many indigenous people in the Americas say that this is merely a new phrase to describe what has been a traditional value of indigenous cultures for generations. Sustainable development demands careful stewardship of environmental resources, in contrast to mainstream theories of economic development, which promote rapid exploitation of the environment to support short-term financial gain.

On the other hand, some poor people may consider the sale of natural resources to be a necessary approach to the development of their communities. Meanwhile, professional "development" experts may try to prevent them from using these resources. Also, local elites, in collaboration with international corporations, frequently try to exploit the resources in ways that do not benefit the poor communities—and often harm them.

Your perspective on development may be quite different from the perspective of the people with whom you want to work. You should know that all too often outsiders define development and set the goals, without giving much thought to the ideas of the local people and their understanding of what is important.

What Is the Path to Development?

In 1998, the United Nations Human Development Report defined human development as people's ability to "lead long and healthy lives, to be knowledgeable, and to have access to the resources needed for a decent standard of living." Even if we agree with this definition, we still can have great disagreements about *how* to create societies where human development is possible. The path toward development that a person sees depends in large part on how that person understands the root causes of underdevelopment.

In sharing our perspective on these root causes, it seems appropriate for us to acknowledge that underdevelopment is a very complicated phenomenon. To really explore the issue would take another entire book—or two. But we strongly believe that volunteers should think critically about development before going overseas. In addition to the information presented here, we urge you to read at least one of the books listed at the end of the chapter, and to visit some of the recommended websites, to explore these issues in more depth.

To begin, let's examine some of the common misperceptions about development.

Many people think that the low-income countries are that way because they lack natural resources. In fact, Nigeria, with an average annual income of only $260, is rich with oil; Hong Kong, with an average annual income of $22,990, has almost no natural resources that it exploits. (Figures are from the World Bank's World Development Report, 1997.)

Overpopulation is sometimes assumed to be the biggest cause of underdevelopment, but in the 1990s, the Netherlands was one of the most densely populated countries on the planet, with 447 people per square kilometer, compared with Bangladesh's 395; Zambia could be considered "underpopulated," with only twelve people per square kilometer. (Figures from the UN Human Development Report, 1995.)

The World Bank has frequently put forth the argument that a lack of free markets causes underdevelopment. However, the World Bank's own pro-free-market "structural adjustment programs" have actually led to *declines* in longevity and education levels in the former Soviet Union, Africa, Asia, and Latin America, according to independent studies based on the World Bank's own data (www.igc.org/dgap).

Newspapers and TV give the impression that natural disasters make the low-income countries the way they are. But a second look reveals that the United States is subject to far more tornadoes, earthquakes, heat waves, blizzards, and cold snaps than most low-income countries and yet relatively few people perish. Natural disasters are "disastrous" in many countries because of the dearth of quality housing and abysmal infrastructure.

Some like to think that many people in Asia, Latin America, and Africa are poor because they don't work hard—but try telling that to a sweatshop worker who labors seventy hours a week in a Nicaraguan *maquiladora,* or a farmer who is up before the dawn to walk to her field in a Cambodian village, or a twelve-year-old boy who washes cars all day in downtown Harare to earn the equivalent of a few pennies.

Obstacles to Development

So if there are holes in all these theories, what does cause underdevelopment? We would argue that poor people are poor because of obstacles to their own efforts to develop themselves and their communities.

The poor in many countries face political obstacles. For example, the lack of democracy in the Congo, North Korea, and Syria means that poor people cannot hold their government accountable if it fails to build schools or maintain roads. The extreme violations of the human rights of women in countries like Afghanistan, and other manifestations of sexism that exist around the world, make it hard for half the population to get the education they need to develop themselves, their families, and their communities. The general lack of human rights in Indonesia, Kenya, and Colombia has created obstacles by preventing workers from organizing unions to bargain for fair wages. This problem is exacerbated when high-income countries provide economic, political, and military support to non-democratic regimes and those that abuse human rights.

Local and international financial policies can also impede people's efforts to develop their communities. In countries like Bangladesh, where moneylenders charge up to ten percent interest *per week,* the lack of affordable credit creates obstacles for farmers who want to grow more food, or small shop owners who want to expand their inventory. Whenever the International Monetary Fund requires governments to restrict access to credit, it makes these obstacles even bigger. Rising costs of agricultural inputs such as seeds and fertilizer along with decreasing prices for agricultural commodities present other obstacles to farmers' abilities to develop their communities and nations. This challenge is an especially heavy burden in countries that depend primarily on a single staple or export crop, such as Zambia (corn), Fiji (sugar), and Burkina Faso (cotton).

Policies to open a country to global trade, especially if introduced suddenly, often lead to local markets being flooded by international goods, providing a significant obstacle to the development of local business enterprises. Small business owners in countries including India, Russia, and Peru have suffered devastating losses as policies imposed by the World Bank and International Monetary Fund required the overnight elimination of laws designed to encourage domestic production. Multinational corporations in Nigeria, Ecuador, Brazil, and other countries have destroyed forests that local people had depended on for their livelihoods.

Military policies also create obstacles to development. In Angola, Mozambique, and Cambodia, land mines create an obstacle for farmers who are prevented from cultivating certain fields. Worse yet, when people are so hungry that they farm despite the risk, land mines maim and kill the very farmers who provide their families' main source of income and food, making it even harder for the rural poor to improve their economic status. Armed conflict sucks up resources that could otherwise be used for health care and education. War disrupts production by forcing large numbers of people to become soldiers and by creating refugees. Liberia, Democratic Republic of the Congo, Sierra Leone, and other countries have had devastating setbacks to development because of wars fueled in part by the international diamond trade.

Many of these obstacles are rooted in the way that the majority of people have been systematically deprived of their power—they lack the power—to stop elites from appropriating their land, they lack the power to prevent large businesses from tearing down their forests and polluting their water, they lack the power to force their government to build schools, they lack the power to make the United States stop selling land mines to rebel groups, and they lack the power to negotiate favorable terms of global trade. In our analysis, then, there are two ways to approach development. One is to address the symptoms of underdevelopment; the other is to shift the balance of power.

Treating Symptoms vs. Removing Obstacles

Addressing the symptoms of underdevelopment isn't necessarily a bad thing. In a crisis, for example, people may need emergency food or housing. And in the long run, development for a particular community may require steps such as building schools, training health educators, or promoting integrated pest management. Unfortunately, it can be quite tricky to provide relief or promote development in an effective way. In the aftermath of a major earthquake, a glut of donated grain can prevent local farmers from selling their crops, forcing them to go bankrupt and lose their land. A new school may crumble if the agency that built it did so without meaningful local participation and therefore without a sense of ownership and responsibility for maintenance. Many international aid projects end up benefiting foreign consultants and local elites, sometimes even making the lives of the poor more difficult, such as a large dam that forces thousands to be relocated and permanently lose their land. The most successful projects are usually ones initiated by local people: a soup kitchen in Peru started by women in a shanty town, a bakery in Costa Rica run by blind women, a school in India built by a local village, or a community-based tree-planting project in Kenya. To learn more about successful development projects, we recommend the books *Reasons for Hope: Instructive Experiences in Rural Development* (Anirudh Krishna, Norman Uphoff, and Milton J. Esman, West Hartford, CT: Kumarian Press, 1996) and *Hope's Edge: The Next Diet for a Small Planet* (Frances Moore Lappé and Anna Lappé, New York: Tarcher/Putnam, 2002).

If projects that attempt to address the symptoms seem hard to implement successfully, shifting the balance of power can be even harder, because there are many entrenched interests eager to maintain the status quo. But people in countries like the United States have an incredible opportunity to shift the balance of power by participating in acts of solidarity—working for a ban on land mines, for example, or cutting off international financing of undemocratic regimes. People can join campaigns to reform the World Bank and the International Monetary Fund (currently controlled by the United States, Western Europe, and Japan) or get involved in "fair trade" activities to purchase goods directly from producers abroad. Shifting the balance can also mean working with groups like Oxfam that support people around the globe who have come together to create institutional change in their communities—indigenous groups demanding access to education, mothers' organizations working against cuts in their country's health budget, or a farmers' union demanding affordable credit. (See Chapter 10, "Staying Involved after You Get Back," for more ideas on working to shift the balance of power by attacking the root causes of underdevelopment.)

Combined, local, and international efforts can make a real difference, but true development is difficult, precarious, and long term.

So What Is a Volunteer To Do?

In our overseas research, we found that few programs give volunteers the opportunity to work on removing institutional obstacles to development. The vast majority of programs place volunteers in positions where they will provide direct services to a small number of people. Most volunteers work in schools, clinics, business development centers, training programs, or community organizations, while a smaller number work in emergency relief programs. Only a few work in human rights, democracy building, or advocacy.

We believe that in the long term, development can occur only when power is shifted and societies function with political and economic democracy that eradicates dictatorship, war, and economic exploitation. We think, however, that it is entirely appropriate that most volunteers in their first experience overseas focus on directly responding to the symptoms of underdevelopment by addressing community needs. We urge you to read Chapter 9, "How to Be an Effective International Volunteer," so you can carry out this direct service with minimum harm and maximum benefit. We also urge you to read the resources recommended in this chapter and Chapter 8, "What to Do before You Go." But most important while you volunteer overseas, seek to probe the root causes of underdevelopment. Ask yourself—and others—what are the structural problems that create poverty in the country where you volunteer? When you visit the capital city, seek out human rights, advocacy, and social justice organizations to learn from their analyses and actions. What do women's groups, environmental organizations, and neighborhood associations see as the obstacles to their efforts to develop their communities? Do external forces impose these obstacles? What is the history of current problems? What are the organizations doing to create change? What can you do to support them in the long term?

When you bring your volunteer experience home, you will be able to use this knowledge to participate effectively in removing obstacles to development and shifting the balance of power. You may also bring back tools to confront underdevelopment, "maldevelopment," and even "overdevelopment" in your own community or nation. We believe so strongly in staying active after volunteering that we have devoted a whole chapter to the topic.

Beyond Good Intentions

We know that the information presented here can be disheartening at first. Development is a difficult process. But our conclusion is not to tell you to give up and stay home. In fact, the very challenges of development make it urgent for more people to gain experience overseas, to become knowledgeable about global problems, and to participate in working for solutions.

We also don't want you to think that participating in the process of development is depressing. In fact, many of the volunteers we interviewed found great joy in their work overseas—learning, sharing, living fully, while doing something proactive to heal the planet.

Your chances for having a positive experience are much better if you are well prepared. In upcoming chapters, we will show you ways to go beyond good intentions by helping you prepare for your experience and advising you on how to be an effective and responsible volunteer. First, we'll help you choose the organization that best matches your interests, skills, and special needs.

WHAT TO CALL THEM?

"Developing countries," "the Third World," "less developed countries," "poor countries," "the Global South." The list could go on, but each and every one of these terms is riddled with contradictions and inaccuracies.

"Third World" is widely recognized but implies an inherent superiority of the so-called "First World" and ignores the fact that the "Third World" comprises the vast majority of the land and population of our earth. Also, the "Second World" (the Soviet Union and Eastern Bloc) no longer exists.

The terms "underdeveloped countries" and "less developed countries" ignore the fact that many communities overseas are developed—in literature, social relations, and environmental stewardship, for example. Calling countries like the United States "developed" implies that conditions are improving, while in many of these countries the majorities are experiencing greater misery. The term erroneously implies that countries like the United States have already "arrived" and do not need to develop.

The term "poor countries" is quite misleading. Many so-called poor countries are in fact quite wealthy in terms of natural resources, although the majority of the people are impoverished, thanks to human-made policies. "Low-income countries" is a little more accurate because it refers to average income, not resources, but not everyone in a low-income country has a low income. There are wealthy people and neighborhoods in so-called low-income countries—and, of course, impoverished people and neighborhoods in so-called wealthy countries.

"The Global South," abbreviated to "the South," was introduced to overcome these problems, but is not generally recognized. And, although many of the low-income nations are in the Southern Hemisphere, there are notable exceptions such as New Zealand and Australia, and a number of countries in Asia. In addition, the phrase does not include Eastern Europe.

Even the shorthand list of regions that we sometimes use, "Latin America, Asia, and Africa," is incomplete because it leaves out the Caribbean, Middle East, Pacific Islands, and Eastern Europe. Also, some countries in Asia and the Caribbean have average incomes that approach or exceed those of countries in Europe and North America.

We try to avoid the problem by referring to specific regions or countries where possible, recognizing that the available global labels all subtly distort our understanding of reality.

Resources

ON INSTITUTIONAL OBSTACLES TO DEVELOPMENT AND CRITIQUES OF CONVENTIONAL FOREIGN AID:

A Fate Worse than Debt: The Third World Financial Crisis and the Poor. Susan George. New York: Grove, 1990.

World Hunger: Twelve Myths. Frances Moore Lappé, Joseph Collins, and Peter Rosset. New York: Grove Press, 1998.

ON THE HISTORY OF UNDERDEVELOPMENT:

A History of the Philippines. Renato Constantino. New York: Monthly Review Press, 1975.

Inevitable Revolutions: The United States in Central America, 2nd Edition. Walter LaFeber, New York: W.W. Norton, 1993.

King Leopold's Ghost. Adam Hochschild. Boston: Houghton Mifflin, 1998.

The Log of Christopher Columbus. Robert H. Fuson, tr. Camden, Maine: International Marine Publishing, 1992.

See the resource list at the end of Chapter 9, "How to Be an Effective International Volunteer," for information on more effective development projects.

See page 154 for websites of organizations working for sustainable development.

Action Steps for Looking at the Big Picture

1. *Educate Yourself.* Once you have decided the region where you want to volunteer, pick a country and research the history of its relationship with Europe and the United States. How have colonialism, the World Bank, the International Monetary Fund, regional conflict, international trade, and human rights impacted the country's development?

2. *Clarify Your Vision.* Write down how you would define development in general and specifically what development would look like for the community where you live.

3. *Challenge Your Perspective.* Think outside of the box and try to imagine how the following groups might analyze your community's development needs: child laborers from a carpet factory in India, a women's union of small farmers from Nigeria, or a group of elders from the Kuna nation of Panama.

4. *Keep Learning.* Read one or two of the books and resources listed in this chapter to gain a deeper understanding of the development issues that interest you.

CHAPTER 4

CHOOSING AN ORGANIZATION

Researching your organizational options is an essential step on the path to international volunteer service. The number of international volunteer programs is growing, and it can be difficult to make your way through all the brochures and websites describing the myriad of options. But it is worth taking the time to consider the various programs that are available. Many volunteers we spoke with offered the following advice: "Don't just select the first program that comes along, as I did. Investigate the different options." This chapter will help you heed their advice and make an informed decision about which international volunteer program is right for you.

Assessing Your Interests and Particular Needs

There are a number of issues to consider when assessing your interests and needs as a would-be volunteer. This section will introduce you to some of the key factors that define the international volunteer experience, such as where you volunteer and for how long, the type of work you do, the type of organization you join, the costs and benefits of the program, and the living situation that a program offers.

Reading this section should help you clarify the issues that are important to you, and may give you some food for thought by introducing issues that you had not previously considered.

Where to Volunteer?

One obvious way to begin choosing among the various organizations is to look at where they send volunteers. Which organizations have a program in a region you have always wanted to visit? Which organizations place volunteers in a country where you have cultural ties or already speak the language?

Most allow volunteers to select the country of service, but a few organizations, such as the Peace Corps, do not.

The region where you choose to volunteer will have a great impact on your experience; volunteering in Poland, for example, might feel in some ways like volunteering in Western Europe, while some neighborhoods in Latin America may feel like working in a Latino neighborhood in the United States. In parts of sub-Saharan Africa and Asia you are likely to witness the most extreme contrasts between wealth and poverty. Of course, even within regions there is great diversity; Haiti and the Dominican Republic, for example, share the same island but have vastly different languages, histories, cultures, and economies. South Korea and Bangladesh are both in Asia but are worlds apart. Costa Rica, one of the most stable and more developed countries in Latin America, shares a border with Nicaragua, one of the lowest-income nations, frequently plagued by external military intervention and internal conflict.

In addition to culture and language, think about climate—how well you tolerate heat or cold, high altitudes, and rain. Check weather patterns, not only in the country where you want to work, but also in the local area where you would volunteer. The Galapagos Islands are radically different from the highlands of Quito and the rain forest of Lago Agrio, although all three are in Ecuador. Also, remember that summertime in the Northern Hemisphere is wintertime in the Southern Hemisphere!

You may want to find out how long an organization has been working in a specific country or region. We spoke with Operation Crossroads volunteers who faced major challenges as the first Crossroads volunteers to work in a remote rural area in northern Kenya. The organization had not made adequate arrangements to provide for some of the basics such as food and water, and this added to the emotional and physical challenges of being in such an isolated region. On the other hand, we met Global Routes volunteers in rural Ecuador who didn't mind being a curiosity for a community that was hosting foreign volunteers for the first time.

You may have a different experience if you are part of an annual or regular presence of foreign volunteers in a community. Sidney Coulter and Bouapha Toommaly, who volunteered in Tanzania with AHEAD, a health care services organizations, told us about the warm reception they received as a result of the long working relationship the organization had with local people.

Rural vs. Urban Placements

Rural and urban assignments are likely to be significantly different experiences. "There is such a big difference between the city and the village in Bolivia," Peace Corps volunteer Stephanie Ediger told us. "It's like two different countries." Rural placements often offer more opportunities for integration into the local culture, while urban posts tend to provide more conveniences familiar to volunteers, although, as Denis Barre of Doctors without Borders in Cambodia pointed out, "You can live in Phnom Penh and be integrated into Cambodian society, and you can live in the village and be totally isolated."

Joy Sanders, a Peace Corps volunteer in Kenya, told us that the Peace Corps's rule of thumb is that the more rural and isolated the volunteer, the happier he or she usually is. A Cambodian working for Food for the Hungry International told us, "to do development work, the volunteer must understand the life of the villager," while another

Cambodian said that he was encouraged that people "were waking up to the fact that there are also important urban development issues."

Volunteers coming from an urban background may experience, in addition to the culture shock of being in another country, the shock of being in a rural environment for the first time in their lives. Likewise, volunteers from small towns may experience shock if volunteering in a large city. This double shock is not always a bad thing, but should be taken into consideration when choosing an organization.

How Long to Volunteer?

The length of time you volunteer will profoundly affect your experiences. On one end of the spectrum, there are volunteer programs lasting from one to four weeks that consist of work on specific projects such as building clinics or repairing trails. On the other end of the spectrum, there are programs that last two years or more in which volunteers live and work side-by-side with local people, virtually becoming a part of the community and its daily rhythms. Programs of different lengths lend themselves to achieving different goals.

Short-term Volunteers

Short-term programs, those that last from one to four weeks, are geared toward exposing volunteers to other cultures but don't always give them the satisfaction of seeing a project completed. Involvement in short-term programs can also foster solidarity and deepen the understanding of issues by introducing volunteers to groups and individuals dedicated to human rights and social change.

In Slovakia, Andre Luptak of INEX, a short-term work camp organization, told us: "These types of exchanges are unabashedly about cultural exchange. The experience places the volunteer somewhere between a tourist and a local. The best projects involve the local community in a meaningful way, but this does not always happen, because of the language barrier and short time commitment."

In our fieldwork we found that projects that last from one to four weeks can also be appropriate for professional placements and training seminars. For example, reconstructive surgeons from around the world have organized short-term clinics that involve both training and direct service to remote communities that otherwise would not receive the same high level of medical attention.

Some volunteers and community members, however, are critical of short-term volunteer programs. Critics suggest that short-term volunteers primarily feed their own ego and sense of importance while burdening the local community that hosts them. Serge Dumortier of Handicap International in Cambodia, argued, "The problem with short-term volunteers is that every new person who comes reinvents the wheel, and it's the Khmer (Cambodian) staff that has to adjust to the foreigner's style and teach them things." Other people point to the tendency of short-term programs to aim for a top-down quick fix, a strategy that frequently does not work.

Long-term Volunteers

With short-term programs you know what you are getting into. It's cut and dried. You might come to build a church or a school, and get some cultural interaction. But when you are doing long-term volunteering things open up that you never dreamed you would be involved in.—Bernard Butkiewicz, Maryknoll Lay Missioners, Bolivia

Long-term placements, those lasting more than six months, offer volunteers more of a chance to take on responsibilities and to integrate into their host organizations and communities. Many long-term volunteers spoke about the profound changes that took place once they had lived in a community long enough to speak the local language more fluently and become immersed in local culture.

Most recommend that people volunteer for at least one year and many suggest even longer stays when possible. Thida Khus of SILAKA in Cambodia commented, "One year is too short. Only after six months do you even start to understand where you are and what you can do."

Long-term placements can also give volunteers opportunities to go beyond the clearly defined projects they are assigned. Volunteers are not in as much of a hurry to make an impact; they have time to listen and learn from local people, and, unlike short-term volunteers, they might have the chance to apply something they learned months earlier by going slowly and taking the time to ask, listen, and observe.

Medium-term Volunteers

Medium-term volunteers, who work from one to six months, often find themselves able to get more deeply involved with the language, culture, and community than short-term volunteers. At the same time medium-term volunteers experience the tension between what they hope to accomplish and what is possible, and tend to struggle with this tension more than long-term and short-term volunteers. As medium-term volunteers pass the two-month mark, they often relax and their experience becomes more similar to that of long-term volunteers.

Keep in mind that short-, medium-, and long-term volunteer programs all have their place. In general, we recommend that you volunteer for as long as you can. Our experience suggests that the longer you volunteer the more meaningful the experience, but even a week-long immersion experience can be profound.

What Type of Work?

Another significant dimension of the international volunteer experience is the type of work you do. Many volunteers choose to put their professional experience to work overseas, while others use volunteering as a way to explore different career options and life paths. Shiela Palza, Interim Peace Corps Director in Costa Rica, thought she had the ideal placement for an incoming volunteer who had a background as a financial analyst with Chase Manhattan, but when he arrived he declined the placement, explaining that he joined the Peace Corps "in order to do something different." If you have a strong preference for the type of work you would like to do, make sure to communicate that with your potential placement organization.

Here are some of the more common types of work that international volunteers undertake.

Education, Teaching, and Training

Many volunteers find themselves in a variety of teaching situations ranging from classroom instruction to individual tutoring to the training of teachers. We met scores of teachers like Eric Lee of Volunteers in Asia, who taught English to Vietnamese government employees in Hanoi, and Sahar Khoury of Global Routes, who taught children in a one-room schoolhouse in rural Ecuador.

Some development practitioners question the strategy of teaching English because they think that rather than meeting community needs, it serves the needs of multinational corporations who want to hire people at low wages who know some English. In some cases, students probably won't have any chance to use their English skills, such as the isolated villagers in the Andes taught by a Peace Corps volunteer we met. But many people overseas see English as an essential skill in today's global economy. Also, teaching English can be part of a sustainable development plan. In the Yucatán region of Mexico we met WorldTeach volunteers who were teaching local fishermen English so that they could supplement their dwindling earnings from fishing by guiding tourists through a rare flamingo habitat. Our advice is that you think through your perspective on this issue if you plan to teach English.

English language instruction may be the most common form of teaching that volunteers undertake, but volunteer teachers instruct in a variety of subjects from basic math to history and ethics. Volunteers who have had previous teaching experience can often make a more significant contribution than those without it, although they must be flexible for they will certainly find the local system of education different from what they are used to.

Education is also a tool that is used in many types of community work. Many volunteers work as trainers in health or environmental education. Volunteers also teach various vocational skills, both in and outside of the classroom, in areas ranging from food processing and manufacturing to physical therapy and carpentry. Training others can have a greater long-term impact than just providing a direct service. If you want to train others, we suggest you try to get some experience as a trainer before you go overseas, or seek an organization that will help you learn how to teach.

Health

The field of health care often provides opportunities for volunteers to make a real difference for people in impoverished communities. Volunteers range from trained professionals, such as surgeons, doctors, physical therapists, and nurses placed through organizations such as Health Volunteers Overseas (HVO), to non-professional volunteers who weigh babies, work on sanitation projects such as constructing ecological latrines, or provide basic health education talks through programs like Amigos de las Americas. Some programs, such as Concern America, focus on building local capacity through teaching, while others, such as Flying Doctors, treat patients directly. In selecting an organization, think about which strategy you prefer.

Volunteers must have a high degree of flexibility, as the conditions and methods can differ dramatically from those typically found in medical practice in North America. In many countries abroad traditional medicine, alternative therapies, and spiritual treatment may be much more commonly practiced. Clinics and hospitals may lack basic equipment, medicine, and staff. You are likely to encounter diseases that are rarely seen in the West such as intestinal worms, malaria, and tuberculosis. Diseases such as malnutrition and diarrhea are often the results of poverty and thus cannot be cured with a strictly medical approach. Medical student Eric Stein said that as a volunteer he learned that "food is medicine."

There are several useful websites with information on volunteering in the medical field, especially if you are a health professional or student, including International Medical Volunteers Association (www.imva.org), The American Society of Plastic Surgeons (www.plasticsurgery.org), or the American Medical Student Association (www.amsa.org).

We also highly recommend David Werner's wonderful book, *Where There Is No Doctor* (Teaching Aids at Low Cost, www.rgp.man.ac.uk/gp/talc/), for all those who will work in the health care field, even doctors!

Human Rights

Working on human rights issues is a courageous form of international voluntary service. In some cases, volunteers with organizations like Peace Brigades International act as human shields accompanying individuals that face threat of imminent harm. In other cases, volunteers are involved in documenting human rights violations. Some human rights volunteers focus on working with the media or international campaigns. Volunteers do human rights work for a range of organizations from U.N. agencies to indigenous people's organizations. NISGUA volunteers accompany Guatemalan refugees returning from exile in Chiapas, Mexico. Volunteers with Witness for Peace lead U.S. citizens on "experiential learning tours" that explore the effects of U.S. policies on the human rights of people in Latin America, while SIPAZ volunteers facilitate workshops on non-violence, conflict resolution, and helping to bring international attention to the increased militarization of Chiapas and the Mexican government's role in massacres.

Social Work

Opportunities for volunteers to provide direct social services include working with street children, the elderly, orphans, and people with disabilities. Participants in the Jesuit Volunteer Corps, for example, work as counselors in local schools. Volunteers often find themselves providing an extra set of hands to care for basic needs, hold infants, provide supervision and tutoring for children, organize special outings, and lead creative projects.

Micro-Enterprise, Fair Trade, and Business Consulting

Micro-enterprise projects seem to be the latest trend around the world. Every women's group, artisan cooperative, and development organization appears to be looking for ways to build sustainable sources of income to support its work. Small loan funds have sprung up on every continent, allowing needy individuals and small groups to launch new businesses on a modest and manageable scale. Business consulting volunteers work in a range of settings providing insight into product development and design for external markets. We met a Cross-Cultural Solutions volunteer who was producing a catalogue of handicrafts and a Peace Corps volunteer who was helping with the marketing and sale of greeting cards. Retired business professionals working with organizations like the Canadian Executive Service Organization (CESO), International Executive Service Corps (IESC), or ACDI-VOCA are likely to volunteer with midsized and larger producers on more specialized projects such as processing raw agricultural goods into finished products or introducing more efficient manufacturing techniques.

Women's Issues

Volunteers who want to work with women and women's issues can find opportunities in virtually any field including health, education, and social work. Specific opportunities for working with women include maternal health education, women's community groups, micro-credit projects with women's borrower groups, domestic violence prevention and support services, and advocacy for women's rights. Organizations such as Concern America help re-ignite interest in traditional midwifery practices and facilitate the organization of women-run artisan cooperatives.

Working with People with Disabilities

As a result of malnutrition, low industrial safety, environmental regulations, war (particularly land mines), and a lack of immunization, numerous people throughout Asia, Africa, and Latin America have disabilities. Some disabilities, such as those resulting from polio, are rarely seen in North America. Government services for people with disabilities are almost nonexistent in many countries, and there are a variety of opportunities for volunteers to help organizations that serve this community. We met a physical therapist from Handicap International, a business consultant from Mennonite Central Committee, and other volunteers who were involved in working with people with disabilities in activities such as rehabilitation, running a gift shop to generate income, assisting with specialized prosthesis and wheelchair production, and supporting local organizations abroad that focus on assisting people with disabilities. The Mobility International website (www.miusa.org) has extensive information about disability issues and organizations.

Children and Youth

Young people usually suffer the most from the brutal effects of extreme poverty. Whether volunteering with an organization like Childhaven International or Nuestros

Pequeños Hermanos, there are many opportunities to work with children and youth in projects such as after-school tutoring or recreational programs, orphanages, clinics and services for street children. In countries affected by war or a high prevalence of HIV/AIDS, volunteers have found it to be both challenging and rewarding to work with abandoned and orphaned children, who are often extremely hungry for attention. Volunteers can also support children indirectly by working with parents, supporting youth-serving organizations, or working on policy issues and youth advocacy with a group such as Visions in Action.

Environmental Issues

An increasing number of volunteers work on environmental issues, especially environmental education. Many volunteers are also involved in scientific research, maintaining public reserves and parks, habitat restoration, or specific conservation projects such as protecting sea turtle populations. Other volunteers, such as those placed on the Ladakh Farm Project by the International Society for Ecology and Culture, practice sustainable agriculture. Volunteers can support the efforts of people to establish viable ecotourism businesses. In the Galapagos Islands, WorldTeach volunteers teach English to trained naturalists so that they can more effectively communicate their environmental messages to tourists.

What Type of Organization to Join?

Governmental vs. Non-governmental Organizations

Government programs such as the Peace Corps and Voluntary Service Overseas often offer a higher level of financial and logistical support than other programs, providing stipends, health insurance, and end-of-service payments. On the other hand, these programs can be frustrating to volunteers who dislike rules, regulations, red tape, and being part of government. Typically, government programs expect volunteers to represent their home country and culture and to be citizen ambassadors. In some cases, the programs are closely bound up with the foreign policy of the sponsoring government. Therefore, if you have major disagreements with your country's foreign policy, a governmental program probably won't be a good fit for you. (See Chapter 11, "The Peace Corps," for further discussion.) Because they cover expenses and compensate volunteers, the application process for government programs is usually somewhat competitive.

Non-governmental programs, in general, are smaller than governmental programs and less well funded so they frequently charge a program fee. (Exceptions include some of the religious programs.) Most have fewer formalities. Many do not provide as much language training as government programs do. Flexibility and choice are likely to be higher with non-governmental programs, and shorter terms of service are usually available. Some programs, such as AHEAD and Pastors for Peace, are very much influenced by the experiences and interests of their founders. Others, such as the International Executive Service Corps and ACDI/VOCA, get most of their funding from governments and, although they are nominally independent, generally follow the government's foreign policy priorities.

In researching different volunteer opportunities it is worthwhile considering not only if the volunteer placement organization is governmental or non-governmental but also the status of the local host organization. Government programs have a bias toward placing volunteers with the host governments' institutions. A staff member from one such program argued that placements with government institutions are "more sustainable, because you know that the institution is unlikely to lose its funding and disappear tomorrow." A number of volunteers working with U.N. agencies and government ministries spoke to us favorably about their work's potential for having a large-scale impact.

Even government programs, however, are increasingly placing their volunteers with non-governmental hosts. Paul Ledwidge, a staff member in Cambodia with the Agency for Personal Service Overseas, the Irish government's volunteer program, put it this way, "While local groups can be less stable than governmental ministries, they are often smaller and easier to work with, and our volunteer's co-workers at local non-governmental organizations are frequently highly motivated."

NGOS, NPOS, AND PVOS COME IN ALL SHAPES AND SIZES: DEFINITIONS AND A BRIEF TYPOLOGY

The terms "non-governmental organization" (NGO), "non-profit organization" (NPO), and "not-for-profit" are all roughly interchangeable names for a particular type of organization. Typically they are citizen groups that work toward a mission other than that of making money, and are neither government agencies nor political parties. In fact, NGOs are often prohibited from direct involvement in electoral politics. While we use the term NGO, you may elsewhere come across the terms above or others such as "private voluntary organizations" or "civic associations." Academics, politicians, and U.N. representatives commonly refer to the entire NGO sector as "civil society."

There are many different types of NGOs. Examples of NGOs in the United States include the Central Iowa Young Farmers Association, the Red Cross, and the National Rifle Association. Some have multimillion dollar budgets and some operate on a shoestring. Some are right wing, some are left wing, and others are apolitical. Some are composed entirely of volunteer staff, while others have only paid staff. Most have both. Some are religiously affiliated and some are secular. NGOs truly come in all shapes and sizes.

Religious and Secular Organizations

Secular and religious organizations often work on similar types of projects overseas, but their underlying philosophies and approaches to volunteering may be profoundly different. Some religious organizations send volunteers who are exclusively focused on converting local people to their faith. We have not profiled organizations of this kind. A number of organizations, however, combine social services with missionary work. Elena Raykowski, a Latin Link volunteer in Bolivia, explained that mission work is about going "into the world and making disciples." "But," she said, "you cannot evangelize someone who is dying from hunger."

Many more religiously affiliated volunteer placement organizations are looking for volunteers who derive their personal motivation from a specific religious background but do not want to evangelize. Paul and Nancy Hamalian explained that they got involved as international volunteers with Habitat for Humanity in Nicaragua and Ecuador because, in their own words, "We were called by the Scriptures to work with the poor." They did not, however, focus on converting people.

Some volunteer organizations seek to build a community of faith either within one religion or in a non-denominational group. The Jesuit volunteers we met in Tanzania, for example, came from diverse religious backgrounds but shared a commitment to building a faith-based community.

Christian Peacemaker Teams and some other volunteer programs are associated with ecumenical Christian movements that emphasize peace and justice issues. In Latin America, volunteers have been inspired by the teachings of "liberation theology," which emphasizes the centrality of social and political transformation as well as spiritual change and the necessity of discerning the gospel through the eyes of impoverished and oppressed peoples.

Many volunteers from secular as well as faith backgrounds choose to work for secular organizations because they do not want to "impose their religious agenda" on local people. It is worthwhile remembering, however, that secular organizations can also "impose their agenda" on a community.

The affiliation of a volunteer program with a particular religion does not necessarily dictate its approach to international volunteer work. A religious organization that focuses on charitable acts and social service, for example, may have more in common with a secular organization with the same focus than it does with a religious organization that focuses on human rights.

Several volunteers explained that they are content, in the words of one of them, "to have the love of God work through them without putting any particular religious label on it." Such volunteers may find spiritual fulfillment even in working with a secular organization.

You should be aware that you don't necessarily have to be a member of a particular religious faith or denomination in order to serve in its volunteer program. Habitat for Humanity, for example, a non-denominational Christian organization, places Christians and non-Christians alike in its short-term volunteer programs.

You may want to ask yourself the following questions: What role, if any, does religious faith play in my motivation for being an international volunteer? Is faith part of my definition of community? Do I feel comfortable volunteering with people of a different faith? Questions such as these can help you figure out if you would rather serve with a religious or a secular organization.

For more information on Catholic faith-based programs try consulting St. Vincent Pallotti Center (http://pallotti.cua.edu, 877-VOL-LINK) or Catholic Network of Voluntary Service (www.cnvs.org, 800-543-5046).

Types of Organizations: Different Approaches to Social Problems

Different organizations have different ways of defining social problems and use diverse strategies for responding to these problems. The Center for Third World Organizing (CTWO) has developed a typology of organizations based on the following different approaches to social problems:

> **SERVICE**—*meeting people's immediate needs*
> **ADVOCACY**—*speaking on behalf of someone else's interest*
> **SELF-HELP**—*developing alternative institutions*
> **ELECTORAL**—*using the political system*
> **ORGANIZING**—*fighting for institutional change based on collective action*

Taking the problem of hunger as an example, a *service* organization might get involved in feeding hungry people at a food pantry or soup kitchen. An *advocacy* organization might work with people who have enough to eat and want to work on behalf of hungry people so that they have access to healthy diets, while a *self-help* organization might create a community garden as a way for hungry people to grow their own food. An *electoral* organization might run a candidate or sponsor a bill to change food policies, and an organization with an *organizing* approach might facilitate hungry people to work together and collectively demand fundamental changes in the policies and structures that create and perpetuate hunger.

Using the categories above as a guide, ask yourself which approach to social change suits you best. Seek a program that can match you with an organization overseas that shares your approach to social problems.

You should be aware, however, that most volunteer programs focus on service and self-help. This is true in part because advocacy, political work, and organizing can be dangerous in the unfamiliar context of a foreign country. Some people question whether it is appropriate for international volunteers to do this type of work. A mistake you make doing political work could have much more serious negative ramifications for your co-workers abroad than a mistake you make doing service. One alternative for volunteers who believe in this type of work but wonder about their role in it, is to work for a human rights group such as Peace Brigades International, which helps create safer civic space for local people to change the institutions of their own society. Another approach is to do direct service overseas, and then get involved in working for structural change when you return home.

How to Compare the Costs of Different Programs

Many people are surprised to find that it often costs money to become an international volunteer. As we discuss in Chapter 7, "Overcoming Financial Obstacles," many of the better volunteer programs charge participants a fee. It takes resources to run effective volunteer programs, and though many organizations receive support from donors, volunteer fees often still comprise the major source of revenue for recruitment, preparation, and in-country support.

One of the best ways to assess the financial value of a program is to look at what you get for your fee. Program fees may or may not include the following benefits:

- *International transportation*
- *In-country transportation*
- *Room and board*
- *Health insurance and health services*
- *Emergency medical and evacuation insurance*
- *Stipend for living expenses*
- *Tourist or non-work excursions and retreats*
- *Language instruction*
- *Technical training*
- *Passport and visa fees*
- *Pre-departure information and support*
- *In-country orientation*
- *In-country staff support*
- *Registration fees to institutions offering academic credit*
- *Assistance securing academic credit for volunteer work*
- *Post-service debriefing, job counseling, and re-entry support*
- *Re-entry or post-service relocation stipend*
- *Assistance with loan deferrals*
- *Benefits for families such as education funds for children, living stipends for dependents, health insurance for entire family, or volunteer placement for spouse*

Don't just look at a program's price tag. Consider, for example, that a $1,000 program that appears to be a bargain may actually be comparable in cost to a $1,700 program that provides health insurance the $1,000 program does not; a one-year program that costs $6,000 but provides a $400 monthly stipend for living expenses would be equal in value to a program that costs $1,200 but provides no stipend.

Be sure to get a sense of the cost of living in the country where you will be posted.

Compare this to the volunteer's average monthly out-of-pocket expenses and the amount of your monthly stipend if you will receive one. Though in many places the cost of living is lower than at home, don't assume you will be rolling in dough. Many organizations provide volunteers with stipends just large enough for volunteers to get by.

In some cases, high program fees are justified by the benefits and support offered by the program. There are definitely cases, however, in which volunteers are frustrated to find out how much they paid merely for the reassurance and information that got them to the volunteer site. We met Global Service Corps volunteers working in Costa Rica, for example, who were angry that they had paid what they felt was a high program fee and yet had received very little support from the volunteer program's staff. Before you pay your fee, find out what you are getting for your money, including the amount of money rebated if you drop out before completing the program.

Don't be discouraged if financial constraints are an issue for you. Ask the volunteer organization you are interested in if it can help you fundraise, defer student loans, or offer you full or partial scholarships. (See Chapter 7, "Overcoming Financial Obstacles," for ideas on fundraising and affording international voluntary service.)

Receiving Academic Credit

Academic credit is another benefit that some international volunteers are able to arrange. One option is to serve with a volunteer and study program such as the International Partnership for Service-Learning (IPS-L) or Minnesota Studies in International Development (MSID). If you are not volunteering with a for-credit service-learning program, ask the organization if it offers any assistance or has any experience in securing academic credit for participants, or consider being a trailblazer and convincing your school that they should give you credit for participating in the program.

What Kind of Living Situation?

Your living situation may well be a major determinant of the quality of your international volunteer experience. One common option is a home-stay in which you live with a family. The experience in a home-stay can range from feeling like an adopted member of the family to feeling like a temporary boarder, with a source of income, but no more. While some volunteers living in home-stays feel constrained by a loss of independence and freedom, others speak of their home-stay as the highlight of their experience abroad, an invaluable window into a culture and the family system of the host country.

Another common living situation is group housing. Norris Friesen, who volunteered in Jamaica with Christian Service International, commented on the drawbacks he experienced in such an arrangement: "Some would argue that we were too self-contained; that is, we were housed together and ate our meals together. As a result, we had minimal contact with Jamaicans in the evening." Volunteers who live in a group house with other volunteers who speak the same language often find it hard to learn the local language or integrate into local culture.

On the other hand, living with other volunteers can have the advantage of providing you with a supportive and understanding network of people. Leslie, a volunteer with SIPAZ in Chiapas, Mexico, commented that one of the things she liked most was the "communal aspect of the experience."

Living with local housemates is another living option. You can learn a great deal from having daily informal interactions with local housemates and their friends. Some volunteers set up their own housing arrangement in apartments that offer them the privacy or independence that they may be used to at home.

Think about how you would like to balance your desires for cultural integration, privacy, and community.

Special Needs and Considerations

There is a wide range of special needs and considerations that may arise for prospective volunteers. By first asking yourself to identify what your needs or concerns are, you will be prepared to ask organizations direct, specific, and meaningful questions. (See the Index of Profiled Organizations to identify organizations that match your special needs.)

High-School Students and Youth

A summer group program is the predominant model for student and youth programs. In choosing among the programs for young people you might want to pay particular attention to the amount of support and training provided by the organization. You may be interested in whether or not young people are included in decision-making components of the program and are able to develop their leadership skills through participation. Another common issue for young people is whether the program satisfies service requirements for high school graduation, and whether time spent abroad can also earn them credit in their language studies. Some programs are open to participation by children and youth who are accompanied by an adult.

Couples and Families

Couples interested in volunteering abroad should find out if there are volunteer positions for only one of them or for both of them. Would they be working on a single project together or on totally different projects? Do they have to be married to be treated as a couple? Some programs do accept volunteers with children, though most of these programs have age restrictions for the children. Volunteers should also inquire about health services and educational opportunities, or any additional benefits for their children.

Seniors and Retirees

International volunteer programs that focus specifically on opportunities for older people are growing steadily. Established international educational groups for seniors, such as Elderhostel, offer an increasing number of international trips with service components. Finding out the age composition of a volunteer group can help you figure out where you might feel comfortable in the age spectrum. If you volunteer for a program not specifically designed for seniors, find out about the age distribution among volunteers by asking about both the age range of the group as well as the age of the typical volunteer. In the profiles of volunteer organizations we include in this book we provide that information. We met a number of older Peace Corps volunteers who missed having more people their age in the program. You may also want to inquire about the accessibility of health services as well as the level of physical exertion required for any given program.

People with Disabilities

While access is expanding, international volunteer programs have a lot of work to do to integrate people with disabilities into their programs. The best resource for people with disabilities is Mobility International (www.miusa.org, 541-343-1284, v/tty). Mobility International provides the opportunity for people with disabilities to participate in overseas delegations that focus on disability and access issues. It also provides organizations with support in the form of consultations, resources, and technical training. Ask the staff of the organization you are interested in working with if it provides work for volunteers with disabilities. If it does not, suggest that the staff get in touch with Mobility International.

Women and Men: Gender Issues in International Volunteering

Gender roles and relations are a constant source of discussion, reflection, challenge, and learning for international volunteers. International volunteers are more often women than men. You may want to know the gender composition of a sending organization's staff and specifically if women are represented in leadership roles within the organization. You may also want to request to speak with past volunteers of your gender to find out what it was like for them as women or men in dealing with the placement organization as well as living and working overseas. Both male and female volunteers should try to get as much information as possible about gender relations in the country where they are considering volunteering. (See Chapter 9, "How to Be an Effective International Volunteer.")

People of Color: Ethnicity in International Volunteering

The field of international volunteering has a long way to go until it becomes representative of the diversity of our planet, or even of North America. As a potential volunteer, you may be interested in how the organization addresses issues of race in international volunteering, and you may want to know more about the ethnic composition of its volunteers. A number of volunteers of color whom we interviewed suggested that prospective volunteers from non-European backgrounds ask the organization for contact information of alumni who come from similar ethnic backgrounds.

Specifically, you may want to get these alumni's impressions on how sensitive the organization was to issues that they faced and whether there were particular challenges or opportunities that they found as people of color during their time abroad. Don't assume that if you look the same as the local people where you volunteer that race and ethnicity will not be relevant. One returned volunteer, for example, told us that African Americans should not expect to be immediately embraced as brothers or sisters in Africa; your reception will depend on many factors including whether the local community has met African Americans before, your style of dress, your behavior, and even the color of your skin.

Gay/Lesbian/Bisexual/Transgender: Sexual Identity Issues in International Volunteering

We met gay/lesbian/bisexual/transgender (GLBT) volunteers in a range of countries. You may wish to ask the volunteer placement organization if it has had openly GLBT volunteers in the past. Ask to speak with alumni from GLBT backgrounds who can share their experiences both with the organization and with living overseas. Find out if you will be able to be "out" to your host family or local colleagues during your service overseas. Be aware that a "no" answer may merely be an honest assessment based on concern for your safety and might not indicate that the placement organization is homophobic. If an organizational profile in the Index of Profiled Organizations indicates that unmarried couples are accepted, same-sex couples are included unless otherwise noted.

Your Interests and Special Needs

Having read about the key factors to consider while choosing an international volunteer program, we suggest that you complete Worksheet II: Assessing Your Interests and Special Needs. After responding to these questions, place an asterisk next to the answers that are most important to you. In addition, you may want to prioritize your interests and special needs. That way you can refer to this list as you begin to narrow down your choices of organizations.

ASSESSING YOUR INTERESTS AND SPECIAL NEEDS

Where do you want to volunteer (in which country or region)?

Are you interested in an urban or a rural placement?

For how long do you want to volunteer?

What type of work do you want to do (e.g., educational, environmental, human rights)?

Do you want to work with a governmental or a non-governmental organization?

_____

_____

_____

_____

_____

_____

Would you prefer a religious or a secular organization?

_____

_____

_____

_____

What type of organization would you like to volunteer with (e.g., helping people directly, teaching or training, social change and advocacy)?

_____

_____

_____

_____

Are you willing to pay to volunteer? What is the maximum amount you are willing to spend? (See Chapter 7, "Overcoming Financial Obstacles," before you rule out paying.)

_____

_____

_____

_____

_____

_____

What is your preferred living/housing situation?

_____

_____

_____

_____

Do you have any special needs or concerns as a volunteer (e.g., serving together with a spouse or dependent children, a medical condition, etc.)?

_____

_____

_____

_____

_____

_____

Other Considerations

Daily Work Life

Another way to compare different international volunteer opportunities is to think about your daily work life abroad. Your typical day may include sleeping until ten, reporting to a health center at eleven, working until seven, then staying out late with local friends. You may rise before dawn to spend a hot, sweaty, long day counting bugs with a team of rain forest scientists. Or you may work nine to five in an office and spend the evening cooking, eating, talking, and praying with the staff and fellow volunteers of your placement organization.

You may be surprised to find that, contrary to certain romantic images (and some volunteer organizations' promotional materials) that show volunteers surrounded by loving children or bushwhacking through the jungle, many volunteers actually work in offices. These volunteers find that office work is the area in which they are needed and have tangible skills to contribute. What do you envision as your work environment? What type of tasks would you like to be doing on a day-to-day basis? Perhaps you are willing to do almost anything, but these are important questions to ask yourself if you want to increase your chances of finding an international volunteer program that fits in with your dream.

Staff Support in the Field

Organizations vary in terms of the amount of support they provide to volunteers in the field. Some have dedicated full-time staff, while others have a more informal network of unpaid advisors and collaborating organizations. Do you want an organization with in-country staff or project leaders from home? Or would you prefer an organization that plays the role of simply connecting you directly to a local organization overseas?

Team vs. Individual Volunteering

If you are volunteering by yourself in a community, you'll probably find cultural integration and language acquisition to be easier, but there may be moments of extreme loneliness. Solo volunteers can find that the highs are higher and the lows are lower, compared to volunteering with a group.

Many volunteers find that working with a team of international volunteers offers great benefits: the chance to experience culture shock together instead of in isolation, relief from the stress of communicating in a foreign language, and the joys of team spirit. However, if the team leader is not effective, groups can break down and members can become openly hostile. Also, team spirit can be draining if it means countless meetings. So if you're the kind of person that hates sitting in a circle "processing" everything, you probably should avoid team volunteer programs.

Digging Deeper: Examining the Values and Philosophies of International Service

> *Volunteers should examine the development philosophy of their placement organization. This requires them to think for themselves about their own philosophy of development.*—Larry Groff, Mennonite Central Committee, Cambodia

One way to identify the volunteer organization that is right for you is to try and match your own personal approach to development with those of the organization. It's not always easy to discern the philosophy of an organization, and the buzzwords in mission statements can be a little numbing. Moreover, it's likely that your own ideas about development are still forming. Perhaps Chapter 3, "The Big Picture," has given you some initial ideas. Answering the following should help you continue to formulate your ideas: What does development mean to you? What do you see as your role in promoting this kind of development?

We realize that volunteer placement organizations' staff members are often very busy, but we nevertheless encourage you to ask them a lot of questions. As Jen Sauber, a volunteer with Global Service Corps in Costa Rica, put it, "Don't think you're a pain. Try to grasp what the situation there is really like by asking lots of questions. Then make an educated decision." The following questions may not be questions that staff field every day, so be patient and willing to wait for someone to respond to your specific questions and concerns.

WORKSHEET III

QUESTIONS TO ILLUMINATE AN ORGANIZATION'S PHILOSOPHY OF DEVELOPMENT

Do volunteers work on projects of the international volunteer organization, or are they placed with local organizations? For volunteers that are placed with local institutions, what type of groups are they placed with?

_____

How does the organization define development?

_____

Is the organization's field staff, if any, native or foreign-born?

_____

Whose idea was the project, and who requested volunteers to work on the project?

_____

What are the roles of volunteers and other outsiders?

_____

_____

How are local people or the intended beneficiaries involved in the project?

_____

What are the financial relationships between the international volunteer program and locals? Does a portion of the volunteer's program fee go to local organizations or people?

_____

_____

Beyond Your Service Overseas

Does the program have a structured post-service component or support for individualized post-service projects? Chapter 10, "Staying Involved after You Get Back," discusses the issues involved in re-entry and staying involved. Many people find that, while they intend to follow up on their experience overseas, the process of re-entry overwhelms them and their intentions to follow up are lost in the shuffle. Structured follow-up programs can assist volunteers in readjusting to life at home, integrating their experiences abroad into their daily life at home, continuing to reflect on what they learned, and staying connected with people with whom they built relationships while overseas. Some follow-up programs give volunteers a chance to support the organizations they worked with and to address the root causes of the injustices they witnessed overseas. In addition to the structured follow-up time, find out what services and activities a program offers for its alumni.

Before You Sign on the Dotted Line

Even if you have selected an organization that would let you volunteer in the country of your dreams doing the work you've always wanted to do, don't sign up until you have spoken with some past participants. Get contact information of past alumni from a program staff member and ask real live people about their experiences. If an organization won't share this information with you, that should be a red flag. Every program is going to have its fans and its critics, but it is essential to talk to alumni to get the straight story on the program. Find out what advice they have for you as a prospective volunteer. Ask them hard questions about the ups and downs of volunteering with the organization. When you get in touch with alumni, who will most likely be the satisfied customers since they were referred by the organization, ask them for the telephone numbers or e-mail addresses of other volunteers who may have had different types of experiences.

Do the Right Thing

As you contemplate all of the various aspects of selecting a volunteer program, remember that you are at a crossroads, ready to consider both what the world has to offer you and what you have to offer to the world.

Since no volunteer program will be perfect for you, we recommend you prioritize those characteristics that are most important to you. It is important to realize that there is always room for improvement in the field of international volunteering. If you do not want to wait for the field (or even one particular program) to change its approaches to match your ideal, then ask yourself: What things do I think are essential for an organization to provide and what things might I be capable of providing for myself?

Remember that, ultimately, your experience as an international volunteer will be your own responsibility. So choose wisely. Most programs are vehicles for service. It is up to you to create meaning out of the service itself.

After considering the various factors that differentiate volunteer programs, you will face an exciting and important decision. Then, after selecting the program that you believe is right for you, you will have a chance to turn your attention to other important factors that define the international volunteer experience. The way you prepare yourself, interact with people while you are overseas, and incorporate your experiences into your life when you return home, will all build upon your decision to choose the volunteer placement organization that is right for you.

Action Steps for Choosing an Organization

1. ***Assess Your Interests.*** Consider the major issues in choosing a program like where and for how long you volunteer, the type of work you do and the type of organization that you work with, your living situation, and the costs and benefits. Complete the questionnaire in this chapter.

2. ***Think about Your Special Needs and Aspirations.*** Consider the various components of your identity like age, ability, race, and sexual orientation and identify the factors that are most important to you. Also think about your vision of volunteering. How much staff support do you need? What are you looking for in your daily work environment? Do you want to volunteer alone or in a group?

3. ***Examine Your Approach to International Service.*** Think philosophically about different approaches to volunteering and your role as a volunteer. Try journaling about these issues.

4. ***Read Chapter 5, "The Ideal Volunteer Organization."*** Think about which qualities are most important to you.

5. ***Refer to the Index of Organizations.*** For example, if your goal is to work in Africa for a year or more in the educational field, see the Index of Profiled Organizations and create your own list of groups that have all or most of the characteristics that you are looking for.

6. ***Read the Profiles.*** The profile section of this book will give you the "flavor" of your top organizational choices. You may want to rate each organization on a one-to-ten scale in terms of how closely it matches the type of opportunity you seek.

7. ***Narrow Your List.*** Figure out the top two to four organizations. If you don't find any groups that meet all your specifications, you may want to broaden your search by choosing one or two primary factors to judge organizations. You may also want to read Chapter 6, "Doing It without a Program," as well as check the websites of organizations in Bonus Section B, "Additional Volunteer Organizations Not Profiled."

8.   ***Gather Preliminary Information.*** Check the web or call the organizations to verify that the organizations still operate in the country where you want to go, and note any changes in fees or programs.

9.   ***Create a List of Questions.*** Based on any concerns you have from the profiles, the questions we suggest in this chapter, your personal values and special needs, and the preliminary information that you receive from the organization, create a list of questions for the organization's staff and alumni.

10. ***Contact the Organization to Ask Your Questions.*** These days, e-mail may be the best way to communicate. Ask your questions and request contact information for program alumni as well as information regarding the application process.

11. ***Contact Alumni.*** Ask them hard questions about their experiences and try to get contact information for people whom they volunteered with who might be more critical of the program than they are.

12. ***Choose.*** Select the organization that most closely matches your interests and aspirations and begin the application process.

13. ***Get It in Writing.*** No matter how nice the organization's representatives you talk to are, get a written document explaining fees, benefits, insurance issues, and refund policies.

CHAPTER 5

THE IDEAL VOLUNTEER ORGANIZATION AND THE STATE OF THE FIELD

Over the course of our research, we came up with certain standards that we agreed would characterize an ideal volunteer placement organization. Keep in mind that a volunteer's experience of a volunteer placement organization greatly depends, in the final analysis, on the volunteer. A volunteer program may delight one person because it offers challenging work and a supportive team environment, but it may frustrate and disappoint another person because it does not offer full cultural immersion or quality language instruction.

While it is instructive to compile the hallmarks of the ideal international volunteer organization, no single organization can meet all of the standards. None of the organizations we researched possess all of these qualities, and many high quality programs only posses a fraction of them. We therefore encourage you to review the following list and think about which qualities are most important to you.

The Ideal Volunteer Placement Organization

1. **Is honest about expenses, activities, and challenges in its promotional materials.**

2. **Provides potential volunteers with names and contact information for previous volunteers.**

3. **Makes an effort to recruit a wide range of volunteers, diverse in their ethnicity, class, religious belief, age, and physical ability.**

4. **Recruits highly skilled volunteers.**

5. **Does not accept all prospective volunteers but screens for maturity and psychological health.**

6. **Assists volunteers with fundraising as needed.**

7. Is transparent about the use of program fees.

8. Provides fair, prorated rebates to volunteers who drop out.

9. Provides orientation materials and preparation suggestions to volunteers well before they leave home (including, for example, information on culturally appropriate clothes to pack).

10. Encourages critical thinking about development and the role of volunteers before departure overseas.

11. Provides extensive orientation to region, country, community, and customs for volunteers on or before arrival in-country.

12. Includes a home-stay during the first weeks in-country to help volunteers "imprint" with a local family and have a home base within the community.

13. Includes professional language training if needed.

14. Has staff with long-term connections and commitment in the community.

15. Places volunteers, whenever possible, with indigenous organizations rather than initiating its own projects.

16. Incorporates a sustainable development perspective into its work (see Chapter 3, "The Big Picture.")

17. Offers a volunteer period of substantial length.

18. Supports local hosts with financial resources as well as human resources.

19. Engages volunteers in critical reflection of their experiences through discussion, journal writing, and other reflection exercises.

20. Encourages volunteers to experience the cultural wealth of the host country.

21. Provides opportunities for volunteers to learn about the root causes of poverty and oppression.

22. Provides formal opportunities for written and oral evaluation of the placement organization and uses this feedback in ongoing program development and innovation.

23. Helps volunteers document their experiences for sharing back home.

24. Creates opportunities for volunteers to make parting "group" gifts that will benefit the community and not just individuals.

25. Has a concrete support structure (retreat, workshop, or residential program) to help volunteers adjust to the challenges of returning home.

26. Provides formal opportunities for volunteers to share their experiences upon return.

27. Helps volunteers remain connected with, and supportive of, the people and organizations they worked with overseas.

28. Provides support for returned volunteers who want to get involved in addressing the root causes of underdevelopment and/or bring the new knowledge from their international experiences to address local problems of injustice.

29. Provides support for an alumni network so volunteers can stay in touch with each other and the organization.

30. Involves alumni in fundraising, recruitment, and training of new volunteers.

As mentioned above, none of the organizations we researched meets all of these standards; most meet less than half. To make sense of the list and find the program that is best for you, we encourage you to circle the points that are most important to you.

International Volunteering: State of the Field

Just as international volunteering takes place in the larger context of history, individual international volunteer programs function in the context of the larger field of international exchange. Our research gave us a unique opportunity to assess the overall state of the field of international volunteering, and our conversations with volunteers and staff gave us a window on the things most organizations do well, and things most do poorly.

Most organizations do the following things well:

Placing Volunteers with Local NGOs

The majority of volunteer placement organizations recognize that it is essential to place volunteers with local NGOs and to ensure that their volunteers are supporting ongoing local efforts to improve communities.

Collaboration

The International Volunteer Programs Association (IVPA) was founded in 1998 to promote collaboration among international volunteer programs, pool resources, and share best practices. The initial response has been encouraging and the more than fifty members have been quick to set aside competition and realize the benefits of cooperation, a trend we hope will continue in years to come.

Increasing Visibility

International volunteer programs have received increasing visibility both in the print media and public television as well as on university campuses, especially among staff members working with international centers and education abroad programs.

Using the Internet and Other Media

Many organizations are becoming sophisticated in the use of the Internet to promote overseas volunteer opportunities, decrease the delay time in volunteer placements, and improve the amount and quality of information available to potential volunteers including directly linking them to alumni and volunteer coordinators overseas.

We also found areas where the majority of organizations fell short:

Limited Volunteer Screenings

Except for groups that pay volunteers, most organizations have a weak screening process for volunteers. Most seem to accept almost anyone who can pay. This lack of screening can cause problems for the host community and other volunteers. One person who is mentally unstable, culturally insensitive, or simply immature can wreak havoc on group dynamics and begin to unravel efforts to create positive cross-cultural experiences as well as harm the organizations that the volunteer program is supposed to support.

Insufficient Training

A surprising number of volunteer placement organizations do not provide adequate training for their volunteers. Very few offer thorough language training. Some groups expect volunteers with no previous knowledge of HIV or sexual health, for example, to become AIDS educators; others place volunteers with no previous agricultural experience in positions where they are supposed to train lifelong farmers; some even ask young women with no parental experience to train women as mothers. Many organizations could vastly improve the quality of their work if they provided training materials for volunteers before they leave home and more extensive in-country training.

Limited Critical Reflection on Root Causes of Underdevelopment

Virtually all international volunteer organizations claim to address some of the problems of underdevelopment: poverty, malnutrition, lack of health care, or lack of education. Almost none, however, promote critical analysis of the causes of underdevelopment or examine the systems that are at the root of underdevelopment. This lack of reflection means that many volunteers never gain exposure to ideas about going beyond Band-Aid approaches to solving global problems. The net result is that volunteers may feel self-congratulatory on the work they do—or frustrated and powerless—but they never make connections to the variety of ways they can support institutional change and long-term, sustainable solutions.

Lack of Support for Post-Service Activities

Returning home can be very traumatic. Yet many organizations do not provide any support for volunteers after they return home. Nor do they coach returned volunteers on ways they can share their experiences with their home communities. Very few groups help volunteers find ways they can support sustainable development and human rights after they return home. (Joining the Returned Overseas Volunteers (ROVE) is one good way to compensate for the lack of support from placement organizations. See page 471 for more information.)

Lack of Evaluation

Few volunteer placement organizations evaluate the overall progress of their development projects or the work of individual volunteers. This severely limits opportunities for improving the projects in terms of the benefits for local people or helping volunteers learn from their mistakes.

Limited Diversity

The vast majority of U.S. volunteers are young, white, middle class, and from the north or coasts of the United States. This demographic reality means that not only do people overseas fail to learn about the diversity of the United States, but the rich experiences and ideas from overseas are only brought back into a limited set of communities.

Improving the Field

It is our hope that this book can be part of the process of improving the field of international volunteering by presenting honest evaluations of volunteer placement organizations. We also hope to help you become part of the solution by choosing an appropriate organization, becoming an effective volunteer, and, most important, staying involved after you get back.

CHAPTER 6

DOING IT WITHOUT A PROGRAM

If you set up your own volunteer experience, you must be persistent. Many people show a superficial interest in volunteering. You have to prove that you are serious.
—Eric Stern, volunteer, American Jewish World Service, Kenya

Many prospective volunteers find themselves a little discouraged or frustrated after examining various volunteer placement organizations. Some suffer from sticker shock and others just can't find their ideal program. In response to this frustration, quite a few people consider arranging their own volunteer placement. While volunteering independently may appeal to you, you should be aware that it's not as easy as it might sound. Even the most hands-off organized programs provide vital support and contacts for their volunteers. Independent volunteers, on the other hand, assume total responsibility for their own experience. You may think that you don't need an organization to help you become an international volunteer—and you may not—but keep in mind that coordinating your own placement overseas entails a lot of hard work.

Before reading further in this chapter, we suggest that you ask yourself a few questions to determine if you are a strong candidate for creating your own overseas volunteer experience:

> **Does travel excite you more than it scares you?**
> **Are you comfortable when you don't have a precise plan?**
> **Are you good at reaching out to people and building personal relationships?**
> **Do you consider yourself to be a person with considerable life experiences or skills that would be relevant to people and organizations overseas?**

If you answered yes to most or all of these questions, then you may be a good candidate for creating your own overseas volunteer experience. Even more than volunteers who join existing programs, independent volunteers must be confident (but not cocky), self-reliant, and comfortable with uncertainty. They must also be patient (yet persistent), sensitive to cross-cultural issues, and able to build personal relationships and their own support network.

People who are well equipped to volunteer on their own also tend to have specific assets or experiences that contribute to successful volunteering, such as extensive foreign travel experience and competency in a foreign language. Independent volunteers also often have contacts or a local support network in the country where they are volunteering, as well as work experience and skills that are relevant overseas.

This is not to say that an independent volunteer has to be superhuman. Rather, independent volunteers need to be ready to face the challenges that all international volunteers face—and face them on their own.

Even if you are a strong candidate and would probably be able to pull it off, what will creating your own volunteer placement mean in terms of the quality of the experience for everyone involved? Would your effort have been better spent learning a language or fundraising to participate in an organized program, or is there something unique that you can gain or give by organizing your own overseas placement?

THE PROS OF VOLUNTEERING INDEPENDENTLY

- You often are able to immerse yourself in the local culture and experience more quickly and completely than volunteers who go with formal volunteer programs.

- You can combine extensive travel and exploration of another culture with volunteer work, and you can and balance the two according to your personal preferences.

- You may be able to do work with local organizations that are more explicitly political or progressive, work that many international volunteer programs avoid.

- You don't have to worry about what the volunteer who preceded you did or did not do.

- You have a better opportunity to tailor your experience more precisely to fit your own skills, values, interests, and learning objectives.

THE CONS OF VOLUNTEERING INDEPENDENTLY

- It's a lot of work to organize, and there are no guarantees.
- You may feel isolated. Even the strongest and most independent volunteers often long for the companionship and understanding of other volunteers.
- It's much easier to have misunderstandings with hosts. You will not have the support of program staff, who are often people with strong language skills and working relationships with the host organization that have developed over years.
- You won't have the opportunity to learn from the trials and errors of the volunteers who have come before you on a program.
- You won't have someone in the country trained and responsible for helping you when you are sick or having serious problems.
- You may never make a serious commitment to volunteering, especially if you are trying to combine travel and volunteering. (Do you want to be a traveler or a volunteer? Can you do both?)
- You may harm or let down the organization hosting you if your volunteer stint doesn't work out. (Is anyone holding you accountable for your commitments? Can you hold yourself accountable?)

Usually, volunteers who work with programs appreciate the support they receive, while independent volunteers typically relish the flexibility of the independent route.

Arthur Silver with Project Concern suggested that "Going with a program is far better than having to deal with foreign governments or organizations without sponsorship. Having a sponsoring organization can make life much less complicated by clarifying living conditions and other issues before the fact."

On the other hand, an independent volunteer we met in Ecuador found that "Going on your own really lets you tailor your experience. It allows you to be passionate about what you are doing and doesn't burden you with the history, bureaucracy, or agenda of a North American organization."

Laura Parsons liked volunteering independently so much that she did it twice. She told us, "I arranged to volunteer in Nicaragua and India independently and both worked out very well. The freedom fit my style. Going without a placement organization meant that my relationship with my supervisors was a direct one and what they said was all I had to concern myself with. The rest was up to me."

While we hesitate to recommend this option to most people, we discovered in our research that for some people arranging an independent volunteer experience is an excellent choice.

Getting Organized to Volunteer Independently

There are two variations on arranging your stint as an independent volunteer. Some pursue the make-it-happen-once-you-are-there option, in which you arrange your volunteer work while you are overseas. Others use the organize-it-before-you-go approach, doing more advance work on researching and contacting organizations, and making specific arrangements with a particular organization abroad before departing.

Regardless of your approach, as an independent international volunteer you will be responsible for preparing for service—making travel arrangements, packing, securing visas, financial planning, health preparations, language study, and cross-cultural awareness preparation. You will also be responsible for earning or raising the funds to pay for travel, insurance, room, and board while overseas. You will face the additional demands of meeting your own housing, health, nutritional, and social needs, as well as adjusting to a new culture, a new work environment, and possibly a new language, not to mention determining your role within an organization. In order to handle all of these responsibilities it is essential to get organized. And organizing any independent international volunteer experience begins with connecting with overseas organizations.

Assessing Your Personal Network

There are many questions that you can ask yourself when considering the independent route to international volunteering and beginning to reach out to potential hosts. A quick survey of your personal network and experience can give you some valuable perspective on where you stand with regard to putting all the pieces together. One of the most complicated parts of being an independent volunteer is arranging for your actual volunteer placement overseas. Ask yourself the questions in Worksheet IV: Assessing Your Personal Network as a first step toward arranging a placement. You should also review the worksheets in Chapter 4, "Choosing an Organization."

ASSESSING YOUR PERSONAL NETWORK

Do you know any people or institutions overseas that could help you find a place to volunteer?

_____

_____

_____

_____

_____

Do you have any friends, or friends of friends, who have volunteered or worked overseas? Do they have any direct contacts with potential host organizations abroad?

_____

_____

_____

_____

_____

Perhaps you have volunteered locally with a solidarity or international development organization. Do these organizations have partner organizations overseas that might be interested in hosting a volunteer?

_____

_____

_____

_____

_____

Are you a member of a church or other religious organizations that have links with people or projects abroad?

_____

_____

_____

_____

_____

_____

Do you know the issue area in which you would like to work? Are there any local organizations working on these issues that have international connections?

_____

_____

_____

_____

_____

_____

Making Connections: "Networking" Is Not a Dirty Word

Once you have assessed your network it is time to start doing the networking. Being an independent volunteer means following up on all the leads that you can identify and developing additional leads where none yet exist. Use techniques you might employ in a job search, such as conducting informational interviews or attending events where you can meet people who share your interest in international issues. Even if it isn't clear how the meeting or event will lead to a volunteer opportunity, always try to make connections and open the doors of possibility. Leave each informational interview with at least two additional leads and each event with information about the next event.

Be careful not to overlook associations; they are a proven way to gain access to a range of international volunteer possibilities. Associations of non-governmental organizations (NGOs) both within and outside the United States are generally organized according to the particular issues they focus on. You may be able to locate an association that serves as an umbrella organization for a number of U.S.-based NGOs. The Society for International Development (www.sidint.org) has working groups for individuals involved in health, the environment, and other fields. InterAction's website (www.interaction.org) lists dozens of international development organizations. Given the dramatic increase in computer literacy around the world, you can discover vast networks of organizations from the comfort of your own home. As technology expands and becomes more accessible, you can expect a dramatic increase in the number of listings of volunteer opportunities on the Internet.

While you may get lucky and find a great option on the Internet, the tried-and-true method is to start your search with your own personal network. Zhara Langford succeeded in arranging a volunteer post in Zimbabwe by following a lead from a friend. Zhara mentioned to her friend that she wanted to volunteer abroad. Her friend told her about a Zimbabwean youth organization he learned of at a public event. Zhara communicated with the organization through a combination of phone calls, letters, and e-mail and discovered that the organization was willing to host her as a volunteer and had some projects that interested her.

Laura Parsons told us that she spoke to anybody and everybody about her hope to volunteer independently overseas. "You would be surprised at who might have a connection to an organization that could host you," she said. "I would have never thought that this guy at a place where I did volunteer yardwork would lead me to my volunteer placement in Nicaragua. But that's what happened."

Another successful networking strategy is to specifically seek out returned volunteers or people who have lived abroad and ask them for contacts to organizations overseas. Take out an advertisement in your local paper to find returned volunteers or check in with a local cultural center to meet people from overseas who are living in your community. Yet another option is to volunteer with an organization in the United States that is working on international issues and has relationships with groups abroad.

Whatever networking strategy you employ, be persistent and keep track of any leads. We recommend keeping all your notes in one notebook—not on little scraps of paper— and writing your phone number prominently on the notebook in case you misplace it.

Arranging the Placement Before You Go

Once you have discovered an organization with which you might volunteer, you have to reach out and communicate with the group. Avoid putting all of your eggs in one basket. While you may think that you have found the perfect group, we recommend that you communicate with several organizations before you depart so that you have more than one option. Aim for a goal, for example, of sending out ten letters or e-mails, receiving four responses, and finding at least one or two that seem to match your interests.

When you mail or e-mail an organization don't assume that they will be interested in hosting you as a volunteer. Make sure you include the following information:

- *Why you are interested in volunteering, and especially what interests you in the organization you are contacting.*

- *Your relevant work experience and skills.*

- *The approximate dates that you will be available.*

- *The estimated number of hours per week you will be available.*

- *All your contact information, including phone number, fax number, e-mail address, and mailing address.*

Part of your responsibility as an independent volunteer is not only to find a host organization but also to evaluate the organization, and determine whether it would be an appropriate place to volunteer. As you try to learn more about a potential host organization, consider asking questions such as:

- *Have you hosted volunteers in the past? If so, what type of work did they do?*

- *Will you provide contact information for previous volunteers?*

- *What skills would be most useful for a volunteer to contribute to your organization?*

- *Can your organization provide help in finding low-cost or donated housing?*

- *What are your organization's hours of operation?*

Davis Broach sent out detailed letters to thirty Central Asian embassies and organizations. He heard back from two places. The Uzbek embassy urged him to pay to come and study the Uzbek language. Davis, however, could not afford the language program. Someone from the Kyrgyz embassy in Washington wrote him back a detailed letter with contact information for the International University of Kyrgyzstan. He wrote to the Director of Educational and Cultural Affairs at the University, and she invited him to come to teach English. Davis bought his ticket to Kyrgyzstan, but the letter of support he needed for his visa never came through.

Finally the people in the embassy in Washington took pity on me and gave me a visa, even though I did not have the letter of support. I flew to Kyrgyzstan, and nobody was there to pick me up at the airport. I figured out how to go downtown, and then found a newspaper. I used my knowledge of Polish and the Cyrillic alphabet to figure out which ads in the newspaper were for apartments, and somehow I found an apartment by evening. The next day I found out where the university was located. When I got to campus, I wandered around until someone directed me to the office of foreign affairs. When I walked in the door, the Director of Educational and Cultural Affairs looked up at me and said with great surprise, "Davis!" I ended up working in the Development Planning Office as well as teaching English. I earned a salary equivalent to the local salary and was able to get by, living simply and shopping where the local people shopped in the bazaar.

Davis had a fantastic experience in Kyrgyzstan through a combination of chutz-pah and luck. Even this success story, however, demonstrates that just because you think you have set up everything in advance, things still may not go according to plan. You may arrive and find that the person you communicated with has left the city or the country, and that no one is expecting you. The school in which you were planning to teach may no longer have any students. The organization you contacted may suddenly be in crisis and unable to accommodate you. Therefore, once you arrive, you should al-ways be mentally and financially prepared for dramatic changes—that is, prepared for the worst-case scenario. The next section might help you create a plan B, should your initial plans fall through.

Making It Happen Once You Are There

> Everyone told me that I wouldn't have trouble finding volunteer opportunities once I arrived in-country. I thought to myself, "What? Me not plan until I am already there?" But they turned out to be right.—Michelle Bloomberg, volunteer, Amigos Del Hogar, Bolivia

Yes, it's true, you can make it happen once you arrive overseas. Don't be foolish, however, and fail to prepare yourself at all. Even if you have not organized all the de-tails before you go abroad, we strongly recommend that you do some research and net-working before arriving in a foreign country. As a volunteer we met in Cambodia advised, "Have at least one idea, a place to start your search." This can be as simple as a phone number—and a physical address in case the phone number doesn't work—for an organization that has hosted volunteers before, or a place where volunteers congre-gate. Even if you are a go-with-the-flow type of person, having at least one lead can help you to arrive on the tarmac in a foreign land feeling confident, knowing that at least you have an idea of where to start looking for volunteer work.

We also met quite a few people who, after backpacking around and enjoying the freedom, spontaneity, and adventure of traveling, began to look into some options for volunteering. Whether following the advice of their travel guide, networking with other foreigners, asking locals for advice, or just staying open to what they stumbled upon, they were actually able to arrange a volunteer placement after arriving overseas.

It is hard to predict how long it will take to find a volunteer position once you are in-country. One lead, an outgoing attitude, and a little luck might be all it takes to get you started. The address of a friend in Hanoi was all that one volunteer needed to meet dozens of NGOs working throughout Vietnam. But not everyone is so lucky, and not everyone is in a hurry to find a placement. After traveling and studying Spanish for al-most three months, Elizabeth Beak spent over two months looking for volunteer op-portunities in Ecuador as she continued to travel. She called numerous organizations, hung out at language schools, and visited several projects before she happened upon a women's cooperative that was located next to a tourist café. She heard some beautiful music, wandered in, and ended up volunteering there for about five months. "I went at my own pace," she told us. "That was how I felt comfortable and that is why it took me so long to find the right place to volunteer."

Some people go abroad with travel or education in mind only to end up changing their plans or extending their stay to pursue other options. DeAnna Blair was registered in a study abroad program in Ghana, but when she realized that it was not going to be satisfactory, she withdrew from the program and set off for the capital. In Accra, DeAnna explained, "I knocked on doors and talked to anyone and everyone as I looked for volunteer work in exchange for housing." Eventually she found what she was looking for. She volunteered at a school and village health clinic and lived for four months with a local nurse.

VOLUNTEERING ON HER OWN

Meghan Gombos made up her mind to go to Costa Rica for three months to travel, learn Spanish, and do some eco-volunteering. She was surprised to learn that most programs required a program fee, and she could not find a program that matched her interests, so she decided to do it on her own, and booked a ticket to the Costa Rican capital, San José.

Meghan admits that "It was very exhausting in the beginning not knowing anything or anyone." But this did not prevent her from working toward her goal. "I immediately signed up at a Spanish school to improve my language skills and to meet people. I found the school in the phone book at the hotel, and I was in school and a home-stay by the second day."

Meghan was also able to contact the friend of a friend who was volunteering with the Peace Corps in Costa Rica. By chance, they passed a tourist fair where they met someone who told them about the National Park Service. Meghan found out that, for a small fee, the park service offered trail maintenance work along with room and board. "I showed them my resume and explained that I had studied island conservation in Baja California and that I really wanted to be placed in the Cocos Islands. I got the run around for about a month, but with persistence they finally assigned me to go out there."

In summing up her volunteer adventure in Costa Rica, Meghan reflected, "It took courage, patience, and persistence to get to do the things I did. It can be very intimidating to get off a plane and not have a clue as to what your next move is, especially when you can't speak the language that well. And to find an internship you have to actively look and talk to many people about your interests as well as be patient when things aren't happening. I considered it like a job search, but I made sure to enjoy that time while I was searching by traveling and meeting new people."

Many independent volunteers, especially in Latin America, start off with language study, and then do a little volunteer work in the town or area where they are studying and living. Many language schools now run their own volunteer projects or refer students to local volunteer opportunities. Students might start with a single-day project sponsored by the school and decide to continue volunteering on a regular basis, while building their language skills. Students can take advantage of these low-risk volunteer opportunities to try out different projects. After exploring what interests them, students can use their new connections to strike out on their own and arrange a medium- or long-term volunteer position. (See section on language schools in Alternatives to Volunteering Overseas.)

In some countries there are well-known organizations that are accustomed to placing independent international volunteers. In India, the Sisters of Mercy in Calcutta are world famous for their work and the attention garnered by Mother Theresa. Many volunteers come to Calcutta from around the world, and check themselves into a cheap hotel on Ida Scudder Street when they arrive. There they are able to meet other volunteers and become part of an informal community of folks who have decided to hang up their backpacks for a while and try their hand at volunteering.

In Cambodia in the late 1990s, there was a rapid and massive influx of international resources, and many international organizations had a great need for English and French speakers. A prospective volunteer could start by visiting the offices of various organizations or spending time at restaurants and cafés frequented by foreigners. A volunteer could easily get in contact with hundreds of organizations working in and around the capital by contacting a local umbrella organization for NGOs, the Cooperation Committee for Cambodia.

Lessening the Burden on Your Local International Hosts

We prefer interns to come within a structured program. We've actually had quite a few who haven't been part of any program as such, and we've found that those are not the desirable ones. Those who come as part of a program tend to work harder and have better qualities, and they are accountable to some other structure back in their homes.—Ranjit Purshotam and Mahendra Thetty, Legal Resources Center, Durban, South Africa

Imagine that a foreign visitor arrives at your organization's doorstep and says that he wants to help out. He is very enthusiastic, but speaks almost no English. In addition, he doesn't have a place to stay and doesn't know anyone in your city. In fact, it is clear that he also needs help getting around and taking care of basic errands. Does this sound absurd? Will he really be able to help, or will he be a drain on your organization's resources?

THE TRAVELING VOLUNTEER

In 1997, Jered Lawson left his work as an advocate for community-supported agriculture to travel the world and find a way to make a difference. He knew that a structured program was not right for him, but he was also realistic and felt that "In order to really learn and make a meaningful contribution, I couldn't just keep moving all the time. I'd have to settle down at some point."

Before leaving the United States, Jered researched several international networks of people and organizations working on agricultural issues. By the time he left the United States for Asia, Jered had contacts in half-a-dozen countries, a plan for the first several weeks, and an open-ended plane ticket.

Jered's combination of traveling and volunteering offered him a wide range of experiences. For example, he spent a month volunteering with an organic farm cooperative in Japan. "In exchange for four to five hours a day of mostly harvesting and weeding, I got to witness firsthand how their model for small-scale sustainable agriculture worked. The rest of the time I was immersed in their homelife, community meetings, and even their local *teiko* drum festival."

While in Bombay, en route to another farm-stay, Jered went out to a theater performance. During the intermission he struck up a conversation with a person who happened to be the leader of the Clean Bombay campaign. "Early the next morning," Jered told us, "they were leading a urban worm composting and greening project and invited me to join. What a great opportunity. I don't think I could have planned this experience if I tried."

The highlight of his trip, however, started on the airplane to Ladakh, a region located high on the Tibetan plateau. "I asked the woman in the seat behind me if she was interested in sharing a taxi ride into town." It turns out that she was a professor from Switzerland who had been coming to Ladakh on numerous occasions to work on sustainable development projects. She offered me a ride and suggested that I stay at her friend's guest house until I figured out my plans." Based on the professor's contacts, Jered arranged to volunteer at a local nunnery, where he grew vegetables and herbs that could be dried and sold as a soup mix as a way to earn extra income for the nuns' studies and amenities.

Based on his experiences, Jered suggested that "Whatever social change work you find compelling, there's bound to be countless groups in every corner of the world that would appreciate a helping hand. If you are self-reliant, motivated, and have skills to offer, many groups will be happy to make arrangements that meet both party's needs."

Many international organizations find themselves in this situation when independent volunteers arrive. In societies where there is an emphasis on hospitality it can be difficult for organizations to turn away volunteers, even if they think the volunteer may be a burden.

Many overseas organizations may be unaccustomed to hosting volunteers and may be financially or structurally ill prepared for them. As Eva Galabrau of LICHADO in Cambodia explains, "Volunteers need to understand that not all non-governmental organizations have the capacity to absorb international volunteers," and not all organizations want to host volunteers.

Ben Mongi of Uvikiuta in Tanzania said we should warn organizations that it isn't always easy to host volunteers. Indeed, organizations should realize that taking on volunteers will cost them a lot of precious time to plan work schedules, supervise, arrange visas, and provide adequate food and shelter. The fee that volunteers pay, if any, may not be enough to cover the direct expenses of hosting them, such as food, transport, and communication.

Here are some suggestions for avoiding being a burden on your hosts:

- *Consider paying your host organization a modest administrative fee for the staff time required to respond to your needs. Or, make a contribution to one of their projects when you depart.*

- *Be flexible, adaptable, and open-minded.*

- *Work and contribute in whatever ways are requested and appropriate.*

- *Be dependable, conscientious, and work a little extra (or work some overtime) to compensate for the organization's investment of time.*

Furthermore, independent volunteers should consider the various tips and issues discussed in Chapter 9, "How to Be an Effective International Volunteer."

There is no one right way to organize your own independent volunteer experience overseas. You might take the organize-it-before-you-go approach or you might embrace the make-it-happen-once-you-are-there philosophy. Regardless, you should think seriously about the pros and cons of independent volunteering. In this chapter, we have provided you with examples of volunteers who lived their dream of volunteering overseas, and did it on their own. Should you decide to take their inspiration to heart, take the time to do your homework so you can make the experience as positive as possible for you and for the organization you hope to support.

Action Steps for Doing it without a Program

1. *Evaluate Your Candidacy.* Reflect on the pros and cons of being an independent volunteer to determine if this is a viable option for you. Ask yourself the questions in the beginning of this chapter. Would the effort to organize your own experience be better spent learning a language or fundraising, leaving the logistics to an organization?

2. ***Assess Your Existing Network.*** Use the worksheet in this chapter to examine your own personal network and the various leads that you might build on.

3. ***Get Organized.*** Decide whether you will make it happen once you are there or organize it before you go.

4. ***Go Out and Start Networking.*** Build on your existing network by reaching out to returned volunteers, associations, international organizations, and others who share your interests. Be proactive in following up on leads and making personal connections.

5. ***Arrange Your Placement.*** Initiate contact with organizations overseas and communicate regarding the timing, responsibilities, and other specific parameters of your volunteering. Conduct further research on the organizations to determine which is the best fit. Finalize arrangements, but make sure you have a backup plan.

6. ***If You Decide to Make It Happen Once You Are Overseas.*** Consult travel guides, network with other foreigners, ask locals for advice, visit potential host organizations, and link with volunteer opportunities through language schools. Arrive in the country with at least one lead for starting your search. Be patient, persistent, and organized.

7. ***Lessen the Burden on Local Hosts.*** Consider making a donation or paying a modest administrative fee to your host organization. Be flexible, adaptable, and open-minded. Work and contribute in whatever ways are requested and appropriate. Work a little extra to compensate for the organization's investment in you, and follow through on your commitments.

CHAPTER 7

OVERCOMING FINANCIAL OBSTACLES

I was a struggling business owner, so I had to come up with a fundraising plan. I used frequent flier miles and raised money within my community. I offered the citizens of my hometown the opportunity to sign a big friendship banner that I had made that would be presented to the citizens of Alma-Ata, Kazakhstan. As people signed it, they made a contribution. I went on the radio, spoke at civic clubs and church groups, and presented my volunteer work as a representation of our community. The community funded one hundred percent of my trip.—Ronald Kensey, volunteer, Global Volunteers, Kazakhstan

Financial challenges are often the biggest obstacles to international volunteering. Common sense suggested this to us at the outset of our research and hundreds of interviews and surveys confirmed our hunch.

Lack of funds shouldn't stop you from living your dream of volunteering overseas. With a little advanced planning, some strategic thinking, and lots of hard work, you can make your dream a reality.

Certainly there are options for volunteering overseas without spending money. A few organizations, such as the Peace Corps, not only have no program fee but also cover your expenses while you are overseas and may even pay you a stipend. Many of the better programs, however, do charge a program fee and require that volunteers cover some or all of their own costs.

Even if financial constraints are a significant concern, do not get discouraged or limit yourself to the programs that offer financial support. Pick the program that is right for you. Most likely, this will require you to make a financial investment in your volunteer experience, but, invariably, the return on your investment will be immeasurable.

Financially investing in your volunteer experience, however, does not necessarily mean that you have to come up with all the funds out of your own pocket. In fact, you may be surprised to discover that many volunteers succeed in raising all their funds from other sources. Before you can begin to raise the funds to support your volunteering abroad, however, you need to understand why you often have to pay to volunteer.

Why Pay to Volunteer?

As we mentioned in Chapter 4, "Choosing an Organization," prospective volunteers are often surprised to learn that many programs charge their volunteers a fee to participate. At first, this can seem ridiculous—Why should you pay money to work for free? Aren't you already forgoing income you could be making? Here are a few things to keep in mind while trying to understand why the vast majority of programs charge international volunteers a fee:

- **The costs of recruiting volunteers, producing literature, answering the phones, sending mailings, developing a website, and interviewing potential volunteers are significant.**

- **Identifying appropriate host organizations overseas and working with them is time-consuming, takes resources, and requires an experienced and professional staff.**

- **The process of preparing, training, transporting, housing, feeding, and supervising volunteers is not cheap. Additional services such as health care, funding of overseas projects, volunteer re-entry assistance, and alumni networks all add to the expenses of a program.**

- **The local organizations and projects with which you volunteer overseas have limited resources and are seldom able to subsidize your trip or cover the costs of hosting you. If they did have the financial resources to pay an international volunteer, it would almost certainly be more beneficial and cost-effective to hire a local person instead, someone who already knows the language and culture.**

Every volunteer program needs a source of funding to cover operational costs. Aside from the few programs that receive religious, corporate, foundation, or government support, most rely on their participants to cover the costs. If you want to get a more precise idea of the costs of running a volunteer program, ask a volunteer program for an annual report or an accounting of how they spend program fees. (You should be suspicious if they refuse to show it to you.)

Now that you have a sense of *why* it often costs money to be an international volunteer, we'll give you some tips on how to raise the funds you may need to make your dream of volunteering a reality.

General Suggestions for Fundraising

Here are a few suggestions to help you achieve your fundraising goals. These broad tips should help you get into the right frame of mind to succeed as a fundraiser.

Focus on Individuals, Not Foundations

According to the American Association of Fundraising Council's 1998 report, "Giving USA," total charitable giving in the United States in 1997 amounted to $143 billion. 76.2 percent came from individuals, while 9.3 percent came from foundations, 8.8 percent from bequests (as specified in a will), and the remaining 5.7 percent from corporations. Make sure, therefore, that individuals figure prominently in your fundraising plan.

In general, we discourage you from putting energy into fundraising from foundations. According to the Foundation Center's "Foundation Giving, 1998," donations to the broad category of "international affairs" comprise only three percent of all grants. In addition to a foundation's specific guidelines for grants, there are often prohibitions on contributions to individuals, not to mention a lengthy review process. There are a few fellowships and scholarship programs described below that may apply to your circumstances, but don't let that distract you from pursuing individual donors and organizing events that will generally be your most reliable and important sources of support.

If you do decide to raise funds from foundations and other institutions like corporations, start with places where you have personal connections. Despite all of the systems in place to make philanthropy objective and accessible, it still often hinges on whom you know. In terms of businesses, try approaching local businesses that you frequent, not the corporate headquarters of a giant chain. Don't discount non-monetary donations from businesses, such as airfare or a backpack. Think creatively about how you can use product donations to raise additional dollars, for example, through a raffle or auction.

Think about Your Fundraising Angle

We have a great deal of personal experience fundraising for nonprofit organizations, and we know it is easy to talk about needing x dollars to meet a budget. A donor, however, is going to be much more interested if you talk about the needs in the community where you will volunteer, and how the work you plan to do will help address those needs. Don't shy away, however, from being open about what you hope to get from the experience, as well as what you hope to do with all the things you learn. Invite people to invest in your personal development, but be careful not to focus exclusively on raising funds for *your trip*. Remember to talk about the bigger issues that your volunteer work hopes to address, and how you will share your experience with others and give back to your own community after returning home.

Ask your volunteer placement organization to send you fundraising tips, examples of the type of work you will do when you are overseas, and sample fundraising appeals from previous volunteers. There is nothing wrong with developing your fundraising strategy based on successful techniques of volunteers who have come before you.

Remember: Fundraising Can Be Fun

Those of you with little previous fundraising experience should not despair; fundraising can actually be fun. Fundraising is a "contact sport," a chance to connect with people. In the process of fundraising, you have the opportunity to involve others in your work as an international volunteer. You have a chance to tell people why you want to be a volunteer and why you care about things happening in other parts of the world. Through the connections you create with donors, you can educate them (before, during, and after your experience overseas) about international volunteering and other international issues. You may be surprised how many people are interested to find out what you are doing, why you are doing it, and how they might be able to help you.

The Six Steps of Successful Fundraising

Whether you have never raised money before or you were the champion of Girl Scout cookie sales, following these six steps will shift your fundraising effort into high gear:

1. **Clarify your goals and reasons for volunteering.**
2. **Outline a budget.**
3. **Establish a support committee.**
4. **Develop a fundraising plan.**
5. **Create your promotional materials.**
6. **Start fundraising.**

Clarify Your Goals and Reasons for Volunteering

Clarifying your reasons for becoming an international volunteer is an essential precursor to inviting others to support your efforts. Ask yourself a few questions and be prepared to discuss them with others:

What do you hope to get from the experience?

What do you hope to contribute to the community overseas?

What are the needs you will be addressing?

What are some of the anticipated outcomes?

Outline a Budget

When fundraising, you must have a clear financial goal. Work out a budget and begin to plan accordingly. Find out from your volunteer organization or previous volunteers how much things cost and how much you are likely to need to spend out of pocket. Start with the big-ticket items like international travel and program fees. Then work your way down the list to smaller items, such as vaccinations and purchasing a few presents to bring home with you. If you get stuck on a particular item (e.g., visa fee or airport departure tax), your volunteer placement organization can probably help you fill in the blanks.

WORKSHEET V

FIGURING OUT WHAT YOU WILL NEED AND SETTING YOUR BUDGET

	1st Estimate	2nd Estimate*
Round-trip international airfare		
International volunteer program fee		
Passport application fee		
Visa fee		
Travel gear (backpack, clothing, equipment, etc.)		
Medical insurance		
Vaccinations and medications		
Travel insurance		
Travel to airport in the United States		
Travel from airport overseas to host site		
Food costs		
Housing costs		
Spending money		
Departure tax from overseas airport		
Travel from airport to home		
Rest and relaxation expenses		
Communications (fax, phone, e-mail, and postage)		
Other:		
subtotal		

Remember to check carefully to find out which expenses will not be covered by program fees.

EXPENSES AT HOME WHILE YOU ARE AWAY	1st Estimate	2nd Estimate*
Rent		
Student loans		
Storage space		
Credit card payments		
Other:		
subtotal, expenses at home		
subtotal, direct expenses		
total expenses		

*Try doing a second estimate of your expenses after considering some cost-saving measures, including:

- Giving up or subletting your apartment/housing

- Finding a friend or family member to store your possessions for free

- Securing a deferment on your student loan

- Consolidating all of your debt to a single credit card with a lower interest rate

- Getting a ride to and from the airport at home

- Selling some of your stuff, especially your car (if you have one)

Establish a Support Committee

Don't do it alone. You might be surprised to find that people are eager to help you. Maybe they don't see themselves volunteering abroad in the near future, but are excited to help you get there. Enlisting a group of supporters can enrich and enliven your fundraising experience. This committee can help you develop and implement a fundraising plan. Seek committee members who are outgoing, positive, and sensible. Invite people from different parts of your life and bring together diverse viewpoints and experiences. Meet with your fundraising committee regularly and use this as motivation to stay on top of your fundraising plan. Make sure to get the addresses of your committee members so you can stay in touch with them while you are away.

Develop a Fundraising Plan

One of the most important steps in fundraising, developing a fundraising plan, requires that you figure out which strategies you will use to raise funds. In addition, you'll need to get specific about your prospects, targets, and time frame. Aim high; you can always amend your plan. Remember to check on your progress regularly.

Make certain that your plan includes individual donors. Start by writing down the names of family members, family friends, friends from school, and co-workers. Keep this list accessible and add to it over several days as more names come to mind. Add to your list by including teachers, professors, doctors, ministers, and other professionals in your community. Then select your top fifty to one hundred prospects and integrate them into your fundraising plan. You may want to categorize your prospects in terms of how much you think they can donate.

You should also seek support from local institutions. Groups to approach include your church, synagogue, mosque, or local ethical society, as well as an array of civic organizations and businesses. The leader of the congregation, organization, or business may be able to make a contribution, set up a display for collecting donations, or allow you to do a "pitch" during services or in the newsletter. Several volunteers we met succeeded in raising the majority or all of their funds from this type of offering.

Another effective strategy revolves around organizing and hosting events. We suggest a number of creative ideas below (see "The ABCs of Creatively Financing Your International Volunteer Experience"), but don't forget some of the more simple events like a dinner or garage sale. Ask your friends to contribute books, clothes, and other surplus items to a garage sale or auction, and seek their support in staffing the event. It's amazing how much money you can raise from cleaning out your closets. One volunteer raised her airfare in a single afternoon.

THE ABCS OF CREATIVELY FINANCING YOUR INTERNATIONAL VOLUNTEER EXPERIENCE

a. arts and crafts fair, approaching your place of worship

b. bake sale, benefit breakfast

c. car wash, canvassing door-to-door, coffee house

d. dance, display in the student union

e. educational event (a lecture or movie)

f. friends and family letter, fashion show

g. garage sale, grant from your school

h. *hula-hoop-a-thon (or any kind of dance-athon, walk-athon, bowl-athon, etc.), hunger banquet*

i. *ice-cream social, information table*

j. *juggling or another type of street theater or performance*

k. *Kiwanis, Rotary, chamber of commerce, or other civic clubs (making presentations at their meetings)*

l. *lighten your load (sell your car, TV, VCR, and other possessions), loans from relatives*

m. *musical concert (approach a band or a club and ask them to donate a percentage of the door/bar)*

n. *network (ask supporters to recommend others who might be interested)*

o. *odd jobs (washing windows, mowing lawns, painting, etc.)*

p. *poetry reading, presentation to a community group*

q. *quiche dinner party (pass a hat, charge at the door, and try a potluck or donated food)*

r. *raffle (get donations from local businesses and have a party for the drawing)*

s. *street theater*

t. *theme party, telephone campaign*

u. *underwriting from local businesses (especially ones you frequent regularly)*

v. *vending (working with a wholesaler to sell anything from grapefruits to orchids)*

w. *workshops (on topics like knitting, cooking, quilting, theater, or calligraphy)*

x. *Xena theme party, X-men or other old comics for sale*

y. *yourself (any money from your savings or extra money you can earn)*

z. *zany events such as a cow pie tossing contest, or a karaoke party*

Some donors may want to make a tax-deductible donation. Find out in advance if donors can write a check directly to your volunteer placement organization, and get a letter confirming that the donation is tax deductible. Note that if the donor receives something in return for the donation, it is not fully deductible. For example, if a donor gives you $50 at a fundraising dinner where the food is worth $10, only $40 of the donation is tax deductible. Raffle tickets are not tax deductible—even if you lose!

Worksheet VI (Developing a Fundraising Plan) can help you assess your financial situation. After looking at your resources, assets, and anticipated income, the worksheet will help you set some goals in different fundraising categories. Adjust your fundraising goals so that the total expense from Worksheet V: Figuring Out What You Will Need and Setting Your Budget equals the total financing available in Worksheet VI . Then identify the key activities you will use to meet your fundraising targets.

WORKSHEET VI

DEVELOPING A FUNDRAISING PLAN

RESOURCES AND ASSETS	1st Estimate	2nd Estimate*
Regular income set aside (what you can save between now and departure)		
Previous savings		
Loans from friends or family		
Income from sales (e.g., car, books, VCR, etc.)		
Scholarships, fellowships, or awards		
Other		
ANTICIPATED INCOME WHILE OVERSEAS		
Living stipend		
Other income		
Subtotal, personal contribution		

FUNDRAISING INCOME: INDIVIDUAL DONORS Individuals @$500+		
Individuals @$250		
Individuals @$100		
Individuals @$50		
Individuals @$25		
Individuals @$10		
Individuals @		
FUNDRAISING INCOME: CIVIC GROUPS AND LOCAL BUSINESSES Group/Business #1:		
Group/Business #2:		
Group/Business #3:		
Group/Business #4:		
FUNDRAISING INCOME: EVENTS AND ACTIVITIES (SEE CREATIVE FUNDRAISING SUGGESTIONS) Event/Activity #1:		
Event/Activity #2:		
Event/Activity #3:		
Event/Activity #4:		
Event/Activity #5:		
FUNDRAISING INCOME: RELIGIOUS, SCHOOL, OR WORK CONNECTIONS Religious/Academic/Work #1:		
Religious/Academic/Work #2:		
Religious/Academic/Work #3:		
Religious/Academic/Work #4:		
subtotal fundraising		
subtotal, personal contribution		
Total financing available		

Sample Fundraising Plan

Here's a sample plan for Nanette, who selected a volunteer program in December and figured from her budget sheet that she needed to raise $4,000 by the end of July.

Nanette's contribution from her own resources and assets (savings plus waiting tables two nights per week): $1,500

January: Form a fundraising committee. *Nanette and four friends form a committee. Nannette creates a fact sheet on her volunteer program and develops her fundraising plan.*

February: Send mailing to friends and family members. *Nanette writes a letter, Juanita edits, and Nancy helps with addressing envelopes and mailing. Nannette estimates that fifty percent of the fifty people that she asks will donate an average of $25. Total: $625. The fundraising committee holds a meeting where everyone practices asking for a donation face to face.*

March: Approach businesses. *The committee approaches ten neighborhood businesses with a request that they sponsor at $250 each. One says yes, and one donates $100. Total: $350. Walter makes a thank-you certificate for the two sponsors to display at their stores or offices.*

April: Hold a fundraising party. *Ask a local supermarket to donate spaghetti and sauce. Each person on the fundraising committee must bring ten people. Ben agrees to host the party. Suggested donation: $10. Total: $500.*

May: Contact religious organizations. *Each person on the fundraising committee contacts the social action committee of two religious congregations of his or her own denomination. Five of ten congregations invite Nanette to speak at their meetings. Three make contributions averaging $100. Total: $300.*

June: Contact civic clubs. *Each person on the fundraising committee contacts one civic club, e.g., Kiwanis, Optimists, Rotary, Chamber of Commerce, Jaycees. Two clubs agree to have a presentation at their June luncheon. Nanette makes presentations. The groups donate $150 each. Total: $300.*

July: Organize a big garage sale. *Fundraising committee members clean out their closets. Nanette visits her neighbors and asks them each to donate their extra stuff. Fundraising committee members send notice to newspaper and help Nanette put up fliers around their neighborhood. Total: $500.*

Nanette's contribution:	*$1,500*
Friends and family letter:	*$625*
Local businesses:	*$350*
Fundraising event #1, spaghetti dinner:	*$500*
Religious organizations:	*$300*
Civic clubs:	*$300*
Fundraising event #2, garage sale:	*$500*
TOTAL RAISED:	**$4,075**

Juanita creates a database with the names and addresses of everyone who makes a donation. While in Africa, Nanette writes a letter every two months and sends it to Juanita. Juanita copies it and mails it to everyone on the list, using the extra $75 raised for postage and copying expenses. When she gets back home, Nanette sends a thank-you letter with a photograph to everyone.

Your plan to overcome the financial obstacles to volunteering will invariably involve hard work and creativity. In addition to your other fundraising activities, consider hosting educational fundraising events that enlighten and inspire participants who support you financially.

EDUCATIONAL FUNDRAISING: A HUNGER BANQUET

A hunger banquet is a great example of how volunteers can raise awareness while raising funds. The basic idea is that participants donate $5 to $50 to take part in a community dinner that simulates the inequality of global food distribution. Proceeds are then donated to support outgoing volunteers like you, as well as to local and international anti-hunger or community development organizations.

As people arrive at the event, each person selects a card randomly. Each card represents one of three different income groups. Roughly seventy percent of the cards represent the lowest income group and entitle the bearers to only rice during the dinner. Twenty-four percent represent the middle-income group and entitle the recipients to rice and beans and maybe a little cheese, while six percent represent the highest income group and entitle the lucky few to a five-course meal. Organizers then might have everyone eat in one large room, with the rice eaters sitting on the floor or in simple chairs, and the five-course meal people at a beautiful table with servers toting fine wine. After the meal, a facilitator helps participants reflect on the simulation and the issues it raises about international hunger and the distribution of food. Questions include: How did it feel to be eating rice while some had a five-course meal? How did it feel to eat a five-course meal while some ate only rice? Did anyone share? Did anyone steal? Why or why not? Use your creativity to adapt the simulation. You can, for example, give each attendee a character sketch for an individual they will represent and act out during dinner.

Oxfam America has done an excellent job of developing ideas and logistics for organizing hunger banquets. You can call them at 800-77-OXFAM, check them out on the web at www.oxfamamerica.org, or send an e-mail to info@oxfamamerica.org. They offer a great organizer's kit including fact sheets and action alerts to further involve participants.

Create Your Promotional Materials

We wrote a first draft of our letter, and it was edited by the folks at Trees for Life. We actually sent out 450 letters, which included a flyer about our first trip to India that explained more about the school where we would be volunteering. In the letter I told the story of one of the girls we had met in India. The little girl, Raika, wanted to be a doctor. She had big aspirations, and the school where we worked provided her with an opportunity for her dreams to come true. Many people who received the letter said they were sorry they could not go, but were happy to be a part of our trip in some way. We estimated we would raise about $6,000 but, in fact, we raised $12,000.—Kathy Miller, volunteer, Trees for Life, India

Deciding which promotional materials to create will depend on your fundraising plan. You can copy and personalize the promotional materials from your volunteer program. Flyers are effective for distributing to individuals, while larger visual displays can be more effective in catching people's attention in public places. Don't forget that this is also a chance to educate people. Facts about the country, projects, organizations, and people you will work with can help capture people's imagination and get them excited about your volunteer work.

Fundraising Letter

You will probably want to write a dear-friends-and-family letter requesting a donation. Draft a one-page letter and ask your committee members to read it and give you feedback. When drafting your letter, keep it brief and to the point. Talk about the needs your volunteer service will address. Be specific about what you will be doing (or give examples of what previous volunteers have done), and ask for a specific amount (some volunteers have created various sponsorship categories to give donors a range of options). We recommend that you offer to send donors periodic reports from overseas. Also, always make it easy for people to donate; enclose a self-addressed return envelope.

We have provided a sample fundraising letter below. Don't hesitate to ask your program for examples of letters from previous volunteers.

SAMPLE FUNDRAISING LETTER

Dear Friends:

Please excuse the impersonality of this letter, but I am writing to many people and don't have much time. I have just been accepted to be a volunteer for WorldTeach, a nonprofit organization that places American volunteers as teachers in countries that need assistance.

I have been accepted to the program in Costa Rica and will be traveling there in five months. Having studied Spanish and worked with Central American immigrants all through college, I am extremely excited about this opportunity, but I might not make it there without your help. Unlike other Central American countries, Costa Rica has a long history of democracy and peaceful development. Despite its relative prosperity, however, this nation faces serious problems including a huge foreign debt and increasing unemployment. In addition, the education system cannot meet the needs of the population, and only a half of Costa Rican children attend school past the sixth grade level.

As a WorldTeach volunteer, I will be teaching English to primary school students. Knowledge of English is very important to Costa Rica's development plans. For many students, it is required to find a job or qualify for higher education. By helping to improve the standard of English instruction, I can contribute to Costa Rica's development, give some kids a better chance of getting a job, and, on a very small scale, help improve relations between the United States and Central America.

I will be living with a Costa Rican family during my entire stay and will be subsisting on traditional Costa Rican foods, such as rice, beans, fried plantains, and tropical fruits. The Ministry of Public Education will also give me a small allowance (about $35 per month).

As with any such venture, there is a cost involved. That's where you come in! The cost of this program is $3,400, which is more than I can afford on my own. This is to cover my airfare, health insurance, training, and field support costs.

I have saved $1,700 of my own money. Now I need to find a few big sponsors or lots of people willing to give me smaller donations. If I could get thirty of my friends and acquaintances to contribute $50 each, I'd be in great shape.

Time is of the essence, though, since my departure date is fast approaching!

In return for your contribution, I promise to share my experience with you; I'll take pictures, write letters, and give slide shows when I return next year.

I have enclosed a fact sheet about WorldTeach and a pledge card. Please return it as soon as possible. Thank you in advance for all your help. I am truly grateful for the opportunity you are giving me.

Your ambassador to the world,
John Q. Volunteer

Reprinted with permission from WorldTeach

When you finalize your letters you may also want to make a list of people capable of giving the most. Contact them by phone as a follow up to the letter. Mentioning in your letter that you will be calling is a good idea and lets people know that they should expect a call. Whenever possible, meet people face to face, but a direct request by phone can increase your rate of return on a fundraising letter substantially.

Start Fundraising

There are so many different ways to raise funds that it is hard to know where to start. Experience suggests that, as already mentioned, focusing on individuals is the best way to go, and a good place to begin your fundraising. Set a timeline and follow your fundraising plan. Persistence is the most important thing.

Though you should not delay in contacting family and friends, don't be daunted if you are short of your optimal goal when it is time to leave. It is possible to fundraise even while you are overseas. One volunteer we spoke with told us that she "received some donations from friends and family because I wrote a newsletter that was disseminated in the United States during my time in Nicaragua."

Basic Principles of Fundraising

Whatever strategy you use to fundraise, remember the following basic principles:

- *Diversify. Don't put all your golden eggs in one basket. Use several different techniques so, if one fails, you will still be able to raise the money you need.*

- *You have to ask to receive. Don't just tell people you need to raise money; ask them for a specific amount.*

- *People are much more likely to make a contribution if they know the person who does the asking and share some of the values of the organization they are being asked to support.*

- *Don't take "no" personally. Some people who might want to support you just can't afford it. If someone says "no," don't feel they are rejecting you, and don't hold it against them. It's just part of fundraising; you have to go through the "no's" to get to the "yes's."*

- *Ask at least one person for money every day.*

- *Thank and thank again. Make sure your sponsors know how much you appreciate their support. Thank you calls and notes are always well received.*

Additional Resources and Considerations

Sources of Fundraising Information

There are many good sources of fundraising information in print and online. The American Medical Student Association's website (www.amsa.org) includes an excellent online guide to fundraising, "Creative Funding for International Health Electives," that is useful for all students. Both Amizade (www.amizade.org) and Visions in Action (www.visionsinaction.org) have excellent fundraising suggestions posted on their websites.

Fellowships, Scholarships, and Funding Resources

Experience suggests that fundraising from individuals is the best bet for meeting your financial goals. There are, however, some scholarship and fellowship opportunities that may also assist you. Start by asking the volunteer program of your choice about any scholarship opportunities they have. If it's a local group, maybe you can volunteer in their office in exchange for a reduced fee. Next, you may want to do some research about other opportunities. Here are a few suggestions:

- *Institute of International Education (IIE)* publishes some of the best directories of scholarships for overseas opportunities, which include grants for all levels of students as well as postdoctorates and professionals. IIE's databases are available on their website (www.iie.org), but only if you have access to an IIE member organization's password. If not, you can find the directory at most college libraries. Search terms such as "work," "internship," "practical," "teach," and "research" all yield a good number of listings.

- *The University of Minnesota International Study and Travel Center (ISTC)* Scholarships database (www.istc.umn.edu/study/scholarships.html) is an excellent, free online database of scholarships. Search categories include "study," "research," and "internships," as well as "location" and other variables.

- *Reference Service Press (RSP)* publishes "Financial Aid for Study and Training Abroad" and "Financial Aid for Research and Creative Activities Abroad" (Reference Service Press). The RSP databases (www.rspfunding.com) are also available to America Online subscribers (keyword: RSP) or through some university libraries.

Don't forget to also approach funding opportunities that are closer to home:

- *Invite your high school principal, department chair, and college president to support you by contributing discretionary funds or nominating you for an award. This has worked for several students we met. Discretionary funds are often not widely publicized, so make sure to ask around regarding different sources of* funding. To seal the deal, offer to make a presentation to the school upon your return. Even if you don't get discretionary money, you may secure an individual donation in the process.

- *Ask parents and family members if any of the organizations they belong to have scholarship programs.* Some workplaces will support the good deeds of employee family members. If that doesn't pan out, you may discover that the company has a matching program where they will match an employee's individual donation to your trip.

While scholarships explicitly for international travel and volunteering are not common, there are several that target individuals from under-represented cultural groups, or those heading to non-traditional travel destinations.

- *Council on International Educational Exchange (CIEE) has two scholarships for United States students (www.ciee.org, 888-COUNCIL):*

  The Bowman Travel Grant is for high school or undergraduate students participating in a CIEE program or program of a CIEE member institution. Awards toward travel to non-traditional destinations range from $500 to $2,000. In most cases, awards are issued as vouchers to Council Travel, to be used toward the purchase of the student's airline ticket to their program destination. Application deadlines are usually in April and October.

  The Bailey Scholarship is intended to promote increased participation in Council's International Study Programs by members of groups that have traditionally been underrepresented in study abroad, especially ethnic minority students.

In addition, there are two notable options for San Francisco Bay area residents:

- *The BRIDGES Fellowship (Building Responsible International Dialogues through Grassroots Exchanges)* offers an International Fellowship combining a summer of volunteer work abroad with volunteering in the San Francisco Bay area during the spring and fall. It is designed for people of color and individuals from low-income backgrounds who have not previously traveled and are interested in exploring the links between local and global issues. The eight-month program includes extensive training before and after the international experience. All expenses are covered and participants receive a stipend. Applications are available in the fall. (www.bridgesfellowship.org, 415-551-9728. Reviewed in Chapter 12, "Organizational Profiles.")

- *World PULSE (Program for Understanding, Leadership, Service, and Exchange)* is a part-time program that involves San Francisco Bay area residents between the ages of 18 and 26 in community service, cross-cultural learning, and leadership development, both at home and abroad. Participants are from low-income

backgrounds and have not had extensive international travel experience. Most program-related costs, including international travel, are paid for by World PULSE. Applications are available in January or February each year. (www.worldpulse.org, 510-451-2995. Reviewed in Chapter 12, "Organizational Profiles.")

Scholarships and fellowships are few and far between, so remain focused on your original fundraising plan even while researching these other funding options.

Student Loan Deferrals

Deferring student loans is another way to make your international volunteer experience financially feasible. Your ability to defer your loans depends on a number of factors, and it's best to pose questions directly to your loan agencies. If you are currently a student, talk with someone in the financial aid office at your school. If you are already repaying loans, get in touch with the bank or lending institution directly.

Start by requesting a deferral form, which is issued by the organization that made or validated the loan. The deferral form usually calls for a U.S. Department of Education school code. Although it appears on the form that students have to be doing the program either through a U.S. college or an overseas institution that has received such a code number, this is not always true. Howard Berry of International Partnership for Service Learning told us that "We often sign such forms for students in our programs even though we do not have a code, and some of our overseas affiliates do not either. Loan companies seem to accept our status as a nonprofit educational organization."

Another consideration is whether or not to pursue deferment or utilize a loan's hardship provision. One of the differences is that when you secure a loan deferral, you *may* not have to pay the interest on your loan for the time of your service, and you still have an ability to use the hardship provision in the future. If you claim a hardship, you typically do have to pay the interest that accrues on the loan, and it may be more difficult, or impossible, to claim hardship in the future. Often debtors prefer to use the deferment option. With some loans, however, it may be more difficult to get the lender to agree to deferment, and therefore utilizing the hardship provision may be the most viable option.

Some organizations, such as Volunteers in Asia, can help you get a deferral on specific student loans including Perkins Loans. As of 2000 Stafford Loans could no longer be deferred, but if your income is a certain amount annually there are hardship provisions available. If you apply for a loan deferral, you must explain your need in writing to your lending agency. Your volunteer placement organization may be able to help you compose this letter. The organization may also send you documentation about what you will be doing as a volunteer, how much you will be paid, and verification of its nonprofit status. All this information should be included with your letter for deferment.

Restructuring Consumer Debt

If consumer debt is one of the constraints that you face in realizing your dream of volunteering overseas, you are not alone. Millions of Americans have chronic credit card debt. Going abroad may be just the motivation that you need to get your finances in order. Restructuring and consolidating your debt and creating a plan for getting out of debt can be integrated into your fundraising plan. On the simplest level, you may decide to take advantage of offers to consolidate various credit card debts onto a single credit card with a favorable interest rate. If your needs are more involved, there are many programs run by local and national consumer organizations. Helpful organizations include the Center for Debt Management (http://center4debtmanagement.com/) and Myvest.org (formerly Debt Counselors of America, www.dca.org).

You Can Do It

Although the thought of raising thousands of dollars, postponing student loans, and getting your finances in order can be daunting, you *can* do it. If you allow yourself enough time, make a good plan, get others to help you, and follow the suggestions in this chapter, you'll be sure to succeed at fundraising.

Action Steps for Overcoming Financial Obstacles

1. ***Focus on Individuals, Not Foundations.*** Individuals account for over three quarters of all charitable dollars given in the United States. Develop a list of potential individual donors to figure prominently in your fundraising plan.

2. ***Think about Your Fundraising Angle.*** Get clear on what you are fundraising for and invite others to invest in you as well as the broader work that you are undertaking.

3. ***Remember, Fundraising Can Be Fun.*** Incorporate educational and creative events and activities into your fundraising efforts.

4. ***Follow the Six Steps of Successful Fundraising.*** Clarify your goals and reasons for volunteering; Outline a budget; Establish a support committee; Develop a fundraising plan; Create your promotional materials; Start fundraising.

5. ***Keep the Basic Principles of Fundraising in Mind.*** Diversify; Be proactive; You have to ask to receive; Don't take "no" personally; Be specific in your request; Ask every day; Thank and thank again.

6. ***Incorporate Additional Resources and Considerations into Your Fundraising.*** Look for additional fundraising resources and investigate scholarships and fellowships, student loan deferrals, and ways to restructure your consumer debt.

CHAPTER 8

WHAT TO DO BEFORE YOU GO

No matter how much time you have before you depart for your destination country, there is no shortage of useful things you can do to be better prepared. Some are things that you must do before you go. Others, while optional, will enrich your experience and make you a more effective volunteer. Whether dealing with the essential yet mundane task of getting your passport and visa or throwing yourself into learning a new language and studying the history of the country where you will volunteer, your investment in being a well-prepared volunteer will certainly benefit you and your colleagues overseas.

Obtaining a Passport

Travelers to most countries in the world need a valid passport. Exceptions for U.S. citizens include short-term travel between the United States and Mexico or certain countries in the Caribbean. Your travel agent or airline can tell you if you need a passport for the country in which you plan to volunteer.

Warning: Even if you are not required to hold a passport to visit the country to which you are traveling, U.S. authorities require you to prove your U.S. citizenship and identity when you re-enter the United States. Make certain that you carry adequate documentation to pass through U.S. Immigration upon your return. A U.S. passport is the most convincing evidence of U.S. citizenship. Other documents to prove U.S. citizenship include an expired U.S. passport, a certified copy of your birth certificate, a certificate of naturalization, a certificate of citizenship, or a Report of Birth Abroad of a citizen of the United States.

Beware of a passport that is about to expire! Certain countries will not permit you to enter and will not place a visa in your passport if the validity of your passport is for less than six months. Also, be aware that if you return to the United States with an expired passport, you are subject to a passport waiver fee of $100, payable to U.S. Immigration at the port of entry—and that doesn't even get you a new passport. Therefore, if you are abroad so long that your passport will expire before you return home, you are much better off applying for a new one at the U.S. consulate abroad (see the section in this chapter on U.S. consulates).

You must apply for a passport *in person* if you are applying for the first time, if you are renewing a passport issued over eleven years ago, or if you were under eighteen when you got your last passport. You can apply at one of the thirteen U.S. passport agencies or at one of the several thousand select U.S. post offices, federal or state courts authorized to accept passport applications. You should be able to find the addresses of passport acceptance facilities in your area in the government listings section of your telephone book, the web at http://travel.state.gov/passport_services.html, or your local library. If you have already held a passport within the past twelve years, you may be eligible to apply by mail. You will have to submit your old passport. You will need to obtain Form DSP-82 ("Application for Passport by Mail") from one of the offices accepting applications, from the website, or from your travel agent, and complete the information requested.

The fee for applicants ages eighteen and over who are required to appear in person (see above) is $65. Their passports will be valid for ten years. Applicants under age eighteen pay $40 for a passport that is valid for five years. If you are eligible to apply for a passport by mail, the fee is $55. Peace Corps volunteers are issued no-fee official passports, which they turn in to the Peace Corps at the end of employment.

Two identical recent photographs (the precise specifications are on the application form) and proof of U.S. citizenship must accompany properly completed applications. A previously issued U.S. passport or a certified copy of your birth certificate showing you were born in the United States is readily accepted as proof of citizenship. A list of other acceptable proof is obtainable from passport agencies and acceptance facilities. If you are applying in person, you will need to prove your identity by a previous U.S. passport, a valid driver's license with a photograph, a certificate of naturalization or citizenship, or a government identification card.

Do plan ahead, for it can take up to a few months to process an application, especially for new passports. Demand for passports becomes heavy in January and begins to decline in August. If you need a visa from the country you are going to visit (more on this below), you will first have to receive your passport before you can apply for the visa and then plan to wait up to two weeks for each visa. Tip: put a date of departure on the passport application form; if you don't, the passport agency might assume you are in no hurry.

Sign the passport as soon as you receive it. It is not valid until you do so. If you send an unsigned passport to an embassy requesting a visa, it may be returned to you without the visa. After signing your passport, fill in the personal notification data page.

Safeguard your passport. U.S. passports fetch a pretty price on illegal markets. Losing your passport could cause you unnecessary travel complications as well as significant expense (getting yourself to the nearest U.S. consulate, a fee for a replacement passport, more photographs, etc.). Should your passport be lost or stolen abroad, report the loss immediately to the local police as well as to the nearest U.S. embassy or consulate. If you can provide the consular officer with the information contained in your passport (such as the serial number), it will facilitate issuance of a new passport. Therefore, photocopy—we suggest in color—the data page of your passport (that's the page with your name, birth date, birthplace, place of issuance, etc.) and keep it in a separate place. In addition, leave the passport number, date, and place of issuance (or another photocopy of the data page) with a relative or friend in the United States whom you can contact in case you lose your passport while volunteering overseas. Caution: there may be a freeze on the issuance if you owe the federal government money or are on the lam. The consulate must run the data through a computer back in the United States to get authorization for the issuance of a new passport.

Securing Any Necessary Visas

Some countries require that you obtain a visa. A visa is an endorsement or stamp placed in your passport by a foreign country that permits you to visit that country for a specified purpose and a limited time—for example, tourists up to six months. Some countries may issue a "multiple entry" visa; this is desirable if you will be on a long-term assignment and may leave the country to visit a neighboring country on a vacation. If you are being placed by an organization, ask if it provides assistance with any necessary paperwork for legal entry to your host country. It should be the best source of information on whether a visa is required and what kind to request:

- *A tourist visa or a work visa or both?*
- *A single- or a multiple-entry visa?*
- *A temporary stay or indefinite residence visa?*

If you are not being placed by an organization, you can inquire with the embassy in Washington, D.C., or the nearest consulate of the country you are preparing to go to, whether a visa is required of U.S. citizens. To obtain the number of an embassy, you can check a telephone directory for Washington, call directory assistance, conduct an Internet search, or consult your local library. Be aware that the embassy may give you inaccurate information. You may be told that you must get a visa in advance when in reality you can get one at the airport or border upon arrival. Worse, you may be told you can get the visa at the airport when you arrive only to arrive and be turned away (deported) for not having a visa. Recent travelers to the region may have useful information, but (as always) it is better to err on the side of caution and get the visa in advance.

The U.S. Department of State operates the Overseas Citizens Services that provides regularly updated Consular Information Sheets that contain passport and visa information for every country in the world. The Consular Information Sheets are available at the thirteen regional passport agencies; at U.S. embassies and consulates abroad; or by sending a self-addressed, stamped envelope to Overseas Citizens Services (Room 4811, Department of State, Washington, D.C. 20520-4818). Be sure to mention the country to which you will travel.

You can access Consular Information Sheets (as well as travel warnings and public announcements) twenty-four hours a day in several ways:

- **By telephone.** *To listen to them, call 202-647-5225 from a touch-tone phone and select the appropriate options.*

- **By fax.** *Using the handset on a fax machine as you would a regular telephone, dial 202-647-3000. You will be prompted on how to proceed.*

- **On the Internet.** *The address is http://travel.state.gov/overseas_citizens.html.*

The Consular Information Sheets are also available through the computerized reservations system of any airline you might use to travel overseas.

Because a visa is generally stamped directly onto a blank page in your passport, you will likely need to give your passport to an official of the foreign embassy or consulate (in person during the often limited hours or by mail, preferably certified mail). You will also need to fill out a form, and you may need to attach one or more photographs. Many visas require a fee. Allow at least three weeks to be on the safe side.

Some countries do not require a visa of U.S. citizens but only a tourist card. If this is the case, you should be able to obtain one from the country's embassy or consulate, or an airline serving the country, or at the port of entry. There is a fee for most tourist cards.

Some countries require that upon arrival at the port of entry you present an airline ticket out of the country and/or a certain minimum amount of money (in cash or travelers checks). Again, you can check with the foreign embassy or consulate in advance or with the organization that is placing you.

If you are being placed by an organization, you should ask what status—"tourist," or "business," or something else—you should put on any application for a visa or a tourist or landing card (immigration card). This can be a little sticky. You may not want to think of yourself as a "tourist," but putting anything else on the card in some countries may open the door to a myriad of questions and delays. On the other hand, if you are caught volunteering on a tourist visa, you may risk fines and even deportation (one of us once had that memorable experience in Zambia!). In Mexico, the long-term volunteers we met were on six-month tourist cards because they could obtain nothing else; every six months they had to leave the country, if only for an hour, and then re-enter.

U.S. citizens are often surprised to learn that many countries have strange and stringent requirements for granting visas, such as showing your bank account and a letter from your employer. Before you get resentful, you should know that these countries' visa laws often mirror, or pale in comparison to, U.S. visa requirements for their citizens; the U.S. government creates many hoops that people (especially Africans, Asians, and Latin Americans) must jump through in order to obtain visas.

Preparing for a Healthy Experience

Before you go to your destination country, you should find out about the health conditions and challenges there. If an organization is placing you, it may (and should) provide you with relevant information. Another key source you should tap into (as your own doctor probably would) is the Centers for Disease Control and Prevention (CDC), the U.S. government agency based in Atlanta. You may contact the CDC's international travelers hotline at 888-232-3228, the center's fax service at 888-232-3299, or its Internet site at www.cdc.gov. You can obtain country-specific advice regarding what inoculations are necessary or advisable as well as other medications you should take with you. There is also non-drug advice on preventing infectious diseases endemic in many tropical areas such as malaria and dengue fever (such as using mosquito repellents containing DEET). There are some countries that require that you have an HIV antibodies test before you enter, showing a negative result. You may also turn to the International Association of Medical Assistance to Travelers (www.sentex. net/~iamat, 716-754-4883) for information about health challenges and care abroad.

It is also advisable to get a general checkup from your physician and from your dentist. You will want to make sure you are in good health as well as get advice on a range of health topics such as preventing diarrhea. Also, if you are going to a malaria area, you will need a prescription if you plan to take an anti-malarial drug. It is a good idea to arrange the medical checkup a few months before you plan to depart, if possible, since the doctor's recommendations may include any of various inoculations to ward off hepatitis, yellow fever, and typhoid. Some of them (for instance, the relatively new ones against hepatitis) may need to be spaced over a period of time, and the most commonly prescribed anti-malarial drug should start to be taken two weeks before you arrive at your destination. Your physician should record any shots you have received over the past several years in the yellow booklet printed by the U.S. Department of Health and Human Services. It should be carried with your passport and other documents. Some countries will examine the booklet when you are entering. Your physician probably has the booklet or it can be obtained through the CDC at the hotline number above.

Since the geographic area of diseases and the appropriate resistance drugs change rapidly, it is difficult for most general practitioners to keep up. Another option is to visit a travel clinic staffed by specialists in international travel health services. There are hundreds of travel clinics now in the United States and Canada, and the number has been growing. Most are found, of course, in metropolitan areas. Check your local telephone directory.

If you wear glasses and/or contact lenses, it is advisable to pack an extra pair, as well as any lens care products you use. In an increasing number of countries contact lens care products are sold in the larger cities, but these already pricey items may cost considerably more and possibly be beyond the expiration date. It is a good idea to have your eye doctor give you a copy of your prescription; it's a small thing to carry and could save you the trouble of getting an eye exam (in a language you may not be comfortable in).

For many countries it is advisable to pack enough of any prescription drugs you are taking to last you for your stay. It's wise to keep them in their original containers and clearly labeled. If any of your prescriptions are narcotics or other controlled substances, we recommend that you bring a letter from your physician explaining your need for the medication. If you have any essential medications, always carry them with you, in case your luggage is lost. While overseas, you may also want to divide medication into two portions stored separately in case one is lost or stolen.

You should be prepared to treat such problems as diarrhea, blisters, sunburn, cuts, sprains, skin rashes, insect bites, headaches, and colds. Does the organization you will be with provide a first-aid kit? If not, you should make your own kit, unless you are going to be where such supplies are readily available. Here is what you should consider including:

- [ ] **Blister pads (moleskin)**
- [ ] **Sunscreen**
- [ ] **Sunscreen lip balm**
- [ ] **Insect repellent (The CDC recommends that it contain DEET.)**
- [ ] **Antibiotic ointment**
- [ ] **Band-Aids**
- [ ] **Adhesive tape and gauze**
- [ ] **Ace bandage**
- [ ] **Antihistamine**
- [ ] **Aspirin, ibuprofen, or equivalent**
- [ ] **Pepto-Bismol tablets (The generic is cheaper.)**
- [ ] **Antibiotics and other anti-diarrhea drugs (Get advice from your doctor and any required prescriptions.)**
- [ ] **Skin-related over-the-counter medications for irritations like rashes, cold sores, athlete's foot, and hemorrhoids**
- [ ] **Anti-malarial medication, if needed (as discussed above)**
- [ ] **Hydrocortisone cream**
- [ ] **Acidophilus (Available at health food stores. Many recommend taking at every meal to prevent diarrhea and maintain intestinal bacterial balance.)**

Speaking of first aid, if you don't already have first-aid skills, you may want to get them before you leave. Inquire at the local chapter of the Red Cross (www.redcross.org).

If you think you will be sexually active, bring a supply of condoms and lubricants. Check expiration dates before packing them! (See the discussion of responsible sexuality in Chapter 9, "How to Be an Effective International Volunteer.") Heterosexual couples volunteering together should be sure to bring birth control. If you use pills, be aware that they may become less effective if you get a case of traveler's diarrhea, so bring backup.

Female travelers should be aware that tampons might not be available, especially in rural areas. Check with the program you're volunteering with, and, if necessary, bring supplies. Ob tampons don't take up much space in your luggage and are recommended. Also, if you'll be living in a rural area for an extended period, you may want to bring treatment for yeast infections if you are susceptible.

Dirk Schroeder's *Staying Healthy in Asia, Africa, and Latin America* is an excellent resource. It is a Moon Travel Handbook that discusses prevention, treatment, what to do before you go, and what to do when you return from overseas, as well as common health problems, infections, and diseases (Emeryville, CA: Avalon Travel Publishing, 2000).

Finally, there is the whole area of health insurance. If you have health insurance, will you be continuing it and, most importantly, what medical services will it cover when you are living abroad? Note that Medicare and Medicaid do not cover medical care outside the United States. If your health insurance policy does provide coverage outside the United States, don't forget to carry both your insurance identity card as proof of such insurance and a claim form (or two). If you are being placed by an organization, is health insurance provided? If so, does the coverage appear adequate? Although many health insurance companies will pay "customary and reasonable" medical and hospital costs abroad, very few will pay for medical evacuation from a remote area or from a country where medical facilities are inadequate. Medical evacuation can easily cost $10,000 and up, depending on your location and medical condition. If either your personal insurance or the organization's insurance is inadequate, we highly recommend that you purchase one of the short-term health and emergency assistance policies designed for travelers. If you are going abroad in conjunction with a faith-based organization, you may be eligible to purchase a policy for missionaries. The Peace Corps, with its enormous taxpayer-funded resources, is an example of an organization that does provide medical evacuation.

See the excellent website www.travelhealth.com for a list of international health insurance providers and a variety of coverage options. Some policies include medical evacuation. The website also has links and extensive information on other overseas health care issues.

Making Your Travel Arrangements

If your international travel is not being arranged by an organization, you will probably be interested in how you can travel as cheaply as possible. There are too many ins and outs to even summarize here, so we thought the best way was to point you in the direction of some of the resources we have found:

You Can Travel Free, by Robert W. M. Kirk (Gretna, LA: Pelican, 1998), has chapters titled, "Free or (Really) Cheap Courier Flights" and "Flying: Bonuses, Bumps, and other Freebies."

The Courier Air Travel HandBook, by Mark I. Field (Okemos, MI: Perpetual Press, 1999), discusses the pros and cons of air courier travel and includes lots of tips on subjects such as how to book flights and how to find the right companies.

Frommer's What the Airlines Never Tell You, by Maureen Clarke (Indianapolis, IN: Hungry Minds, 2000), has chapters such as "Ticketing Pitfalls: Know Your Rights before the Flight" and "Cheap Fares: Easy Ways to Cut the Cost of Air Travel."

Fly Cheap, by Kelly Monaghan (Branford, PA: The Intrepid Traveler, 2000), is another useful book. Also check out *Air Courier Bargains: How to Travel World-Wide for Next to Nothing* (1998) and other books by the same author. The publisher, Intrepid Traveler, has its own website that can help you find useful information on travel, including cheap tickets. The website is www.intrepidtraveler.com.

Also check out some of the following websites for information on lower-cost travel:

- **www.cheaptickets.com**
- **www.expedia.com**
- **www.travelocity.com**
- **www.bestfares.com**
- **www.webflyer.com**

You can also join, for a fee, the Air Courier Association (800-282-1202, www.aircourier.org). They will send you a folder with information on the different courier companies and where they fly. No companies listed in this folder, however, are singled out for recommendation, so it's up to you to flip through the listings and make calls.

In addition to flying as a courier, you can fly standby. There are bargains to be found here, but there are also a number of disadvantages. You may find yourself spending the money you would have spent on a normal flight ticket just trekking back and forth from the airport, and hoping that this will be the day they will have a seat for you on the plane. (We speak from experience!) Whole Earth Travel is one company that offers information about standby tickets. It is located in San Francisco and can be contacted by calling 800-834-9192, or by checking the website www.airhitch.org.

Packing Your Bags

WorldWorks in Vancouver has some memorable advice that should serve you well when you pack: "When in doubt, leave it out." They go on to suggest that you try to think of the worst-case scenario if you left out an item and ask yourself, "Could I buy it locally? Could it be sent to me? Could I do things differently without it?"

Global Exchange in San Francisco suggests that you pack your bags and "then walk up and down a flight of stairs or around your neighborhood. If you get tired, reconsider what you are bringing and try to pare it down to the bare minimum."

Traveling light always enhances safety. If you travel light, you can move more quickly and more likely have a hand free. You will also be less tired and less likely to set your luggage down, leaving it more vulnerable, even unattended. Packing a small bag that fits in a plane's overhead compartment also ensures that the airline won't lose it (Again, we speak from painful experience!). If you are really pressed for space, wear or carry your bulky clothes rather than pack them in order to save valuable space in your bag.

If you are traveling by plane and plan to check your luggage, also pack a small bag that fits in a plane's overhead compartment. You should include in it anything that is vital for the first few days—important documents, medications, addresses and other contact information, and even such things as contact lens fluid. Thus if the airline misplaces or, God forbid, loses your checked luggage, you will at least be able to cope (Yes, again, we speak here from some sorry experiences!). You should study the list of items not covered by the airline's automatic insurance on your checked luggage; one such item of note is camera equipment. Therefore, we advise you to keep any such items in your hand luggage. Carry your tickets, passport, credit cards, and cash on your person at all times.

You will want to find out about the climate where you are going so that you can bring appropriate clothing. If you are going through an organization, it should be able to help you. Guidebooks for the country invariably give information about what weather to expect, often month by month. Be careful not to base your clothing decisions on a generalization about the climate and weather of an entire country. For instance, the climate of Ecuador's capital, Quito, at 8,000 plus feet above sea level is much cooler than that of its largest city, Guayaquil, on the tropical coast. Moreover, seasons can make an important difference. Contrary to popular myth, many parts of Africa are cold at certain times of year. You should also consult your organization, or even guidebooks about local dress codes. We recommend that you plan to dress more conservatively than you do at home. For example, for women, sleeveless shirts and those that show your midriff are inappropriate in most of rural Africa. If adults do not show their legs in the area where you will be working, even though it is warm, you should think long skirts and light pants instead of shorts. In many places in the world, a man will not be treated with respect if he wears shorts because only little boys wear shorts.

You will want to take clothes that do not require special care. Cotton-polyester blends dry easily, don't wrinkle much, and are more comfortable than a hundred percent synthetic. Global Exchange wisely suggests you should "select clothes with the knowledge that they may be lost or ruined" during the course of your time abroad.

Communicate with the organization you will be with about what you might expect to be able to buy locally. This is especially important if you are preparing for a long stay. Don't bring what you can buy locally at reasonable prices. We spoke with one volunteer in Costa Rica who thought she had better bring a year's supply of shampoo with her from the States, only to discover to her chagrin that shampoos, most coming from the same multinationals as at home, were readily available in even the smaller towns. It's also better to think ahead about whether there are some things you think you need that you really don't.

Even though most people going abroad to volunteer probably wish they had packed less rather than miss things they left behind, a few of the things to consider packing you may not readily think of are:

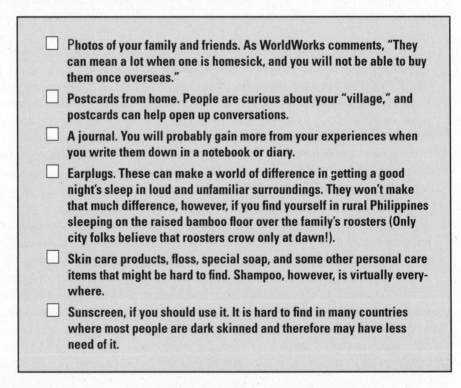

☐ **Photos of your family and friends. As WorldWorks comments, "They can mean a lot when one is homesick, and you will not be able to buy them once overseas."**

☐ **Postcards from home. People are curious about your "village," and postcards can help open up conversations.**

☐ **A journal. You will probably gain more from your experiences when you write them down in a notebook or diary.**

☐ **Earplugs. These can make a world of difference in getting a good night's sleep in loud and unfamiliar surroundings. They won't make that much difference, however, if you find yourself in rural Philippines sleeping on the raised bamboo floor over the family's roosters (Only city folks believe that roosters crow only at dawn!).**

☐ **Skin care products, floss, special soap, and some other personal care items that might be hard to find. Shampoo, however, is virtually everywhere.**

☐ **Sunscreen, if you should use it. It is hard to find in many countries where most people are dark skinned and therefore may have less need of it.**

☐ **A small gym bag or daypack (which might go empty and folded up in your suitcase). This can be handy when you have a short trip to make from your new home and want a bag that can fit easily overhead in a bus, which will probably be your most common mode of transport. It also may be useful if you acquire some things while overseas that you want to bring home.**

☐ **For women, a simple ring that you wear as if it were a wedding ring may prove invaluable in situations such as long bus rides on which you may get unwanted attention from single men.**

☐ **Plastic bags for liquids such as shampoo and sunscreen, and for storing documents during the rainy season.**

Always carry valuables on your own person, not in a backpack. Also avoid carrying valuables in fanny packs, handbags, and outside pockets. All are easy targets for thieves. By valuables, we mean your passport, air tickets, travelers checks, cash, credit cards, and medications. Leave jewelry at home.

If you are traveling with someone, consider packing half of your clothes in his/her bag and carrying half of your companion's in yours. If one of your bags is stolen or lost, you at least have half your things.

A final note: Don't take chocolate bars to the tropics, unless you like chocolate soup, or, perhaps, chocolate over everything in your bag.

Money: Figuring Out How Much You Will Need and How You Are Going to Carry It

First, you will need to estimate how much money you will need to take with you. If you are going through an organization, it should be able to advise you. If the organization covers expenses and even provides you with a stipend, you should not need much at all.

But if you are required to cover your own expenses or if you have created your own program, you will need to take money with you. If you are not working through an organization and therefore cannot ask how much you might need, you can look at a budget-minded guidebook for the country and check out the estimates (Lonely Planet, www.lonelyplanet.com, or Moon Handbooks, www.moon.com, are good for this purpose). Of course, living somewhere as a volunteer is not the same as traveling around (which may well cost more), but at least consulting a budget-minded guidebook gives you a starting point.

Once you've figured out how much you need and somehow have pulled it together (suggestions for how to raise the money can be found in Chapter 7, "Overcoming Financial Obstacles"), you'll need to ask yourself, How should I keep it safe while overseas?

One of the safer places to carry money and other valuables such as tickets and passport is in a pouch worn under your clothing. You can also find in some men's clothing stores leather belts that double as money belts with a zipper on the inside opening up a compartment for folded-up large bills. If you zip up one hundred dollar bills in the belts we have used, you can carry up to $2,000. The advantage of these money belts over traditional money belts is that they don't look like money belts and therefore don't attract the attention of thieves. Take money out of your money belt only in places where no one can see you, such as a restroom stall or hotel room.

Traveler's checks, because they are insured against loss or theft, are the safest way to carry your money. The ones issued by the well-known companies such as American Express or Thomas Cook are accepted in most countries. In some places you get a slightly higher rate of exchange because they are safer to handle and transport than cash for those who are buying them from you. In other places, the rate is lower. The automobile associations (e.g., AAA, CSAA) will sell American Express traveler's checks to members without charging the customary one percent commission. Some banks will do the same for customers; if your bank doesn't do so automatically, speak with the manager, explaining that you are volunteering overseas—she or he may be moved to help you by waiving the commission. Keep a copy of serial numbers of the checks in a separate place from the checks themselves and cross off the ones you use as you cash them. Also leave a copy of the numbers with a friend or relative at home, just in case you lose both your checks and the serial numbers.

Traveler's checks are not accepted in some countries and in others they may be accepted only in urban areas, and it can be a hassle, for instance, to wait in a long line at the bank to cash them. If your volunteer placement organization doesn't know if traveler's checks are accepted in the country they are placing you in, you can try checking with the country's embassy or consulate in the United States. In some countries you will have no choice but to take cash, and in any case you should take some cash for emergencies. In such countries, you might find that $100 bills command a higher exchange rate than smaller denominations. Smaller bills can be handy when you want to exchange only a small amount of money as you pass briefly through a country en route to another country, to renew your visa for example. Keep in mind when you are at your bank at home to insist on bills that are fresh, that is, without any writing, other marks, or tears on them since in some countries only perfectly clean bills are accepted.

Even when you are planning on receiving a stipend or salary, remember that unforeseen problems can arise. Electronic equipment can be out of order, agreements with host institutions can come undone, volunteer organizations can face cash-flow problems, and political instability can close banking institutions. Even the Peace Corps experiences delays when Congress fails to pass a new federal budget in a timely fashion. So bring some of your own money for emergencies and don't get caught without a backup plan.

In many countries, licensed money exchange houses offer the same or better rates than banks and almost always are quicker. Even simple transactions in a bank in some countries can take hours (literally). Generally, hotels offer the worst rates.

A good rule of thumb is that if you need local currency upon arrival, change only somewhat more than you think that you will need until you've had a chance to compare rates and have a sense of what a good rate is.

Whether you change money in a bank or at a money exchange house, be sure to inquire first if a commission is charged and, if so, what is it and what is the minimum commission charged. Armed with this information, you will not only be sure you are accurately comparing competing options, but you also can calculate what is the minimum amount of dollars you should probably change in a single transaction. For example, if the commission is five percent, with a $5 (or equivalent) minimum commission, then you know that it wouldn't make financial sense to change less than $100 at a time. Another way to compare exchange rates is to simply ask, for example, "How much will I get for $50 American?" You can then compare that response with that of another money exchanger and make your decision as to which is the better option.

In an increasing number of Asian, African, and Latin American countries, the globalization of finance means that you can and may sometimes want to use a credit card for purchases, especially of sizeable items such as airplane tickets. Of course, using your credit card implies that you have figured out a way to deal with your monthly statement or to have it dealt with for you. Credit cards often offer a favorable exchange rate because of the high-volume exchange rate negotiated by the credit card company, plus you don't have to carry as much money around with you. Some credit card issuers (such as Citibank) now charge cardholders a commission on foreign currency charges, so you may want to compare the various credit cards and look for one that does not charge such a commission. Another advantage of paying by credit card is that you can dispute the payment through the credit card company if you do not receive what you paid for. In considering using a credit card, however, be aware that in many countries throughout Africa, Asia, and Latin America, some of the businesses that advertise that they accept your credit card will add on a percentage (we've seen as high as six percent) to cover the fee they pay to the credit card company. In some countries, particularly in Asia, our experience suggests that in businesses such as travel agencies, it is a good idea to ask for both the "cash price" and the "credit card price" when you are negotiating a major purchase.

Sometimes if you are using your credit card in a country with a high incidence of credit card fraud, approval for a particular charge may be denied. If that happens, telephone collect to the number on the back of your card. You will be switched to the credit card company's fraud department. You will be asked questions (e.g., your mother's maiden name or your social security number) in order to ascertain that it is indeed you using the card in, say, Nicaragua. Seemingly, it is then noted in your account that you are in this "shady country" and that ordinary charges made there should be approved. (Some make a proactive move here and contact the credit card company before going overseas and notify it that they will be in such-and-such country for such-and-such time.) Just as at home, you will want to take precautions to see that the name, account number, and expiration date on you card do not fall in the hands of anyone intent on fraud.

A final note on credit cards: if you lose yours or if it is stolen, you should telephone collect as soon as possible to the number in the United States on the back of your card. Hence, it makes sense to write that number down somewhere else, including leaving it with someone back home. Many credit card companies will express mail you a replacement card, using FedEx, DHL, or the equivalent.

In an increasing number of countries you now can use your ATM card. Of course, the money will come out of the machine in the local currency. In our experience, the ATM exchange rate is quite good, and you don't have to stand in line at a bank or currency exchange house. Of course, both your bank at home and the one you are using abroad might charge ATM fees, but they seem to be no greater than those charged at home (under $3 total). This option is particularly appealing if you fear you may run out of money during your volunteer stint (and if you have money in your account or a good friend who will make a deposit for you). This is considerably easier and far less expensive than the old standby, the wire transfer by bank to a local bank or by a company such as Western Union. In some countries you can avoid the ATM fees by buying something with the card and requesting cash back.

If there is a "black market" in money, dare you use it? In general, we recommend that you do not. In addition to possible legal risks, there may be ethical as well as practical considerations. As always, you should take your pointers here from the organization that placed you as well as the local organization with which you are working. There are some countries (fewer than before the free-market era) where "everyone" uses the extra-legal market to change money rather than banks since official rates are absurdly low. There may be a few countries where you might choose not to use the extra-legal market to change your money because you think it is undermining the fiscal policies of a government you support.

As for the practical considerations, the danger in quite a few countries (but by no means all) in using the extra-legal market to change money is that you can be cheated or robbed by the marketer. Some operators in these markets are sleight-of-hand artists. You'll swear that you watched with unswerving eagle eyes the local currency counted out in front of you before accepting it and placing it in your pocket (hurriedly, of course, because of fear of the authorities) only to get back to where you are staying and find to your disbelief that you have a nice stack of plain paper, covered with a single real bill (we speak from experience). Other operators in these markets may try to rob you (yeah, we've been there, done that, too). Always, therefore, receive into *your* hands and count the local currency before handing over your dollars. If the operator with whom you're dealing doesn't want to play by this rule, find another operator. Also be aware that in some countries money exchangers on the street pass off counterfeit bills. Another rule is that you should exchange money only in public, established places such as stores and squares and never in alleys or woods. Be forewarned that black marketers who are out to cheat you will invariably try to stir up in you a fear of the police. They are thereby likely to distract you with anxiety and coax you to go with them down some dark, deserted alley in order to be out of sight of the police. We have never known the police to trouble foreigners using the extra-legal market; but again, persons with the organization you work with and other foreigners are your best guides. Whenever possible, go with a friend; don't go alone. It is also better to change money extra legally with a shopkeeper since she or he is unlikely to cheat you since you can come back and cause a stink, unlike a streetwalker whom you may never see again. A final tip for changing money on the extra-legal market: if traveler's checks are accepted, they're always safer. If you discover that despite taking all precautions, you have been cheated, you could report the checks as stolen.

What if you are a U.S. citizen overseas and you urgently need to have money sent to you? If you are able to get to a U.S. Embassy or Consulate, money sent for you by someone in the United States to a Department of State trust account in Washington, DC, can be forwarded to you. This service of the Overseas Citizens Services costs only $15. The person sending the money for you will have to do so in the form of a cashier's check, bank check, or money order—not a personal check. Overnight mail to Washington speeds up the process, as would a wire transfer to NationsBank, Department of State branch, but NationsBank charges an additional $25 fee for handling. Inquiries at OCS can be made at 202-647-5225 (8 AM to 10 PM weekdays; 9 AM to 3 PM Saturdays. Note that the funds are normally disbursed in the foreign country's currency, not in U.S. dollars. That could be a problem if the official exchange rate is very unfavorable compared to the street market rate.

For some countries, there may well be commercial possibilities (for example, through Western Union: 800-325-6000), but these options might well be more costly.

It is worth repeating here that if you are going to be working in a country where the banks have ATMs, the ATM option described above will probably be quicker, less expensive, and safer than changing traveler's checks or cash.

Educating Yourself about the Country Where You Will Volunteer

Once you know which country you are going to, you should take advantage of any opportunities you have to learn about the country before you depart. You will want to learn about the country's history, economy, current events, customs, beliefs, and gender and sexuality issues. Westerners, and U.S. citizens in particular, are widely thought to be ignorant, indeed uninterested, in knowing about the rest of the world. The more you can learn before you go, the more, once you are there, local people will experience you as eager to learn and will help you learn much more. (Of course, once you are there, be prepared to keep modifying—even radically—what you thought you had learned before you arrived.)

In addition to any suggested reading list provided by your organization, there are a number of sources for learning before you go.

The Internet

Local newspapers, tourism ministry propaganda, and overseas organizations are all on the web these days. You may be amazed by how much your searches come up with. Many returned Peace Corps volunteers have created websites that they use to share their experiences. Even though you may not be going abroad through the Peace Corps, you might find useful the website of a Peace Corps volunteer whose assignment was in the country where you are preparing to go.

The Radio

The good old-fashioned radio offers a number of sources for information on current events around the world, though some provide better analyses of these events than others do. National Public Radio (NPR) provides international news coverage in more depth than most stations and is carried on most local listener-sponsored stations. The British Broadcasting Corporation (BBC) out of London has even better international coverage; it is notably strong in its coverage of the former British colonial areas in Africa and Asia (as well as cricket!). The BBC Worldservice is rebroadcast on some listener-sponsored stations in the United States as well as available through its website (www.bbc.com). The Pacifica Foundation's radio stations are another special source of in-depth international news. Check the website (www.pacifica.org) for stations in your area.

Libraries

Libraries offer a vast array of educational materials on countries around the globe including novels, reference books, newspapers, periodicals, and both audio and video recordings. Most university and public library catalogues are now online.

United Nations Publications

The United Nations Development Program (UNDP), UNICEF, and the World Bank all publish annual reports that have numerous tables comparing virtually all the countries in the world by different development indicators (e.g., health indicators, economic indicators, social well-being, and inequalities). Any good library should have them. The UNDP's annual Human Development Report is a good resource. It also can be found at the library or on the Internet at www.undp.org/hdro/. See also www.unicef.org and www.worldbank.org.

Guidebooks and Travel Literature

Few guidebooks to off-the-beaten-track countries were published before the late 1970s. Now there are the pioneering guides in the Lonely Planet series plus those of Moon Publications and Passport Press (Box 1346, Champlain, NY 12919). They are researched with the "budget" traveler in mind. In addition to recommendations about inexpensive lodging and eating, they provide a useful historical, political, economic, and environmental overview. After browsing through guidebooks in a local bookstore's travel sections, you'll surely want to buy at least one and possibly read in the bookstore and take notes from some of the others. (Remember you want to travel light, so you can't carry lots of guidebooks.) There are so many guidebooks out there that

Greg Hayes and Joan Wright have compiled *Going Places: The Guide to Travel Guides* (published by Harvard Common Press, 535 Albany Street, Boston, MA 02118). Books Passage is a mail-order house specializing in travel literature (51 Tamal Vista Boulevard, Corte Madera, CA 94925, 800-321-9785, www.bookpassage.com). It markets an enormous listing of travel guides, literature, and maps for developing countries organized by country and region. This "living, breathing, independent bookstore" (we're quoting from its website) has over 500,000 titles on their website and a staff of fifty to respond to your e-mailed queries. Regardless of the country where you plan to volunteer, we recommend L. Robert Kohl's *Survival Kit for Overseas Living* (Intercultural Press).

There are also number of specialty guidebooks including those emphasizing a gay and lesbian perspective. The *Spartacus International Gay Guide,* updated and published annually, covers virtually every country in the world. Under each country, it summarizes the local laws that affect sexual minorities, gives some general heads-up advice, lists relevant local organizations (if any), and places where gay men and lesbians meet one another. It is more up to date and comprehensive on some countries than others, probably depending on information received from travelers. A web search might also be helpful.

There are also a number of excellent websites and guidebooks addressing travel issues specifically for women. You may want to start with Women Travelers Resources (www.bootsnall.com/cgi-bin/gt/sidetalk/women/index.shtml), Maiden Voyages (http://maiden-voyages.com), or Journeywoman (www.journeywoman.com). Check out either "Gutsy Women," full of travel tips from women for women, or "A Woman's World," both from Travelers' Tales (www.travelerstales.com).

Be sure to visit the travel literature section of your local bookstore, usually distinct from the travel guides section.

Literature from Overseas

Short stories and novels can be windows on a culture. Some literature is so widely known in a country that being familiar with it gives you another common reference point with people you will meet. If you live near a university, check if it offers courses on the literature of your destination country. If so, ask the department for copies of the course syllabi and start reading. You may want to contact a professor recommended by the department, perhaps by e-mail. Many syllabi from universities around the world are on the web; search using "syllabus" and the country or region where you will volunteer.

Newspapers and Magazines

Certain periodicals provide current news and information you won't be able to obtain from books. The *New York Times* and *London Times* cover at least some international news. If the country you are going to is in the former French colonial world and you can read French, consult the daily *Le Monde* and the monthly *Le Monde Diplomatique,* both at good bookstores and, one hopes, any university library. For the Spanish-speaking world, you should consult *El País,* the Madrid daily. *La Jornada,* arguably the best daily in Mexico, is available in quality bookstores in the United States and can be read online at www.jornada.unam.mx. For the former British colonial world, keep an eye on the major English daily *The Guardian.* Then there are magazines worth checking out such as *The Economist,* a conservative and business-oriented publication with many articles and interesting data about "developing" countries; it is published in England but widely available in the United States. To get an idea of the interests multinational companies have in the country you are going to, you should check the annual indexes for recent years of *Business Week* and the *Wall Street Journal.* Of course, every publication has a viewpoint and should be read with that in mind. Still you can learn a lot by reading even a publication whose editorial viewpoint you might fundamentally disagree with. Also, look in your local library for back issues of "alternative" publications such as *Mother Jones* (www.mojones.com), *The Nation* (www.thenation.com), *The Progressive* (www.progressive.org), *Multinational Monitor* (www.essential.org/monitor/), and *Z Magazine* (www.zmag.org). Look up country names in their annual indexes. *Transitions Abroad* (www.transabroad.com) is one of the best publications for information about work, travel, and study abroad. Articles cover everything from teaching English in Chile to biking through Africa. Even the ads are valuable sources of information about health insurance, discount plane tickets, and volunteer programs.

CultureGrams, a division of Mstar.Net, publishes briefings for nearly every country in the world. Formerly produced at Brigham Young University, each four-page "culturegram" summarizes a nation's economic and other statistical data, highlights aspects of the culture of which the foreign visitor should be aware, and provides information about entry requirements and the like. You can download free samples at www.culturegrams.com or order by calling 800-528-6279.

Computerized periodical indexes such as Current Topics are available online and you can browse them for free through major public universities.

U.S. Government Publications

We have already mentioned the Consular Information Sheets issued periodically by the State Department for virtually every country in the world. In addition to detailing entry requirements for U.S. citizens, these documents inform travelers about currency regulations, health conditions, the crime and security situation, political disturbances, areas of instability, special information about driving and road conditions, and drug penalties. They also provide addresses and emergency telephone numbers for U.S. embassies and consulates (you may want to print these out and take them with you). Normally, the Sheets do not give advice. Instead, they describe conditions and issue public announcements so travelers can make informed decisions about their trips. However, if the State Department considers a situation to be dangerous for U.S. citizens, it issues a travel warning that recommends that they defer travel to that country.

People Who Know Your Country of Interest

Seek out others in your area who have spent time in the country you are traveling to. If you are going through an organization, you will want to ask for the names and contact information of others who have been volunteers through the organization in the country or region where you are headed. Also seek out citizens of the country you will be visiting who live in the United States, for instance, at a local university or college. You can even place a classified ad in your local newspaper saying, "Have you been to 'xyz' country recently? Traveler seeks your advice. Call Jane Doe at 555-1212."

Volunteering Here before You Go

If you first volunteer at home with a local organization, you'll probably be a much more effective international volunteer. By volunteering before you go, you can develop specific skills you can use overseas, such as teaching or carpentry. You may gain an understanding of some of the challenges that organizations face virtually everywhere. You may also pick up valuable ideas that you can share with an organization overseas. Visit www.volunteermatch.org for information about volunteering locally. See Chapter 10, "Staying Involved after You Get Back," and Bonus Section A, "Alternatives to Volunteering Overseas," for further suggestions of how to get involved with different domestic volunteer programs.

Educating Yourself about Development

As part of your preparation, we suggest you read and think about development. In Chapter 3, "The Big Picture: International Volunteering in Context," we offered some critiques of prevailing ideas about sustainable development. There we also offer some suggestions for further reading.

Learning the Language

In our fieldwork we found that volunteers who had not achieved ease in the local language were among the most frustrated. If you need to learn a language, there is no time like the present for getting started, even if your program abroad begins with language training. Especially if the language is one likely to be taught where you live, such as Spanish, you should start right away. One man we know who was waiting to start his volunteer work in Indonesia, advertised on local bulletin boards that he wanted to exchange English conversation lessons with lessons in Indonesian. He found a local family that had recently emigrated to California. By visiting them in their home he learned not only some Indonesian but also some helpful things about the culture.

Communicating with Home

Check if you will have access to the Internet. Cybercafés are increasingly common throughout Asia, Africa, and Latin America, partly because it is such a relatively inexpensive way to communicate internationally and because so few people can afford their own computers and connection. You can find out about cybercafés in the country you'll visit at www.cybercafes.com. It's a good idea to set yourself up with a free e-mail account with Hotmail, Yahoo, or one of the equivalents before you depart. You can even have your mail forwarded from your regular e-mail account. See Chapter 9, "How to Be an Effective International Volunteer," regarding avoiding excessive use of e-mail while overseas. Be aware that Internet access in some countries can be expensive and excruciatingly slow, especially at times of the day that correspond to morning and afternoon in the United States.

Sign up with your long-distance carrier for a travel phone card, if you don't already have one. Carriers such as Working Assets also offer for a nominal monthly fee ($4 at the time of this writing) an international plan. The plan gives you steeply discounted rates on international calls.

Note that some long-distance telephone companies such as MCI and AT&T block calling card calls from certain countries because of high levels of fraudulent use of such cards in those countries. We experienced this in trying to use an MCI calling card in Peru. You may wish to check before you leave home whether you will be able to telephone with your calling card from the country you will be in and how much it would cost to do so, so that you can compare with rates charged by a telephone company where you are volunteering.

Although it may sound obvious, remember to write down important phone numbers and addresses so that you can call or write home. Don't forget to leave an emergency phone number and contact information for you overseas even if you won't necessarily be reachable there at all times. This way if someone needs to contact you, at least they know where to start.

Plan to register with your embassy or consulate after you arrive, especially if you are in an area experiencing unrest or a natural disaster. This will make it easier if someone at home needs to locate you urgently or in the unlikely event that you need to be evacuated.

Finally, it may be a good idea to settle in your mind what level of a personal loss or crisis back home would bring you back home. Your father, facing a life-threatening illness? Perhaps, yes. Hard financial times for your siblings? Maybe not. You decide, but give some thought to it ahead of time.

Managing Your Expectations

Now that you have handled all of your travel logistics, received your shots, organized your finances, decided what to pack, started to learn about the country and the language of your destination, begun volunteering with a local nonprofit organization and made arrangements to communicate with home, it is time to take a deep breath and a step back.

By now you have probably built up an incredible list of expectations and it is important to start managing those expectations before they get out of control. Expectation management is one of the most important but difficult parts of being an international volunteer. Start by trying to become aware of the expectations that you possess, and take the time to question the validity and usefulness of these expectations. You might find that some expectations are easily discarded while others are stubborn companions for your journey abroad. Whatever the case, do your best to avoid having your expectations sneak up on you for the first time when you are overseas and facing the additional pressures of arrival and culture shock.

One strategy for actively managing your expectations is to try to imagine your life overseas. What do you envision yourself doing? What setting do you see yourself in? What type of people do you see yourself interacting with and on what terms? As you create a mental picture of your life abroad and outline your expectations, you will have an opportunity to uncover the assumptions underlying these expectations. You may find that certain expectations are based on ignorance, stereotypes, or idealistic visions of life overseas. Is your expectation to show people how to build better houses based on the assumption that your knowledge of building houses in the United States is applicable to building houses abroad? Is your desire to live in a grass hut predicated on the assumption that most Africans live traditional rural lifestyles? Is your expectation to "help people" based on the assumption that people need or want your help? Ask yourself which of your current expectations are realistic? Which are not? Which expectations might set you up for disappointment? Which expectations are you willing to let go of? In Chapter 9, "How to Be an Effective International Volunteer," we will suggest ways that you can "check in" on your expectations, and modify them according to the reality of the situations you encounter.

Summing Up: You've Got Your Work Cut Out for You

As you can see, you have a lot to do. Some of this preparation is necessary but tedious. Some of it is necessary but exciting. Try to set a realistic preparation schedule for yourself so you don't feel unduly anxious in the months before your departure. And remember, like so many things in life, the more you prepare, the better your volunteer experience will be.

Action Steps for What to Do before You Go

1. *Get Your Documentation.* Obtain a current passport and any necessary visas.

2. *Take Care of Your Health.* Visit a health care professional and pack for a healthy experience. Buy necessary health and evacuation assistance.

3. *Buy Your Tickets.* Make your travel arrangements if your travel is not being arranged by an organization.

4. *Pack, Then Repack.* Figure out what you really need to pack and what you can and/or should leave at home.

5. *Deal with Your Finances.* Figure out how much money you will need to bring and how you are going to carry it. Create a system for how your student loans and other bills will be handled when you're gone. Make a plan for how you would get emergency funds if needed.

6. *Educate Yourself about Life Overseas.* Learn about the country through publications, the Internet, and by talking to others, who are from, have volunteered in, or have traveled in the country you're heading to.

7. *Beef Up Your Skills.* Volunteer here before you go.

8. *Study the Big Picture.* Educate yourself about international development.

9. *Aprenda el idioma.* Learn the language.

10. *Plan Your Communication.* Arrange how you are going to communicate with home.

11. *Reflect on What You Expect.* Manage your expectations.

HOW TO BE AN EFFECTIVE INTERNATIONAL VOLUNTEER

As an international volunteer, you should know that you will live a considerably different life than you would at home. You need to build trust and understand what locals think and know. You may have to drink a lot of tea and eat a lot of rice. And you should always have the attitude that you are learning.—Larry Groff, volunteer, Mennonite Central Committee, Cambodia

So, you've found a volunteer placement organization that matches your skills, interests, and budget. You raised enough money for your program and plane ticket and have been preparing yourself for volunteering abroad. Now you need to know how to be the best possible volunteer. In our research, we found that technical skill alone will not determine whether a volunteer will have a positive impact. A nurse may volunteer at a small clinic and help train the staff, educate patients, and, in the process, become a lifelong friend of the clinic director. Another, equally qualified nurse might volunteer at the same clinic and anger the staff, scare the patients, and create crises that drain the director's precious time and energy. In this chapter, we will share strategies for making your volunteer experience a positive one for you, your co-workers, and the people you hope to serve.

Moving from Culture Shock to Cultural Integration

Arrival

For most international volunteers, especially those with little or no previous international experience, arriving in a foreign country is a dramatic experience. Typically, the smells, the climate, the buildings, the action on the street, the traffic, the language, the people, and the very ambience are radically different from those at home. These differences can be quite staggering, and both exciting and overwhelming.

When you first arrive in a new country, a single day can seem like a week. Activities as simple as following directions to an office or getting food at a market can be intense adventures. The drive to experience everything is exhilarating, yet the combination of jet lag and the fact that nothing is routine can be exhausting.

Generally, people experience a "high" after their arrival in a new country. The images of foreign lands they have held close to their hearts suddenly come to life before their eyes. Some people are disappointed or frustrated upon arrival, but the sheer volume of new stimuli tends to push aside, at least temporarily, any disappointments that a volunteer might have. Most new arrivals are optimistic and upbeat.

Culture Shock

At some point during the first several hours, days, weeks, or months of their volunteer term, international volunteers experience culture shock. Culture shock is a term that describes the variety of emotions such as stress, frustration, anger, isolation, confusion, anxiety, and loneliness typically experienced by individuals traveling, living, and working in a foreign environment. Culture shock often stems from ignorance about how to do things "correctly" in a new environment. Behavior that is normal and accepted at home may be frowned upon in your new surroundings. Communication can be difficult even if there is a common language, which there frequently is not. Due to different cultural norms, your "strange" behavior can elicit negative reactions, as well.

Our goal in discussing culture shock is not to prevent it. That would be impossible. Our goal is to help you to be conscious of it and avoid being surprised when you experience the first symptoms. If you catch yourself getting easily frustrated with your hosts, your host country, and yourself, recognize it as a sign of culture shock.

Reactions to culture shock vary widely, but there are several common patterns. Research by CUSO and Canadian Crossroads International suggests that individuals tend to respond to culture shock in one of four ways:

- *Participators* tend to enthusiastically embrace the culture of the host country. They assimilate quickly and often integrate certain aspects of local culture into their own behavior. They get very involved with the new things around them, and this helps them to overcome the initial confusion and isolation of culture shock.

- *Adjusters* tend to be less enthusiastic about the local culture than participators, but they do not reject it completely. Instead, adjusters identify the positive and negative sides of the culture in which they are immersed and learn to appreciate the positive while finding ways to simply endure the negative.

- *Escapers* are people that seek, often unconsciously, to avoid things about themselves or their lives at home. While being in a new culture can offer a new way of being in the world, it can also increase the very stress that escapers are trying to avoid. Some escapers who serve as long-term volunteers completely adopt the local culture and deny their own culture. Some escapers find that the problems that they were trying to avoid continue to plague them.

- *Non-adapters* never adjust to the local culture or conditions of life in the host country. They may be obsessed with how much better things seem at home and may be unable to make any positive connections with the people in the host community. For some non-adapters, the stress of being in another culture may precipitate severe depression (or on rare occasions a psychotic episode). Non-adapters often leave the work site and return home quickly, which is usually the best solution for them and others. Those who stay constantly criticize the host country and its people while romanticizing life back home.

You should be aware that some people do not experience culture shock until as late as one or two years after arriving in a new culture. Don't be surprised if it sneaks up on you. Your type of reaction to culture shock is not predetermined, and you always have the opportunity to move from culture shock to cultural integration.

Cultural Integration

Throughout your volunteer experience, you have the chance to determine to what degree you will integrate yourself into the local culture and to what degree the local culture will become a part of you.

Hanging out by the pool at a downtown hotel? Socializing exclusively with other volunteers? We call this behavior "hiding in little America." Cultural integration often depends on your avoiding little America. As globalization accelerates the export of Western culture and all its trappings, volunteers may be tempted to seek refuge in expatriate enclaves. We were surprised and somewhat disturbed by the number of volunteers we met who were frequently eating hamburgers and drinking Budweiser as they lost themselves in replicas of life in the United States.

Expatriate enclaves and familiar chain stores can also reinforce the messages of the mass media, which elevate consumption above all other values. Is that the message you want to send to your hosts? Try to limit your trips to the mall (if there is one) and refrain from socializing exclusively with expatriates. Instead, ask yourself what you can do to become more involved in other social realities. Carla Blunpschli, a volunteer trainer in Haiti, suggested that you "make personal relationships with people immediately. Go to their gardens, listen to them sing and talk, and wash clothes with them, carry water, interact as much as possible." Here are a few additional suggestions for becoming more integrated into local culture:

- *Learn a local craft, song, or dance.*

- *Eat meals with local friends rather than with other volunteers. (If eating out, be sensitive to their budgets.)*

- *Attend a local church or other religious institution, even if it's not your religion. Many congregations are very open to visitors.*

- *Spend time with your co-workers outside of the workplace.*

- *Offer to make a presentation at a local school.*

- *Enlist the support of local children in learning the language. They will probably be happy to tell you the names of different objects, and may be easier to converse with than adults, even though they may laugh at your mistakes. The children you meet can often connect you to adults who may become friends or allies.*

- *Ask a local person to teach you how to cook a traditional dish.*

- *Offer to help with daily work, even if it takes you an hour to do what your host can do in ten minutes. If nothing else, your attempts at plowing a field with a water buffalo or transplanting rice will be entertaining to the community.*

- *Use local transport.*

- *Opt for local cuisine served in mom-and-pop style eateries over the increasingly ubiquitous franchise fast food. (See p. 133 for tips on eating safely.)*

Your warmest memories of your experience may be the wedding you attended, a grandmother you met on the bus, or the day you spent with a first-grade class. Making efforts to participate in local cultural activities can go a long way toward helping you become integrated into the community.

The Limits of Cultural Integration

> There are good and bad in all societies. You need to create a balance after seeing another culture and another way. You can decide to absorb certain things, but when you see the bad, don't be so quick to criticize.—Sudha Datar, Academic Director, Minnesota Studies in International Development, India

As you begin to adapt to your new surroundings, don't forget that you are not a local. Despite all of the common ground that volunteers may find with local people, there will always be differences in values and behavior that may become points of contention. In many cases, regardless of the number of months spent in a community or their mastery of the local language, volunteers may still be considered guests or outsiders. Be careful of raising too high your expectations of "going native."

Try not to idealize the host culture. While you may feel that people in a small humble rural village are happier and live less stressful lives than people back home, remember that many of these communities may lack basic human needs such as clean water or adequate sanitation. On the other hand, don't demonize the local culture—seek to understand it. You will most likely discover some elements of the culture that you will want to embrace, and others that you will want to challenge.

The Art of Crossing Cultures, (Yarmouth, ME: Intercultural Press, 1990) written by Craig Storti, is recommended reading; it discusses culture shock, cultural integration, and cross-cultural communication.

Five Character Traits of Highly Effective Volunteers

Different people will take different approaches to volunteering. As we spoke with people in the field of international volunteering, however, it became clear that there is consensus around the most important traits of effective volunteers: flexibility, patience, openness, dependability, and humility.

Flexibility

You must be flexible. You may arrive at a volunteer post with a written job description, but when it comes time to start doing things, you may discover that your job description is largely irrelevant. No volunteer ever knows exactly what he or she will experience or what will be required of him or her in the workplace, but, as Lee Cridland of the Andean Information Center in Bolivia told us, "Being a good volunteer is about doing what is necessary." Doing what is necessary often means letting go of grandiose plans and undertaking more basic tasks. Ranjit Purshotam of the Legal Resource Center in South Africa explained, "It's actually impossible to find exciting, high-profile work for volunteers every day. At some point you have to do the run-of-the-mill stuff. Fighting for someone's old-age pension, for example, may not seem exciting at first, but it's of the utmost importance to that person." Being flexible involves adapting to what is going on around you, even if it is dramatically different than what you are used to.

Patience

International volunteers must learn to be patient and go slowly. Almost everyone we interviewed noted that the pace of life in Asia, Africa, and Latin America is slower than back home. Tom Benevento, with the Brethren Volunteer Service in Guatemala, suggested that you "Focus on the process rather than the successes, and try not to do too much."

In many countries, when people say they will meet you at a certain time, you can expect them to be late or not arrive at all. Punctuality is not always highly valued, and this can be a great test of a volunteer's patience. People in Asia, Africa, and Latin America can also be much less project oriented than their North American counterparts. Many volunteers working in community development come in with the attitude that they have a project to complete; they must realize that meaningful community development is a long and slow process. We were asked repeatedly, by volunteers and hosts alike, to advise future volunteers to "avoid forcing their agenda," and to "let things develop at their own pace." Many projects proceed much more slowly than they would in North America. A community organization in Haiti, for example, may lack computers, filing cabinets, phones, and even electricity. In Nepal, some villages may be accessible only on foot. All of these things can slow down a project, and a healthy dose of patience is necessary to help you keep going.

Openness

> *Volunteers should either have a really open worldview or have a willingness to have their worldview opened. Don't be afraid to acknowledge your prejudices. If you think that you do not have any, then you are pretty naïve.*—Mary Helen Richter, volunteer, Mennonite Central Committee, Vietnam

Respect and tolerance are essential for international volunteers. You will be going into situations that you will not understand right away. Be careful not to judge too quickly. Be willing to see things through others' eyes. You may have the opportunity to do things you would never do at home: drink yak butter tea, make a fool of yourself dancing in public, attend a traditional healing ceremony. Take the chance.

Dependability

We interviewed hosts who felt they had wasted time orienting, supervising, and befriending international volunteers who ended up abandoning posts, taking holidays whenever they wanted, or just hanging around doing no work at all. Volunteers should not abuse the hospitality and warmth of their hosts. Follow through with your commitments and respect the time and energy of your host organization and host community.

Humility

International volunteers have a unique opportunity to realize how little they know. In situations where the language is unfamiliar, the rules are new, and the culture is different, volunteers are often reduced to feeling childish. Some have revelations that, while they may be accomplished professionals and community leaders at home, in their new environment they are novices. Often volunteers have to ask a lot of questions and carefully observe their surroundings in order to accomplish even the most basic tasks. Fighting your occasional feelings of helplessness with stubbornness and pride will invariably lead to frustration and conflict.

Humility does not come easily to many volunteers. One simple exercise that you might consider completing while in the field is a life experience assessment. Look around at the people with whom you are living and working, and ask yourself a few simple questions:

Life Experience Assessment

- **What knowledge and skills do the people from this community possess that I do not?**

- **What life experiences do they have which are different from mine?**

- **What are some of the obstacles they have had to overcome in their lives?**

- *What challenges do they face daily that I do not?*
- *What are some of their personal and professional strengths?*
- *What can I learn from them?*

These questions can help you humble yourself and temper some of the arrogance and frustration that so easily enter the psyche of many volunteers. They can also assist you in the process of opening yourself to what Kelly Reineke, who volunteered in Brazil, calls "two-way empowerment," learning from and being changed by the people you intended to help.

Ten Things Effective Volunteers Do

In addition to nurturing the five character traits discussed above, international volunteers can also take concrete steps to increase their efficacy in the field. Here are ten things that volunteers can do to increase their chances of success.

Ten Things You Can Do to Become an Effective Volunteer

1. *Learn the language.*
2. *Listen before you act.*
3. *Be friendly.*
4. *Live simply.*
5. *Find allies.*
6. *Dress appropriately.*
7. *Exercise extreme caution in friendship, love, sex, dating, and marriage.*
8. *Work for sustainability and local control.*
9. *Reflect on your experience.*
10. *Share with people at home.*

Learn the Language

No single factor can alter your international volunteer experience more profoundly than your ease in the local language. With proficiency in the local language, new worlds will open up to you. You will be able to interact with people more directly, your conversations unfiltered by translators. As soon as possible after arriving overseas, take classes, find a tutor, or exchange lessons in a foreign language for lessons in your own native tongue. Don't be afraid to make mistakes—just try to find someone who will correct your mistakes so that your skills will continue to improve.

Listen before You Act

Take the time to listen. Some programs instruct their volunteers to do nothing more in the first few months than try to observe and adjust to the pace of life in the host community. While this "go-slow" period may be frustrating, putting time into building relationships and developing cultural sensitivity can help make it easier for you to accomplish things down the road.

Volunteers that focus solely on teaching, telling, ordering, or directing will miss out on a lot of valuable learning experiences. As one volunteer host in Cambodia exclaimed: "Don't come in and tell people what to do! Americans are so bossy." Many overexuberant volunteers have devised projects that made sense on paper, but were inappropriate or ineffective because they violated local cultural practices. A bicycle-operated water pump, for example, devised by volunteers but intended for use by women in West Africa was installed in a region where there was a taboo against women riding bicycles. In Fiji, Peace Corps volunteers who sought to help island villagers gain access to micro-enterprise loans did so in a culture where people are supposed to share excess money with friends. In order to use the micro-enterprise loan model, the villagers had to go against one of their most important cultural values. Taking the time to listen before you act can help you avoid working on projects that are either inappropriate or destined to fail.

One common mistake volunteers make is failing to listen to women. In some societies, it may be especially difficult to get to hear women's voices. In many cases male volunteers will do better working with a female colleague who can get close to women more easily to hear and pass on what they have to say.

Be aware of polite agreement. In some cultures, negative feedback is considered to be extremely impolite (especially if it is directed at someone perceived to have more power or status). Just asking for an opinion may not guarantee an honest answer.

Be Friendly

Remember that there is a lot of room for non-verbal communication to augment the spoken language you are learning. Being friendly can be an important part of relating with people in another culture. As Case McCrea, a YMCA World Fellow in the Philippines said, "A big smile . . . can get you further than almost anything else."

Be aware, however, of the cultural context of non-verbal communication. A big smile can mean different things in different cultures. Take your cues from the locals, and learn to be friendly in appropriate ways and at the appropriate times. This is especially important in male/female interactions, where your friendliness might be misinterpreted, as discussed below.

TO SMILE OR NOT TO SMILE?

The following are typical reactions of three foreign students to one non-verbal behavior that most North Americans expect to bridge gaps—the smile.

Japanese student: On my way to and from school I have received a smile from non-acquaintance girls several times. I have learned they have no interest for me; it means only a kind of greeting to a foreigner. But if someone smiles at a stranger in Japan, especially a girl, one can assume he is either a sexual maniac or an impolite person.

Korean student: An American visited me in my country for one week. His inference was the people in Korea are not very friendly because they don't smile or want to talk with foreign people. But most Korean people take time to be friendly with people we know. We just never talk or smile at strangers.

Vietnamese student: The reason why certain foreigners may think that North Americans are superficial is that they talk and smile too much. For people who come from cultures where non-verbal language is used, silence, a smile, and a glance each have their own meanings. It is true that North Americans speak a lot. Their superficiality can also be detected in their relations with others. Their friendships are, most of the time, ephemeral compared to the friendships we have at home.

For more details on this discussion, see WorldWork's web page www.vcn.bc.ca/ idera/wworks/ww.htm.

Live Simply

I recall that, when I was a child, the missionaries from the States always talked about how we were all brothers. Yet when I visited them in their homes, I saw that they lived in another world. In the bathroom, everything—the soap, shampoo, and toothpaste— would be from the United States. I asked myself, "Isn't this a contradiction?"—Lalo (Eduardo) Rodriguez, Mennonite Central Committee, Mexico

Though many volunteers live in luxury relative to local people, some live in luxury even compared to their lives at home. Even if you have the financial resources and access to the amenities of home (as might be the case in large cities or regions such as Eastern Europe), we suggest you try to live simply.

You may have choices regarding not only where you live, but also whether you live with local people or with other foreigners, with domestic help or not, with or without air conditioning. You may also have choices about what kind of food you eat—imported pasta and deli food or local staples purchased in the market. While taxis may be convenient, and even essential for certain types of work, nothing compares to riding a local bus.

Take time to think about how your lifestyle will affect your interactions with people in the community. David Chaske, a volunteer with the Overseas Development Network in India, recalled that, "Children began to recognize their poverty in the value of my belongings." Hopefully, you will consider this before you arrive overseas, but, if not, you can still choose to simplify your life. Many volunteers find great joy in simple living. Global Service Corps volunteer Elizabeth Kikuchi told us, "One of my favorite parts of living in Kenya is the simple pleasure of washing my clothes by hand."

In some countries, Peace Corps volunteers may be surprised to find that they are expected to hire a "house boy" or "house girl" to cook, clean, and wash clothes. Doing your own housework may actually require making a "statement" or defying others' expectations of you. When Peace Corps volunteer Jeff Silverman chose to do all his own cooking and cleaning in Kenya it was "seen as a strange thing for a white person to do." Jeff's decision helped him feel better about his service and possibly challenged certain assumptions in the local community. (On the other hand, we met volunteers who argued that hiring local people to do certain domestic chores is a boost to the local economy.)

Another aspect of simple living involves decisions about the amount of contact that you have with home. A number of programs discourage or forbid travel home during vacations while in service. Volunteers told us how they experienced a second and more severe wave of culture shock when returning to their volunteer site after a short trip home. We recommend that you avoid travel home even if your program allows it.

E-mail and fax machines have recently become much more available to international volunteers. They are especially accessible to volunteers serving in capital cities, and even volunteers in many rural areas can get their hands on a computer and a modem periodically to tap out an e-mail message. This ease of communication can lead volunteers to try to exist in two worlds at once. You may want to consider simplifying your life by focusing on where you are and limiting your contact with home.

Find Allies

> The best advice that I was given before my service was to endear myself to the people I worked with. I took that advice to heart, and it has probably given me my greatest sense of accomplishment concerning my service.—Laura Vogel, volunteer, YMCA World Fellows Program, Trinidad and Tobago

Befriend someone from the local community with whom you have a connection. A local ally might be able to help you become a more effective international volunteer. Spend time with someone who can offer you advice and support on how to handle relationships or issues at work, or how you can navigate in their culture. Such a relationship could prove to be the most rewarding part of your volunteer experience. Due to the possibility of the community misinterpreting the relationship, we suggest that you choose a friend of your own sex. Also, remember that there are people overseas, just as there are at home, who are untrustworthy; exercise caution in choosing your friends and allies.

You may also find support from someone of the same cultural background. He or she might offer you a break from the constant cross-cultural challenges and help you reflect on some of your experiences. Remember, however, not to spend too much time with other foreigners—you risk isolating yourself from local people.

As a foreign volunteer, it may be a challenge to gain the confidence of your hosts, colleagues, or students. "Hanging out" can be a good way to get to know local people, but think about whom you are hanging out with and where, and what message that will send to others. If you are working at an orphanage and are therefore responsible to act as a role model for the children, your supervisor will probably be upset if she finds out that you spend your days off in a local bar.

Dress Appropriately

> *Please advise female volunteers not to wear sleeveless shirts and to keep their legs covered. Males should wear long pants; in our society, only young boys wear shorts. When volunteers dress here the way they do at home, they set a bad example for our youth.—Frank Matoro Nyatiwa, community member, Tanzania*

We urge you to pay attention to local norms about dressing. It does not matter if you do not feel like yourself unless you are wearing a miniskirt and low-cut top, or shorts and a T-shirt. In many communities, if you wear such an outfit, people will form a negative impression of you based on their own cultural norms. You may be insulting their religion, or culture, or both. You may inadvertently feed stereotypes that all Westerners are insensitive or sexually available, and you will make it more difficult for future volunteers. Women should leave their halter tops and short skirts behind and buy some comfortable skirts that fall below the knees. Men should bring long pants (of lightweight cotton if you are going to the tropics). We suggest leaving your tongue and other body piercings in your backpack, and covering your tattoos with clothing. In general, take your hints from the locals. You may even consider investing in some local garments.

Exercise Extreme Caution in Friendship, Love, Sex, Dating, and Marriage

> *Single Western men often go crazy over Asian women . . . but dating does not necessarily exist. A couple of dates and it is assumed that you have slept together, that you are engaged . . . and, if the Westerner casually breaks it off, then that woman can be viewed as "polluted" and unmarriageable.—Jeff Stebbins, staff, English Language Institute, Vietnam*

Few volunteer organizations offer formal advice or support dialogue concerning issues of sex, dating, and marriage. The people we interviewed, however, agreed that international volunteers should exercise extreme caution when dealing with romance in a cross-cultural context. Cultural understandings of friendship, dating, love, and sexual relations vary greatly. There is always the potential for serious miscommunication. As an international volunteer, you have to realize that your reason for being involved in a romantic relationship may be quite different from that of your foreign partner.

In many countries, friendships between men and women are rare. Spending a lot of time with someone of the opposite sex, even if you avoid physical contact, may be interpreted by that person (or the community) as a romantic relationship. In some cultures, for example, when a woman lets a man walk her home, they are considered to be romantically involved. The perception of a romantic or sexual relationship—even if unfounded—may hurt you, the organization you work with, and your friend. Some advise that under no circumstances should you date or have sexual relations with anyone on the staff of the organization where you work. We recommend that you avoid casual sexual relations, especially if you are living and working in a small rural community. If you do want to pursue a romantic relationship, be sure to be very clear about your boundaries. Don't let your partner assume that a willingness to kiss means a willingness to have sexual intercourse.

Many people in developing countries are desperate to get out of their own countries and go to countries like the United States, and this can have a direct impact on your relationships overseas. We heard of volunteers getting romantically involved with foreign nationals only to discover (sometimes after getting married) that the relationship they thought was about love was really about their partner's aspirations to get a foreign visa. A Peace Corps volunteer we met in Nicaragua said that she realized her position as an American when, as she put it, "A man with whom I'd had a good working relationship started telling me that I should help him get a visa to the States. 'If you really wanted to help me,' he would say, 'then you would marry me.'"

While we met some volunteers who fell in love and married across national boundaries, we also talked with those whose relationships did not survive the volunteer's time overseas. We heard about relationships and marriages that fell apart in the process of trying to move back to the volunteer's home. We also met some volunteers who developed a relationship with a local person and never moved back home.

One volunteer who married an Egyptian she met in West Africa—and then went through a painful divorce after moving with him to the United States—said that in retrospect, her decision to get married was "like denying everything that had been an important part of me up until that point." She suggested that we remind our readers that it's easy to lose perspective on reality when you're in a totally different culture, and suggests that a major decision like marriage should not be made until you have gone back home and had time to reflect.

Some volunteers see dating and romantic relations as the ultimate form of cultural integration, but remember that there is more at stake than just the volunteer's ability to become a part of the culture. As Andrew Wells, a staff member of Catholic Relief Services in Vietnam, explained, "Traditionally, when a Vietnamese (or Chinese) person has married a foreigner—and it's almost always a woman marrying a foreign man—

IT COULDN'T HAPPEN TO ME, BUT IT DID

If you have any doubts about issues of sex and love,
listen carefully to "Alison's" story:

"The very first day I arrived in town, I met Samuel. I liked him right away; he was thoughtful, kind, and funny, not to mention exceedingly handsome. The day before school started, he spent hours helping me set up my classroom, and he gave me price-less advice on dealing with the fifth graders I was to work with all year. We ended up meeting every day; he tutored me in the local language, and I helped him with his French.

"Within a few weeks, I realized I was starting to fall in love with him. I kept my feel-ings to myself until, three months after I arrived, he confessed his love for me, and we became more than friends. We truly loved each other. After getting tested for HIV, we began a sexual relationship that continued throughout my two years in Cameroon.

"While I knew AIDS was a big problem in Cameroon, I saw and heard no signs of it in the small town where we lived. I didn't even think of it much, especially since Samuel and I had been tested and we used condoms. But one time the condom broke, and a couple of times we were careless.

"Near the end of the second year I got a terrible vaginal infection and high fever that would not go away. My organization arranged for me to be admitted to the best hospital in the capital, and the doctors prescribed heavy doses of antibiotics. The in-fection persisted, and I was finally sent back to the States, without even saying good-bye to the students. Samuel took me to the airport, and we cried as if our lives were falling apart. In a way, they were.

"When I arrived home, I was diagnosed with genital herpes. In a panic, I wondered if Samuel had been unfaithful to me. If so, he might also have become HIV positive.

"After three days of living hell, my HIV test came back negative. I now thank God with all my heart that I only have herpes. I'll never know if Samuel cheated on me, or if, as he claims, he was infected before he met me and did not realize it. But I do know that true love does not protect you, innocence does not protect you, being young does not protect you, being middle-class does not protect you, and being a good person does not protect you. Only safe sex or no sex protects you."

While we've changed the names and some details, this is a true story.
Don't let it happen to you.

she has been cut off from her culture and 'lost' to the larger community, even to family and friends. But times are changing." We suggest that you avoid getting intimately involved with anyone at least until you gain your bearings in the culture in which you are volunteering.

Work for Sustainability and Local Control

Put simply, teach rather than do it yourself. Teach what you know and what you have been requested to teach. Though it may be faster or easier to do something yourself, the lasting impact will most likely be greater if you pass your knowledge on to the local people. Many of those we interviewed stressed the importance of focusing on capacity building and sustainability. As Belinda Forbes, staff member of the Committee for Health Rights in the Américas in Nicaragua, suggested, "As soon as you arrive, pick someone local to replace you." If the volunteers alone develop and implement projects, then the local people will become dependent on foreign aid. Many agree ardently with Francis Potter, a volunteer with Institute for International Cooperation and Development in Angola, who commented that it is "disempowering to have foreigners run the projects."

Be responsive to local needs and be aware of who is defining what those needs are. Just because someone is a local does not mean he or she is necessarily working for the interests of the community. Local landowners may have learned how to ensure that volunteers' projects work solely to their benefit. One of the boons of volunteering overseas is that it provides the opportunity to reflect on who benefits from development projects. Try thinking more critically about local power structures. Learn how you can ally yourself with those grassroots organizations that prioritize the needs and aspirations of people with less social, economic, and political power.

Even projects that appear to be uncontroversial may have unintended side effects. An influx of foreign doctors can disempower local women who work as midwives, unless the doctors find ways to collaborate. Teaching exclusively in European languages can decrease literacy and fluency in local languages. "Green Revolution" seeds can deplete soil, displace locally adapted varieties, and sharply increase poor farmers' cash costs for chemical fertilizers and other inputs that these seeds require. Think through your action's potential impact on people's ability to take care of themselves in the long term.

Issues of sustainability and local control also relate to the means by which various projects are accomplished. The desire to help can lead to an unwitting undermining of local efforts and culture. Steve Rosenthal, founder of Cross-Cultural Solutions (CCS), told us that "Volunteers often say 'I wish you had told me what exactly my work was going to be, so I could have brought this or that from the States,' but we think it's better to get things from here in India, so we don't teach people to think that things from the United States are better."

Reflect on Your Experiences

International volunteers deal with many different types of experiences, and they need time to process it all. Many volunteers told us that their lives as volunteers were very conducive to thinking, reflecting, and journal writing. You might find it interesting not only to write about everything that is going on around you, but also to chart the ups and downs of your volunteer experience. Volunteers themselves benefit from personal reflection first and foremost, but your journal can also be a great resource for sharing your experiences when you return home.

Ellen Donaghue, a volunteer with Minnesota Studies in International Development, who we met in India, kept three journals. "One is for weird things that happen every day," she told us, "like my trip to the post office." The second was for stream-of-consciousness writing about her feelings, and the third was reserved for use as a day-by-day accounting of what she did, where she went, and whom she met. Regardless of how you organize it, journal writing is an invaluable practice while you are an international volunteer.

International volunteers also benefit from organized group reflection. Group discussions and retreats can provide volunteers with feedback on their experiences and help them place these experiences more deeply in context. Through group reflection, volunteers can examine some of the root causes of the problems their projects address, and increase their sense of commitment and accountability to others.

There are many broad topics that you might reflect on, from understanding your new culture and your cross-cultural experiences, to examining your personal development as a volunteer. Issues of identity such as gender, race, class, sexual orientation, and nationality are also important subjects for individual and group reflection.

Here are some possible questions for journal writing or group reflections:

- *What are the problems that my work here is addressing, and who has defined these as problems?*

- *What are the immediate causes of the problems my work is addressing? How have these immediate causes influenced the strategies employed to address the problems?*

- *What are the root causes of the problems my work is addressing? How have these root causes influenced the strategies employed to address the problems?*

- *What role does the global economy play in the problems and opportunities facing the local community?*

- *What power and privileges do I have that local people do not?*

- *What power and privileges do local people have that I do not?*

- *What do I gain from my work here?*

- *What do local people gain from my work here?*

- **What will happen here after I leave?**

- **How can I nurture the positive changes I've made in myself here once I return home?**

- **What can I do when I return home to continue to support people here, or to confront the root causes of the challenges they face?**

Share with People at Home

Through reflection, many volunteers identify ideas and experiences they want to share with people they care about. Many volunteers send periodic letters to their family, friends, and supporters. In fact, writing letters can be another way of reflecting on your experiences. Some volunteer programs assist volunteers in organizing a system to distribute a single letter to a large group of people, or maybe you have a friend or a family member who would agree to do so. One volunteer used carbon paper to copy letters to friends into his journal; you could photocopy yours or ask friends to keep them for you. While constant e-mail use can detract from a volunteer's cultural integration, periodic distribution of letters to an e-mail group can be a great way to keep people informed. It's never too early to take a few pictures of your host family or interview your colleagues at work. These documents will be invaluable for sharing your experience, as well as keeping your memories alive.

Self-Awareness and Effective Volunteering

Managing Your Expectations

Go in with high expectations of yourself and with very few expectations about the direction your service will take you.—Laura Vogel, volunteer, YMCA World Fellows Program, Trinidad and Tobago

The best advice we can give you about expectations is to be willing to let them go. To start letting go, nothing is more helpful than admitting to yourself that you do have expectations. Belinda Forbes advises volunteers to write down their expectations. "Don't say, 'I don't have expectations, I am open to anything,'" she says. "It's better to try to dig out what your expectations are, articulate them, and then realize that they might not be met."

We can tell you in advance that you should work hard to let go of the expectation that you'll be doing exactly what your job description says. Also do your best to drop the expectation that you'll be able to fix all the problems you'll encounter.

Reining in your expectations, or at least becoming more aware of them, can help you to move beyond your initial motivations for becoming an international volunteer. The reasons that you are interested in international volunteer work today may not be the reasons that guide your volunteer work three months or three years from now.

Many volunteers begin to look for volunteer experience with one set of expectations and motivations, depart for overseas with another, and return home with a totally different set of experiences and lessons learned. We frequently heard volunteers say things such as, "I volunteered for all the wrong reasons and with too many expectations, but luckily I was able to change my approach as I went along."

We suggest that throughout your time abroad you reexamine your expectations and ask yourself which expectations have been fulfilled, which you are willing to abandon, and which you still want to work to fulfill. Looking back on some of your expectations may even give you a good laugh.

If you didn't write down your initial expectations as suggested in Chapter 8, "What to Do before You Go," take the time to do so now. Then choose any or all to analyze in the following "Expectation Analysis Chart."

WORKSHEET VII

EXPECTATION ANALYSIS CHART

What you expected?

What you found?

What's the difference?

Why is there this difference?

How do you feel about it?

Was/Is this expectation a burden or an asset?

Let go or hold on and continue to work to realize this expectation?

You will probably wrestle with your expectations throughout your tenure as a volunteer, but if you are willing and open, you can begin to transform the values, beliefs, attitudes, and assumptions they are rooted in.

Identifying Your Skills and Making a Contribution

I feel that, in some ways, I was a burden for the people I worked with because of my limitations with language and culture. I hope that my contributions made the burden worth it.—Rachel Cornwell, intern, United Methodist Mission, Japan

Many volunteers vacillate between feeling that they have made a concrete contribution and feeling that they have been a burden on their hosts. If you doubt whether you are making a contribution, try reminding yourself about some of the skills you possess that may be valuable to the people and organizations you are working with by completing a quick "Skills Inventory."

In addition to valuing technical skills in areas like health, agriculture, and education, organizations overseas often look for help in the following areas: English, report writing, proposal writing, public relations, computers, customer service or sales, organizing office systems, research, communications, organizational management, and website design.

Some volunteers overlook the "soft skills" they might have. As Debbie Hurst, a Peace Corps volunteer in Bolivia, reflected, "At first I thought that technical skills were what was important, that maybe I could use these skills to help improve people's health. But I soon realized," she told us, "the most important thing a volunteer can possess is people skills."

WORKSHEET VIII

SKILLS INVENTORY

List some of the skills that you possess that might be helpful to the organization and people you are working with. Consider your education and work experience. Don't forget to also list personal characteristics and talents that might be useful.

_____

_____

_____

_____

_____

Using Your Contacts

In addition to the skills that you bring into your placement, you also bring your own personal and cultural network and set of contacts. Tammy Sharp, a volunteer with the Zimbabwe Cycle Against Unemployment, explained how being a foreigner gave her "easy access to the media, to local dignitaries and to sources of funding" that were previously not accessible to the organization. Elizabeth Beak, a volunteer with the Pusanga Women's Cooperative in Ecuador, used the local network of foreign travelers to help translate promotional materials about the cooperative's products into several different languages. Eric Stern, an American Jewish World Service volunteer in Kenya, commented that "As a foreigner, your biggest contribution may be the contacts that you bring to the organization." By the time you leave, other people in the organization should have relationships with your contacts so that the benefits don't walk out the door when you do.

Using Good Judgment

Use your good judgment, especially concerning the use of alcohol and recreational drugs. It is always a bad idea to ignore local laws. Remember that while you are developing a reputation for yourself, for better or worse, you are also developing a reputation in the local community for the volunteers who will come after you.

WHAT NOT TO DO: VOLUNTEERS FROM HELL

We hope you read this chapter carefully so you don't end up written up under this heading in future editions of this book!

After six months in Zimbabwe, Bob invited all the teachers of the school where he volunteered to go out to dinner at a fancy hotel as his guests. The bill totaled hundreds of dollars. He claimed to have forgotten his money, borrowed it from the principal, then left town without paying it back, never to be seen again.

Ricky, a Peace Corps volunteer, worked as an agronomist in the Ecuadorian rain forest. He was responsible for teaching members of the community agricultural techniques to grow more nutritious food and utilize economically and environmentally sustainable farming practices. On his own plot, however, Ricky chose to grow marijuana, and he tried to support the local economy by buying an additional half-pound from a local drug dealer. Ricky was caught and sent to jail. The community was left without an agronomist.

Recognizing the Umbilical Cord of Privilege

Our economic background makes it hard for us to understand the degree of financial struggle most people in developing nations endure. Volunteers eventually come to realize how fortunate we are and usually how spoiled we are.—Andrea Foster Crna, volunteer, Health Volunteers Overseas, Guyana

Many volunteers do not think of themselves as privileged; however, the mere act of volunteering abroad suggests that a volunteer has the time and resources to travel and not be working to meet his or her family's basic needs. As Rani Deshpande, a volunteer with International Development Exchange, commented, "The very ability to take a few months or years of one's life, usually unpaid, to work supporting social change outside of one's own community must be recognized as a form of privilege." Volunteers often think that no one can see their privilege. But their possessions, food, and clothes, as well as the vacations and short excursions that they take, are all part of the "umbilical cord of privilege," a term coined by volunteer Kelly Reineke. Even those who live simply have this umbilical cord, which at a moment's notice can meet their desires for comfort, health care, and entertainment. This umbilical cord also provides volunteers with an escape if things get uncomfortable, dangerous, or overwhelming; they can always pull on the cord and bounce back to life at home. "The volunteer must always keep in mind that their ability to retreat to a comfortable First World existence," Rani told us, "is a fundamental difference between volunteers and people in developing countries who do not have that option."

Volunteers, therefore, must negotiate a fine line between supporting and learning from the community in which they are working and never assuming that a stint as volunteers enables them to truly understand the problems and situations of people living in that community.

The most important advice we have about the umbilical cord of privilege is that you be aware that it exists and realize that others can see it even when you cannot.

Remember that you have the protection of a Western passport and of a government that could evacuate you if a violent political unheaval occurs. The local worker that you think should confront his boss, for example, about the illegal use of pesticides may be fired, jailed, or even worse should he challenge certain entrenched interests. Jim Tuite, a Maryknoll volunteer in Korea, was horrified when his roommate was violently attacked because of his involvement in the labor movement. Jim realized he could never be in the same predicament as the people he worked with because, as a foreigner, he never would have been attacked that way.

Most people will assume that you are rich. In fact, in relative terms you probably are. Recognize that, although you may be living at a level that would be well below the poverty line at home, you will most likely still be living far above the level of the local poor. You may be asked for money either directly or indirectly. You may be a target of thieves or simply of people who charge you higher prices for the same goods and services. Such experiences can be disheartening. One volunteer we interviewed had decided to quit after her money was stolen by one of the children in an orphanage where she worked.

Understand that, because you are a foreigner, especially if you are white, you may be given power and status that you do not deserve. But, as Suzanne Nickel, a Mennonite Central Committee volunteer in Egypt reflected, "With this power comes the responsibility to use it properly." You may not want the power, but it's up to you to make some conscious decisions about what you want to do with it.

Staying Safe and Staying Healthy

Accidents

Traffic accidents are perhaps the biggest threat to a volunteer's safety. Lower safety standards and bad road conditions make accidents more frequent in Africa, Asia, and Latin America. Exercise caution when driving during the day, and avoid driving at night. Remember that, in many countries, pedestrians do not have the right of way. Also, pedestrians and drivers should take special care in former British colonies where vehicles drive on the left.

Staying Healthy

Thoughtful preparation (see Chapter 8, "What to Do before You Go") and conscious living can go a long way toward helping you stay healthy while in the field.

Heed the advice of local people as well as fellow volunteers and travelers. Here are a few ideas for staying healthy that we have learned during our travels:

- *If you did not get all your necessary shots before you left home, go to an embassy-referred doctor in your host country.*

- *Eat consciously. Choose hot food over cold, fruits with a skin or peel that you can remove, and bottled beverages. In many countries, it is not safe to drink the water. Boil it, drink bottled water, or use iodine pills if you will be in an area where bottled water is not available. Avoid non-bottled juice as well, as it may be diluted with tap water, and ask for drinks without ice.*

- *Volunteers often face the challenge of trying to eat safely and at the same time not insult their hosts. Try talking with your hosts before meals are prepared. If you decide that you don't want to eat a particular dish, be polite in asking for something else. We found that volunteers often succeeded with phrases such as, "Unfortunately, I have a very weak system, and I often don't feel well after I eat such-and-such."*

- *Experiment with preventative tips from other volunteers and locals. We have heard suggestions such as eating yogurt, taking acidophilus daily, or adding hot chili peppers to your meals.*

While many diseases, such as polio, hepatitis, tetanus, and yellow fever can be avoided through vaccines, other serious diseases can only be avoided through careful behavior. Avoiding being bitten by mosquitoes and/or taking prophylactic pills can prevent malaria, a serious and potentially fatal disease. (See Chapter 8, "What to Do before You Go," for more information.)

While abstinence is the surest way to avoid sexually transmitted diseases, using a condom correctly is a highly effective safe-sex strategy. In addition to practicing safe sex, you can limit your chance of contracting any sexually transmitted disease by avoiding IV drug use and contact with blood. Health workers should use the same precautions they would at home. Blood transfusions should be avoided if at all possible, and any shots you need should be given with a new syringe, even if you have to buy one from a local pharmacy.

If you get diarrhea, you can avoid dehydration by drinking bottled water or juice with salt added. Boiled water with sugar and salt will work in a pinch. Bananas, plain rice, crackers, or toast are good options if you need some energy as you are trying to get your stomach back to normal.

If you do become very ill, seek medical treatment. Bloody urine or diarrhea, diarrhea that is severe or does not go away, yellowish skin or eyes, and high fevers are all potential indicators of serious illness, and should be treated *immediately*. Err on the side of caution. We encourage you to use the privilege and power of your money and/or nationality to get the best treatment you can find. Often this will mean contacting your embassy to get a list of recommended doctors.

Crime

Street crime is a concern almost everywhere in the world today. Whether you find yourself in the largest city in North America or the smallest village in South America, you could be the victim of petty theft or a more serious crime. Especially in many urban areas, crime is on the rise, and some places are extremely dangerous. Volunteers cannot make themselves immune to the extra attention that a foreign face or clothing often attracts, but a few precautions can help you avoid some unpleasant incidents and minimize the loss in others.

- *Don't carry around a lot of money. Carry only enough money to purchase what you might need for the day.*

- *Wear a money belt with your valuables under your clothes and next to your skin. Never open your money belt in public.*

- *Be aware of your surroundings. Be especially on your guard in or near public transportation hubs like airports and bus terminals. In crowded situations, try wrapping a strap from your luggage around your arm or straddling larger bags.*

- *Try to avoid arriving at your destination at night, especially in a new town or country.*

- *Don't carry any valuables in a fanny pack. If you wear a fanny pack wear it in front, not on your fanny. Also be aware of carrying valuables in your backpack. If you are in a crowded area try carrying your backpack either in front of you or at your side with one arm over the zipper.*

- *Don't wear jewelry or watches. Even something that is not especially valuable to you could attract unwanted attention.*

- *Never walk down poorly lit streets or alleys at night, even if accompanied by a local. (One of us learned this the hard way.)*

Safety Issues for Women

> Women will feel uncomfortable at times because of unfamiliar sex roles. My advice: take men's come-ons lightly but refuse firmly. Never lose your dignity or sense of humor. Say no assertively, and they will get the point. Getting all worked up about it will not help.—Rebecca Grossberg, volunteer, Joint Assistance Center, India

Women are frequently warned against going to the "developing" world. Unfortunately, it is true that women are much more likely than men are to be the victims of sexual harassment and sexual assault. In virtually every country we visited, we heard from female volunteers who had been subjected to "frequent come-ons, unwanted touching, or inappropriate comments," in the words of one Peace Corps volunteer. Harassment and assault range from verbal harassment, to crude propositions, to groping (especially by men in buses or trains), to, in rare cases, rape.

One of the challenges for female volunteers overseas is that they may focus so intensely on being helpful, open-minded, or culturally sensitive that they inadvertently allow their personal safety to become a secondary issue. When almost all cultural norms are different, it can be hard to discern a person's true motives. One volunteer let her host father put his arm around her when they walked around the village, which he interpreted as a green light to initiate a sexual relationship. Listen to your intuition about a situation and always err on the side of caution—it's better to risk offending someone than to risk being assaulted.

Remember that there are various ways to respond to harassment. Responses can range from saying "no" firmly but nicely, to screaming, fighting, and/or running away. Modify your response according to the situation. In some cultures, a simple "no" is a polite way of saying "maybe." Some situations may require a more forceful message.

"Bay Watch" is the most watched television show in history, and European and American porn flicks are shown to audiences around the world. It is not surprising, therefore, that many people overseas think Western women are "loose." This assumption almost inevitably leads to harassment and misunderstanding. When you fight back against harassment you are fighting years of Hollywood imagery as well.

Unfortunately, you will need to modify your behavior to combat these stereotypes and avoid unwanted attention. Most women volunteers act more conservatively overseas than they might at home, giving up certain freedoms in exchange for an enhanced sense of safety. In many cultures, smoking cigarettes, barhopping, or simply drinking beer, for example, could put you in the "sexually available" category. As mentioned, we suggest leaving your skimpy clothes at home. Avoid sexual dancing and sexual flirting. Behavior you might consider normal at home may be scandalous or even dangerous overseas.

Women abroad, as well as at home, are much more likely to be sexually assaulted by men they know than by strangers.

In many places, if a woman invites a man to her home, he thinks that she is inviting him to have sex, especially if she is an American. If you do not want romantic involvement with someone, be sure to avoid compromising situations where you might be alone in a suggestive context with that person. Also be aware of situations in which you would be especially vulnerable (e.g., where it would be difficult to get out if you felt endangered).

There are a number of strategies that women volunteers have used to avoid harassment. Some women wear a wedding ring to discourage would-be suitors. Many volunteers learn strategies from local women. In Mexico, for example, women often sit together in public parks and other public spaces, even if they don't know each other, in order to avoid the harassment they would experience if they sat alone. Other tips, in the voices of previous volunteers, include:

- *"Be careful about letting your guard down while on vacation."*
- *"Travel with a group if you go out at night."*
- *"Before you leave home, talk to other female volunteers that served in your country of service."*
- *"The in-country program director cautioned us against looking or staring at the men for too long at a time because this could be misinterpreted since the women in the local villages were taught not to make eye contact with the men."*
- *"Be ready to give up some freedoms that you are used to in the United States."*
- *"Females must take care with their dealings with any male older fourteen and younger than seventy-five. I was often misunderstood at first and didn't realize that plain speaking and looking at a man directly when speaking to him could be misinterpreted as flirting. I learned quickly to be very formal and to always involve several people in any given conversation."*
- *"Don't be afraid to ask about the security situation where you are posted, and find out about any prior incidents that may have occurred in the area."*
- *"When it comes to your life, you can't be too cautious."*

No matter what you do or don't do, remember that it is not your fault if you are assaulted. If you are raped or assaulted, it is most important to get to a safe place, then seek medical care and emotional support. The Peace Corps cautions that the local police station may *not* be a safe place; a friend, neighboring family, or hospital may be safer. If you feel comfortable with them, you may want to notify your host family or organization's staff for support. You are not alone, and you deserve support.

For more information for survivors of sexual assault, try contacting:

- **National Alliance of Sexual Assault Coalitions** *(www.connsacs.org/alliance.htm)*

- **National Coalition against Sexual Assault** *(717-728-9764, ncasa@redrose.net, www.ncasa.org)*

- **Rape Abuse and Incest National Network Hotline** *(800-656-HOPE)*

Dealing with Challenges in the Field

Why Do People Lie to Me?

In many cultures "no" is considered impolite and, therefore, you have to be on alert to the ways "yes" is said to really mean "no." Bernard Butkiewicz, a Maryknoll volunteer in Bolivia, commented that people do not want to make you feel rejected. "If they say yes to you when they know that they are not going to be able to make it," he told us, "later they can apologize and the relations are not broken. If they just say no to your face, then relations are broken." In time you will learn how to distinguish a "yes" from a "no."

Dealing with Government Bureaucracy

For some volunteers, the government bureaucracy of the host country creates frustrating barriers to effective work. For example, permission to proceed with a project may hinge on the agreement of two government agencies that, apparently, don't communicate with each other. A bureaucrat may expect a bribe that you are not willing to pay. Try to deal with these challenges with persistence, humor, and patience. If bureaucracy makes plan A impossible, invent plan B.

Face It . . . You Are Going to Make Mistakes

We heard countless stories of volunteers who, in their eagerness to "fit in," played the part of the fool. You might actually say, for example, in the attempt to say in Spanish that you are "embarrassed," that you are "pregnant" (*embarazada*). Though you may be horrified at the moment, you often later can look back on such an incident and laugh. In some cultures everyone will laugh out loud at your mistake, especially a physical one like tripping, as a way to say that you didn't really trip by mistake but just wanted to give everybody a good laugh. That way you don't look bad. Some mistakes will have more serious consequences. Whenever you do make a social blunder, try to learn exactly what it was so you can avoid a repeat performance.

Why Don't They Stop Staring at Me?

> *Don't take yourself too seriously. You will be stared at, laughed at, and you most likely will start with the vocabulary of a two year old. You should be comfortable being the center of attention. Don't be afraid to make mistakes and make a fool of yourself. Be funny with people. Sometimes I think that maybe my purpose in the village is to enter-tain people.* —Katrina Donovan, volunteer, Peace Corps, Bolivia

People stare at foreign volunteers, especially in places where foreigners are sel-dom seen. Foreigners tend to look a lot different than the average person on the street, and they actually might be kind of entertaining. Try to let go of your desire to be anonymous. With the exception of some larger cities, international volunteers tend to attract a lot of attention, so don't expect to blend in. In a small town all eyes are on you.

Why Won't People Give Me Some Privacy?

Many Americans long for privacy when they're abroad. People in other cultures may assume that if you are alone you are sad, and your host may think it is their re-sponsibility to make sure you are never alone. Try to explain to your hosts that you would like some time alone, that you won't be lonely, but that you appreciate their con-cern. Take some time for yourself when you can. Take a long walk, but don't forget to tell your hosts where you are going. "If you get overwhelmed and want a place to run and hide, arrange for your own sanctuary—either a place, or within yourself—somewhere that you feel safe," suggested Carol M. Hansen, who volunteered with Cross-Cultural Solutions in India. A short weekend away once in a while may help you maintain your sanity and need not undermine your participation in the local commu-nity. As for the kids whose favorite pastime is looking in your window, the concept of "privacy" may be lost on them.

To Give Gifts or Not?

> *It is very important that North American volunteers not bring things to give the local people. One problem with having North Americans as volunteers is that the locals think that the North Americans don't really expect them to pay back the loans. They say, 'But the North American padrinos (godparents) wanted me to have this house, they gave it to me.'* —Carlos Mejía, staff, Habitat for Humanity, Guatemala

Many volunteers harbor a strong desire to share with their hosts and to try in some way to repay the generous hospitality offered to them. But gift giving can be problem-atic. Gifts given by one set of volunteers creates expectations of gifts from the next set of volunteers. Gifts given to one person or group may create jealousy on the part of others. Gifts of items representing North American culture may feed into a devaluation of local culture. Why not try showing your appreciation in more non-material ways such as writing a song or poem for your friends? If you feel you must give a gift, try giving something that can benefit the broader community as opposed to just one individual or family.

Reducing Negative Impact and Danger for Local People

Local people have to live with the long-term impacts of your actions. What for you might be merely a frustrating work experience for them could mean life or death. The effects of your presence and your work may alter social relations in a given community, changes that continue to play themselves out long after you depart.

In one community, corn may have for years been ground at an individually owned mill. A volunteer's effort to establish a cooperative corn mill that charges a lower rate will be a direct challenge to the already existing mill. There are always some winners and some losers as local economic arrangements change, such as the fee for grinding corn. Foul play or even violent responses are not unheard of. Volunteers should be cautious about taking the lead on a project. If local people and their leaders are committed to starting a cooperative mill, and seem mindful of the risks and challenges, then it may be appropriate for a volunteer to be a part of the effort.

In communities entrenched in struggles for social change such as for indigenous people's rights, agrarian reform, or labor organizing, retaliation from established interests is commonplace. Stop to consider if your presence is endangering local people. On the other hand, your status as an international volunteer may offer them some protection. If this is the case, ask yourself, What are the plans for their protection after my departure?

Gender Roles and the International Volunteer Experience

> *Being a woman will certainly present limitations in most parts of the world in issues of safety, equality, or independence. But it may also present positive opportunities in cultures where the goddess is worshipped, where deities are female, where mothers are respected and honored as almost sacred, where expectations and standards for beauty are different and, perhaps, more realistic.—Mara Kaufman, student, Study Service Term at Goshen College, Costa Rica*

Don't forget that gender roles may be more rigidly defined overseas. Certain dances, religious practices, drinks, and spaces may be designated as the exclusive realm of men or women. Some cultural practices may surprise you or strike you as sexist. Women, for example, may be expected to wait until the men finish eating before they may begin a meal. Girls may be prohibited from going to school. And in some countries, female genital mutilation is still practiced. You must, as a volunteer, make a decision about what things you will accept and what things you will challenge. Examine the difference between accepting cultural relativism and tolerating injustice. If you decide to rock the boat, do so gently.

Some female volunteers are informally granted "honorary male" status, and the ability to participate in some activities that are usually exclusively male. Other female volunteers, however, may be expected to confine themselves to the female realm.

Whether or not they are able to explore traditionally male activities, female volunteers do have a key advantage over male volunteers—they have access to the women's world. The informal cross-cultural exchange that takes place while cooking, walking to market, or preparing a bride for a wedding could be the most fulfilling part of your volunteer experience. Most development practitioners will tell you that women are pivotal to the development of any nation. Female volunteers' special access to women can increase their project's chances of success and make the work more personally satisfying.

Spend time with local people of your own sex to see how they view gender roles and relationships, including friendships, between the sexes. Find local people you trust and ask their opinions before you take a step that you suspect might not be generally acceptable.

Race and the International Volunteer Experience

Race relations differ dramatically from country to country. Xavier Livermon, an African-American volunteer in Lesotho, found that "in some contexts, I was referred to as a Basotho (local African), other times I was considered to be South African or even white." In South Africa, he might be labeled "colored," while in the Dominican Republic, he could be labeled "mulato." Each of these racial labels carries its own connotations in the different cultures. White skin privilege is a reality in many countries around the world. If you are white (or perceived to be white) pay attention to the ways you may be granted privileges, and seek to understand historical reasons for this special treatment. (The website www.prisonactivist.org/cws has interesting essays and resources on this issue.) In rare cases, white people may be openly resented; seek also to understand the roots of these attitudes.

Racial stereotypes abound in all parts of the world. If you are Asian American, some people may not believe that you are from the United States. If you are Chicano, everyone may expect you to speak Spanish fluently. If you are African American, people in the community where you volunteer may expect you to play basketball. If you are a Native American, you may face ridiculous stereotypes based on Hollywood images.

Talk to locals and other volunteers of various ethnic backgrounds so that you can become aware of the ways that others may view your ethnicity. Many volunteers told us that they benefited from not only reflecting on race but also the ways that racial identity intersects with issues of national origin. Lucius Walker, the founder of Pastors for Peace, shared his experience with us. "In Latin America, people call me 'gringo.' So I had to learn to either own up to or somehow deal in my own psyche with the fact that I was being seen as an American, not as an African American. The distinction between Americans and black Americans was clearly not being made." Explore the privileges or challenges your ethnic identity can create for you while volunteering.

Homophobia and the International Volunteer Experience

In many parts of the world homophobia is much more extreme than in the West. Some political and religious leaders in developing countries claim that homosexuality is a colonial import. Even otherwise open-minded and progressive people may not be accepting of gays and lesbians. Under these conditions we recommend that the default option for gay/lesbian/bisexual volunteers is to stay in the closet, at least until you can assess the community's values on sexual orientation. In some countries, people can be jailed for homosexuality.

Barry Bem, a staff member at Peace Corps headquarters, a former Peace Corps volunteer in Brazil, and deputy country director in Ecuador, himself an out gay man, cautions that all volunteers "have to make cultural adjustments of all sorts in order to live and work effectively in another culture." For gay/lesbian/bisexual volunteers, "going back into the closet, or at least being much more circumspect about one's sexual orientation than in the United States, is one of the possible adjustments."

Having said that, in some communities, the people may be more tolerant than their religious and political leaders. One volunteer in a small community in Mexico found out that there was a street corner where gay men socialized. A woman who dressed in men's clothing was present at many community events and was tolerated as if she was someone's eccentric aunt. Still, as outsiders, volunteers should use extra caution.

Working with the Accidental Manager

Because people who do a good job usually get promoted, a volunteer teacher may end up directing a school. Another common scenario is for a visionary person to see a need in the community and start an organization dedicated to meeting that need. In both cases, the person suddenly finds himself responsible for raising money, training and supervising, or spending most of their time behind a desk instead of working with clients. Such a person can be called an "accidental manager."

He or she may be highly skilled in teaching literacy to street children, for example, but may have great difficulty in creating a budget, writing a proposal, or supervising someone else at teaching.

If you find yourself frustrated because your boss is an accidental manager, you may want to try to keep focused on the project. Don't let the fact that the administrative office is in total chaos distract you from your primary goal of, for example, caring for the children at the orphanage. If you have management experience, you may want to offer to help improve management systems. Keep in mind that any systems you set up must work for the organization's staff and continue to function after you leave.

Perhaps you can assist the staff in finding existing resources in their community in the form of other volunteers or training workshops. You might want to "manage your boss" by writing out your priorities as you perceive them and reviewing the list with him or her. You may also find it useful to write your list with five columns to create maximum clarity:

"What I will do"	"Expected results"	"What if" (trouble-shooting)	"By when"	"What next"

Try to distinguish accidental managers from corrupt ones. There are many dedicated visionaries who are doing the best they can, given their lack of training and resources. Unfortunately, there are also individuals who are downright corrupt. If you cannot in good conscience continue to volunteer for a group, look for an alternative placement and calmly resign.

Remember that many accidental managers are doing a lot with scarce resources, and are making headway despite facing serious obstacles. Steve Arnold and Kelly Reineke explore the dilemmas facing accidental managers in an article in the journal *Grassroots Development* (Volume 20, No. 1, 1996).

Early Departure: If It Just Isn't Working Out

All volunteers go through significant ups and downs during their service. It is not uncommon, especially for long-term volunteers, to consider returning home during one of their lows. While most volunteers successfully wait out and learn from these low periods, some realize that volunteering abroad just isn't for them. Others discover that the project they are working on is in conflict with their values. Even if your volunteer program is a good match for you, illness, a traumatic experience, war, or an emergency back home could cut your trip short.

While each case will be different, we can make a few general suggestions. Don't be rash. Ask yourself if you have really given the volunteer experience a chance. Find someone to talk with and consider your options. If you do decide to cut short your volunteer time, find out as soon as possible the financial implications of withdrawal: Will you get a refund? How long will your health insurance benefits last? When will you get your final stipend and how much will it be? If you are leaving because of an issue specific to the site, is another placement possible? Be sure to get contact information for anyone you will want to stay in touch with, including fellow volunteers and local friends.

If you are leaving due to illness, do not cut corners in your treatment. Certain diseases can be life threatening, so see a specialist, even if you have to borrow money to do so.

Remember that leaving early does not mean that you are a failure. There are still many things you can do to stay involved. (See Chapter 10, "Staying Involved after You Get Back.") Reflect on what you have experienced and learned during you time abroad, even if you didn't stay as long as you expected.

End of Service

The end of service is often a time of mixed emotions. Volunteers may be both happy to return home to friends and family, and sad to leave new friends and host families.

For those volunteers who are considering returning overseas to work, begin networking and exploring possibilities for other overseas positions before going home. If you are interested in helping future volunteers, ask your organization how you can offer feedback.

Whether volunteering for two weeks or four years, all volunteer experiences come to an end. You will experience radical changes as you transition from your life overseas as a volunteer and re-enter your old world. Don't forget that your life is not the only one that will change. Your departure will also affect your host family and community, as well as your local co-workers. Remember to say goodbye to everyone. Get the names (with the correct spellings) and mailing addresses of friends and consider leaving some self-addressed stamped envelopes to make correspondence feasible. Some have suggested hosting a going-away celebration. Whatever you decide to do at the end of your service, remember that endings are also beginnings.

Resources on Effective Development Projects

Challenging the Professions: Frontiers of Rural Development. Robert Chambers. London: Intermediate Technology Publications, 1993.

Rural Development: Putting the Last First. Robert Chambers. Reading, MA: Addison-Wesley, 1995.

Two Ears of Corn. Roland Bunch. Oklahoma City, OK: World Neighbors, 1995.

When Aid Is No Help: How Projects Fail and How They Could Succeed. John Madeley. London: Intermediate Technology Publications, 1991.

Action Steps for Being an Effective International Volunteer

1. *Arrival.* After you come down from the initial high of arrival, get settled and oriented in your new environment.

2. *Culture Shock.* Seek to move from culture shock to cultural integration and be aware of the different stages you might move through.

3. *Cultural Integration.* Avoid "little America" and seek to immerse yourself in the lives and culture of the local people. Learn a local craft, eat meals with local friends, and dance at a local dance.

4. *Limits of Cultural Integration.* Try not to idealize the local culture—seek to understand it.

5. ***Keep in Mind the Five Character Traits of Effective Volunteers.*** Flexibility, Patience, Openness, Dependability, and Humility.

6. ***Learn the Ten Things You Can Do to Be an Effective Volunteer.*** Get comfortable in the language; Listen before you act; Be friendly; Live simply; Find allies; Dress appropriately; Exercise caution in relationships; Work for sustainability and local control; Reflect on your experiences; Share with people at home.

7. ***Manage Your Expectations.*** Re-examine your expectations throughout your time abroad and ask yourself which expectations have been fulfilled, which you are willing to abandon, and which you still want to work to fulfill.

8. ***Identify your Skills and Making a Contribution.*** Identify both your soft and hard skills. Work at resolving the conflict between the feeling that you have been a burden on your host and that you have made a concrete contribution.

9. ***Use Your Contacts.*** Bring your personal and cultural network of contacts into your work as a volunteer. Remember that "your biggest contribution may be the contacts you bring to the organization."

10. ***Use Good Judgment.*** Remember that you are developing a reputation in the local community for the volunteers who will come after you. Don't leave a bad legacy.

11. ***Recognize the Umbilical Cord of Privilege.*** Be aware that you have it and that others can see it even if you cannot.

12. ***Recall How to Stay Safe and Healthy.*** Remain aware of how to avoid accidents, crime, disease, and illness. Women should note the additional precautions we have listed.

13. ***Review How to Deal with Challenges in the Field.*** Think through issues such as whether or not to give gifts, how to deal with the fact that people may "lie" to you or not give you enough privacy, and how to remain aware of the impact of your gender, race, and sexual orientation on your experience.

14. ***Be Prepared for the End of Service.*** Don't forget that your life is not the only life that will change upon your departure. Remember to say goodbye to everyone and smooth the way for a peaceful departure and safe return to your home country.

CHAPTER 10

STAYING INVOLVED AFTER YOU GET BACK

Coming home can be the most joyful part of your volunteer experience—and the most painful. You may feel elated, confused, empowered, depressed, or all of these things at once. You are a different person from the wide-eyed volunteer that stepped onto that plane months ago. You undoubtedly have a new perspective on your place in the world, and, quite possibly, a new perspective on your own country. The insights you gained volunteering abroad can help you work for positive changes both in your own life and in the world. Many volunteers tell us that it is only after returning home that they are truly able to begin making the world a better place.

We'll look into the return process in three stages: immediate re-entry, staying connected, and long-term involvement. We've also included several worksheets at the end of the chapter to help you with personal planning in these different areas.

Immediate Re-entry:
Hometown Hero or Stranger in a Strange Land?

Your first days at home can be as intense as your first days abroad. As you catch up with family, visit your favorite restaurant, get together with an old friend, or go back to work, you are almost certain to experience conflicting emotions. Expect to feel a little off-balance, and don't be surprised if you have dramatic emotional swings.

For some, reverse culture shock is even more unsettling than the culture shock experienced abroad. In general, the longer you are away from home, the more challenging your return will be. The transition will probably be more difficult if you worked as the only volunteer in a rural village than if you were part of a group of Western volunteers in an urban center.

Reverse culture shock can take many different forms, but it often involves the feeling that you don't understand others and they don't understand you. You may find yourself getting frustrated with little things at home that you never even noticed before. Normal features of life may seem absurd, overwhelming, or even upsetting. One volunteer told us, "It took a year before I could go into a supermarket without being shocked by all the choices compared to the market in Zambia, which sold only tomatoes, cabbage, and sun-dried caterpillars." Another volunteer said that because she saw her home with "different eyes," she felt like she had moved to a strange new country. Many volunteers have trouble adjusting to the hectic pace of life back home.

Even if you do experience some form of reverse culture shock, be assured that you are also likely to experience moments of joy and gratitude at your homecoming. It may be a real relief to be able to communicate freely in your native language, enjoy the comforts of home, have a sense of belonging, or feel deeply loved by friends and family.

Robert O'Donovan, who volunteered in Kazakhstan, was thrilled to be able to do laundry in less than five hours, to turn on the tap and have hot water come out, and to eat the pepperoni pizza he had been craving for two years.

While you may be happy to see your loved ones, they may not understand what you've experienced. You have to be patient and remind yourself that it can take time for people to understand how you have changed. In fact, some of your friends may not be happy with these changes.

Remember, when you return home you are a different person than you were when you left home. Important parts of your former life may no longer fit. The wasteful consumption of your suburban neighborhood may horrify you. Your friends and family may seem overly materialistic. Your wardrobe, your hobbies, even your career may no longer feel "right."

Although it may feel difficult at first, this change is almost always a positive thing. You have probably developed a better understanding of yourself. You have new skills and knowledge of your own strengths. You have a better understanding of the world and, perhaps, an even stronger commitment to making the world better. The ultimate goal of a successful re-entry is to gain mental and emotional stability while staying true to the ways you have changed while overseas. You might find yourself waiting to feel like you are back to normal, but eventually you may realize that you will never be your "normal" (i.e., "old") self again, and that is okay.

Here are several strategies you can adopt to help in the re-entry process.

Realize That the Transition May Be Hard

I was only in Latin America for a year, but it took me two years to readjust to being back in the United States. In fact, I think I'm still adjusting.—Jamie Foster, independent volunteer, Ecuador

Feeling strange and even depressed is a normal part of re-entry. If your depression seems severe, or lasts more than a few weeks, see a counselor. (The Peace Corps sometimes provides counseling, and other volunteer programs may at least be able to recommend someone.)

Peace Brigades International volunteer Michael Mogensen warns that "If you had an intense experience, like working with torture victims or working in a war-torn area, be prepared to deal with some emotional issues, because sooner or later, they will crop up."

Keep Processing Your Experience

As far as short-term adjustment, I would recommend sitting down one day just to write. Get all of your emotions and memories out on paper. Do nothing else that day, except think about how you are feeling and what you have just gone through. I did that and felt much better after doing it. I also had a nice essay about my experiences abroad. I think this should be done a few days to a week after returning. Bask in the enjoyment of returning home for a few days to let your mind settle. Then sit down to write.—Mark Dunn, Princeton in Asia, China

If your volunteer organization offers a re-entry retreat, take advantage of it. If the organization does not offer a post-volunteer program, set aside some time to reflect on your homecoming. Continue to write in your journal and put your ideas and emotions on paper. Establishing a routine and being active when you return home is important, but don't get so busy that you don't have time to think, write in your journal, and process your re-entry.

Whatever you write can be summarized and sent to friends and family. If a group of donors supported your trip, remember to send them a letter about your experience within a few weeks of returning home.

Take Care of Your Health

You may have accidentally brought home more than memories and handcrafts. Your body may be carrying some dangerous stowaway microbes. We recommend that you schedule a physical exam upon your return. If you've been so foolish to have engaged in unsafe sex, get tested for HIV and other STDs. And seek immediate medical attention if you have any unusual physical problems such as blood in urine, persistent diarrhea, yellow skin or eyes, fever, chills, or unexplained headaches.

Create a Supportive Environment for Yourself

Creating a positive environment is essential to staying balanced during the re-entry process. Returned Peace Corps volunteer Allison Nowlin found that her close connections with other returned volunteers helped her during a difficult transition. "Knowing that I could call one of them on the phone, and they knew exactly what I was going through, helped me through that time. Also, anything I did that connected me to my life overseas helped—listening to Latin music, dancing merengue and salsa, speaking Spanish, all eased the sadness a little."

E-mailing the friends you worked with overseas can help, too. If you lack access to the Internet, consider picking up the phone and calling your host family or colleagues abroad. Members of your community, faith tradition, or any clubs you belong to may also be supportive, especially if you share information with them about how the experience affected you.

You may also want to take the best elements of your life overseas and merge them with your own culture. Try something as simple as taking your shoes off before you enter the house or saying hello to strangers you pass on the street. Maura Kaufman wanted to hold on to some of the simplicity she experienced in Costa Rica, so she cooked rice and beans every night and made her own tortillas.

Sharing experiences with friends at home is one of the best ways to work through reverse culture shock. Even if you aren't suffering from reverse culture shock, sharing your stories can help you reflect on and continue to learn from your experiences. Going through your photographs with friends can be entertaining for them and therapeutic for you. Perhaps you can share some parts of your journal with others. Many people share their experiences by inviting friends to a dinner or hosting a small party at which they share photos, handicrafts, and slides. We discuss this topic in more detail below in "Telling Your Story Publicly."

Some friends may not want to hear about your experience in depth, especially if it was traumatic in any way. When people talk with you about your experience, expect them to ask vague questions, such as, "How was your trip?" How do you answer that? "Fine?" Several volunteers suggested developing a very brief explanation of your experience, such as, "I worked with street children in Brazil. It was extremely challenging, but I had a very positive experience." If people want more detail, they will ask. Another idea is to choose an anecdote that exemplifies a meaningful issue or a poignant personal moment from your experience. Telling a personal story can give people a glimpse of your life abroad and even share with them a lesson from your journey.

You may also want to seek out more permanent communities of people who understand you and your experiences. This network can help you keep alive and build on the lessons you learned while volunteering. For starters, you may want to see if you can meet others in your community who grew up or lived in the country where you volunteered. Is there a language class or a group of people who speak the language socially where you can keep up the language skills you worked so hard to develop? Try finding a music or dance class where other cultural enthusiasts and artists congregate. Keep your eyes open for lectures, seminars, or conferences that focus on the region or issue most prevalent in your volunteer experience. Build community with other returned volunteers, North Americans who have lived abroad, and immigrants who have come from overseas to live in and around your hometown.

Even if you were not a Peace Corps volunteer, the National Peace Corps Association (NPCA) may be able to link you with people who volunteered near where you did. The Returned Overseas Volunteers (ROVE) may also be able to do so (www.returned volunteers.org). The NPCA website (www.rpcv.org, 202-293-7728) also has excellent resources on how to be an effective advocate for sustainable development. If you can't find people in your local community, try sending e-mail to friends who volunteered with you and build some virtual community.

Canadians may be interested in the Vancouver-based WorldWorks (www.vcn.bc.ca/idera/wworks/ww.htm, 604-732-1496) and their Returnee Network that helps volunteers integrate and share their overseas experiences.

> *Sometimes I felt like I couldn't talk to anyone because all the conversations I had with my friends were one sided. They had been doing the same things, but I had changed. It felt strange, like I had nothing in common with them. They would say "Did I tell you that chicken is on sale at the supermarket?" and I would want to say, "No. Did I tell you about the time I was followed by soldiers, interrogated, and given a military escort out of town?"—Ilisa Gertner, independent teacher, South Korea*

Some Additional Re-entry Suggestions

Here are suggestions for North American volunteers from the Institute for Central American Development Studies (ICADS) culled from advice from returned volunteers:

- *Don't feel sorry for yourself.*

- *Don't constantly compare your home with your host country abroad.*

- *Don't live in the past.*

- *Continue your willingness to learn.*

- *Be prepared for a certain amount of pressure from friends, family, and peers to become your predictable "old self" again and give up the "new" parts that you have come to cherish.*

- *Be tolerant and accepting of others just as you would like them to be of you.*

- *Go easy on yourself. Give yourself a break. This time of transition is both emotionally and physically demanding.*

- *Don't expect things to be the same back home; actively look for changes instead of allowing them to take you by surprise. Changes might have occurred in social customs, language, etiquette/dress, music, morals, technology, etc.*

- *Be prepared for a possible emotional, physical, psychological, spiritual "let down" after you have been back home for weeks or months.*

- *Expect your readjustment to take some time (more than just a few days).*

- *Expect not to be able to re-identify fully with your own culture; realize that you have absorbed some of the host culture where you volunteered and that you will probably not be able to return fully to your past way of life.*

- *Expect your own personal values to have changed. The extent of change can only be realized after you've returned home. Attempt to define the changes that have taken place.*

- *Don't jump right into an intense job, school, or relationship. If possible give yourself a few weeks or even months to see friends, reflect, and rest.*

- *Don't judge others negatively for not having had your international experience.*

- *Remember that your friends, family members, and colleagues did not go into hibernation while you were gone. They have changed, too.*

We also refer you to *The Art of Coming Home* by Craig Storti (Yarmouth, ME: Intercultural Press, 1997).

Staying Connected

You may miss certain aspects of the overseas culture that you had embraced during your tenure as a volunteer. You may long for the less hectic pace of life that you knew abroad, or perhaps you miss the warmth and closeness of a more communal culture—a stark contrast to the individualistic culture of home. Even if you have a relatively easy re-entry experience, there is a great deal to gain from staying connected with your experience during the several months following your re-entry. Staying connected means maintaining the ties with the people you met overseas, the organization you volunteered with, and the lessons you learned while volunteering.

Maintain Contact with Friends Overseas

The people you met overseas can become lifelong friends. It is possible to stay in touch, even with those who don't have access to fax machines and e-mail. We strongly urge you to not lose contact with people you met while volunteering. As we interviewed community members overseas and people who hosted volunteers, we discovered that staying in touch was one of the simplest and most meaningful things volunteers could do after returning home. We also found, unfortunately, that very few volunteers seem to keep their promises to stay in touch.

Good old-fashioned letters may be a great way to communicate with your host mom, a student you tutored, a co-worker who took you under his wing, or a friend who made you laugh. Make sure the people you write to have your full permanent mailing address and the correct spelling of your name. Even if you are a poor correspondent, keep them on your once-a-year holiday card list.

If any of your friends have access to e-mail, try sending your letters electronically and ask one person to share them with others or print them out and deliver them. Make sure to find out if the cost is too burdensome since your friends may have to pay to receive and print e-mail messages. Consider making arrangements to cover the costs if that will make a difference in being able to keep in touch.

If you stay involved with the organization that sent you abroad, you may be able to give future volunteers letters and photos to deliver to your friends overseas.

Get Involved with Your Volunteer Organization

Providing feedback to the headquarters of your volunteer program is important. Personal feedback is the main force driving the innovations and development of most volunteer programs. Whether you are frustrated with the program or elated, pick up the phone or schedule a meeting. This is an important way to process your experience, get closure on certain issues, and stay connected to the people and the place where you volunteered. Limited budgets often mean that volunteer program coordinators spend a lot of time in the home office and not nearly as much time in the field as they would like. Your stories and experiences can bring things to light and help staff to see the strengths and weaknesses of their programs. Remember to use diplomacy and respect when you provide your feedback.

Recruiting and training new volunteers are concrete ways to be involved with your volunteer organization. Let the organization know if you are willing to take the time to talk to prospective volunteers about your experience. Working on volunteer orientation and preparation allows you to put your knowledge to use, so that future volunteers will be as well prepared as possible. Good training means that volunteers can get the most out of their experience while creating the least burden on, and contributing the most to, their host community.

Some organizations have active alumni networks. If yours does, be sure to share your new address and contact information so the organization can be in touch with you and you can stay involved with friends you met during your overseas service.

Staying Involved in the Long Term:
Personal Transformation and Concerted Action

A Mennonite Central Committee (MCC) worker in Zaire (Democratic Republic of the Congo) went back to Kansas for a couple weeks to attend a wedding. Someone in his home church community said, "When these MCC workers come home they are sort of strange at first, but we get them straightened out after a while." Within MCC, our hope for volunteers is that we do not ever get straightened out; we want to stay "crooked!" We want to maintain the sensitivity we have been privileged to receive. This "crookedness" is one of the gifts people have given us to bring back to our home communities.
—Fremont Regier, MCC, Zimbabwe

For many people, volunteering overseas is a once-in-a-lifetime experience. Fortunately, there are many things you can do to stay "crooked" and stay involved, even if you never leave your hometown again. Read this section and see which approaches could work for you.

Continue to Seek Knowledge

Many people return home with more questions than answers. You may have witnessed firsthand the effects of globalization. Perhaps you saw some of the inequities of the modern world and are wondering what exactly are the root causes of this "underdevelopment." There are a variety of ways that you can educate yourself about these deeper issues. One method is to seek "alternative" sources of news. You will probably find upon your return that the media coverage of the region where you worked is insufficient or even misleading. You can find a list of alternative newspapers, magazines, and websites, as well as other recommended resources, in Chapter 8 in the section "Educating Yourself About the Country Where You Will Volunteer."

Most newspapers are online. You can probably find an online version of the major papers from the country where you volunteered. Papers in the local language can help you stay fluent as well as keeping you informed.

Seek out the literature produced by writers from Asia, Africa, and Latin America, fiction as well as nonfiction. Food First (www.foodfirst.org), Global Exchange (www.globalexchange.org), and Kumarian Press (www.kpbooks.com) all have first-rate publications analyzing causes of global poverty and strategies for creating change.

Focus on the country or region where you've now had some direct experience. By deepening your knowledge you will come to grasp the root causes of underdevelopment everywhere, and the links to policies and institutions in your own country. This knowledge can make you a more credible and effective advocate for change.

Become an Advocate

The anti-apartheid movement in the United States and Canada accomplished much more to help the South African people than did any North American volunteering in South Africa. As South Africa rebuilds in the post-apartheid era, we will still need this type of international advocacy. If ten volunteers return home and work to limit the power of the World Bank and World Trade Organization, they will help more South Africans in the long run than a hundred volunteers doing direct service in South Africa.—Dennis Brutus, former political prisoner, South Africa

A well-known parable describes a small village located next to a river. One day, while walking near the river, a villager sees a baby in the water. He rushes into the river and rescues the baby. An hour later, the villager sees another baby, which he also rescues. Then another baby floats by. Eventually he organizes all the adults of the village to stand by the river to rescue babies. But after a week of rescuing babies, one young woman leaves the other villagers and starts walking upstream. The other villagers ask, "Where are you going? We need you to help save the babies." The young woman tells them, "I'm going upstream to find out who is throwing the babies in the water."

DEMOCRACY ADVOCATE

Hoping to tame their wild fourteen year old, Beverly Bell's parents sent her to Haiti for a summer to volunteer with a church group. Coming from an upper middle-class background in Louisiana, Bev had never witnessed the kind of poverty she saw in Haiti. As soon as she graduated from high school, she moved to a small Haitian village for a year to work in community health and education. Soon she realized that the crushing poverty she witnessed could not change until Haiti got rid of the dictators that made it impossible for people to organize themselves and improve their conditions. Bev co-founded the Washington Office on Haiti to educate people about human rights abuses and to lobby Congress to end U.S. support for the dictatorship there. After many years of hard work in coordination with the grass-roots movement of Haiti, she celebrated the election of Jean-Bertrand Aristide, Haiti's first democratically elected president. Then, after the coup that ousted Aristide, Bev worked with his government in exile to promote the return of democracy. When Aristide finally returned to power, Bev wrote a book about Haitian women in the struggle for democracy. Bev now directs the Center for Economic Justice, and works to change international economic policies that threaten democracy and human well-being in Haiti and other low income countries. Says Bev, "I believe that the most important work I have to do is in the United States, the site of so many of the institutions that create obstacles to justice around the world. But I couldn't do this work without having been schooled by the very best teachers: the Haitian peasant women I first met in high school."

Many volunteer placement organizations specialize in direct service, which is an important element of development, but can be considered a form of pulling babies out of the river. Volunteers often realize that there are forces throwing the babies into the rivers, such as non-democratic governments, war, unfair trade policies, and corporations that hurt the environment. These systems operate upstream so it can be hard to see their direct impact. Returned volunteers can become effective advocates for making changes "upstream."

An important first step in this process is to join a network of people working on sustainable development or global justice issues, so you don't have to go at it alone. Effective networks operate on local, national, international, and virtual levels. A local network will provide the opportunity to meet face-to-face with other members, conduct community-based education, and participate in grassroots advocacy campaigns. National networks provide information on upcoming legislation and campaigns. International campaigns usually have national and local organizations you can contact, and may also provide opportunities for networking, conferences, emergency alerts, and actions. No matter what their geographic level, campaigns these days utilize the Internet as an important organizing tool. Check out www.igc.org for links to current campaigns.

There are several different types of networks. Some networks unite multiple constituencies to work on a broad range of sustainable development goals. These networks include:

- **Development Group for Alternative Policies (DGAP) (www.igc.org/dgap, 202-898-1566)**
  DGAP works to ensure that the knowledge, priorities, and efforts of the women and men of the South inform decisions made in the North about their economies and the environments in which they live.

- **Food First (www.foodfirst.org, 510-654-4400)**
  Food First is a "people's think tank" and education-for-action center. Food First highlights root causes and value-based solutions to hunger and poverty around the world, with a commitment to establishing food as a fundamental human right. By joining the Food Information and Action Network (FIAN), members get free e-mail alerts about ways they can get involved.

- **Global Exchange (www.globalexchange.org, 415-255-7296)**
  Global Exchange is a human rights organization dedicated to promoting environmental, political, and social justice around the world. Global Exchange programs include reality tours, campaigns for fair trade, public education, and support of community groups overseas.

- **Oxfam America (www.oxfamamerica.org, 800-77-OXFAM or 617-482-1211)**
  Oxfam America creates long-term solutions to hunger, poverty, and social injustice through partnerships with poor communities around the world.

Other networks are organized by the country or region of their focus, such as:

- **Asia Pacific Center for Justice and Peace (www.apcjp.org, 202-543-1094)**
  The Asia Pacific Center for Justice and Peace works with the peoples and organizations of Asia and the Pacific to strive for political, social, cultural, and economic justice.

- **Network in Support of the People of Guatemala (NISGUA) (www.nisgua.org, 202-518-7638)**
  NISGUA educates the public about Guatemala, supports grassroots organizations in Guatemala, and responds to human rights emergencies.

- **Washington Office on Africa (WOA) (www.woaafrica.org, 202-547-7503)**
  WOA is a church-sponsored advocacy organization seeking to promote a just American policy toward Africa.

- **Washington Office on Latin America (www.wola.org, 202-797-2171)**
  WOLA promotes human rights, democracy, and social and economic justice in Latin America and the Caribbean.

Others are focused on a particular issue:

- **Amnesty International (www.amnestyusa.org, 202-544-0200)**
  Amnesty International promotes human rights around the world.

- **Bread for the World (www.bread.org, 202-639-9400)**
  Bread for the World focuses on lobbying to support policies that address the root causes of hunger and poverty worldwide.

- **The Center for Economic and Political Research (CEPR) (www.econjustice.net, 202-265-3263)**
  CEPR is coordinating a campaign to get universities, unions, and religious groups to sign a pledge not to invest in World Bank bonds.

- **Fifty Years Is Enough Campaign (www.50years.org, 202-463-2265)**
  Fifty Years is a coalition of 200 U.S. organizations working to fundamentally transform the World Bank and the International Monetary Fund.

- **Friends of the Earth International (www.foei.org, 31-20-6221369)**
  Friends of the Earth International is an international federation of autonomous environmental organizations.

- **Human Rights Watch (www.hrw.org, 212-290-4700)**
  Human Rights Watch is dedicated to protecting the human rights of people around the world.

- **The International Campaign to Ban Land Mines (ICBL) (www.icbl.org, 612-925-9418)**
  ICBL calls for an international ban on the use, production, stockpiling, and sale, transfer, or export of antipersonnel land mines.

- **The International Forum on Globalization (IFG) (www.ifg.org, 415-561-7650)**
  IFG is an alliance of sixty leading activists, scholars, economists, researchers, and writers formed to stimulate new thinking, joint activity, and public education in response to economic globalization.

- **Jubilee USA Network (www.j2000usa.org, 202-783-3566)**
  Jubilee calls for definitive cancellation of debts owed by impoverished countries in order to support investment in human needs.

- **Peace Action (www.peace-action.org, 202-862-9740)**
  Peace Action works against nuclear weapons and arms trafficking.

- **RESULTS (www.action.org, 202-783-7100)**
  RESULTS promotes grassroots citizen action to eradicate world hunger and poverty.

- **Sustainable Communities Network (SCN) (www.sustainable.org)**
  SCN links citizens to resources and to one another to create healthy, vital, sustainable communities.

Many other groups are organized by the region or characteristics of the members, such as:

- **Church World Service (www.churchworldservice.org, 888-297-2767)**
  CWS is a non-denominational Protestant organization that raises funds for grass-roots development overseas and advocates for policies that would benefit the poor in other nations.

- **JustAct, Youth Action for Global Justice (www.justact.org, 415-431-4204)**
  JustAct has programs for youth to get involved in working for global justice.

Links to these and other groups can be found at our website, www.volunteerover-seas.org. You can also find many of the U.S.-based organizations involved in international development work through Interaction, the American Council for Voluntary International Action (www.interaction.org, 202-667-8227).

Once you have joined a network, you'll get updates on legislation, conferences, campaigns, and business issues that affect people overseas. Your voice can make a difference. Elected officials get very few letters or calls from constituents about foreign policy issues. Corporations are sensitive to their public relations images. A network can also keep you in touch with like-minded individuals, inform you about upcoming events, and share ways that you can be involved in supporting the struggles of people overseas.

Tell Your Story Publicly

You have had an international experience that many people will never have. In addition to sharing your experience with those who are close to you when you first return, we encourage you to share your experiences with as broad an audience as possible. Public education is the basis of most social change.

The following groups are usually very open to presentations about the rest of the world:

- **Schools.** *Approach a local principal or teacher you know. Find out which classes might include academic subjects that connect with your presentation.*

- **Religious Institutions.** *The social action committee of your local church, synagogue, or mosque might help you organize a presentation for its congregation, or you can approach the leader of the congregation directly.*

- **Universities.** *Contact the chair of any area studies program to see if there might be interest in your presentation. Most universities also have community service programs, career centers, education abroad programs, and international studies departments that could help you schedule an event.*

- **Businesses and Volunteer Clubs.** *Rotary, Kiwanis, Lions, and Optimist clubs are often very open to lunchtime or evening presentations to inform their members. Check your local phone book.*

As you create a structured presentation try completing Worksheet VIII: Deciding What I Am Going to Share with Others. Make your presentation as engaging as possible by including maps, cultural artifacts, music, and photos. Prepare questions for the audience so you can make the session interactive. Be sure to include a handout with action suggestions and contact information for at least one organization such as your volunteer program, overseas host, or an advocacy group so that participants who are inspired by your presentation can leave with one concrete thing that they can do.

COMMUNITY EDUCATOR

In 1987, David Bryden volunteered on a construction project in Nicaragua. To travel to the project required a long ferry ride across Lake Nicaragua. The ferry David took on his way home was transporting a soldier wounded in the U.S.-backed Contra war. "For twelve hours, I was face-to-face with his suffering," David told us. "I knew that I had helped pay for the bullet that shot him when I paid my taxes, and that policymakers in the United States had a far too simplistic view of events in Nicaragua." David's experiences in Nicaragua influenced him in many ways. He found that he had renewed sympathy for immigrants and refugees from Central America, now that he had seen firsthand the war and deprivation they were fleeing. So he began volunteering with Central Americans in his community, and eventually got a job teaching English to Latino parents of children attending a local elementary school. In addition, he helped to form a local volunteer chapter of the Network in Solidarity with the People of Guatemala to educate people about the little-known U.S. support for the armed conflict in Guatemala. He finds that a combination of acting locally and acting globally provides the satisfaction of helping people directly and of knowing that he is participating in long-term change that addresses the root causes of the war he witnessed in Central America.

Work with the Media

When you come home from working overseas, you will probably read the newspaper with new eyes. The U.S. media provide precious little coverage of the non-Western world. Many articles portray poor people as passive and ignorant victims of storms, earthquakes, and landslides. Other stories focus on violence. You can help to portray a more accurate image of life overseas, and educate other citizens, voters, and policymakers.

The editorial page is the most widely read page of the newspaper, after the front page. Use your I-was-there status to write a convincing letter to the editor. Challenge the misleading attitudes of the popular press and give examples of how local people are working to solve their own problems. The letters that get printed usually are concise (under 250 words), timely, and reflect a unique view of a current issue. Remember that printed letters are not only seen by the general public; they are also clipped by Congressional staff to inform policy decisions. Unprinted letters to the editor are also essential because they help inform the editorial board of issues important to their readers. Letters can have a cumulative effect, eventually inspiring editorials and opinion editorials (op-eds). Don't forget to contact the editors if you see something you like or dislike in the coverage of the country or issue of your interest; that way your next criticism may be better received. Most newspapers today have websites with e-mail addresses for the various editors. These can be useful for quick responses.

THE INSTANT EXPERT

Recognize that even if you volunteered only for a short period of time, you will often be considered an expert on a certain region just because you were there. Use this status carefully. To deal with your "expert" status, continue to educate yourself about the issues, be prepared with some stories that will illustrate your experience, and be honest if asked to comment an on issue beyond your range of expertise.

Use "hooks" in the news to write timely op-eds. In addition to something already in the news, a "hook" can include an anniversary, a historical marker, or something that ties into the season, holiday, or major annual event (like the Superbowl). We Interrupt This Message (interrupt@igc.org, 415-537-9437) suggests: "In your op-ed, make an argument. Be for or against something. Propose action." Relatively few op-eds submitted get published, however. Many more letters to the editor do. Even if your article or letter is not published in a major newspaper, however, perhaps you can get it printed in your employer's newsletter, a church bulletin, or a local paper.

The audiotape "Living Media: Media Training Designed to Bring Your Third World Experience Home to Your Community," has more excellent suggestions for dealing with the media. The tape is available from GW Associates (www.accucom.net/pwirth).

WORKSHEET IX

DECIDING WHAT I AM GOING TO SHARE WITH OTHERS

There were many themes, lessons, and interesting aspects of my international volunteer experience. The following questions and answers highlight some of the key aspects of my experience:

My daily life overseas consisted of:

_____

_____

_____

_____

My work overseas involved:

_____

_____

_____

_____

_____

_____

I learned many lessons including:

_____

_____

_____

_____

I learned a lot about my host culture and country. Some examples are:

_____

_____

_____

_____

My most inspiring experience/the most inspiring person I met overseas was:

_____

_____

_____

_____

I saw people face the following challenges, and this is how they responded:

_____
_____
_____
_____

I personally faced the following challenges and responded to them in the following ways:

_____
_____
_____
_____

I recognize the following connections between local and international issues:

_____
_____
_____
_____

I had these expectations going into the experience and found that the reality was different in these ways:

_____
_____
_____

I learned that the policies of the United States and other wealthy countries affect the people I was with in the following ways:

_____
_____
_____
_____

From all of these ideas, I choose this theme/aspect of my personal experience to emphasize in telling my story:

_____
_____
_____

The reason I want to emphasize this theme/aspect of my experience is:

_____
_____

I'd like my audience to consider taking the following actions after hearing my presentation:

Support Fair Trade

Many people who volunteer overseas see the devastating impact of the "free market" on the people and environment overseas. When there is great inequality in the distribution of wealth, the "invisible hand" of the market often ends up making the rich richer and the poor poorer.

FAIR TRADE PROMOTER

Janine Johnston learned how to teach English as a second language at the New World teachers school in San Francisco. But the first village where she planned to teach in Nepal was under threat from rebel soldiers, and the second village had no students of the age group she planned to teach. She tried training teachers but became frustrated because she realized that English wasn't really what the villagers needed: "They needed economic development. Parents invited me into their homes and asked me to do one of two things: help get their kids out of the village, or help bring funds into the village." She ended up assisting the community with the promotion of a paper-making business, and she also bought local handmade carpets for resale in the United States. Once she was back home, Janine enrolled in a Master's degree program at American University, focusing on international development and fair trade. She was soon elected to be president of the Fair Trade Student Association. Janine plans to stay involved in trade issues: "I see fair trade as a way to link the grassroots in the United States with the grassroots in other countries. These connections tap the creativity of different cultures while making a concrete difference in people's lives overseas."

This is most tragically evident in the area of food production, where despite long-term increases in agricultural output per person in many countries, the percentage of the population in many of those countries who go hungry has also increased. For example, from 1970 to 1990, as Chile focused on developing its export economy, it became the world's number one exporter of grapes. At the same time, the poverty rate in Chile rose from 20 percent of the population in 1970 to 41 percent in 1990. (For a more detailed discussion consult *World Hunger: Twelve Myths,* by Frances Moore Lappé, Joseph Collins, and Peter Rosset, New York: Grove Press, 1998).

Some businesses take advantage of the lack of enforcement of fair labor and environmental laws overseas. Yet, if conducted properly, trade can raise the quality of life for people abroad. An alternative to "free trade" is "fair trade." Fair trade is based on the idea that business can be truly empowering for low-income people, without harming the environment or negatively impacting future generations.

Let your dollars do the talking and buy fair trade products. If you are like millions of other Americans and start each morning off with a cup of coffee, why not drink coffee grown under fair trade conditions and start your day with purpose. Fair trade groups include:

- **Fair Trade Federation (www.fairtradefederation.com, 660-665-8962)** *is a network of businesses and organizations that work to create a just and sustainable economic system through fair trade.*

- **TransFair Canada (www.transfair.ca, 888-663-FAIR)** *has a website that includes lots of useful links, such as where to find fair trade coffee.*

Some people work on laws to make sure "regular" trade has fewer negative effects. For example, the Nike Boycott Campaign (c/o Vietnam Labor Watch, (www.saigon.com/nike, 202-518-8461) works to promote labor rights in Nike factories. Multinational Monitor (www.essential.org, 202-387-8030) tracks corporate activity in areas of exports of hazardous substances, workers' issues, and the environment.

You can find out about the broader movement for social responsibility in commercial ventures by contacting Business for Social Responsibility (www.bsr.org, 415-537-0888), which promotes innovative products and services that help companies be commercially successful in ways that demonstrate respect for ethical values, people, communities, and the environment.

Fundraise for Development

Many returned volunteers become volunteer fundraisers for international development organizations. Our favorite organizations that are effective in promoting grassroots development are Oxfam, Grassroots International (www.grassrootsonline.org, 617-524-1400), IDEX (www.idex.org, 415-824-8384), and Food First. Most of the suggestions in Chapter 7, "Overcoming Financial Obstacles," can be used to fundraise for these and other organizations. We would, in general, advise you to stay away from supporting groups that get a large portion of their budgets from the U.S. Agency for International Development (USAID). The interests of the U.S. government often dictate their projects and priorities, and not the interests of the people they are supposed to help.

Some people fundraise for the organization that placed them or to directly support community projects overseas. We met several returned volunteers who established scholarship funds to make the volunteering experience accessible to others. Susan Yee, a volunteer with Cross-Cultural Solutions, contacted all the former volunteers who worked in Himachel Pradesh, India, to rally them to raise funds to purchase a computer for the non-governmental organization with which she volunteered.

Fundraising for development can also support your other efforts to stay involved in the long term. Instead of exchanging dozens of gifts for the holidays why not make a family contribution to an organization. Even children, when given a chance to participate, will often be excited about helping other people. And as you support others you can actually simplify your own life.

Voluntary Simplicity

Living overseas can make you see that having lots of things is not a prerequisite for happiness. Some find great joy in the simpler lifestyles they experience volunteering overseas, and bring home this attitude to help simplify their lives in the "developed" world. A simple lifestyle can also help reduce pressure on you to find the job that will pay you the most and enable you to seek employment that will bring you the most satisfaction.

Reducing acquisitions and increasing happiness can mean walking, biking, or taking the bus instead of buying a car. It can mean eating a very simple meal once a week. Brown rice cooked with a few vegetables and served with soy sauce makes a healthy, low-fat, and inexpensive meal. Joining a network of people seeking voluntary simplicity can provide other ideas and support.

Organizations promoting simplicity include the **Center for the New American Dream** (www.newdream.org, 877-68-DREAM) and **The Simple Society** (www.simsoc.org).

Books and magazines on voluntary simplicity and related topics include:

Freedom of Simplicity. Richard J. Foster. San Francisco: Harper, 1989.

Hope's Edge: The New Diet for a Small Planet. Frances Moore Lappé and Anna Lappé. New York: Tarcher/Putnam, 2002.

Living More with Less. Doris Janzen Longacre. Scottdale, PA: Herald Press, 2000.

More with Less Cookbook. Doris Janzen Longacre. Scottdale, PA: Herald Press, 1976.

Your Money or Your Life. Joe Dominguez and Vicki Robin. New York: Penguin, 1999.

Volunteer Locally

Many volunteers sign up to go overseas with the notion that the most profound troubles are "over there," outside of their own community, only to find that there are similar problems at home. Returned volunteers can bring home new ideas and strategies for facing these problems. Volunteering locally can also help returned volunteers remain connected to the values and issues that were important during their time overseas. See the "Doing Good at Home" section of Bonus Section A, "Alternatives to Volunteering Overseas," for a more detailed discussion of volunteering at home.

International Careers

Many people have meaningful long-term international involvement without making a career out of it, but some volunteers return home and realize that they want to make it their vocation. If you think global work may be your calling, this section provides some food for thought.

International careers include:

- ***Working for a nonprofit organization doing international development, advocacy, human rights, or environmental work (Oxfam, DGAP, Amnesty International, or the Environmental Defense Fund).***

- ***Working for the for-profit sector such as a small or large business or a "fair trade" organization.***

- ***Teaching in the United States about international issues (The Center for Teaching International Relations at the University of Denver).***

- ***Teaching overseas.***

- ***Working for the government as a policymaker or in the foreign aid establishment (U.S. Congress, State Department, or USAID).***

- ***Working for the United Nations (UNICEF, UNDP, UNESCO).***

- ***Working for a multi lateral bank (World Bank, IMF, development banks, etc.).***

- ***Translation.***

- ***Tourism, including eco-tourism.***

- ***Working with immigrants or refugees.***

Here are some questions to ask yourself as you decide which of these options is best for you:

Is my goal to work overseas or to do international work while based at home?

Do I prefer working in an office or in the field?

What type of work do I want to do—direct service, advocacy, economic development, policy/electoral, or community organizing?

Do I want to work for a small organization where I may have more hands-on work, or a larger organization that may be more stable?

In our analysis, there are far too many international organizations that contribute more to the problems of underdevelopment than they do to the solutions. The World Bank, International Monetary Fund, and other multilateral lending institutions (MLLIs) often make ill-advised loans to undemocratic governments, then force governments to cut social spending to pay back the loans, even if the projects or reforms fail to bring about the benefits promised by the MLLIs. Many contractors with USAID are more accountable to the U.S. Congress and businesses than to impoverished people overseas. Large international businesses such as oil and timber companies frequently harm the environment and exploit local workers. In general, we would urge you to stay away from these types of organizations, unless you seek to change them from within. Fortunately, there is a growing number of groups promoting a sustainable approach to development. Unfortunately, almost all groups claim that they promote sustainable development, so try to analyze all organizations with a critical eye.

For a more detailed analysis of the sometimes negative role of international development organizations, we refer you to Chapter 3, "The Big Picture," as well as *Aid as Obstacle* by Joseph Collins, Frances Moore Lappé, and David Kinley (Oakland, CA: Food First Books, 1981).

With the rise of the Internet, finding international job openings is much easier than it used to be. We recommend visiting the following websites, many of which can be found on the resource page of www.volunteerinternational.org, published by the International Volunteer Programs Association:

- *Human Rights Internet (click on Human Rights Job Board, www.hri.ca)*

- *International Career Employment Weekly and International Employment Hotline www.internationaljobs.org, 804-985-6444) Over 500 current job openings every week.*

- *International Employment Gazette (www.angelfire.com/biz/resumestore, 800-882-9188) Biweekly paper with over 400 current job openings around the world.*

- *www.backdoorjobs.com*

- *www.ciee.org*

- *www.idealist.org*

- *www.interexchange.org*

- *www.jobsabroad.com and www.teachabroad.com*

- *www.overseasjobs.com offers job search options as well as links to other relevant sites.*

- **www.reliefweb.int (select Humanitarian Vacancies for relief work positions in different parts of the world)**
- **www.transitionsabroad.com**

Even with a volunteer experience overseas, it can be hard to get your first international job. The best technique we can suggest is building your network through informational interviewing. The organization you volunteered with can probably provide you with a few names of people to interview in your field of interest. Any college career center can probably provide you with suggestions on setting up informational interviews. The book *What Color Is Your Parachute* (Richard Bolles, Berkeley: Ten Speed Press, 2001) has a helpful section on how to get the most out of these interviews. In fact, we recommend the book or the website www.jobhuntersbible.com for great career advice no matter what type of career you seek. Other recommended books include:

> *The Directory of Work and Study in Developing Countries.* Toby Milner. Oxford: Vacation-Work, 1997. Includes information on jobs, volunteer work, and academic opportunities in the developing world. Targeted to a U.K. audience.

> *Work Your Way Around the World.* Susan Griffin. Princeton, NJ: Peterson's Guides, 2001. Extensive country-by-country information and firsthand stories.

See Bonus Section A, "Alternatives to Volunteering Overseas," for more ideas and resources on work abroad.

Continuing Your Education

Many volunteers realize that in order to continue their international career they will need to gain further education. A particular skill, language, or certification may help them move forward on their path of international work. For graduate schools that can help you develop skills that you'll need for international careers, we recommend the following resources:

- **Association of Professional Schools of International Affairs (APSIA) (www.apsia.org, 202-326-7828) APSIA is an association of twenty-three graduate schools of international affairs and fifteen affiliated institutions based in the United States and abroad. The APSIA website has links to all the member universities.**
- **Education for Action: Undergraduate and Graduate Programs That Focus on Social Change. 3rd edition. Sean Brooks and Alison Knowles. 3rd edition. Oakland, CA: Food First, 1995 (www.foodfirst.org).**

Our favorite graduate programs include the School for International Training (for educational careers), the University of Denver Graduate School of International Studies (for human rights), and American University School of International Service (for international development).

In the field of international careers, you will find some individuals who chose international work because they saw it as a good way to make money while traveling the world, and others who chose it because they are committed to helping create a more just world. Although we see nothing wrong with making a living while doing good, we hope that the ideas in this chapter will help you stay committed to the ideals that led you to volunteer in the first place. (See page 422 for more resources on international work options.)

Go Forth and Change the World

There is so much important work to be done in the world. International volunteers have the opportunity to put the lessons they learned overseas into practice when they return home. We should not underestimate what the community of returned international volunteers can do if we get organized and commit ourselves to going forth and changing the world.

> *One of the most important things you can do with your experience is to get involved with solidarity work. Solidarity means people coming together in a process of changing the power structure to benefit the disenfranchised and create a more equitable system. It's a process in which you're learning and growing as much as you are giving back. Solidarity is ultimately an expression of love, a commitment to yourself and to other people for whom you want a better future.—Ron Garcia, National Organizers Alliance*

Action Steps for What to Do When You Get Back

1. ***Realize that the Transition May Be Hard.*** Allow yourself time to process your overseas experiences and to readjust to life at home.

2. ***Take Care of Your Health.*** Schedule a physical exam upon your return. You may have brought home a microbial souvenir.

3. ***Create a Support System.*** Seek out friends, family, and/or groups with whom you can discuss your experiences.

4. ***Stay Connected.*** Maintain contact with friends overseas, get involved with your volunteer organization, and build community with those who share your interest in the region from which you have returned.

5. ***Continue to Seek Knowledge.*** Many people return from overseas with more questions than answers. Educate yourself about the root causes of the "underdevelopment" and poverty you may have experienced.

6. ***Get Involved with Advocacy or Solidarity Work.*** Join a network of people working on sustainable development or global justice issues.

7. ***Share Your Story Publicly.*** Public education is the basis of most social change. Use your status as an "instant expert" to make a presentation to schools, religious institutions, universities, businesses, volunteer clubs, and the media.

8. ***Practice Voluntary Simplicity.*** Living overseas may make you aware that having a lot of things is not a prerequisite for happiness. Find ways to simplify your life.

9. ***Volunteer Locally.*** Recognize the similarities between the problems overseas and those in your own community. Apply the ideas and strategies you learned overseas to local issues.

10. ***Research International Careers.*** Investigate ways that you can make international development, advocacy, human rights, or environmental work a vocation or a topic for further education.

11. ***Go Forth and Change the World.*** Remember one of the main points of this book: what you do after you return home may be more important than what you do while overseas. Your work has just begun.

CHAPTER 11

THE PEACE CORPS

Peace Corps

1111 Twentieth St., NW
Washington, DC 20526

phone (recruitment office): **800-424-8580**
e-mail: **volunteer@peacecorps.gov**
web: **www.peacecorps.gov**

The Peace Corps dwarfs all other organizations that place U.S. volunteers overseas. Surely it crosses the mind of almost anyone in the United States considering international volunteer service. After four decades, Peace Corps alumni are spread out all across the country and the world, and official Peace Corps recruiters can be found at many university campuses. We even have met second-generation Peace Corps volunteers whose parents or uncles or aunts had been with the Peace Corps and who grew up thinking they'd join the Peace Corps someday, never really considering any other options.

It's not just its sheer size that makes the Peace Corps stand out among organizations offering volunteer placements abroad. While the Peace Corps is one of several international volunteer programs funded by U.S. taxpayers, it alone is *part* of the U.S. government. This fundamental reality, unique to the Peace Corps, has numerous implications that surfaced repeatedly in our research on the Peace Corps.

Our fieldwork for this guide included visits to Peace Corps programs in fifteen countries—countries in Eastern Europe, Africa, Latin America, and the Caribbean. We interviewed and surveyed more than one hundred Peace Corps volunteers and staff in the field and at home. To round out the picture, we interviewed a sampling of staff members of local organizations overseas that host Peace Corps volunteers. We also consulted websites, government evaluations, and books about the Peace Corps.

Because the Peace Corps is so huge, volunteer experiences range from horrible to stupendous. We found that the quality of the experience depends in great part on the country, local staff, placement site, and individual volunteer. Throughout our research, however, certain common themes, both positive and negative, emerged. After presenting a factual overview of the Peace Corps, we will lay out its strengths and weaknesses as we see them.

The Peace Corps: An Overview

The Peace Corps is huge by any yardstick. Since its founding by Congress in 1961, with a mandate from President John F. Kennedy, the Peace Corps has placed well over 150,000 U.S. citizens as volunteers in 134 countries around the globe. By century's end, the Peace Corps operated with 7,300 volunteers and trainees in eighty countries, with an annual budget of $241 million.

The Stated Mission of the Peace Corps

- **To promote world peace and friendship by making available to interested countries Americans willing to serve overseas who will help the people of these countries to meet their needs for trained men and women.**

- **To help promote a better understanding of Americans on the part of the peoples served.**

- **To help promote a better understanding of other peoples on the part of Americans.**

Volunteer Profile (2000)

- **Number of volunteers and trainees:** 7,300

- **Gender:** 61 percent women; 39 percent men

- **Marital status:** 92 percent single; 8 percent married

- **People of color:** 14 percent (5 percent Asian American, 3 percent Latino, 3 percent African American)

- **Age (median):** 25 years old

- **Volunteers over age 50:** 7 percent

- **Education:** 82 percent have undergraduate degrees, 13 percent have graduate studies/degrees

- **Work experience:** 3 out of 4 have less than one year of out-of-school experience

- **Drop-out rate (voluntary or involuntary "early termination"):** approximately 30 percent

Volunteers normally serve for two years following three months of in-country training. Service can be extended for a third and even a fourth year, possibly in a different country. The Peace Corps, under certain circumstances, may authorize an early date for completion of service (up to three months prior to the normal two years and three months) without considering it a resignation or "early termination."

Volunteers by Region (2000)

- **Central and South America, the Caribbean, and Pacific Islands:** 33 percent
- **Eastern Europe, Asia, and the Mediterranean:** 32 percent
- **Africa:** 35 percent

Volunteers by Sector of Their Assignments (2000)

- **Education:** 39 percent
- **Environment (includes teaching environmental studies):** 17 percent
- **Health:** 18 percent
- **Business:** 13 percent
- **Agriculture:** 9 percent
- **Other:** 4 percent

In each country, the local Peace Corps staff, in collaboration with host government agencies and non-governmental organizations, selects and sometimes develops projects for Peace Corps volunteers to assist. While the Peace Corps contributes human resources (both volunteers and their supervisory staff) to such projects, it does not (with rare exceptions) finance such projects or contribute material resources such as vehicles or building materials.

Peace Corps volunteers may also develop their own "secondary projects" in the sites to which they are assigned. Some examples of secondary projects include small income-generating projects with women's groups such as raising guinea pigs or rabbits to improve nutrition and income; recycling with school kids to teach environmental lessons and generate a little money; teaching English to interested adults; drawing a world map on a school wall to involve the kids in discussions about the world; advising locally owned restaurants in a tourist area on menus that would appeal to foreign tourists; starting a demonstration vegetable garden using organic methods. Volunteers whose primary assignment is teaching are required to organize activities during vacations; they may not take vacations when their students take them.

Requirements to Be a Peace Corps Volunteer

- **Be a U.S. citizen prior to joining the Peace Corps.**
- **Be at least eighteen years of age (although few applicants under twenty-one are judged to have the skills and experience to qualify); there is no upper age limit.**
- **Married couples without dependent children may be accepted, but both spouses must qualify and serve as Peace Corps volunteers. Anyone with a dependent**

child should not apply. A married person without a dependent child may serve without her or his spouse; but the spouse that stays at home must sign a document agreeing to this, and the couple must document the means of support for the remaining spouse.

- *Meet the health requirements. Applicants must undergo a comprehensive medical and dental assessment "to determine if and where they can safely serve in the Peace Corps." A lengthy list of health conditions that may affect medical clearance or the country of placement, along with related information, is available through the Peace Corps Office of Medical Services at 800-424-8580, ext. 1500, or through the website.*

- *Meet the legal and security requirements. Legal clearance includes ascertaining whether there are any outstanding legal issues, such as debt repayment or child support, and, if so, that they all have been dealt with properly. The FBI conducts a security check.*

The Peace Corps claims that it is seeking candidates with a university degree or work experience in one of its areas of focus: environment, agriculture, community health, education, and business. A degree combined with work experience would, of course, be "ideal," a Peace Corps spokesperson told us. "We look at the whole person. . . . We even are interested in what the applicant's hobbies are." She noted that "We even work with people to help them qualify for the Peace Corps by telling them where in their area of the country they might volunteer and gain the needed work experience." In practice, however, many Peace Corps volunteers have neither a degree nor experience in the focus areas.

Costs to the Volunteer

There are no costs to the volunteer.

Benefits to the Volunteer

Peace Corps volunteers receive numerous benefits, including:

- *Living expenses, including an allowance for modest housing.*

- *Medical and dental care, including medical evacuation if needed.*

- *Vacation time (two days per each month served) and small vacation allowance, if requested (approximately $20 per month of service).*

- *Transportation to and from assignment.*

- *$6,000 "readjustment allowance" upon completion of twenty-seven months in the Peace Corps ($225 per month for volunteers who leave the Peace Corps early).*

- *Possible deferral of student loans. (Information about such possibilities is available through Peace Corps recruiters and the lending institution. For certain types of loans, interest will continue to accrue; for others, there are partial or complete deferments of interest.)*

- *Non-competitive eligibility in federal hiring; that is, for up to one year after completing service (or in the case of an early termination, if you volunteered for at least one year and the departure was for reasons beyond your control), a Peace Corps volunteer may be hired for a federal job for which he or she meets at least the minimum qualifications ahead of someone who is more qualified but does not have non-competitive eligibility.*

- *No-fee official passport (surrendered at the end of service).*

Training

Volunteers travel to their assigned country for three months of training. Training includes language, technical skills, cross-cultural issues, health, safety, and an accompanied visit to the placement site.

Education Credits

The Peace Corps has a program that allows you to combine graduate study and Peace Corps work. If interested in this Master's International Program, you must apply to both the Peace Corps and the participating graduate school of your choice. If accepted by both, you complete all or most of your on-campus studies prior to entering the Peace Corps. Your Peace Corps assignment will be related to your graduate studies. After completing your Peace Corps service and any remaining on-campus studies, you will receive your degree. In effect, your work in the Peace Corps becomes your fieldwork in your chosen discipline.

Application Process

Potential applicants should contact the nearest Peace Corps recruitment center for a complete information and application packet. Detailed and extensive forms must be completed. A recruiter from the nearest center interviews each applicant. The recruiter then makes a recommendation to the Peace Corps headquarters. Medical and legal clearances must be obtained and three letters of reference, sent directly to Peace Corps headquarters.

On the application form, one can request a specific country or region of the world, or state that he/she does not want to go to certain countries. The more restrictive the applicant is, however, the less chance he or she has of being accepted. If an applicant will only go to one or two places, his or her chances are not very good, we were told.

If Peace Corps headquarters decides to invite the applicant to join, an invitation is issued. The invitation is usually for a specific project in a particular country ("You are invited to join a water and sanitation project in Nicaragua starting on March 3rd. Enclosed are background materials to help you decide. . . .").

An applicant may decline an invitation to a particular assignment. He or she may (or may not) be offered another assignment. Another opportunity is offered, we were told, if and when there is another "match of skills to project and time availability of the applicant." There is no stated rule regarding how many times an applicant can turn down an assignment invitation. A senior staff member at Peace Corps headquarters informed us, however, that "the Peace Corps feels it knows best how and where to place applicants and would question someone's motives after more than a couple of invitations are declined."

In 1998, there were some 10,000 completed applications. Approximately 3,000 applicants were placed.

The application process often plays out over what seems like an eternity to an eager applicant. With the screening, medical clearance, legal clearances, waiting for an appropriate training class to begin, etc., applicants should expect the process to take a year or more. It is not unheard of, however, for an applicant to be placed in as little time as six months or less. Moreover, the Peace Corps told us they are streamlining the process.

Applications are accepted throughout the year. However, seventy percent of Peace Corps trainees depart for their assigned countries between April and October.

Living Arrangements

Living with a local family has become part of the three-month Peace Corps training and is now considered to be an important component of the volunteer's initial immersion in the local culture and language. Those trainees who become full-fledged Peace Corps volunteers then move to their assigned sites where they must find their own housing. The local organizations to which they are assigned may help with this. The Peace Corps country office must approve the housing arrangements.

No housing situation or standard of living can be said to be typical, especially given the diversity of standards of living within the host countries. Even within the same country the difference between rural and urban sites can be dramatic. In all situations, we were told by Peace Corps headquarters, volunteers are expected to live on the level of their local colleagues and never in a way that is luxurious or ostentatious. The truth is that while Peace Corps volunteers do not live in luxury by U.S. standards, many do live at a level that is much more comfortable than that of most local people. In rural Africa, it is even common for volunteers to employ servants to wash their clothes, houseclean, and/or cook for them. Peace Corps volunteers are supposed to live within their monthly living allowance, which varies from country to country according to the estimated cost of modest living. Reportedly, most volunteers do so, some even saving money out of their allowance. In general, volunteers placed in or near cities tend to spend more since they have more opportunities to do so. Today almost all Peace Corps volunteers live in housing with electricity.

Safety has become an ever more serious concern in many countries for virtually everyone and certainly for foreigners. Peace Corps volunteers have been victims of theft, rape, and, in very rare cases, murder. In each country in which the Peace Corps operates, the staff establishes guidelines aimed at ensuring the safety of the volunteers yet allowing them to become integrated into their communities. In some countries, Peace Corps volunteers are encouraged—and in a few countries even required—to live with a host family or within a family compound (in a separate dwelling on the same property) so that someone is always likely to know their whereabouts. Peace Corps volunteers may live with other volunteers, if stationed in the same town. In some places, living together is required because of isolation, lack of housing, or reasons of safety. In some countries, Peace Corps volunteers (other than married couples) are not allowed to live together.

A very small number of Peace Corps volunteers live in a relationship with a local person. Marriage, if allowed by local law, is possible with the permission of the Peace Corps country director.

Sample Peace Corps Placements

The image of a Peace Corps volunteer living in a mud hut in an isolated village is outdated. While a small number of volunteers do live in isolated villages with no electricity or plumbing, the following examples give a better idea of the diversity of placements.

- **Janet Line** *worked in an office of a nonprofit organization in Slovakia. Her assignments focused on helping the staff with English skills, including editing papers they wrote in English.*

- **Valerie Silensky,** *as a health care educator in Ghana, gave presentations on hygiene, nutrition, and HIV/AIDS prevention at schools, in community meetings, and with local commercial sex workers. She lived in her own room within the enclosed compound of a local family.*

- **David Ermisch** *worked as an environmental educator in schools in northern Ecuador near the Colombian border where the organization he was assigned to managed an eco-reserve. He also carried out educational activities in the community such as creating a demonstration organic garden, composting with worms, promoting land reclamation projects, and planting native trees as windbreaks.*

- **Patrick,** *a retired policeman from southern California, worked with troubled city youths in the Costa Rican capital, San José, involving them in sports activities. He lived alone in a one-room cottage in the backyard of a local family's home.*

- **Stephanie Donlon** *went to Uganda with a teaching credential and worked as a teacher trainer. She took over the house of a Peace Corps volunteer whom she replaced. The highlight of her experience was organizing with a local teacher a gender awareness day for over 1,000 young girls.*

- **Robert O'Donovan Jr.** *had experience as a teacher before joining the Peace Corps. He received a Peace Corps assignment as a "university lecturer" but the Kazakhstani town where he was sent had no university. Instead, he taught*

English to high school students, trained teachers in teaching English, and helped to start an English teachers' association.

The Pros and Cons of the Peace Corps

The Pros

Volunteering with the Peace Corps doesn't cost you any money.

Uncle Sam covers all your transportation and living expenses plus a vacation allowance. You even receive a stipend of $6,000 at the completion of twenty-seven months of service. If you are saddled with student loans you will be pleased to know that they might be deferred while you are in the Peace Corps.

The Peace Corps's health benefits are first class.

Many potential volunteers—and their loved ones—are legitimately concerned about health issues when they contemplate volunteer life overseas.

You and your loved ones may well be relieved to know that if you fall sick while in the Peace Corps you will have access to one or more staff doctors, fluent in English and trained in the United States. Dr. Ann Lifflander, one of the two Peace Corps staff doctors in Nicaragua, told us that she has at her beck and call "an unbeatable back-up" in the United States. "Within less than an hour I can have a phone consultation with a leading specialist in the United States, such as a State Department tropical disease specialist." She also noted that since health care is totally free "some volunteers seek out health care for the slightest ailment, more than they would back at home where they'd have to pay." The Peace Corps tends to err on the side of caution if you do become seriously ill and may require you to go home, even if you do not want to do so. Should you ever need it, medical evacuation (which can be very expensive) is available and paid for.

In short, while you will be at much higher risk for becoming ill than if you stayed home, your health care benefits will be comparable to those available to only the elite in the country in which you are working or, for that matter, in the United States.

The Peace Corps is a long-established, experienced organization with enormous financial and human resources dedicated to the well being of its volunteers.

Your parents and/or friends back home need not worry (as much) about you. As becomes evident in times of personal need or a crisis in the host country, you come attached to an "umbilical cord of privilege," as discussed in Chapter 9, "How to Be an Effective International Volunteer." If there is a serious crisis in your family back home, you will be on the next plane out. If political unrest or even a natural disaster strikes in the country where you are a Peace Corps volunteer, the U.S. Embassy will be looking after you, and your loved ones back home will be able to phone Peace Corps headquarters in Washington and obtain special up-to-the-hour information.

If the going truly gets rough, you will get going. When Hurricane Mitch's torrential rains pounded Honduras in late 1998, Peace Corps volunteers were whisked out of the country—often by helicopter—to the poolside of a luxury hotel in Panama, leaving behind, often in desperate straits, the people with whom they were working. In Uganda in 1999 after several bombs went off in the capital as part of a protracted civil war, all the Peace Corps volunteers were evacuated. The downside of the "umbilical cord," in the view of some Peace Corps volunteers we spoke with, is that it markedly sets you apart from the people with whom you are working.

Jamie Bond, Peace Corps staff in Poland and former Peace Corps volunteer in Romania, summed up the overall feel for us when she told us that the Peace Corps is especially suited to young people because "it is mothering and full of lots of safe support." You should know, however, that after the three-month training period, the "mothering" will not be there in normal times on a daily basis, especially if you are in a rural area. Usually, however, the Peace Corps will provide support if you seek it out or if problems arise.

A stint in the Peace Corps can make you more attractive to potential employers and help your career in many fields.

Potential employers are sure to have heard of the Peace Corps and probably think positively about someone who has been in the Peace Corps. A foreign language and cross-cultural experience might also get your application special attention in today's global economy. The same goes for graduate schools, and each Peace Corps country office is equipped to help you find out about graduate schools and take admission tests. Peace Corps country directors told us they know the Peace Corps is an important reference for employment and graduate school because they receive a large number of requests for letters of recommendation. If you pursue employment with the federal government, you get preference in federal hiring; this applies even to those who have completed only one year in the Peace Corps, as long as their early departure was considered "beyond their control."

Returned Peace Corps volunteers receive an exclusive newsletter with extensive information about job openings. Peace Corps headquarters in Washington, DC, has an office dedicated to helping returned Peace Corps volunteers find jobs. In addition to the formal assistance provided by the Peace Corps, the informal network of returned Peace Corps volunteers can be very helpful during a job search.

You can get accepted into the Peace Corps even if you are only a generalist; you need not have specific skills.

Many volunteers have only a liberal arts undergraduate degree. Three out of four volunteers have from zero to less than one year of outside-of-school experience. Good health and strong motivation seem to be key. Many other volunteer placement organizations require applicants to have relevant training and experience, as well as some language skill. The Peace Corps takes you and trains you, at taxpayers' expense.

The Peace Corps provides you with intensive language training by experienced professionals in small groups.

Most, though by no means all, of the volunteers with whom we spoke gave the Peace Corps language training high marks. Feeling comfortable in the local language is a key factor in a positive volunteer experience. The Peace Corps language training is superior to that of most other volunteer programs. (Occasionally we have heard of volunteers who were taught a language that was not used in the region where they were sent to volunteer.)

Peace Corps training now takes place in the country where volunteers are assigned.

For decades Peace Corps training was in the United States or some other country. Now it takes place in the country where you are assigned. Moreover, since the mid-1990s in a growing number of countries the training is largely "community-based." There are variants of community-based training in the different countries where the Peace Corps uses it. With community-based training in Bolivia, for example, the first four weeks of training are still done in a group setting; this, among other things, makes it easier for the staff to give talks on safety, health, cultural issues, and the like. During the remaining two months of training, the volunteers are split up into groups of only three to five, according to the sector in which they have been assigned to work (e.g., education or agriculture), and trained in different communities. Everywhere we spoke with Peace Corps volunteers and staff about community-based training, they clearly saw it as a positive step forward. Matthew Thompson, a Peace Corps volunteer in Bolivia, commented, "Since this type of training is in a setting more similar to your eventual volunteer site it gives you a setting in which you can decide whether or not you want to commit to two years."

The Peace Corps used to conduct the entire three-month training in a group setting, and in quite a few countries this is still the case. Some think that an advantage of this style of training is that it allows the volunteers to form strong relationships with other volunteers who in turn support them throughout their service. However, Dwight Roskos, another Peace Corps volunteer in Bolivia, was critical of the group training: "When I arrived here we did a group training, and I did not enjoy it. It kind of felt like high school." He noted that there was not a lot of interaction with the locals: "We were an island of gringos." Phil Stantial, the Peace Corps Training Officer in Slovakia, made similar observations about the group model. "You might as well have been in the States," he said. He found that cliques developed: "The atmosphere could easily turn collegelike, with volunteer behavior sinking to the lowest common denominator." Fortunately, according to a senior staff member at Peace Corps headquarters, "Community-based training would seem to be the wave of the immediate future."

The Peace Corps operates in a wide range of countries.

In contrast, many other volunteer placement organizations are working in only one or, at most, a handful of countries. Whatever region, language, or level of economic development piques your interest, you have an excellent chance of finding those preferences represented within the Peace Corps portfolio of countries.

Most applicants do not list specific countries where they wish to work; they are more likely to specify a region of the world. Some applicants indicate a region where they do *not* want to go. The Peace Corps, we were told, tries to comply with such requests.

Keep in mind, however, that the Peace Corps frequently invites applicants to serve in a country or type of work not on their list of top choices. As was already mentioned, the more restrictions an applicant puts on where he or she will serve, the less likely the applicant will be invited to join the Peace Corps.

The Peace Corps offers a significantly long period of service: two years, plus a three-month in-country training.

For some, such a long-term commitment might be a reason *not* to consider the Peace Corps. During our research on international volunteering, however, we were told repeatedly that many volunteers find that only with at least two years' experience do they begin to feel that they are comfortable enough in the language, culture, and the work to make a contribution. Stephanie Donlon, Peace Corps volunteer in Uganda, told us, "Two years is not as long as you think. The first year you are only getting your feet wet." A senior member of the Peace Corps staff in Nicaragua told us that she had come to think "a three-year assignment would be more appropriate than the Peace Corps's two-year model." In fact, you now may opt to extend for one or two additional years and even "re-up" for another country.

The Peace Corps helps volunteers with the re-entry process and comes with an active alumni network.

Many organizations and programs do not. As a group of volunteers is nearing completion of service, the Peace Corps provides workshops on readjustment that include coping with reverse culture shock, landing a job, and identifying appropriate schooling. Each Peace Corps office overseas has materials about graduate schools and admission tests. In addition, the Peace Corps pays a readjustment allowance of $225 for each month of service and provides job search assistance, as mentioned above. Moreover, in many areas of the United States there are regional networks of returned volunteers; most now have websites, easily found through an Internet search or by contacting the national office of Returned Peace Corps Volunteers at 202-692-1428 or www.rpcv.org. Returned volunteers can also access low-cost health insurance through the Peace Corps.

The Peace Corps seeks diversity.

While people of color are still quite underrepresented in the Peace Corps, efforts to increase minority presence appear to be meeting with some success. The Peace Corps has a higher percentage of people of color than most of the other international volunteer placement programs we researched. Peace Corps recruiters across the country have been trained to be sensitive and responsive to minority and diversity issues, including those of gay/lesbian/bisexual people.

A senior staff member at Peace Corps headquarters, himself an openly gay man, assured us that gay/lesbian/bisexual individuals may be "out and up front" during the recruitment process. Their sexual orientation should not have any influence on where they are sent, he said, because there is really no "safe" Peace Corps country to be openly gay. Lesbian/gay/bisexual persons interested in the Peace Corps may want to get in touch with the organization Lesbian, Gay & Bisexual RPCVs, based in San Francisco. It has an informal network for applicants to contact and attempts to provide support in any way possible. Their website, among other things, posts letters from current and past volunteers (www.geocities.com/WestHollywood/Village/1457/).

In some countries, a Peace Corps volunteer may help a local group she or he is working with to submit a proposal for a Small Projects Assistance (SPA) grant, usually from USAID, the U.S. Government foreign aid agency.

True to its name, an SPA grant is invariably small—approximately $2,000 maximum. Some see the small size of these grants to be their virtue, well suited to management by small community-based organizations or ad hoc committees or groups that have organized themselves to accomplish specific goals. USAID, we are told, likes Peace Corps volunteer involvement in these projects because it means there is someone in the community but not of the community monitoring the project. USAID, like other large bureaucratic aid organizations, does not monitor small projects since the costs of monitoring would exceed the grant. It is, therefore, unlikely to make grants to community-based organizations if there are no Peace Corps volunteers in the area.

We were told that some people in Peace Corps headquarters do not like SPA grants because they believe the grants lead people to associate the Peace Corps volunteers with money. Making financial grants is contrary to Peace Corps's official philosophy that local communities should view Peace Corps volunteers as a technical resource, not a source of funding. On the other hand, in countries we visited with a sizeable stream of official and non-governmental foreign assistance, some Peace Corps volunteers reported that local people are disappointed to find that they, as Americans and part of the U.S. Government, do not have dollars to back up their ideas and make things happen.

In many sites, Peace Corps volunteers are relatively independent and scarcely supervised.

Some Peace Corps volunteers told us that they appreciate this freedom to find and create their own projects and not have someone breathing down their necks. Indeed many warn that the Peace Corps is not for those who seek a program with structured work assignments. Teaching assignments may provide the most notable exception to this generalization since teaching in a school by its very nature is structured with defined tasks, but supervision may still be lax.

The Peace Corps encourages and helps volunteers to share their experiences with people throughout the United States.

The World Wise Schools program links Peace Corps volunteers with K–12 teachers back home. Volunteers send letters for the teachers to share with their classes, and some even set up pen pal programs. World Wise Schools also helps returned volunteers visit classrooms to help promote international awareness among the students. The Peace Corps website has detailed information for both volunteers and teachers about how to get the most out of the program.

The Cons

The Peace Corps is part of the U.S. Government.

As a Peace Corps volunteer, you are an employee of the government of the United States. Most of the pluses of the Peace Corps, such as health and other benefits and good language training, are possible because of its extraordinary resources. Being part of the U.S. Government, however, carries with it a host of troubling implications.

The Peace Corps is a government-to-government program based on a formal agreement between the government of the host country and the U.S. Embassy. As a Peace Corps volunteer, you represent not yourself but the U.S. Government, and you come under the control of the U.S. Embassy. You are not permitted to publicly criticize U.S. policies or U.S. businesses in the country. Alexis Eakright, assigned to teach environmental education in a grade school on Costa Rica's Atlantic coast, learned about this prohibition the hard way. Along with some of her students, she got involved with a local environmental organization. For this grassroots organization, the biggest local polluter was a big U.S.-owned banana company that injected tons of pesticides into the environment. One day, she joined some of her students in a protest action against the company organized by a local environmental organization. "This was a real problem," she told us. "I am with the U.S. Government, and this is a big U.S. company. I am not supposed to be involved in protests." Reflecting more on what had happened, Alexis complained, "It's a big tease when the Peace Corps says you are going to be out there on your own, but in fact you are part of the U.S. Government. You are a little ambassador." As she discovered, this has the potential to be a head-on collision if you are working on environmental issues since in many countries U.S.-based multinational companies cause big environmental problems. Alexis told us that she was an activist when she was a university student but that in the Peace Corps she can't be. "I feel ridiculous telling my students to be active to make a better world when they see that I am not allowed to act."

Indeed several Peace Corps volunteers complained to us, "You can't be yourself." Shiela Palza, the Peace Corps director in Costa Rica, told us she agreed that a drawback of the Peace Corps is that you represent the U.S. Government, not yourself. "This means," she said, "you aren't allowed, to cite just one example, to be a member of an organization such as Amnesty International. And, as a U.S. Government employee, you are forbidden to tell anyone who asks how you vote."

In countries where the United States has a history of military or political intervention, resentment of U.S. policies may be turned on you. In Bolivia, a number of Peace Corps volunteers spoke to us of the considerable anti-American sentiment there because of the U.S Government's "war on drugs" that has victimized many peasant coca producers. Some Peace Corps volunteers in Bolivia have been run out of the communities that they were assigned to because they were thought to be from another part of the U.S. Government, the Drug Enforcement Agency.

In a number of countries, especially in Latin America and Africa, the Peace Corps has not lived down widespread allegations in the 1960s and '70s of collaborating with the CIA, no matter what may be its current reality. Although the Peace Corps denies that it ever collaborated with the CIA, you, as a Peace Corps volunteer, might be held in suspicion by some of the more socially aware and active people in the country.

Because the U.S. Government wants the public image of the Peace Corps to be "non-political" and "non-partisan," the training systematically leaves out local political history and current politics. "That's a pretty big hole in a country like this," noted Heather Gardner, a Peace Corps volunteer in Nicaragua, a country in which the United States has repeatedly intervened, militarily and otherwise.

As a Peace Corps volunteer you might want to dig deep and get at the root causes of the distorted development that generates much of the needless suffering that you witness firsthand. In other words, you might not want to address only symptoms. You may view the concentration of money and political power in the hands of a few to be a cause of problems with the local agricultural, health, and education systems. You may believe that local poverty is caused in part by militarism, violations of human rights, and plunder by foreign corporations. You may come to consider some of the locally based organizations that take on these issues to be allied with the impoverished majority and truly helping them to improve their lives. But you will be prohibited from associating with these organizations because your employer, the U.S. Government, will surely label such work as "political."

Genuine development work often threatens established economic and political interests. But the unwritten Peace Corps rule is: "Don't rock the boat." As a Peace Corps volunteer, you are forbidden to be associated with any organizations that are perceived to oppose the local government. This penchant for the status quo goes with the government-to-government nature of the Peace Corps.

The government-to-government structure also means that the Peace Corps's local networks tend to be official and elitist, for instance, with government officials in a ministry or with well-to-do business people in the local Chamber of Commerce. As a result, volunteers sometimes find themselves working with people they had not imagined they would be working with. This appears to happen particularly to volunteers assigned to work in the business sector. In Fiji, for example, a Peace Corps volunteer assigned to work as a computer specialist found that he was assigned to work at a for-profit telephone company with business professionals who had just privatized Fiji's telecommunications industry. The government-to-government nature of the Peace Corps also can mean that the volunteers' "counterparts" in a government ministry can be so high up that they neither have time for nor interest in them.

Precisely because it is a government agency, the Peace Corps is quite bureaucratic. Many Peace Corps volunteers we spoke with complained about how bureaucratic the organization is. Decisions are made top-down. When asked what she liked least about the Peace Corps, one volunteer replied, "Being a government employee is a headache because of red tape and late payments when Congress hasn't passed a new federal budget."

In many parts of the world the United States has been long identified with military and economic interventions on behalf of the interests of wealthy people, and with the imposition of social and economic policies that are truly devastating for the poor majorities. The dilemma of the politically conscious Peace Corps volunteers, especially in such countries, is that the more they work to be caring, helpful, and likeable persons, the more they risk "putting a happy face sticker on their government's inhuman policies toward the third world," in the words of Doug Hellinger, a former Peace Corps volunteer in Brazil. Alexis Eakright, the Peace Corps volunteer in Costa Rica, told us that she resented "being a tool—a cheap one at that—for public relations for the U.S. Government." Senator Ross Adair (R-IN) highlighted a crucial truth when he said, "If there is a person in the Peace Corps who feels he cannot support U.S. foreign policy, then he ought not to be in the Peace Corps."

The Peace Corps application process is extensive and drawn out.

It can easily take more than a year to get an invitation to work in a particular country and sector. Moreover, with the Peace Corps you can't specify when exactly you would like to join. All this might wreak havoc on your planning. (At this writing, the Peace Corps claims it is trying to speed up the process through an early admission program.)

The Peace Corps has a long and daunting list of disqualifying medical criteria.

If you do have special health challenges but feel confident you can manage them, you may find it easier to be accepted by other organizations and programs or to create your own program.

With the Peace Corps you can't choose to work in a particular country or even a region.

If you are accepted, the Peace Corps invites you to work in a specific country in a specific sector (for example, Mozambique, in business). You either accept or decline. Since the Peace Corps works in so many countries around the world you might well be asked to serve in a different region than you had in mind. Interestingly, it is Peace Corps policy not to assign volunteers to countries where they have extensive prior personal contacts, based on the notion that such contacts could interfere with work, adjustment, and appropriate lifestyle. Most other organizations place volunteers in the country or region of their choice. Thus if you have your heart set on, say, sub-Saharan Africa, you may want to apply to an organization specializing in that region. Many organizations allow you to choose at the time you apply from among the countries in which they place volunteers. On the positive side, an offer by the Peace Corps may allow you to discover, and fall in love with, a place where you never even dreamed of volunteering.

The Peace Corps excludes anyone with a dependent child or anyone who would wish to bring along a partner or a spouse unless the spouse is also separately invited to be a Peace Corps volunteer.

Thus, if you are a married couple, you must both qualify and then wait until the Peace Corps finds situations for both of you in the same place in the same country. An unmarried couple (same gender or mixed gender), we were told, "will not be invited to serve together." Children accompanying a volunteer are strictly prohibited, and you should not bother applying if you have a dependent child you would be leaving at home.

The Peace Corps is overwhelmingly made up of young, inexperienced people fresh out of college.

Most Peace Corps volunteers lack expertise and experience. One older Peace Corps volunteer in Costa Rica complained to us about some of his fellow Peace Corps volunteers, "They are girls who never have been mothers themselves and yet they are assigned to teach young mothers how to parent." Mark Line, a Peace Corps volunteer in his sixties in Slovakia, told us that local people do not find the young Peace Corps volunteers credible. "In this country, age is automatic credibility. You must be wise if you're older. And if you're older with gray hair, you're even smarter." Most of the older Peace Corps volunteers we interviewed, such as Patrick, a retired policeman assigned to Costa Rica, told us that they miss having colleagues their own age. "I feel like an old man here with some kids."

The Peace Corps has lots of rules.

The Peace Corps tends to be very protective. Be prepared to be treated like a student in an intensively managed private college. One older volunteer complained to us, "The Peace Corps says it is looking for people of competence, and yet it treats you like a college student." Since the Peace Corps always wants to know where you are, you will be required to check in frequently with the country office. You are required to report whenever you leave your site, even if it is on a day that you would not be expected to be working (and when you do report your absence, it might count against your vacation time).

Many chafe at the rules. More than a few Peace Corps volunteers in Eastern Europe reportedly want to use their days off to travel around Europe, but doing so is strictly against Peace Corps policy, unless it is on vacation time. Most, according to Peace Corps volunteers we interviewed, evade some of the rules. Some get caught and are sent back home. Mark Line found the rules "a bit childish" but admitted he understood where the Peace Corps was coming from. "If I were responsible for eighty people, I might want some pretty hard and fast rules, too." And Daune Neidig, a Peace Corps volunteer in Nicaragua, also older, told us she likes the rules: "Hey, I'm glad someone cares where I am!"

The rules, including those governing the grounds for the termination of service, may be founded on concern for volunteers' well being. Unfortunately, however, they can sometimes contribute to a lack of trust and openness necessary to address genuine problems. A Peace Corps volunteer in Bolivia told us that she had experienced "many times" Peace Corps volunteers who are "afraid to reveal drug/alcohol problems, psychological problems, rapes, assaults, etc., for fear of being sent home."

In all too many countries Peace Corps volunteers have gained a reputation for raucous partying, heavy drinking, rowdiness, insensitivity to the locals' norms in dress and behavior, and an overall lack of maturity.

Volunteers in urban areas shared stories with us about how the reputation of rural volunteers who come into the cities to party negatively affects their ability to build relationships and to do serious work. In Spanish-speaking countries, some people inside and outside the *Cuerpo de Paz* have dubbed it the *Cuerpo de Paseo* (the Leisure Corps). Deborah Hurst, a Peace Corps volunteer in Bolivia, talked with us about the impact of the Peace Corps's ill fame: "I've had some Bolivians say to me, 'Oh, Peace Corps volunteers, they are just here to party. They get paid and do not do anything.' And there is some truth to that. I had a good friend whom I invited over to dinner at my house, but her son told her not to go, not to get involved with Peace Corps people. It turned out that her son worked in a bar where a lot of Peace Corps volunteers went on the weekends, and I guess a lot of crazy things happened there." Obviously, it is up to the individual volunteer to be responsible and to take advantage of the special opportunities the Peace Corps offers. The problem is that you still have to consider whether you want to be associated with such a reputation—and if you will regret not having more responsible colleagues.

The Peace Corps is not for you if you expect a detailed job description awaiting you when you get off the bus in your assigned village.

If, however, you relish the challenge of figuring things out on your own, Peace Corps may work for you. Before you really get down to work with a Peace Corps assignment, you will need to get to know people in the community and the "counterpart" agency, figure out how things get done in the culture, what might motivate people to work with you, and what on earth your contribution might be. Peace Corps works best for self-starters, people who can be patient and realize that all this figuring things out can take a long time. If you aren't a self-starter and/or want something with more structure but nevertheless want to make a go of the Peace Corps, your best shot is a teaching assignment since, as we have said, more of a job description and structure are built into most teaching assignments.

Numerous Peace Corps volunteers complained to us that their assignments were not appropriate for their backgrounds and interests.

The Peace Corps director in Costa Rica told us that one of the drawbacks of the Peace Corps is that you have no choice about what your assignment is. She admitted that one of the biggest complaints of the volunteers is that what they are assigned to do is not what they were told that they would do when they were invited to join the Peace Corps. Some Peace Corps volunteers believe their assignments were based on a superficial look at their resumes. Anthony Gilbert, a Peace Corps volunteer in Guatemala felt that, even though he had studied dairy sciences in Pennsylvania, he was assigned to help apple farmers to market their apples because his resume showed he was from Washington state, the "apple state." Many complain that their assignments are given to them late in their training, which often means that they do not know what they are training to do. On the other hand, many volunteers commented that the Peace Corps is open to changing your assignment once you are in your site for a while and if you find something that you think is better to do. Some volunteers told us that they think this flexibility is positive, with some noting that they had changed their projects as many as five times. Host organizations, however, disagreed and thought the willingness of the Peace Corps to let volunteers change their assignments led the volunteers to not take their assignments seriously and go back on their commitments. Father Finnbarr O'Leary who has hosted volunteers from several different programs in Santo Domingo, Ecuador, told us he was "not enthusiastic" about the Peace Corps: "I had one volunteer who stayed four days and then found other work. I think that the Peace Corps management is questionable for letting the volunteers do that."

The technical training (as distinct from the language training) is often reported by Peace Corps volunteers to be weak, vague, irrelevant, led by someone who didn't know much about the subject, and/or not specific to the assigned site and work (which usually is not revealed until very late in the training).

The executive director of a local development organization in the Dominican Republic with years of experience with Peace Corps volunteers told us, "The main problem with the volunteers is that when they come here they don't know what they're supposed to be doing." One group of Peace Corps trainees in Costa Rica was called upon to train some of their fellow trainees in environmental education. The "trainers" had majored in environmental studies in college, but they had no experience in teaching and were unfamiliar with tropical environmental issues. Some volunteers complained to us that their technical training was done in English because some of the trainees had low competence in the local language; the volunteers felt that the training therefore was less useful at their work sites. Others commented that the Peace Corps tends to assume that because you speak English you can teach English. Weaknesses in the technical training are especially problematic since so many of the Peace Corps volunteers join with little if any relevant technical skills.

Ironically, volunteers who do have technical expertise become frustrated because assignments often do not seem to take advantage of their skills. Some of them asked us to warn technically expert persons considering the Peace Corps that the thrust of the Peace Corps is teaching in schools and not hands-on work outside the classroom.

Despite Peace Corps rhetoric, in practice most volunteers, instead of helping local people learn how to do a job, end up doing the job themselves.

Most volunteers wind up assigned to teach, generally teaching in schools rather than training teachers. Frankly, few would have the expertise to train teachers since they themselves lack teacher training and experience. Host organizations seldom see the Peace Corps volunteer as a person to build local capacity; the volunteer is there to work and indeed perhaps to free someone else up from his or her work. A Peace Corps volunteer in Nicaragua assigned to give health talks in the schools told us she did not feel that she was building the capacity of local teachers. "They take my coming into the classroom as an opportunity to take a break."

The Peace Corps's program of local "counterparts" for its volunteers seems poorly thought out and rarely works satisfactorily.

The Peace Corps now assigns each Peace Corps volunteer to a local counterpart. The official rhetoric about "counterparts" is fuzzy. Is the role of the counterpart to mentor the Peace Corps volunteer or to be trained by the Peace Corps volunteer? In our research we found that the counterpart program generally does not work effectively. In many cases, the counterpart is a more senior person with many more responsibilities—not by any stretch a true "counterpart." Moreover, she or he is likely to be poorly paid and overworked, with no incentive to add yet another component to his or her job description. In all likelihood, the assignment to be a "counterpart" for a U.S. volunteer came from on high, even from a government ministry. In many cases, the designation of a counterpart is simply a prerequisite for getting a Peace Corps volunteer assigned to your site; once the volunteer is there, meaningful interaction seems rare.

The support in the field by the Peace Corps's in-country staff, in some countries at least, is experienced by many volunteers as lacking and even perfunctory.

While some volunteers had strong praise for the staff, most agree that the quality of Peace Corps personnel is inconsistent. Alexis Eakright, the volunteer in Costa Rica, reported that, while she had three visits from the program director, a Costa Rican almost twenty years on the Peace Corps staff, "He just came and shot the breeze. He didn't really talk over with me what I was doing." The local staff especially in countries where the Peace Corps has operated for many years often appears to be entrenched and burnt out. Interestingly, the Peace Corps sets a five-year limit on U.S. citizens as staff members but has no limit on foreign nationals in Peace Corps country offices. Some question whether U.S. staff members are able to develop serious expertise in view of the mandatory staff turnover. In some countries it seems that the local supervisory and support staffers are simply overloaded, especially given the tendency of the Peace Corps to scatter volunteers around a country. We also heard complaints about some country directors who are obviously political appointees lacking the needed language and/or management skills.

While some Peace Corps volunteers we interviewed said they appreciate the lack of day-to-day supervision because they feel freer to be creative, this freedom can make the Peace Corps a haven for "slackers." A few Peace Corps volunteers we interviewed complained that the slackers among their numbers give the Peace Corps a bad name. Matthew Thompson, volunteering with the Peace Corps in Bolivia, noted that, "The Peace Corps is not especially critical of the work their volunteers do. They do, however, encourage big-time slackers to go home. They ask volunteers to turn in bimonthly reports of work done and work in progress for Washington and also to identify slackers."

The Peace Corps does not carry out substantive evaluations of the projects in which volunteers work or even of the effectiveness of the individual volunteer's work.

Issues of effectiveness and who truly benefits do not seem to be a priority of the Peace Corps.

In practice, the priorities of the Peace Corps are (in order of importance): (a) look after the Peace Corps volunteers; (b) promote the image of the Peace Corps with the American public and secure future Congressional bipartisan funding for the Peace Corps; and (c) respond to the needs of the host communities in which the Peace Corps volunteers are working.

It should not be surprising, therefore, that the Peace Corps does not do any critical evaluations of the impact and actual beneficiaries of projects in which Peace Corps volunteers work. There is a tendency, we were told, for Peace Corps senior staff, both in the field and in Washington headquarters, to be more concerned with quantity than quality. They look for numbers that will justify with the White House and Congress the big budget it gets—and the budget increases it wants. Critical evaluations could be risky.

Usually, what passes for evaluation seems to be a general monitoring of the individual volunteer's experience. Peace Corps volunteers are periodically visited at their sites by the local Peace Corps program staff, and the volunteers are required to submit reports to the local Peace Corps director. Upon completion of the volunteer's service, the Peace Corps country director decides whether or not to replace the outgoing volunteer with a new volunteer in the same position.

An external evaluation carried out by the U.S. Government's General Accounting Office (GAO) took the Peace Corps to task for several key aspects of its performance in Eastern Europe and Central Asia. Quite possibly, such a negative review reinforced the Peace Corps apparent reluctance to carry out its own evaluations. The 1994 GAO review found that "many of the new programs were poorly designed and faced a host of other problems, including the lack of qualified staff, the assignment of volunteers to inappropriate or underdeveloped projects, insufficient volunteer training, and volunteer support systems that did not work." The study reported that "volunteer sites were not visited, assignments were ill-defined, and host country sponsors were not identified. Host country officials were often uncertain what the Peace Corps's goals and philosophy were, what volunteers had to offer, and what the Peace Corps expected of host country officials." The GAO found language training to be insufficient, technical training to be "of little use," and, in Uzbekistan, instances of physical and verbal assaults on women during their placements. (The full GAO report is available at www.concentric.net/~jmuehl/fofm/fofm08.htm.)

The Peace Corps spends a lot of money.

While the volunteer pays nothing, the taxpayers' tab for each Peace Corps volunteer works out to be $37,000 a year. That means U.S. taxpayers underwrite over $80,000 for a single volunteer's training and service! We tried to put that in perspective. The most common assignment of a Peace Corps volunteer is to teach in a school, even though most volunteers appear to have little or no experience in teaching, a considerable number have never wanted to teach, and almost all are struggling with the local language in which they try to teach. At the same time, in many countries where the Peace Corps operates, less than $2,000 would double the miserable salary of an experienced local public school teacher. With $80,000, therefore, at least a score of appropriate persons could be hired locally and trained to be teachers. So, while the Peace Corps might be a desirable experience for the individual U.S. volunteer, is it an even remotely sensible way to begin to help address a country's basic needs? Our visit to Ecuador brought these realities into sharp focus for us. During 1999 to 2000, over 15,000 experienced Ecuadorian school teachers, together with many other professionals, migrated to the United States and to Europe because the "Structural Adjustment Programs" mandated by the IMF slashed the purchasing power of their salaries (approximately $2,000 a year for the most experienced). During the same period the Peace Corps was telling U.S. citizens to congratulate ourselves for supplying a couple dozen inexperienced, yet high-priced, Americans to teach in Ecuador. From what we saw of the Peace Corps in country after country, we were hardly surprised when a Peace Corps volunteer, about to wrap up his two years in Honduras, confided to us, "I'm glad I did the Peace Corps, but as a taxpaying citizen I am not sure I would support it."

It can also be charged that so much money spent amounts to a subsidy for privileged Americans. The vast majority of Peace Corps volunteers come from middle- and upper-class backgrounds, the very people who would still travel the world, Peace Corps or no Peace Corps.

Women in the Peace Corps are likely to experience sexual harassment.

In our interviews with dozens of female Peace Corps volunteers, we heard all too many stories of sexual harassment, ranging from annoying comments to dangerous physical assault and even rape. To be fair to the Peace Corps, female volunteers in all the programs we researched are liable to be harassed due to the overt forms of sexism that exist in the very countries where people are likely to volunteer. Peace Corps volunteers, however, seemed to suffer disproportionately from sexual harassment, and the forms of harassment sometimes seemed to be more severe than what women in most other programs endured.

Peace Corps volunteers in Africa, Latin America, and Eastern Europe reported a high level of on-the-job harassment, such as a government worker making inappropriate comments, a fellow teacher crudely asking for sex, or a driver groping a volunteer while visiting an isolated region. Many Peace Corps volunteers were harassed or even assaulted while traveling alone on public transportation. Some suffered from daily harassment by strangers in the villages or towns where they worked. Although none of the volunteers we met or surveyed reported being raped, a very small number said they knew of volunteers who had been raped. Some said they were never harassed at all.

Why did we hear so many stories from Peace Corps volunteers who were harassed? Because of the Peace Corps's size, we interviewed more Peace Corps volunteers than those from any other program, so perhaps it's to be expected that we heard a higher number of harassment incidents from Peace Corps volunteers. However, after much discussion and reflection, we became convinced that there are also other reasons that a high level of harassment was reported by Peace Corps volunteers.

The Peace Corps generally spreads out its volunteers throughout a country, with many volunteers working and living apart from other volunteers. As a result, they do not have the protection of being in a group. The vast majority of Peace Corps volunteers are young, single, and eager to make friends, and may unintentionally send misleading signals in cultures where it is not customary for a woman to be friends with a man. Some volunteers, in an attempt to be trusting and culturally sensitive, disregard warning signs that seem to indicate potential danger. Peace Corps volunteers are often placed within schools and organizations that do not have a long-term relationship with the Peace Corps; therefore, they may not be embraced as quickly or taken "under the wing" of an organization or community. Because the Peace Corps is not a religious program, volunteers do not have the benefit of affiliation with a local church and therefore do not have the respect that nuns or female lay missioners may receive. One Peace Corps former staff member told us that alcohol is a factor in many reported assaults. Of course, none of these observations are meant to blame volunteers for the bad behavior of harassers.

The Peace Corps takes sexual harassment and assault of its volunteers very seriously. If a volunteer is harassed at her job, she will probably be offered a transfer. In more serious cases of sexual assault or rape, the Peace Corps provides medical and psychological support. Harassment is discussed in the training period (although some volunteers feel that the training is not extensive enough, and that it "tiptoes" around the issue of sexual harassment and sexual relations in general). Overall, the Peace Corps has more resources than other programs and is, therefore, better able to respond when there are problems. Of course, not all country offices are the same, and a few volunteers said they did not notify staff of harassment because they did not think they would be given appropriate support.

The challenges women face in the Peace Corps do not mean that we think women should rule out volunteering with the Peace Corps, especially since some harassment is common with virtually all volunteer programs.

As mentioned in Chapter 9, "How to Be an Effective International Volunteer," "Baywatch" and movies portraying American women as "loose" have been disseminated to the far corners of the world. We encourage women who volunteer with the Peace Corps and other programs to avoid feeding this stereotype and/or becoming a victim of it. Behavior modifications we recommend include dressing much more conservatively than you would at home (e.g., never wearing tank tops, shorts, or short skirts), avoiding bars or drinking in public, following local norms such as avoiding eye contact with men, and not inviting men into your home. See Chapter 9, "How to Be an Effective International Volunteer," for additional suggestions.

Don't let fear of harassment deter you from volunteering; just know that it may occur, and take precautions to protect yourself. If you are particularly concerned about this issue you may wish to consider programs that place volunteers in a group living situation, are religiously affiliated, or have a long-term relationship with a particular community.

Observations and Commentary

The size and complexity of the Peace Corps make it difficult to evaluate it comprehensively. For almost any finding, there will be a number of exceptions. We have tried hard to present what *generally* seems to be the case for the Peace Corps today. In order to assess the overall program, however, it is helpful to look beyond the individual pros and cons and examine the broader goals and context of the Peace Corps.

Does the Peace Corps Succeed in Its Own Stated Mission?

From the viewpoint of the Peace Corps's mission, we can see that the agency has met with mixed success. The first part of the Peace Corps's stated mission is "to promote world peace and friendship by making available to interested countries Americans willing to serve overseas who will help the people of these countries to meet their needs for trained men and women." If we take at face value this mission, the Peace Corps falls short in several respects. Unlike volunteers in several other organizations we profile, very few, if any, Peace Corps volunteers do work that relates directly to peace building. In fact, the "apolitical" nature of the Peace Corps prevents volunteers from working on most types of peace building, or even inter-group conflict resolution. One could argue, however, that friendship indirectly helps promote peace, and certainly most Peace Corps volunteers do develop friendships in the country where they are assigned.

The Peace Corps gets poor marks for helping foreign countries meet their needs for trained men and women. As we have already pointed out, the vast majority of volunteers lack the work experience or the education to be considered "trained men and women." Most volunteers we spoke with said their technical training was seriously lacking. There is no reason to assume just because most Peace Corps volunteers are Americans with bachelor's degrees that they possess the skills and training necessary to contribute to their host country.

The second part of the Peace Corps's mission is "to help promote a better understanding of Americans on the part of the peoples served." The Peace Corps certainly has helped people in other countries understand *some* Americans. In many ways, sending idealistic volunteers puts our country's best face forward. The Peace Corps volunteers that people in other countries meet, however, do not accurately represent the diversity of our country; they are overwhelmingly young, white, middle class, and do not generally include people with disabilities. Finally, as discussed below, sometimes the image of Peace Corps volunteers is exploited to give a positive impression of Americans in countries where U.S. policies have been harmful.

The Peace Corps has probably had the most success in the third and final part of its stated mission: "promoting a better understanding of other peoples on the part of Americans." While the understanding of other peoples that volunteers gain depends on their vantage point and their level of involvement, most of the volunteers do learn a great deal about other cultures. Friends, relatives, and young people involved in the World Wise Schools program may also learn about other people and cultures. We hope that more Peace Corps volunteers take responsibility for sharing their experiences so that more people in the United States can learn about the lives of peoples overseas.

Many Peace Corps volunteers and some staff told us that the Peace Corps is better understood as a cultural exchange program, not a development program. We would agree with this assessment, although $80,000 per volunteer seems like a lot of money to pay for cultural exchange. High school exchange or college semester abroad could accomplish this goal at a fraction of the cost.

Peace Corps in the Context of U.S. Foreign Policy

Given that many people join the Peace Corps because they want to support development, we feel that it is important to analyze the Peace Corps in the overall context of U.S. policies toward the "developing" world. When we examine the Peace Corps along with other U.S. Government programs and agencies, some strange contradictions emerge.

A prime example of what we mean is in the area of schooling in those countries in which the Peace Corps places the majority of its volunteers as teachers. Simultaneously, however, the U.S. Government supports policies that harm the educational systems of some of the same countries. For instance, the World Bank and the International Monetary Fund, institutions in which the United States has the greatest voting power, have worked together to condition lending on policy packages known as Structural Adjustment Programs. Frequently these policy packages require governments to slash their education budgets and impose school fees. In many countries like Zambia, the World Bank's own data shows that school enrollment has dropped since the imposition of structural adjustment.

In this context, for the U.S. Government to send teachers to Zambia is like shooting someone with your right hand while your left hand puts a bandage on her. A more effective way to promote the patient's health would be not to shoot her. Similarly, if the United States is genuinely concerned about education of the poor overseas, it could use its clout to change the policies of the International Monetary Fund and World Bank that often require countries like Zambia to cut funding for education as a condition for financial assistance. This strategy would be many times more effective than sending mostly untrained teachers. There are other U.S. Government policies that create problems for impoverished people overseas, including sending military support to anti-democratic governments, providing economic support to governments that repeatedly abuse human rights, and using embassy resources to promote U.S. oil companies that endanger rain forests where people live. We feel strongly that before spending money to send Americans overseas to help poor people, the United States should stop spending money on programs that sabotage impoverished people's efforts to help themselves.

Clearly, just because one branch of government is doing the wrong thing doesn't mean *all* parts of the government are negative. But people considering the Peace Corps should realize that they would be part of a government that helps to create many of the problems they are trying to address. Chapter 3, "The Big Picture: International Volunteering in Context," explores these issues in more detail.

The Peace Corps as a Public Relations Agency of the U.S. Government: Image vs. Reality

To understand the image that the Peace Corps promotes, consider what was going on in the world and in U.S foreign policy when the Peace Corps was created. The United States was at the height of its Cold War rivalry with the Soviet Union, fighting for allies and seeking to overcome its "military bully" image. The Peace Corps was explicitly created to win the hearts and minds of people around the world. Even now, in the post-Cold War era, U.S. militarism and economic domination generate anti-U.S. sentiments that the U.S. Government seeks to counter. The United States has found a powerful public relations instrument in the image of smiling young Americans helping needy people in foreign lands. In fact, this image is not realistic; the Peace Corps, as mentioned, is far from an effective tool for helping poor people in other countries.

Nonetheless, the Peace Corps continues to promote the image of the volunteer helping to bring about development. A 1999 U.S. postage stamp issued in honor of the Peace Corps captured the absurd notion that impoverished people overseas need Americans to teach them to develop. The stamp is a Norman Rockwell painting of a young, white American teaching black Africans how to plow. The Africans stand passively watching, not working, as if plowing and hard work are new concepts to them. In reality, most Africans could plow circles around most Americans, including most

Peace Corps volunteers. This misleading image of the American "helping" is part of the Peace Corps's attempt to win broad public, and thus bipartisan, support in Congress. Prospective volunteers should know that the "volunteer as savior" image is unreal. The Peace Corps should stop perpetuating this stereotype.

Lessons from Programs of Other Governments

We believe that the Peace Corps could benefit by learning from the volunteer programs of other governments. While we did not conduct extensive research on such organizations, we think they offer some lessons for how the Peace Corps could become more effective. In Australia, the Overseas Service Bureau's Volunteers Abroad Program, for example, focuses on identifying locally initiated projects overseas rather than recruiting large numbers of relatively unskilled volunteers for undetermined projects. Once it has indentified such projects, the Bureau puts energy into recruiting highly trained volunteers whose skills match the specific needs of the projects. Sweden's Forum Syd, Canada's CUSO, and England's Voluntary Service Overseas all utilize a model of responding to requests from foreign non-governmental organizations for assistance for a particular project or task by recruiting volunteers with the appropriate skills. In addition, a number of organizations like New Zealand's Volunteer Service Abroad have devised effective strategies for attracting experienced professionals such as offering short-term volunteer options as well as longer placements.

Many Peace Corps Volunteers Do Make a Contribution

Our critical perspective is not meant to negate the hard work of many Peace Corps volunteers. Although we met and heard of far too many volunteers who were unproductive, we also met volunteers who were doing good work, often in quite challenging situations. We also met many volunteers who were idealistic, caring, and eager to learn about the local culture, and trying hard to make a contribution.

Making Your Decision

In making your own decision about the Peace Corps, consider carefully the pros and cons discussed earlier in this chapter. To be fair, several (but by no means all) of the "cons" of the Peace Corps are weaknesses shared by most other volunteer placement organizations. We are referring here to weak technical training, potential for sexual harassment, spotty and deficient support in the field, and, most of all, a lack of meaningful evaluations of the projects on which volunteers work. At the same time, as we have said, the primary drawback most unique to the Peace Corps—its being part of the U.S. Government—is, ironically, the very reason why it is able to offer so many benefits to the volunteer that most other programs cannot provide.

In the end, of course, you will need to make your own decision about whether or not you want to be a part of the U.S. Government, with all the privileges and drawbacks we have discussed. If you want to explore other options that have some of the benefits of the Peace Corps, we refer you to specific sections of our Index of Profiled Organizations including "Organizations That Pay Your Expenses" and "Organizations Offering Long-term Programs."

We also refer you to the chapter on fundraising, so you won't think that the Peace Corps is the only financially viable option for you to volunteer overseas.

If You Do Choose Peace Corps

Robert Kleinhaus, who volunteered in Ghana, says he always tells new Peace Corps recruits: "Be realistic about expectations, question things, and stand up for yourself if you think Peace Corps staff is wrong." In addition, we suggest that people who choose to volunteer with Peace Corps take the following advice:

- *Get some relevant work experience before joining Peace Corps instead of signing on just out of college.*

- *Use your own initiative to create a better situation if you don't like your initial placement with Peace Corps once you are in-country. Give yourself time to assess the situation; don't just bail out on a placement, but, for instance, if the school where you are assigned doesn't need you, perhaps you can bike to a more rural school that does. If you can't get a new gardening club started, perhaps there is an existing club that could use your support—or could teach you different outreach strategies. If the people in your area don't really need to study English, gather materials in their language on more relevant information such as self-help in primary health care. You can also request an official reassignment. According to one volunteer in Fiji, Nick Bartoli, "My reassignment turned my Peace Corps experience from a job I abhorred to one that was more than I could have hoped for."*

- *Avoid becoming part of the Peace Corps "party crew."*

- *Take advantage of Peace Corps's support for the third part of its mission—sharing what you learn overseas with other Americans. During your time in the Peace Corps, have the Peace Corps match you with a public school class in the United States. After you return home, volunteer to make presentations in schools.*

- *Use some of your time in the Peace Corps to explore the root causes of poverty. Specifically, learn as much as you can about the history of U.S. policy toward the country, the role of the IMF and World Bank, and ways that various international forces, especially those based or greatly influenced by the United States, have helped or hindered the development of political and economic democracy. When you return home, you can use this learning to join with others in addressing some of the root causes of underdevelopment.*

You may also want to do your own research about the Peace Corps, its history and what it has meant to volunteers. One good resource is the unofficial website "Peace Corps Crossroads" (www.concentric.net/~jmuehl/links.shtml), which contains a wealth of links to other Peace Corps–related websites, including a site that discusses the reasons why one may not want to join the Peace Corps.

http://clubs.yahoo.com/clubs/peacecorps is a chatroom "Where prospective Peace Corps volunteers and returned Peace Corps volunteers can come together." And in a similar vein, the Peace Corps Information Network (www.concentric.net/~jmuehl/pcinfon.shtml) is a database that helps potential volunteers get connected with returned or current volunteers.

Edwin Staples's "Reinventing the Wheel?: The Peace Corps and Organizational Memory" (http://picante.net/text/memory.htm) is a bit academic but discusses the Peace Corps's failure to pass on to its volunteers the "institutional memory" of its projects.

www.geocities.com/MeagsDream features journal entries of Meagan's experiences from signing up, to working in the field. Her entries are a window onto the life of a Peace Corps volunteer and are more revealing of the shortcomings of the Peace Corps than perhaps she realizes. The website also contains some good packing advice.

In addition, out of the hundreds of books written about the Peace Corps, we recommend reading:

> *All You Need Is Love: The Peace Corps and the Spirit of the 1960s.* Elizabeth Cobbs Hoffman. Cambridge, Massachusetts: Harvard University Press, 1998. A fascinating analysis of the creation and early days of the Peace Corps.

> *Dear Exile: The True Story of Two Friends Separated for a Year by an Ocean.* Hilary Liftin and Kate Montgomery. New York: Vintage Books, 1999. Reads like a cross between *Bridget Jones's Diary,* a National Geographic travelogue, and a Kafka novel.

For information on other books by former Peace Corps volunteers try www.peacecorps.gov/about/facts/books.html.

Conclusion

Given the high degree of bipartisan Congressional support for the Peace Corps and the limited number of volunteer placement organizations that offer total financial support for volunteers, the Peace Corps is likely to continue to be a popular option for U.S. citizens considering long-term volunteer work overseas. If you are considering the Peace Corps, be sure to compare it with other organizations discussed in this book. If you do choose the Peace Corps, enter the experience with your eyes open to its structural challenges and take personal responsibility to make the most of the experience. Perhaps in the long term, you can help the Peace Corps do justice to the idealism of its volunteers and the goodwill of the American people who want their government to support international peace and development.

The Peace Corps is the easiest way to volunteer in another country if you don't have the money to fund your own expenses.—Matthew Thompson, Peace Corps volunteer, Bolivia

My grandmother said that she thinks the Americans are very smart to have this Peace Corps program. They send their young people here to Africa so that our elders can educate them.—Coumba Touré, Institute for Popular Education, Mali

The independence the Peace Corps gives you is a blessing and a curse. You can sometimes be very creative because there's no one telling you what to do. But it's also extremely frustrating because sometimes you just don't know where to start.—Robert O'Donovan, Peace Corps volunteer, Kazakhstan

We think the volunteers get more from the Peace Corps than the people here do. —Meredith Smith, Peace Corps Associate Director, Guatemala

What I like least about the Peace Corps is having to be a representative of a government whose motives I question and whose policies I don't always support.—Tamara Stenn, Peace Corps volunteer, Bolivia

What I liked best about the Peace Corps was that I felt safe working in Kenya with them as an organization. They were like a security blanket for me. They did, however, give us a lot of flexibility and freedom, which was good, since we could do our work without always wondering what they would say. It was sometimes bad, however, since I saw a lot of people take advantage of the situation.—Christopher A. Galaty, Peace Corps volunteer, Kenya

CHAPTER 12

ORGANIZATIONAL PROFILES

How We Did Our Research

In researching volunteer placement organizations, we wanted to go beyond what any organization said about itself. We also sought to include a wide range of organizations, recognizing that different people look for different things because the skills, interests, and time frame of prospective volunteers vary enormously.

We therefore initially cast our net quite broadly, creating a database of well over 300 organizations from various publications, websites, and networks. We narrowed the list by excluding programs that were purely study or travel, however praiseworthy their purpose or excellent their reputations; programs that were exclusively proselytizing or missionary; and most organizations that targeted primarily Europeans, deciding to focus on organizations that recruited mostly North Americans.

Working with this refined list, we first communicated with each organization's headquarters to gain factual information. We then planned our site visits, with the goal of interviewing not only volunteers in the field, but also local staff and community members. As mentioned in "Our Stories," along with our research assistants, we visited twenty-five countries in over a dozen trips overseas. Whenever our resources permitted, we visited more than one site for each volunteer placement organization in order to assess the organization's consistency. It was not possible, however, to visit all the sites of all the volunteer placement organizations.

We complemented our field research with hundreds of surveys of returned volunteers. We did not use random sampling; our research was not quantitatively oriented, but instead focused on qualitative assessment.

In the beginning stage of our research we planned to rate volunteer programs according to their quality. After our fieldwork, however, we realized that virtually all of the programs did some things well and all had areas for improvement. Rather than rating programs, therefore, we decided to make recommendations about which programs, given their strengths and weaknesses, might be better for certain types of volunteers. We included even organizations that we felt were generally of low quality, both to warn our readers and to illuminate some of the challenges of volunteering. We also decided to give readers suggestions for evaluating programs according to their needs and interests. (See Chapter 4, "Choosing the Right Organization.") As we prepared this book for publication, we reconnected with the headquarters of each volunteer placement organization in order to confirm and update the factual information in each profile.

We included only commentary on organizations for which we had enough data; if we did not have a sufficient number of interviews and/or surveys, we list only factual information or mention in the commentary the limited nature of our research. Of course, programs can vary from country to country and change year to year. To complement the profiles of organizations we have also included contact information for more than 130 organizations in "Additional Volunteer Organizations Not Profiled." We were not able to research these organizations more thoroughly. We encourage all users of this guide to supplement and update the information in the guide with Internet research and by talking to recently returned volunteers.

Because we plan to issue future editions of the book, we hope you will help us keep our research up to date. If you volunteer with an organization listed here (or even one not listed), take the time to fill out and mail or e-mail the survey starting on page 467. You can also find the survey online at our website, www.volunteeroverseas.org. Let us know what aspects of the profiles were most helpful, any details that no longer apply, and additional information you think we should include in future profiles.

ACDI/VOCA

50 F St. NW, Suite 1075
Washington, DC 20001

phone: 800-929-8622; 202-383-4961
fax: 202-626-8726
e-mail: volunteer@acdivoca.org
web: www.acdivoca.org

While ACDI/VOCA may be working largely on macro projects throughout the world, it is the interpersonal connections that really make the ideas and work stick. It is the impact on the individuals on both sides of the Atlantic that make it worthwhile.—James Thibeault, volunteer, Slovakia

Countries where volunteers are placed: Armenia, Azerbaijan, Belarus, Bolivia, Bulgaria, Croatia, Egypt, Ethiopia, Georgia, Honduras, Indonesia, Kazakhstan, Kosovo, Kyrgyzstan, Macedonia, Mongolia, Mozambique, Romania, Russia, Rwanda, South Africa, Thailand, Uganda, Ukraine, and the West Bank/Gaza

Field(s) of Work: Volunteers provide short-term technical assistance in agribusiness (e.g., agricultural production, food processing, and marketing), cooperative and association development (agricultural cooperatives, craft cooperatives, etc.), or natural resource conservation. Volunteers also provide assistance in banking, business planning, feasibility studies, strategic planning, micro-enterprise development, and rural finance.

Requirements or special skills necessary: ACDI/VOCA volunteers typically are mid-career or retired U.S. professionals with at least ten years of professional experience. ACDI/VOCA has a growing need for volunteer specialists in the following fields: banking, rural finance, small and medium enterprise development, information technology and e-commerce, business management, farm/rural credit systems, food and meat processing, baking and bakeries, agricultural cooperatives, post-harvest handling, agricultural trade associations, and commodity marketing and development. ACDI/VOCA offers a limited number of volunteer opportunities for non-U.S. citizens.

Duration and dates: Volunteer assignments last from two weeks to three months with start-up dates year round. Volunteers are typically placed within eight weeks of a client organization's request for assistance.

What volunteers pay and what they receive: All project-related expenses are covered, including medical inoculations, airfare, in-country travel, housing, and meals. ACDI/VOCA also provides medical insurance, emergency evacuation insurance, and in-country orientation and support. ACDI/VOCA receives support from the U.S. Agency for International Development (USAID) (in particular the Farmer-to-Farmer program), the U.S. Department of Agriculture, multilateral banks, and other sources.

Typical volunteer responsibilities: Volunteer responsibilities vary with the type of work but include developing strategic plans and marketing strategies, evaluating production efficiencies, conducting feasibility studies and seminars, training staff, meeting with government officials, and preparing asset valuations.

Number of volunteers sent abroad annually: 621 (2000)

Age range: Adults   **Typical age:** Mid-Career Adults

How to apply: Prospective volunteers should submit an application and resume by visiting the ACDI/VOCA website. If qualified, they are entered into a database of skilled professionals. When ACDI/VOCA receives requests from overseas, it searches the database for specialists that meet the project criteria. Information on current openings, updated regularly, is available on the website as is an online application.

Stated mission: "ACDI/VOCA identifies and opens economic opportunities for farmers and other entrepreneurs worldwide by promoting democratic principles and market liberalization, building international cooperative partnerships, and encouraging the sound management of natural resources."

History: ACDI/VOCA is a nonprofit international development organization that was created through the consolidation of Agricultural Cooperative Development International (ACDI) and Volunteers in Overseas Cooperative Assistance (VOCA). The U.S. agricultural cooperative community founded both organizations in the 1960s with the "humanitarian goal of globalizing the successes of American agriculture." Prominent U.S. cooperatives and farm credit banks are members of ACDI/VOCA and are represented on its board of directors. Funding from the U.S. government, member cooperatives, and other sources has enabled ACDI/VOCA to apply experience in more than 128 nations to "helping emerging and transitional economies grow."

Observations and commentary: ACDI/VOCA (VOCA for short), as mentioned, was founded with the "humanitarian goal of globalizing the successes of American agriculture." The millions of American family farmers who have been forced out of business might wonder what successes VOCA is referring to.

In general, we found VOCA staff and volunteers to be professional, positive, and friendly. We are troubled, however, by VOCA's tendency to "follow the money" and conduct whatever projects are paid for by USAID. As one volunteer put it, "Wherever USAID funding goes, there will go VOCA." This means that VOCA runs a risk of serving the interests of multinational agribusiness over the interests of low-income people in the countries where they work.

On its website, for example, VOCA announced a volunteer position titled "Fast Food Café Management." The volunteer was to have "practical experience in the U.S. fast food business, like McDonalds, Burger King, or Taco Bell," and was to assist Allegro Food, "the biggest and dynamically developing chain of fast food cafes" in Russia, to develop a training program for Allegro's sales people. Corporations such as Allegro Foods have much more buying power than mom-and-pop eateries and small cooperatives. Helping them expand directly benefits the large U.S. agribusiness corporations that USAID supports by boosting international market demand for U.S. agricultural products. The downside, however, is that a project of this type further concentrates wealth in the hands of a few corporations, not to mention the lamentable promotion of fast food.

Ninety percent of VOCA volunteers, we were told, work in some aspect of the development of agricultural cooperatives, though this ratio is changing as VOCA increasingly offers positions in non-agricultural areas such as assisting businesses in the fields of medicine, veterinary science, and tourism. Many VOCA volunteers are farmers, but as many are professionals in the fields of finance and business management who help fledgling cooperatives and other businesses get on their feet. VOCA also assists in the building of institutions and associations.

Glen Blumhorst, a VOCA representative we met in Bolivia, told us that VOCA has a commitment to capacity building in Bolivia. One example he gave us was of a project in which an organization of llama ranchers enlisted one of the senior economists at the USDA to assist them in capturing a larger portion of a market dominated by Peru. "The volunteer," Glen commented, "was here to help develop the external and internal markets for pre-spun wool and yarn."

James Thiebault, a VOCA volunteer we met in Slovakia, seemed to be the ideal person to help develop craft cooperatives in the town of Tolcik in Slovakia. He brought years of experience helping artisans, specifically quilt makers, preserve their craft and make a decent living. Interestingly, James gained this experience years earlier when he volunteered with VISTA, the precursor to Americorps. His VISTA placement was in Cabin Creek, West Virginia, and involved going into homes to conduct water pollution surveys. "During my trips into people's homes," he told us, "I noticed quilts, beautiful works of art." The families asked James if he would sell some of the quilts when he went back to Boston. "They told me: 'We don't have any other source of income.'" The challenges facing many populations in the Appalachian Mountains mirror those faced by populations in Slovakia, which parallels West Virginia in topography and economics; both are coal mining areas with strong craft cultures looking for market outlets.

For professionals in the fields of business, finance, and agriculture, who have a desire to improve the "economic self-sufficiency" of people and cooperatives in developing countries, and can live with the organization's limitations, VOCA would be a good choice.

Overall, I was extremely impressed with the ACDI/VOCA people I met in Slovakia. They are enthusiastic, energetic, intelligent, community-minded individuals, who are very much adding value to regional tourism in Slovakia.—Christine Weiss Daughtery, staff, Slovakia

The best thing about the VOCA program is rediscovering my talents and remembering that, having lived fifty years, I've learned a few things that could be interesting to someone else. It's renewing and reinvigorating.—James Thiebault, volunteer, Slovakia

---

Adventures in Health, Education, and Agricultural Development (AHEAD Inc.)

PO Box 2049
Rockville, MD 20847-2049

phone: 301-530-3697
fax: 301-530-3532
e-mail: aheadinc@erols.com
web: www.aheadinc.org

The thing I liked best about AHEAD is the relationship that they have with the people of Tanzania. They have been there a long time, working at the grassroots level and teaching people to help themselves.—Bouapha Toommaly, volunteer, Tanzania

Countries where volunteers are placed: The Gambia and Tanzania

Field(s) of work: Primary health care, health education, construction/renovation, youth leadership development, environmental education, micro-enterprise, and water and sanitation

Requirements or special skills necessary: Volunteer opportunities are open to college students, professionals, retirees, and other interested persons. No specific skills are required, although some special projects may require medical training.

Duration and dates: Volunteers serve from one month to a year, but most participate in the Summer AHEAD Volunteers to Africa Program that lasts six to eight weeks. Volunteers are expected to travel to Washington, DC, for a four-day orientation before departing for Africa.

What volunteers pay and what they receive: Participation in the Summer AHEAD Volunteers to Africa Program costs $4,000. This fee includes round-trip international airfare, in-country travel, departure taxes, visa fees, all tips, taxes, and gratuities in-country, and room and board. A down payment of $500 (part of the program fee) is due upon acceptance into the program. Volunteers are responsible for covering their own travel costs to Washington, DC.

Typical volunteer responsibilities: Volunteers work with ongoing projects that emphasize teen pregnancy prevention, HIV/AIDS and STI prevention, immunizations, nutrition, women's health, family planning, and youth leadership development. Volunteer responsibilities range from weighing babies and assisting health professionals with immunizations, to helping youth prepare and perform presentations with social messages.

Number of volunteers sent abroad annually: 5–15

Age range: 22–70   **Typical age:** 25

How to apply: Interested individuals should contact AHEAD via e-mail or telephone.

Stated mission: "Adventures in Health, Education, and Agricultural Development (AHEAD) is a nonprofit, non-government organization. Its purpose is to work with underserved communities in developing countries and in the United States to improve the quality of life by implementing programs that lead to self-sufficiency and self-reliance in health, education, and agriculture. The goals of the organization are to: (1) reduce and eliminate disease and premature death; (2) cultivate and advance healthy living; and (3) foster sustainable environmental activity."

History: In 1974, Dr. Irving Williams moved with his family to Tanzania to work as a pediatrician. The observation of deprivation and suffering of children dying of preventable diseases prompted the Williams's family to commit their lives to helping combat malnutrition, diseases, poverty, and other conditions that have an adverse effect on the health and welfare of peoples in developing countries.

In 1981, Dr. Williams and his wife Elvira founded AHEAD to provide direct, hands-on, people-to-people assistance to underserved communities in Africa. Since 1987, AHEAD has provided opportunties for more than 150 U.S. citizens and others to live and work in African communities.

Observations and commentary: In Tanzania, AHEAD has focused its attention on the Shinyanga Region in the north central part of the country, eighty miles south of Lake Victoria. The organization has several distinct programs in the region including school health programs, women's micro-enterprise groups, village-based primary health care committees, and general health outreach. The outreach teams work with village health workers to provide a range of services such as health education, growth monitoring, nutrition, and immunization. It is not uncommon for volunteers to drive to remote rural areas and set up afternoon clinics in schools to attend to the needs of women from the surrounding area who have walked miles to receive health care services.

In the Gambia, volunteers work with urban youth, exploring issues such as health and fitness, environmental awareness, first aid, AIDS/HIV, and substance abuse. A major project is the AHEAD/PAS Youth Leadership Camp, a three-week residential camp for youth from around the country that includes intensive community service projects, recreational activities, and cultural and historical outings. AHEAD volunteers serve as camp counselors, facilitating workshops on topics such as life planning, conflict management, adolescent health issues, and communication and study skills. The camp community service projects vary from year to year. Ruth Kimball, who served as a camp counselor in 2000, for example, worked with villagers to repair a well.

Volunteers typically live together in groups of three to six. Some volunteers appreciate the comfort of having other volunteers around, but others feel that the accommodations separate them from the community in which they are living.

AHEAD has been a leading organization in terms of connecting African Americans with Africa. While participation is open to all concerned U.S. citizens, the organization is notable for its inclusion of African Americans as both trip leaders and participants. It has also done a good job of making opportunities accessible to older volunteers. Younger volunteers should be aware that the age composition of the group has been a challenging aspect of the experience for some younger volunteers who struggled to try and establish equal and respectful relationships among their group composed of primarily older volunteers.

AHEAD has earned a reputation, particularly in Tanzania, as an organization that gets results. One of its recent successes, for example, was a program that immunized ninety-eight percent of the children in the Meatu District of Shinyanga. Successes such as this, more than a decade of continual presence in the region, and the personal relationships that have been built between the organization and local people have earned the organization great respect and notoriety.

Volunteers play an assisting role in this ongoing work, but at times can feel like they are not doing a lot. One volunteer told us that "the program is doing a lot, but the volunteers are not." Another recommended the program for individuals who like to "go at a slow pace."

Several volunteers felt that AHEAD did not provide adequate information prior to their departure overseas, including disclosing that their volunteer work would last only several weeks and that the remaining weeks were unscheduled. Others commented that there was a lack of clarity on what expenses were to be covered by the organization.

The orientation in Washington, D.C. also received mixed reviews, leaving some feeling "totally clueless" as to what they should expect in the field. On the other hand, most volunteers we spoke with felt that the orientation in Tanzania was quite informative.

We recommend the Tanzania program for people who want to gain experience working in rural health care with a well-established and respected organization and the Gambia program for those who want to work at a youth camp. AHEAD is welcoming of older volunteers and is a good choice for those who want a small group experience, but not for those who want to volunteer alone or in a large group.

AFS

310 SW 4 Ave., Suite 630
Portland, OR 97204-2608

phone: 800-AFS-INFO
fax: 503-248-4076
e-mail: info@afs.org
web: www.afs.org

Countries where volunteers are placed: Argentina, Australia, Austria, Belgium, Bolivia, Brazil, Canada, Chile, China, Costa Rica, Czech Republic, Denmark, Dominican Republic, Ecuador, Egypt, Finland, France, Germany, Ghana, Guatemala, Honduras, Hong Kong, Hungary, Iceland, Indonesia, Ireland, Italy, Jamaica, Japan, Latvia, Malaysia, Mexico, the Netherlands, New Zealand, Norway, Panama, Paraguay, Peru, Portugal, Russia, Slovakia, South Africa, Spain, Sweden, Switzerland, Thailand, Turkey, United Kingdom, and Venezuela

Field(s) of work: AFS (formerly American Field Service) offers three programs with volunteer opportunities overseas: the Summer (or Intensive) Program, the Community Service Program, and the Educator Program. The Summer Program for high school students includes an optional community service opportunity with non-profit organizations in addition to cultural exchange and language study. The Community Service Program offers young adults the opportunity to work with nonprofit organizations such as orphanages, health care centers for the disabled, community organizations, environmental protection groups, and schools. The Educator Program provides teachers and administrators with the opportunity to meet and work with their counterparts and students in other countries.

Requirements or special skills necessary: Participants in the Summer Program must be 16 to 18. Participants in the Community Service Program must be at least 18. Both the Summer Program and the Community Service Program require no special skills, simply a desire to learn from and participate in another culture. Those who volunteer in the Educator Program must be teachers or administrators with the appropriate experience and credentials.

Duration and dates: Placements in the Summer Program run from one to three months. Placements in the Community Service Program range from four months to one year, but the typical placement is six months. The Educator Program offers placements ranging from a semester to a full school year.

What volunteers pay and what they receive: Fees for the Summer Program range from $3,500 to $4,500. Fees for a typical six-month placement in the Community Service Program range from $4,795 (Bolivia) to $5,995 (Costa Rica). Fees cover round-trip airfare, travel within the host country, in-country orientations, language training, accomodations with a host family, and 24-hour emergency phone assistance. Fees do not cover the cost of mandatory AFS medical insurance.

Fees for the Educator Program vary from $1,500 (summer short program to China) to $3,200 (semester program to Argentina). Fees cover pre-departure orientation, travel within the host country, room and board, and activities. Volunteers are responsible for round-trip airfare, personal expenses, and the mandatory AFS medical insurance.

Typical volunteer responsibilities: Volunteers in the Summer Program, as already noted, are involved in various cultural and/or community service activities. Volunteers in the AFS Community Service Program work with a variety of local nonprofit organizations. Responsibilities vary but may include administrative work, teaching, environmental restoration, working with children in orphanages, or assisting with animals in zoos. Volunteers in the Educator Program participate in cultural lessons and events, family home stays, observations of local educational practices, and teaching in schools in the host country.

Number of volunteers sent abroad annually: 84 (Community Service Program)
230 (Summer Program volunteers involved in community service)
12 (Educator Program) (2000)

Age range: 15–29 (Community Service Program)
14–18 (Summer Program)
23+ (Educator Program)

Typical age: 18 (Community Service Program)
14–18 (Summer Program)
23–60 (Educator Program)

How to apply: Contact the AFS Info Center in Portland for an application or download one from the Internet.

Stated mission: "AFS-USA works toward a more just and peaceful world by providing international and intercultural learning experiences to individuals, families, schools, and communities through a global volunteer partnership."

History: "In 1947 AFS created a student exchange program that now places students from the United States in fifty-four countries worldwide. In 1995 AFS launched the Community Service Program, which provides the opportunity for students to broaden their knowledge of a new culture and develop marketable skills while they work with local nonprofits."

Observations and commentary: AFS is arguably the most well known and successful high school exchange program. Many thousands of high school students have gone overseas as a part of AFS's student exchange program, and now, as mentioned, hundreds are volunteering with AFS's Community Service Program. The Community Service Program provides more serious volunteer placements for individuals eighteen and over. Although in the Summer Program the community service activity is optional, most students opt to do it.

Guadalupe Prado, who works with AFS in Mexico City, told us that volunteers in the Summer Program and the Community Service Program work with both governmental and non-governmental organizations. Some volunteers work with the DIF, the Mexican government organization that serves families and children. Nongovernmental organizations include those that work with homeless children or children in orphanages and day care centers teaching them to read and write, plant trees, speak English, play musical instruments, and use proper hygiene.

The dominant thrust of both the Summer Program and the Community Service Program is cultural and educational exchange. The website says, "Volunteers are exposed to new customs, morals, ethics, and values that challenge them to reflect on their own cultural norms." The programs also provide students with the opportunity to learn a foreign language while living with a local host family.

AFS chapters in each country are organized to both send and receive students, a notable example of reciprocal exchange that is often lacking in international volunteer programs.

Guadalupe told us that she believes the typical six month placement of the Community Service Program is too short of a period. As many overseas hosts have told us, she stated that organizations often don't want to invest in volunteers who are staying for such a short period. We suggest that AFS consider longer placements for volunteers that desire to be involved in community service.

AFS conducts evaluations after six months and at the end of a volunteer's placement. The AFS support structure consists of offices in each country where volunteers are placed, pre-departure and arrival orientations, and an AFS support network within the United States.

For high school students, young adults, and current or retired school administrators and teachers with a desire to study abroad, experience another culture, and participate in community service, we recommend AFS. Based on the AFS history and reputation, and our limited research, we believe that the Community Service Program would be a good choice for college age students who want to work for a medium length of time with an NGO.

American Friends Service Committee (AFSC)

1501 Cherry St
Philadelphia, PA 19102-1479

phone: 215-241-7295
fax: 215-241-7026
e-mail: info@afsc.org
web: www.afsc.org

Countries where volunteers are placed: Mexico and the United States

Field(s) of work: Agriculture/farming, appropriate technology, construction, environmental conservation, and work with youth

Requirements or special skills necessary: AFSC and its partners offer two opportunities: the Summer Project in San Luis Potosí, Mexico, and the Joint Service Projects on Native American Reservations and in Mexico.

Volunteers with the Summer Project must be at least eighteen years old, be able to demonstrate maturity and leadership potential, have prior experience in community service and organizing, and possess a commitment to issues of social and economic justice. Conversational ability in Spanish is required, as are skills in one of the needed areas such as construction, farming, or work with youth. Required skills vary from project to project. (See the program descriptions posted on the website.)

Joint Service Projects are organized for groups, while volunteers with the Summer Project apply as individuals. Neither program requires applicants to be "Friends" (members of the Quaker church).

No special skills are required for the Joint Service Projects.

Duration and dates: The Summer Project lasts seven weeks from late June through mid-August. After a brief orientation, followed by a three-day home-stay with a local family, volunteers proceed to the project site where they spend the duration of the seven weeks.

Placements with the Joint Service Projects last one week, typically during school holidays.

What volunteers pay and what they receive: A program fee of $1,250 for the Summer Project covers room and board, travel while in the host country, medical insurance, in-country staff support, written materials, project supplies, and an orientation. Volunteers cover their own round-trip airfare. A limited number of scholarships are available.

Arrangements for the Joint Service Projects are worked out on a case-by-case basis.

Typical volunteer responsibilities: The Summer Project is managed by SEDEPAC (Service, Development, and Peace), an AFSC partner organization in Mexico. The project, formerly known as the Youth for Peace and Sustainable Community (*Semilleros de Futuros*), allows volunteers to assist SEDEPAC and the local people in appropriate technology projects or in the organization of workshops and cultural exchanges with local youth. There are also a limited number of expenses-paid facilitator positions that have additional responsibilities.

Volunteers in the Joint Service Projects assist in the construction of latrines, schools, clinics, roads, small stores, irrigation, and water supply systems in communities in rural Mexico and on Native American reservations in the United States.

Number of volunteers sent abroad annually:
> 50 (Summer Project)
> Varies (Joint Service Projects)

Age range: 18–26 (Summer Project)   **Typical age:** None
13+ (Joint Service Projects)

How to apply: Potential volunteers with the Summer Project send a written application and letters of reference to the headquarters in Philadelphia. Receipt of the application is followed by a phone interview. Potential volunteers can directly contact project staff at the following e-mail address: mexsummer@afsc.org.

For information on applying to the Joint Service Projects contact the project coordinator at 2852 W. Gamez Road, Benson, AZ 85602; phone: 520-212-4696. For application information or project dates, consult the AFSC website.

Stated mission: "The American Friends Service Committee is a Quaker organization that includes people of various faiths who are committed to social justice, peace, and humanitarian service. Its work is based on a belief in the worth of every person and faith in the power of love to overcome violence and injustice."

History: AFSC was founded in 1917 to provide conscientious objectors with an opportunity to aid civilian victims during World War I. The Summer Project has been carried out since 1939. The Joint Service Projects have been carried out since 1990 as a project of the American Friends Service Committee (AFSC) and Intermountain Yearly Meeting (IMYM) of the Religious Society of Friends.

Observations and commentary: AFSC is a well-known and respected development organization with innovative programs worldwide. The organization assists local NGOs in organizing, for example, small-scale irrigation projects in Laos, or the training of grassroots and union leaders in northeast Brazil in leadership, organizing, political, analytical, and advocacy skills. The Joint Service Projects and the Summer Project, however, are the only AFSC programs with volunteer opportunities. AFSC programs in countries other than the United States and Mexico are carried out by AFSC staff.

We did not have the opportunity to interview volunteers in the field, but on the basis of our familiarity with other AFSC programs, we would expect them to be of high quality. If you are considering one of AFSC's volunteer programs, we encourage you to contact returned volunteers to help you assess whether or not the program is for you.

AFSC sees that volunteers needs are met. The support provided for volunteers is adequate, but there can be a tension for those who live outside of the Quaker ideology of simplicity.—Bob and Helen Clark, staff, Cambodia

American Jewish World Service (AJWS)

989 Avenue of the Americas,
Tenth Floor
New York, NY 10018

phone: 800-889-7146
fax: 212-736-3463
e-mail: jvcvol@ajws.org
web: www.ajws.org

There was a time when we Jews needed help and there were people who helped us. Now we need to be there for others. I really wanted to serve with a Jewish organization, and I like the AJWS commitment to helping non-Jews.—Eric Stern, volunteer, Kenya

Countries where volunteers are placed: Belize, Cameroon, El Salvador, Ghana, Honduras, India, Israel, Kenya, Malawi, Mali, Mexico, Nicaragua, the Philippines, Russia, Senegal, South Africa, Ukraine, and Zimbabwe

Field(s) of work: AJWS has two programs, the Jewish Volunteer Corps (JVC) and the International Jewish College Corps (IJCC). JVC volunteers are placed as individuals with local non-governmental organizations where they provide technical assistance as computer specialists, small business consultants, public health professionals, teacher trainers, agriculturists, and many other professionals. IJCC volunteers are involved with group construction projects such as rebuilding houses in Honduras in the aftermath of Hurricane Mitch or building an elementary school in Ghana.

Requirements or special skills necessary: JVC volunteers must be Jewish and experienced professionals who can provide training in their area of expertise. IJCC volunteers must be Jewish and college students or recent graduates.

Duration and dates: JVC volunteers sign up for one to twelve months. Most volunteer for two to three months. Start dates vary. The seven-week IJCC volunteer program is a group experience that starts in late June and runs through early August. It begins with an orientation in New York and continues with a four-week placement in a rural village in either Ghana or Honduras. Volunteers then visit Israel, completing community service projects and continuing the dialogue about international development and its relation to Jewish texts and traditions. The program continues after volunteers return to the United States; this part of the program includes educational seminars, retreats, public speaking engagements, and volunteer service opportunities. After returning home, IJCC volunteers meet three times for discussion, presentations, and events.

What volunteers pay and what they receive: AJWS pays for JVC volunteers' airfare and other transportation to the site (as well as evacuation insurance) and provides limited staff support (mostly pre-departure). Volunteers must cover their own room and board expenses. Participants in the IJCC program pay $3,500, which covers all travel expenses, staff support, housing, food, orientation, and evacuation insurance. Financial aid is available.

Typical volunteer responsibilities: JVC volunteers are placed as individuals with local non-governmental organizations with which they provide medical services at clinics, research human rights issues, assist with fundraising and administration, and provide instruction in English, business, and management skills.

During their four-week placement in rural villages, IJCC volunteers are involved in a variety of group construction projects such as rebuilding houses in Honduras in the aftermath of Hurricane Mitch or building elementary schools in Ghana.

Number of volunteers sent abroad annually: 33 (JVC in 1999)
29 (IJCC in 1999)

Age range: 21–75 (JVC)
18–24 (IJCC) **Typical age:** 29–55 (JVC)
20 (IJCC)

How to apply: The JVC and IJCC programs require a written application with letters of reference, and an in-person or phone interview. Contact JVC/IJCC for an application or download one from the website.

Stated mission: "JVC sends highly skilled Jewish men and women to volunteer in health, education, agricultural, and economic development projects throughout the developing world. JVC provides humanitarian relief in the form of technical assistance to grassroots non-governmental organizations, enables Jewish men and women to renew and strengthen their bonds to Judaism by giving them the opportunity to fulfill the ethical ideal of *tikkun olam* (healing the world), and communicates to the world the Jewish commitment to the well-being and dignity of all people."

History: AJWS was founded in 1985. JVC began in 1994 and IJCC in 1998.

Observations and commentary: The two AJWS programs are quite different. JVC is distinguished by three characteristics: the quality and skills of its volunteers, the innovative grassroots organizations in which volunteers are placed, and the example it provides as a faith-based organization that does not engage in proselytizing.

JVC volunteers are among the most skilled volunteers we met during the course of our research. Instead of seeking idealistic but inexperienced volunteers, AJWS accepts only those with technical skills and/or significant work experience, as well as previous intercultural exposure. Volunteers include medical students and doctors, experienced nonprofit staff, and small business owners. The volunteers we met also shared appropriately modest expectations about what they could accomplish and a general openness to learning from those in their host community.

The in-country organizations where volunteers work are impressive, and the volunteers' assignments are challenging. Emilie Barnett, a volunteer in Zimbabwe, provided management training for the Organization of Rural Associations for Progress (ORAP), which reaches tens of thousands of rural Zimbabweans. Medical student Eric Stern helped develop AIDS education programs for a clinic in a slum of Nairobi and for a network of organizations that serve street children. Volunteer Joyanne Bloom created a feasibility study for expanding funding of tortilla factories run by women in Cuetzalán, Mexico. The organizations with which volunteers work often function without modern conveniences such as computers or telephones, and projects often do not proceed according to the expected timeline. Volunteers must be able to work with little supervision or support from AJWS, figuring out how they can be most useful, and be disciplined in their work habits.

JVC volunteers appear to be motivated by the Jewish faith. Most are placed with non-Jewish organizations, except for placements in the former Soviet Union where they provide training to isolated Jewish communities. Emilie Barnett commented, "I didn't have a great Jewish education, but the one thing that stuck with me was that Judaism is a religion of deeds, not words. All my adult life, I have felt that I have to live in that fashion."

According to AJWS, volunteers are often "the first Jews encountered by project partners and the people they serve. Because there is great curiosity about Judaism, a JVC volunteer is not only a representative of AJWS, but also an unofficial 'ambassador' of the Jewish people everywhere."

Volunteers often have the opportunity to get to know the local community. Joyanne Bloom was hosted by local families and took the *colectivo* (local bus) to the office each morning. After her workday of meetings and research, she would shop in the local market. "In the evening I helped prepare tortillas for dinner, then spent the remainder of the evening playing games with the kids and teaching others to knit."

JVC does not provide extensive support for its volunteers while they are in the field. Eric Stern would recommend JVC "highly, but only for people who are self-sufficient and can figure out their own logistics of housing, etc." Since AJWS does not provide language training, potential volunteers must take responsibility for learning the local language.

Joyanne Bloom would recommend JVC for "people who could say, 'Yes, I would sleep in a local's home on their dirt floor and eat their food out of a communal dish.' If that sounds offensive then this is not the right organization for you. You shouldn't expect to live better than they do." We agree with Joyanne's assessment and recommend JVC for Jewish people who have significant professional experience, a disciplined but flexible approach to work, an ability to thrive in other cultures, and a desire to work with grassroots organizations.

IJCC is a relatively new program that appears to be based on innovative ideas for linking Jewish faith with community service. Unlike JVC, IJCC has no skills requirements, and volunteers generally have little previous work experience. They provide unskilled labor for basic sanitation and construction projects, but since there is not really a shortage of unskilled labor in Honduras or Ghana, for example, the emphasis is more on cultural exchange than filling vital developmental needs. Volunteers we surveyed felt that they had meaningful interactions with local people and learned important things about themselves, Judaism, and social justice. Volunteer Daniela Zeltzer said that her main critique was that the program was too short. Daniela told us that "the two very professional leaders on our team helped us in every way," and that the experience changed her tremendously. Corinna Proffitt said, "I have never felt so alive, so purposeful, or so strong, before or since."

We recommend IJCC for flexible Jewish young adults who want to explore international development as it relates to Jewish traditions.

"My years of work and nurturing a family taught me the patience to wait and settle into the rhythm of life in this remarkable land. I could see beyond the daily frustrations of appointments not kept, broken telephones, and the absence of plumbing to the extraordinary depth of commitment that the people with whom I worked brought to the endeavor. I learned from my colleagues and friends the primacy of their families, their ability to manage well with very little, and their unfailing courtesy."—Emilie Barnett, JVC volunteer, Zimbabwe

I successfully raised funds for a very important project: the eradication of child labor in the silk-weaving industry. As a result of the work of the organization I helped, hundreds of children will make the change from work to school, and their families will be involved in alternative income-generation programming. This work will make both an immediate and long-term difference in the lives of these families.—Jessica W. Meistrich-Gidal, JVC volunteer, India

---

Amigos de las Américas

5618 Star Ln.
Houston, TX 77057

phone: 800-231-7796
fax: 713-782-9267
e-mail: info@amigoslink.org
web: www.amigoslink.org

The biggest summers of my life have been with Amigos and they keep getting bigger. I have never been this challenged or learned so much from an experience. I have learned to be flexible, how to find solutions, how to use my support system, and how to delegate. I have never worked harder.—Christina Martin, former volunteer and project director, Ecuador

Countries where volunteers are assigned: Brazil, Bolivia, Costa Rica, Dominican Republic, Honduras, Mexico, Nicaragua, and Paraguay

Field(s) of work: Volunteers provide short-term public health and development services in communities, schools, and clinics.

Requirements or special skills necessary: Volunteers must be at least sixteen years of age by the departure date for Latin America. Amigos requires a minimum of two high school years of Spanish or Portuguese, or equivalent ability, and a willingness to live in rustic conditions. Volunteers must also complete the training program either with a local chapter or as correspondents prior to departure, provide proof of health insurance, and successfully fundraise their share of expenses.

Duration and dates: Four to eight weeks during the summer.

What volunteers pay and what they receive: The basic participation fee is approximately $3,300. This covers round-trip transportation, training, food, lodging, transportation within the host country, project supplies, short-term international medical insurance, and 24-hour emergency communications support. Additionally, volunteers must cover airfare to the U.S. gateway city, immunizations, and passport/visa fees.

Typical volunteer responsibilities: Building "ecological" latrines, stove construction, home construction for rural school teachers, reforestation and other environmental projects, promotion of health and dental hygiene, and facilitating youth leadership development programs.

Number of volunteers sent abroad annually: 600–700

Age range: 16–24   **Typical age:** Two-thirds are high school students

How to apply: Application forms can be downloaded from the website or requested from headquarters.

Stated mission: "Amigos de las Américas builds partnerships to empower young leaders, advance community development, and strengthen multicultural understanding in the Americas."

History: Amigos de las Américas grew out of the experiences of members of a church youth group who spent part of the summer of 1965 in rural areas of Honduras fighting a growing polio epidemic. Amigos soon became a national organization working to deliver public health services to underserved areas in Latin America while encouraging young people to get involved in community health and development. Over the years, Amigos has sent approximately 20,000 volunteers abroad to work on a variety of public health projects such as community sanitation, human immunization, animal rabies vaccination, oral rehydration, and dental hygiene education.

Observations and commentary: Amigos operates a well-organized and supervised program based on four decades of experience. Most volunteers, we were told, enjoy the program and many return year after year as volunteers or staff.

Amigos is rightfully proud of its achievements in youth leadership development. We commend Amigos for providing their field staff with extensive training on communication and conflict resolution. Amigos leadership development exercises include role-playing followed by discussion of the participants' performance in the activities and how they can improve. Through these exercises, staff are given the opportunity to consider potential problems and find solutions before they reach the field. We are also impressed by how many people involved in international issues have told us that they got their start through the Amigos program.

We also commend Amigos for expanding the involvement of Latin American youth in Amigos projects. In the Dominican Republic, for example, local youth are collaborating with Amigos volunteers to create an ongoing Amigos chapter in the Dominican capital of Santo Domingo. In the Mexican State of Oaxaca, local medical students partner with Amigos volunteers to conduct community health projects. In many other projects local volunteers are actively involved in promoting leadership and community service among youth in rural communities. "The success of these programs, coupled with the enthusiasm and support expressed by volunteers, staff, and our part-nering agencies," says Emily Untermeyer, President and CEO of Amigos, "has led to more permanent and long-term involvement of Latin American youth in Amigos."

Amigos is to be credited for taking the pre-trip training of volunteers seriously. Training includes instruction on fundraising, language, safety and health, as well as a review of the history, politics, and culture of the area of service. The written materi-als are extensive and useful. Those living near one of the eighteen local chapters re-ceive their training through the chapters. Those who do not live near a chapter receive training through correspondence with the headquarters. Not surprisingly, the training of those who live near a chapter, we were told, more adequately prepares volunteers for the field. Personal contact with knowledgeable staff members seems to vastly in-crease the quality of instruction.

We asked field staff members in the Mexican state of Oaxaca, April Miller and Tanya Saboun, to describe a typical day in the field for an Amigo's volunteer. They gave us the example of two female volunteers who taught English to members of their host community. The girls woke up at around seven a.m. and had breakfast. After breakfast, they taught a few English classes, took a break, taught a different age group, broke for lunch, and taught again between four to seven in the evening. At seven they went back to their host families. April said that many of the girls in the host community told her they had learned a great deal from the two volunteers. These Amigos volunteers were exceptionally dedicated, but most Amigos volunteers, we were told, do work hard sev-eral hours a day.

In the field Amigos supervisors conduct volunteer evaluations that help volunteers continually improve their relationships with their host communities. Before their return to the United States, volunteers are debriefed about their strengths and weaknesses as volunteers. This is particularly important given that many Amigos volunteers return to the organization as volunteers or supervisors or continue international work elsewhere. Amigos does not, however, conduct evaluations of the projects themselves, and this is one of the shortcomings of its program. Project evaluations would create the opportu-nity for discussions about important topics such as the degree to which members of the host community are included in the creation and implementation of projects.

Both volunteers and staff have commented that two years of high school language instruction may not be enough preparation for volunteers. Carmen Lopéz, a staff mem-ber with CENIFE, a Costa Rican government agency responsible for the educational infrastructure in Costa Rica and one of the agencies that facilitates Amigos work, told us that language is the biggest weakness of Amigos training. We agree with CARE staff in Ecuador who told us that the experiences of volunteers would be richer if the volunteers were more proficient in Spanish.

Amigos has understandably strict rules about behavior, dress, sex, and alcohol. Volunteers who violate rules are subject to expulsion and, in that case, they may be subject to a fine. During a mid-term retreat in the summer of 1999, several volunteers drank alcohol. All those who drank, whether or not they became drunk, were sent home. Ostensibly, Amigos did this to make a point to current and future volunteers—

Amigos will not tolerate volunteers who break the rules. Some believe that the abundance of rules is stifling to volunteers. Amigos trustee Audelia Chiriboga says, "I am concerned for the future of Amigos. What makes the program great is that the kids get to make the decisions. And they get to make mistakes and learn from those mistakes. If everything is written down in the rule book then they won't have a chance to grow." Most of the rules, however, appear to us to be prudent and provide a structure that makes the Amigos program more successful in the long run.

One of the most important questions about Amigos, and all volunteer programs for that matter, is whether they benefit the host communities. Many volunteers believe they are giving back to the community, in a sense repaying the community with their skills. But, as one Amigos staff member puts it, "Most people assume that just coming with some skills is enough. But what skills does a sixteen year old have? There is no comparison between the manual labor that a gringo can do and a campesino. Even after I was in the Peace Corps two years, when I went out to hoe my garden I wasn't a tenth as strong as the local women I worked with." Despite their relative lack of skills, however, most Amigos volunteers are reportedly willing to work hard, sweat, and get their fingers dirty. Yet even the most well-intentioned labor can cost the impoverished host community more in food and housing than they receive. Amigos's policy of requiring host communities to feed and house volunteers has resulted in some resentment among impoverished host communities, who, in addition to their normal workload, feel they are being asked to babysit rich kids. Perhaps volunteer organizations like Amigos should consider paying host organizations/communities as educators since this is the role they are inevitably playing with young North American volunteers.

For high school students with an interest in other cultures and in public health, Amigos provides a well-established and structured program that serves as an excellent introduction to work in developing countries.

Currently, many volunteers and Amigos constituents view their experience primarily as a "service" activity. However, my research shows that the most significant impacts of the experience are manifested in the personal growth of volunteers. Amigos should thus promote the experience increasingly as an opportunity to grow personally and develop skills rather than as an opportunity to "help" others or teach skills. The promotion of the "helper" mentality can perpetuate paternalism and undermine efforts at solidarity.—Kirsten Tobey, former Amigos volunteer and leader (quote from Kirsten's undergraduate thesis for Brown University)

I like the fact that I wasn't a tourist but rather a part of the community. There were a lot of tourists coming to see the turtles and they were oblivious to what was going on in the community while we were a part of it. It was a beautiful thing to be a part of a family and a community and to know that you were significant in their lives and they were significant in your life. As a tourist, you never have that experience.—Jen Dominguez, volunteer, Costa Rica

Amigos is a fantastic opportunity to become a leader for young people who have strong language facility and interest in development issues.—Wendy Phillips, volunteer, Dominican Republic

Amity Institute, Amity Volunteer Teachers Abroad (AVTA) Program

10671 Roselle St., Suite 100
San Diego, CA 92121-1525

phone: 858-455-6364
fax: 858-455-6597
e-mail: avta@amity.org
web: www.amity.org

Countries where volunteers are placed: Argentina, Brazil, Dominican Republic, Ghana, Mexico, Peru, Senegal, and Venezuela

Field(s) of work: Teaching various subjects including English, mathematics, science, computer applications, technical drawing, and agricultural science

Requirements or special skills necessary: Participants in the AVTA Program must be at least twenty-one years of age and possess a relevant undergraduate degree. They should have some teaching or tutoring background, experience working with children or adolescents, and previous experience working, traveling, or studying abroad. A working knowledge of Spanish is required for assignments in Latin American countries.

Duration and dates: Full academic year, semester, and summer assignments are offered. The academic year in Argentina, Brazil, Peru, and Venezuela begins in March and runs through mid-December; second semester assignments begin in July. In the Dominican Republic, Mexico, Ghana, and Senegal the school year begins in late August and runs through June.

What volunteers pay and what they receive: Volunteers are responsible for round-trip airfare, health insurance for the duration of the stay, and at least $150 per month in personal spending money. An administrative fee of $500 for positions in Latin America and $1,200 for assignments in Africa is payable once an applicant accepts an assignment. AVTA participants are provided either with free room and board in the home of a host family or independent housing. Volunteers may have the opportunity to attend classes or workshops at the institution where they teach, or at a nearby university or teacher training college. In some cases a weekly spending allowance of $15 to 25 is also provided.

Typical volunteer responsibilities: Each Amity volunteer is involved in twenty to twenty-five hours of classroom instruction and activities each week. Class size varies from ten to twenty-five students. Students range in age from preschool through adult.

Number of volunteers sent abroad annually: 20–30 (2000)

Age range: 21-65   **Typical age:** 23–30

How to apply: Contact the Amity office for an application. Applications are accepted year-round and should be received by Amity Institute at least three months prior to the start date of the assignment.

Stated mission: "Amity Institute, founded in 1962, is a nonprofit educational exchange program giving young people around the world the opportunity to represent their countries, by sharing their languages and cultures in language classrooms of all levels. By offering students close contact with these informal ambassadors, Amity strives to encourage and enhance international understanding and friendship through the study of world languages and cultures."

History: "In 1962, Dr. Ernest and Emily Stowell of Eau Claire, Wisconsin, founded Amity Institute to meet the needs of American foreign language teachers and students for direct and personalized contact with world languages and cultures. Amity continues to bring together Americans and volunteers from more than forty other countries, creating international friendship through language learning."

Amizade

367 S. Graham St.
Pittsburgh, PA 15232

phone: 888-973-4443
fax: 412-648-1492
e-mail: volunteer@amizade.org
web: www.amizade.org

I went with an Amizade group for two weeks to the Brazilian Amazon to build an orthopedic workshop for children with disabilities. We spent half of our time working with local volunteers on the project and the other half enjoying the rich environment and culture of the Amazon.—Volunteer, Brazil

Countries where volunteers are placed: Australia, Bolivia, Brazil (the Amazon), Nepal, and the United States

Field(s) of work: Most of the projects focus on the construction of schools, health clinics, and environmental centers.

Requirements or special skills necessary: No special skills are required, just a willingness to help. Local masons and carpenters instruct Amizade volunteers on every aspect of the project. Children from 12 to 18 are accepted when accompanied by an adult or legal guardian. Married and unmarried couples may volunteer together.

Duration and dates: Programs last two weeks but volunteers may participate in consecutive programs.

What volunteers pay and what they receive: The cost of a two-week program in Brazil is $1,290, Bolivia $1,185, and Nepal $1,655. The U.S. programs include the Greater Yellowstone Region at $455 and the Navajo Nation at $450. For all programs, fees cover room and board, recreation and cultural activities, transportation within the project area, and Amizade staff support. Amizade also provides an orientation to the country, region, project, and partner organizations. Volunteers must provide their own health insurance and travel to the program site.

Typical volunteer responsibilities: Amizade is a fifty-fifty mix of volunteer service and recreation. About six hours a day are spent working on construction projects and the rest is spent eating, socializing, and exploring.

Number of volunteers sent abroad annually: 200

Age range: 21–90 **Typical age:** None

How to apply: Volunteers can obtain applications by visiting the Amizade website or by contacting the Amizade office. Applications and deposits are due forty-five days before the start of the program; medical forms and liability waivers are due thirty days before the start of the program. Volunteers are accepted in the order in which their applications and deposits are received. If a particular project is full, volunteers are placed on a waiting list.

Stated mission: "Amizade is a nonprofit organization dedicated to promoting volunteering, providing community service, encouraging collaboration, and improving cultural awareness in locations around the world."

History: Amizade was founded in 1994 with the idea of "saving the rain forest by helping the people in the rain forest." For their first project, volunteers traveled to Santarém, Brazil, to build an orthopedic shoe workshop for a Brazilian nonprofit organization that provides health, education, and social services to low-income children with disabilities. For its second project, Amizade helped construct a vocational training center for street children. The success of these programs led to the development of additional programs in Santarém as well as the creation of programs in Bolivia, Nepal, the Navajo Nation, and the Greater Yellowstone region.

Observations and commentary: Santarém, the site of Amizade's original program, is a bustling river town at the confluence of the Amazon River and one of its largest tributaries. Located in the heart of the Amazon, it is not an easy place to reach, but for those who can afford the airfare, this is a pleasant place for what Dan Weiss calls a "volunteer vacation." Weiss, Amizade's founder, says the work is never overwhelming and there is always plenty of time for walks into the jungle or boat rides down the Amazon. Dan told us that he "likes the volunteers to have a sense of completion in their projects. Therefore we try to have realistic goals."

A typical day on an Amizade project begins at 7 a.m. with a breakfast of fruit, bread, and coffee. Between 8:30 and 11:30 volunteers work. Lunch is served around noon and is followed by siesta. Volunteers wake from their siesta just before 2 and work again from 2 to 5:30. Dinner is served at 6:00 p.m. The evenings are generally free time for volunteers to go into town to listen to music or visit with new friends.

In Santarém, Amizade works in close partnership with Esperança, an organization that provides dental and medical services to both the rural and urban poor of the Amazon. In 1995, ten volunteers worked for two weeks building an orthopedic workshop for Esperança's health professionals, some of whom perform orthopedic surgery.

One of the most positive aspects of this program is the exchange between the local young people and the young volunteers. Dan Weiss says that he tries "to make it clear that you come to experience, not to help." This shift of focus helps diminish, in Dan's words, "the North-South superiority," and creates an atmosphere in which the building of friendships is the priority (the word "amizade" itself means friendship in Portuguese). One volunteer recalled how a walk through town to the ice cream parlor turned into a sort of festival: "The walk required numerous stops to chat with people we knew. Others were curious about us and stopped to ask us what we were doing in Santarém. We felt we had really become a part of this society and culture." The same volunteer said that her time in Santarém ended with "a joyous celebration at a large outdoor restaurant along the banks of the Amazon. There was samba dancing and joy and stirrings of nostalgia."

In some cases, Amizade organizes group volunteer projects. In one instance, Amizade brought twenty-two university students from Pittsburgh to Carracollo, Bolivia, to work with a local non-governmental organization and local volunteers from Radio Bahai. Together they built an adult education facility. Local community members laid the foundation ahead of time, and the group from the United States completed the walls. Julia Costas, who coordinates Radio Bahai, told us it was "beautiful" for the local community to see a group of "gringos" working on construction projects using local materials.

Amizade volunteers receive a modest degree of information in preparation for their project. Julia Costas found that the volunteers who came did not have a deep knowledge about Bolivia but knew basic information on the culture. "They were as prepared as they could have been for something so different," she said. "They knew that they would be sleeping on the floor and that they had to let go of comforts they were used to."

Volunteers live in a group housing situation. In Brazil volunteers live with one to two people per room and two rooms per bathroom. In Bolivia two to six people share a room and there are men's and women's communal bathrooms. In Peru there are six people to a room and men's and women's communal restrooms; and in Yellowstone, volunteers live in simple cabins with outhouses and solar showers. In South America the rooms are cleaned every day and laundry is done every other day. Ironically, the most rustic living conditions are in the U.S. program.

If you are looking for a short-term service program that combines meaningful work with cultural exchange, and especially if you are interested in the Amazon, Amizade may be an excellent choice for you.

Within hours, I was mixing cement by hand, cutting timber posts with a handsaw, and laying bricks, all under the supervision of a Brazilian construction worker whose only language was Portuguese, of which I knew not one word at the time.—Volunteer, Brazil

Through Amizade I learned that to save the rain forest, we must help the people of the rain forest. I can't say enough about Amizade. I wish I could go every year.—Kim Palmer, volunteer, Brazil

---

ARCAS

Section 717
PO Box 52-7270
Miami, FL 33152-7270

phone: 502-476-6001
fax: 502-476-6001
e-mail: arcas@intelnet.net.gt
web: www.rds.org.gt/arcas

Volunteers are our salvation.—Fernando Martinez, Director of the Animal Rescue and Rehabilitation Center, Peten, Guatemala

Countries where volunteers are placed: Guatemala

Field(s) of work: Volunteers work with endangered tropical animals.

Requirements or special skills necessary: No prior experience is required, but ARCAS (Asociacíon de Rescate y Conservación de Vida Silvestre) gives priority to volunteers with backgrounds in marine biology, ecology, or other environmental sciences, as well as those with prior experience in the fields of education or development. Spanish language ability is recommended but not required.

Duration and dates: The minimum stay in an ARCAS program is one week, but most volunteers stay a month or longer. Projects are ongoing.

What volunteers pay and what they receive: Volunteers at the Animal Rescue and Rehabilitation Center pay $80 per week for food and lodging. Transportation from the Flores airport costs $5. Volunteers pay $50 per week for lodging at the Sea Turtle and Caiman Conservation Center but are responsible for their own food as well as transportation to and from the site.

Typical volunteer responsibilities: Volunteers at ARCAS's Animal Rescue and Rehabilitation Center in Flores, in the Peten region of northern Guatemala, follow a specific daily schedule. Volunteers feed animals, clean cages, and clean and maintain the shelter.

At the organization's Sea Turtle and Caiman Conservation Center (near the town of Hawaii on the southern Pacific coastline of Guatemala), volunteers participate in egg collection and hatchery management, construction, environmental education, mangrove restoration, caiman breeding, and various community projects.

Number of volunteers placed annually: 50–60 stay for more than a month, while approximately 200 work for a shorter period.

Age range: 18+   **Typical age:** 30

How to apply: Prospective volunteers should contact the volunteer coordinator at the e-mail address above at least two weeks before the date of desired departure. Guidebooks and registration forms are available for a fee of $15.

Stated mission: ARCAS (the acronym in Spanish for the Wildlife Rescue and Conservation Association) is a Guatemalan nonprofit, non-governmental organization. "ARCAS's objectives are to strive for the conservation, preservation, protection, and research of wildlife; to rescue, rehabilitate, and reintroduce into their natural habitat wild animals seized from animal traffickers; to promote and assist in the creation and management of protected habitat areas for wild animals; to support tropical wild animal veterinary research; to reproduce and reintroduce animals in danger of extinction; to raise awareness among Guatemalans about the need to conserve natural resources through a program of education and information dissemination; and to develop and promote economic alternatives to the unsustainable consumption of natural resources in rural communities."

History: ARCAS was founded in 1989 by a group of Guatemalan citizens who became concerned about the rapid depletion of their natural heritage, especially their wildlife. ARCAS was created with the specific purpose of building a rescue center to care for and rehabilitate animals that the Guatemalan government confiscates before they are illegally exported.

Observations and commentary: Most of the work at ARCAS's centers is done by volunteers. "These volunteers," ARCAS's 1999 Annual Report says, "not only have helped out with manpower and technical expertise, but have also improved ARCAS's financial self-sufficiency." Volunteers from overseas are particularly important to ARCAS because few Guatemalans have the luxury to be involved in this volunteer work, and apparently most of those that do don't seem to be interested.

The Animal Rescue and Rehabilitation Center is a pioneer project in Latin America and ARCAS's "keystone project." Fernando Martinez, a veterinarian who directs work at the rescue center told us that it typically houses 350 animals at one time (we were impressed by the number of animals and the amount of noise!). Volunteers are kept busy performing health checks (observing and recording the health of the animals), cleaning cages, feeding (each species requires a different method of feeding), and performing other duties such as improving cages and constructing bird perches. Volunteers usually work four times a day, six days a week. They can choose to take off either Tuesday or Friday (these are the days Fernando drives into the town of Flores to purchase supplies). The months with the most intensive work are April, May, June, and July because this is when animals have their young. Arieh, a volunteer from Israel, told us that the work at the rescue center "is interesting without being exhausting." The climate, however, can make the work more exhausting than you might expect, especially during November and December when the humidity can be unpleasant.

The food served to volunteers at the rescue center is primarily beans, veggies, and tortillas. Meat is only served once a week—obvious this is a suitable assignment for vegetarians! On weekends the cook does not come, so volunteers must prepare their own meals.

The Japanese Embassy in Guatemala and the Japanese government's Community Projects Assistance Fund are supporting the construction of a new rescue center. When completed, it will be the largest and most complete rescue center in Latin America. It will include new facilities for the animals, a kitchen, dining hall, and a volunteer house. The volunteer house will accommodate approximately thirty-two volunteers, researchers, and eco-tourists, and will include full bathrooms, solar electricity, and a large porch. As stated, ARCAS believes that the participation of volunteers and eco-tourists are key to the long-term sustainability of the rescue center so building a spacious and comfortable facility is a high priority. The facility should be completed by the time of the publication of this book.

We recommend ARCAS to people who love animals and enjoy caring for them. It is bound to be a rewarding choice for those concerned with the protection of wildlife.

Brethren Volunteer Service (BVS)

1451 Dundee Ave.   *phone:* 847-742-5100; 800-323-8039
Elgin, IL 60120   *fax:* 847-742-0278
                            e-mail: bvs_gb@brethren.org
                            web: www.brethrenvolunteerservice.org

I chose Brethren Volunteer Service because of its philosophy of accompanying people, respecting cultures and religions while at the same time being a faith-based organization. The work becomes a way of life, a life of simplicity and service, especially with the marginalized.—Tom Benevento, volunteer, Guatemala

Countries where volunteers are placed: Belgium, Belize, Bosnia-Herzegovina, Croatia, Czech Republic, Dominican Republic, El Salvador, England, France, Germany, Guatemala, Honduras, Ireland, Japan, Mexico, the Netherlands, Nicaragua, Nigeria, Northern Ireland, Poland, Serbia, Slovakia, Switzerland, and the United States

Field(s) of work: Volunteers provide community service and advocacy work in agriculture, hunger, homelessness, peace, domestic violence, housing, health care, outdoor ministries, education, and the environment. Clients include children, youth, senior citizens, farm workers, people with disabilities, prisoners, or refugees.

Requirements or special skills necessary: Volunteers must have a college degree or equivalent life experience and be at least twenty-one years of age. All projects in Latin America require fluency in Spanish and experience in Latin American issues. Volunteers come from many different faith backgrounds and do not need to be members of the Church of the Brethren.

Duration and dates: Most domestic projects require a one-year commitment; overseas projects require two years. Assignments of as little as six months are available for volunteers over fifty. All volunteers begin their term by attending one of the three-week orientations offered every summer, fall, and winter.

What volunteers pay and what they receive: Volunteers pay a fee of $400 and provide their own transportation to the orientation site (in the United States). BVS covers all additional costs, including transportation within the project area, room and board, a monthly stipend of $50 to $70, medical insurance, and an annual retreat for volunteers in the United States and Europe. Volunteers may live with other volunteers in group housing, independently in an apartment, or with a host family. In many cases student loans can be deferred during the volunteer period.

Typical volunteer responsibilities: Responsibilities vary from working with the homeless or with youth, providing technical services, facilitating resolution of conflict, producing publications, teaching English, and supporting NGOs through public relations, networking, administration, communications, translation, fundraising, and research.

Number of volunteers sent abroad annually: 11 (1999)

Age range: 18–85 (21+ for overseas projects)   **Typical age:** 22

How to apply: Contact the BVS office to request an inquiry packet.

Stated mission: "The BVS mission is to bring hope to shattered lives, offer food and shelter to those in need, and build understanding between individuals, groups, nations, humanity, and the world we share. BVS was established to provide an avenue for sharing God's love through these acts of service."

History: "The Church of the Brethren was founded in 1708 and is considered to be one of the pacifist 'peace churches.' The denomination has a special concern for the poor and oppressed and recognizes a cost as well as joy in Christian discipleship. BVS was established in 1948 out of this tradition."

BRIDGES (Building Responsible International Dialogue through Grassroots Exchanges)

333 Valencia St., Suite 325   *phone:* 415-551-9728
San Francisco, CA 94110   *fax:* N/A
                                 e-mail: info@grassrootsbridges.org
                                 web: www.grassrootsbridges.org

---

I feel my nationality needs to rhyme with my rationality—that is, I belong to a global pueblo that is mobilizing around the universal ghetto to create community that is pro-people.—Otto Perez-Arana, 2000 fellow, India

Countries where volunteers are placed: Africa, Asia, and Latin America

Field(s) of work: Youth development, environmental justice, public health, and education

Requirements or special skills necessary: In order to qualify volunteers must demonstrate financial need, be at least eighteen years old, and have previous experience working for positive change in their communities. Applicants can be either U.S. citizens or residents and should come from a background in which they have had limited opportunity to travel, work, study, live, or volunteer abroad. Couples are not accepted, whether married or unmarried.

Duration and dates: The fellowship is an eight-month program, beginning in late March and ending in late November. The actual time abroad runs between June and August.

What volunteers pay and what volunteers receive: Fellows receive a stipend, a travel grant to cover the costs of their international volunteer experience, and extensive training prior to and following international service.

Typical volunteer responsibilities: The responsibilities depend on where volunteers choose to work overseas. They have ranged from teaching English in a one-room schoolhouse to coordinating a rally for a town clean-up campaign, to working in a traveling health clinic.

Number of volunteers sent abroad annually: 10 (2000)

Volunteer age range: 18–40   **Typical age:** 21–28

How to apply: Applications are available on the BRIDGES website.

Stated mission: "The BRIDGES Fellowship is a unique eight-month program that provides individuals who have been historically underrepresented in international exchanges with the opportunity to build a bridge between social justice work abroad and the struggles for social and economic justice in their local communities. Fellows who have demonstrated a commitment to strengthening their own communities are given a financial grant, educational training, mentoring, and service-learning overseas.

"The program supports the fellows to explore how their own communities, handle issues affecting their well-being, share this information with communities overseas, learn how communities overseas approach similar issues, and share this knowledge with their own community upon their return home."

History: Since it was founded in 1997 as a program of the LaFetra Operating Foundation, the BRIDGES Fellowship has sent more than thirty low-income San Francisco Bay area leaders to developing countries around the world including Brazil, Ecuador, India, Kenya, Tanzania, and the Gambia. In 2000, BRIDGES became a fiscally sponsored project of JustAct.

Observations and commentary: BRIDGES is one of the few organizations offering scholarships to people of color and people from low-income backgrounds to participate in international volunteering. The organization offers a high level of support for its participants throughout the eight-month program. We commend BRIDGES for the depth of its training both before and after volunteers go abroad as well as its efforts to link community activism in the United States with community activism overseas.

In a short time, BRIDGES has built a collaborative network of twenty-five community organizations in the San Francisco Bay area that provide fellows with a range of trainings, internship opportunities, and mentoring services. On a global level, the fellowship has partnered with several international volunteer programs, sending fellows around the world with such organizations as Cross-Cultural Solutions, Global Routes, AHEAD Inc., and Operation Crossroads Africa.

If you are active in your community in the San Francisco Bay area and interested in volunteering overseas but have limited options to do so on your own, then BRIDGES is a good choice for you. The program is especially suited to individuals who want to internationalize their vision of social change.

Canadian Crossroads International (CCI)

National Office
66 Gerrard St. East, Suite 300
Toronto, Ontario
M5B 1G3
Canada

phone: 416-967-1611
fax: 416-967-9078
e-mail: info@cciorg.ca
web: www.cciorg.ca

Countries where volunteers are placed: Bolivia, Botswana, Burkina Faso, Cameroon, Canada, Costa Rica, Ecuador, Fiji, Ghana, Grenada, Guatemala, Guyana, India, Indonesia, Ivory Coast, Kenya, Mali, Mexico, Nepal, Niger, St. Vincent and the Grenadines, Senegal, Surinam, Swaziland, Togo, Tunisia, and Zimbabwe

Field(s) of work: Individual and group volunteers work in the following sectors: youth/children; basic education; sustainable resource management; and rural development. Netcorps interns work in information technology.

Requirements or special skills necessary: Applicants to the Overseas Individual Program and Overseas Group Program must be Canadian citizens or Canadian-landed immigrants, be nineteen years of age or older, and have demonstrated cultural sensitivity, adaptability, and tolerance as well as experience in one of CCI's fields of work. Applicants for the Overseas Group Program must have French language skills.

Netcorps applicants must be Canadian citizens or permanent residents between the ages of nineteen and thirty, be unemployed or underemployed, and never have participated in the Youth Employment Strategy program funded by the Canadian federal government. They should have training or solid experience in Information Technology. Netcorps provides support to organizations and agencies in CCI partner countries in their efforts to strengthen their Information Technology (IT) capacity as well as provide relevant work experience to young underemployed or unemployed IT professionals within an international context.

The Qualifications for the Interflow Program and the To-Canada Program are the same: applicants must be 19 years old or older with limited or no overseas experience, demonstrated cultural sensitivity, adaptability and a commitment to volunteering, and must reside in one of CCI's partner countries.

Married and unmarried couples can be accepted to volunteer together if both partners qualify and if CCI is able to place them both in the same project.

Duration and dates: Placements last four to six months (two months for the Overseas Group Program). Recruitment for the Overseas Individual Program takes place across Canada during the winter and spring months and departures are in May, September, and December/January of each year. Netcorps internships last six months.

What volunteers pay and what they receive: The Overseas Individual Program costs $2,250 (Canadian) and the Overseas Group Program costs $1,800 per volunteer (Canadian). CCI covers airfare, a modest living allowance, in-country support, and a pre-departure orientation. Volunteers typically live with a host family. CCI provides returned volunteers with support in reintegrating and developing ways to contribute to their home communities. CCI also provides fundraising support. There are no costs to volunteers who participate in the Interflow Program or the To-Canada Program.

Typical volunteer responsibilities: Responsiblities for assignments with the different programs vary from placement to placement. Volunteers work with local NGOs to address specific community needs. One volunteer, for example, brought her research and documentation skills to work with "Comisaría de la Mujer y la Familia," a national Ecuadorian organization that seeks to help women and their families leave abusive situations, and to inform them of their legal rights and the types of social support available to them. Another volunteer, who had studied nutritional sciences, traveled to St. Vincent and the Grenadines to help develop seminars and evaluation tools with staff of the Nutrition Unit, a division of the Ministry of Health.

Netcorps interns are generally involved in training staff of local organizations in a variety of computer software programs, in the use of the Internet and e-mail, as well as working with local staff on databases, designing networks, and website development.

Number of volunteers sent abroad annually: 200

Age range: 19+   **Typical age:** 23+

How to apply: CCI has offices in Ontario, Quebec, Nova Scotia, and British Columbia. Consult the website or contact the national office for the contact information of the office nearest you. Applications can be requested from the national office or downloaded from the website. Group volunteers must apply to the Quebec office in the fall for the following year. Netcorps applications are due in the spring for summer departures.

Stated mission: "To build a constituency of global citizens committed to volunteering, international development, and social action. We do this by developing partnerships with southern countries, organizing two-way volunteer work placements and internships, and educating the public on development issues."

History: CCI grew out of its American counterpart, Operation Crossroads Africa, founded by Dr. James H. Robinson in the 1950s. Throughout the 1960s, small groups of Canadian volunteers coordinated similar placements for Canadians, and in 1969, Canadian Crossroads International was founded to continue the pursuit of Dr. Robinson's "one world" vision. Dr. Robinson believed that by living and working together, we create a "crossroads" of cultures and personal experience—the birthplace of both individual and societal change.

Observations and commentary: CCI is at the cutting edge of international voluntary exchange. In addition to its programs for Canadian citizens, CCI provides opportunities for individuals in its partner countries to become international volunteers themselves. The Interflow Program allows individuals from partner countries to volunteer in any one of CCI's other partner countries and the To-Canada Program is specifically designed to bring volunteers from CCI partner countries to Canada. Few volunteer placement organizations offer this opportunity, and we encourage other organizations to follow CCI's example.

Although we did not complete extensive research on CCI while in the field, the organization seems to take development education seriously. One of CCI's goals is to promote "understanding of the root causes of inequitable development and to encourage constructive involvement in addressing these injustices." Local CCI committees assist volunteers in coordinating both fundraising and development education activities. Despite this support, the responsibility for being active especially upon return from overseas is still up to the volunteer and not built in to the program.

CCI's Overseas Individual and Overseas Group Programs are both particularly good choices for young Canadian adults with specific skills who are looking for medium-term volunteer experiences. The To-Canada and Interflow Programs provide rare opportunities for young adults from Africa, Latin America, Asia, and the Pacific to gain experience as international volunteers, without the barrier of an expensive program fee.

Casa de los Amigos

Ignacio Mariscal 132
Mexico, D.F., Mexico 06030

phone: 52-5-705-0521; 52-5-705-0646
fax: 52-5-705-0771
e-mail: friends@avantel.net

Countries where volunteers are placed: Mexico

Field(s) of work: Administration/clerical, environment, human rights, women, youth, street children, and indigenous issues

Requirements or special skills necessary: Volunteers working at the Casa Guesthouse must have a working knowledge of Spanish, enough to handle the telephone and to be able to communicate with staff and guests who do not speak English. Volunteers placed outside the Casa Guesthouse should have some knowledge of Spanish in order to be useful to the local organizations that they work with. For all volunteers, technical skills are useful but not required. Young people under the age of 18 can participate with either parental permission or accompaniment. Unmarried as well as married couples are welcome to participate.

Duration and dates: There is no fixed time commitment, but the typical volunteer period is at least three months.

What volunteers pay and what they receive: Volunteers working at the Casa Guesthouse must cover their own transportation to and from the Casa, as well as all personal expenses. They receive a private room, breakfast Monday through Friday, a small stipend, and may utilize Guesthouse facilities, which include a kitchen, community breakfast room, library, and conference room.

Volunteers placed outside the Casa with a local organization pay an initial program fee of $50 to cover administrative costs. They are responsible for travel to and from the casa and must provide their own medical insurance. The Casa provides assistance in identifying a suitable host organization, and a post-service evaluation.

Typical volunteer responsibilities: Volunteers working at the Casa Guesthouse are expected to dedicate thirty-five hours per week to the Casa. Some of this time is spent assisting guests in the reception area; the rest is spent working on one (or more) of the Casa's programs/projects.

Volunteers placed outside the Casa de los Amigos in local organizations are involved in a variety of tasks such as organizing activities for street youth at the Fundación Pro-Niño.

Number of volunteers sent abroad annually: N/A

Age range: 18–80   **Typical age:** N/A

How to apply: Those interested in volunteering at the Casa Guesthouse or with a local organization in Mexico, D.F., should contact the Casa for an application.

Stated mission: "The Casa de los Amigos, a Quaker service center and volunteer-operated guesthouse in Mexico City, works through volunteer service for greater international understanding."

History: In 1956, the Casa was formalized, creating a guesthouse for volunteers who were coming to Mexico to work on Quaker workcamps. The Casa receives over 2,500 visitors each year from all over the world, and its community is made up of long-term staff (largely Mexican), and medium-term volunteers (international) combined with short-term guests.

Catholic Medical Missions Board (CMMB)

10 West 17th St.
New York, NY 10011-5765

phone: 800-678-5659; 212-242-7757
fax: 212-242-0930
e-mail: rdecostanzo@cmmb.org
web: www.cmmb.org

Countries where volunteers are placed: 26 countries in Africa (including Ethiopia, Lesotho, Namibia, Nigeria, South Africa, Swaziland, and Zambia), 14 countries in Asia (including China, East Timor, and India), seven countries in Eastern Europe (including Armenia), and a number of countries in Latin America and the Caribbean (including Dominican Republic, El Salvador, Guatemala, Mexico, Nicaragua, and Venezuela)

Field(s) of work: Healthcare

Requirements or special skills necessary: Volunteers must be licensed health care professionals with a strong desire to serve overseas. CMMB does not have placements for students. Volunteers need not be Catholic. A "non-medical spouse" may accompany a medical volunteer, although work opportunities for the spouse may be limited. Children and teenagers may accompany their parents, but schooling is not always available. Unmarried couples may not volunteer together.

Duration and dates: Long-term placements are six months to one year, although longer placements may be arranged. Short-term brigades or volunteer placements with host organizations last up to six months. Placements are made year-round.

What volunteers pay and what they receive: For those who volunteer one year or more, CMMB covers all trip-related expenses including round-trip airfare, local transportation, medical supplies, and a small stipend. All volunteers, regardless of the duration of service, receive Medivac insurance and room and board, which is provided by the host organization in remuneration for service.

Typical volunteer responsibilities: Some volunteers provide direct care to patients while others provide medical training for local healthcare providers. Volunteers are encouraged to make maximum use of locally available equipment and supplies. Training of local health care providers focuses on local pathologies and medical problems. CMMB aims at making the practices and procedures it teaches both relevant and realistic. "The ultimate goal of all our volunteer placements," according to the CMMB website, "is to assist local personnel to assume the role of educator and provider, thus continuing the learning process."

Number of volunteers sent abroad annually: 35 long term and 300 short term (2000)

Age range: 21–74   **Typical age:** 25–35; 50–60

How to apply: Contact the coordinator of volunteer programs by telephone, fax, e-mail, or mail.

Stated mission: "CMMB provides pharmaceuticals and health care supplies for distribution, coordinates the placement of volunteer professional and paraprofessional health care providers, supplies emergency/disaster relief for medical emergencies, and supports short-term health-related training of individuals in developing countries. The CMMB Medical Volunteer Program is an important component in CMMB's quest to improve the quality and increase the accessibility of health care throughout the developing world.

"CMMB also strives to raise consciousness in the United States about basic health care inequities throughout the world. It is involved in several international groups that seek to effect changes in policies, guidelines, and regulations regarding the distribution of donated drugs. CMMB also publishes *Medical Mission News,* a quarterly publication that focuses on its work and on international health care issues."

History: CMMB was founded in 1928 by Dr. Paluel Joseph Flagg, then a young anesthesiologist who wanted to help the poor throughout the world have access to basic medical care. Since its inception, CMMB has provided "medicine and health care supplies to the needy in developing countries worldwide."

Central European Teaching Program (CETP)

Beloit College
700 College St.
Beloit, WI 53511

phone: 608-363-2619
fax: 608-363-2449
e-mail: dunlopa@beloit.edu
web: www.beloit.edu/~cetp

For a lot of the students I was the first American they had ever met. It turned out to be a lot of fun teaching them English, and by the end I cried when I had to leave.—Lindsay Amsberry, volunteer, Poland

Countries where volunteers are placed: Hungary, Latvia, Lithuania, Poland, Romania, and Slovakia

Field(s) of work: Most volunteers teach conversational English in local Central European schools and colleges. A small number of volunteers teach French conversation, German conversation, British/American literature, British/American history, or English for special purposes (scientific/legal/medical/business English, according to one's specialty).

Requirements or special skills necessary: Candidates must hold a bachelor's degree or be scheduled to receive one by the spring before departure. They must have experience in teaching English as a second language or be willing to acquire such experience through volunteer work or TESL/TEFL certification prior to their placement. Volunteers must also be willing to commit to one full school year in a Central European school, though half-year assignments are available. Volunteers must exhibit flexibility, patience, maturity, and sensitivity to cultural differences. Married as well as unmarried couples may volunteer together. Children may accompany adults who are volunteering.

Duration and dates: Placements last approximately ten months, starting on or around September 1 (for primary and secondary school positions), September 15 (for secondary school positions in Romania), or October 1 (for tertiary/university-level positions). All CETP volunteers should plan to arrive in the host country approximately ten days before commencement of the program to participate in the orientation session. CETP has also begun to offer mid-year placements lasting from January to June. Fees for this program are approximately half that of the one-year program.

What volunteers pay and what they receive: Volunteers pay an application fee of $50, a placement fee of $2,000, a deposit of $200 (refunded upon successful completion of the teaching contract), and airfare ranging from $500 to $1,000 (depending on departure city and season). CETP also recommends that volunteers also bring at least $300 as "settling in" money. There is an optional Hungarian language-training course in Hungary that costs approximately $1,000; at Beloit College the course costs approximately $2,900. Optional international medical emergency insurance ranges from $20 to $500 per year, depending on the plan. Financial aid is sometimes available; more often, however, CETP provides applicants with a list of fundraising suggestions and applicants raise their own fees through grassroots efforts.

Volunteers are provided with a full-time contract in a public school. They receive a salary in the local currency (equivalent to that of local teachers), housing in private apartments or hostels, national health insurance, a work permit, and a temporary residency permit in the host country. CETP also provides a week-long in-country orientation, a cross-cultural handbook, teaching materials, in-country meetings, and a monthly newsletter. Each country has a director who is available to offer advice and help negotiate with school administrators if conflicts arise.

Typical volunteer responsibilities: Teachers are typically responsible for giving between eighteen and twenty-two forty-five minute classes per week. In addition, fifteen to twenty hours per week are devoted to various administrative, clerical, and teacher-related duties such as lesson planning. Teachers are responsible for enhancing students' oral fluency in English through conversation practice, classroom drills, games, audio-visual instruction, and listening comprehension, as well as through working closely with local teachers to emphasize important grammar concepts.

Number of volunteers sent abroad annually: 53 (2000)

Age range: 21–60+   **Typical age:** 25

How to apply: Obtain an application form through the CETP office. A phone or in-person interview will follow receipt of the application.

Stated mission: "CETP exists to benefit young people in the formerly socialist countries of Central Europe by providing regional public schools with native-speaking English teachers. CETP offers North Americans and others a meaningful long-term professional and cross-cultural experience and a unique opportunity to become an active part of a Central European community."

History: CETP was founded in 1990 at Beloit College by Lesley Davis. Lesley had taught English in Hungary and, while there, directors from other schools asked her if she knew any other volunteers who might want to teach at their schools. When she returned to the United States she founded CETP to respond to these requests. CETP expanded to Romania, Lithuania, and Latvia in the late 1990s. Expansion to other Central European countries such as Slovakia is in the planning stages.

Observations and commentary: One of CETP's strengths is its success in arranging teaching positions throughout Central Europe, in towns that are somewhat off the beaten track. The placements in both small towns and cities offer volunteers a chance to gain unique experiences that they probably would not be able to arrange on their own and give them a chance to be much more than just teachers. As former volunteer and director Alex Dunlop explained, "Since some of our volunteers are the only program participants in their town, teachers take an active role in the school community, participating in sports and extracurricular activities."

CETP does a good job of organizing its placements and preparing volunteers. They handle the logistics of the visas and orientation, and effectively negotiate teaching positions. Most volunteers said they were adequately prepared for their specific school placements and teaching in general, as well as for living overseas. Others mentioned that they needed more information and preparation that would help them with their teaching role. Richard Reinneccius, the program coordinator in Poland, agreed that volunteers could benefit from training in lesson planning. He observed that some volunteers lack confidence in the classroom and are not prepared to deal with fifteen-plus students. He was quick to note, however, that CETP is not necessarily looking for experts, just people genuinely interested in teaching. "Host schools," he told us, "want volunteers to be themselves, share what they know, and make lessons relevant to their students' lives."

CETP has a mixed record of supporting its volunteers. Some volunteers reported that the in-country orientation was a "great start," but that afterward they were primarily left on their own. CETP does provide a network of colleagues and introduces its volunteers to other teachers, but there is not a lot of ongoing support. Former CETP teachers are available to assist with teaching and cultural integration, and a part-time program director (usually a national) is available to respond to requests for help in resolving conflicts that arise between volunteers and their host institutions. This may be sufficient for volunteers who don't want a lot of support or others, like Brian Schwarz, who happen to live and teach in the same town as the program director. Others, however, have found that they did not receive much support. The program seemed to work better for independent individuals.

CETP is a lean operation with a single full-time director in the United States and part-time staff overseas. According to Alexis Northcross, who volunteered in Hungary, an advantage of CETP is that it is "not as rigid as some other programs." The lack of bureaucracy gives the organization a familial feel. This means that CETP is more likely than a larger organization to respond to a request, for example, for two friends to be placed in the same town. This also means that the organization's resources are limited.

We recommend CETP for independent folks who are looking to become part of a school community while teaching high school or college in Central Europe. CETP is probably not right for the first-time traveler or volunteer seeking substantial organizational support.

Child Family Health International (CFHI)

2149 Lyon St., #5
San Francisco, CA 94115

phone: 415-863-4900
fax: 501-423-6852
e-mail: students@cfhi.org
web: www.cfhi.org

Countries where volunteers are placed: Ecuador, India, and Mexico

Field(s) of work: Health care

Requirements or special skills necessary: CFHI coordinates Medical Exchange Programs in three countries. Each Medical Student Exchange Program has slightly different requirements of its volunteers. In India the rural Himalayan rotation is open to medical students and premedical students while the integrated medicine program is open to medical professionals, medical students, premedical students, and alternative health students.

The clinical rotation in Quito, Ecuador, is open to medical students and premedical students and requires basic Spanish. The mobile surgical unit in Cuenca, Ecuador, is open to medical students conversant in Spanish while the Amazon jungle rotation in Ecuador is only open to medical students with near fluency in Spanish. The Mexico program in Cuernavaca is open to medical students and public health students conversant in Spanish.

All volunteers must provide proof of active health insurance. Third and fourth year medical students and residents must, in addition, provide proof of medical liability insurance. Married and unmarried couples may volunteer together.

Duration and dates: Volunteers on the Medical Student Exchange Program are required to participate for a minimum of four weeks (with the exception of the integrated medicine program in India, which lasts three weeks). Longer terms of service are recommended when possible. There are no deadlines for applications but potential volunteers should apply two to three months in advance of desired departure dates to ensure space availability. Volunteers can sign up for two successive rotations, or, in the case of the program in Cuernavaca, Mexico, extend for up to twelve weeks.

What volunteers pay and what they receive: Program costs vary, ranging from $850 for a four-week clinical rotation in Cuenca, Ecuador, to $1,950 for a three-week rotation in integrated medicine in India. Program fees cover room and board with a host family, airport pick-up, and in-country support. Volunteers are responsible for airfare, visas, and travel insurance, daily transportation in-country, and personal and tourist related expenses. Volunteers' program fees help support the clinics that serve local people at little or no costs to patients.

Typical volunteer responsibilities: Volunteers assist local counterparts with primary and preventative care and the training of local health care promoters in rural and urban clinics and hospitals. Volunteers involved in hospital and clinic rotations are under the supervision of local physicians.

Number of volunteers sent abroad annually: 150–200 (2000)

Age range: 21–30   **Typical age:** 23

How to apply: Fill out an application and send it along with a non-refundable $35 application fee to CFHI. Application forms are available on the CFHI website, www.cfhi.org.

Stated mission: "Child Family Health International supports long-term sustainable health care projects, and conducts educational programs in international health for U.S. medical and premedical students. CFHI provides free surgery, immunizations, and primary health care as well as recycling necessary medical equipment.

"CFHI volunteers are encouraged to examine the uneven distribution of health care. CFHI actively encourages students to develop an awareness of community health and to examine the ways in which every health system is socially and culturally constructed."

History: While traveling as a medical student in Ecuador, South America, Dr. Evaleen Jones of Stanford University, saw many parallels between health issues in developing countries and the medically underserved in the United States. She also realized that speaking Spanish was a very useful skill for primary care physicians. To encourage and facilitate U.S. medical students to work abroad and learn Spanish, she created Child Family Health International.

Observations and commentary: CFHI as an organization has two distinct parts: on one hand it supports clinics in urban and rural areas that provide services to underserved communities in India, Ecuador, and Mexico, and on the other it runs the Medical Student Exchange Program. Through the Medical Student Exchange Program, CFHI encourages medical, premedical, public health, and alternative health students to get involved in primary health care. CFHI programs in Mexico and Ecuador are also designed to develop these students' Spanish literacy, a skill that they can use as they continue to practice medicine in the United States.

CFHI has recently streamlined its volunteer program, targeting volunteers with a specific interest in careers in medicine. If you are interested in developing your skills as a medical practitioner by observing and assisting professionals working overseas, then CFHI is worth considering.

Child Haven International

RR1, Maxville, ON
K0C 1T0
Canada

phone: 613-527-2829
fax: 613-527-1118
e-mail: fred@childhaven.ca
web: www.childhaven.ca

This is a small organization with a core of committed volunteers and donors that accomplishes a lot in India and Nepal.—Christine Victorino, volunteer, India

Countries where volunteers are placed: India and Nepal

Field(s) of work: Childcare and tutoring

Requirements or special skills necessary: Volunteers should have a love of children, openness to other cultures and religions, and the ability to live a simple, vegetarian lifestyle while overseas. Married couples may volunteer together. Children may accompany their parents who are volunteering, but it is generally not recommended. Unmarried couples are not accepted due to "cultural reasons." Volunteers must be self-directed and enthusiastic.

Duration and dates: Volunteer programs last a minimum of three months.

What volunteers pay and what they receive: A $25 fee covers the application cost and a processing fee of $175 is due upon acceptance into the program. Volunteers are responsible for their own airfare. Child Haven provides volunteers with a weekend orientation in Maxville, Ontario, room and board while overseas (volunteers share a room with other volunteers), and pick-up from the host country airport upon arrival.

Typical volunteer responsibilities: Volunteers help with children at the Child Haven homes and are responsible for a range of tasks including tutoring, doing arts and crafts with the children, taking them to medical appointments, reading to them, walking them to school, and doing any other tasks that may be needed.

Number of volunteers sent abroad annually: 10–100

Age range: 21–80 (but this is flexible)   **Typical age:** None

How to apply: Request an information package from the Child Haven headquarters. After reviewing the information package volunteers must attend a 24-hour orientation session at the farm of Bonnie and Fred Cappuccino in Maxville, Ontario.

Stated mission: "Child Haven was established to assist children and women who are in need of food, education, health care, shelter, clothing, and emotional and moral support. Child Haven is based on the Gandhian ideals of no recognition of castes, equality of the sexes, non-violence, vegetarian meals, respect for the culture of others, and simple living."

History: Child Haven International was founded by Bonnie and Fred Cappuccino and Dr. N. H. Shah in 1985. Since then it has opened four homes—three in India and one in Nepal—and received over 500 children in these homes. CHI is building another home outside Mumbai, India, and CHI operates a soymilk program and women's and children's program near New Delhi. They also support an orphanage and school in Tibet.

Observations and commentary: Volunteers can work individually with local staff or, at any given time, be joined by as many as six other volunteers. Local, in-country staff members are reportedly helpful and supportive. As one volunteer put it, "Volunteers contribute as little or as much as they are willing to give." Volunteers often mention that the founders, particularly Bonnie Cappucino, "is truly an inspiration."

At the time we wrote this, the volunteer program in India was suspended due to concerns about visas used by students. Bonnie and Fred were working with the Indian High Commission in Ottawa and officials of the Indian government to work out an agreement acceptable to everyone. Volunteers are still being sent to the home in Nepal.

If you are interested in a firsthand account of volunteering with Child Haven consult Patricia Paul-Carson's book, *Into the Heart of India.* Paul-Carson spent three months in the Gandhinagar Home in India and the book tells her story—the highs and lows, joys and frustrations, new-found friendships and loneliness—as a Child Haven volunteer. To obtain a copy, visit the Child Haven website. We recommend Child Haven for responsible, self-motivated and flexible individuals who have experience and a commitment to working with children.

Christian Foundation for Children and the Aging (CFCA)

One Elmwood Ave.
Kansas City, KS 66103

phone: 913-384-6500
phone: 800-875-6564
fax: 913-384-2211
e-mail: mail@cfcausa.org
web: www.cfcausa.org

The strength of the program is how much we provide for the kids. The weakness is the looseness of the program, which could be a strength for the right person.—Tania Mikaitis, volunteer, Bolivia

Countries where volunteers are placed: Bolivia, Brazil, Chile, Colombia, Costa Rica, Dominican Republic, Ecuador, El Salvador, Guatemala, Haiti, Honduras, India, Jamaica, Kenya, Liberia, Madagascar, Mexico, Nicaragua, Nigeria, Peru, the Philippines, Sri Lanka, Uganda, and Venezuela

Field(s) of work: Translating from English into the local language and vice-versa, teaching, childcare, health care, or parish work

Requirements or special skills necessary: There are no specific skills required to serve as a CFCA volunteer except a desire "to serve and live with the poor." Knowledge of the local language and experience in a specific field such as health care or agricultural are preferred but not required.

Duration and dates: Programs last six months to a year.

What volunteers pay and what they receive: Volunteers are responsible for travel, health insurance, and personal needs. CFCA provides room and board. The average cost for a nine-to-twelve-month period in Latin America or a six-month period in India, for example, would be about $3,500. Most volunteers do their own fundraising.

Typical volunteer responsibilities: Volunteers are placed in orphanages, schools, parishes, and clinics. Responsibilities in these placements vary but include teaching, childcare, and nursing. Married couples may be accepted together, and CFCA also can sometimes place friends together as volunteers at the same site. Same-sex couples, however, would only be accepted "under certain circumstances." Children may accompany parents who are volunteering.

Number of volunteers sent abroad annually: 62

Age range: 20–65   **Typical age:** 33

How to apply: Contact the office for an application.

Stated mission: "The Christian Foundation for Children and Aging is a lay Catholic organization serving the poor at mission sites around the world. Through sponsorship of children and aging we build relationships of mutual respect and support while raising awareness in our own country of the needs and gifts of the poor and the mission outreach of the church."

History: CFCA was founded in 1981 by Catholic lay people and has experienced dynamic growth ever since. Currently the CFCA "family" includes over 200,000 sponsors, hundreds of missionaries, staff, volunteers, and a twelve-member board of directors, serving more than 200,000 needy children and aging at Catholic mission sites around the world.

Observations and commentary: CFCA is not primarily a volunteer placement organization; it is a humanitarian organization that involves thousands of individuals in child sponsorship programs. Robert Hentzen, founder of CFCA, told us that the foundation did not set out to start a volunteer organization. The first volunteers were people who contacted CFCA in search of ways to help. In time, CFCA identified sites with sufficient infrastructure to receive volunteers and today continues to carefully assess proposed volunteer projects before placing volunteers there.

CFCA is a lay Catholic institution. It works in collaboration with the Catholic church but is autonomous. A religious affiliation is not required of volunteers; however, not being Christian may limit your placement choices. Non-Christian volunteers, for example, may not be comfortable escorting orphans to church or participating in children's faith groups.

Living arrangements include living in a parish house, a group house with other volunteers, or with a host family.

CFCA provides an in-person, two-day orientation/training/interview in Kansas City. Tania Mikaitis, a volunteer we spoke with in Bolivia, told us that the orientation covers topics such as "how you can do the most good for those around you, how to put yourself into service for others, and how to learn about yourself through this service." The two-day in-person meeting in Kansas City helps volunteers decide whether CFCA would be a good fit for them, and if there is a particular program that would be an especially good match.

Volunteers are involved in a wide range of activities while in the field. Paola Gabarino taught English to primary and junior high school students, and participated in a children's faith group. Tania Mikaitis worked as a nurse with two to six year olds, assisted staff in improving sanitary conditions, and wrote letters to the sponsors from the children's point of view.

CFCA conducts evaluations of its own and its partner organizations' projects.

As mentioned, the foundation does not place volunteers in a given site without first assessing whether it is an appropriate site. Ongoing projects are continually evaluated in terms of how well they are serving the community; if a project is not working, CFCA pulls out. Some volunteers, however, told us that the evaluations are not systematic.

Volunteers we spoke with in Bolivia and Guatemala told us that CFCA is an excellent introduction to living in a developing country. If you are a self-directed but flexible person, committed to direct service and comfortable working as part of a Catholic organization, CFCA may be a good choice for you.

> *Our culture is so fast paced. Here life is laid back. A lot of people expect to make a big change but you just have to start the ball rolling. We can be goal-oriented but realize we might not build five wells in two weeks.—Tania Mikaitis, volunteer, Bolivia*

> *One thing I realized through my year in Guatemala is that their world is entirely different than ours. Just because it's not as developed as ours doesn't mean it should be. Development doesn't necessarily improve a culture.—Christopher Jacob Loynd, volunteer, Guatemala*

Christian Peacemaker Teams (CPT)

PO Box 6508
Chicago, IL 60680

phone: 312-455-1199
fax: 312-666-2677
e-mail: cpt@igc.org
web: www.prairienet.org/cpt/

> *As I lived among the Palestinians, I learned to know many of them and was frequently impressed by their knowledge, their dignity, their integrity, and their courage in dealing with the day-to-day hardships of life under an oppressive occupation. But I had an American passport, and the Israeli settlers and soldiers didn't want an international incident, so they tended to be somewhat careful not to hurt us badly.—Esther Ho, volunteer, Palestine*

Countries where volunteers are placed: Canada, Colombia, Israel, Mexico, Palestine, Puerto Rico, and the United States

Field(s) of work: Human rights accompaniment and non-violent intervention in conflict areas

Requirements or special skills necessary: Long-term volunteers must be willing to commit to three years of service and be at least twenty-one years old. They should be Christians who understand the principles of non-violent direct action and conflict resolution, are "grounded in faith," and free enough from responsibilities that they can work in potentially life-threatening situations. CPT prefers applicants who have had significant cross-cultural experience. CPT also has programs for "Reservist" volunteers, and offers short-term education and action delegations.

Duration and dates: Full-time volunteers spend approximately two-thirds of their time on assignment in North America or overseas and one-third of their time in their home communities educating people about the conflict in which they have worked. When they are not on assignment volunteers also go on speaking tours or write or help staff in the Toronto and Chicago offices. Reservists go through the same training as full timers, but serve for shorter periods of time, when they are able, and pay for their own expenses. The primary training takes place in Chicago in January, but CPT has conducted regional trainings in Ontario, Colorado, and Cleveland at the request of local groups in these locations. Delegations last twelve days and are offered several times throughout the year.

What volunteers pay and what they receive: Volunteers raise $1,000 to $2,000 to participate in a short-term delegation, and help raise additional funds if they join a long-term team. Friends Peace Team Projects (www.quaker.org/fptp) may be able to provide members and attendees of Friends Meetings and Churches with support (logistical, training, and financial) for their service with Christian Peacemaker Teams. Once placed on a delegation or a long-term team, all expenses are covered, including housing, food, and insurance. Full-time volunteers receive a very modest monthly stipend (from $30 to $75 per month). CPT covers room and board and health insurance for volunteers when they are not on assignment, according to their needs. Many volunteers have housing provided to them by support communities. Canadian volunteers do not need health insurance because of Canada's health system.

Typical volunteer responsibilities: CPT corps members accompany people threatened by human rights abuses, document human rights violations, intervene non-violently in conflicts, train and support non-violent activists, and promote media coverage of non-violent resistance. "Teams of two to twelve persons join the efforts of local peacemakers facing imminent violence." Volunteers also have fundraising and administrative responsibilities. While at home, members make themselves available for short-term organizing, speaking, training, or other peace work within their community.

Number of volunteers sent abroad annually: 20 full-time and 100 reserve volunteers (2000)

Age range: 22–72   **Typical age:** 22–26; 60–70

How to apply: After submitting a written application with letters of recommendation, potential volunteers must participate in a CPT short-term educational delegation. If they are still interested in joining the team, they participate in a three-week intensive training on peacemaking skills, after which there is a "mutual evaluation" and decision about whether to join.

Stated mission: "CPT offers an organized, non-violent alternative to war and other forms of lethal inter-group conflict. CPT provides organizational support to persons committed to faith-based non-violent alternatives in situations where lethal conflict is an immediate reality or is supported by public policy."

CPT is an organization committed to "getting in the way," challenging systems of domination and exploitation as Jesus Christ did in the first century. CPT responds to invitations from grassroots movements seeking to rectify injustice in non-violent ways. "We rely on the Biblical witness, the power of the Holy Spirit, and the prayers of our church constituency to sustain us in the difficult work of peacemaking."

History: Christian Peacemaker Teams was founded in 1986 by the historic peace churches (Mennonites, Quakers, and Brethren in Christ). CPT was a response to evangelical author and professor Ron Sider's call for Christians to follow "Jesus's call to be peacemakers," even if it means risking their lives to promote peace and justice. Over the years CPT has greatly expanded both its full-time and reservist programs while initiating plans for the development and training of local reservist groups. By 1992, CPT had organized a series of delegations to Haiti, Iraq, and the West Bank of Israel; in 1995, it had begun a project in Hebron; and by 1998 was operating two full-time projects. In 2001, CPT added a project in Colombia. CPT has also sent delegations to support activists working against the bombing in Vieques, an island off Puerto Rico.

Observations and commentary: For the right type of person, CPT can provide an incredible opportunity to put faith and a commitment to non-violence and peacemaking into action, but the CPT experience is quite risky and therefore is not one we would recommend for most people seeking a volunteer program.

CPT volunteers work in situations of intense conflict, most notably in Hebron and Chiapas. In Hebron, volunteers visit and pray with Palestinians whose homes have been targeted for demolition by the Israeli Government's Defense Force. CPT makes its presence in Hebron visible, so the Defense Force knows their actions are being observed. Volunteers document the destruction of Palestinian homes and publicize human rights abuses.

In Chiapas, volunteers document human rights abuses and prepare information for dissemination in the United States. CPT has had a hard time recruiting volunteers who speak Spanish, and this deficiency limits the effectiveness of the program there.

The controversial nature of CPT's work as well as the situations of conflict in which volunteers are placed put CPT volunteers at high risk of becoming targets of violence. Applicants must sign a waiver that says, "I am aware that I will be entering situations that may be tense at the present time and that there may be danger of war or other violent conflict while I am overseas. . . . I could be imprisoned, taken hostage, injured, or even killed." Potential volunteers should reflect on their initial attraction to this organization in order to be certain that their interest does not come out of a desire for extreme adventure. CPT needs volunteers who are committed to non-violent conflict resolution, not "danger junkies."

While no CPT volunteers have been killed or kidnapped, some have been involved in other dangerous situations. Cliff Kindy, for example, was visiting a family in the Gaza Strip when seven Israeli soldiers broke into the home. According to Cliff, "Two and a half hours of roughshod terror ended in a miracle—none of the seventeen people were killed, injured, or arrested."

Despite the dangers, the volunteers we met were quite positive about their CPT experience. They praised the CPT staff members, who, according to CPT volunteer Esther Ho, are "dedicated and personally concerned about the welfare of each volunteer and about the project."

Another strong point of CPT is the team experience. Cole Hull, who volunteered in Haiti, Palestine, and North America, said that the intensity of the team was the best part of volunteering: "You literally depend on your teammates for your life at times." But this same intensity created challenges due to team turnover and different motivations and skills among members.

Strong faith seems to be a necessary part of a volunteer's ability to survive very challenging situations. As Esther Ho said, "The strong sense that we were being led by God was very necessary for us to be able to carry on in a difficult setting." For Esther, "asking friends and acquaintances for money" was harder than the actual volunteer experience in Hebron.

CPT is a low-budget organization; stipends are kept low, and living conditions are humble. For example, volunteers in Palestine live above a chicken market that is loud and smelly.

We recommend CPT for brave Christian people with a strong commitment to non-violence. If you have dependents, are not religious, or do not cope well with tension and conflict, we suggest that you find another program.

We have been re-invited by the municipality, welcomed and praised in the streets, rated above the international observer presence of 140 people because we live in the conflictive neighborhoods; we interfere with injustice, create and participate in non-violent alternatives to the present conflict, and respond to their requests. What I liked best about CPT was the challenge of being in difficult, dangerous situations and the opportunity to be changed by these experiences. The Palestinian people are initially wary of U.S. citizens, but Israeli soldiers and police have respect for carriers of U.S. passports. That respect is a tool we can use to help the people in occupied Palestine.
—Cliff Kindy, volunteer, Palestine

Citizens Democracy Corps (CDC)

Suite 1125
1400 I St., NW
Washington, DC 20005

phone: 800-394-1945
fax: 202-872-0923
e-mail: info@cdc.org
web: www.cdc.org

Countries where volunteers are placed: Azerbaijan, the Balkans, Central Asia, Russia, Thailand, and Ukraine

Field(s) of work: Business-related tasks in all sectors including sales, accounting, and manufacturing

Requirements or special skills necessary: Volunteers must have expertise in areas such as production, distribution, customer service, marketing, advertising, and/or management. Required skills vary with the industry and project. Volunteer advisors should have a minimum of ten years senior level management experience.

Duration and dates: Most volunteers spend three weeks abroad; some work for up to two months. Start dates are offered year round.

What volunteers pay and what they receive: Volunteers cover daily expenses such as meals and laundry. CDC pays for airfare, visas, and any expenses incurred enroute to the project site. The local enterprises receiving the volunteers provide housing, lunches, local transportation, and translation.

Typical volunteer responsibilities: Volunteers act as consultants to help modernize manufacturing processes and financial reporting systems, increase sales and productivity, facilitate mergers of client companies, and build markets for United States and regional partners, buyers, and suppliers.

Number of volunteers sent abroad annually: 500 (2000)

Age range: 30–65+   **Typical age:** 50

How to apply: Send the CDC office a resume that "highlights recent work and volunteer experience." In order to help CDC make the best possible match between company and volunteer, be sure to include the following information in your resume: education, employment history (listing major responsibilities and accomplishments), expertise, volunteer projects, and language capabilities.

Stated mission: "CDC supports and develops small-and medium-sized businesses in Central/Eastern Europe and Russia by placing volunteer advisors in foreign companies. Volunteers assist in the growth of market economies. They provide new market opportunities and jobs for the region's companies and citizens."

History: CDC was formed in 1990 to support the transition to free market economies in Central Europe and Newly Independent States (former Soviet Union) "where decades of government control and central planning have left people and institutions poorly prepared to compete in a market-driven economy."

Concern America

2015 N. Broadway
PO Box 1790
Santa Ana, CA 92702

phone: 714-953-8575; 800-CONCERN
fax: 714-953-1242
e-mail: concamerinc@earthlink.net
web: www.concernamerica.org

Since working with Concern America, issues dealing with Guatemala and Latin America are not something I can block out. I will be following developments. I will be active.
—Danna Karash, volunteer, Guatemala

Countries where volunteers are currently placed: Guinea and Mozambique in Africa, and Mexico, Guatemala, Honduras, El Salvador, Bolivia, and other countries in Latin America

Field(s) of work: Public health, nutrition, agriculture, engineering, education, sanitation, and community organizing

Requirements or skills necessary: Volunteers must have experience in one of the needed professions, be fluent in Spanish (Portuguese for volunteers in Mozambique), or be able to learn the language at their own expense. Volunteers also must be at least twenty-one years old, have work experience abroad, and make a minimum commitment of two years. Children under the age of 18 may accompany adults who are volunteering. Married and unmarried couples can volunteer together, provided that both partners qualify.

Duration and dates: Volunteers make a commitment of two or more years. There is no particular start-up date.

What volunteers pay and what they receive: Concern America provides room, round-trip transportation, an annual trip home, health insurance, a monthly stipend of

$350, support services, and a small repatriation allowance. Volunteers also receive a three-day orientation at the headquarters in Santa Ana, California, prior to departure.

Typical volunteer responsibilities: Volunteers help build local capacity in health care and midwifery, in appropriate technologies, and in the organization and operation of craft cooperatives. Volunteers may also work on ecological projects such as reforestation or community-based development projects such as literacy programs. Volunteers may be involved in the training, technical assistance, and material support of refugees.

Number of volunteers sent abroad annually: 20–25

Age range: 21–55   **Typical age:** 28–34

How to apply: Send a resume, a personal statement, and a cover letter to the recruitment coordinator at the office in Santa Ana. There is no application deadline.

Stated mission: "Through the work of volunteers who are professionals in the fields of health, public health, nutrition, education, sanitation, and community organizing, Concern America assists impoverished communities and refugees in developing countries in their efforts to improve their living conditions. Concern America programs emphasize the training of community members in order to impart skills and knowledge that will remain with the community long after the volunteer is gone."

History: Concern America was founded in Stockton, California, by the relatives of a group of Irish clergy who had been expelled from Biafra, Nigeria, in 1968. Concern was incorporated as a nonprofit organization in California in 1972.

Observations and commentary: Concern America strives to increase the capacity of its host communities to address their own problems. Concern believes that once a handful of people are empowered to work as health promoters, for example, they act as "multipliers," continuing the work and spreading the knowledge to neighboring communities long after Concern has departed. This approach to development is potentially more self-sustaining than other development models in that it does not create a situation in which the continued presence of foreign organizations is necessary. One volunteer told us that "Our vision is that we will not be here forever. We are helping to build sustainability."

Concern's volunteer training begins, as mentioned, with a three-day orientation. Volunteers, however, are accepted one at a time, on a rather ad hoc basis; this works against Concern investing in longer pre-departure orientations. Volunteers do, however, receive training in the field during a month-long overlap in which an incoming volunteer works with an outgoing volunteer.

Concern's small size enables it to operate without an extensive bureaucracy. Volunteers are therefore able to have direct contact with staff and participate in some of the organization's decision-making processes. For example, volunteers are at times involved in the selection of their replacements.

In Guatemala, income-generating projects connect volunteers with indigenous artisan cooperatives. The goals of this project are to help artisans market their goods in the United States, receive a fair price for their goods, and preserve their artistic traditions. Most of the cooperatives are comprised almost entirely of women, often widows, who are offered training in organization, production, and marketing.

We spoke with Dr. Mary Bryson, a volunteer in the midwifery program in the remote Peten region in Guatemala. She told us that the Mayan women who have participated in the program have grown in self-confidence. As an example, she told us that when a local doctor was consistently late to a teaching course, the women simply started the meetings without her. Some of the midwives, however, sometimes called Dr. Bryson "Mama María," a nickname she hated. "They were saying we were teaching them how to walk," Dr. Bryson commented to us. "It seemed so paternalistic." This type of relationship is an inherent danger in development work catalyzed by foreign organizations, but we commend Concern for being aware of this issue and continually seeking to reduce local people's dependence on foreign knowledge and resources.

Concern is a good option for professionals with skills in public health and community development who want to dedicate two years or more of their lives to working at the grassroots level. If you have skill and experience as a teacher or trainer, and desire to help build long-term capacity of less developed communities rather than providing short-term services directly, this would be a good placement for you.

Council on International Educational Exchange (Council)

International Volunteer Projects
633 Third Ave.
New York, NY 10017

phone: 888-COUNCIL
fax: 212-822-2649
e-mail: info@councilexchanges.org
web: www.councilexchanges.org

Council volunteer projects are short-term projects that are primarily intended to give all participants an intercultural experience. The project, however important or enjoyable, becomes secondary.—Steven Brillon, volunteer, East Germany

Countries where volunteers are placed: Belarus, Belgium, Bulgaria, Canada, Czech Republic, Denmark, Ecuador, Estonia, Finland, France, Germany, Greece, Italy, Japan, Lithuania, Mexico, Morocco, the Netherlands, Poland, Russia, Slovakia, Spain, Turkey, the United Kingdom, Ukraine, and the United States

Field(s) of work: Construction/renovation, nature conservation, cultural programs, social work, and archaeological projects

Requirements or special skills necessary: There are no special skills required. Work in all projects involves simple tasks that unskilled volunteers can be taught to do in a day's time. On most projects, no foreign language skills are required of native English speakers as English is the primary language.

Duration and dates: Projects last from two to four weeks. Most projects take place between June and September, but some are available year round.

What volunteers pay and what they receive: Volunteers pay airfare and a program fee of $300 in addition to $35 for thirty days of Council's "Peace of Mind" insurance coverage. Some projects require additional fees. Council provides a placement, contact information for returned volunteers, newsletters, e-mail updates, a volunteer handbook, pre-departure support, room and board, and some group activities.

Typical volunteer responsibilities: Typical construction and renovation tasks include hammering, mixing and pouring cement, transporting building materials, and scraping and painting walls. Volunteers in conservation projects can expect tasks such as weeding, cleaning riverbanks, and mapping pollution sources. Volunteers in cultural projects assist members of host communities in preparation for national festivals or setting up an exhibit on an important current issue. Social projects (not as abundant as manual labor projects due to language barriers) offer an opportunity for volunteers to assist in the planning and supervision of games for children, distribute meals and read to hospital patients, work around the house or garden of elderly people, or accompany people with disabilities on excursions. Typical tasks in the limited number of archaeological projects include digging slowly with spoons, hands, and brushes to remove dirt and artifacts from the site, as well as sorting and labeling finds.

Number of volunteers sent abroad annually: 300

Age range: 18+   **Typical age:** 20–25

How to apply: An online calendar of summer projects is annually posted on the Council website at the end of March. To apply, visit the Council website, select your project choices, and print an application. After mailing in the application and payment, Council typically responds to applications within three weeks. Placements are made on a first come, first served basis.

Stated mission: "The Council on International Educational Exchange (Council) is committed to help individuals gain understanding, acquire knowledge, and develop skills for living in a globally interdependent and culturally diverse world. Founded in

1947, Council believes that an international perspective is best developed through the firsthand experience of other cultures."

History: Council's International Volunteer Projects program was founded in 1982.

Observations and commentary: Council on International Educational Exchange's International Volunteer Projects' focus is workcamps. These international volunteer projects bring together young people from different countries to live and work together to benefit the community in which they are working.

As mentioned in the other profiles, one of the main advantages of volunteering on a workcamp is that you can choose from a wide array of projects that present different working and living conditions. There are literally hundreds of workcamps to choose from. Workcamps take place worldwide; the majority are located in Europe, North America, and Asia.

Council gets good marks from former volunteers. The organization is reportedly responsive to requests for assistance from volunteers in preparing to go abroad and being available to answer questions as they arise. Although Council is a part of a large travel organization with a variety of priorities, the International Volunteer Projects staff remains dedicated to volunteer exchange.

Since there is such a range from workcamp to workcamp, it is hard to make general comments about any of the workcamp placement organizations. Potential workcamp volunteers should focus their search by looking for camps in the country of their choosing, then seeking those camps that feature the type of work, languages, and volunteer composition that fits their interests. In order to get firsthand details about a specific camp, we suggest that prospective volunteers contact past volunteers who have worked at a specific camp or with a particular overseas host institution. Council does a good job of providing contact information for past volunteers. If you don't find the right contact on the website, ask the staff for additional suggestions of former volunteers to contact.

Competition for some workcamps can be intense. Our advice is to identify more than one workcamp that interests you and to put in your requests as quickly as you can after the project is listed.

In comparison to many short-term volunteer programs, Council is an inexpensive option. The trade-off is that Council volunteers don't have their hands held and often receive very little training or preparation before they arrive overseas. The quality of the experience is often dependent on the host organization, the project of the camp, the chemistry of the group, and the skill of the group leader.

Council is a good option for volunteers interested in short-term projects. Certainly the highlight of the workcamp experience is getting to know the team of volunteers, most of whom will probably come from Europe. Council is also a good option for those who would like to combine travel and volunteering. If you are a loner, or if you think you'd like to be the only foreigner on a project, Council is not for you. First-time travelers with a sense of adventure and a desire for intercultural exchange are likely candidates, but the program is probably less than ideal for a volunteer interested in total immersion in the local culture since your primary peer group will be the other volunteers.

Crispaz

1555 Massachusetts Ave.   *phone:* 617-354-9645
Cambridge, MA 02138   *fax:* 617-354-9648
                                 e-mail: crispaz@igc.org
                                 web: www.crispaz.org

Countries where volunteers are placed: El Salvador

Field(s) of work: Literacy, health care, pastoral work, community organizing, education, agriculture, appropriate technology, women's issues, substance abuse, earthquake reconstruction, and work with youth

Requirements and skills necessary: Volunteers in the Long-Term Program must have a college degree and be able to make at least a one-year commitment. There are no special skills required for the Summer Immersion Program. Crispaz recommends but does not require that volunteers not comfortable in Spanish undertake an intensive Spanish course prior to placement.

Duration and dates: The Summer Immersion Program lasts three months, from June through August. Long-Term Program placements are one to three years; placements are made in March and September.

What volunteers pay and what they receive: A program fee of $1,500 for the Summer Immersion Program covers all in-country costs, in addition to personal and international travel costs.

Long-term volunteers must raise funds to cover their own airfare and living expenses in El Salvador. They do not pay a fee to Crispaz. The estimated cost of room and board for long-term volunteers is $250 to $300 a month. Health insurance may be available. Long-term volunteers must be sponsored by an institution or a network of individual supporters from their home country who provide volunteers with financial, spiritual, and moral support. Typically, this support comes from faith communities, but this is not a requirement. "This sponsorship," says the Crispaz website, "serves to create important ties of solidarity between Salvadorans and the volunteer's home community." Crispaz provides volunteers with orientation, project placement, team building, ongoing support throughout the placement, and, when needed, assistance in fundraising and/or identifying sponsors. Many volunteers live with local families in their community settings. Living conditions in the countryside can be quite basic and may require an adjustment on the volunteer's part.

Typical volunteer responsibilities: The Summer Immersion Program is "an intensive learning and service experience in a poor community in El Salvador." Summer Immersion Program volunteers accompany rural low-income Salvadoran families in their daily lives and work.

Long-term volunteers assist in the work of local NGOs, cooperatives, rural parishes, and urban social service organizations. Volunteers live with families in rural low-income communities and occasionally at the Crispaz team house in San Salvador.

Number of volunteers sent abroad annually: 16

Age range: 21–75   **Typical age:** 22–45

How to apply: Potential volunteers should contact the Crispaz office for an application. Upon receipt of the completed application and three references, Crispaz arranges an interview between the applicant and a Crispaz board or staff member who assesses the applicant's motivation, maturity, skills, and understanding of the Salvadoran reality. Volunteer placements are based on a combination of the volunteer's interests and Salvadoran NGO and/or other community needs.

Stated mission: Crispaz (Christians for Peace in El Salvador) is a faith-based organization dedicated to mutual accompaniment with the church of the poor and marginalized communities in El Salvador. In building bridges of solidarity between communities in El Salvador and those in our home countries, we strive together for peace, justice, and human liberation. As an organization, we are politically non-partisan and committed to non-violence."

History: In 1984, Crispaz began providing volunteers with the opportunity to witness the civil war in El Salvador and its impact on the people of El Salvador and, upon returning home, to act in response to what they had experienced. Volunteers were sent into communities to accompany Salvadorans who were displaced physically and spiritually by the prolonged and brutal conflict and who bore an enormous burden of loss and suffering, from which many still struggle to recover after nine years of peace. Today, through its volunteer and educational programs, Crispaz continues to support the long-term efforts of the Salvadoran people and their communities to live with dignity, hope, and empowerment.

Cross-Cultural Solutions (CCS)

47 Potter Avenue
New Rochelle, NY 10801

phone: 800-380-4777, 914-632-0022
fax: 914-632-8494
e-mail: info@crossculturalsolutions.org
web: www.crossculturalsolutions.org

The things that I liked most about the program were the way that we were integrated into the community and the evening discussions about social justice and other issues affecting developing countries.—Erin Connolly, volunteer, Ghana

Countries where volunteers are placed: China, Ghana, India, Peru, and Russia

Field(s) of work: Healthcare, education, and community development

Requirements or special skills necessary: CCS offers both skilled and unskilled placements. Unmarried as well as married couples may volunteer together. Under special circumstances, in some countries, teens and preteens can accompany parents who are volunteering, but this option is not always available. Parents who are potential volunteers should contact the staff.

Duration and dates: Duration of programs ranges widely, from the one-week "Insight Program" to six-month-long volunteer programs. Many volunteers serve for as few as two or three weeks, while others extend their stay to a year. Start dates are offered year-round.

What volunteers pay and what they receive: Costs range from $1,750 for two weeks in Russia to $5,220 for 20 weeks in Peru. Fees do not include airfare but CCS provides volunteers with airport pick-up and transportation to local volunteer sites. CCS also provides room and board as well as staff support. Volunteers must pay a $275 non-refundable deposit to confirm their registration and must pay the program fee no later than ninety days prior to program start date to secure their place on a program. Volunteers also must provide their own health insurance.

Typical volunteer responsibilities: Volunteers work with a wide range of local healthcare, education, and social development organizations. We met volunteers who worked with children in orphanages facilitating arts and crafts projects, teaching English, and providing basic computer training. We also met volunteers who worked in women's groups, in health clinics, and in sanitation and waste management campaigns.

Number of volunteers sent abroad annually: 1,000 (2001)

Age range: 18+ (Some programs accept younger children if accompanied by an adult.)

Typical age: 35 percent college age, 35 percent retired, and 30 percent mid-career professionals

How to apply: First, submit your registration form noting the program, country, and date of the project that interests you. Then fill out the full application documents, which include personal information, job history, and health forms. The CCS "Skills and Interests Survey" is truly a model personal skills inventory form. It is used by the organization to match volunteers with placements, taking into consideration not only their current skills and the type of work they are interested in, but also the balance they seek between service and cultural exchange. Applications are typically submitted three months prior to departure but can sometimes be processed more quickly.

Stated mission: "Cross-Cultural Solutions is a non-profit, public-benefit organization that employs volunteer humanitarian action to empower local communities, foster cultural sensitivity and understanding, and contribute grassroots solutions to the global challenges of providing healthcare, education, and social development." CCS believes that "the people of each culture know and understand what is appropriate for their community. Because local people are the experts, we assist them in carrying out the objectives they deem important, rather than impose Western ways."

History: The most rewarding part of Steve Rosenthal's travels through Asia and Africa was the time he spent assisting a friend and Peace Corps volunteer in the building of a healthcare clinic in a village in Kenya. He was inspired by this experience but realized that many people are unable to make the approximately two-year commitment that the Peace Corps and other long-term organizations require. In 1995 he founded CCS to provide international volunteer opportunities that were accessible to people who could make only limited time commitments. CCS launched its first program in India and within several years inaugurated projects in Ghana and Peru. CCS has also organized humanitarian programs such as the Kosovo Refugee Relief Service program that operated in Kosovo in 1999 at the height of the humanitarian crisis there. CCS has since developed volunteer programs in China and Russia and has added "Insight Tours"—one-week educational tours—to Cuba and each of the countries where volunteers are currently placed. In 2001, CCS also initiated a strategic alliance with CARE, a development agency with projects around the globe.

Observations and Commentary: Volunteers tend to agree that CCS provided them with a great deal of support. This intensive support leads many participants to the conclusion that they "get their money's worth."

CCS in-country coordinators and other staff are nationals with significant experience in the non-profit sector. Country coordinators make themselves available for informal conversation with volunteers and organize formal presentations and discussions. Interacting with the country coordinator can be, as one volunteer put it, "the best part of the experience." Staff members reportedly are skillful in handling logistics such as daily transportation to volunteer sites, household management, and the volunteer placements themselves.

The official orientation takes place on the first day in-country and primarily serves as an introduction to the local culture. Informal conversations among the volunteers and staff as well as formal evening programs allow for continued orientation and reflection. Volunteers are encouraged to interact with the local culture throughout the program. As Bela Singh, the Country Coordinator in India, tells volunteers: "Go and get fruit at the market, ask questions and strive to understand the rich culture, the family systems, and the big gap between the rich and the poor."

CCS's extensive network of partner organizations means many work options for volunteers. Volunteers, however, are responsible for finalizing their volunteer placement once they arrive in-country. While information on placements is provided prior to arrival, placements are considered tentative until the volunteer and organization meet and work together to define the specific duties.

While the staff is careful to warn volunteers that living quarters are not five-star-tourist hotels, all accommodations, whether in group compounds or collections of cottages or houses, are very comfortable. In addition, meals are prepared for the volunteers. According to several of the younger volunteers who we spoke with, the accommodations and food are "nicer than they are at home."

The CCS program, as mentioned, assumes that volunteers don't have much time to go overseas and therefore is built around three-week segments. This three-week cycle of arrivals and departures of short-term volunteers, however, can create difficulties for long-term volunteers who end up feeling obligated to play an informal leadership role with the short-term volunteers.

Although CCS has attempted to meet the needs of its local partners by placing volunteers throughout the year, the types of projects that volunteers undertake are almost always defined by the three-week cycle of short-term volunteers. Nonetheless, many local NGOs agree that the support CCS provides for volunteers reduces the burden on the NGOs. In the words of Dr. Tooly of Amar Jyoti, a school in Delhi for differently abled children, "CCS gives volunteers a good orientation, motivates them, and helps them both to understand the culture and show respect."

The Amar Jyoti school is a good example of a CCS placement. It contains an extensive medical clinic with physical therapy, surgery, and prosthesis production facilities. There is also a carpentry shop, a craft shop, an art and music space, and a printing and paper-making facility. CCS volunteers have been involved in a myriad of activities such as decorating classrooms, designing, packaging and marketing cards, creating a manual of the Amar Jyoti Occupational Therapy System, and documenting the school's history.

Overall, we commend CCS for living up to its philosophy of supporting people in other societies as they promote the development objectives of their own communities. We believe that the high quality of CCS programs is a result of the organization's careful matching process that links volunteers with appropriate placements. CCS has expanded its programs rapidly, but thus far it appears to have been able to maintain a solid infrastructure and a high level of personal attention to individual volunteers.

CCS seems to be meeting both the needs of its volunteers and the needs of the local NGOs it works with. Overall, we highly recommend CCS for volunteers interested in short-term to medium-term volunteering.

Cultural Restoration Tourism Project (CRTP)

c/o Mark A. Hintzke
722a Liggett Ave.
San Francisco, CA 94129

phone: 415-563-7221
e-mail: crtp@earthlink.net
web: home.earthlink.net/~crtp/

Countries where volunteers are placed: Mongolia

Field(s) of work: Construction and restoration of Buddhist temples

Requirements or special skills necessary: Volunteers do not need any construction experience, but should be in good physical health.

Duration and dates: Volunteer programs last from ten to twenty days. The first tour begins in June and the last group returns at the end of September. Tour groups are made up of five to seven volunteers with overlapping schedules so that two groups are always present at any given time.

What volunteers pay and what they receive: Program fees range from $1,500 to $3,200. Volunteers live in *gers*, the traditional housing of the nomadic Mongolians, and eat local meals prepared by a Mongolian cook. Participants are permitted to practice with the monks during many of their ceremonies. Program fees help to support the costs of supplies as well as support a full-time year-round coordinator and a local staff of twenty during the building season.

Typical volunteer responsibilities: While at the site, the participants are involved in many aspects of the restoration projects. Tasks are assigned according to the individual's experience and physical limitations. Work ranges from light to arduous. Typical tasks vary from scaffolding construction and masonry to sewing and painting.

Number of volunteers sent abroad annually: 20 (2000)

Age range: 19–58   **Typical age:** 22–25

How to apply: Contact the office to further discuss the project and inquire about openings on the various tours.

Stated mission: "CRTP was established to restore temples and other artifacts in Central Asia. Lack of money and infrastructure is leading to the decay of many beautiful and significant buildings in the region. CRTP provides assistance to local communities at no cost to them. CRTP provides support to communities, enabling them to restore culturally significant structures. CRTP is a self-supporting effort aimed toward the needs of the local communities in Central Asia. We hope to establish a relationship of trust with communities that will enable us to help in the restoration of temples and other structures."

History: The Baldan Baraivan temple, located about 300 kilometers east of the Mongolian capital city of Ulaan Bataar, is full of history. Like many monasteries in Mongolia, destruction and persecution have left only the ruins of buildings that were once magnificent cultural centers. With the fall of the Soviet Union and the changes throughout the country, there has been a revival of interest in Buddhist lamaism in Mongolia.

During a trip to Mongolia, CRTP founder Mark Hintzke, who has a professional background in construction, was asked by the lama of the temple to assist in rebuilding the temple. In the summer of 1999, restoration began with the arrival of the first group of tourists to work alongside local people to restore the temple. Today, as the reconstruction and renovation moves forward, one lama still lives at the temple in a newly constructed wooden house at the site of the old monastery and maintains important cultural and religious tradition by guiding the monastic education of younger monks.

CUSO

500-2255 Carling Ave.
Ottawa, Ontario
Canada, K2B 1A6

phone (in Canada): **888-434-2876**
phone (from U.S): **613-829-7445**
fax: **613-829-7996**
e-mail: **cuso.secretariat@cuso.ca**
web: **www.cuso.org**

CUSO calls their volunteers "cooperants," a phrase that in the minds of Canadians means that people are involved in two-way cooperation, whereas the word volunteer has the connotation of charity.—Gabriella Labelle, staff, Mexico

Countries where volunteers are placed: Antigua, Bangladesh, Barbados, Belize, Bolivia, Burkina Faso, Chile, Colombia, Costa Rica, El Salvador, Ghana, Guatemala, Indonesia, Jamaica, Kenya, Laos, Malaysia, Mexico, Mozambique, Nicaragua, Nigeria, Papua New Guinea, Peru, Saint Vincent, St. Lucia, South Africa, Solomon Islands, Tanzania, Thailand, Togo, Vanuatu, and Zimbabwe

Field(s) of work: Human rights and legal advocacy, rural development, natural resources management, institutional capacity building, skills development, and other fields aimed at improving livelihoods in developing countries

Requirements or skills necessary: CUSO seeks out volunteers with experience with social justice organizations that meet the needs of their overseas partners. Volunteers must be Canadian citizens or Canadian immigrants with significant experience in a specific profession as well as experience living and/or working overseas. CUSO generally does not accept young people just out of college. Volunteers must be willing to make a two-year commitment and must share the vision of CUSO. They should also have a commitment to social causes in Canada, CUSO believes that before volunteers get involved in a foreign country they should have a commitment to social justice in their own country. Volunteers are prohibited from involvement in partisan political activity in their host country but are encouraged to become involved in political activity upon their return to Canada. Children may accompany their parents who are volunteers. Married couples may volunteer together; it may be possible for unmarried couples to volunteer together in certain countries.

Duration and dates: Assignments last for two years. Volunteers are placed year-round.

What volunteers pay and what they receive: CUSO or the host organization provides housing, airfare to and from the host country, and a stipend that allows volunteers to live a "modest and healthy life" overseas. In certain instances, CUSO might provide medical insurance and other health benefits as well as assistance with departure expenses, resettlement allowance and a small contribution toward ongoing financial commitments, such as loans or credit card payments, while on a CUSO placement. Placements begin with in-country orientations that are aimed at helping volunteers integrate into life in the host country. The orientation includes discussions of how to live in the host country on the budget CUSO provides. It also provides volunteers with an introduction to their particular host organization.

Typical volunteer responsibilities: Responsibilities vary from assignment to assignment. One advertised placement called for a volunteer to assist host organization staff with writing, illustration, and layout of a magazine. Another position called for a community forester to work on "participatory community mapping and a community-based natural resource management forestry project."

Number of volunteers sent abroad annually: 405 (2000)

Age range: 18–75   **Typical age:** 30–50

How to apply: "An application for a CUSO placement means more than simply applying for a job in another country. Your decision reflects a commitment to live, work, learn, and share under very different expectations, conditions and levels of support than you may have ever faced before. It will be an experience that will challenge your personal as well as your professional resources. As such, the CUSO selection process is thorough, and can be lengthy; in fact, it can take months to confirm a placement. Application deadlines vary from project to project; consult the website for postings."

Stated mission: "CUSO is a Canadian organization which supports alliances for global social justice. We work with people striving for freedom, gender and racial equality, self-determination, and cultural survival. We achieve our goals by sharing information, human and material resources, and by promoting policies for developing global sustainability."

History: Since its founding in 1961, CUSO has placed more than 12,000 Canadian volunteers in communities around the world. Their commitment to this mission is a principal reason CUSO has become a Canadian success story. The Canadian government's Canadian International Development Agency (CIDA) has been a major donor since CUSO's inception. CUSO originally was an abbreviation for Canadian University Service Overseas but now only the acronym is used since there is no longer a university affiliation or focus.

Doctors Without Borders/Médecins Sans Frontières (MSF)

6 E. Thirty-Ninth St., Eighth Floor
New York, NY 10016

phone: 212-679-6800
fax: 212-679-7016
e-mail: doctors@newyork.msf.org
web: www.doctorswithoutborders.org

Humanitarian aid to warring countries unfortunately can actually free up resources to be used to continue fighting. Doctors Without Borders works in crisis or conflict areas so it is important that it be conscious of how aid is used. It wants its work to be in line with what it stands for.— volunteer, Cambodia

Countries: Afghanistan, Albania, Algeria, Angola, Armenia, Azerbaijan, Bangladesh, Belgium, Benin, Bolivia, Bosnia and Herzogovina, Brazil, Bulgaria, Burkina Faso, Burundi, Cambodia, Central African Republic, Chad, China, Colombia, Congo-Brazzaville, Costa Rica, Cuba, Democratic Republic of Congo, East Timor, Ecuador, Egypt, Equitorial Guinea, El Salvador, Eritrea, Ethiopia, France, Georgia, Guatemala, Guinea, Guinea-Bissau, Haiti, Honduras, India, Indonesia, Iran, Italy, Ivory Coast, Kazakhstan, Kenya, Kyrgyzsta, Laos, Lebanon, Liberia, Luxembourg, Madagascar, Malawi, Mali, Mauritania, Mexico, Mongolia, Morocco, Mozambique, Myanmar (Burma), Nicaragua, Nigeria, Palestine, Panama, Papua New Guinea, Peru, the Philippines, Romania, Russia/Chechnya, Rwanda, Sierra Leone, Spain, Somalia, South Africa, Sri Lanka, Sudan, Tajikistan, Tanzania, Thailand, Turkey, Turkmenistan, Uganda, Ukraine, Uzbekistan, Vietnam, Yemen, Yugoslavia/Kosovo, and Zambia

Field(s) of work: Medical volunteers provide emergency medical assistance and offer training in preventive health care to "endangered communities," conflict zones, refugee camps, and areas of natural or manmade disasters. Doctors Without Borders, best known by its French acronym MSF (Médicins Sans Frontières), also provides long-term assistance to governments developing health care infrastructures. Non-medical volunteers look after the administration and logistics of medical projects.

Requirements or special skills necessary: MSF recruits medical, administrative, and logistics volunteers. Medical volunteers (nurses, doctors, midwives, psychotherapists, and physicians' assistants) must have a valid license, at least two years professional experience in their areas of specialization, and preferably some experience in tropical medicine. All volunteers should have some experience living or working overseas and the ability to work in a high-stress environment. A good knowledge of English or French is required, and knowledge of a second or third language such as Portuguese, Spanish, Russian, Arabic, Chinese, or Swahili is useful. There are no positions for students in the field but internships are occasionally available in the United States or European offices.

Duration and dates: The minimum commitment for a first-time volunteer is six months, although nine months to a year is more typical.

What volunteers pay and what they receive: MSF covers all costs including living expenses, round-trip airfare, and other travel costs, as well as health insurance. First-time volunteers receive a stipend of approximately $700 per month. Volunteers are responsible for personal expenses such as souvenirs. One volunteer told us that living conditions are sometimes quite basic and offer little privacy.

Typical volunteer responsibilities: Responsibilities depend on profession, country, and project. Tasks range widely and include setting up and staffing operating rooms and clinics, implementing vaccines, conducting public hygiene and epidemic control campaigns, distributing water, food, and medical kits in disaster zones, and training local medical and support staff.

Number of volunteers sent abroad annually: 125 from the United States and 2,000 from countries worldwide (2000)

Age range: 18+   **Typical age:** 35

How to apply: Contact the MSF office in your country of residence or visit the website for information on becoming a volunteer. A personal interview is required for all applicants. For the interview, prospective volunteers must travel to New York, Los Angeles, or one of the recruitment sessions MSF organizes throughout the United States.

Stated mission: "Doctors Without Borders/Médicins Sans Frontières (MSF) is an independent international medical relief organization that aids victims of armed conflict, epidemics, natural and man-made disasters, and others who lack healthcare due to geographic remoteness or ethnic marginalization. Each year the organization sends more than 2000 doctors, nurses, other medical professionals and logisticians to provide medical aid in more than 80 countries."

History: MSF has set up emergency medical aid missions around the world since 1971.

Observations and commentary: MSF owes some of its fame to winning the 1999 Nobel Peace Prize. To those, however, who have been following its work since its founding in 1971, it has long been known as an effective human rights advocate and a provider of medical support for what it calls "endangered communities" (including conflict zones and areas of public health emergencies). The volunteers we spoke with had, for the most part, good things to say about the organization. Anna Sophie Lindahl, a volunteer we met in the Mexican state of Oaxaca, for example, told us that "One of the organization's greatest strengths is its humanity, its values. There is also a wonderful feeling of esprit de corps."

In many countries, MSF medical volunteers supervise and support local medical professionals who are paid staff. In Oaxaca, for example, medical volunteers are not involved in the hands-on provision of medical services, except in cases in which there is an insufficient number of local doctors to meet project needs. Mauritz, a volunteer we met in Cambodia told us, "Here volunteers are not substituting for what Cambodians can do. Its not really hands on but rather is about encouraging Cambodians, transferring skills, helping build basic health services through training and discussion, and assisting trainers and providers to create curricula."

Medical volunteers who are given the opportunity to do hands-on medical work perform a multiplicity of tasks while in the field. For example, Molly Savitz, a volunteer physician's assistant, visited jungle communities along tributaries of the Amazon River. She trained indigenous health workers to read expiration dates on medication labels, gave talks on diarrhea prevention, started a course on sexually transmitted diseases at the community's request, and reorganized the community pharmacy. On another trip she spent much of the week visiting houses up and down the river to find cases of malaria, and working with indigenous health workers and other health professionals to diagnose and treat the disease.

MSF, as mentioned above, offers positions for both medical and non-medical staff. Volunteers who work as administrators, according to the organization's website, "are usually based in the country capital, although in large project countries administrators with bookkeeping functions sometimes work with teams in the field." This was confirmed by Anna Sophie. Although she worked as an accountant in the capital of Oaxaca, she frequently traveled to the field with the doctors to provide supervision and other kinds of support. She told us that the doctors she worked with treated her with respect. She never felt like an outsider in the field with the doctors.

MSF's provision of emergency medical aid to "endangered communities" is primarily in regions where, as the website puts it, "health structures are insufficient or even nonexistent." In most cases, MSF works in a region at the request of agencies of the host government such as the Ministry of Health. In other cases, such as in Brazil, projects are initiated at the request of, and with the assistance of, indigenous political organizations.

The public image of MSF is that it works primarily in war zones. This is due in part to high-profile cases involving the kidnapping of volunteers. Indeed, volunteers who work in conflict zones and refugee camps may not only live in primitive conditions in a chaotic environment but also risk their own personal safety. Dates, locations, and job descriptions in these project areas may change rapidly. Volunteers may have to carry out emergency mass vaccination campaigns against cholera and measles, diagnose and treat psychological problems, and construct sanitary facilities out of the rubble of war.

Increasingly, however, MSF is focusing on providing primary health care training, especially in hard-to-reach communities. As Molly Savitz wrote in one of her letters home, "We held a meeting with about twenty-five women in the health post. It was part of MSF's overall effort to focus more on health promotion and community involvement." The meeting was held to discuss women's health concerns such as birthing and urinary tract infections and to share ideas about how to prevent diarrheal illness and treat various problems with *remedios do mato* (local remedies from the jungle). No one knows how much of what gets talked about in a meeting like this is or becomes part of people's actual health practices, but Molly did notice that over the course of the next few days the women were bringing in their sick children more readily and mentioning the *remedios* they had already used.

One of the thrusts of the MSF program is advocacy, which it defines as "being present among the victims to bear witness and speak out about their plight in order to improve their basic living conditions and protect their fundamental human rights." MSF requires, however, that volunteers remain uninvolved in partisan political movements.

After being accepted into the MSF program, volunteers attend a two-and-a-half-week orientation. This orientation includes role-playing and discussions on topics such as how to overcome cultural differences. Anna Sophie felt that the orientation was quite professional. Medical volunteers must attend six weeks of training in tropical medicine prior to departure, and some projects require higher degrees of training above and beyond the six-week course. Language training is arranged in the host country.

Volunteers and staff are evaluated every six months, sometimes by organizations other than MSF. As one staff member told us, "MSF has a desire for transparency."

We repeatedly experienced a very hard time reaching MSF staff in New York and Europe; they rarely (or never) returned our phone calls or e-mails. We cannot say, however, whether this is a common experience or whether it had more to do with MSF's desire to focus on communicating with potential volunteers to the exclusion of researchers.

We recommend MSF to volunteers with the required skills and experience, a commitment to human rights advocacy, and an ability to work effectively in extremely stressful situations. If you prefer working in a more routine environment, we suggest you explore other programs.

Earthwatch Institute

3 Clock Tower Place
PO Box 75
Maynard, MA 01754-0075

phone (U.S./Canada): **800-776-0188**
fax: **978-461-2332**
e-mail: **info@earthwatch.org**
web: **www.earthwatch.org**

For me, Earthwatch is a kind of intellectual Outward Bound adventure. It presents an opportunity to work closely with people you have never met, in a place where you have never been, and on a research subject you know little about.—Susan Gartner, Panama, Kenya, Costa Rica, and Turkey

Countries where volunteers are placed: Argentina, Australia, Bahamas, Barbados, Belize, Bermuda, Bolivia, Borneo, Botswana, Brazil, Cameroon, Canada, Chile,

China, Costa Rica, Czech Republic, Ecuador, England, Falkland Islands, Ghana, Hungary, Iceland, Italy, India, Indonesia, Ireland, Israel, Italy, Kenya, Madagascar, Malaysia, Mauritius, Mexico, Namibia, Nepal, Nevis, New Zealand, Peru, the Philippines, Romania, Russia, Scotland, South Africa, Spain, Sri Lanka, Tanzania, Thailand, Turkey, the United States, Uruguay, Venezuela, and Zambia

Field(s) of work: Most projects undertake the study of endangered ecosystems, biodiversity, and resource management, though a few each year focus on public health, historical preservation, or sustainable development.

Requirements or special skills necessary: No special skills are required on most projects as Earthwatch conducts extensive training in the field. A few projects require diving skills (certification and dive logs are required for these projects).

Duration and dates: Volunteers serve between one to three weeks on projects arranged year round. Most projects are filled on a first come, first served basis and popular projects do fill up. The deadline for financial aid applications for teachers and students is February 15.

What volunteers pay and what volunteers receive: Project contributions range from $700 to $3,500, but most volunteers pay approximately $1,750. Contributions cover in-country transportation, food and housing, and in-country orientation and staff support. Volunteers cover their own international travel and insurance costs. Most of the project donation as well as international travel expenses may be tax deductible for U.S. taxpayers. Living arrangements vary widely, from university dorms or comfortable guesthouses to wilderness camping. About 250 K–12 teachers and 100 students each year receive fellowship support to cover their project expenses. Some fellowships also include a travel stipend.

Typical volunteer responsibilities: Volunteers assist university scientists on research projects with ecological or social foci. Responsibilities may include tracking and monitoring endangered animals, cataloguing botanical diversity, participating in archaeological excavations, evaluating sustainable farming systems, surveying medicinal herbal practices, or printing and preserving historic photographs.

Number of volunteers sent abroad annually: 4,000 (2001)

Age range: 16+   **Typical age:** None

How to apply: For a list of Earthwatch projects, volunteers should consult the Earthwatch website or request an annual expedition guide. A $250 advance project donation holds your place. A brief written application and a doctor's note attesting to the volunteer's physical health are also required.

Stated mission: "The Earthwatch Institute promotes sustainable conservation of our natural resources and cultural heritage by creating partnerships between scientists, educators, and the general public."

History: Since its founding in 1971, Earthwatch Institute has mobilized more than 54,000 volunteers to support more than 2,000 projects around the globe.

Observations and commentary: Earthwatch is one of the most popular volunteer vacations available. The variety of projects and locations provide a myriad of options to would-be adventurers. Many volunteers we spoke with have worked on more than one project, trying out new Earthwatch projects during their regular vacations. As one volunteer commented, "I learned much more from the Earthwatch experience than the safari which I also did in Kenya."

The program focuses on scientific research with an emphasis on the environment. Most projects focus on endangered ecosystems, wildlife, oceans, and biodiversity. There are also a number of archaeology and anthropology projects. More recently Earthwatch has introduced programs that examine world health issues and their connection to economic and environmental health. But as previously mentioned, programs such as the world health program that focus on social issues are eclipsed by the number of programs that focus on environmental concerns.

Environmental projects include weighing sea turtles in Baja California, taking a "census" of whales off the Australian coast, banding birds in Ecuador, and observing howler monkeys in Brazil. Cultural projects include interviewing tourists in Guatemalan markets, photographing Russians at folk festivals, and videotaping Buddhist monks. The Earthwatch booklet describing these projects rivals a coffee table hardcover for colorful photos and "exotic" locales. Earthwatch notes that the day-to-day scientific work, such as counting birds, can be tedious.

Volunteers join a team composed of volunteers who are led by "principal investigators." These investigators are professional scientists who are at times joined by graduate students. Often they are not nationals of the country where the project is taking place. Whether conducting a forest census or an archaeological dig, teams usually receive "excellent training" from the principal investigator on their various responsibilities in the field. But as one volunteer commented, "Scientists who are inexperienced in leading volunteers in the field can be a weakness of the program."

On many projects, volunteers' interactions are primarily with other members of the group. Volunteers work with local counterparts on some projects but some of the remote project locations preclude much contact with local people. Earthwatch refused to allow us to visit their teams working in the field, and we were unable to interview local people about their perspective on the projects. In terms of benefits to local people we heard reports from volunteers that they believed locals were educated about various environmental issues and the need for conservation. Others thought that the benefit to local people was limited to "an infusion of cash into the economy, or some paid employment for local people."

Despite these factors, many volunteers, even on projects that didn't have an explicit goal of linking volunteers to local people, still managed to introduce themselves to another culture. As volunteer Ron Kratzner remarked, "Experiencing a totally different ethnic viewpoint was perhaps the highlight of the trip." Some volunteers, like Gayle and William Bauer, whose project involved interviewing villagers about what type of education would be most beneficial in their valley, had more contact with local people. In the case of the Bauers, this contact helped them "to understand the problems and needs of developing countries."

On the other hand, some volunteers seemed to have been very sheltered from local realities. One volunteer told us that it wasn't until she left the project and traveled to other parts of the country that she noticed that many Panamanians were poor.

Earthwatch gets high marks from its volunteers for the briefing booklet it sends out ahead of time detailing what volunteers should expect during their trip. There also seems to be a consensus that Earthwatch appears to take project evaluation seriously. Volunteers provide feedback through surveys, and staff members from headquarters conduct field site visits to evaluate a project. One volunteer reported signing up for two trips, both of which were cancelled because they did not meet staff expectations.

Accommodations are functional with volunteers sharing the typical life of the field scientists, ranging from condos to castles to college dorm rooms. You may sleep in a bed, cot, or hammock. Food ranges from basic to luxurious, depending on the project. Earthwatch offers a master-class program with more comfortable accommodations.

If you have the funds and are excited about environmental issues, Earthwatch may be a good program for you. It's well organized and the projects are interesting and constructive. If you want to work closely with local people to understand and respond to the challenges and opportunities that they face, either select one of the few Earthwatch projects with a focus on human needs, or choose another volunteer program. We encourage teachers and high school students to apply for Earthwatch fellowships, but be aware that most fellowships do not cover travel expenses.

For people who want an active and productive vacation without worrying about a lot of details, Earthwatch is great. It's like going to camp for two weeks.—Melody Reynolds, volunteer, England and Ireland

---

Elderhostel Inc.

11 Avenue de Lafayette
Boston, MA 02111-1746

phone: 877-426-8056
fax: 877-426-2166
e-mail: registration@elderhostel.org
web: www.elderhostel.org

Countries where volunteers are placed: Argentina, Australia, Austria, Belize, Belgium, Bermuda, Bhutan, Bolivia, Botswana, Brazil, China, Cook Islands, Costa Rica, Cuba, Czech Republic, Denmark, Ecuador, England, Estonia, Fiji, Finland, France, French Polynesia, Germany, Ghana, Guatemala, Greece, Hungary, Iceland, India, Indonesia, Ireland, Israel, Italy, Jamaica, Japan, Jordan, Kenya, Latvia, Lithuania, Luxembourg, Malta, Mexico, Midway Atoll, Monaco, Mongolia, Morocco, Namibia, Nepal, the Netherlands, New Caledonia, New Zealand, Nicaragua, Norway, Paraguay, Peru, Poland, Portugal, Russia, Samoa, Solomon Islands, Spain, Suriname, Sweden, Switzerland, Syria, Tanzania, Tonga, Tunisia, Turkey, Uruguay, U.S. Virgin Islands, Uzbekistan, Vanuatu, and Zambia

Field(s) of work: Volunteers work in construction, environmental and biological research, environmental conservation, teaching and tutoring, historic preservation, archaeology, community development, and water and sanitation projects.

Requirements or special skills necessary: Most projects do not require any specialized skills, simply a willingness to participate and help. Some projects, however, include physical work, so being physically fit is beneficial.

People under fifty-five can participate only if they register with a spouse, parent, or friend fifty-five or older; couples are welcome and do not have to be married (although the younger partner must be at least 21!). Elderhostel offers intergenerational programs for grandparents and grandchildren to participate together, but most of these programs are "learning adventures" rather than volunteer programs. The age range for the younger participants in these programs is usually 9–17. Volunteers do not have to be U.S. citizens.

Duration and dates: Project duration ranges from one to three weeks. Departure dates are offered year-round.

What volunteers pay and what they receive: Program fees vary from country to country (and depend on departure city and season when airfare is included) but range from $972, which includes seven nights in the Caribbean (without airfare) to $3,900 for three weeks in China (including airfare). Project costs include lodging, meals, international airfare (except the Caribbean), supplies, emergency evacuation insurance, in-country staff support, and rudimentary-level language instruction.

Typical volunteer responsibilities: Day-to-day tasks depend on the location and type of work. Responsibilities may include manual labor, assisting with scientific research, teaching children and adults English as a second language, or helping with archaeological digs. In India, volunteers work with community organizations, and in Nicaragua volunteers work on water and sanitation projects.

Number of volunteers sent abroad annually: N/A

Age range: 55+   **Typical age:** 65

How to apply: Volunteers may register via mail, phone, fax, or online. Projects are listed on the website or in Elderhostel's seasonal international catalogue. Registration usually closes six weeks prior to departure so early registration is encouraged.

Stated mission: "Elderhostel is a nonprofit organization committed to being the preeminent provider of high-quality, affordable, educational opportunities for older adults: An Elderhostel Service Program is a short-term, residential experience for hostelers that engages them in responsible and challenging actions for the common good." Each project must involve both learning and doing, and the educational component relates to and enhances the service work.

History: Elderhostel was founded in 1975 at the University of New Hampshire by Marty Knowlton, a social activist and former educator, and David Bianco, a university administrator. During a trip to Europe, Knowlton was impressed by the youth hostel concept, and the folk schools where older adults handed down age-old traditions. Using these ideas as a springboard, Knowlton founded Elderhostel to create educational adventure opportunities for older adults from North America. The Elderhostel Service Program was initiated in 1993.

Observations and commentary: Elderhostel's study and travel programs are well established and widely respected. The service programs are a relatively new component of Elderhostel's work but have become a regular year-round option for Elderhostelers.

Many of Elderhostel's Service Programs are offered through partnerships with Amizade, Caribbean Volunteer Expeditions, Global Volunteers, Habitat for Humanity, and Oceanic Expeditions Society. Partner organizations are mentioned in the project descriptions on the Elderhostel website. We encourage you to read our profile on the partner organization if the Elderhostel program you're interested in has one.

Esperança

Caixa Postal 222
Santarém, Para 68040-100
Brazil

phone: 55-91-523-1940
fax: 55-91-523-1951
e-mail: fesperan@ax.apc.org

Esperança provides high-quality medical services to the people of Santarém, Brazil, at a lower cost than other local medical facilities.—Linda Rames, volunteer, Brazil

Countries where volunteers are placed: Brazil

Field(s) of work: Health care

Requirements or skills necessary: Volunteers must have a sense of humor and a valid license as a medical doctor or dentist.

Duration and dates: Doctors and dentists come for one month or more.

What volunteers pay and what they receive: Esperança provides room and board. If volunteers bring a spouse the cost is $25 a day, which includes room, board, and laundry. Families with children are not accepted. Esperança also provides an in-country orientation and ensures that doctors are always accompanied by a nurse, dentists by a dental assistant, and all volunteers by a translator (when needed). Volunteers are responsible for airfare, which ranges from $800 to $1,200, and must carry their own health insurance. Scholarships are available to Rotarians who volunteer for one month or more.

Typical volunteer responsibilities: Doctors and dentists see patients from 8 a.m. to 11:30 a.m. and again from 2 p.m. to 5 p.m., Monday through Friday.

Number of volunteers sent abroad annually: 110 (2000)

Age range: 25–85   **Typical age:** N/A

How to apply: Contact the office in Brazil for further information on the program.

Stated mission: "Esperança is saving children's lives . . . because every child deserves a healthy life. We heal children by providing medical treatment to heal the sick; we restore children by sending medical volunteer surgeons to give young bodies new life through reconstructive surgery; we prevent the tragic death of children due to malnutrition, dehydration, and pneumonia."

History: "Esperança was founded in 1970 to support the work of Friar and Doctor Luke Tupper, who worked in the Amazon Basin between 1969 and 1975. In 1972, Esperança purchased a riverboat, christened the *Esperança,* which was transformed into a mobile clinic to serve people living in hard-to-reach places along the Amazon River. After ten years the *Esperança* was retired, and the medical and surgical facilities were moved on shore. Today, Esperança occupies a full city block with up-to-date medical facilities." Dr. Tupper was killed in a motorcycle accident in 1978, but many stellar staff members and volunteers continue his legacy.

Observations and commentary: Esperança's work in Brazil consists of long-standing medical centers in the Amazon river town of Santarém. The township of Santarém is approximately the size of the state of Maryland.

We find it laudable that Esperança uses local volunteers in all aspects of their work in Brazil. We encourage other volunteer placement organizations to follow this example.

Esperança conducts extensive evaluations of their organization and the departments within it. Volunteers are evaluated through an informal interview.

Esperança has a ten-room dormitory. There are typically one to two volunteers per room. All rooms have both beds and hammocks, and several have air conditioning. Each two rooms share a bathroom. Three meals a day are served in the Esperança kitchen by arguably the best cook in Santarém.

For medical professionals with a desire to share their skills with the people of the Amazon Basin and experience the rich culture of this region, Esperança is a good choice.

FFA Organization

FFA Global
6060 FFA Dr.
PO Box 68960
Indianapolis, IN 46268-0960

phone: 317-802-5215; 317-802-6060
fax: 317-802-5214; 317-802-6061
e-mail: global@ffa.org
web: www.ffa.org/international

Countries where volunteers are placed: Worldwide, including programs in Australia, Costa Rica, Europe, and New Zealand

Field(s) of work: Agriculture

Requirements or special skills necessary: The FFA Explorers Program: Participants must be fifteen to twenty-four years old and have experience and/or interest in international agriculture.

The Australia Homestay Program: Participants must be sixteen to twenty-four years old and have interest in agriculture in Australia.

The World Experience in Agriculture Program: Participants must have moderate to extensive experience in at least one area of agriculture (e.g., dairy, production livestock, crops, horticulture, greenhouse, soils, fruits/vegetables).

Volunteers considering placements in Europe must be eighteen to twenty-four years old, and nineteen to twenty-four for placements in Australia and New Zealand.

Language skills are not necessary for any FFA programs except the program in France, which requires one year of French.

Duration and dates: The FFA Explorer Program has placements of six weeks, or three or six months in one of twenty-five countries. The Australia Homestay Program lasts four weeks starting in mid-June. The World Experience in Agriculture Program usually lasts three, six, or twelve months.

What volunteers pay and what they receive: FFA Explorers pay between $2,950 and $4,200. The Australia Homestay Program fee is approximately $3,300 to $3,700, while the World Experience in Agriculture Program price is approximately $2,500 to $4,500. All program fees include international air travel, a pre-departure telephone and mail orientation, and health, accident, and cancellation insurance. Most programs include room and board through home-stays. Volunteers in longer programs receive a monthly stipend. Volunteers are responsible for their own passport and visa fees as well as any personal expenses.

Typical volunteer responsibilities: Volunteers contribute agricultural labor and exchange ideas about different agricultural methods. Explorers, in addition, must assist in youth projects.

Number of volunteers sent abroad annually: 300

Age range: 15–24   **Typical age:** 21

How to apply: Applications for the World Experience in Agriculture are accepted year round. Applications to all other programs are due by March 1.

Stated mission: "To provide quality global education to teachers, students, and others through agriculture."

History: FFA, previously known as Future Farmers of America, has been one of the preeminent organizations promoting youth involvement with agriculture in the United States.

Flying Doctors/ Los Medicos Voladores

PO Box 445
Los Gatos, CA 95031

phone: 800-585-4LMV (toll-free in CA)
e-mail: info@flyingdocs.org
web: www.flyingdocs.org

You come back tired and hungry and say you're never going to do that again. And then you think of the people you helped and you say, OK, I'll go back one more time.—Bill Stover, volunteer, Mexico

Countries where volunteers are placed: Mexico, especially the states of Baja California and Sonora in northwest Mexico

Field(s) of work: Volunteers provide medical care to the people of rural Mexico. A team of three to four—one to two health professionals, a pilot, and a Spanish interpreter—are present on every trip.

Requirements or special skills necessary: Flying Doctors has positions for optometrists, dentists and dental assistants, hygienists, physicians, and other professionals in health-related fields. Pilots and Spanish interpreters are also needed. Physicians must be currently licensed by a U.S. state. Pilots must have at least 500 hours of PIC time and current FAA medical certification. All positions have specific requirements; prospective volunteers should check the Flying Doctors website for details.

Duration and dates: Trips generally last four days. Volunteers depart from northern California on Thursdays, typically the Thursday following the second Wednesday of every month. Friday is a full workday in the field and Saturday can be a full or half workday. Saturday evenings and Sunday mornings are free time for relaxation. Volunteers depart late morning on Sunday and usually return by late evening.

What volunteers pay and what they receive: Volunteers pay a $35 membership fee, a $200 flight fee, and incur an additional $50 to $100 in food and lodging expenses. Health professionals must bring their own medical supplies. Optometrists, for example, should bring their own eye charts. Flying Doctors owns, and is able to provide upon request, certain equipment, such as an auto-refractor, and also provides supplies such as approximately 120 pairs of eyeglasses for each trip staffed with an optometrist.

Typical volunteer responsibilities: Friday and Saturday, as mentioned, are workdays and volunteers are expected to work with the team leader to meet the goals of the trip. (See the observations and commentary for more information.)

Number of volunteers sent abroad annually: 150 (2000)

Age range: 18–84   **Typical age:** None

How to apply: All volunteers must first become members of the Flying Doctors by filling out a membership form and paying the $35 membership fee. They must also fill out a trip planning form, sign a liability waiver, and mail a $200 check to Flying Doctors. Space on trips is limited, so volunteers are encouraged to call or e-mail the trip coordinator at least one to two months in advance of departure.

The toll-free number listed above works in California only. For those outside California, even for California residents, Flying Doctors recommends email.

Flying Doctors recommends that members who live outside of Northern California plan to join trips in the good weather months of April through October, as winter trips can be canceled on short notice when storms blow through.

Stated mission: "The Flying Doctors sends medical teams on four-day trips to Mexico each month to provide health services and education to the people of northern Mexico. The Flying Doctors' long-term goal is to help villages in which we work become self-sufficient, so that they can provide their own medical, dental, and optical care."

History: Flying Doctors was founded in 1974.

Observations and commentary: Flying Doctors teams return each month to a number of clinics in Mexico. Teams only travel to already established clinics, although Flying Doctors is continually expanding into new regions and adding new villages to their list. Teams remain in one village for an entire weekend. Volunteers begin to work immediately upon arrival because their work time in the village is limited to two days. One volunteer described the work as grueling but rewarding. It is not unusual for a single medical volunteer to see as many as three dozen patients in a day.

Flying Doctors visits clinics in a number of villages south of Ensenada, in Baja California, such as Buena Vista, Chapultepec, and Maneadero. In Buena Vista the doctors have worked at both the local orphanage and the school that houses and serves several hundred students and approximately fifty orphans. Chapultepec has two well-equipped examining rooms and some supplies that the clinic allows the Flying Doctors to use to treat patients. While in Chapultepec, the doctors also visit the local elementary school. Six miles south of Chapultepec is the small town of Maneadero, which consists of several small encampments that house migrant farm workers, most of whom are indigenous peoples that have migrated to the area from Chiapas and other parts of Mexico to find work.

In October 2000, there was a tragic accident in which a plane operated by a Flying Doctors volunteer pilot and carrying five other volunteers went down near the town of Ensenada in Baja California. The volunteers were returning from a day of providing medical services in the town of St. Ignacio.

We believe that Flying Doctors is a well-organized program providing effective short-term services to impoverished Mexicans. Flying Doctors, however, does not seem to question why there is so much poverty among their clients, many of whom have fled rural Mexico to look for agribusiness jobs. We cannot help but observe that the policies of Mexico's elite-controlled government, as well as low wages paid by U.S. agribusiness, contribute to poor living conditions in northern Mexico. We therefore hope that long-time volunteers also become advocates to help create more justice in the lives of the people whose poverty they witness. We are also not sure of how well Flying Doctors is achieving its own mission of promoting self-sufficient villages.

Despite these caveats, we recommend Flying Doctors for professionals with the required experience and licenses who have a desire to donate their skills for a few days to provide medical services to impoverished communities in northwest Mexico.

Flying Samaritans

1203 E. Meda Ave.
Glendora, CA 91741

phone: 800-775-9018
fax: 626-914-1585
e-mail: caroljonmarco@hotmail.com
web: www.geocities.com/flyingsams/index.html

Countries where volunteers are placed: Mexico (Baja California)

Field(s) of work: Healthcare

Requirements or special skills necessary: Medical volunteers include doctors, nurses, chiropractors, physician's assistants, optometrists, and dentists. Non-medical volunteers include pilots, translators, and "general helpers."

Duration and dates: Most trips last two to three days

What volunteers pay and what they receive: Volunteers share the cost of travel and cover the cost of their own room and board. Flying Samaritans is an all-volunteer organization; there are no paid employees.

Typical volunteer responsibilities: Volunteers provide primary health care, specialty care, education, and emergency treatment at free clinics in underserved communities in Baja California.

Number of volunteers sent abroad annually: 2,400 (2000)

Age range: 18–80   **Typical Age:** N/A

How to apply: Call the toll-free number for an application or complete one on the website.

Stated mission: "The Flying Samaritans offer free medical assistance and education to people in rural areas of Mexico. Volunteers do not get involved with politics or religious issues in Mexico."

History: In 1961, a group of Californians were flying home from Baja. A windstorm forced an emergency landing in a Mexican village. The people of the village provided food and shelter. A medical doctor in the party had his bag with him; he treated some of the villagers, and the Flying Samaritans was born. Currently, the Flying Samaritans has nine chapters in California and Arizona, and clinics throughout Baja California.

Food for the Hungry

7729 E. Greenway Rd.
Scottsdale, AZ 85260

phone: 800-2-HUNGER
fax: 602-998-9448
e-mail: go_now@fh.org
web: www.fh.org

Countries where volunteers are placed: Twenty countries worldwide

Field(s) of work: Evangelism in combination with childcare, construction, emergency relief, agriculture, computers, education, and business management

Requirements or special skills necessary: Volunteers must be Christians who are committed to "submitting their lives to the Lordship of Christ" and evangelism. Participants in mission teams do not need any special skills, although construction skills would be helpful. Intern requirements vary. Hunger Corps volunteers must have a career "motivated by Christ's love" and must feel "called by God" to help the Food for the Hungry mission. Hunger Corps placements have other specific requirements, such as experience in curriculum designs, agronomy, or medicine.

Duration and dates: "Missionary team" projects last for about two weeks. Internships last one to six months. "Hunger Corps" positions last three to four years. Start dates vary.

What volunteers pay and what they receive: Volunteers must fundraise to cover their expenses. Most volunteers get financial support from their church, friends, and families making monthly donations. Living expenses vary widely ($25 to $1,600 per month).

Hunger Corps members receive a six-week training in Colorado before placement. Mission team members pay $35 to $45 each per day for room and board; airfare is not covered. Construction project team members pay an additional $200 to $300. Some intercultural training is provided, as well as pre-departure advice on health and logistics.

Typical volunteer responsibilities: All volunteers participate in evangelism. Mission teams usually work on construction projects. Most interns work with youth at a neighborhood ministry in Phoenix, Arizona. Tasks of Hunger Corps volunteers vary widely, but may include social work, agricultural development, office management, or pastoral service.

Number of volunteers sent abroad annually: 500 (Mission teams); 5–10 (Interns); 25–30 (Hunger Corps) (2001)

Age range: 18–adult (Mission teams)   **Typical age:** 25–35
18+ (Interns)
21+ (Hunger Corps)

How to apply: Fill out the online application or call headquarters.

Stated mission: "Motivated by Christ's love, the international partnership of Food for the Hungry exists to meet both physical and spiritual hungers of the poor."

History: Larry Ward founded Food for the Hungry in 1971.

Observations and Commentary: Food for the Hungry (FH) is best understood not as a volunteer placement organization, but as an evangelical organization with a volunteer component. We recognize that all development organizations promote their worldview, but we find the effort to change peoples' religion to be particularly intrusive. We are troubled by the implication in FH materials that non-Christians live in "spiritual darkness and bondage." We also noted that FH gets part of its funding from child sponsorship, a controversial form of fund-raising that frequently contributes to paternalistic ideas about people overseas.

We also observed positive aspects of the program. FH is upfront about its mission and the challenges of working in the field. FH assignments were substantial: treating patients in a refugee camp, working in an orphanage with HIV-positive children, and helping communities drill wells. (Wells sometimes have undesirable environmental impacts, but we were not able to research the details of the FH program.)

Hunger Corps members raise their own monthly stipends from donations from their home communities. One volunteer reportedly subsisted on $25 a month; yet a couple in Kenya lived in a gated community in a beautiful apartment that seemed more like the lifestyle of a United States suburb than that of an African capital.

We hesitate to recommend FH as a volunteer program because of our concern about the organization's development approach and emphasis on proselytizing.

FUNDECI

Apartado Postal 2694
Managua, Nicaragua

phone: 011-505-266-4373
fax: 011-505-266-3381
e-mail: fundeci@ibw.com.ni
web: www.fundeci.org

I chose FUNDECI because of their focus on human rights issues. I wanted to help in community development rather than just teaching English.—Diana Bernal, volunteer, Nicaragua

Countries where volunteers are placed: Nicaragua

Field(s) of work: Community organizing activities in the fields of agriculture, carpentry, education, legal aid, leadership training, political delegation, public health, youth development, and women's issues

Requirements or skills necessary: FUNDECI seeks professionals with technical skills in hydrology, engineering, architecture, and planning, and at least intermediate Spanish skills. FUNDECI also accepts generalists to support a wide range of projects. FUNDECI organizes several short-term brigades each year for carpenters and health-care workers; contact the organization for specific requirements.

Duration and dates: There is no limit to how long one can volunteer, but the average duration is three months. The duration of one's stay depends upon the type of work. Work in care-giving fields will require a longer stay, and academic work requires at least a semester-long commitment. FUNDECI realizes that it takes time to get acclimated to any kind of volunteer work and therefore encourages longer stays. Most FUNDECI projects operate year round, though some follow a specific schedule. Volunteers who work in the school system, for example, follow the academic schedule, which runs from March through November. One- to two-week brigades are offered four to five times per year.

What volunteers pay and what they receive: Volunteers pay for the cost of round-trip airfare, their visa, and other documents. Volunteers also pay a program fee of $300, which is due at least two weeks prior to arrival in Nicaragua. Monthly living expenses, including room and board with a Nicaraguan family, run a maximum of $400 a month.

Volunteers receive an on-site orientation to the FUNDECI program and to living in Nicaragua. They also receive transportation to and from the airport and to and from the job site during orientation. FUNDECI provides on-the-job support and an educational program that includes field trips to points of interest and reading material.

Typical volunteer responsibilities: Volunteers in the Social Action Program work in women's education, support for children and adults with disabilities, counseling, and youth education such as auto mechanic workshops. Volunteers in the Legal Aid program offer services to lower-income groups. Some volunteers assist FUNDECI in helping to strengthen grassroots community organizations through providing leadership training and organizational support. Other volunteers work in community kitchens, community preschools, or on reforestation projects in areas destroyed by Hurricane Mitch.

Number of volunteers sent abroad annually: 12 (2000)

Age range: twenties   **Typical age:** 25

How to apply: Prospective volunteers are encouraged to apply two to three months in advance of the desired date of departure. An application and resume (if possible, a resume translated into Spanish) are required. FUNDECI matches the skills, interests, and availability of volunteers with the needs of Nicaraguan host organizations. Placements are made with an appropriate Nicaraguan organization or with FUNDECI itself. Once placements are made, the office will notify volunteers and begin the process of arranging housing with Nicaraguan families, educational trips and meetings, and other services to facilitate the volunteers' travel and work.

Stated mission: "The mission of FUNDECI (The Nicaraguan Foundation for Integral Community Development) is to strengthen democracy at the local and national level through alternative development methods, which offer equitable and sustainable solutions to the problems of Nicaragua's poor, to contribute to the empowerment of community organizations through leadership training and organizational support, to promote development in Nicaragua based on the International Covenants of Economic, Social, and Cultural Rights as well as Civil and Political Rights, and to provide medical attention, legal advice, and material aid to disadvantaged communities in Managua and rural areas in western and northern Nicaragua."

History: FUNDECI was founded in the aftermath of the 1972 earthquake in Nicaragua. FUNDECI's original purpose was to help relieve the housing crisis that resulted from the earthquake. Since then, FUNDECI has grown from a small relief organization into a Nicaraguan non-governmental organization that works with grassroots community organizations to provide them with the technical knowledge necessary for the implementation of local development projects. In recent years, FUNDECI has been assisting in the aftermath of Hurricane Mitch, which ravaged the Central American coast in 1998.

Observations and commentary: FUNDECI, as a Nicaraguan NGO, is not geared exclusively toward the facilitation of volunteer service but welcomes the participation of foreign volunteers in a number of its programs.

FUNDECI operates many of its own programs, such as the Social Action program, which provides support for children and adults with disabilities, as well as educational programs for teenagers and young adults. FUNDECI has also been increasing its work with a number of partner organizations, such as Casa Materna and Casa de la Mujer. FUNDECI's programs, together with the projects of other Nicaraguan NGOs, provide volunteers with a cornucopia of work possibilities.

FUNDECI volunteers live with Nicaraguan families. At the inception of FUNDECI's volunteer program, homestays were in poorer communities. However, the dirt floors, outhouses, lack of running water, street crime, and number of people per household (i.e., a lack of private space) were an overwhelming culture shock to volunteers. Volunteers are now placed in middle-class households with fewer people and more modern conveniences such as running water.

Diana Bernal, a volunteer we interviewed after her return to the United States, said that being Latina and a fluent Spanish speaker improved her relationship with her homestay family. She was taken in as family and entrusted with the care of the daughters and cousins. "Most of the volunteers who work with FUNDECI," as one FUNDECI spokesperson told us, "are non-Latino because of the history of the solidarity movement, the cost of the program, and the lack of program promotion in Latino communities in the United States."

One strength of the volunteer program is that FUNDECI is experienced at placing volunteers in programs that fit their skills and personalities. A weakness is that it interviews volunteers by mail. This has resulted in FUNDECI choosing a couple of volunteers who proved to be people with emotional and psychological problems. We recommend that FUNDECI rethink its application process to screen out emotionally unstable people.

The strong historical presence of the solidarity movement in Nicaragua has had some negative impacts on local community development. Volunteer coordinator Carolina Espinoza Ruiz commented: "One of the problems is that Nicaraguan people have gotten used to getting handouts. They are used to seeing volunteers as money. We try to get them to see volunteers not as money but as professionals."

In Nicaraguan culture, people talk a great deal about politics. This can be especially educational for volunteers from a non-politicized culture like that of the United States.

In addition to its long-term programs, FUNDECI hosts short-term "brigades" of health professionals and carpenters who bring skills and supplies to Nicaragua and work on one- to two-week projects. There are four to five of these "brigades" every year, each with fifteen to twenty volunteers. There are at times collaborations between the long- and short-term programs. Diana Bernal, for example, provided translation assistance for a delegation.

FUNDECI provides a good opportunity for volunteers to learn about community development and work in solidarity with the people of Nicaragua—a solidarity that goes beyond the mere provision of material aid.

Global Citizens Network (GCN)

130 Howell St.
St. Paul, MN 55104

phone: 800-644-9292
phone: 651-644-0960
e-mail: gcn@mtn.org
web: www.globalcitizens.org

Countries where volunteers are placed: Guatemala, Kenya, Nepal, and Arizona, New Mexico, and South Dakota in the United States

Field(s) of work: Agriculture, conservation, community development, community organizing, construction, teaching/tutoring

Requirements or skills necessary: No specific skills are required, only a willingness to serve and an ability to accept and appreciate other cultures. Some projects are open to families and couples; participants under the age of 18 must be accompanied by a parent or guardian.

Duration and dates: GCN programs last one to three weeks. Trips are ongoing throughout the year, with visits to each site about two to three times a year.

What volunteers pay and what they receive: The program fee, which ranges from $650 to $1,650, covers room and board, informational material prior to departure for the host country, in-country orientation and staff support, outings in the project region, and a debriefing prior to the return home. Airfare is not covered. Volunteers stay with host families or live with other volunteers at community centers. Most trip-related costs are tax deductible for U.S. citizens.

Typical volunteer responsibilities: Volunteers assist local residents on locally initiated projects such as building a health clinic, planting trees, or renovating a youth center. Volunteers also make visits to the homes of local families, take tours of local farms or factories, and go on hikes in the surrounding area. Volunteers participate in local life and eat communally with other volunteers and the local people.

Number of volunteers sent abroad annually: 150 (2000)

Age range: All ages are welcome.   **Typical age:** None

How to apply: Prospective volunteers should contact headquarters for an application. The application process typically takes two months.

Stated mission: "Global Citizens Network seeks to create a network of people who are committed to the shared values of peace, justice, tolerance, cross-cultural understanding, and global cooperation; to the preservation of indigenous cultures, traditions, and ecology; and to the enhancement of the quality of life around the world."

History: GCN was founded 1992 by a group of volunteers, many of whom had participated in Global Volunteers programs, and has grown to include two part-time staff and a network of trip leaders who are previous GCN participants.

Global Routes

1814 Seventh St., Suite A
Berkeley, CA 94710

phone: 510-848-4800
fax: 510-848-4801
e-mail: mail@globalroutes.org
web: www.globalroutes.org

Global Routes gave me complete immersion into the culture. I lived with a host family, went to the market and church with them on Sundays, helped in the fields and the kitchen, taught elementary school Monday through Friday, and taught adult English classes four nights a week.—Danielle Reese, volunteer, Ecuador

Countries where volunteers are placed: High school programs are in Belize, Costa Rica, Dominican Republic, Ecuador, Ghana, Kenya, Nepal, St. Lucia, Thailand, and Vietnam. College programs are in Costa Rica, Ecuador, Ghana, India, Kenya, Navajo Nation, and Thailand.

Field(s) of work: Primarily teaching and community service

Requirements or special skills necessary: Programs in Latin America require a background in Spanish for high school students and proficiency in Spanish for the college program. College program participants must be at least seventeen years old and have finished high school.

Duration and dates: High school summer programs last one and a half to two months, and college programs from ten weeks to three months, with start dates year round.

What volunteers pay and what they receive: High school volunteers pay a program fee of $3,300 to $4,300 (depending on program); college program volunteers pay $3,950 to $4,250. Fees cover room and board, travel while overseas, in-country orientation, and support from a group leader. The fee also covers adventure activities such as river rafting and trekking. Volunteers are responsible for their own airfare to the host country. Global Routes offers a few partial and full scholarships, with at least one significant scholarship in each group. Volunteers are encouraged (but not required) to raise an additional $300 to finance a secondary project. College credit may be available.

Typical volunteer responsibilities: College-age volunteers in the college program teach English and other topics like environmental issues independently in a village school. High school volunteers work together in a group to build a school, community meeting house, or clinic. All volunteers also have a chance to initiate a small secondary project like painting a mural and fixing desks at a school or expanding a village water system.

Number of volunteers sent abroad annually: 350 (2001)

Age range: 14–17 (high school program)   **Typical age:** 16 (high school program)
18–27 (college program)   19 (college program)

How to apply: Global Routes requires a written application, a letter of reference, a phone interview, and a physical exam/waiver. Applications have been processed in as little as thirty days but should be submitted up to five months prior to the start of the program.

Stated mission: "As peoples of the world become increasingly interdependent we must all recognize that we live in a global community. The future of this community depends upon our self-knowledge as well as upon mutual understanding and respect among diverse cultures. Global Routes deepens these roots of our shared community as we foster personal and international development. By giving North American youth and their hosts the opportunity to push past stereotypes and misconceptions to build strong relationships, self-understanding, as well as buildings, we help our global community to flourish."

History: Before founding Global Routes, Kenneth Hahn and Andrew Rivin worked as co-directors of Interlocken, an organization specializing in adventure travel in the United States and abroad for high school youth. After designing numerous programs for Interlocken, they founded Global Routes as a nonprofit organization that could focus exclusively on trips for high school and college students that incorporated community service. Global Routes led its first community service trip for high school students to Kenya in 1986.

Observations and commentary: High school volunteers travel to their destination country with a group of about seventeen participants and accompanied by a group leader. College volunteers travel independently, meeting their group leader and the other four to fourteen volunteers at their destination.

In the high school program all of the participants usually live in the same village where they are working on a construction project. In the college program volunteers are placed in clusters of villages surrounding a larger town. Typically two volunteers are placed with different families in a single village and they teach in schools in and around their homes. According to Carole Lester, a college group leader in Kenya, "Anyone can get a ticket and go to a country to travel, but the most amazing part of being in Kenya with Global Routes is staying with a family. Being part of the community is irreplaceable."

Volunteers agree that there is a high level of staff support in all of the programs. Whether visiting volunteers at their home-stays, accompanying them to seek medical attention at a local hospital, advising them about teaching, or communicating with local officials, the group leaders are "on the job 24/7." Each high school group has two leaders, and each college group has at least one. Group leaders participate in staff training in Berkeley before the program starts and usually travel to the local community ahead of the other volunteers in order to finalize arrangements. Group leaders also arrange the living and working placements for each individual volunteer. Jen Friedman, a volunteer in Ecuador, thought that "Global Routes delivered on matching our interests and priorities" with appropriate housing and work assignments. Many of the group leaders we met had led numerous Global Routes trips, both high school and college and in a variety of countries.

As one high school participant said, "This program is not just about community service. The group is a big part of it." This is especially true for the high school program, but it also applies to the college program. College volunteers have some independence, but also receive a lot of supervision. The group leader organizes trips, meetings, discussions, and informal gatherings each weekend to give people a chance to come together and bond as a group. As Colin Wood explained, "With Global Routes you can have as little or as much group interaction as you want." But not all volunteers agree. Commenting on the group experience and staff support Karina Ostoich wrote, "The staff was excellent. Although the support was comforting, there was almost too much supervision for me. . . . If you already have experience in travel, teaching, and living on your own I would suggest a program where you have more freedom."

Group leaders organize the in-country briefing for new volunteers. Participants get to know one another while receiving an introduction to the country, its culture, and environment, as well as some language instruction. Participants also have a chance to discuss strategies for establishing themselves in the communities where they are to be placed. College-age volunteers come away with teaching ideas and lesson plans for their first week of classes. While the briefings received generally high marks, there were some instances in which they came up short. Learning about the vegetation, agriculture, and environment of the high mountainous region of Ecuador did the volunteers little good when they went to their villages in the coastal lowlands. Receiving an introduction to Ecuadorian politics from a North American who worked for the World Bank gave volunteers a much more limited perspective than might have been the case if there had been greater local participation such as a presentation by an Ecuadorian national with a more community-based perspective. And, while Global Routes has made a significant commitment to diversity through scholarships, it could do more to facilitate exchange of ideas, perspectives, and experiences among a more heterogeneous group of volunteers.

The ability of Global Routes to identify and sustain relationships with local allies is impressive. In both Costa Rica and Kenya we met local people who had been working with Global Routes for more than a decade. These relationships give the Global Routes staff reliable insight into the communities and appropriate locations and activities for their programs.

High school groups work primarily on construction projects. The students generally do menial labor while local laborers do the more technical tasks. Unlike many other programs, Global Routes not only brings the human resources to the communities to help complete projects, but it also commits financial resources to these projects. This means that schools and clinics can be built in isolated and impoverished communities. It also means that Global Routes can have a dramatic impact on local politics and social relations.

Another aspect of the Global Routes program is a secondary project. Volunteers organize a small project in the community where they are living or working. Secondary projects we saw included expansion of a village water system, renovation of a classroom, painting murals, establishing a library, building a teacher's house adjacent to a school, and working with a women's group. While secondary projects need not be "bricks and mortar" projects, usually they do involve a financial contribution from the volunteers. Global Routes gives volunteers the option of raising funds before they leave the United States with the target being about $300 for a secondary project. Volunteers who exceed the fundraising target often choose to share funds with volunteers who have fewer funds for their secondary projects. Group leaders and local contacts provide guidance in the implementation of the secondary projects, but they require significant initiative from the volunteers. While funding a project can be beneficial to the community it can also cause friction among competing interests. Secondary projects are not always easy to implement and challenge volunteers to reflect on their role in the community as well as different philosophies of community development. It's not uncommon for volunteers to find themselves with a lack of knowledge and experience necessary to develop their secondary project. In one instance we sat in on a meeting of one of the high school groups that was attempting to decide what to do with the funds it had raised above and beyond the costs of constructing the school, their primary project. The discussion of where to invest was educational for the students, but with limited language ability and only several weeks living in the area, they had only a superficial sense of the community's needs and their discussion seemed to take place in a vacuum. While group leaders provide support in this process of selecting and implementing a secondary project, more guidance from them and greater input from the community would help insure that the projects truly meet community needs.

Global Routes programs also include an adventure travel component, typically at the end of the trip. This is an opportunity for volunteers to see other areas of the country outside of their villages and towns. Some volunteers felt in retrospect that, because of the limited time of the program, the week of travel would have been better spent in their own villages and continuing their work there. Volunteers who were clear that their priority was to learn and make a contribution to community development felt that the "resort-style" adventure travel did not fit well with the rest of the program. Other volunteers enjoyed the trips and appreciated having the informal time to talk with other volunteers about their village stay. For many, the travel served as a debriefing period, which lessened the reverse culture shock of returning home.

Overall, we recommend Global Routes to would-be volunteers ages eighteen to twenty-seven who want to experience living with a family and teaching in a rural village. If you want the security of staff support and a well-run program along with some independence to create your own experience and initiate a secondary project, then Global Routes might be right for you. We also recommend Global Routes for high school students who are excited about volunteering in a group and working on construction projects in rural areas.

The goal of Global Routes is to create a safe environment where students can challenge themselves and learn. The students' goal is to make a difference in the community and grow themselves.—Carole Lester, college group leader, Kenya

Global Service Corps (GSC)

Earth Island Institute
300 Broadway, Suite 28
San Francisco, CA 94133-3312

phone: 415-788-3666, x-128
fax: 415-788-7324
e-mail: gsc@earthisland.org
web: www.globalservicecorps.org

As a GSC participant, I lived with a Costa Rican family on a farm. I worked on trails, did light construction work, and taught English in the local kindergarten and elementary school.—Paul Englander, participant, Costa Rica

Countries where volunteers are placed: Costa Rica, Tanzania, and Thailand

Field(s) of work: GSC provides short- and long-term placements in health, education, national park maintenance, and sustainable agriculture.

Requirements or special skills necessary: Volunteers must be twenty years of age or older. Specific skills are useful but not required. Children under the age of 18 can participate if accompanied by an adult. Married as well as unmarried couples are accepted.

Duration and dates: Short-term programs, lasting from seventeen to twenty-seven days, depending on the country, start at various times throughout the year. Long-term placements, for those interested, take place after the completion of a short-term program.

What volunteers pay and what volunteers receive: Short-term programs cost $1,795 to $1,995, depending on the country and length of placement. Long-term placements require prior paid participation in a short-term program. Long-term participants must also pay $595 for each month of a long-term placement. In addition to these fees, all participants must pay airfare to the host country and insurance. Participant fees cover airport pick-up, accommodations (usually a home-stay), meals, in-country transportation, and a sightseeing excursion. College credit is available.

Typical volunteer responsibilities: Preparing and giving an HIV/AIDS presentation in a school, clearing trails in a rain forest preserve, helping women's groups develop community projects, teaching English to a class of fourth grade pupils, doing inventory and writing up in English biographies of artisans in a women's cooperative craft shop, and harvesting coffee.

Number of volunteers sent abroad annually: 114 (2000)

Age range: 20–72   **Typical age:** 25

How to apply: Potential participants must fill a short application form and return it to GSC, together with a $300 deposit. For those desiring a long-term placement, a resume or curriculum vitae must also be included, by e-mail if possible. Once this is received, GSC will send more thorough application materials. For short-term projects that still have space available, acceptance is "automatic." For long-term volunteers, GSC will attempt to find a placement based on the applicant's wishes and skills. Once a placement is found, GSC will inform the applicant, at which time the applicant can either accept or decline the placement. For short-term volunteers, all forms and deposits must be returned to GSC at least sixty days before the departure date. For long-term placement, the deadline is ninety days before the desired departure date.

Stated mission: "GSC seeks to create opportunities for adult volunteers to live in developing countries and work on projects that serve Earth's people and her environment."

History: Programs in Costa Rica began in late 1993, Kenya in 1994, Thailand in 1995, and Tanzania in 2001 (replacing Kenya). In 1995, GSC became a project of Earth Island Institute, an umbrella organization that sponsors more than thirty environmental and social projects. In 1999, San Francisco State University began offering credit for GSC programs.

Observations and commentary: At the time of our site visits to Costa Rica and Kenya (1999), it was apparent that the GSC program suffered from significant weaknesses. The GSC program was lacking, for the most part, in orientation, training, project selection, and, especially support of its volunteers in the field. Given that its volunteers, both short- and long-term, pay a substantial fee, these shortcomings were particularly glaring.

A few of the volunteers who participated only in short-term programs spoke more positively of their projects but the emphasis was on cultural exchange. Other short-term volunteers, however, complained about the lack of orientation, misleading information given by GSC, lack of support, and the price paid.

We were also taken aback by GSC's placement of short-term volunteers in Kenya. Volunteers there gave HIV/AIDS prevention talks in some rural schools. While HIV/AIDS is an extremely serious problem in Kenya, it has been abundantly demonstrated around the world that changes in intimate behavior have a chance of being undertaken only in the context of peer education. Is it not naïve to think that well-off young people from the United States are the "peers" of the rural Kenyan secondary school students whose "awareness" of sexuality and sexually transmitted infections they are going to "raise"? Perhaps GSC's young well-meaning volunteers are only a few years older than African rural high school students but the differences in culture (including gender norms) and life situations are glaring, and these are critical in changing sexual behavior. Moreover, effective HIV/AIDS/ sexuality work has long since moved beyond talks in schools to helping people develop "life skills" (self-esteem, assertiveness, negotiation skills, knowing whether it is appropriate to get tested, and so forth). To do this effectively takes a good amount of training, experience, and familiarity with the culture. The Kenya short-term volunteers had no training in HIV/AIDS prevention except for reading some brochures, and had no orientation on sexuality in Kenyan culture. As volunteer Natalya Marquand said, "The training we received was totally inadequate."

The GSC volunteers in Kenya we interviewed generally enjoyed the host family arrangement and the opportunity to learn about Kenyan culture. They did not, however, feel that their actual work was that effective.

Many long-term volunteers, all of whom first had to sign up for short-term programs, repeated the same complaints. Especially, given the sums they were paying, they were miffed that GSC headquarters was so unsupportive of them in the field that it wouldn't even respond to e-mails. Long-term volunteers we interviewed in Costa Rica concluded that they wound up appreciating their placements through the local host organization but felt that they could have come to the host country and directly organized their work through the host organization. Jen Sauber, a GSC volunteer working with the Family Life project of the Quaker-inspired Monte Verde Institute expressed frustration with GSC: "I like what I am doing here. But I could have gotten a flight to Costa Rica and taken a bus here and gotten off and walked into the Monte Verde Institute. I didn't need Global Service Corps."

Be aware that immediately before we were going to press GSC told us that they have improved their program in response to complaints of many past volunteers. While they did select and fax us three evaluations from satisfied volunteers, we, of course, did not have the time to do a more adequate sampling, let alone follow-up site visits. We did note that GSC now has an in-country coordinator in Costa Rica; that should help address the lack of support felt by the volunteers we interviewed there. GSC also informed us that they were in the process of shifting their work from Kenya to neighboring Tanzania. There the volunteers, under the auspices of the Catholic Church, will receive a three-day training on HIV/AIDS prior to doing "prevention education" in high schools. The Church's stance against condoms should make that work especially challenging. Moreover, we question the wisdom and the cost-effectiveness of sending young well-off Americans to educate impoverished African adolescents on sexual behavior.

As with every organization, we recommend that you ask for names of recent volunteers and contact them in order to seek out their views of the pros and cons of the organization's program. Given GSC's announced efforts to improve its program, this advice is particularly relevant.

I felt that Global Service Corps deceived us about where we were going and what we would be doing. Or we didn't ask enough questions. Global Service Corps should have said, Hey, this is not what you think. Challenge our fantasies. But they don't want to lose paying customers.—Jen Sauber, volunteer, Costa Rica

Global Volunteers

375 E. Little Canada Rd.
St. Paul, MN 55117

phone: 800-487-1074; 651-407-6100
fax: 651-482-0915
e-mail: e-mail@globalvolunteers.org
web: www.globalvolunteers.org

I liked the way that the program was organized. The hosts and other local people utilized us to the maximum. I also liked the fact that even though I was only in-country for two weeks, my work will be carried on by the next team, and the next, for years to come.—Ronald Kensey, volunteer, Kazakhstan, Poland, and Ukraine

Countries where volunteers are placed: China, Cook Islands, Costa Rica, Ecuador, Ghana, Greece, India, Indonesia, Ireland, Italy, Jamaica, Mexico, Poland, Romania, Spain, Tanzania, Ukraine, the United States, and Vietnam

Field(s) of work: Volunteer teams work on short-term human and economic development projects.

Requirements or special skills necessary: No specific skills or languages are required unless you are working with specific health care or business programs. Teaching or construction experience is helpful in other projects.

Duration and dates: Programs last from ten days to three weeks; most volunteers stay two weeks. Programs are offered year round.

What volunteers pay and what they receive: Volunteers pay fees ranging from $450 to $2,395 depending on the length and location of the program. Fees include travel within the host community, housing, food, emergency evacuation insurance, in-country orientation, in-country support, project materials, and an experienced team leader. Volunteers pay for their own travel to the project site.

Typical volunteer responsibilities: Volunteers teach subjects such as English or business, or help to construct village water systems, group homes, or other community development projects.

Number of volunteers sent abroad annually: 1,500 (1998)

Age range: All ages   **Typical age:** 50+

How to apply: Volunteers must complete a written application and provide three character references. There is no formal interview requirement, but volunteers usually speak with Global Volunteers staff members via phone. If a volunteer has a particular health issue, he or she may need to supply a letter from a physician. Applications can be processed in as little as two weeks but we recommend that volunteers apply three months before their planned departure date.

Stated mission: "Global Volunteers strives to wage peace throughout the world by helping establish mutual understanding between people of diverse cultures. Global Volunteers sends teams of short-term volunteers of all ages to sites worldwide to work on development projects determined by community leaders to be important to the community's long-term development. Volunteers work alongside and under the direction of local people."

History: Burnham J. Philbrook founded Global Volunteers in 1984. The first volunteer projects focused on underserved rural areas in the "developing world." Over the past decade and a half Global Volunteers has expanded to work in emerging democracies and communities in the United States as well.

Observations and commentary: Global Volunteers is one of the most popular international volunteer options, especially for volunteers fifty and older. We met quite a few volunteers who decided that Global Volunteer trips are better than tourism, choosing regular volunteer vacations as an ongoing part of their lives. The regularity with which some volunteers participate in Global Volunteer programs is testament to their satisfaction.

Global Volunteers is well organized and, according to volunteers, provides its volunteers with "good pre-departure information." The volunteer placements are quite varied but often bring volunteers into relatively remote rural areas.

One of Global Volunteers' guiding principles is that volunteers are "servant learners." As one volunteer explained, volunteers give their labor and actively learn while they "work alongside people in host countries to accomplish something the local people deem worthwhile." Global Volunteers has a "one-to-one" policy—one local volunteer for each international volunteer—intended to guarantee local involvement in projects. In some cases, however, other work responsibilities have precluded extensive involvement of local people in the volunteer project. Sometimes local volunteers work on the project only a fraction of the time that the volunteers are there, and in one case we heard that local laborers were being paid. While the one-to-one policy is not strictly applied, it is reported to have been successful not only in keeping Global Volunteers focused on having local participation in projects but also in facilitating interaction between volunteers and local people.

Global Volunteers programs differ from country to country. In many cases volunteers serve with host organizations and in countries where Global Volunteers has been before. According to one volunteer, "Global Volunteers lets you know if it is the first time they are sending volunteers to a particular site." Local organizations such as schools, churches, government agencies, and a wide range of nonprofit organizations host each project. The level of support offered by local host organizations pleased most volunteers, but varied by project and country.

The Global Volunteers experience is a group experience. Teams live as a group in modest accommodations, work together during the day, and "spend a lot of time in group process meetings." Each group has a team leader. Leaders are typically former volunteers who have participated in a week-long leader training session. Leaders do not get paid but they have all of their costs covered. We heard many positive comments about group leaders including praise for their availability, language skills, and motivational influence. While most team leaders live in the United States, Global Volunteers has recently established some in-country coordinators who live abroad, coordinate with local groups, and then lead trips. Unlike some other organizations, leaders tend not to work side by side with volunteers, but act exclusively as coordinators and facilitators.

Global Volunteers has a policy of limiting gift giving to gifts of books and supplies to schools so as not to create feelings of favoritism or a "hand-out" mentality in the local community. We support this policy, but apparently it is not always followed, as we heard several complaints from volunteers who were upset by the extent of excessive gift giving to children by other volunteers on their trips.

We recommend Global Volunteers for older volunteers who seek a challenging but structured work environment. Global Volunteers will be a better fit for people who flourish in a team environment. Those who want a deep immersion experience and want to be the only foreigner working in a particular community should seek another program.

Habitat for Humanity International

121 Habitat St.
Americus, GA 31709

phone: 229-924-6935; 800-HABITAT
fax: 229-928-3655
e-mail: GVWC@habitat.org; IPP@habitat.org
web: www.habitat.org/gv/

A country with poverty like ours needs an institution like Habitat that helps people. It makes me proud to provide real help for families. To see the smile, the joy of a family as it receives a house—that is priceless.—Erwin Miranda, El Alto regional director, Bolivia

Countries where volunteers are placed: Armenia, Bolivia, Botswana, Brazil, Cambodia, Cameroon, China, Colombia, Costa Rica, El Salvador, England, Ethiopia, Fiji, Guatemala, Hungary, India, Jamaica, Malawi, Mexico, Nepal, New Zealand, Nicaragua, Papua New Guinea, Paraguay, the Philippines, Portugal, Romania, South Africa, Trinidad, Uganda, Venezuela, and Zambia

Field(s) of work: Construction and rehabilitation of houses

Requirements or skills necessary: Habitat offers two volunteer programs: the Global Volunteers (GVs) and the International Partners (IPs). Global Village (GV) volunteers must be at least eighteen years old. They are sometimes involved in strenuous manual labor, at times at high altitudes or in hot climates. GV volunteers donate time and money to the host affiliate. Unlike International Partners (IPs), GV volunteers are not required to have a specific faith commitment. Although it is not required, GV volunteers often sign up as an organized group from one church or community.

Strong applicants for IP positions will have a willingness to communicate and affirm the Christian roots and principles of Habitat; a bachelor's degree or its equivalent; experience living at least one year in another culture; a relevant second language and work or volunteer experience in areas such as resource development, community development, adult education/training, volunteer coordination, and finance. Skills in creative problem solving, group facilitation, and leadership are also helpful. Volunteers may be single or married, with or without children.

Duration and dates: Habitat's GV volunteers work for two to three weeks with teams of eight to fifteen volunteers. Prospective volunteers should request a schedule or check the website for availability of countries and programs. IP positions require a three-year commitment. Open positions are posted on the website.

What volunteers pay and what they receive: The cost of the GV program depends on the location of the project and the requests of the local Habitat affiliate. Approximate costs are $2,500 to $3,500 for Africa; $1,800 to $3,000 for Asia and South America; $1,200 to $1,800 for Central America and the Caribbean; and $1,800 to $2,000 for Europe. Fees include airfare, room and board, travel insurance, and a donation toward the construction cost of houses built in the host country.

Compensation for IPs includes a stipend of $425 per month, housing/utilities, health insurance, an allowance for dependent children, an education allowance for dependent children, relocation allowance, escrow account, pension plan, assistance with student loans, and other benefits.

Typical volunteer responsibilities: The Global Village (GV) program is a short-term international program with an educational focus. It helps to raise funds and construct houses in countries worldwide. When GV volunteers return to the United States they share their experiences by presenting slide shows, speaking at public events, and publishing articles.

International Partners (IPs) volunteer for three years, living and working in another country to help advance the work of Habitat for Humanity. They work in partnership with host country nationals to develop local skills, train others to carry out Habitat for Humanity's mission and support or manage programs. Responsibilities may include training, resource development, special event coordination, accounting, community development planning, and assessment.

Number of volunteers sent abroad annually: Approximately 4,000 GVs and approximately twenty IPs.

Age range: 18–80 **Typical age:** 30–40

How to apply: Prospective GV volunteers may apply individually or with a group from their home church or community. Applications may be requested from headquarters or downloaded from the website.

Prospective IPs are asked to submit a resume, cover letter, and answers to a set of application essay questions that can be found on the website. These documents should be sent to:

e-mail: IPP@hfhi.org

mail: 322 W. Lamar St., Americus, GA 31709

fax: 229-924-0641

Stated mission: "Habitat for Humanity International is a nonprofit, ecumenical Christian housing ministry. Habitat seeks to eliminate poverty housing and homelessness from the world, and to make decent shelter a matter of conscience and action."

History: Millard and Linda Fuller founded Habitat for Humanity in 1976. Since then, Habitat has constructed over 95,000 homes worldwide. The nearly 1,900 Habitat affiliates around the world, composed of local community members, are responsible for organizing the construction of new homes and the selection of new homeowners (those who are going to receive a home after it is constructed).

Observations and commentary: Habitat and its international affiliates provide partner families (families that are members of a local affiliate) with the opportunity to become homeowners. In the words of a Habitat brochure, "Habitat offers a hand-up not a hand-out." While Habitat homes are subsidized in a number of ways, partner families become homeowners by participating in the construction of both their own homes and the homes of other members of the affiliate, and by making payments on the mortgage of the homes they receive. Habitat makes homes affordable for partner families in four ways: the organization 1) sells homes at no profit with long-term interest-free mortgages; 2) solicits individuals, corporations, and faith groups to provide financial support; 3) provides free volunteer labor; and 4) organizes partner families to assist in the construction of their own home and the homes of others in the affiliate.

Habitat uses a revolving loan fund system. This means that when partner families repay their loans they are providing funds for other families to build homes. One Habitat volunteer, Paul Hamalian, told us, "It is true Habitat does not work with the poorest of the poor, but with the sector that has the ability to pay. If Habitat chose families that did not have the ability to pay and these families were forced to take money out of their family's food budget, Habitat would be doing them a disservice." Homeowners are chosen by the local affiliate according to their need, their ability to pay, and their willingness to work in partnership with Habitat and help Habitat in the construction of affiliate homes. "Most international affiliates," states a Habitat brochure, "operate in areas of the world where local financial resources are inadequate to meet the critical need for housing."

In Nicaragua, Habitat has had a problem with families not making payments on mortgages and a major reason is the presence of foreign volunteers on Habitat projects. This is one example of a situation in which, by their mere presence, well-intentioned volunteers can do more harm than good. Scarlett Palacios Miranda, administrator of Habitat Nicaragua told us, "I'll be frank with you and point out that Habitat Nicaragua is not very open to receiving short-term volunteers." Some people maintain that because foreign volunteers are often so nice and because Nicaraguans believe it is the volunteers who are funding the mortgages, the Nicaraguans think their new friends do not really expect them to repay the loans. We commend Habitat's policy that volunteers are not to give gifts to individuals because of the disruptive role these gifts can play. Volunteer teams can, however, make collective gifts to the communities in which they work.

Habitat is a faith-based organization that requires IPs to sign a statement of faith that says they agree to participate in a faith community and express their faith in mutual respect. Volunteers we spoke with, however, said that discussions about faith come up mostly when describing and defining Habitat. A Habitat staff member told us that, "Habitat believes that to live a truly Christian life your actions have to show that you care about other people in the world." For most Habitat volunteers, this means that one expresses their faith through actions rather than words. Though Habitat is, as one volunteer told us, "unashamedly Christian," it is not a vehicle for religious proselytizing. Paul Hamalian, himself a graduate of an evangelical seminary said that, "If you are an evangelist, you should search for another volunteer program."

Habitat is well organized and demonstrates a unique and successful approach to reducing the amount of poverty housing in the world. If you meet the criteria for the GV or IP programs and are not turned off by the idea of working for a Christian organization, then Habitat may be an excellent choice for you.

> *In each of the fourteen African countries in which Habitat works, Habitat uses different building styles. We try to do what works locally. Each affiliate creates its own designs. In Zambia, for example, people build houses in a circle, whereas in Uganda they only provide roofs because the people build their own walls.—Kirt Firnhaber, IP volunteer, South Africa*

> *Habitat does not want groups to come for more than a few weeks because their visits are too disruptive to the host community. At the same time, it causes great enthusiasm when GV volunteers come to work; it inspires more locals to get involved.—Shadrack Mulembi, national partner, Kenya*

In the big scheme of Habitat, volunteers serve a couple of different purposes: their presence adds an element of cultural exchange and is also a significant means of fundraising.—Doug Dahlgren, regional representative, Hungary

It's a good experience for families. Our kids are growing up understanding different points of view, and they have the advantage of being bilingual.—Nancy Hamilian, IP volunteer, Ecuador

---

Health Volunteers Overseas (HVO)

PO Box 65157
Washington, DC 20035-5157

phone: **202-296-0928**
fax: **202-296-8018**
e-mail: hvo@aol.com
web: **www.hvousa.org**

HVO provides good communication, good support, good office infrastructure. I enjoyed the satisfaction of returning to the site of my previous work, being welcomed, and finding that the impact of the work continues.—volunteer, Uganda, South Africa, and Guyana

Countries where volunteers are placed: Bangladesh, Belize, Bhutan, Brazil, Cambodia, El Salvador, Ethiopia, Guyana, Haiti, India, Indonesia, Jamaica, Kenya, Malawi, Nepal, Peru, the Philippines, St. Lucia, South Africa, Tanzania, Uganda, Vietnam, and Zimbabwe

Field(s) of work: Training local health care providers, including doctors, dentists, nurses, physical therapists, and medical/nursing and other students

Requirements or special skills necessary: Volunteers must be licensed (in the United States or Canada) health professionals such as MDs, nurses, dentists, physicians' assistants, or physical therapists. Teaching experience is beneficial, but not required.

Duration and dates: Most HVO programs require a minimum service of one month; some, however, require only two weeks. Some volunteers stay longer, up to one year. Assignments are available year round.

What volunteers pay and what they receive: Volunteers cover their travel to and from the program site. Most sites provide free room and board; those that don't usually charge $10/day. Volunteers also cover health insurance and incidental costs.

HVO provides written orientation materials. Volunteers keep track of their expenses, and HVO sends a letter of acknowledgment, certifying that expenses are tax deductible.

Typical volunteer responsibilities: Volunteers lecture, conduct rounds, and demonstrate medical techniques in classrooms, clinics, and operating rooms.

Number of volunteers sent abroad annually: 350 (2000)

Age Range: 30–80   **Typical age:** None

How to apply: Become a member of HVO, then fill out a volunteer profile form. Suggested donation for membership is $100 for doctors and dentists and $50 for nurses and allied health professionals.

Stated mission: "HVO is dedicated to improving the quality and availability of health care in developing countries through education."

History: HVOs predecessor, Orthopedics Overseas, was founded by a small group of doctors in 1959. In 1986, HVO was founded as an umbrella organization with Orthopedics Overseas as the largest division, and has grown to include divisions for the following specialties: dentistry, general surgery, internal medicine, nursing, anesthesia, oral and maxillofacial surgery, pediatrics, and physical therapy.

Observations and commentary: HVO appears to be a well-managed, effective organization. HVO makes a clear distinction between its work, which emphasizes training people and building local capacity, and other programs that emphasize emergency relief and direct treatment. The emphasis on building capacity is part of what makes its work so effective.

The emphasis on sustainability is evident in HVO's excellent pre-departure booklet, "A Guide to Volunteering Overseas." The booklet includes information on appropriate technology, suggestions on how to teach, contact numbers for insurance, fundraising tips, discussion of HIV prevention, and a checklist for preparation. Potential volunteers receive telephone numbers of past volunteers. Orientation also includes discussions with the U.S.-based country program director, who briefs volunteers on issues relating to their specialties, pathology, equipment, and details of what their role will be.

Once overseas, most volunteers live in compounds and teach doctors, nurses, and medical students at local hospitals with which HVO has ongoing partnerships. Because they are teaching, volunteers do not always attend to patients directly. Our site visits, however, showed that the volunteers do have an impact on the quality of health care in the long term. HVO volunteers have built up the capacity of local practitioners through training and education. As Dr. Raibin Chacko, a host to HVO volunteers in India, explained, "HVO volunteers can help to debunk the high-tech hype. An experienced practitioner can help us to avoid wasting our limited resources by giving us a realistic picture of them and helping us judge and discern new advances." In addition, HVO volunteers have facilitated donations of medical equipment and expanded existing facilities. At the Christian Medical College in India, dental volunteers have helped local practitioners start a dental assistant program that uses donated books, videos, and a video player. In Uganda, they inspired local doctors to start their own volunteer program to reach underserved rural areas.

Overall, we found volunteers to be highly satisfied with their placements. According to Dr. David Francisco, who volunteered in South Africa, "HVO provides very good insight into Third World medicine." The volunteers' biggest frustration was the sometimes rudimentary conditions of the hospitals and clinics where they worked.

HVO encourages returned volunteers to make presentations at conferences and hospitals. The organization also involves past volunteers as recruiters for future volunteers. Their newsletter, "The Volunteer Connection," features articles by and about volunteers and is sent to alumni as well as potential volunteers. This newsletter helps potential volunteers picture what volunteering is like. HVO also seems to have a relatively high number of repeat volunteers.

Overall, we found HVO to be one of the best organized programs that we researched, with remarkable local hosts (mostly local doctors, some of whom have studied in the United States). The main disadvantage to HVO is that volunteers have to pay all of their travel and out-of-pocket expenses. They are, however, tax deductible. HVO keeps other costs down by relying on a network of volunteers in the United States to recruit and orient overseas volunteers. HVO does not accept health professionals still in training, which is an advantage for its overseas partners, but it is a disadvantage if you are a medical student.

The overseas partner organizations we spoke with appreciate the fact that most HVO volunteers are experienced practitioners. Some hosts liked the older volunteers the best because they were better able to function without all the high-tech machinery found in modern U.S. hospitals.

HVO could improve its program by involving volunteers more in international health care advocacy. For example, many orthopedic volunteers treat polio; HVO could inform returned volunteers of ways they can support worldwide vaccination efforts. While HVO does work with the same institutions over the years and sends volunteers back to the same sites, they could do more follow-up work and not rely exclusively on the local hosts for post-surgery work such as speech therapy after cleft palate surgery. HVO focuses on a curative rather than a preventative approach. We hope that in the future they will provide more opportunities for volunteers to work on prevention.

If you have experience as a health professional, an interest in teaching, sufficient funds for a plane ticket, and two weeks to one year available, we highly recommend HVO for your consideration.

Himalayan Explorers Club (HEC)

PO Box 3665
Boulder, CO 80307-3665

phone: 888-420-8822; 303-998-0101
fax: 303-998-1007
e-mail: info@hec.org
web: www.hec.org

Countries where volunteers are placed: Nepal

Field(s) of work: English language teaching

Requirements or special skills necessary: Prior experience camping and/or traveling in an underdeveloped country is encouraged. Volunteers who have not previously taught English are requested to complete twenty-five hours of training in ESL teaching before their departure for overseas.

Duration and dates: Programs last three months and operate twice a year. The spring program runs February through April and the fall program runs September through December. The fall semester extends into December because of a holiday break in the middle.

What volunteers pay and what they receive: A $1,000 program fee covers school supplies, assistance from a trained ESL teacher/trainer throughout the program, and an excellent volunteer manual geared toward foreign volunteers in Nepal; it does not include the home-stay or orientation costs. Volunteers are responsible for their own transportation costs to Nepal and should expect to spend approximately $1,000 on other costs such as visas, a local flight, language instruction, and the home-stay with a Sherpa family.

Typical volunteer responsibilities: Volunteers teach elementary school English classes six days a week, six hours a day.

Number of volunteers sent abroad annually: 25 (2000)

Age range: 22–69   **Typical age:** 22–35

How to apply: Contact the office for an application. You may request an answer sheet to frequently asked questions.

Stated mission: "The Himalayan Explorers Club is a nonprofit organization that seeks to promote a better understanding of and respect for the environment and culture of the Himalayan region." Volunteer Nepal Himalayan teachers "provide Sherpa students with exposure to native English speakers who will help to enable primary school children to learn basic English, thus stimulating their desire for an advanced education and increasing employment opportunities. Because teachers live in the villages with families, the community can learn first-hand about the pros and cons of Western culture, rather than being solely influenced by tourists."

History: The Himalayan Explorers Club was founded in 1996 in Boulder, Colorado, and later opened clubhouses in Kathmandu, Nepal, and Islamabad, Pakistan. The membership organization provides many different benefits to its members, including the Volunteer Nepal Himalayan Teaching Program, which was created by HEC to provide native English speaking teachers to schools in the Everest (Solu-Khumbu) region of Nepal. Pasang Sherpa, the Nepali coordinator, who earned his bachelor's degree in the United States in 1989, grew up herding yaks in the region, and helped HEC establish the program as a way to give back to his country.

Institute for Central American Development Studies (ICADS)

San José, Costa Rica
c/o Dept. 826, PO Box 025216
Miami, FL 33102-5216

phone: 011-506-225-0508
fax: 011-506-234-1337
e-mail: icads@netbox.com
web: www.icadscr.com

Countries where volunteers are placed: Costa Rica, Nicaragua, and Panama

Field(s) of work: ICADS offers intensive Spanish language training combined with volunteer community service opportunities. Volunteers are engaged in work and internships in the fields of environmental studies, women's studies, public health (people with disabilities, women, children), education, primary health care, English teaching, wildlife conservation, and animal shelters.

Requirements or special skills necessary: There are no prerequisites for the Spanish language training, offered on a month-to-month basis; training is for all levels of students from beginners to advanced. Particular volunteer placements, however, are related to the volunteer's language skills.

The semester internship and research program is open to undergraduates and students in between high school and college with at least one year of college Spanish (two years recommended), or three years of high school Spanish. Students in this program must also demonstrate a serious interest in the issues addressed by the program and possess a strong desire to participate in community service activities.

The summer internship program is open to students who, upon arrival, have a working knowledge of Spanish. No other previous work or study experience is required.

Duration and dates: ICADS offers three programs (with volunteer opportunities) of different duration:

The Spanish language immersion program is a four-week program that begins the first Monday of every month. The program includes four-and-a-half hours of daily instruction, five days a week, in a group setting of no more than four students. Students with adequate Spanish language proficiency may choose to participate in a group community service activity in addition to the scheduled afternoon fieldtrips and activities that the school offers. Students with more limited Spanish skills have the option of doing one community service activity per week.

The semester internship and research program is a full-semester program (fourteen weeks) that begins with intensive language training and specialized seminars and is followed by an eight-week supervised volunteer internship in Costa Rica, Nicaragua, or Panama.

The summer internship program is a non-credit ten-week volunteer internship program. The program includes sixty hours of intensive language training before students go into the field to begin an internship in either Costa Rica or Nicaragua.

What volunteers pay and what they receive: The $1,500 fee for the Spanish immersion program in Costa Rica covers the cost of all classes, books, room with partial board (breakfast and dinner), field trips, activities, afternoon lectures, internship placements, laundry service, and an airport pick-up.

The semester internship and research program fee of $7,200 covers the same services as the Spanish immersion program (but for fourteen weeks) and, in addition, includes structured academic onsite supervision, transportation to and from internship sites, site visits by ICADS staff, and a group trip to either Panama or Nicaragua. It also offers students the opportunity to choose among three countries for their eight-week internship experience: Costa Rica, Nicaragua, or Panama. The program is affiliated with Hampshire College in Amherst, Massachusetts. Students are granted fifteen semester hours of college credit for successful participation.

The summer internship program fee of $3,500 covers room, partial board, laundry service, and airport pick-up, as well as internship monitoring, consultations, language instruction, and all necessary transportation to and from works sites.

Volunteers are encouraged to budget $350 to $500 per month for personal travel and expenses. All volunteers receive a detailed guide to help them prepare for the trip (includes information on personal security, health, packing, cultural differences, etc.), an extensive orientation upon arrival, I.D. cards, and emergency telephone numbers. ICADS also provides storage facilities and free e-mail service, and will, at the volunteer's request, provide a list of faculty affiliations at colleges and universities in the United States as well as names and addresses of past ICADS students.

Typical volunteer responsibilities: ICADS has relationships with a large number of organizations in Costa Rica, Nicaragua, and Panama so there are many placements to choose from. Each placement, of course, has its own responsibilities. At Madres Adolescentes in San José, Costa Rica, a shelter for adolescent mothers (often victims of incest) that offers educational and vocational programs, volunteers assist with tutoring, teaching English, providing emotional support, or vocational training (e.g., handicrafts). At Niños Trabajadores de la Calle in Matagalpa, Nicaragua, volunteers participate in projects such as tutoring and helping to maintain this center for children forced to work in the street to support their families. In Panama, students may chose to volunteer at the Parque Nacional Marino Isla Bastimentos, established in 1988 as Panama's first nationally protected marine park. Located in Bocas del Toro, Panama, students can tag sea turtles, help with studies on coral reefs, or design environmental education projects with local school children.

Number of volunteers placed annually: Approximately 135

Age range: 17–70   **Typical age:** 28

How to apply: In order to enroll in the Spanish immersion program participants must send in an enrollment form and a $250 deposit at least one month before their date of arrival in the host country. Participants should apply two months in advance for the summer months and the month of January. Students may register online at ICADS's website.

Applications for the semester internship programs are due by May 1 (fall term) and November 1 (spring term). The summer program application deadline is April 1. Prospective volunteers should log on to the ICADS's website to apply or write to ICADS's Miami address for an application.

Stated mission: "ICADS, a nonprofit foundation, is a center for study, research, and analysis of Central American social and environmental issues. We focus on women's issues, economic development, environmental studies, public health, education, human rights, and wildlife conservation."

History: "ICADS was created in 1986 to fill the information gap in foreign policy between U.S. citizens and their government, promoting a deeper understanding of the Central American region."

Observations and commentary: In addition to our research visit to ICADS to check out some of their community service volunteer opportunities, one of us returned the following year for a month-long Spanish intensive course. Our observations, there-fore, are based on an exceptional amount of experience.

ICADS offers quite possibly the highest-quality Spanish language training in Latin America. ICADS is extraordinarily well managed. The staff seems strikingly well qualified, dedicated—and happy. The volunteer opportunities, both the short-term and internship ones, appear to be carefully selected.

All ICADS programs are presented so as to offer the participants opportunities to discuss and understand development issues in the Central American region.

For a combination of Spanish language training, community service opportuni-ties, and orientation in development issues, we could not more highly recommend ICADS.

Institute for International Cooperation and Development (IICD)

PO Box 520
Williamstown, MA 01267

phone: 413-458-9828
fax: 413-458-3323
e-mail: iicd@berkshire.net
web: www.iicd-volunteer.org

IICD is bizarre. In my group, we always wondered if we were joining a cult. I certainly think positive experiences can come out of IICD, but be wary! You are joining a precon-ceived way of being—the IICD person.—Tanya Pearlman, volunteer, Nicaragua

Countries where volunteers are placed: Angola, Brazil, El Salvador, India, Mozambique, Nicaragua, Zambia, and Zimbabwe

Field(s) of work: Fundraising and community health and education development projects, primarily in rural areas

Requirements or special skills necessary: Volunteers must be 18 or older. (You must be 18 by the time you go abroad, which means that you can begin the training at age 17 if you turn 18 by the time the project begins.) Married and unmarried couples are accepted into the program. No formal academic background or skills are required.

Duration and dates: Programs range from six to nineteen months. The typical length is one year. Programs begin in January, February, May, July, August, and No-vember. Most programs include several months of training in the United States, three months to a year overseas, and several months of follow-up upon return to the United States.

What volunteers pay and what they receive: Volunteers pay $3,800 to $5,500 for programs ranging from six months to over a year and a half. In addition, during the preparation period volunteers are required to fundraise up to $5,600 each by seeking donations. In some cases this can bring the total cost to over $10,000. The only additional out-of-pocket expense is health insurance for the training and follow-up period. The fees cover the training and follow-up periods, airfare, international health insurance, and room and board. Affiliated organizations in the host country provide housing and a weekly living allowance. Partial scholarships may be available. During the training period, volunteers live at the IICD residential campuses in rural Massachusets, Michigan, or California.

Typical volunteer responsibilities: Volunteers work on agricultural or environmental development projects, mobilize community members to improve sanitation and health, organize preschools and children's clubs, do research, and, upon return to the United States, educate North Americans about international issues. One volunteer described herself as a "community organizer, project motivator, liaison to agricultural agencies and prospective buyers, lease payment collector, basic health care administrator, and teacher *shamware* (the problem solver)."

Number of volunteers sent annually: 70 (1999)

Age range: 18–80   **Typical age:** 23

How to apply: Call or e-mail for a brochure and application form. Receipt of application will be followed by a phone or in-person interview.

Stated mission: "IICD promotes global understanding and solidarity through cross-cultural exchange and working hand in hand with peoples of different cultures to improve living conditions."

History: IICD was founded in 1986 by two Americans as part of a controversial Danish organization known as "Tvind." After approximately two years, Danish members of Tvind took over the operation of the school.

Observations and commentary: IICD is a strange and complex organization with some commendable ideas and a massively flawed program. IICD provides some positive examples that other groups can learn from and many examples of what not to do in the field.

The staff of IICD, including those who lead teams of volunteers, belong to an international collective known as the Teachers Group. Many ex-members and other critics consider the Teachers Group to be a cult. Indeed, the Teachers Group and its parent organization, Tvind, do have several characteristics of cults. Tvind is led by a charismatic and secretive Dane, Mogens Amdi Petersen, who is alleged to have fled Denmark to escape tax evasion charges. Members of the Tvind collective forgo personal income and personal time; everything belongs to the group.

As a Teachers' Group web site states: "The Joint Economy means that you will share your income and expenses with everyone in the Teachers Group. . . . The Joint Time means that together we determine the best use of our time, that is, what each of us should do. We want to ensure that we: valuable [sic] human resources, utilize our time and efforts in the best possible way. . . . The Joint Work means that we have a common responsibility for the work we do. Together we decide where and who to do what, and when. . . . You don't join the Teachers Group part time and with conditions. It is a full time commitment involving all parts of your life, day and night, work and leisure, private as well as common issues." "Full-time commitment" translates into frequent sleep deprivation, according to some ex-members of the Teachers Group, and "all parts of your life" includes your relationships and any pregnancies. All of the staff of IICD live under these rules, which ex-members say create a psychologically unhealthy environment wherein "group-think" and "peer pressure" replace critical thinking.

All three IICD sites are self-contained "campuses"; students don't have to go off-campus to get any of their needs met, except for fundraising (see below). Some argue that the living situation serves to isolate volunteers from friends, family, and the outside community, another characteristic of cults, according to experts.

Tvind is a multimillion dollar business that owns, among other things, a shipping company, according to a 1993 investigation by *The Guardian*. Ex-members of the Teachers Group in Europe have formed an international Movement Against Tvind and have created websites detailing what they consider to be the organization's abuses (www.netby.net/Syd/Andantevej/Movement AgainstTvind/ and www.tvindalert.org.uk). As we were going to press, the Danish police force conducted a raid on all Tvind offices in Denmark, alleging a variety of tax-related offenses. Essentially, the Danish government alleged that Tvind members claimed millions of dollars as tax writeoffs for "humanitarian" donations that the government said have gone to Tvind and to Tvind businesses.

The TvindAlert website argues that Tvind is primarily a moneymaking venture, earning income from volunteer programs, resale of secondhand clothes, and plantations in the developing world. Based on our firsthand experience with Tvind in Massachusetts, Zambia, and Zimbabwe, we are inclined to agree with this assessment.

Volunteers with IICD do not have to join the Teachers Group. Most are not even aware of the Teacher Group's affiliations, but they do have to follow some of the group's rules, including the rule that all their time is group time and the rule forbidding consumption of alcohol. Several volunteers told us that they were pressured to join the Teachers Group soon after signing up to volunteer. This tactic appears to be especially common on the California campus.

Despite the unusual affiliation, IICD has a program that makes sense on paper: the volunteer experience includes an extensive preparation period in the United States, several months working and traveling overseas, and a period of four to eight weeks during which participants return to share their experiences with others in the United States. Unfortunately, the reality of IICD is not as smooth as their brochures suggest. In fact, one group of former students filed a complaint against IICD for false advertising. Participant dissatisfaction with IICD often begins during the preparation stage, during which all the students must solicit donations from strangers on the streets of various East Coast cities. According to volunteer Sarah Troemel, "A lot of people drop out because of the fundraising since it is so difficult. I have sat down and cried on a street corner because no one would give me money." In another group, participants dropped out after discovering that the money they were raising went to construction at the IICD campus in Massachusetts, not to the projects in Africa and Latin America.

The actual volunteer experience can be equally frustrating. Most volunteers in Africa are placed with projects coordinated by Development Aid from People to People (DAPP), a Tvind program. DAPP projects are often closely linked to government programs and are rarely developed with a high level of local input or environmental consideration. DAPP's Zimbabwe program, for example, is training a small number of African farmers to qualify for the government's land reform program. This project, called "communal to commercial," encourages farmers to grow cotton, eucalyptus, and paprika as cash crops. DAPP's strategy is based on the government's promise of land redistribution and the hope for high prices for agricultural goods in the international market. The Zimbabwe government, however, has been promising land redistribution for twenty years without delivering on that promise, and with the instability of the Zimbabwean currency the farmers might find their profits decrease while the burden of loan repayment escalates. If DAPP's strategy backfires, the farmers and their families won't be able to eat the eucalyptus trees. In addition, the trees may have depleted the soil and lowered the water table, threatening the farmers' ability to switch back to crops that are the basis of their food security.

In Zambia, DAPP's development strategy did backfire. IICD volunteers worked with local farmers to plant fruit trees. After the volunteers left, DAPP fired all but six of the 160 Zambian workers on the project. Virtually all of the thousands of trees that they had planted died. The farmers who were counting on DAPP are now without the income or the fruit trees they had hoped would help feed their families.

Frequently, IICD students who experience the mismanagement of these programs drop out, forfeiting thousands of dollars. One volunteer team in Angola started their nine-month program with seventeen volunteers and ended with four. A Nicaragua program began with eighteen participants; not one remained for the full course.

IICD volunteers in Africa work in AIDS awareness clubs and in other projects intended to prevent the spread of AIDS. IICD says that almost all of its volunteers in Mozambique "can expect to be involved in AIDS prevention and education." We did not have the opportunity to observe IICD's HIV/AIDS projects. We do know, however, that, while HIV/AIDS is an extremely serious problem in much of sub-Saharan Africa, it has been repeatedly shown there and elsewhere that changes in intimate behavior have virtually no chance of being effectively promoted except in the context of education among peers. Yet, only the naïve could consider IICD volunteers "peers" of the Mozambicans they seek to "educate" about sexuality.

Many volunteers, even those with a critical perspective, also said positive things about their experiences. According to one volunteer, "Everyone had an exceptional experience of living with a family in a tiny Sandinista town in Nicaragua." Molly Dowling, an IICD volunteer in Zimbabwe, said, "I'm immersed in this awesome culture. Everything is beautiful. You look around and it's all gorgeous. Everything I see and everyone I talk to, I learn from." Participants in IICD's non-volunteer travel programs often agree with Debra Farkas that "despite challenging group dynamics and frequent disagreements with our leader, the program offered us an incredible learning experience, which opened our eyes to the impact of U.S. foreign policy and militarism." Some claim, however, that these positive experiences occurred not because of IICD, but in spite of IICD. Those volunteers who stick with the program are frequently those who are determined to make the best of a bad situation.

One participant we know cancelled his check to IICD when he found out about Tvind. Others stuck with the program long enough to get to Africa, then created independent volunteer activities. (See Chapter 6, "Doing it without a Program.")

Prospective IICD volunteers should ask themselves what is the potential damage to the communities where they will work, and whether it is worth the benefits they will receive. Since you can volunteer overseas with a more reputable organization, why join IICD?

Despite the problems with DAPP, IICD has two program elements that other volunteer placement organizations could learn from:

- *IICD has one of the few structured post-volunteer programs in existence. Volunteers who complete the program travel around the United States sharing information with a wide range of people, from elementary school children to Congresspeople, from Rotary Club members to prisoners.*

- *IICD sends volunteers to Angola and Mozambique. It is very important for North Americans to learn about these countries, which have been greatly impacted by U.S. foreign policy but are off the map of most volunteer programs.*

Overall, IICD is an organization to be avoided.

The fundraising was one of the most awful things I've ever had to do.—Molly Dowling, volunteer, Zimbabwe

Sometimes I feel that they [IICD's partner groups in Zimbabwe] want to grow so fast; they just want to have more students and are not really looking at what do they want the students to learn. It's like they're running and they don't have the ball.—Sara Troemel, volunteer, Brazil and Zimbabwe

It's been complete disorganization. When I arrived I was in culture shock city. But there was no one here telling me what to do. The two people I am here with were completely unsupportive.—Jennifer Comeley, volunteer, Zimbabwe

International Executive Service Corps (IESC)

333 Ludlow St.
PO Box 10005
Stamford, CT 06904-2005

phone: 203-967-6000
fax: 203-324-2531
e-mail: iesc@iesc.org
web: www.iesc.org

IESC gave me the chance to help emerging companies and entrepreneurs in a country moving from state control to private enterprise. It was a wonderful experience to partic-ipate in one of the great events of our time: the transition of the ex-Soviet bloc to democracy. I recommend it to anyone with real experience of value to the host company and the ability to communicate well.—Zvi Eiref, volunteer, Kazakhstan

Countries where volunteers are placed: Argentina, Armenia, Botswana, Brazil, Bulgaria, Chile, China, Columbia, Costa Rica, Côte d'Ivoire, Czech Republic, Ecuador, Egypt, El Salvador, Ghana, Jordan, Honduras, Hungary, India, Indonesia, Jamaica, Kazakhstan, Kenya, Lebanon, Madagascar, Mexico, Mongolia, Namibia, Panama, Paraguay, Peru, the Philippines, Poland, Romania, Rwanda, Senegal, South Africa, South Korea, Tanzania, Thailand, Tunisia, Turkey, Uganda, Ukraine, Uruguay, Venezuela, Zambia, and Zimbabwe

Field(s) of work: Consulting with businesses, government organizations, or non-profit organizations

Requirements or special skills necessary: Applicants must have extensive expe-rience as corporate managers, public administrators, information technology experts, association executives, business support organization executives, business owners, en-trepreneurs, or as professionals in other fields. Spouses of volunteers may join them on their placement.

Duration and dates: Assignments can be anywhere from two weeks to three months. Longer-term assignments are also available. Placements occur throughout the year.

What volunteers pay and what they receive: Volunteers incur virtually no out-of-pocket expenses. IESC covers passport and visa expenses, immunizations, airfare, health insurance, modest hotel accommodations, and a per diem to cover the cost of food and incidentals. Spouse's expenses are also covered if a project lasts a month or longer.

Typical volunteer responsibilities: Volunteers meet with business executives, government leaders, and NGOs. They analyze management and production problems, work with organizations to create plans for improving operations, and assist executives with the implementation of business development plans.

Number of volunteers sent abroad annually: 500 (2000)

Age range: 25–75   Typical age: 60

How to apply: Volunteers fill out a registration form online at the IESC website, www.iesc.org, which includes detailed questions about professional skills and experience, which is entered into a volunteer database. IESC contacts volunteers from their database as they receive requests, matching needs overseas with volunteers who possess the desired skills.

Stated mission: "The International Executive Service Corps is a private, voluntary, not-for-profit organization. Our mission is to contribute to global stability by assisting in the development of free-market economies and democratic societies. We provide expertise to strengthen private sector enterprises and government entities to enable self-sufficiency and participation in the worldwide economy. As a consequence, we also strengthen the U.S. economy through trade, investment, and alliances between overseas companies and American businesses."

History: IESC was founded in 1964 by a group of American business people, led by David Rockefeller, then president of Chase Manhattan Bank. The U.S. Agency for International Development (USAID) originally funded IESC and continues to be its primary financial sponsor.

Observations and commentary: IESC is a well-organized volunteer placement program, notable for its ability to recruit highly skilled volunteers for placements with for-profit businesses in countries worldwide.

IESC's mission is clear: it seeks to help overseas businesses compete in the global marketplace and to help countries make a transition to privatized market economies. IESC, as mentioned, recruits high-level volunteers, usually retired business people, to provide consulting services for foreign companies. The volunteer program focuses on providing human resources, but as one staff member explained, "Volunteers can take the initiative to bring other resources" such as identifying potential sources of investment.

IESC maintains a large database of potential volunteers and is usually able to match businesses with volunteers who have relevant industry expertise, such as manufacturing, agribusiness, chemical processing, or hotel and tourism management.

IESC's system for recruiting, screening, and placing volunteers gives them an edge over most other programs. Their placement is client-driven, that is, it is focused on the needs of the overseas company, not the needs of the volunteer. In fact, only 500 to 1,000 volunteers (out of 13,000 in the database) are placed each year.

Most volunteers seem to be satisfied with the support offered by IESC. The country directors, we were told, generally do a good job of welcoming and orienting the volunteers. The per diem stipends are sufficient to cover basic needs, and the hotel accommodations, while not luxurious, are adequate. Interpreters are available if needed. IESC also provides a per diem for the spouses of volunteers and can often find ways for them to be involved in volunteer work, such as teaching English at a local community center.

IESC does not, however, hold their volunteers' hands. R. Jerry Hargitt, who worked with IESC in Egypt, Barbados, Indonesia, and Manila, told us that, "You should not get involved in this if you need constant guidance or counsel. You must be a self-starter." Volunteer Conrad Peterson thought the IESC support staff were "well trained and motivated," but warned that some assignments are in the "boondocks where volunteers may be on their own."

The volunteer's specific work will depend on the assignment but will likely involve providing managerial advice and training to small, medium, or large business. Volunteers essentially serve as consultants helping upper-level managers improve their business performance by reducing costs, streamlining production, and developing new products. Some volunteers also help businesses identify sources of financing and new markets for their products. Zvi Eiref, for example, who volunteered in Kazakhstan, helped raise a $3.5 million loan for a local company from the European Development Bank. Others assist their clients in assessing important business decisions. In Ecuador, for example, a company was planning to purchase a $100,000 piece of machinery for their T-shirt and blouse manufacturing plant but changed its plans after working with an IESC volunteer. The staff of the business appreciated the assistance of the volunteer because he had helped them, as one staff member put it, "to achieve a twenty-five to thirty percent increase in production without purchasing new machines, saving $100,000."

In some ways, IESC provides a model for other volunteer placement organizations such as the Peace Corps. IESC recruits people with relevant experience, screens them carefully, and places them where their skills will be used most effectively. IESC evaluates the volunteer at the end of the placement and evaluates the project six months after completion. This careful placement and monitoring can result in what one volunteer called a "perfect" placement.

IESC does not, however, provide extensive cross-cultural training. Most volunteers do not learn the local language and therefore rely on translators for most of their communication with the local people. This limits their immersion into the local culture and makes cross-cultural understanding, one of the primary benefits of volunteering abroad, much more difficult. It also can lead to misunderstandings between the consultants and the staff of the businesses they consult with.

IESC has a reputation as a "man-to-man" volunteer program. The majority of volunteers are retired men, although in recent years IESC has begun to recruit a higher proportion of women.

Our main concern with IESC is the premise behind the organization's mission. IESC was founded during the Cold War with the express purpose of promoting private enterprise. IESC projects do seem to help the businesses that are its clients, but we question whether this form of assistance "trickles down" to help workers and other local people. IESC seeks to strengthen democracy, but in some countries where they work, business interests have undermined democracy rather than promoting it. In addition, some of the businesses they have helped, such as shrimp harvesting, have been known to engage in practices harmful to the environment. Our concern is exacerbated by the fact that in recent years, three of IESC's nine top executives were retired from oil companies with questionable environmental and human rights records overseas.

On the other hand, some volunteers share industrial environmental technology. In Ecuador, for example, one volunteer analyzed a plastic production facility, and made suggestions for how to recycle and filter water before emitting it into a local river.

Most of IESC's clients are middle-sized and large businesses that can afford the fees IESC charges its clients. Occasionally, the fees paid by large businesses subsidize work for small businesses that cannot afford the fees, such as small bakeries in Ecuador.

IESC has recently expanded its work to include opportunities for volunteers to serve as advisors to government agencies. We welcome this expansion of IESC's mission, since improved government efficiency can create better outcomes for local people. (We did not, however, have the opportunity to visit volunteers in this program and are therefore unable to comment on it.)

Overall, we recommend IESC to potential volunteers with extensive management experience, a belief in the "free market," and a desire to share their skills with the businesses and governments of "emerging democracies."

International Foundation for Education and Self-Help (IFESH)

5040 E. Shea Blvd.   phone: 480-443-1800
Suite 260   fax: 480-443-1824
Phoenix, AZ 85254-4687   e-mail: fellows@ifesh.org; teachers@ifesh.org
                            web: www.ifesh.org

This is an extraordinary experience because of the people I work with, like Owen, who was in exile for about twenty years. I feel like I'm part of an effort that is bigger than me.—Umi Howard, IFESH Fellow, South Africa

Countries where volunteers are placed: Benin, Ethiopia, Ghana, Guinea, Liberia, Malawi, Namibia, Nigeria, South Africa, and other countries in sub-Saharan Africa

Field(s) of work: Volunteers in the Teachers for Africa program: Teaching a wide variety of subjects, such as special education, English and ESL (including training of teachers of English and ESL), business, health, medicine, library science, computer science, mathematics, engineering, and sciences, as well as teacher training (e.g., curriculum development, pedagogy, methodology, planning, and administration).

International Fellows: Implementing health (including HIV/AIDS), education, agriculture, micro-finance, small-scale business development, and other types of community-based self-help projects; working on grant development and coordination; assisting with project administration and monitoring of development projects.

Requirements or special skills necessary: Volunteers in the Teachers for Africa program must be U.S. citizens or permanent residents in good health, and should have a college degree and at least three years teaching experience. French is required for placement in Benin or Guinea. IFESH specializes in placing people of color, especially African Americans, but all qualified individuals are encouraged to apply.

International Fellows must be U.S. citizens who are in their senior year of college, recently graduated, or enrolled in graduate school. They must be in good health and should possess excellent communications skills. Students with backgrounds in areas such as health, computer science, business administration, literacy, and education are particularly encouraged to apply.

Duration and dates: Teachers for Africa programs usually begin in late August or September (although a few positions begin in January) and last one academic year. The International Fellows program lasts nine months beginning in late August.

What volunteers pay and what they receive: IFESH covers most costs including pre-departure and in-country orientations, health/evacuation insurance, airfare to the host country, and visa and work permits. IFESH also provides allowances to help cover pre-departure and settling-in costs as well as a stipend of $800 per month. Housing is not always provided.

Typical volunteer responsibilities: Teachers for Africa are assigned to teach or advise at universities, colleges (especially colleges of education), government educational agencies, and secondary schools and occasionally primary schools in sub-Saharan Africa. IFESH International Fellows are assigned to work with various international organizations such as Africare, CARE, UNAIDS, Save the Children, UNICEF, and Opportunities Industrialization Centers International (OICI). Fellows work on a variety of development and community-based self-help activities in both urban and rural settings.

Number of volunteers sent abroad annually: 50

Age range: 25–70 (Teachers for Africa)   **Typical age:** 35 (Teachers for Africa)
21–40 (Fellows)   22–26 (Fellows)

How to apply: Contact IFESH for an information package and application form. Applications for both the Teachers for Africa and International Fellows programs are due six months prior to the start of the programs. Applicants are notified two to three months after the receipt of their application.

Stated mission: The mission of the Teachers for Africa program is "to provide technical and educational tools to improve the educational systems of sub-Saharan Africa and foster sustainable development." The mission of the International Fellows program is "to empower the poor, particularly women and children, to become self-sufficient in the areas of health, literacy, skills training, and agriculture. This is done through the support of community-based projects developed by the Africans in cooperation with U.S. nongovernmental organizations."

History: IFESH was founded in 1984 by Reverend Leon Sullivan, a prominent member of the African-American business and philanthropic community.

Observations and commentary: IFESH's two volunteer programs (International Fellows and Teachers for Africa) are notable for their success in recruiting people of color, especially African Americans, to volunteer in Africa.

Participants in the International Fellows program work for nine months in paid internships, usually with international organizations. The program's strengths are that it provides a relatively generous stipend of $800 a month, and places fellows with groups that are established enough to be able to utilize their skills and yet grassroots enough to benefit from the skills the fellows offer. Fellows generally work in office jobs; some do more hands-on project management. Tasks include writing proposals, doing research, providing administrative support, and doing some fieldwork.

Umi Howard, a recent college graduate from Philadelphia, worked for a job training program in South Africa. According to Umi, "The majority of what I do is what I learned in school: how to research and how to write." Kim Yates was placed in the IFESH office in South Africa and spent most of her time on writing and administrative tasks. The excitement of the IFESH placements isn't the type of work that fellows do so much as the type of organization with which they are placed.

The Teachers for Africa program places U.S. teachers and professors in African schools, training programs, and universities. The emphasis is on teacher training, although some volunteers are placed in positions where they end up teaching students instead of training teachers.

The Teachers for Africa program appears to be a family-friendly program; many volunteers are accompanied by spouses, and some bring children.

Many of IFESH's strengths are the result of the charisma, commitment, and connections of its founder, Reverend Leon H. Sullivan. Sullivan, an important member of the African-American elite, involved a range of institutions in IFESH partnerships, from USAID and Tuskegee University to Chase Manhattan Bank. Like Sullivan, IFESH tends toward coordination with upper-level government entities and business executives. Sullivan was very controversial in the anti-apartheid movement because he encouraged business involvement in South Africa, as long as the businesses complied with his "Sullivan principles."

Prospective volunteers should know that Sullivan's ideological background was conservative and pro big business—he was on the board of General Motors—and these beliefs seem to guide the big picture of the organizational policy. This ideology, however, does not appear to impact the day-to-day work of the volunteers. We met progressive volunteers who did not feel that their own values were compromised by the affiliation. Reverend Sullivan's death occurred shortly before we went to press; it is not clear how his death will impact the organization.

The main drawback of IFESH is that the U.S. office seems to be somewhat disorganized and does not provide a high level of training or support for volunteers in the field. Their competitive application process seems to enable the selection of volunteers who thrive in independent environments, and take initiative to make a difference.

The Teachers for Africa program is a good option to consider if you are an experienced teacher who can work independently in a potentially challenging environment. The International Fellows program is recommended for mature college seniors and graduates who have some experience working with community-based organizations and who are willing to spend at least some time in a desk job. All three programs are particularly recommended for people of color or those who need financial support in order to be able to volunteer, and who are willing to create a positive experience without receiving a great deal of organizational support.

I would definitely recommend it for someone who is interested in having a new experience and immersing themselves in a different culture because nine months is a long time. If this were my first time coming, I'm sure it would be even more overwhelming than it already is, and sometimes it's something extraordinary to deal with. You need to be very organized and adaptable. You can't come in with one set of ideas about what is going to happen, and if it gets changed, you're shaken at the roots.—Umi Howard, South Africa

The International Partnership for Service-Learning (IPS-L)

815 Second Ave., Suite 315   *phone:* 212-986-0989
New York , NY 10017   *fax:* 212-986-5039
    e-mail: pslny@aol.com
    web: www.ipsl.org/

IPS-L is an ideal program for college students to incorporate service and academic study abroad.—Claire Barret, volunteer, Ecuador

Countries where volunteers are placed: Czech Republic, Ecuador, England, France, India, Israel, Jamaica, Mexico, the Philippines, Russia, Scotland, the United States (South Dakota with native Americans), and Vietnam

Field(s) of work: Academic study combined with community service with local agencies in a wide range of fields, primarily in social services. IPS-L also offers a master's degree in International Service.

Requirements or special skills necessary: All volunteers must be high school graduates and be either native English speakers or have scored above 550 on the TOEFL examination. Volunteers in Ecuador, Mexico, and France must have two years of high school or one year of college Spanish/French. In Quito, Ecuador, the requirement is three years of high school Spanish or one and a half years at the university level and a general ability to succeed in classes taught in Spanish. Participants in the Glasgow, Scotland, program must have at least a 3.0 GPA. Married and unmarried couples are accepted; IPS-L stresses that both partners should participate in the program. Unmarried couples probably will not be able to room together during homestays because of sensitivity to cultural norms.

Duration and dates: There are several options: three-week India sessions in January and August, summer-long programs, semester-long programs and full-year programs. Applications to the master's program are due March 1. Application dates for other programs vary. Check the website for the most current deadlines.

What volunteers pay and what they receive: Summer-long programs cost from $3,000 to $4,900, semester-long programs cost between $6,600 and $8,900, and year-long programs cost from $12,900 to $17,100. These costs cover instruction, administration fees, volunteer placement, supervision, orientation, accommodation, and some in-country travel expenses. These costs do not include international airfare. Meals are also included except in the Israel and Scotland programs. The three-week program in India costs $5,300 and includes airfare. For an additional $3,600, participants can extend the three-week India program for a semester. The master's degree program costs $28,000.

Participants may apply for financial aid to IPS-L programs, provided they remain enrolled at their home college/university. There are a limited number of IPS-L scholarships to assist with program fees. Participants in the South Dakota program might be eligible for membership in Americorps.

Typical volunteer responsibilities: Volunteers are individually placed with one of an array of local agencies and work between fifteen to twenty hours per week. Volunteers may work as English teachers or in community health, recreation, rehabilitation, community development, cultural preservation, crisis intervention, human rights, teaching adults and children, or work with women and people with disabilities.

Number of volunteers sent abroad annually: 200–250 (2001)

Age range: 18+   **Typical age:** 21

How to apply: Participants may apply directly or through their campus study abroad office. The application includes an application form, essay, a transcript (where applicable), two photos, an insurance form, a medical form, two recommendations, and a $250 deposit. Interviews are not required. Applications are due two months before the start of a program, and admissions are made on a rolling basis.

Stated mission: "IPS-L's mission is to offer intercultural service-learning programs for academic credit to college students and other interested individuals and to promote service-learning research and curriculum development while advocating for international service-learning. Through service-learning programs, participants continue formal study and at the same time work with others to meet human needs, the service making the academic study relevant and the academic study informing the work.

"The International Partnership for Service-Learning believes that the joining of study and service is a powerful means of learning, addresses human needs that would otherwise remain unmet, promotes intercultural/international literacy, advances the personal growth of students as members of the community, gives expression to the obligation of public and community service by educated people, and sets academic institutions in right relationship to the larger society."

History: Since its inception in 1982, more than 4,000 students from over 400 American and foreign universities have participated in IPS-L programs.

Observations and commentary: IPS-L is a well-established undergraduate and graduate program with a clear commitment to the principles of service-learning that the organization describes as "uniting the values of academic study and service to the world."

Participants receive printed materials before they depart overseas, but the program doesn't truly begin until they are met at the airport by the in-country program supervisor. In-country orientations vary. In Quito, much of the cultural orientation is handled by the Ecuadorian students from the Universidad de San Francisco. In South Dakota, professors from South Dakota State University, visiting Native American scholars, and the program director facilitate the orientation.

The India program is based in Calcutta, West Bengal. Amitava Roy, the in-country program coordinator in India, described the beginning of the program: "We pick up the group from the airport, provide them with an orientation on culture, and give them a chance to meet the faculty. We take them to several social service agencies, and then they choose which to serve with." During the three-week sessions in India the schedule is very structured with an intense combination of group living, cultural immersion, and community service projects. The semester program allows for more flexibility.

Sean Pelky started with the three-week program and extended to the semester-long program. While in Calcutta, he received independent study credit from Boston University. On a typical day, Sean worked in the mornings with dying and destitute people at Perna Dahn, an institution affiliated with Mother Theresa's Missionaries of Charity. At midday he returned to his home-stay for a meal with his host family before catching public transportation to his afternoon volunteer teaching position at the Gandhi school. He told us that the children at this school most of all needed "patience, affection, praise, and understanding." Between 3 and 7 P.M., Sean attended classes in which he studied Bengali culture and ancient Hindu beliefs such as the existence of a mother goddess through the mediums of theater, film, and Indo-European literature. His other areas of study included modern history, British rule, post-independence, and modern religion in India.

The IPS-L instructors try to respond to the students' interests. As Professor Krishna Sen commented, "I gave a talk on gender and law, and we ended up having a one-hour discussion about the NGO and labor movements. We talked also about labor in the family and domestic help and had to organize another evening meeting just to discuss these issues further."

A typical day in the Guadalajara program in Mexico begins with a class from 8 to 9 A.M. about Mexican institutions and society at the Universidad Autonoma de Guadalajara (UAG). From 9 to 1 participants attend an intensive Spanish course. After class they eat their lunches (often prepared by their host families) and in the evening work with their host organizations. The IPS-L participants we met generally work a modest fifteen hours per week on community service projects.

Guadalupe Delgadillo, head of the UAG's exchange program, has worked directly with the IPS-L program in Mexico for thirteen years. When we spoke with Guadalupe at the university she had good things to say about IPS-L participants. She emphasized that they compare favorably to other foreign exchange program participants and attributed this to the fact that they had chosen an organization with a community service component. She says that even the Spanish language instructors say that most of their better students are the partnership students.

Guadalupe has a favorable impression of IPS-L as an organization. "They are serious," she says. "I can e-mail headquarters several times a day and always get an immediate response." Unlike a handful of organizations we profiled whose headquarters staff seems to be virtually unavailable while their volunteers are in the field, IPS-L seems to be online (literally) for its participants.

Guadalupe meets once a week with the partner organizations that the participants work with. These meetings help Guadalupe evaluate the organizations' projects and gain insight into the performance of the volunteers from the organizations' perspective. She told us that many organizations do not take all participants that apply to their programs. Some organizations insist that the volunteers be Catholic; others that they know Spanish well. She also meets weekly with the volunteers themselves.

The Guadalajara program has seen some exceptional participants. One young man, a law student who was slightly above the average age of IPS-L participants, worked with an organization interviewing families to identify those that had needs for legal services. He later connected them with faculty in the Law Department of UAG. Another participant set up a scholarship fund, using her own money, to help street children she thought had potential.

Several participants in IPS-L programs said that volunteering did not seem to be the priority or the most developed part of the program. While others were satisfied with the volunteer component, as a volunteer you may have to take the initiative to make the service aspect of the program work for you.

IPS-L also offers a unique master's degree in International Service. The program involves a fall semester either in Mexico at UAG or in Jamaica at the University of Technology followed by a spring semester in England at the Roehampton Institute in London.

There is an active alumni network that publishes a newsletter, "SEQUEL," and there are plans for an online alumni directory. In "SEQUEL," alumni share the long-lasting effects of the IPS-L experience on their lives. "My experience with IPS-L," one volunteer wrote, "brought me into the field of development, and I am now preparing for my fifth overseas job as a local NGO advisor."

Overall, we were impressed with IPS-L, and strongly recommend it for people for whom academic study and credit, as well as cultural exchange, are the highest priorities. We do not recommend it for those who want to focus primarily on volunteering.

International Service for Peace (SIPAZ)

(Servicio Internacional para la Paz [SIPAZ])   *phone:* 831-425-1257
PO Box 2415   *fax:* 831-425-1257
Santa Cruz, CA 95063   *e-mail:* volcom@sipaz.org
                                                  web: www.sipaz.org

Countries where volunteers are placed: Chiapas, Mexico

Field(s) of work: Conflict transformation and peace and human rights advocacy

Requirements or special skills necessary: SIPAZ is looking for volunteers who are fluent in Spanish, have good political analysis skills and prior international work experience, and are willing to make a minimum of a one-year commitment. Volunteers should have experience with nonviolent peace-building or conflict resolution, a commitment to the principles of nonviolence, and excellent communication skills. Volunteers must be mature and be comfortable working with faith-based groups.

Duration and dates: Placements last one year or more.

What volunteers pay and what they receive: There is no volunteer fee. All living expenses are covered. Volunteers receive a modest stipend, health insurance (if needed), and are reimbursed for some travel expenses.

Typical volunteer responsibilities: Volunteers work under the supervision of the coordinator of the Chiapas office; tasks vary widely.

Number of volunteers sent abroad annually: 4–7

Age range: 23+   **Typical age:** 25–35

How to apply: Contact the international office in Santa Cruz, California.

Stated mission: "The uprising in Chiapas was sparked by indigenous resistance to deep-seated injustice. It continues today in a low-intensity conflict marked by complex negotiations, a tense military situation, and the deep polarization of communities throughout the region.

"International Service for Peace (Servicio Internacional para la Paz or SIPAZ) is a response from the international community to the shared sense among many Mexican sectors that international opinion can contribute to the search for peaceful solutions, through dialogue, to the conflict. SIPAZ was organized at the invitation of Mexican human rights and church contacts. Grounded in a commitment to active nonviolence, SIPAZ reflects the support for a dignified, just, and lasting peace of its member groups around the world."

History: SIPAZ was formed as a response to the Zapatista uprising in Mexico that began on January 1, 1994. SIPAZ is a coalition of over fifty organizations from North America, Latin America, and Europe, with offices in Chiapas and Santa Cruz, California.

International Society for Ecology & Culture, Ladakh Farm Project (ISEC)

PO Box 9475
Berkeley, CA 94709

phone: 510-548-4915
fax: 510-548-4916
e-mail: isecca@igc.apc.org
web: www.isec.org.uk

The best part of the Farm Stay project was the opportunity to work and live closely with a Ladakhi family. It was a very deep and rich experience of a more earth-centered and community-based culture. The many personal challenges and eye-opening experiences taught me how we can shift our own lives and societies away from an obsession with consumerism, central control, and economic growth.—Rodney Vlais, volunteer, India

Countries where volunteers are placed: Ladakh region of northern India

Field(s) of Work: Agricultural work and cultural exchange on family farms

Requirements or special skills necessary: None, but farming experience is beneficial

Duration and dates: Volunteers serve for at least one month from June to October. It is best to arrive on the 26th of the previous month to allow for time to acclimatize to high altitude and to be ready to participate in the two- or three-day orientation and language workshop, which starts at the beginning of each month.

What volunteers pay and what they receive: Volunteers pay $350 for the first month and $40 per month thereafter. Volunteers cover their own travel expenses. They receive basic room and board during their stay with their host family, but are responsible for all other costs including, but not limited to, travel expenses and accommodations during meetings in the capital.

Typical volunteer responsibilities: Volunteers live with families and assist in various tasks in agriculture and household maintenance. Volunteers are also expected to follow a brief curriculum and participate in group meetings before, during, and after their stay.

Number of volunteers sent abroad annually: 70 (2001)

Age Range: 18+   **Typical Age:** 25

How to apply: Request an application and more information from ISEC, review the materials, and return a completed written application to ISEC.

Stated mission: "ISEC works on three continents to promote ecological regeneration, community renewal, and economic localization. ISEC's primary goal is to promote critical examination of the foundations of modern industrial society, while at the same time examining the principles necessary for the emergence of more sustainable and equitable patterns of living."

ISEC focuses on several key issues such as:

- *The crucial link between cultural and biological diversity.*
- *Food and agriculture, with an emphasis on small farmers and rural society.*
- *The importance of strong local economies.*
- *The psychological benefits of community and having a connection to nature.*

History: ISEC has over twenty years of experience working for "counter-development" in Ladakh, and has helped to found two leading Ladakhi community organizations, the Ladakh Ecological Development Group (LEDeG) and the Women's Alliance. In 1986, ISEC founder and director Helena Norberg-Hodge shared the Right Livelihood Award or "Alternative Nobel Prize" with LEDeG. ISEC has a main office in England and another in Berkeley, California, and has produced a variety of public education materials including a book and a movie titled *Ancient Futures: Learning from Ladakh.* In addition to its involvement in public education in the United Kingdom and United States around globalization and alternative models of development, ISEC continues to work directly in Ladakh, operating a tourist education program as well as the Farm Project. The Farm Project has grown steadily since its inception in 1996.

Observations and commentary: Farm Stay volunteers perform manual labor. They work closely with family members to care for crops, soil, gardens, and animals on small-to modest-sized farms where barley is the staple. By all accounts volunteers work hard.

In the words of one recent volunteer, "The objectives of the farm-stay are to provide volunteers with an experience of simple living, sustainable and local socioeconomic systems, and a deep connection with the Earth," and, in addition, "to provide the host family with labor as well as a less romanticized perspective of Western culture. "

The project exposes participants to the tension that exists between traditional and modern ways of life. The program seeks to demonstrate alternative forms of development that are built upon a foundation of traditional culture. The program also intends to validate Ladakhi culture through the presence of Westerners who choose to live as Ladakhis. However, there are inherent tensions between program intentions and outcomes. Some volunteers grappled with the question of whether exposure to Westerners, even those showing respect for traditional Ladakhi culture, can succeed in promoting traditional ways of life. As one volunteer explained, "Despite the best intentions, volunteers may be furthering admiration for the Western way" by their inanimate possessions or unconscious actions.

The main suggestion from volunteers for improving the program is to provide more preparatory support to volunteers. ISEC has taken this feedback from former volunteers to heart and has added "language workshops and improved program briefing." The improved briefings include more training on "counter-development communication techniques." ISEC not only provides volunteers with encouragement to volunteers to return home and "get involved in activities that help our own culture move in more human and ecologically sound directions," it also provides "workshops and contacts during meetings in Ladakh."

The Farm Project coordinator, who lives in residence from May to October, supports volunteers in various ways including working with the Women's Alliance to select and match volunteers with families. Volunteer's experiences seem to vary depending on the family with which they are placed. As one volunteer commented, "families differ in how traditional they are." Some volunteers found the "long working hours and harsh climate" difficult, while others seemed to thrive in this environment. Still others felt isolated in the remote villages in which they were placed. In addition to the remote placements, some volunteers found the language barrier a great challenge.

Volunteers agreed that one of the best things about the program was its philosophical approach that combined a deep respect for Ladakhi culture, a humble learning role for the volunteers, and an openness and honesty about the downside of modernization and Western culture. If you are interested in living and working with a family on a farm, learning about traditional culture, and being a voice for "counter-development," then this could be a great match for you. If you don't want to do manual labor and are not comfortable living in a rustic and somewhat isolated situation, then you'd be better off with another program.

International Volunteer Expeditions (IVEX)

2001 Vallejo Way
Sacramento, CA 95818

phone: 510-496-2740, x-4550
fax: 510-496-2740, x-4550
e-mail: ivexinformation@espwa.org
web: www.espwa.org

Countries where volunteers are placed: Primarily the Americas, and occasionally other parts of the world

Field(s) of work: Agriculture/farming, appropriate technology, arts, construction, education, environmental conservation, filmmaking, and health

Requirements or special skills necessary: Ability to speak and understand some English—English is the language of the programs. A few projects require some French or Spanish. Technical skills may be useful but are not required.

Duration and dates: Most projects are short-term group projects of two to four weeks. Alumni are eligible for independent placement with projects for up to one year. Special programs of variable length can be designed for preexisting groups interested in volunteering in the Americas

What volunteers pay and what they receive: Volunteers pay for their airfare, incidental expenses, insurance, and a registration fee that ranges from $200 to $1,500. IVEX provides meals, lodging, and project materials. A portion of the registration fees go to the partner NGOs. Accommodations are simple—tents, village schoolhouses, home-stays, or dormitories. IVEX accepts children under the age of 18 if they are accompanied by an adult, and accepts both married and unmarried couples.

Typical volunteer responsibilities: Responsibilities vary widely and can include tasks such as developing trails, photographing animals, creating videos, designing educational displays or websites, constructing an irrigation system, or researching and documenting environmental conditions. Volunteers usually work six to eight hours a day, five days a week. Programs are organized in partnership with local host organizations. Placements may involve volunteering in more than one country.

Number of volunteers sent abroad annually: Varies

Age range: All ages (Participants under age eighteen must travel with adult family member.)

Typical age: None

How to apply: Download application from the website or call the office.

Stated mission: IVEX has "two compatible and equal goals: (1) to provide motivated individuals a meaningful and unique service experience; (2) to provide service and financial support to organizations and agencies working for sustainable communities."

History: "After life-changing trips to East Africa in 1993, two San Francisco Bay area attorneys were determined to resume their travels on a meaningful and involved level, to gain a better understanding of life as lived by local people, and to lend a hand with projects of importance to those people. Unable to find the type of experience they sought, they founded IVEX, thus creating new opportunities to travel, even for a short time, in a meaningful, responsible, and significant way."

Interns for Peace (IFP)

475 Riverside Dr. Suite 240
New York, NY 10115

phone: 212-870-2226
fax: 212-870-2119
e-mail: ifpus@mindspring.com
web: www.internsforpeace.org

Countries where volunteers are placed: Israel

Field(s) of work: Peace-building between Arabs and Jews through shared community-building activities

Requirements or special skills necessary: Participants must be Jewish or Arab, proficient in advanced Hebrew, and must have lived in Israel for six months or more. A college education is required, as is prior work experience and a track record of involvement in promoting peace. Volunteers must be able to take direction, accept authority, and live a conservative lifestyle. Applicants should demonstrate strong interpersonal skills in a multicultural environment.

Duration and dates: The program lasts for one year.

What volunteers pay and what they receive: Volunteers must help raise funds in collaboration with IFP to cover their expenses, including travel to Israel. While the cost per intern is high ($25,000), IFP has a record of success in raising funds from synagogues and United Jewish Appeals. Volunteers are expected to help IFP with this outreach. Room and board are provided. Volunteers also receive training in community peace work.

Typical volunteer responsibilities: Volunteers work on community development programs, most of which involve young Arabs and Jews. Tasks might include partnering Arab and Israeli schools, developing a joint training for children on bicycle safety, tree planting, or working with youth business clubs. Most volunteers are placed in Arab villages where they either work on preexisting projects or develop their own.

Number of volunteers sent abroad annually: 4 (2000)

Age range: 22–50   **Typical age:** 22–35

How to apply: Contact the IFP office in New York and then send a résumé and an essay on why you would like to volunteer with IFP. Application forms are available online or from headquarters.

Stated mission: IFP's mission is to "train professional coexistence leaders, Jews and Arabs, who actively foster cooperative intercommunal action that meets the needs of both communities. As a community work program, Interns for Peace is non-political and non-ideological."

History: IFP was founded in 1976. Since then, IFP has helped over 200 interns (community peace workers) engage 80,000 Jews and Arabs in business, athletic, cultural, educational, women's, and community development projects. IFP is considering developing projects in the Balkans.

Interplast, Inc.

300-B Pioneer Way
Mountain View, CA 94041-1506

phone: 650-962-0123
fax: 650-962-1619
e-mail: IPnews@Interplast.org
web: www.interplast.org

Countries where volunteers are placed: Bolivia, Brazil, Ecuador, Honduras, Laos, Myanmar (Burma), Nepal, Nicaragua, Peru, the Philippines, Tibet, and Vietnam

Field(s) of work: Reconstructive surgery

Requirements or special skills necessary: Volunteer medical teams consist of board certified/eligible plastic surgeons, anesthesiologists, pediatricians, and operating room and recovery room nurses. Some teams also include nurse educators. Senior plastic surgery and anesthesia residents may also be eligible to go on some Interplast trips. In addition, one team secretary/translator is typically assigned to each trip. All medical volunteers must be credentialed by Interplast's medical committees before being considered for trip assignments.

Duration and dates: Trips last from one to two weeks and take place throughout the year. In recent years there have been approximately forty trips annually.

What volunteers pay and what they receive: Volunteers pay $325 toward transportation and accommodation costs, and Interplast covers the remaining travel and accommodation costs. Volunteers pay for their own meals during the trip. Interplast provides medical supplies and arranges for housing either with local families or in hotels.

Typical volunteer responsibilities: Volunteer teams complete seventy-five to a hundred surgeries on an assignment. In addition to providing direct medical care, volunteers train local doctors and nurses in advanced surgical techniques and related care. Interplast volunteers may also be asked to bring slides and other educational materials, and to prepare lectures to present to the host country's medical personnel.

Number of volunteers sent abroad annually: 500

Age range: All ages   **Typical age:** None

How to apply: Potential volunteers should refer to the Interplast website or call the Interplast office for specific application requirements. Completed application packets should be mailed to the Director of Volunteer Staffing and Recruitment at the address above.

Stated mission: "Interplast's mission is to provide free reconstructive surgery for people in developing nations, and to help improve health care worldwide. The organization's goals are to establish, develop, and maintain host-country, domestic-patient, and educational programs with the following objectives: provide direct patient care, reconstructive surgery, and ancillary services to those with no other resources; provide educational training and medical interchange; assist host-country medical colleagues toward medical independence; enable recipients of care to become providers of care to new sites."

History: Interplast was founded in 1969 under the leadership of plastic surgeon Dr. Donald R. Laub, who at the time was Chief of Plastic and Reconstructive Surgery at Stanford University Medical Center in Palo Alto, California.

Dr. Laub was inspired by Antonio, a fourteen-year-old boy who had come to Stanford from his home in Mexico to receive surgery to repair his cleft lip and palate. Since this first successful surgery, Interplast has grown into an organization that takes forty surgical trips annually and, together with medical colleagues around the world, performs more than 3,000 surgeries every year. Interplast gained public recognition when the film *A Story of Healing,* produced during an Interplast trip to Vietnam, won the Academy Award for Best Documentary Short Subject. Interplast's work is also profiled in the book *The Gift* by internationally acclaimed photographer Phil Borges.

Japan-U.S. Community Education and Exchange (JUCEE)

Nichibei Pathfinding Opportunity
Program (NPOP)
1440 Broadway, Suite 501
Oakland, CA 94612

phone: **510-267-1920**
fax: **510-267-1922**
e-mail: **info-us@jucee.org**
web: **www.jucee.org**

Countries where volunteers are placed: Japan

Field(s) of work: Community development, education, the environment, civil rights, immigration, public health, women's issues, mental and physical disabilities, fair trade, and more

Requirements or special skills necessary: Preference is given to those with at least two years experience in the U.S. nonprofit sector and the demonstrated vision and potential to promote change in their communities. Proficiency in Japanese language is not required by most host organizations, but Japanese is the primary spoken language in most projects, Nichibei Pathfinding Opportunity Program (NPOP) accepts both married and unmarried couples provided that both are selected to be participants.

Duration and dates: NPOP participants are placed in five-week placements with nonprofit organizations throughout Japan. Placements are made once a year in the fall (usually September through October).

What volunteers pay and what volunteers receive: The program fee is $500, with the majority of costs per participant such as airfare, accommodations, local transportation, and international health insurance subsidized by external funding sources.

NPOP participants are partially reimbursed for additional program-related expenses such as pre-trip Japanese language training, meals, research, and materials, but are wholly responsible for their personal travel and entertainment expenses. NPOP provides participants with an introductory training session in Tokyo and ongoing support in their placement in other regions of Japan. At the end of each placement, host organizations and participants hold local public events to present the results of their work together. During their final week, NPOP participants are given the opportunity to take part in a three-day learning tour including some sightseeing and a trip to see community mobilization in action. Upon their return to the United States, NPOP participants are asked to write a report of their findings and present their experiences in Japan to their home communities through small-scale public events.

Typical volunteer responsibilities: NPOP participants work five days per week with their host organizations. Participants are also encouraged to pursue their own interests and to take the opportunity to meet with other organizations and individuals in their field.

Number of volunteers sent abroad annually: 6–8 (2000)

Age range: 21–62   **Typical age:** None

How to apply: Participants are required to submit a written application with a resume and other supporting documents by the end of May. Telephone interviews take place the first week of June, and selected applicants will be notified by the end of June. Matching of participants and host organizations will take place no later than late July.

Stated mission: "Japan-U.S. Community Education and Exchange (JUCEE) is an agent for change. We promote civil society by strengthening and linking the nonprofit sectors in the United States and Japan. We do this through bilateral nonprofit internships, fellowships, organizational exchanges, and professional training."

History: In 1996, JUCEE launched the Japan-U.S. Nonprofit Internship Program to bring people from Japan to work in nonprofit organizations in the United States. Since then, JUCEE has helped establish organizational collaborations between nonprofit organizations in the two countries. In 1999, JUCEE established the Nichibei Pathfinding Opportunity Program (NPOP) to bring diverse groups of people from the United States to work as volunteers in Japan, especially those with experience in the nonprofit sector.

Jesuit Volunteer Corps/ Jesuit Volunteers International (JVC/ JVI)

PO Box 3756
Washington, DC 20007-3756

phone: 202-687-1132
fax: 202-687-5082
e-mail: jvi@JesuitVolunteers.org
web: www.jesuitvolunteers.org

This community is great. The orientation was informal, but done with a lot of care. The other volunteers are amazing people. The sites chosen are well supported and organized.—Ted Eull, volunteer, Tanzania

Countries where volunteers are placed: Belize, Chile, Marshall Islands, Micronesia, Nepal, Nicaragua, Peru, Tanzania, South Africa, and the United States

Field(s) of work: Community organizing, education, health, and social work

Requirements or special skills necessary: Volunteers must be at least twenty-one years old and have a desire to "grow in the values of spirituality, justice, community, and simplicity." They should hold a college degree or applicable work experience. Some teaching positions require certification, and some placements require fluency in Spanish. Married couples without dependents may apply to volunteer together. Although the Jesuit Order is Catholic and exclusively male, volunteers with JVC/JVI do not have to be either male or Catholic. (In fact, the majority of domestic volunteers are female.) International volunteers do not even have to be Christian, but most are.

Duration and dates: Overseas volunteers work for two years. The U.S. program requires a one-year commitment. All volunteers begin with a one- to two-week orientation in late July through early August.

What volunteers pay and what they receive: All volunteers' travel, insurance, and living expenses are covered. Domestic volunteers (members of the Jesuit Volunteer Corps [JVC]) pay their way to the orientation site in the region where they will serve. Domestic volunteers receive a stipend of $75 per month. International volunteers (placed by Jesuit Volunteers International [JVI]) receive the equivalent of $60 per month. JVI provides a two-week orientation, retreats (including an end-of-service retreat), and an in-country coordinator. International volunteers are asked to undertake some fundraising efforts before they leave, but acceptance is not contingent on this fundraising.

Typical volunteer responsibilities: Most international volunteers teach English, computer skills, math, liberal arts, business, or journalism. Social workers work with the homeless, people with physical or mental disabilities, the elderly, children, refugees, prisoners, or migrant workers.

Number of volunteers sent abroad annually: 70 abroad, 500 in the United States (2000)

Age range: 21 or older   **Typical age:** 23

How to apply: JVI recommends that you submit your applications by February 15, although applications are accepted through July, or until all placements are filled. Most international placements are filled by April. JVI requires a "spiritual reference" in addition to other letters of reference.

Stated mission: JVI and JVC "offer women and men an opportunity to work full-time for justice and peace. Jesuit Volunteers are called to the mission of serving the poor directly, working for structural change in the United States, and accompanying people in developing countries. The challenge to Jesuit Volunteers is to integrate Christian faith by working and living among the poor and marginalized, by living simply and in community with other Jesuit Volunteers, and by examining the causes of social injustice."

History: The Jesuit Volunteers program began in 1956 in Alaska. Since its inception, over 7,000 people have volunteered with JVC/JVI.

Observations and commentary: Jesuit Volunteers International (JVI) is centered on four principles: spirituality, community, simplicity, and justice. These principles distinguish JVI from other organizations that place volunteers as teachers. In some ways, living these principles is a more important part of the experience than the actual work done by the volunteers. The volunteers we interviewed report that the JVI does a relatively good job of weaving these four principles into the volunteer experience.

The principle of spirituality is promoted through a weekly meeting for communal prayer. Even non-Christian volunteers are expected to join in prayer and spiritual reflection. Retreats and reflection discussions are used to help volunteers integrate their faith into their work.

To promote community, volunteers live in a group situation and share household responsibilities such as cooking and cleaning. The group collectively decides how to spend money, resolve conflicts, and organize the weekly prayer meetings.

Simplicity means living a modest lifestyle. To achieve this, volunteers are asked to limit their spending to the amount of their stipends. Volunteers may not work for outside pay. What Americans consider a modest lifestyle, however, may be well above the local standard of living.

Most volunteers' work involves providing a direct service, not advocating for social justice. The idea of justice, however, is incorporated into reflection discussions.

We commend JVI for its strong emphasis on reflection. Regular reflection is an essential part of a complete volunteer experience, but is often ignored by other volunteer placement programs. Denise Bennet, a volunteer in Tanzania, felt that "the best part of JVI is the community of volunteers, to bounce ideas and feelings off each other."

Ted Eull, on the other hand, who taught computers and coached basketball in Dar Es Salaam, told us that while he greatly appreciated the emphasis on community spiritual reflection, it sometimes took away from his ability to have time to get to know local people.

JVI provides a high level of support for volunteers. The orientation period in the United States includes not only cross-cultural training, but also time to create group goals, learn consensus decision-making skills, and engage in a two-day silent retreat to reflect on the four principles.

JVI also provides more training than many other programs. Katie Quirk, for example, a volunteer in Tanzania, was trained by JVI in teaching techniques with an emphasis on understanding students' different learning styles before being assigned to her post.

JVI does a better job than most other volunteer programs of keeping past volunteers active and in touch with one another. JVI has an active alumni network that plans frequent activities for alumni in many different parts of the United States and maintains a lively listserve. Their tongue-in-cheek motto is "ruined for life" since many volunteers are transformed by their experience and are unable to return to business as usual. Judging from the listserve, a high number continue to work in community service and social justice.

We did not research JVC, the domestic volunteer program.

Overall, we found JVI to be a good choice for spiritually inspired volunteers who want to integrate their faith into their volunteer experience without proselytizing. If you are interested in living in a community, participating in spiritual discussions, and working as a teacher, we recommend that you consider JVI. If you do not like participating in group meetings to make collective decisions, then JVI is not for you.

Living in a community is awesome and challenging. Like family, you don't get to pick your fellow community members.—Denise Bennet, volunteer, Tanzania

Joint Assistance Centre, Inc. (JAC)

PO Box 6082
San Pablo, CA 94806-0082

phone: 510-464-1100
fax: 603-297-3521
e-mail: jacusa@juno.com
web: www.jacusa.org

> *JAC is a relatively easy and low-commitment way to get an authentic experience of village life in India. It's good for someone who wants to visit the country with the security of an airport pick-up and a place to stay upon arrival.—Rebecca Grossberg, volunteer, India*

Countries where volunteers are placed: Bangladesh, India, Nepal, and South Korea

Field(s) of work: Agriculture, disaster preparedness and reconstruction, construction, education and literacy, environmental conservation, public health and sanitation, and children and women's welfare

Requirements or special skills necessary: For short-term volunteers, there are no requirements other than a willingness to participate in cross-cultural learning and to contribute to the work of the camp. Long-term volunteers should gain basic language skills in one of the local languages spoken where JAC works, such as basic Hindi and Nepali. Intensive week-long Nepali language training can be arranged in Kathmandu for Nepal participants. JAC accepts children under the age of 18 if accompanied by an adult. They accept married and unmarried heterosexual couples, but were not able to tell us whether they accept same-sex couples as volunteers.

Duration and dates: Programs are available year round. Workcamp programs last for one to four weeks; long-term placements for individuals last three months with the possibility of an extension.

What volunteers pay and what they receive: Workcamp programs cost $230; long-term programs cost $550 for the initial three-month placement and $125 for each monthly extension. Registration for all programs is $50 in addition to the program fee. Fees include room and board, orientation, and airport pick-up. Volunteers are responsible for their own round-trip airfare.

Typical volunteer responsibilities: Most short-term volunteers participate in workcamps with non-governmental organizations operating at the village level, and they assist local people with herbal gardening, managing tree nurseries, running awareness campaigns on disaster preparedness, and playing games with youth at rural schools. Volunteers also prepare and attend conferences on development, disasters, and environmental issues, take part in environmental treks in the Himalayan region, and participate in yoga, meditation, and natural health care training programs.

Long-term volunteers have responsibilities similar to those of short-term volunteers, but their work allows for greater depth. Long-term volunteers assist host organizations in projects such as organizing workcamps, or publishing and editing written materials. Volunteers with medical backgrounds are sometimes placed in medical centers. Volunteers who want to work with children can stay at a school or home for children and teach English.

Number of volunteers sent abroad annually: 50

Age range: 18–55   **Typical age:** 20–30

How to apply: Contact the headquarters by e-mail, phone, or fax.

Stated mission: "The international volunteer programs of JAC are intended to provide opportunities for visiting friends from abroad to see India and learn about its people and their concerns while traveling. They help enrich the outlook of those whom they meet and in turn develop a better understanding of these new friends. This way each one is an ambassador of peace and international understanding."

History: The Joint Assistance Center (JAC) in India was established in 1978 in response to a hurricane that struck the Indian state of Andhra Pradesh, killing more than 10,000 people. JAC India focuses on preventing and responding to disasters and has facilitated volunteer placements in India for over 3,000 individuals from around the world.

JAC in the United States was created to work in collaboration with JAC India and other organizations that share a commitment to international exchange. Over time, JAC in the United States has expanded beyond its initial collaboration with JAC India and has developed partnerships with organizations throughout Asia, particularly those involved with the international workcamp movement.

Observations and commentary: JAC is part of the global network of organizations running workcamp projects. These projects typically bring together volunteers from a variety of countries to live and work together in a host country like India. Volunteers interested in participating on JAC workcamps benefit from the great variety of options to work at camps throughout India. But this range of choice also means that the quality of the workcamps varies significantly depending on the host organization. Feedback from participants ranges from complete satisfaction to frustration that "things were totally disorganized." Reports from volunteers who had participated in a variety workcamps through different sending organizations suggest that JAC projects often afford volunteers a greater immersion in local culture than some of the other workcamp organizations.

JAC's network in the Indian subcontinent is particularly strong due to its close affiliation with well-established local workcamp organizations such as the Joint Assistance Centre in India (an independent organization), the Non Formal Education Service Center (NFESC), the New International Friendship Club (NIFC) in Nepal, and the Bangladesh Work Camps Association (BWCA).

Volunteers may stay at the Sugandha project, a JAC maintained dormitory in

Delhi, when they first arrive and during orientation. This structure made of bamboo, thatch, and mud plaster is similar to those in the Indian villages. Water comes from a hand pump and volunteers help in maintaining the facility. During our research we were told that JAC is developing a home-stay option for the Delhi portion of the program. Accommodation in workcamps is either in homes, schools, or other public buildings, but regardless, expect simplicity.

While volunteers do work, several volunteers told us that the "real purpose of the workcamp was to experience village life and share some of our culture with the local people." JAC is a good bet for independent travelers who don't need a lot of support or want to combine travel with volunteer work as a meaningful way to get off the beaten track. If you want things to be very structured, however, then JAC is probably not for you.

Kibbutz Program Center

633 Third Ave., 21st Floor
New York, NY 10017

phone: 212-318-6133; 800-247-7852
fax: 212-318-6134
e-mail: kibbutzdsk@aol.com
web: www.kibbutzprogramcenter.org

We got up early to prune the banana trees. It was difficult work, and within a few hours our bodies and clothes were stained with purple banana sap. When we finished work in the mid-afternoon, we were free to hang out with our international volunteer group, go swimming, or just watch the sunset.—Lauren G. David, volunteer, Israel

Countries where volunteers are placed: Israel

Field(s) of work: Childcare, food services, and factory and agricultural work on Israeli collectives known as kibbutzim

Requirements or special skills necessary: Applicants must be willing to work hard (seven to eight hours a day, six days per week) and be in good physical condition. Very few kibbutzim accept volunteers older than thirty-five. The religious kibbutzim only accept people who observe Jewish law, but ninety percent of kibbutzim are not religious and have no religious requirements. The Kibbutz Volunteer Program is open to couples, but not to families with children. The organization cannot guarantee unmarried couples will room together and separate from other volunteers—some Kibbutzim have four volunteers to a room. (In terms of public displays of affection for both gay and straight couples—"that depends on the kibbutz.")

In addition to the Kibbutz Volunteer Program, the Kibbutz Program Center offers a wide range of vacation and study programs for families, singles, and seniors, but most do not include a work component.

Duration and dates: Volunteers stay from two to six months with start times year round, although longer stays are possible with visa approval.

What volunteers pay and what they receive: Volunteers pay a registration fee of $150, plus $25 per month for health insurance, and pay their own travel expenses. Living expenses such as room and board are covered, and volunteers receive a very small monthly stipend (about $50 per month) for toiletries and personal items. Local synagogues and Jewish Federations may be able to provide partial scholarships to help fund travel expenses. Some kibbutzim offer special day trips for volunteers so they can visit other parts of Israel.

Typical volunteer responsibilities: Volunteers provide community services such as childcare, laundry, dining hall service, and physical labor such as factory work, gardening, poultry and dairy farming, and other agricultural work (mostly mechanized).

Number of volunteers sent abroad annually: 1,000

Age range: 17½–35 (with some exceptions)   **Typical age:** 18–25

How to apply: Volunteers fill out an application form and include two letters of recommendation. Volunteers are then interviewed in-person by a representative of the Kibbutz Program Center or on the phone if there are no representatives in their region.

Stated mission: "To allow volunteers from all over the world to share in our communal lifestyle while getting to know Israel."

History: The first kibbutz was founded in 1909 as an experiment in Jewish communal participatory democracy. As conditions grew worse in Europe between the two world wars, Jews began to emigrate to Palestine and a movement of kibbutzim was formed. The kibbutzim movement expanded after World War II as Holocaust survivors fled Europe. In the 1960s and '70s, the kibbutzim created a volunteer program to enable people from other countries to experience the cooperative kibbutz lifestyle while contributing their time and labor.

Observations and commentary: Volunteering on a kibbutz used to be one of the most well-known options for working abroad, especially for volunteers with an interest in socialism on a small scale. In recent years, the kibbutz movement has grown smaller, and many kibbutzim are less socialist than in the past. The kibbutz experience can still be a very positive one for volunteers with a desire to work hard and learn from a community that has chosen to live collectively.

Volunteers that register with the Kibbutz Program Center get priority treatment from the office in Israel, but the actual matching with a kibbutz can only take place after a volunteer arrives in Israel. The office in Israel places volunteers according to their timeframe, their interests, and openings at the various kibbutzim.

Volunteers should not expect to be fully integrated into a collectivist utopia. Because of the high volume and turnover of volunteers, most permanent kibbutz members maintain some distance from the volunteers. Volunteers who speak Hebrew or stay for a longer time will find it easier to build friendships with permanent residents.

The work done by volunteers is often manual labor on kibbutz farms or factories. We met volunteers who fed fish, stuffed pimientos into olives, and folded laundry. Other volunteers helped to provide childcare or worked in food service. Most kibbutz agriculture is mechanized, so volunteers are more likely to use agricultural machinery than to weed an organic garden by hand. All the volunteers we spoke with emphasized that kibbutz volunteering is hard work. Most work seven to eight hours a day, six days a week, with Saturdays off. Some find the work to be spiritually satisfying; others are bored numb by mindless repetition of manual tasks. Of course there is an element of luck in the type of assignment a volunteer receives.

The kibbutz experience attracts a diverse range of participants, so volunteers can usually expect to meet some interesting co-workers. Most volunteers are not Jewish. Many come from Europe, especially from the Scandinavian countries, as the Middle Eastern desert climate provides a welcome relief from cold weather—if you can tolerate the heat.

Kibbutzim vary widely not only in the type of products they produce, but also in their size and "personalities." A kibbutz founded by German Jews may have a very different flavor than a kibbutz founded by Russian Jews. Most kibbutzim are struggling to find the right balance between collectivism and individuality; each kibbutz has achieved a slightly different balance. Ninety percent are "secular" (i.e., non-orthodox), but all celebrate Jewish holidays. Many kibbutz members are somewhat left-wing politically and support the Israeli Peace Movement, but there is a wide range of political philosophies that guide the kibbutzim. Kibbutzim located in the Golan Heights or near the border with Lebanon may have a much different perspective on the peace negotiations than those located in the interior. Among both kibbutzim members and volunteers, expect to find great diversity of perspectives regarding Israel/Palestine relations.

The Kibbutz Placement Office also has information about special programs such as Hebrew study at kibbutzim, the Singles Open Border program, the Kibbutz University Program, the Kibbutz Family Adventure, tours of Israel, and other educational programs. Visit the website for details. Some kibbutzim even offer an *ulpan* (language study) for seniors.

Overall, if you are willing to work hard and sweat a lot, are curious about collectivism but not blindly idealistic, and can afford a plane ticket to Israel, the kibbutz experience may be a good option for you.

Volunteers who expect their kibbutz to be an idealistic love society will be disappointed. Those who come willing to work hard within a community, however, can have an incredibly positive experience.—Joel Magid, staff

---

Maryknoll Mission Association

PO Box 307
Maryknoll, NY 10545-0307

phone: 800-818-5276; 914-762-6364
fax: 914-762-7031
e-mail: joinmmaf@mkl-mmaf.org
web: www.maryknoll.org

"Maryknoll, while faith-based, does not proselytize. We have a new vision of Catholic mission that sees our volunteers, whom we call 'missioners,' giving three years or more of their lives to walk with the poor and oppressed in a mutual sharing of faith and commitment to justice. By immersing ourselves in another culture, and living alongside the poor who have been marginalized by the new globalization, our volunteers work together with the communities they serve to bring about a world of justice. For all of us it is a life-changing experience."—Gerry Lee, Co-Director, Maryknoll Mission Association

Countries where volunteers are placed: Bolivia, Brazil, Cambodia, Chile, El Salvador, Kenya, Mexico, Peru, Sudan, Tanzania, Thailand, Venezuela, Vietnam, and Zimbabwe

Field(s) of work: Education, community organizing, grassroots economic development, and direct service to people with HIV/AIDS

Requirements or special skills necessary: Maryknoll lay missioners come from a wide range of professional and educational backgrounds. Applicants must be Catholic and U.S. citizens or permanent residents. They must have personal maturity, adaptability, good physical and psychological health, and a college degree or needed skill. Volunteers must be willing to learn a foreign language and make an initial three-and-a-half-year commitment. Families with children eight years old or younger (at the beginning of volunteer service) are also welcome to apply; Maryknoll has found that cross-cultural adaptation becomes much more difficult for a child after the age of eight. Unmarried couples are not accepted.

Duration and dates: Volunteers first participate in a four-month orientation that is in addition to the three-and-a-half-year overseas commitment. The orientation takes place every year from mid-August to mid-December in New York near the town of Ossining. The first six months to a year in the host country consists of language instruction and classes on the culture and history of the country and region. Maryknoll occasionally offers short-term delegations and volunteer opportunities through its affiliates.

What volunteers pay and what they receive: Maryknoll Mission Association covers all costs. Volunteers are expected, however, to participate in fundraising. They receive round-trip airfare, room and board, full health care, and a stipend of $200 a month. They also receive a four-month orientation, training in a foreign language, and a month-long re-entry program. Maryknoll allows, but does not pay for, a return visit to the United States during the service term.

Typical volunteer responsibilities: Responsibilities vary from country to country and site to site and depend on the talents of the volunteers and the needs of the local people. Sometimes a country team has very specific work for volunteers, and sometimes it has a more of a general plan of action.

Number of volunteers sent abroad annually: Approximately 20

Age range: 21–55 (flexible)   **Typical age:** 35

How to apply: The application process includes a written application, a personal interview, a psychological examination, letters of recommendation, a medical exam, and approval by the Admissions Board. Applicants do state their country of preference, but Maryknoll assigns them according to the needs abroad (see "Observations and commentary" below for more on this process). The application deadline is December 31, although applying earlier is encouraged.

Stated mission: "We are a Catholic community of lay, religious, and ordained people, including families and children. We participate in the mission of Jesus, serving in cross-cultural ministries in order to create a more just world in solidarity with the poor."

History: In 1911, the Catholic bishops of the United States founded Maryknoll as a missionary society of priests, sisters, and brothers. While over the years there was the occasional lay associate, in 1975 Maryknoll established a program for lay volunteers who would make a three-year commitment. In 1994, the Maryknoll Mission Association became legally independent of the Maryknoll Fathers and Brothers.

Observations and commentary: The Maryknoll Mission Association offers one of the most challenging and well-organized programs we reviewed. The orientation, re-entry program, evaluation, guidelines, benefits, and support are among the best one could hope for in a volunteer placement organization.

The orientation includes cultural and cross-cultural studies, country studies with an emphasis on socioeconomic conditions, scripture and theology, and discussions of questions such as, "What does it really mean to be a missionary?" The orientation is also a period during which the volunteers and staff together determine if the Maryknoll program is right for the prospective volunteer.

The minimum commitment, as already noted, is three-and-a-half years with the possibility of renewing for another three years. Bernard Butkiewicz, a volunteer we met in Bolivia, told us that approximately sixty-five percent of the volunteers extend beyond the first service term. We were told that nearly half of volunteers have been in the program for six years and approximately thirty-five percent have been in the program for ten years or more. There is no maximum commitment; some volunteers have been with Maryknoll for as long as twenty-five years.

Although Maryknoll has no formal short-term volunteer program in place, it is exploring the possibilities for establishing one. It does offer occasional short-term opportunities through its affiliates, such as teaching English in China and other countries. Maryknoll also sponsors two-week delegations to the U.S./Mexico border, where several volunteers are currently working. Participating groups visit economically poor communities on both sides of the border; learn about the history, demographics and other aspects of the border reality; and partake in prayer, debriefing, and community reflection. Similar "exposure trips" or delegations are offered as well to Latin America, Asia, and Africa.

The Maryknoll Mission Association is one of the few organizations that offer families the opportunity to work overseas. Jean Walsh, a Maryknoll volunteer who served with her husband and children in Mexico, told us that "Maryknoll has twenty-five years of experience working with volunteers with families. They have a lot of accumulated wisdom about bringing families outside of the United States." Maryknoll provides a host of benefits for families, including full health care and a stipend to help cover the cost of the children's education. There are a number of guidelines for acceptance into the program, but these guidelines, we believe, are meant to protect both volunteer families and Maryknoll itself. Prospective volunteers who have recently married, experienced the birth of a child, or been through a divorce or annulment, for example, usually must wait at least one year after that change has been made before Maryknoll will consider them for admission. As mentioned, children must be eight years old or younger at the time the family signs up, but Maryknoll is flexible on the number of children in a volunteer family.

Single applicants also must wait at least a year after a "serious change in lifestyle" before applying to the program. People who have recently made a religious vow, left religious life, or experienced the loss of a spouse, for example, are generally asked to wait one year after these changes before applying to the program. Maryknoll apparently wants volunteers that are in a stable place in their lives, and this works to the benefit of not only the volunteers and the organization but also of the local people they are working with overseas.

Maryknoll usually works in conjunction with a diocese in the host country and volunteers do not get involved in work that the Church opposes such as promotion of birth control or abortion. Maryknoll does not, however, engage in religious proselytizing. Though faith is an important part of the lives of most volunteers, their mission is not to convert. "If a person asks about our faith," said Bernard Butkiewicz, "then we answer but we don't hit them over the head with it. It's not a 'convert-then-help' attitude." Joe Loney, another Maryknoll volunteer we met in Bolivia, told us, "You can't attend to the faith needs of people without attending to their more immediate needs such as food and shelter."

A person's country assignment is decided upon mutually. Working with regional representatives, Maryknoll considers an applicant's country preferences, the type of work that interests them, and the priority needs for that year.

Volunteers annually complete a self-evaluation and participate in two evaluations by others. A person they know well performs an evaluation of their personal growth, using the self-evaluation as a guide, and a supervisor evaluates each volunteer's work performance. Maryknoll is one of the few organizations that evaluate their volunteers, and we believe other organizations can learn from Maryknoll's example.

The month long re-entry program helps returning volunteers re-orient to life in the United States and prepares volunteers who "re-up" for their next three years in the field. The program includes both psychological and job counseling as well as a health checkup. Returning volunteers learn how to stay involved with Maryknoll and continue to work with social justice issues. Bernard Butkiewicz illustrated for us the importance of the program: "When you are going into the field, you are excited about the exotic, the unknown that lies before you. Returning home, however, is a different story. You expect everything to be the same as when you left but in fact it is not. Maryknoll really helps you to prepare for your next step, whether you are transitioning back to the United States or returning to work overseas."

Maryknoll's website offers an abundance of information on its volunteers and programs with stories that provide a window on the lives of Maryknoll lay volunteers. Alison and Davis Purvis, together with their son, Nicholas Diem, whom they adopted in Vietnam, are one volunteer family Maryknoll profiled on its website. They have worked in Vietnam for four years. David runs a program in small business development. His project aims "to enable small traditional artisans to preserve their skills, build a business, and meet the needs of a growing market economy." Alison coordinates a skills-training project for impoverished and physically challenged youth. The project provides these youth with vocational skills in the fields of tailoring, welding, and electrical repair.

Maryknoll works with organizations such as the School of the Americas Watch, the Religious Working Group, and many more that are involved in influencing government policies. Maryknoll puts an emphasis on a strong "option for the poor." In the 1960s, the Second Vatican Council met and, among other things, emphasized the centrality of the poor in the gospel message, and it is in that spirit that Maryknoll designs its work and selects partner organizations.

Maryknoll offers an outstanding opportunity for people who meet the requirements and are deeply committed to long-term volunteer work overseas in social justice programs.

Mennonite Central Committee (MCC)

21 S. Twelfth St.
PO Box 500
Akron, PA 17501-0500

phone: 717-859-1151
fax: 717-859-2171
e-mail: mailbox@mcc.org
web: www.mcc.org

This is MCC: service, friendship, and sharing the peace and love of Christ.—Suzanne Nickel, volunteer, Egypt

Countries where volunteers are currently placed: Afghanistan, Angola, Bangladesh, Bolivia, Botswana, Brazil, Burkina Faso, Burundi, Cambodia, Chad, China, Colombia, Cuba, Democratic Republic of Congo, Egypt, El Salvador, Ethiopia, Guatemala, Haiti, Honduras, India, Indonesia, Iran, Iraq, Jamaica, Japan, Jordan, Kenya, Laos, Lebanon, Lesotho, Liberia, Mexico, Mozambique, Myanmar (Burma), Nigeria, Nepal, Nicaragua, North Korea, Palestine, Paraguay, the Philippines, Rwanda, Swaziland, Syria, Somalia, South Africa, Tanzania, Thailand, Uganda, Vietnam, Zambia, and Zimbabwe

Field(s) of work: Agriculture, health, social service, community development, education, peace, and reconciliation

Requirements or skills necessary: Volunteers must be Christians actively involved in a congregation, but they need not be Mennonites. They should be service-minded and agree with the principles of nonviolent conflict resolution. MCC welcomes married couples who want to serve together.

Duration and dates: Volunteers in the main MCC program commit to three years. MCC also offers programs of shorter duration such as Service and Learning Together (SALT), Adult Exchanges, and Inter/Menno Exchange. (See "Observations and commentary" below for more information on these programs.)

What volunteers pay and what they receive: Most MCC volunteers do not incur any costs, other than some preparation expenses. MCC provides volunteers with round-trip airfare, room and board, a small stipend of $62 per month, and full dental/medical coverage. Volunteers receive a ten-day orientation prior to departure and a field orientation upon arrival in the host country. After their time overseas, volunteers receive a modest re-settlement allowance and dental/medical insurance for a period of up to three months.

Typical volunteer responsibilities: Volunteers serve in agriculture, community development, health, education, social service, as well as religious and peace work. A typical day will include a myriad of different activities. Volunteers may work in offices, fetch water, sit in meetings with church and government officials, talk and eat with people under a tree, teach children how to read, or sign papers so food commodities can be shipped from point A to point B.

Number of volunteers sent abroad annually: 862 (2000)

Age range: 18–99   **Typical age:** None

How to apply: Contact the MCC headquarters in Akron. Applications are accepted year round.

Stated mission: "MCC provides resources and volunteers to meet the needs of people suffering from poverty, oppression, conflict, and natural disasters, serves as a channel for interchange by building relationships that are mutually transformative, and strives for the peace, justice, and dignity of all people by sharing our experiences, resources, and faith in Jesus Christ."

History: The Mennonite churches belong to the "peace churches," denominations known for their rejection of the use of violence to solve conflicts. The Mennonite Central Committee was founded in 1920 as the relief and development agency for the Mennonite and Brethren in Christ churches in North America. As its first mission, the MCC sent volunteers to assist the famine-stricken Ukraine in the aftermath of World War I.

Observations and commentary: MCC is a long-established and highly respected organization that places volunteers in positions with significant professional responsibilities. The type of work varies a great deal from country to country; potential volunteers should visit the website and explore the annual workbooks, which detail the type of projects volunteers are engaged in.

Mary Helen Richer, a volunteer we interviewed in Vietnam, worked with a project called Craftlink. Craftlink was created by Vietnamese MCC staff members, in cooperation with NGOs who saw a need for the production and marketing of traditional handicrafts. Craftlink members began by selling their handicrafts in local bazaars and eventually opened their own retail shop. Craftlink taught women's groups and other collectives how to improve their products in order to meet market demands. Mary's contribution to Craftlink was to give members a perspective on Western tastes while at the same encouraging them to continue using traditional Vietnamese techniques. Mary told us that she saw herself as "a question asker, a facilitator, and idea generator." At the time we interviewed her, Mary had just extended for a fourth year of service.

Most of the volunteers we interviewed gave the long-term program high marks. The word of mouth among Mennonites and other like-minded Christians is very positive. Many MCC volunteers we spoke with said it was the experiences of friends and relatives who had served as MCC volunteers that inspired them to sign up in the first place. The fairly high rate of fourth year extensions also testifies to the fact that volunteers found their first three years to be a positive experience.

Some volunteers felt that their language training had not been thorough enough. More intensive and long-term language training is particularly important for an organization like MCC that emphasizes building relationships with the local people.

Some volunteers we interviewed who lived in relatively remote locations felt that they were not getting all the support from the in-country staff that they would like but understood the travel difficulties involved.

MCC is to be praised for its process of volunteer evaluation, something all too few programs do well. Once a year, each volunteer is evaluated by MCC staff, fellow volunteers, and the volunteer himself. The evaluations are collected and discussed with the volunteer.

Several volunteers told us that MCC provides good support upon return home—something many other organizations fail to do well. MCC's relocation package includes three months of health insurance, vocational and educational assistance, and counseling if needed. MCC staff debriefs returning volunteers, and returned volunteers organize retreats and reunions.

We commend MCC for encouraging its volunteers to share their experiences in the United States. Volunteers are encouraged to write articles for publication during their time overseas. Upon their return to the United States, volunteers are encouraged to give presentations that focus on the impact of U.S. policies on the peoples of other countries. The large network of Mennonite churches is a ready channel for such presentations.

The Mennonite churches believe in simple living. Our field visits confirmed that MCC volunteers tend to live simply, especially when compared with volunteers with some other programs. They do not, however, live as the local poor (for health reasons alone, that would truly not be possible). In the capital of Cambodia, for example, the volunteers lived together in relatively comfortable and spacious compounds, though partly out of security concerns. MCC volunteers in Cambodian provinces were said to live more simply than city-based volunteers, yet still with more comforts than the local poor in one of the world's least developed countries. In Mexico, an MCC volunteer couple we met lived in a rough-hewn wooden shack in a working-class neighborhood. In Nicaragua, volunteers try not to use private vehicles; they take the bus like most people do.

MCC, to its credit, is wary of the often negative impacts of material aid. As MCC coordinators in Nicaragua told us, "Material aid is seldom good. It is divisive and creates dependency. Nicaragua is cursed with material aid." MCC recognizes that there have been times when local people in countries with a significant foreign aid history complain that MCC volunteers "don't give us anything."

MCC programs are not proselytizing in nature; rather they are service-oriented, or what MCC calls a "ministry of presence." In some parts of the world, in fact, MCC cautions volunteers against building new churches. As Fremont Regier, a MCC staffer in Zimbabwe commented: "We realize that Africa's main problem is not a lack of churches."

In addition to three-year programs, MCC also offers several shorter-term international volunteer programs:

1. **Service and Learning Together (SALT):** North Americans, aged eighteen to twenty-four, live overseas in one of sixteen countries on one-year learning and service assignments. Because participants are young people, SALT is much more structured than other MCC programs. SALT applications are due every year on January 31.

2. **The Youth Discovery Team (YDT):** Small groups of youth, aged eighteen to twenty-four, from around the world, come together for three to six months to participate in team activities such as music groups. YDT also provides young people with an experience in cross-cultural living, and educates them on topics such as the impact of multinational corporations on small-scale farmers.

3. **Inter/Menno Training Program:** North Americans volunteer for one year on work assignments in Europe. The Inter/Menno Committee in Europe administers the program and MCC facilitates the placement of North American volunteers.

4. **Adult Exchanges:** Adults from different countries, but similar to identical professions, volunteer to exchange jobs for one year. A teacher from Africa, for example, takes the place of a North American teacher, and the North American teacher travels to Africa.

The main purpose of the SALT program is to provide younger volunteers—most of whom have just finished their first or second years of university—with an experience of another culture. Though there is a service aspect to the program, it is less pronounced than in the long-term program. In SALT, more than the long-term program, the focus is on learning rather than providing a service. "We feel that we're always in the learning mode," said Freemont Regier. "As long as we're on someone else's turf, it behooves us to operate in the learner's mode and not to be pushing from behind or leading from ahead but to be journeying with." SALT volunteers prepare a newsletter called "SALT Tidbits," made up of poetry and stories by SALTers; it is sent out to MCC's members. SALT serves as excellent preparation for the longer-term programs.

Jeffrey Zortman, a SALT volunteer we interviewed in Zimbabwe, taught classes, such as a New Testament survey course, and helped with office work. Jeffrey found his work interesting, but said that the work was not a perfect fit. As an undergraduate in college, he studied computer science and mathematics. As a volunteer with MCC and just out of college, he found his work as an office accountant a bit of a stretch beyond what he was used to doing. "In a way," he told us, "it was challenging. But it was good because I did things I wouldn't normally do, such as teaching." Bruce Khumalo, Jeffrey's supervisor, said he appreciated SALT not only for the service offered to the school, but also because it provides young people from the U.S. with rare, first-hand opportunities to learn from other cultures.

We did not interview participants in the other short-term programs and therefore cannot comment on them, but they appear to be based on the same values as the long-term MCC program. For progressive-minded, pacifist Christians who can make a three-year commitment, this is one of the very best volunteer placement options. The most successful MCC volunteers will be those who agree with the MCC philosophy of simple living, nonviolent conflict resolution, learning from the local people, and promoting solidarity, not proselytism.

MCC started about seventy-six years ago by providing aid to war-torn Europe. Slowly, through the 1960s and '70s, MCC became concerned with what you might call "development." Then it was advocacy work. Then we moved into environmental concerns and justice work.—Freemont Regier, staff, Zimbabwe

People who apply to MCC should remember that it is a personnel placement organization. Applicants should be people who want to work with local organizations, people who want to be flexible, who are interested in the challenge of not knowing exactly what they are going to do, and preferably don't have too rigid an idea about how things should be done.—Susan Lind, MCC staff, South Africa

My purpose here is to live out my Christian faith. Service to others is an expression of this faith, and faith is what has sustained me.—John Means, MCC, Cambodia

Minnesota Studies in International Development (MSID)

c/o Global Campus Study Abroad
230 Heller Hall
271 Nineteenth Ave. South
University of Minnesota
Minneapolis, MN 55455

phone: 612-626-9000
fax: 612-626-8009
e-mail: umabroad@umn.edu
web: www.umabroad.umn.edu

MSID is for people who want to really experience every part of life in the host country. The family stay was the highlight.—Sara Leiste, volunteer, India

Countries where volunteers are placed: Ecuador, India, Kenya, and Senegal

Field(s) of work: Academic study complemented by volunteer placements with grassroots organizations working in wide range of fields related to development. Volunteers work with local organizations in public health, women's issues, micro-business, environmental protection, education, sustainable agriculture, social services, and community organizing.

Requirements or special skills necessary: MSID is primarily for students in their third or fourth year of undergraduate studies but it is also open to graduate students and others who have already earned a university degree. Applicants must have at least a 2.5 GPA. Ecuador participants must have completed the equivalent of two years of university level Spanish, and Senegal participants must have completed the equivalent of two years of university level French.

Duration and dates: MSID offers three enrollment options: a fifteen-week fall semester that runs early September through mid-December, a full academic year consisting of the fifteen-week fall semester and a seventeen-week spring semester that includes a three-week break for travel; and a twenty-one-week spring semester in Kenya that runs from mid-January to mid-June.

What volunteers pay and what they receive: In the 2001 through 2002 school year, costs for Ecuador were $8,700 for the fall semester and $12,400 for the academic year; for India, $7,300 for the fall semester and $10,200 for the academic year; for Kenya, $8,100 for the fall semester, $11,600 for the academic year, and $8,900 for spring semester; and for Senegal, $8,100 for the fall semester and $11,600 for the academic year. Non-University of Minnesota students add $750 to each program fee.

Program fees cover tuition, academic credit, field study/internship and registration fees, accommodations, most meals, and program-related travel and fieldtrips while overseas. Volunteers pay for their own airfare, although they travel on prearranged group flights. Volunteers must also pay for their own pre-departure immunizations, passports and photos, entry visas, health insurance, and any independent travel.

University of Minnesota students may apply most of their financial aid to MSID programs. Students from other institutions are often able to do the same, depending on their universities' financial aid policies; they should consult with their study abroad office. Some partial scholarships are available, including several scholarships reserved for University of Minnesota students.

Typical volunteer responsibilities: The work done by volunteers in both their fall semester field placements and their spring internships varies widely. Responsibilities have included managing a tree nursery, writing a funding proposal for a women's cooperative, developing a marketing plan for local artisans, shadowing a local obstetrician, or observing and assisting at a rural mother and child clinic.

Number of volunteers sent abroad annually: 60–90

Age range: 20+   **Typical age:** 20–24

How to apply: Request a current program brochure and application. Submit an application indicating your country of choice and attaching the required essays, resume, letters of recommendation, and college transcript.

The deadline for priority consideration is February 15. The regular deadline is March 15. Applications submitted after April 16 are considered on a space-available basis.

Stated mission: "MSID is devoted to the preparation of culturally sensitive individuals who are committed to justice and sustainable development for all societies in our interdependent world. MSID seeks to engage students, faculty, and staff in dialogue and reciprocal learning with people from Africa, Asia, and Latin America. MSID's concerns include both local and global problems, with a particular emphasis on development and social change issues. Through grassroots internships and research in economically poor communities, MSID participants gain firsthand understanding of the conditions, needs, and strengths of the countries involved with the program."

History: MSID was founded in 1982 and has taken nearly 800 students overseas. Past countries of operation included Colombia, Morocco, and Jamaica. Although MSID is a program of the University of Minnesota, from the beginning it has also accepted participants who are not University of Minnesota students.

Observations and commentary: The MSID experience begins in the summertime when participants receive readings and assignments and then moves into high gear with the one-week orientation in Minnesota. The orientation includes preliminary discussions of development as well as an introduction to issues such as culture shock, relating to your host family, and safety. As Ellen Donaghue commented, "The time in Minnesota was good. I liked talking to the other country groups and hearing people's reasons for going."

Once overseas, students continue their orientation, moving in with their host families within a few days of their arrival. This family relationship is an essential part of the program. Jed Iverson, a volunteer in India, commented that "MSID has given us time to get comfortable with our families and relax, assimilate, and go shopping so that we can wear Indian clothes. It is nice to have a place to call home and have a connection. It's amazing that people are willing to have you in their home. They are so welcoming."

The academic study is a group experience, with the MSID students taking classes together every day with local instructors. The course of study includes seminars, discussions, fieldtrips, and guest lectures. The emphasis is on reflection and the personal experiences of the students. Some participants like the academic structure for reflection while others find it challenging having to complete academic requirements when they "really wanted to just be part of the scene."

The fall curriculum is the same in all four countries and is comprised of the following classes: Theories of International Development, Cross-Cultural Communication, Topics in International Development, Country Seminar, Development Agency/Project Analysis, and a language course.

While academics are an important part of the program, José Suarez, the administrative director in Ecuador, believes that the most important part of the program is the "strong friendship that the student and the local people develop while working together. In that way, they are able to understand one another, respect different cultural values, and establish a strong solidarity for the communities' efforts." Volunteer Sara Leiste thought that family-stays were the most important part of the experience explaining that "It was a chance to be involved with community life. The experience would have been hollow had I not had a chance to get to know Indian families."

Although MSID offers three enrollment options, everyone we spoke with expressed a preference for the full-year program. While the shorter programs fit some students' schedules, students who leave after the fall have "just begun to adjust." Staying the full year provides more opportunities for learning and makes it possible for the student to contribute something to the communities where they are working.

If only going for the fall semester, then students have a four-week internship placement. January term gives students an opportunity to take a directed research class and extend their internship by another four weeks. Full-year students have even more time to volunteer as they participate in a nineteen-week-long internship broken up by a two-week-long midterm conference and writing period.

Volunteer placements are highly individualized. As Sharmila Godbole, administrative director in India, explained, "Most of the students go into the rural areas since the program is more about grassroots development. . . . Not all students are with NGOs. Some are placed directly in communities. It always depends on the student's interest." Sudha Datar, the academic director in India, added, "They are highly individualized stays; otherwise it is meaningless. They work with grassroots level agencies. They are typically not in the office but having direct contact with the beneficiaries." Working at the grassroots level was frustrating to some students who complained about poor communication with their host organizations and the challenge of waiting around at times with no particular projects or tasks to do. Several students commented that they were mostly observing the work of their agency. As one student emphasized, "The goal of volunteering was learning, not accomplishment." For some, however, the initial volunteer placements were not satisfactory. In these cases the local staff was quite responsive and helpful in arranging an alternative volunteer placement.

The variety of volunteer work is truly impressive. Whether teaching mathematics or adult literacy, working in an orphanage or health clinic, or helping out with women's producer groups, volunteers get to do work that is related to their personal interests. Volunteers have the ability to work with local coordinators to undertake unique projects, like one volunteer we met who was working alongside traditional Maasai healers in Kenya.

MSID is a good program for students who want to combine the challenges of rigorous academic exploration of development issues with experiential learning. The program succeeds at giving participants a thoughtful and critical approach to development, at times emphasizing the learning process above the tangible results of a specific volunteer project. This program is for people with a strong interest in the country or region for which they apply and a desire to explore cultural differences, social justice issues, and international development. If you just want to volunteer, however, and are not excited about studying international development, this program is not for you.

> *My host family in the village was amazing. They taught me so much about my perspective about life and people. I want to go back just to see them.—Angela Crowley-Koch, India*

Mobility International (MIUSA)

PO Box 10767
Eugene, OR 97440

phone: 541-343-1284 (v/tty)
fax: 541-343-6812
e-mail: info@miusa.org
web: www.miusa.org

> *I hope that my story will encourage everyone with a disability who has ever thought about volunteering abroad to apply to any organization that offers the opportunity. Don't wait to be recruited. Just apply. Have an open mind and a few ideas about how you might deal with the differences you might find in another country. Take the chance, and you may have one of the most enjoyable and educational experiences of your life.*
> *—Sarah Presley, who is blind, Peace Corps volunteer, Morocco (from MIUSA website)*

Countries where volunteers are placed: A number of countries worldwide, including Azerbaijan, Bulgaria, China, Costa Rica, Germany, Italy, Japan, Mexico, Russia, the United Kingdom, and the United States

Field(s) of work: Delegations, manual labor, construction, teaching, health care, adaptive technology, advocacy, and leadership training

Requirements or special skills necessary: Most but not all MIUSA participants are people with disabilities, including people who are visually impaired, deaf, or in wheelchairs. Many have been involved in disability rights work in their home communities. MIUSA does not accept people under the age of 18 on its own delegations, but some collaborating organizations do. Both married and unmarried couples may join MIUSA delegations as well as many of the collaborating organizations' delegations.

Duration and dates: MIUSA organizes delegations that last from one week to one month. MIUSA collaborates with a wide range of organizations that offer volunteer placements of one week to two years. Start dates vary.

What volunteers pay and what they receive: MIUSA's own delegations, such as the 2001 summer exchange to Costa Rica, cost approximately $750. Generous partial scholarships are available. Fees cover orientation, transportation from the orientation in the United States to the host country, room, board, excursions, and adaptive assistance such as sign language interpretation (where available).

The fees to volunteer with collaborating organizations vary greatly. Some organizations cover all expenses while others charge fees of up to several thousand dollars.

Typical volunteer responsibilities: MIUSA sponsors a small number of its own delegations through which people with disabilities from the United States have the opportunity to meet with people with disabilities from other countries and explore issues of disability rights. Some of these delegations have a volunteer component such as helping to make a trail in a national park accessible to people with disabilities.

Through the National Clearinghouse on Disability and Exchange (NCDE), MIUSA helps people with disabilities link with a wide range of volunteer placement organizations, offering work opportunities in virtually every field from teaching a first-grade English class to providing medical care for refugees.

Number of volunteers sent abroad annually: Seventeen delegates were sent overseas and thirty-two were hosted in the United States (2000). Many more volunteers are referred to other volunteer placement organizations each year.

Age range: 25–retired   **Typical age:** None
18–24 (MIUSA youth delegations)
25–retired (MIUSA Adult and professional delegations)
(Note: Adult and professional delegations are not offered every year.)
Organizations that collaborate with MIUSA: all ages

How to apply: To participate in a MIUSA delegation, call or e-mail MIUSA for an application form and information. Dozens of collaborating volunteer placement organizations can be contacted through the MIUSA website. Volunteers apply directly to these organizations.

Stated mission: "As a U.S.-based nonprofit organization, the mission of Mobility International USA (MIUSA) is to empower people with disabilities around the world through international exchange, information, technical assistance, and training, and to ensure the inclusion of people with disabilities in international exchange and development programs."

History: Mobility International grew out of Susan Sygall's personal experience as a Rotary scholar in Australia. She returned from her trip convinced that international exchange is crucial for people with disabilities to develop as leaders and in 1981 she founded Mobility International along with Barbara Williams.

In 1995, with funding from the United States Information Agency, MIUSA launched the National Clearinghouse on Disability and Exchange (NCDE) to further promote the inclusion of people with disabilities in international exchange.

Observations and commentary: MIUSA is a pioneering organization and a leader in the movement for diversity in the field of international volunteer exchange. As mentioned earlier, in addition to its own exchange program, MIUSA also manages the National Clearinghouse on Disability and Exchange (NCDE). The NCDE works to educate people with disabilities about international volunteer opportunities, promoting the inclusion of people with disabilities in all types of exchange and service programs. Through the NCDE, MIUSA has helped people with disabilities volunteer with Peace Corps, American Field Service (AFS), the Council on International Educational Exchange, and a variety of other organizations. The NCDE also provides advice and technical assistance to international exchange organizations and universities on how to include people with disabilities in their exchange programs. The NCDE website has a database that can be searched by region, country, or disability type for information about accessible transportation, disability organizations in other cultures, and volunteer opportunities.

While we did not have the opportunity to meet with any of MIUSA's overseas delegations, we have had extensive interaction with their efforts in the United States to make the field of international volunteering more accessible. MIUSA does an excellent job of not only providing exchange opportunities but also challenging other international volunteer organizations to be more inclusive of people with disabilities and then assisting them in meeting the challenge. We most highly recommend MIUSA as a resource for anyone with a disability who is considering volunteering overseas, as well as for others who want to learn more about disabilities and international exchange.

New Haven/Leon Sister City Project (NH/LSCP)

608 Whitney Ave.
New Haven, CT 06511

phone: 203-562-1607
fax: 203-624-1683
e-mail: nh@newhavenleon.org
web: wwwnewhavenleon.org

Countries where volunteers are placed: Nicaragua

Field(s) of work: Construction, agriculture, transportation, play therapy, and prevention of domestic violence

Requirements or special skills necessary: Volunteers must have substantial work experience in their area of expertise, be able to communicate in Spanish, and be prepared to live in a physically demanding climate with minimal comforts and conveniences. Both married and unmarried couples are accepted as volunteers. Children under the age of 18 (usually teenagers) accompanied by adults are accepted into the program.

Duration and dates: Construction delegations go to Nicaragua for ten days in August. Peace and Justice Project volunteers spend from one month to one year in Leon.

What volunteers pay and what they receive: The cost of the program depends on the length of stay. Volunteers pay their airfare, food and lodging, and an administrative fee. They live with host families. Monetary compensation and stipends are not provided.

Typical volunteer responsibilities: NH/LSCP has two different volunteer opportunities: short-term delegations, and long-term Peace and Justice Project assignments for skilled professionals. Delegations are organized according to interest groups, such as university and church groups. Past construction delegations, for example, have helped to build village preschools. Almost all delegations have a work component. Peace and Justice Project volunteers share their expertise in community development programs. Both volunteers and delegates live with host families. Returned volunteers are encouraged to continue to support the program.

Number of volunteers sent abroad annually: N/A

Age range: 16–75   **Typical age:** None

How to apply: Prospective volunteers should contact the New Haven office to discuss the program and their interests and qualifications. They will be sent an application form, which will then be reviewed by a selection committee in New Haven for consideration by the Leon office. Orientation may be minimal (phone calls and e-mail) for short-term construction work, or more extensive for Peace and Justice assignments, with reading assignments and other preparatory work even before volunteers enter an orientation program in Leon.

Stated mission: "The New Haven/Leon Sister City Project is a progressive grassroots organization that fosters a sister city relationship between New Haven, Connecticut, and Leon, Nicaragua. The project promotes mutual understanding, growth, and development in both cities through programs that support just models in the political, economic, social, spiritual, and cultural spheres."

History: Inspired by the 1979 social justice revolution in Nicaragua, the New Haven/Leon Sister City Project formed in 1984 "with the dual purpose of supporting the revolutionary process and exposing the hypocrisy of U.S. foreign policy." Today, the NH/LSCP supports integrated sustainable community development through a variety of programs in Leon.

NISGUA Guatemala Accompaniment Project

1830 Connecticut Ave. NW
Washington, DC 20009

phone: 202-265-8713
fax: 202-223-8221
e-mail: nisguagap@igc.org
web: www.nisgua.org

The training was excellent; it included lots of role-playing. We were asked, for example, "What do you do if a woman comes in with a sick child and says she needs one hundred dollars? What if someone comes to you and says the Army has just come?"
—Melinda Van Slyke, volunteer, Guatemala

Countries where volunteers are placed: Guatemala

Field(s) of work: Human rights monitoring and reporting

Requirements or special skills necessary: Volunteers must be at least twenty-one years old and should be proficient in Spanish. There is no educational requirement, but most applicants have an undergraduate degree. Volunteers must have the ability to undertake human rights monitoring and reporting. They must have good writing and analytical skills, cultural sensitivity and good judgment, and a willingness to live simply in rugged conditions.

Duration and dates: Volunteers are placed for six months to one year. Programs are ongoing; there are no standard start or end dates. NISGUA holds three volunteer trainings a year usually in February, June, and October. The training locations rotate but are always in the United States.

What volunteers pay and what they receive: Each volunteer is linked to a U.S. sponsoring community that provides a monthly stipend of $275 and pays for health insurance. The stipend adequately covers travel within Guatemala, food, living expenses, and an orientation as well as a bimonthly retreat. The Guatemalan host community provides housing. The volunteer is normally expected to fundraise to cover other expenses, including airfare, a training fee ($320), and language school, if needed. There is no set program fee, as costs will be negotiated with the sponsoring community, but a typical fundraising goal is $1,000 to $1,500. Volunteers may arrange to receive academic credit and/or loan deferrals.

Typical volunteer responsibilities: Volunteers familiarize themselves with the life and dynamics of a Mayan community, gather information on the human rights situation and the peace process, write articles and reports, and undertake educational outreach about the Guatemalan Accompaniment Project. Upon return to the United States, volunteers educate their communities about the situation of the displaced Mayans and seek to change U.S. policy toward Guatemala.

Number of volunteers sent abroad annually: 30

Age range: 21 and older   **Typical age:** 25–30

How to apply: The application process includes an evaluation of a written application, a phone interview, a one-week training course, and reference checking. This process takes an average of five weeks to complete.

Stated mission: "NISGUA (Network in Solidarity with the People of Guatemala) supports the social movement in Guatemala for a democratic, multiethnic, and multicultural society, based on socioeconomic justice and full respect for human rights and freedom of expression. In addition, [they] work to educate and empower U.S. citizens in their efforts to influence U.S. policy toward Guatemala in support of the above goals, to build links between social justice initiatives in Guatemala and the United States, and to promote grassroots organizing efforts that forge ties of solidarity and understanding between the peoples of both countries."

History: The Guatemala Accompaniment Project (GAP) was founded in 1995 to respond to requests from Mayan refugee groups for international observers to accompany them as they reintegrated into Guatemalan society. In 1999, GAP became a project of NISGUA, a grassroots solidarity group that has lobbied on human rights and U.S. policy in Guatemala since the 1980s. Together, the two organizations seek policy change while at the same time providing direct on-the-ground support for at-risk Mayan communities.

Observations and commentary: NISGUA volunteers placed through GAP "accompany" Mayans displaced by the civil war in Guatemala. Accompaniers act as human rights observers in Guatemala and help to strengthen relationships between the United States and Mayan communities. NISGUA has cited several reasons why a Mayan community might request accompaniment: a need for protection (not through weapons but through the attention of the international community), a desire to feel more connected to the outside world, and the community's experience that where there have been accompaniers with them there have not been assaults.

One of the unique features of NISGUA is that each Mayan community NISGUA works with is linked with a community in the United States. After volunteers are admitted into the program and pass through training they are sent first to these sister communities to raise funds for their term as volunteers. Upon completion of their time with the Mayan community, volunteers return to the sister communities to educate people there and strengthen their connection with the Mayans.

NISGUA's volunteer training is reportedly excellent. The week-long training includes role playing, an introduction to the philosophy of international human rights accompaniment, and an overview of the Guatemalan civil war. The training also includes instruction in nonviolent action, human rights reporting and monitoring. Upon arrival in Guatemala, the NISGUA staff provides an on-the-ground orientation and accompanies the volunteer to the placement site. Before volunteers depart from their host communities in Guatemala, the communities evaluate them to give volunteers a final opportunity to reflect on how they can improve their skills as accompaniers.

Most volunteers live in difficult-to-reach communities located in hot, humid, low-lying areas where it rains heavily for up to eight months of the year. Volunteers sleep in wooden houses with thatched or tin roofs and dirt floors. They have limited access to running water and electricity. Volunteers should be prepared for these conditions.

NISGUA is a member of the Latin American Working Group (LAWG) and is involved in lobbying and advocacy efforts in both the United States and Guatemala. In addition to volunteer positions in Guatemala, NISGUA also offers unpaid internships in its Washington, DC, office. Interns provide assistance in organizing the Human Rights Rapid Response Network, speaking tours, legislative work, and a news bulletin. They have pressured for the prosecution of participants in massacres of Mayan villagers and have lobbied the Guatemalan government to fulfill its obligations under the 1992 accord on refugee return.

We believe that NISGUA provides an example for other volunteer placement organizations in three ways. First, NISGUA understands that political work, such as human rights documentation, aims to change the structures that perpetuate injustice. While it is harder to train volunteers to do political work than to train them, for example, to dig latrines, the political work has the potential to have a greater impact in the long run. Second, NISGUA is one of the few volunteer programs that creates the space for host communities to evaluate volunteers. Finally, NISGUA does a commendable job of involving volunteers in the education of communities in the United States.

Volunteers have told us that accompaniment is demanding but rewarding work. Volunteers must be ready to report human rights abuses. They must be able to live simply and at times spend weeks without contact with people from their own culture. If you are proficient in Spanish, have a strong commitment to the protection of human rights, and are capable of living under physically and emotionally challenging conditions, NISGUA may be a good choice for you.

Nuestros Pequeños Hermanos (NPH)

Volunteer Coordinator
Apartado Postal 30-500
06470 Mexico, D.F. Mexico

phone: 011 (52-73) 11-26-54; 11-46-00
fax: 011 (52-73) 11-26-55
web: www.nphamigos.org

When you leave here, you realize how important the kids are to you—and you to them.—Jim Shydlowski, repeat volunteer, Mexico

Countries where volunteers are placed: Guatemala, Haiti, Honduras, Mexico, and Nicaragua

Field(s) of work: Work with youth in "orphan homes;" engineering, construction, and repair of NPH infrastructure

Requirements or special skills necessary: The minimum age is normally twenty-one, but younger is possible, if an applicant is mature and has at least a high school diploma. The reason NPH seeks volunteers older than twenty-one is because it wants the volunteers who work with the children to be role models, not peers, with some experience in the world. Nevertheless, in practice, many of the volunteers are young college graduates.

A working knowledge of Spanish is required for all the sites except Haiti where French (or better, Creole) is required. All volunteers are required to study some Creole in their first weeks in Haiti. Working directly with the children demands being at ease in the local language. Those with less fluency in the local language can be assigned to work in the office or on the farm.

There are also positions for engineers (environmental, electrical, etc.), technicians (lab, sanitary, etc.), and tradespeople (plumbers, electricians, painters, etc.). For more information about these opportunities visit the Infrastructure and Engineering Volunteer Opportunities Website, www.alistaraz.org.

While NPH is a Catholic organization, a volunteer may be accepted regardless of his or her religious affiliation (or lack thereof). A volunteer must respect religious faith and, if working directly with the kids, must go with them to church.

Heterosexual couples are encouraged to apply. NPH sees them as role models.

Duration and dates: Positions that involve working directly with children are for a minimum of one year, because stability is critical for the orphans. Volunteers who wish to extend their stay may do so for another year or more, provided the NPH country director agrees. There are possibilities of short-term volunteer work in the offices or farms. Applications should be sent in by April 1 for a July 15 start date and by October 1 for a January 15 start date. Other start-up dates may be possible. There are short-term volunteer opportunities in Haiti (July through August) and Honduras (November through February). Deadlines for applications are April 1 for Haiti and August 15 for Honduras.

What volunteers pay and what they receive: Volunteers pay their own travel expenses. Volunteers who work for more than two years, however, may receive a paid trip home. Volunteers in Haiti, considered a "hardship post," receive an annual trip to Miami. Volunteers are encouraged to purchase their own health insurance (and are referred to a relatively inexpensive policy designed for missionaries). For primary care, the health facilities at the orphanages are available free of charge to the volunteers. NPH provides on-site room and board. Volunteers share quarters, with different quarters for men and women. Separate small quarters are available for married couples. A small stipend is given to each volunteer, except in Mexico where none is provided. Volunteers are encouraged to do some modest fundraising to cover their expenses before departing for their assignments, and NPH provides information about the orphanage to help with the fundraising.

Typical volunteer responsibilities: Volunteer positions vary. During an initial period of up to a few weeks, volunteers work in an orphanage's administrative office in order to adjust to the new surroundings and become more familiar with NPH (as well as the organization with the volunteer). Volunteers are then placed in one of a variety of positions in view of the orphanage's current needs, and the volunteer's talents and fluency in the local language. Positions for volunteers include supervising children (up to age seventeen) as assistant "parents" in the dormitories, facilitating correspondence with the children's sponsors in Europe and North America, teaching and assisting teachers in the schools, preparing meals, and working as health professionals in the orphanages' clinics.

Number of volunteers sent abroad annually: 65 (1998)

Age range: 18–60   **Typical age:** 22–25

How to apply: Inquiries should be made through the volunteer coordinator's office in Mexico. A packet with information on all five sites together with application materials is sent to all that inquire. Applications can also be downloaded from the website. In applying, one may state which country is preferred. Completed applications for work in Mexico, Nicaragua, and Guatemala should be sent to the volunteer coordinator in the Mexico office. Applications for work in Honduras and Haiti should be sent directly to NPH in those countries. Once an applicant has been approved, the application is sent to the NPH director in the country for which the applicant has expressed a preference. The country director then decides whether he or she is interested in the applicant. A health form must be completed by the applicant's physician. Applications that the volunteer coordinator judges to be worth pursuing are forwarded to a psychoanalyst for his decision as to whether the applicant appears suitable to work with children. If the applicant is judged not to be suitable for direct work with the children but is thought to be a good potential volunteer, he/she may be invited to work with NPH in another capacity.

Stated mission: "NPH provides orphaned and abandoned children food, shelter, clothing, health care, and education in a Christian family environment. The care is based on unconditional acceptance and love, sharing, work, and responsibility."

History: Founded in 1954 in Mexico by Father Wasson, a U.S. Catholic priest, NPH is today home and "family" for over 2,500 children, from infants through young adults, in five countries. Over the past forty-five years the NPH orphanages have been home to more than 15,000 orphaned and abandoned children. NPH started only with boys, but now there are boys and girls, as its name in English implies ("Our Little Sisters and Brothers").

Observations and commentary: NPH is an impressive organization. We visited NPH in four of the five countries in which it operates orphanages. The first thing to impress us was that the directors and other key staff are invariably former *pequeños* who now have training and even university degrees in relevant fields. As José Luis Mejía, NPH country director in Nicaragua, once a hungry street kid in Mexico, proudly explained to us, "The kids know that we know where they are coming from."

NPH emphasizes that it is a "family" that an orphaned or abandoned child joins and absolutely not an organization that seeks parents to adopt them.

NPH has a volunteer service philosophy built in. Every *pequeño* has a daily job, from dusting and mopping to cooking and farming. After graduating from high school, each youth is called upon to give NPH a year or more of volunteer service as house directors, medical assistants, or office staff. If they go on for further schooling through NPH, they are expected to give two years of volunteer service. Some of these young adults do this service in other countries; for instance, we found a number of Mexican former *pequeños* working at the orphan home on the island of Ometepe in Nicaragua.

The application process for prospective volunteers is appropriately professional. The essay questions asked of applicants are thoughtful and relevant to the work. Applicants are asked, for example: "Why do you wish to work for Nuestros Pequeños Hermanos?" "In a few sentences, describe a child with whom you have had some experience." "What is your religious background and what does religion mean to you?" "What would you do if you discovered that a child had stolen something highly valued that belonged to another child?"

Volunteers told us they find that they are inspired by the commitment of everyone involved with NPH. They also praised the good working relations between staff and volunteers. "The distinction between staff and volunteer is really blurred," noted Jean-Marc Du Plantier, a volunteer at the NPH orphanage in Haiti.

Volunteers commented negatively, however, on the lack of a good orientation.

NPH staff we interviewed agreed with the criticism and reported they had specific plans to initiate a serious orientation for new volunteers. Volunteers and staff describe training for volunteers as "on the job."

All commented that working with the children is demanding. Long hours are normal. Because of the family atmosphere, volunteers are expected to spend major holidays at the orphanages. Jim Shydlowski, a volunteer with NPH in Mexico, who at the time of our interview was back for his third stint, commented, "A year of giving yourself fully is a lot. It is hard to do. You need a break. Two years is the maximum without a break."

Jim also noted that while Father Wasson's original idea was that the older kids would look after the younger ones, the reality is that many of the kids come from abusive backgrounds. "So there is a role for volunteers. If you're an assistant dorm director and you realize that the older kid who is the director is abusive, you can bring that out. His peers are unlikely to do so."

NPH estimates that out of every twelve volunteers, two to three drop out, while another two to three stay on for more than a year. Occasionally, according to NPH, a volunteer has been asked to leave; the example given to us was that of a volunteer who was found to be too physical in disciplining the children.

Volunteers come from the United States, Canada, and several western European countries, notably the Netherlands and Germany, where NPH maintains offices to solicit donations and sponsorships for the children.

We recommend NPH for mature volunteers, especially those who already have some experience working with kids. It's not for you if you are unsure about your ability to handle a very high degree of responsibility or if you feel uncomfortable in a context of social and Catholic religious rules.

> *It is good for the children that the volunteers come with different ideas and different ways of thinking from the staff. But we also have our own views that we uphold as a program. For example, let's say a volunteer were open to abortion—we wouldn't like that foreigner to have influence on the children in that way.—Alfonso Leon, director of NPH orphanage, Haiti*

> *The children who find their way to NPH have been orphaned, abused, shuffled from one family member to another. Like all children, they are seeking love and security, a place they can call home. When they come to NPH, they are told they will never be asked to leave. The children grow and learn in their culture and language and become contributing citizens in their own countries. Also, many children arrive with several brothers and sisters; NPH wants to keep them together.—Excerpt from a NPH brochure*

> *You have to remember that you're here for a year or two. You can get close to the kids, but you shouldn't make them dependent on you.—Eileen Shydlowski, NPH volunteer, Mexico*

You got to expect that things are going to be slow, that the kids aren't going to be doing everything you want to do. . . . You need the ability to see beyond the immediate problem.—Jean-Marc Du Plantier, volunteer, Haiti

---

Operation Crossroads Africa (OCA)

475 Riverside Dr., Suite 1368
New York, NY 10027

phone: 212-870-2106
fax: 212-870-2644
e-mail: oca@igc.org
web: www.igc.org/oca

I wanted to learn more about myself and how Africans live. The best parts are the opportunities to come to Africa, not as a tourist; the friendships within the group; and facing issues I did not expect. Everything I "knew" about poverty went out the window. —Maury Bonner, volunteer, Kenya

Countries where volunteers are placed: Benin, Botswana, Brazil, Burkina Faso, the Gambia, Ghana, Kenya, Malawi, Mali, Namibia, Senegal, South Africa, Tanzania, Uganda, Zambia, and Zimbabwe

Field(s) of work: Construction, community health, agriculture, reforestation, and education

Requirements or special skills necessary: Applicants must have strong communication skills and a willingness to respect different lifestyles, beliefs, and values. Students of medicine and related fields are encouraged to apply. Knowledge of French, Portuguese, or a local language is beneficial, but not required. All projects involve a component of physical work, so applicants should be in good health. Both married and unmarried couples are accepted into the program, but couples are not encouraged to apply because they alter the group dynamics for other participants.

Duration and dates: Just over seven weeks (mid-June to mid-August) consisting of three days of orientation in New York, six weeks of work overseas, and one week of travel in the host country.

What volunteers pay and what they receive: A $3,500 participation fee covers all program expenses including round-trip airfare. Volunteers are responsible for their own travel to the orientation in New York City. Personal expenses such as souvenirs are not included in the program fee. Crossroaders seeking college credit typically receive five to ten semester credits for their summer experience. OCA provides advice for fundraising, and recently has provided a few scholarships to select participants.

Typical volunteer responsibilities: Tasks vary widely depending on the project, and include teaching English or computer skills, building shelters and community facilities, providing basic medical services, and performing other forms of manual labor.

Number of volunteers sent abroad annually: 165 (2001)

Age range: 17–32   **Typical age:** 21

How to apply: Applications are received year round, but the deadline for summer is February 1. Applications are reviewed on a rolling basis, so the earlier you apply the better. Application requirements include an autobiographical sketch, short answers to several essay questions, two passport photos, a letter from your physician, and an application fee of $25. Make three copies of the application. Send the original and one copy to OCA, and keep one for yourself.

Stated mission: "Operation Crossroads Africa (OCA) promotes cross-cultural sharing and understanding, lending sweat and muscle to build friendship."

History: OCA was founded in 1957 "to combat American ignorance about Africa." OCA founder Dr. James H. Robinson believed all people are "fundamentally more similar than dissimilar," and that by living and working together, we create a "crossroads" of cultures and personal experience—the birthplace of both individual and societal change. American President John F. Kennedy acknowledged OCA as the "progenitor of the Peace Corps." Since its inception OCA has sent over 10,000 volunteers to thirty-five African countries, twelve Caribbean countries, and Brazil.

Observations and commentary: OCA is an important and generally well-respected organization, in part because it is one of the oldest programs placing North American volunteers overseas, and because it has been successful in recruiting a culturally diverse group of volunteers. OCA also places a relatively high number of volunteers in regions of Africa that have been virtually ignored by most other volunteer programs.

Our research revealed that OCA is an organization with a committed staff and a logical program structure but inconsistent program quality due in part to inexperienced group leaders.

A group we interviewed in Tanzania had a positive experience. They were placed with a local cooperative. They learned a great deal from the Africans, as well as each other. Initially, they were surprised that the community was flourishing and self-sufficient; they had expected to find extreme poverty and misery. The "youth" they worked with were twenty to thirty-five years old, older than most of the volunteers, who had thought that they would be working with young children. Their group leader helped them process reasons for their faulty assumptions and helped to turn what could have been a disappointing experience into a positive one. As volunteer Danika Powell stated, "The key to survival was that we communicated among ourselves. When problems arose, we stopped, stepped back, and then came together to discuss the situation. We kept communication open instead of people retreating into their own worlds."

The volunteers we met in Kenya, however, had a very different experience. They were shocked and unprepared for the very challenging physical conditions of their work site. Water was a four-kilometer hike away, and food shopping required a two-hour bus ride. While these challenges could probably have been positive lessons, the group leader was not skilled in facilitating discussions about the difficulties they were experiencing. Their volunteer role at the local orphanage was undefined and this posed another challenge to the group. The volunteers became bitter about their situation and had disagreements that made their experience even more negative. In general, they felt they had not been well prepared for the realities they encountered or the work they conducted.

Luis Monterrosa, who volunteered for the program in Brazil, had similar criticisms. "Our group leader," she said, "had a negative and discouraging attitude. We were not trained for our work assignment, teaching English, and the project was not part of any ongoing program. In addition, no one else in my group spoke Portuguese, which made it very difficult to have meaningful interaction with the local people." Nonetheless, Luis felt that being in Brazil was overall a positive experience, and he enjoyed learning from the dynamic grassroots organizations that OCA connected him with in Brazil. Several other volunteers that we interviewed expressed the sentiment that the local organizations with which they worked were excellent and they had a positive experience, despite Crossroads's weaknesses in terms of group facilitation and support of volunteers.

Most volunteers agreed that the experience opened their eyes to cultural differences and gave them a broader perspective on the world. As Danika Powell said, "This experience opened the world of travel to me. I realized that my home in Bermuda isn't going to change latitude if I'm gone for two weeks. The world has become smaller." This eye-opening was primarily left up to individual volunteers. The mandatory predeparture orientation in New York got mixed reviews; several volunteers, especially those heading off to Brazil, noted that the general nature of the orientation for volunteers going to many different countries undermined its usefulness.

We would agree with the volunteers we interviewed that OCA could improve its program greatly by providing a more thorough orientation that would include more details about specific sites. The written materials sent to students before the orientation should include more information on what to pack, how to prepare, and what to expect, although recent materials suggest that OCA has improved in this regard. OCA should also have a better selection and training process for group leaders and more rigorous screening of volunteers, since one volunteer with a bad attitude can detract from the experience for the whole group.

OCA brochures talk about confronting ignorance in the United States about Africa. Unfortunately, they do not have a formal program to help returned volunteers share their experiences. Still, a number of returned volunteers have stayed involved in African issues after returning home to the United States, and some alumni have become lifelong advocates for Africa.

OCA staff appears to be stretched by their far-flung program sites and limited resources. Recent grant support has allowed the staff to expand, but volunteers voiced concern over OCA's ability to handle difficult situations in more than one program site at a given time. Others questioned the group leaders' abilities to solve problems, whether due to resource constraints or lack of experience.

Anyone choosing OCA should ask to be sent to a site where the organization has worked previously, and with an experienced group leader. Volunteers should also try to speak with a returned volunteer that went to the site where they will go.

In general, we would recommend OCA for young people who want to go to some of the African countries where OCA is one of the few options. We recommend it for volunteers who are really looking for a challenge in terms of the work environment and group process and are willing to deal with some organizational weaknesses in order to be connected to some outstanding local organizations. We agree with Kenya volunteer Mona Badani, who would recommend OCA "to someone not so attached to an American lifestyle, more willing to compromise. Someone who will make the best of any situation."

> *I wanted to be Superman and help the starving kids. At first, I was disappointed to find that I wasn't able to play that role. But now, I'm glad I had this experience. It gives me hope for the future to know that people are making it and that not everyone needs help.*—Rishi Oza, volunteer, Tanzania

---

Operation Smile

6435 Tidewater Dr.
Norfolk, VA 23509

phone: 757-321-7645
fax: 757-321-7660
e-mail: webmaster@operationsmile.org
web: www.operationsmile.org

Countries where volunteers are placed: Bolivia, Brazil, China, Colombia, Ecuador, Gaza and the West Bank, Honduras, India, Jordan, Kenya, Morocco, Nicaragua, Peru, the Philippines, Romania, Russia, Thailand, Venezuela, Vietnam, and the United States

Field(s) of work: Medical (reconstructive surgery)

Requirements or special skills necessary: The following medical professionals are eligible for international medical missions: plastic surgeons, anesthesiologists, nurse anesthetists, pediatricians, pediatric intensivists, biomedical technicians, speech pathologists, child life specialists, nurses, orthodontists, and dentists. There are some opportunities for non-medical volunteers in the United States.

Duration and dates: Each "mission" lasts approximately two weeks with start dates year round.

What volunteers pay and what they receive: Volunteers pay a $400 team fee to defray costs. Operation Smile covers airfare, and room and board. Volunteers are responsible for incidental costs such as visas, phone calls, and airport taxes.

Typical volunteer responsibilities: Medical volunteers perform reconstructive surgery on patients with cleft lip and cleft palate and similar problems. Non-medical volunteers assist with fundraising and awareness, mostly in the United States.

Number of volunteers sent abroad annually: 750 (2000)

Age range: 16+ (Most opportunities for young people will be in the United States.)   **Typical Age:** N/A

How to apply: Contact headquarters for an application form or download one from the website.

Stated mission: "Operation Smile is a private, not-for-profit volunteer medical services organization providing reconstructive surgery and related health care to indigent children and young adults in developing countries and the United States. Operation Smile provides education and training around the world to physicians and other health care professionals to achieve long-term self-sufficiency."

History: Operation Smile was founded by Dr. William P. Magee, a plastic surgeon, and his wife, Kathleen, a nurse and clinical social worker. In 1981, the Magee family traveled to the Philippines with a group of medical volunteers to repair children's cleft lips and palates. They found hundreds of children ravaged by deformities, and although they helped many children, the volunteers were forced to turn away the majority of those who sought help. Bill and Kathy Magee promised those children that they would return the following year to offer more surgeries. They kept that promise and, in 1982, Operation Smile was born. Since then, Operation Smile has helped tens of thousands of children and young adults around the world.

Observations and commentary: Although we did not visit any Operation Smile volunteers in the field, a public controversy about the organization deserves mention.

On April 12, 2000, the *New York Times* reported that a small number of the patients that volunteers operated on had died, and that others had experienced health complications. There was also some evidence of inadequate financial record keeping by the organization. The *Times* reported that, since the incidents, many supporters and volunteers have distanced themselves from the organization.

Operation Smile, while denying many of the allegations in the article, has responded to criticisms by improving some medical and administrative policies. As one of the deaths was apparently caused by an adverse reaction to anesthesia, Operation Smile now requires the use of modern monitoring equipment. Another death occurred because volunteer doctors were misinformed by local hospital staff about the availability of oxygen, so Operation Smile improved the verification process. The board of Directors created two new positions, a CEO to deal with management issues, and a Chief Medical Officer to be responsible for the quality of medical care and training issues. The board also changed the organization's fiscal policies and created a medical oversight committee. Many overseas physicians affiliated with Operation Smile wrote letters of support for the organization, emphasizing the positive impact of the organization on the lives of its patients.

It is important to note that no surgical procedure, in North America or abroad, is risk-free. Operation Smile reports an overall mortality rate of 1 per 2,000, maintaining that this is virtually identical to that of Interplast, a similar organization. As mentioned, we did not conduct any site visits overseas and therefore encourage potential volunteers to do their own careful research and talk with recently returned volunteers before signing up.

Parroquia San Lucas Toliman

c/o Kathy Huebert
1400 Sixth St. North
New Ulm, MN 56073

phone: 507-359-2966
fax: 507-354-3667
e-mail: toliman@intel.net.gt
web: www.dnu.org/service/sanlucas.html

Don't do this to work out personal problems. Don't come to "save the world." It's you that are going to get a lot from this. If you do try to change anything at the Parroquia, you're just going to screw things up.—Dina, volunteer, Guatemala

Countries where volunteers are placed: Guatemala

Field(s) of work: Education, agricultural development, health, and housing

Requirements or special skills necessary: There are no special requirements, but a working knowledge of Spanish is recommended.

Duration and dates: This is a year-round volunteer program. The minimum stay is three weeks, but most volunteers stay several months to a year. Programs are crowded during the summer so it is best to contact the office early if you desire to work during this period.

What volunteers pay and what they receive: The only financial cost to volunteers is travel to and from Guatemala as well as pocket money, as no stipend is provided. The parish provides room and board. Volunteers also have the option of staying with a host family or renting an apartment. The cost of staying with a host family ranges from $50 to $200 a month, depending on the family. Staff at the Parroquia provide an orientation about work possibilities and offer program guidance and insight into political and social realities.

Typical volunteer responsibilities: Volunteers assist in literacy programs, housing projects, health clinics, and in an orphanage called Casa Feliz, the "Happy House." Volunteers also help to develop socioeconomic programs such as the Land Development Program and the Coffee Project that help Mayan farm families meet their subsistence needs or raise cash crops.

Number of volunteers sent abroad annually: 30 (2000)

Age range: 18+   **Typical age:** mid-20s

How to apply: Contact the office in New Ulm, Minnesota, to request an application.

Stated mission: Parroquia San Lucas Toliman is a rural Catholic parish (*parroquia* is "parish" in Spanish) with long-standing community-based programs. Parroquia seeks "to enhance and enrich the whole person spiritually, intellectually, and physically." Its mission is "to fight both the immediate effects of poverty and its underlying causes." A number of programs have been developed in cooperation with the Mayan community. These programs "provide an opportunity to grow together in love of God and neighbor, a value common to both Western and Mayan cultures."

History: In the early 1960s the Diocese of New Ulm, Minnesota, began its support of Parroquia San Lucas. The parish helped start a community association that carries out a wide range of programs and projects.

Observations and commentary: The Parroquia of San Lucas Toliman is located on the shore of the clear waters of Lake Atitlan and is overlooked by three volcanoes. The surrounding countryside is strikingly beautiful; equally striking is the impoverishment of the local people, most of whom are Mayan. The parish has been socially active since the 1960s. It helped to start an association, based on the spirit of Liberation Theology, that in turn has developed a wide range of community-based programs and projects. The Parroquia provides Guatemalans and volunteers the opportunity to work side by side.

One of the unique features of life at the Parroquia is that Father Greg, a parish priest and the effective volunteer program director, regularly gives talks on social and political realties in Guatemala and Central America as a whole. Father Greg is an extraordinary individual, rich in insights into the situation of Guatemala and the impact of U.S. policies on the people of Guatemala. The work of the parish, however, is guided by the lay people who live and work there, not by a church hierarchy. As Father Greg put it, "It is the Community Association that has the ownership. It is an elected and participatory association. Every morning the crew chiefs get together and discuss how things are going." For the gringo volunteers, working at the Parroquia is, as Father Greg told us, "an opportunity to be a minority." By this he means a minority not only in the sense of being a North American among many Guatemalans, but also a minority as a volunteer among the many locals working in the Parroquia and its Community Association.

The Parroquia is a working Catholic parish; it was not established for the purpose of hosting volunteers but, as the Parroquia brochure says, "to give the Guatemalan people the opportunity to express and address their needs." The volunteer program does provide an opportunity to work on projects within the community, but the focus of the volunteer program is more about educating North Americans about another society, the links between U.S. policies and needless suffering in that society, and the efforts of an impoverished people to improve their own lives. The brochure also points out that the role of volunteers is one of solidarity with Guatemalans: "Volunteers play an important role in Parroquia's mission. Their mere presence in the community is an asset. It lets the people of San Lucas know they are valued. The volunteers also benefit—they get to know another culture on a first name basis." The host community benefits from the cultural exchange with volunteers, but they do not depend on volunteer labor to get their work done. As one volunteer explained, "The volunteer doesn't really start anything—many things are underway. The train is already rolling and he or she simply jumps on." Volunteers do at times propose new projects. One volunteer, for instance, proposed an after-school program. However, the decision of whether and how to proceed with a project is in the hands of the Community Association.

One of the challenges of volunteering at the Parroquia is deciding, once you get there, what work to be involved in. "Once a volunteer arrives," Father Greg told us, "she or he is given a very general orientation to the different work possibilities and chooses which program to get involved in. Initiative is therefore key."

We commend Parroquia for its emphasis on local leadership and volunteers as learners. We also believe that Parroquia's exploration of the root causes of underdevelopment provides a model that other volunteer programs could emulate.

Of the three housing options (living with other volunteers in a group house, renting your own house, or staying with a host family), we recommend the host family option. Group housing is provided by the parish and, we were told, is a supportive environment for volunteers, but living with a host family gives volunteers a fuller experience of the life of Guatemalans and is a better environment in which to learn Spanish.

A working knowledge of Spanish will make you more useful as well as enrich your volunteer experience. There are a number of good Spanish language schools in Guatemala, and we recommend attending one of these schools before going to the Parroquia if you are not already proficient in Spanish.

If you possess initiative but are willing to follow local leadership, Parroquia could be an excellent choice. Parroquia will be the best fit for volunteers who wish to learn about the progressive work of a community of Guatemalans and how U.S. foreign policy and U.S.-based companies affect their lives.

Pastors for Peace/IFCO

National Office
402 W. 145 St.
New York, NY 10031

phone: 212-926-5757
fax: 212-926-5842
e-mail: ifco@igc.org
web: www.ifconews.org

The caravan I went on included the most incredibly diverse group of people I have ever worked with. We had black, white, and Latino activists from the United States, as well as participants from England, Iran, Germany, Canada, and Ghana.— Rachel Heckscher, delegation member, Cuba

Countries where volunteers are placed: Cuba, El Salvador, Guatemala, Haiti, Honduras, Mexico, and Nicaragua

Type of work: Material aid caravans, construction brigades, educational delegations, and human rights monitoring

Requirements or special skills necessary: Participants under eighteen must have parent/guardian sign a release form. All applicants should agree with perspective of IFCO/Pastors for Peace and have a willingness to work within a group.

Duration and dates: IFCO/Pastors for Peace programs require a minimum service of one week and a maximum of one month. The typical volunteer stint lasts two to three weeks. Caravans and delegations, depending on the country, start at various times throughout the year.

What volunteers pay and what volunteers receive: Volunteers pay between $600 to $1,800, depending on the project, to cover the costs of international travel, travel while overseas, room and board, in-country orientation and staff support. The fee also covers special non-work excursions where participants learn about local culture and local peoples' grassroots struggles for land, liberty, and democracy. There are partial scholarships available to individuals who can demonstrate a special need.

Typical volunteer responsibilities: In Chiapas, volunteers can be *caravanistas* helping to distribute humanitarian aid to indigenous communities that are suffering due to the protracted military presence. There are also opportunities to live in civilian encampments where volunteers report human rights violations and maintain a source of supplies for civilian populations. The volunteers' most important responsibilities are to monitor the activities of soldiers based in or near the community and to help establish educational programs for young people. In Cuba, Haiti, and Nicaragua, groups of volunteers deliver humanitarian aid and work side by side with local peoples to help rebuild their communities. Most delegations focus on meeting and learning from local community activists, rather than volunteering.

Number of volunteers sent abroad annually: 300 (2000)

Age range: All ages (those under eighteen   **Typical age:** College age and retired with accompaniment of parent or guardian)

How to apply: Volunteers are required to submit a written application three months in advance, however applications have been processed as quickly as one month before the beginning of the program.

Stated mission: "To provide support for grassroots struggles for self-determination in areas/regions negatively affected by U.S. foreign policy."

History: The Inter-religious Foundation for Community Organization (IFCO) was founded in 1967 as a national ecumenical foundation committed to the support of community organizing.

In 1988, founding director, Reverend Lucius Walker Jr. was shot and wounded in a terrorist attack by Nicaraguan contras as he led an IFCO study delegation to Nicaragua's Atlantic coast region. In response to the attack, Walker founded Pastors for Peace, which organizes humanitarian aid caravans to assist the victims of U.S. foreign policy. IFCO/Pastors for Peace has organized aid caravans to Nicaragua, El Salvador, Guatemala, Mexico, and Cuba.

Observations and commentary: Pastors for Peace is essentially a hybrid between a volunteer program and a study tour. The combination of a learning component and a practical volunteer component is both a strength and a weakness of the program. At times some participants reportedly are frustrated by the lack of available volunteer work. But others enjoy the opportunities for meaningful visits with local organizations and political groups.

Pastors for Peace has delivered significant material aid to struggling communities. Whether responding to the needs of communities hit hard by hurricane Mitch or ravaged by a U.S. covert war, Pastors for Peace clearly goes beyond the rhetoric of helping, delivering aid even when it is politically controversial or, as is the case with Cuba, "illegal." Pastors for Peace seems to do a good job of balancing its material aid campaigns with a belief that aid is only a small gesture and that real change is political.

Pastors for Peace gets high marks for diversity among program participants. Unlike many organizations, Pastors for Peace provides scholarships and typically includes people from all walks of life. Several volunteers cited teamwork as the high point of the caravan experience.

We recommend Pastors for Peace for volunteers who have team spirit and would enjoy meeting and learning from people through an intensive short-term program while delivering material aid. Volunteers interested in political history and solidarity movements will feel at home. If you want to do extensive volunteer work or do not want a group experience, then Pastors for Peace is not for you.

Peace Brigades International (PBI)

1904 Franklin St., Suite #505
Oakland, CA 94612

phone: 510-663-2362
fax: 510-663-2364
e-mail: pbiusa@igc.org
web: www.igc.org/pbi/usa.html

After volunteering with PBI my perspective on pain and suffering is completely different. I realize that people with very little can struggle under what seem like insurmountable odds. People in wealthier nations do not realize how easy they have it, and also how incredibly poor their lives are in spite of the amount of riches at their disposal.
—Michael Spiegel, volunteer, Guatemala

Countries where volunteers are placed: Colombia, Indonesia/East Timor, and Mexico

Field(s) of work: Human rights in conflict areas, providing protective international accompaniment for individuals and organizations that have been threatened by political violence.

Requirements or special skills necessary: Volunteers must be at least twenty-five years old and be physically and mentally able to carry out the required work. Volunteers in Latin America must be fluent in Spanish. Strong commitment to nonviolence is required. PBI is open to couples, but both individuals must be accepted into the program.

Duration and dates: Volunteers must commit to a minimum of one year. Start dates vary.

What volunteers pay and what they receive: Volunteers raise their own funds for travel to the worksite. Volunteers share a house and receive a monthly stipend of about $50 to $100, plus a repatriation allowance upon return home. All costs for food, housing, and local travel are covered by PBI. If you are a member or attend a Friends Meeting or Friends Church, the Friends Peace Teams Project may provide you with support. For more information call 301-774-6855 or e-mail *fptp@igc.org.*

Typical volunteer responsibilities: Volunteers escort political activists, are present at offices or homes, accompany refugees returning to their home communities, and observe elections, meetings, and demonstrations. PBI provides a non-partisan presence at negotiations and disputes, as well as initiatives for peace. PBI volunteers also train people in nonviolence, conflict resolution, and human rights documentation. Volunteers write reports, articles, and alerts for distribution worldwide.

Number of volunteers sent abroad annually: 60 (2000)

Age range: 25–60+   **Typical age:** 30

How to apply: Application forms can be obtained from the PBI office in Oakland, California, or from other offices abroad (see website). Applications should be submitted well before the week of intensive project-specific training at which final selections are made. Week-long trainings are held twice a year and are a mandatory part of the selection process. The Colombia project has a more extensive application process requiring several months of communication with staff prior to the training. Trainings are usually held twice a year in Europe and in North America. Typically, volunteers apply three to six months before beginning their volunteer assignment abroad.

Stated mission: Peace Brigades International (PBI) "explores and implements nonviolent approaches to peacekeeping and support for human rights. By invitation, PBI sends teams of volunteers into areas of political repression and conflict. PBI provides protective international accompaniment for individuals and organizations who have been threatened by political violence or who are otherwise at risk. In this way, PBI enlarges the space for local activists to work for social justice and human rights, while at the same time being non-partisan: not telling them what to do or how to do it."

History: PBI was founded in 1981 by a group of people with extensive experience with nonviolent activism. In 1983, PBI's first team of volunteers worked in Nicaragua with the goal of deterring conflict in the Contra war. Since then, nearly 200 PBI volunteers have worked in Guatemala, El Salvador, Mexico, Colombia, North America, Sri Lanka, East Timor, Haiti, and the Balkans.

Observations and commentary: PBI is not for the faint of heart. The PBI experience is intensely challenging for several reasons. The countries where PBI operates are typically torn apart by conflict and violence. PBI volunteers work with human rights activists whose lives are threatened by government and/or paramilitary forces; sometimes these activists are attacked or even murdered. The volunteers themselves have been victims of threats and, on occasion, attacks.

Given these challenges, it may be surprising that most volunteers feel quite positive about their service and the organization. PBI has been credited with saving the lives of several human rights activists, including a winner of the Robert F. Kennedy Human Rights Award. PBI volunteers also accompanied Nobel Peace Prize recipient Rigoberta Menchú when she returned to Guatemala from exile.

PBI's success is due in part to the care they take in screening volunteers. All potential volunteers must participate in a week-long training/screening, where they learn about PBI and are assessed with respect to their maturity, ability to work collaboratively, and language ability. The training/screening includes discussion of conflict resolution and role-plays of the types of challenges volunteers are likely to confront overseas. PBI tries to select volunteers who are politically savvy, but are not "left-wing agitators."

PBI's program is a team experience. Volunteers in each country live together, work together, evaluate each other, make decisions by consensus, and rely on each other in extremely stressful and sometimes dangerous situations. The team is what keeps the program together and sustains the volunteers, although for some volunteers it is also a major source of frustration. U.S., Spanish, and German volunteers, for example, may learn a great deal from each other's political perspectives, but these very differences may make the consensus process challenging.

The actual work performed by volunteers includes accompanying activists to their meetings and events, documenting and publicizing human rights abuses, and keeping diplomats and the international community informed about the human rights situation. Although the work is "political," PBI volunteers must be careful not to take sides. They observe, but do not participate in meetings held by local activists. In Colombia, for instance, PBI supports neither the government nor any of the guerrilla movements. Several volunteers told us that while they understand the importance of a non-partisan approach, at times observing and not getting involved was very difficult.

According to Colombia volunteer Michael Mogensen, "Human rights accompaniment is, in my opinion, probably one of the most valuable things that a foreign volunteer can do. I think that it is, in certain countries, much more beneficial than the typical 'development' volunteer."

We agree that PBI provides an invaluable service. Creating safer space for local activists enables local people to come up with their own solutions to the root causes of the problems they face.

We also commend PBI for having a better follow-up program than most volunteer placement organizations. Returned PBI volunteers are encouraged to spend a month traveling in their home country to educate people about human rights conditions overseas. PBI helps to arrange these presentations as well as meetings with policymakers, an important service that few other organizations provide. Some volunteers feel that the speaking tour can be stressful and PBI should provide more psychological support to returned volunteers, since the overseas experience itself can be traumatic.

Again, while we find PBI's work to be impressive, we must emphasize that it is dangerous. According to the PBI website, "In August of 1989, a hand grenade was thrown into the PBI house in Guatemala (nobody was hurt), and three months later, three volunteers were stabbed in their arms and chests on their way home from the bus stop. In El Salvador five volunteers were arrested, and one of them badly beaten, before being released and asked to leave the country."

The history and philosophy of PBI is documented in the book *Unarmed Bodyguards* by former volunteers Liam Mahony and Luis Enrique Eguren, published by Kumarian Press. The book describes the high stress nature of PBI's work, and is suggested for anyone considering the program.

We recommend PBI to prospective volunteers with a strong commitment to human rights and nonviolence, a high degree of street smarts and common sense, experience living in-community, excellent communication skills, and those who are brave but have small egos. If you match this description—and if your family will not get sick worrying about you—PBI may be for you.

> PBI uses the racism inherent in global politics to achieve its goal of protecting certain people. Because I am foreign, I am "worth" more politically than most Guatemalans and therefore my presence offers them some protection. At times it was strange to be part of that reality in the privileged position when the Guatemalans knew it as well as I did.—Winnie Romeril, volunteer, Guatemala

> PBI is a non-hierarchical international organization. There is a meeting every three years where the strategies are defined and each country has a committee that advises the work of the in-country team. But the work is really defined by the team with the advice of the committee. The older volunteers are in charge of orienting new volunteers when they come.—Alfred Largange, volunteer, Haiti

> I experienced some of the most passionate, beautiful moments of my life and also some very painful ones. Life in Colombia is lived intensely, and that is really wonderful in its own way. You work with people, Colombians, who are incredibly strong and resilient, people who you are going to learn a great deal from. You also work with people who have been through hell. —Michael Mogensen, volunteer, Colombia

Peacework

305 Washington St. SW
Blacksburg, VA 24060-4745

phone: 540-953-1376
fax: 540-552-0119
e-mail: mail@peacework.org
web: www.peacework.org

Peacework is a great introduction to volunteering overseas. The experience affected my views and I went on to further study about Nicaragua and U.S. policy toward Central America.—Julie Brunner, volunteer, Nicaragua

Countries where volunteer groups are placed: Belarus, Belize, Bolivia, Brazil, Cape Verde, China, Costa Rica, Cuba, Czech Republic, Dominican Republic, El Salvador, Ghana, Guatemala, Guyana, Haiti, Honduras, Mexico, Mozambique, Nicaragua, Principe and Sâo Tomé, Russia, Ukraine, the United States, Vietnam, and Zimbabwe

Field(s) of work: Construction, renovations, and repairs to schools, orphanages, and clinics as well as projects in health care and other disciplines

Requirements or special skills necessary: Peacework is looking for people with "flexibility, cross-cultural sensitivity, and a genuine commitment to humanitarian service." Experience traveling or volunteering overseas, proficiency in a foreign language, and construction skills are helpful but not required. Participants under eighteen must provide a parent/guardian release form. Peacework accepts young volunteers as a part of larger sanctioned delegations or well-supervised youth delegations. They also accept married and unmarried couples as volunteers.

Duration and dates: Volunteers serve between one to four weeks with programs arranged year round.

What volunteers pay and what volunteers receive: Costs vary greatly depending on the country and duration but range from $1,000 to $2,500. Peacework arranges accommodations, international and domestic travel, meals, supervisors, interpreters, educational and cultural programs, an orientation, optional health and travel insurance, and excursions.

Peacework is unique in that it works with college, university, community service, and church groups to match groups and their itineraries with locally organized, indigenous relief, and development projects. These arrangements are made in consultation with the leadership of the college or sponsoring organization and the in-country host.

Typical volunteer responsibilities: Typical responsibilities include various jobs in construction or renovation of houses, schools, orphanages, and clinics, or work on agricultural, educational, and health care projects. Work is available for everyone, regardless of their level of skill or background.

Number of volunteers sent abroad annually: 700-800

Volunteer age range: 17–76   **Typical age:** 20–30

How to apply: Organizations that want Peacework to design a special program work together with the office to match an appropriate country and project site. Peacework arranges logistics such as travel, visas, room and board, on-site supervision, materials, and cultural experiences.

Stated mission: "Peacework was created to offer new volunteer opportunities in international development for people around the world and to bridge cultural and political differences through volunteer interaction. By living together and working with local citizens, volunteers expand their knowledge and experience of the world far beyond the classroom or their own community and contribute in a meaningful way to local needs and sustainable development."

History: The first Peacework project was sponsored in Nicaragua in August of 1989 and brought together volunteers from the former Soviet Union and the United States. Together these groups of volunteers built houses for refugees from active Contra war zones in the highlands. From this beginning Peacework activities quickly grew into a larger volunteer program operating in twenty countries and with numerous educational and development partners.

Peacework accepts just about anybody who has sincere interest. My painting, shoveling, and weeding skills were put to use.—Ann Maushammer, volunteer, Mexico

---

Project OTZMA

United Jewish Communities
111 Eighth Ave., Suite 11E
New York, NY 10011

phone: 877-GO-OTZMA (466-8962)
fax: 212-284-6844
e-mail: OTZMA@ujc.org
web: www.projectotzma.org

I learned a great deal about myself, Israel, and my Jewish identity. I met a lot of friends and family, traveled, and experienced different cultures. Most importantly, I learned to appreciate community service, devoting my time and energy to help others. The program also included a one week stint in the Israeli Army, which was intense, but fun.—Eric Lob, volunteer

Countries where volunteers are placed: Israel

Field(s) of work: Manual labor in kibbutzim such as agricultural work; a variety of community service tasks at youth villages, nursing homes, and immigrant centers; as well as civilian service in the Israeli Army

Requirements or special skills necessary: Participants must be Jewish young adults ages twenty to twenty-five in good health. Volunteers do not have to be religiously active or observant. College graduates are preferred.

Duration and dates: The program lasts ten months, from August to June.

What volunteers pay and what they receive: The program cost is approximately $7,700, but each participant receives a small partial fellowship of $5,000. Each participant pays $1,950 plus the cost of round-trip airfare (approximately $1,200). Participants who live in their own apartments receive a very modest living allowance to cover the cost of food and staples. All program participants receive health insurance and most also receive student loan deferrals. Language training is provided, as are study tours and excursions.

Typical volunteer responsibilities: Participants work at four different placements during their ten months in Israel. They spend the first three months in an immigrant absorption center where they acquire Hebrew language skills and other skills necessary for the rest of their placement. Participants then spend three to four months working on neighborhood projects followed by two months either at a youth village or at a kibbutz performing manual labor or service work such as harvesting crops or taking care of children. Finally, they work three weeks on an independent project of personal interest; some work as civilians on Israeli army bases.

Number of volunteers sent abroad annually: 84 (2000)

Age range: 20–25   **Typical age:** 22

How to apply: Contact OTZMA by e-mail for an application form.

Stated mission: "Project OTZMA is a leadership development program in which Jewish young adults in their early twenties come from all over the world to live and work in Israel for ten months." OTZMA, which means "strength" in Hebrew, seeks to build strong links between Israel and Diaspora Jews.

History: In 1983, at a conference on the issue of Israel-Diaspora relations, participants resolved to bridge the gap between Israeli and North American Jewish youth by initiating hands-on projects that would allow American volunteers to spend a year in Israel. OTZMA is a joint program of the North American Jewish Federations, represented by United Jewish Communities, the Jewish Agency for Israel, and the Israel Forum.

Observations and commentary: OTZMA appears to be a well-organized program that provides a supportive environment for volunteers. Participants report working hard, being challenged, and having fun. The four different placements provide a panoramic view of Jewish Israeli society. Volunteers experience the demands, joys, (and, sometimes, boredom) of kibbutz life. They work with immigrants from the former Soviet Union and Ethiopia, witnessing the challenges immigrants face in a new culture. The independent project allows volunteers to dive more deeply into a sector of interest, such as women's issues, job training, or the environment. Each volunteer is matched with an Israeli family to visit on Jewish holidays, so by the end of the program, many volunteers feel like part of the family.

Unlike some of the other programs in Israel, OTZMA does not provide much of a critical perspective or focus on peace building. The study tours include some meetings with Palestinians and the peace movement, but the focus is on developing young people who will generally be supportive of the Israeli government. Some volunteers even spend a week or more in the Israeli Army.

We cetainly cannot recommend OTZMA for any potential volunteers with a commitment to nonviolence and reconciliation. If the thought of you or your peers working for the Israeli Army doesn't offend you, and if you want an immersion experience in Jewish culture in Israel, you should consider OTZMA. If you don't want to participate in a team, or want to focus on peace and justice issues, try another program.

SCI-IVS USA (Service Civil International-International Voluntary Service)

814 NE Fortieth St.
Seattle, WA 98105

phone: 206-545-6585
fax: 206-545-6585
e-mail: sciinfo@sci-ivs.org
web: www.sci-ivs.org

Countries where volunteers are placed: Algeria, Armenia, Australia, Austria, Azerbaijan, Bangladesh, Belarus, Belgium, Botswana, Bulgaria, Croatia, Czech Republic, Denmark, Estonia, Finland, France, Georgia, Germany, Ghana, Great Britain, Greece, Hungary, India, Ireland, Italy, Japan, Kenya, Latvia, Lesotho, Lithuania, Malaysia, Mauritius, Morocco, Mozambique, Nepal, the Netherlands, Nigeria, Northern Ireland, Norway, Pakistan, Poland, Romania, Russia, Senegal, Slovakia, Slovenia, South Korea, Spain, Sri Lanka, Swaziland, Sweden, Switzerland, Tanzania, Togo, Tunisia, Turkey, Uganda, Ukraine, the United States, Yugoslavia, Zambia, and Zimbabwe

Field(s) of work: SCI-IVS USA places North Americans in group volunteer programs known as workcamps. The focus of each workcamp varies, and includes work on environmental, construction, solidarity, and social service projects.

Requirements or special skills necessary: Most workcamps are in English, although some require additional language skills. Volunteers must be eighteen or older to participate in European camps, and at least twenty-one to work in camps in Africa, Asia, and Latin America.

Duration and dates: Workcamps last between two and three weeks, although there are some long-term volunteer opportunities available as well. The majority of workcamps take place from June to October, but there are some options year round.

What volunteers pay and what they receive: SCI volunteers pay $65 for U.S. workcamps, and $125 for most international workcamps. (There are additional fees for camps in Africa, Asia, and Latin America.) Once accepted, volunteers are guaranteed a place in an international team and have their room and board covered while on the project. Volunteers also receive an information sheet from SCI USA with information and directions to their volunteer site. Paying for and making travel arrangements and other preparation, however, are the responsibility of the individual volunteer.

Typical volunteer responsibilities: Volunteers work as a group, building, planting, digging, painting, restoring, assisting children and the elderly, or working in more creative areas such as arts and culture.

Number of volunteers sent abroad annually: 100 (2000)

Age range: 18+   **Typical age:** mid-20s

How to apply: Volunteers first review the different workcamp projects that are available on the SCI website or by ordering the International Workcamp Directory, which is published annually in the springtime. Volunteers then complete and submit an application to SCI USA. SCI USA then sends the application to the SCI branch or branches that coordinate the workcamp selected. Workcamps are filled on a first-come, first-served basis. SCI USA notifies volunteers directly when they receive notice from host organizations overseas of a volunteer's placement. Applications can be processed in as little as three days, although it is more typical to receive a response a week after applying and in some cases as long as three or four weeks.

People with disabilities are encouraged to apply.

Stated mission: "SCI-IVS promotes peace through deeds, not words. SCI believes when groups of people from different countries are living and working together on a project, barriers between them will decrease and international understanding will increase." SCI works to "promote greater understanding and tolerance throughout the world through practical measures. SCI works for fair and just distribution of world resources, and takes appropriate nonviolent measures in situations of tension, injustice, and war in hopes that such work will foster greater confidence between nations and peoples."

History: SCI-IVS USA is the U.S. branch of Service Civil International. It is one of the primary organizations facilitating the participation of people from North America in the international workcamp movement.

The movement evolved out of the experience of a small international team of volunteers working together to reconstruct the war-devastated village of Esnes near Verdun in France after World War I. Pierre Cresole, a Swiss pacifist who participated in the reconstruction in Esnes, went on to found SCI as an alternative to military conscription.

Since its inception in 1920, SCI has grown and currently has thirty-three branches and affiliates primarily in Europe and Asia. SCI USA is run by volunteers from across the United States who have participated in workcamps themselves.

Observations and commentary: The focus of SCI is organizing workcamps—an international volunteer project where people from different countries live and work together on a project that benefits a local community. Typically, workcamps are made up of five to twenty volunteers from various nationalities, ages, and ideologies.

As mentioned in other profiles, one of the main advantages of volunteering on a workcamp is that you can choose from a wide array of projects that present different working and living conditions. In addition to SCI USA, several other North American organizations place volunteers. There are literally hundreds of workcamps to choose from. Workcamps take place worldwide, with the majority located in Europe, North America, and Asia. The number of African workcamps has grown significantly in the past decade, but the network of camps in Latin America is still in its infancy.

SCI is different than several of the other U.S. organizations that place volunteers because it has its own network of affiliated SCI branches around the world. While different workcamp organizations and networks exchange volunteers, SCI volunteers are often placed with projects organized by other SCI branches in other countries. The

U.S. office is run exclusively by volunteers, an example of the commitment of SCI alumni, but this has led some to find it difficult at times to get in touch with anyone at the office.

Since there is such a range from workcamp to workcamp it is hard to make general comments about any of the workcamp placement organizations. Potential workcamp volunteers should focus their search by looking for camps in the country of their choosing, then seeking those camps that feature the type of work, languages, and volunteer composition that fits their interests. In order to get firsthand details about a specific camp, we suggest that prospective volunteers contact past volunteers who have worked there. Volunteers may also want to inquire about the likely national origins of other group members; if you want to practice your German, find a camp in Germany or a camp elsewhere with lots of German volunteers.

We met several SCI volunteers that did not get their first choice of volunteer sites. Our advice is to identify more than one workcamp that interests you and to put in your requests as quickly as you can after the annual International Workcamp Directory is published.

Many people view the decentralized and affordable nature of SCI (and other workcamp programs) very positively. By the same token, however, volunteers often receive very little training or preparation before they arrive in country. The quality of the experience is often dependent on the hosts organizing the camp, the chemistry of the group, and the skill of the group leader.

Certainly the highlight of the workcamp experience is getting to know the team of volunteers, most of whom will probably come from Europe. If you are a loner, or if you think you'd like to be the only foreigner on a project, SCI is not for you. Although there are definitely some exceptions, SCI often does not provide the opportunity for full immersion in the local culture, since your primary peer group will be the other volunteers.

United Methodist General Board of Global Ministries (GBGM)

475 Riverside Dr. Suite 1374
New York, NY 10115

phone: 800-554-8583; 212 870-3825
fax: 212-870-3508
e-mail: voluntrs@gbgm-umc.org
web: http://gbgm-umc.org/vim

I felt that my presence in Okinawa was mainly one of solidarity and that I was there to work with Okinawan people and express to them that their protest of the U.S. bases was not theirs alone.—Rachel Cornwell, Mission intern, Okinawa

Countries where volunteers are placed: Antigua, Armenia, Bahamas, Barbados, Belize, Bolivia, Brazil, Cambodia, Canada, Chile, China, Costa Rica, Cuba, Democratic Republic of the Congo, Dominican Republic, Ecuador, El Salvador, Estonia, France, Fiji, Ghana, Guatemala, Guyana, Haiti, Honduras, Israel, India, Indonesia, Italy, Jamaica, Japan, Kazakhstan, Kenya, Kosovo, Liberia, Lithuania, Mexico, Montserrat, Mozambique, Nepal, Nigeria, Nicaragua, Panama, Paraguay, Papua New Guinea, Palestine, Peru, the Philippines, Poland, Puerto Rico, Russia, Sierra Leone, South Africa, South Korea, Spain, St. Croix, St. Thomas, Tajikistan, Tonga, Turks and Caicos Islands, Uganda, Uruguay, Venezuela, Zambia, and Zimbabwe

Field(s) of work: Construction, healthcare and computer training, among others

Requirements or special skills necessary: GBGM offers a wide range of programs, each with different requirements. Some placements require medical or technical skills, but there are abundant opportunities for generalists. Placements require Christian faith and a few positions require membership in the United Methodist Church. All individual volunteers are expected to attend a volunteer orientation/training the weekend prior to mission service.

Duration and dates: Volunteers in Mission team projects last from one to two weeks. Individual participants in Volunteers in Mission projects make a commitment ranging from two months to a year. Global Justice Volunteers' projects last from two to six months. The Mission Intern Program lasts three years: eighteen months overseas and eighteen months in the United States.

What volunteers pay and what they receive: All participants in Volunteers in Mission projects must contribute to the cost of the program through fundraising; exact costs and benefits depend on the program.

Typical volunteer responsibilities: Participants in Volunteer in Mission team projects typically work on construction and repair of churches, schools, and community centers. Individual Volunteers in Mission provide medical treatment, teach at schools, translate theological works, or serve as pastors. Global Justice Volunteers work in church-affiliated peace and social welfare organizations.

Number of volunteers sent abroad annually: 50,000 (including the United States)

Age range: 12–80   **Typical age:** 30–60 (Individual Volunteers in Mission)
none (Volunteer in Mission teams)
18–25 (Global Justice Volunteers)
20–30 (Mission Intern Program)

How to apply: Download the appropriate application form from the website or request one from headquarters.

Stated mission: "The mission of the United Methodist Volunteers In Mission is to enable people to share their faith in Jesus Christ through utilizing each individual's unique skills and gifts in hands-on mission activities in a global context. Our theme is 'Christian love in action!'" Other GBGM volunteer programs have similar missions.

History: Since the 1940s, members of Methodist churches have volunteered worldwide as individuals and teams. The United Methodist Volunteers in Mission Movement "arose spontaneously out of the local church," and as time went on, conferences and jurisdictions organized to recruit, support, and coordinate projects. By 1980 the grassroots movement of United Methodists in Mission was officially sanctioned by the General Conference, and by 1996 Mission Volunteers became one of the six primary program areas of the United Methodist Church. Today, tens of thousands of United Methodists participate each year as volunteers.

United Nations Volunteers (UNV)

Peace Corps/UNV
International Operations
1111 Twentieth St. NW
Washington, DC 20526

phone: 800-424-8580
fax: 202-606-3298
e-mail: unv@peacecorps.gov
web: www.unv.org

I know that volunteers with other programs receive a whole lot less money. But the reason our stipend is higher is that we come as professionals; you can't come into UNV right out of school. You have to have extensive work experience. For example, here we're working with our South African colleagues to provide top-quality census data that is desperately needed at the national and provincial government levels.—Heather Branson, volunteer, South Africa

Countries where volunteers are placed: 133 countries around the world. Thirty-eight percent of volunteers are placed in Asia and the Pacific, twenty-eight percent in Africa, and the remainder in the Arab States, the Caribbean, Central and South America. There are some newer projects in Central and Eastern Europe.

Field(s) of work: Most UN volunteers carry out functions with UN agencies, government agencies, and non-governmental organizations. They work in the field as relief workers, electoral officers, human rights monitors, engineers, health care providers, or technical specialists, in a wide range of professions including agriculture, city planning, business, and demography.

Requirements or special skills necessary: Volunteers must be at least twenty-five years old and have a university or technical degree as well as a minimum of three to five years of work experience in a relevant profession. The average volunteer has at least ten years of work experience, and substantial professional experience in low-income countries. UN volunteers must be fluent in one of the following languages: Arabic, English, French, Portuguese, Russian, or Spanish and have knowledge of the local language where they are placed (although our research found that some volunteers were not fluent in the local language). Volunteers must also pass a health screening. The UNV application process is extremely competitive, especially for citizens of the United States, Canada, and Europe, since the United Nations focuses on recruiting volunteers outside of these countries. Two-thirds of UN volunteers come from low-income countries.

Duration and dates: Most assignments are for two years. Some assignments can be renewed for up to eight years. There are some short-term assignments (two weeks or more) for elections monitoring or relief work, or advisory services through UNISTAR (United Nations International Short Term Advisory Resources) and TOKTEN (Transfer of Knowledge through Expatriate Nationals). See the website for information on short-term programs.

What volunteers pay and what they receive: Volunteers pay no fees. The United Nations covers travel, housing, medical insurance, and evacuation costs if needed. During service, volunteers receive a "monthly living allowance (MLA)" for food, housing, and utilities. The MLA ranges from $1,000 to $2,700, depending on the country of assignment and the number of dependents of the UNV specialist. Health benefits are provided for up to three dependents. Volunteers receive 2.5 days leave per month and a post-service adjustment allowance of $100 per month of completed service.

Typical volunteer responsibilities: Assignments vary widely. Volunteer projects typically fall under one of four main headings: "technical cooperation with governments; community-based initiatives for self-reliance; humanitarian relief and rehabilitation; and support of human rights, electoral peace, and peace-building processes." Assignments may include such responsibilities as administration, teaching and training, research, project management, planning, and engineering in a variety of fields such as community development, human rights, cultural preservation, and small business development.

Number of volunteers sent abroad annually: 4,780 (2000). Approximately twenty-five U.S. volunteers are placed every year.

Age range: 25–70+   **Typical age:** 39

How to apply: Applicants apply through their in-country UNV or UNDP office if there is one; otherwise they apply through the Bonn office. The application process includes a written form (available online), letters of reference, interviews, and a physical exam. Country offices are listed on the website.

U.S. citizens apply through the Peace Corps office at the address above.

Canadian citizens apply through World University Service of Canada:

> WUSC/UNV
> PO Box 3000
> Postal Station C
> 1404 Scott St.
> Ottawa, Ontario K1Y 4M8

Other country offices can be found on the web or by writing to the international headquarters:

> United Nations Volunteers
> Postfach 260111
> D-53153 Bonn, Germany
> e-mail: enquiry@unv.org

Stated mission: "The United Nations Volunteers program promotes volunteer contributions to development, especially with a community focus, and seeks to influence policy for sustainable results. The program assigns mid-career men and women to various activities and community-based projects, humanitarian aid, and the promotion of human rights and democracy."

History: UNV was created in 1970 by the United Nations General Assembly "to serve as an operational partner in development cooperation at the request of UN member states." Since then, over 20,000 people from over 150 countries have worked as UN volunteers.

Observations and commentary: UNV's main strength—its affiliation with the United Nations—is also its main weakness. The UN affiliation means that volunteers have the support of a very large and fairly well-funded institution. But it adds an element of bureaucracy, which can be frustrating for some volunteers.

UNV participants tend to be experienced professionals, with advanced degrees and extensive work experience. Their assignments are usually in a professional work environment within a UN or government agency, or at a large NGO. The nature of the placements and the relatively high stipend participants receive make the UNV experience appear more like a "real job" than a volunteer position. In fact, one volunteer who worked at the UN Center for Human Rights in Cambodia said the word "volunteer" did not even appear in her job description or business card. Her stipend, while much higher than that of volunteers with other programs, was much lower than the salary of the UN employees with whom she worked.

Overall, the UNV program is to be commended for recruiting hundreds of talented and experienced volunteers, and for placing them in positions where their professional skills are well used. UNV has a wide range of fields of service and one of the widest geographical distributions of any of the programs we researched. Also, unlike almost every other volunteer placement organization, UNV recruits volunteers from low-income countries to serve in their own countries or abroad. As many as seventy percent of UN volunteers come from low-income countries.

UNV posts can be a backdoor (but low salary) entree to employment with UN projects when there has been a freeze on hiring junior project officers.

The UNV experience varies widely depending on whether the volunteer is placed with a government, the United Nations, or a non-governmental organization. In general, the volunteers we met were highly satisfied with their assignments. Architect Stanley Rymaszewski, for example, enjoyed his placement as a town planner in Poland so much that he extended his placement five times, for a total of six years. Stanley contributed to the development of a center for people with disabilities, and assisted with other renovation and town development projects. Stanley told us that being an "ethnic Pole and a Roman Catholic" helped him immensely in his placement.

Unlike many other volunteer organizations, UNV does not offer an orientation before placement or language classes upon arrival. Volunteers like Stanley said that they did not need language or technical training so it did not matter that little training was provided. They recommend UNV for self-sufficient volunteers with previous international experience.

UN volunteer Heather Branson was able to use her five years of experience as a research analyst and her graduate work in demography to help the South African government conduct the first post-apartheid census. Although her day-to-day work consisted of gathering and analyzing data, she found her placement to be "very exciting because I'm working on something historical. This census is different from all the previous censuses that have ever been conducted in the country."

Clearly, UNV did a great job of matching Stanley and Heather's skills with the needs of the host organizations, and we found excellent matches in other countries as well. This success is due in part to the UNV's painstaking matchmaking system, organized by their office in Cyprus. A database of requests for volunteers with specific skills is matched with a database of potential volunteers. Anna Wiktorowska, UNV staff in Poland, gave an example of a center for handicapped children that requested a volunteer. Anna sent the job description to the United Nations Development Program to get approval. Once approval was obtained, the UNDP office in Cyprus matched the job description with the skills of pre-approved individuals in the database. A list of proposed candidates was sent to the requesting organization. If the organization identified an appropriate candidate from the list, then an invitation was made to the prospective volunteer. The downside of this matching process is that it is slow and bureaucratic; organizations requesting volunteers may have to wait up to two years to get one, and volunteers can wait up to two years to get a placement. Occasionally UN volunteers have been placed more quickly, especially in urgent situations such as for the monitoring of elections in Bosnia.

UNV has one of the most generous compensation "packages" for volunteers; the stipend provided is often much higher than salaries of local professionals and allows volunteers to maintain a comfortable lifestyle (although, as mentioned, they make less than other UN professionals, a source of tension when the UN volunteers are doing similar work). In addition, UNV benefits are more family-friendly than any other volunteer program we researched, providing benefits for dependents and sometimes helping spouses make contacts for employment. We heard from several volunteers, however, that finding a post with a dependent can extend the already lengthy process of securing a post.

The UN affiliation can be a problem for volunteers who want to work with small, local, or grassroots NGOs. Most placements are with larger national or international organizations. One UN volunteer in Vietnam who had previously volunteered with Voluntary Service Overseas (VSO) in Kenya told us, "People who are used to being in the field should realize that there are not the same opportunities to connect to local communities." In addition, the relationship with the United Nations can, in itself, separate volunteers from the local community. Ana Lara, a UN volunteer in East Timor, told us, "There is a division between myself and many Timorese because of the power dynamics inherent in my attachment to the United Nations."

Potential Peace Corps volunteers who have graduate degrees and over five years of experience should consider applying to the UNV program. Although UNV is much more competitive than the Peace Corps, those who are accepted by UNV will probably find their placements to be a closer match with their skills. The Peace Corps, on the other hand, provides language training, and Peace Corps volunteers have a better chance of working with smaller organizations. Also, the cultural immersion experience is often much more limited for UN volunteers; some live in a virtual UN world, or even in a UN compound.

If you have extensive work experience and an advanced degree, and want to work for a large organization in a professional environment, we recommend that you consider UNV. If you have your heart set on working with a community organization, or if you are put off by the thought of the UN bureaucracy, you should not apply.

> *I love my work; I work with an incredible team of people, and it is amazing to see the data that we collect put into action, specifically around gender issues, education policy, and economic development. When I arrived, there was no current data. In the past four months, my team has put together the very beginnings of the education, health, population, and refugees databases, and the work only gets more exciting, intense, and fulfilling.—Ana Lara, volunteer research officer, East Timor*

University Research Expeditions Program (UREP)

University of California	*phone:* 530-757-3529
One Shields Ave.	*fax:* 530-757-3537
Davis, CA 95616	*e-mail:* urep@ucdavis.edu
	web: http://urep.ucdavis.edu

Countries where volunteers are placed: Belize, Bolivia, Canada, Chile, Ecuador, Hungary, India, Indonesia, Israel, Kenya, Malawi, Nepal, Russia, the Solomon Islands, South Africa, Spain, Turkey, the United States, and Venezuela

Field(s) of work: Volunteers with the University Research Expeditions Program (UREP) work with university researchers on a wide range of projects focused on animal behavior, archaeology, geology, conservation and environmental studies, and arts and culture.

Requirements or special skills necessary: Wilderness experience and skills in observation, drawing, photography, or diving are useful but not required. Flexibility, adaptability to other cultures, and a willingness to work as a team member are the most important skills for UREP volunteers. UREP occasionally accepts applicants under the age of 18, but 16 is the minimum age (only 2 percent of applicants are under the age of 18). Most projects are extremely rigorous and challenging, and the project leaders take that into consideration when reviewing applications—it is entirely up to their discretion whom they accept to be on a project.

Married and unmarried couples may volunteer together provided that both partners are accepted into the program on their own merits.

Duration and dates: Placements typically last two weeks, with start dates year round.

What volunteers pay and what they receive: Volunteers pay a $200 application fee (which is refunded to applicants who do not end up volunteering). After being accepted, volunteers pay a further contribution toward the costs of food and lodging, transportation, and supplies (except for sleeping bags and diving gear). Contributions typically range from $1,400 and $1,600. In addition, volunteers are responsible for their own airfare or travel costs to the assembly point, as well as visas, passports, inoculations, medical treatment, emergency evacuation expenses, and other personal expenses.

The settings and accommodations of UREP expeditions vary from simple urban living to wilderness camping in remote areas. All participants receive information on field techniques, recommended reading, project conditions, and a list of things to bring.

Scholarships are available to both California teachers and students. California teachers of grades K–12 who teach at least one course in science receive priority in scholarship selection. There are special scholarships for teachers in the Stockton/ Sacramento and Los Angeles areas of California.

Typical volunteer responsibilities: Daily tasks vary widely depending on the project. Volunteers work on projects ranging from archaeological digs for tools from 40,000 B.C. to 800 A.D.; to the monitoring of nests of Orinoco geese before and after hatching; to collecting fruit samples; and collecting, counting, and rearing insects. Each volunteer is responsible for working with his or her team under the direction of a team leader.

Number of volunteers sent abroad annually: 200+

Age range: 18–70   **Typical age:** 18–25

How to apply: Download an application from the UREP website and send it along with the $200 application fee. Applications should be submitted at least sixty days before expeditions depart.

Stated mission: "The mission of the University Research Expeditions Program (UREP) is to improve our understanding of life on earth through partnerships between University of California researchers and members of the general public."

History: "Established in 1976, UREP has supported hundreds of research teams and provided opportunities for students, teachers, and other members of the public to join UC scientists on research projects investigating critical issues of environmental, human, and economic importance, worldwide."

VIA (formerly Volunteers in Asia)

Haas Center for Public Service
PO Box 20266
Stanford, CA 94309

phone: 650-723-3228
fax: 650-725-1805
e-mail: info@viaprograms.org
web: www.viaprograms.org

> *The goal of the volunteer is to provide effective language instruction in communities where there is not access. VIA volunteers provide teaching service in a unique way, a way that emphasizes personal relations, language study, and living at a local level.*
> *—David Joiner, volunteer and field coordinator, Vietnam*

Countries where volunteers are placed: China, Indonesia, Laos, and Vietnam

Field(s) of work: Primarily English language instruction as well as limited opportunities to address pressing social issues like environmental conservation and women's advocacy

Requirements or special skills necessary: Volunteers must speak English with native fluency. Most long-term volunteers must have a BA or BS degree at the time of departure, and all volunteers must participate in all aspects of training in the San Francisco Bay area. Summer volunteers must be continuing undergraduates from the San Francisco Bay area. All volunteers are required to take one class in teaching English as a second language and arrange to practice teaching in a classroom. In addition, participants are required to begin study of the language of the country to which they are placed. VIA accepts children only on a case-by-case basis. Couples are accepted, but each individual must apply separately, and there is no guarantee that they will be able to live together unless they are married.

Duration and dates: There are summer programs, one-year, and two-year posts. Long-term volunteers participate in three weeks of training—half held at Stanford University immediately prior to departure, and the other half held in-country. For summer participants, training sessions are held on four to five weekends between April and June at Stanford. Summer participants depart in late June. Long-term volunteers leave in late July. The varied length of service means that there are always various "generations" of volunteers in the field at any one given time.

What volunteers pay and what they receive: The longer you volunteer the less you pay. VIA summer participants pay $1,425, one-year volunteers pay $1,350, and two-year volunteers pay $950. There are some need-based scholarships available.

For long-term volunteers, the fee covers training at Stanford and in-country, training materials, housing during training and while overseas, visa costs, round-trip airfare, two to three weeks of language instruction in-country, travel costs to their teaching sites, basic health insurance, evacuation insurance, and support from the home office and in-country field coordinator. Long-term volunteers also receive a living stipend, in most cases comparable to a local teacher's salary.

For summer participants, the fee covers training at Stanford and an in-country orientation, training materials, seven days in Japan, housing during the program, visa costs, round-trip airfare, language instruction during the program, travel costs to their site, basic health insurance, evacuation insurance, on-site mentor teacher/coordinator, and support from the home office coordinator. All volunteers must make a $100 deposit to secure their place and pay the balance of their fee by early April.

Typical volunteer responsibilities: Volunteers teach primarily at colleges and universities. In addition, there are several English resource positions in Indonesia and Laos where volunteers help the staff of local organizations build their English language skills and work on community development, environmental conservation, and women's advocacy projects. Summer program participants work in small groups to teach conversational English to middle school students and high school students in China, university students in Vietnam, and high school students in Indonesia.

Number of volunteers sent abroad annually: VIA currently sends twenty-five to thirty-five volunteers each year for one- to two-year posts in China, Indonesia, Vietnam, and Laos. VIA also offers special summer programs in China, Vietnam, and Indonesia for approximately eighteen continuing undergraduates from the San Francisco Bay area each year.

Age range: 18–60+   **Typical age:** 20 (summer programs)
24 (one- and two-year programs)

How to apply: Written applications are due in mid to late February. In-person interviews take place at Stanford during late February and early March. Check the website for specific dates.

Stated mission: VIA provides Asian host institutions with needed resources while offering volunteers the opportunity to become a valued member of an Asian community.

History: Based at the Haas Center for Public Service at Stanford University, VIA has sent over 1,400 volunteers to Asia since its inception in 1963. The first volunteers served in refugee camps in Hong Kong but over the years the emphasis of the work has changed from working with refugees to teaching English, the language of communication between Asian nations. VIA also coordinates the Stanford Program (formerly the Trans-Pacific Exchange), which brings approximately 250 Asian visitors to Stanford each summer for short-term culture and English study.

Observations and commentary: VIA is one of the most established and respected international volunteer programs specializing in placing volunteer English language instructors in Asia.

VIA focuses on English instruction as a way "to provide a much-needed service, which does not displace local workers" and "provide an immersion experience for volunteers."

One of the unique aspects of the VIA program is the training that the organization provides for its volunteers before they depart for work overseas. The training focuses on cross-cultural issues and issues specific to the destination country. In addition, volunteers with no prior teaching experience are required to take classes in teaching English as a foreign language. Volunteers study the appropriate Asian language on their own. Eric Lee, a volunteer in Taiwan and Vietnam, commented that "the training is a good opportunity to meet other volunteers and build relationships so that you can go visit other volunteers in-country. The training also gave me knowledge, and instilled the volunteer ethic. . . . it allows you to see yourself as a volunteer and accept a small stipend."

With the exception of the Laos program, volunteers are supported during their service by a field coordinator based in the capital. As one volunteer explained, "Support from the field staff and the home office was a great help in overcoming problems with my school." Field coordinators provide an in-country orientation for volunteers when they arrive. Field coordinators also visit volunteers at their teaching sites periodically and convene an annual meeting with volunteers and representatives from California to elicit feedback on the program and involve volunteers in making policy recommendations for the future.

Summer program participants are guided by a mentor teacher, a seasoned VIA volunteer, who assists them with all aspects of the program. Afternoons and weekends are spent studying the local language and learning more about culture, history, and social issues.

Many alumni describe VIA as a tight-knit organization with a family feel. Whether providing input for program development, serving in alumni posts, or making financial contributions, alumni are active in the organization. As one alumnus explained, "VIA is a consensus-based organization." Several volunteers commented that staff and alumni had assisted them with things like adjusting to their homecoming and finding employment.

Alumni were active in creating an appropriate technology source book and microfiche library to make a wide range of knowledge about appropriate technology for small-scale community development available to people in even the smallest towns and remotest areas of Asia. After many years under VIA's care, the project is now being managed by the Appropriate Technology Institute (PO Box 797, Ft. Collins, CO 80522, www.colostate.edu/org/ATI/, 800-648-8043, fax 970-491-2729).

VIA offers both rural and urban posts, and tends to offer more rural posts than other organizations in the region. One unique position brings volunteers to teach at Pondok Peastantren, a Muslim boarding school in rural Indonesia.

One downside to the VIA program is that you must either live in or travel to the San Francisco Bay area to participate in the preparatory training.

Volunteers in Asia is an excellent option for would-be volunteers interested in teaching English in Asia. VIA's training, support in the field, and track record make it a very attractive program, especially for San Francisco Bay area residents.

What I most appreciated about VIA was that it taught me to approach living and working in Indonesia in a very modest way. I found that by following VIA's philosophy of living a modest lifestyle and seeking to incorporate oneself as closely as possible into the local culture, my experience was much richer and more rewarding than the experiences of my counterparts who were in Indonesia with other programs.—Brian Murphy, volunteer, Indonesia

Visions in Action

2710 Ontario Rd., NW
Washington, DC 20009

phone: 202-625-7402
fax: 202-625-2353
e-mail: visions@igc.org
web: www.visionsinaction.org

My time in South Africa was among the most stimulating, interesting times of my life. As a Visions volunteer, I represented an organization with values that matched my own. The job and home-stay gave me a great entry into life in South Africa.—Carol Gales, volunteer, South Africa

Countries where volunteers are placed: Burkina Faso, Liberia, Mexico, South Africa, Tanzania, Uganda, and Zimbabwe

Field(s) of work: Volunteers work as interns with local non-governmental organizations in a range of fields including agriculture, children's issues, environment, human rights, education, housing, health care, family planning, refugee relief, journalism/media, and small business development.

Requirements or special skills necessary: Volunteers must be at least twenty years old with a college degree or equivalent work experience. Visions prefers volunteers who speak French (for Burkina Faso) or Spanish (for Mexico), but many volunteers we spoke with in Mexico were not yet proficient in Spanish. Visions accepts married couples as volunteers and can arrange for them to room together. Unmarried couples are also accepted as volunteers, but there is no guarantee of a room together.

Duration and dates: Programs last six months to one year. Visions has six-month programs in Liberia, Mexico, and South Africa, and one-year programs in Uganda, Tanzania, Zimbabwe, and Burkina Faso. Volunteers who will work in South Africa, Liberia, and Mexico depart in January or July, July for Tanzania, January for Zimbabwe, September for Uganda, and October for Burkina Faso. Training while overseas lasts five months for long-term volunteers.

What volunteers pay and what they receive: Program fees, ranging from $3,800 to $4,500, cover housing expenses, medical insurance, language instruction, orientation, home-stay, some in-country support, and a small stipend during service. Partial scholarships are available to people who volunteer in the DC office. Airfare is not included in the program fee. Visions provides fundraising advice and support to volunteers who need it.

Typical volunteer responsibilities: The type of work a volunteer does depends on the needs of the local organization. Tasks include writing proposals and articles, editing reports, doing research, working with children, facilitating workshops, teaching, fundraising, and doing photojournalism.

Number of volunteers sent annually: 43 (2000)

Age range: 20–60+   **Typical age:** 27

How to apply: Request an application from the office or print one from the website. Enclose a $45 application fee and two letters of recommendation with the application.

Stated mission: "Visions was founded out of the conviction that a community of self-reliant volunteers committed to social justice can make a difference in the developing world by working closely with grassroots organizations."

History: Visions in Action was founded in 1989 by Shaun Skelton, after a trip to Kenya. In Kenya, Shaun had been inspired by community-based organizations, doing great things with limited resources, and saw that the groups welcomed qualified volunteers. He knew that many people in the United States wanted to volunteer. Thus Visions was born as an intermediary or matchmaking organization to link volunteers with dynamic NGOs in a variety of fields.

Observations and commentary: Visions in Action is distinguished by its explicit commitment to social justice and the quality of some of the partner organizations with which volunteers are placed. After an in-country orientation, volunteers are interviewed by organizations that match their interests. This approach both allows volunteers to understand more about an organization before accepting an assignment and also gives the organization an opportunity to learn about the volunteers before making a decision to host them. As one host organization spokesperson said, "The interview process helps make sure both sides are happy."

Visions' greatest asset is its network of partner organizations with which volunteers work. These partner NGOs include groups such as South Africa's Weekly Mail, the Kilimanjaro Women's Rights Organization, the Ugandan Foundation for Human Rights Initiative, and Mexico's Metodos Consultora. Visions has experience finding volunteers placements that suit their interests; they can even find placements in specialized fields such as journalism and human rights. Most volunteers feel that they learn a great deal from their placements and at the same time make genuine contributions to their host communities. Because the partners are mostly local organizations, volunteers gain an insider's perspective on local culture, politics, and economics.

The match, however, does not always work. Volunteers with small organizations sometimes feel that they are not given enough supervision or that the organization does not know how to fully utilize them. Visions, we were told, makes it clear to its partner organizations that volunteers are not secretaries. Most volunteers told us that they received meaningful assignments. If the match does not work, however, volunteers can change assignments.

In most countries, volunteers live together with other volunteers in a group housing situation, and in some countries such as Tanzania, volunteers can choose to live in a group house, with a host family, or independently. Group housing is a great way for volunteers to network and share ideas but some find the interpersonal issues that arise between volunteers to be challenging. Some volunteers feel that group housing isolates them from the local community and does not immerse them in the local language. The program does include a week-long home-stay with a rural family as part of the orientation. Some volunteers wanted to stay longer with their host family; others felt that group housing was best for them because of the support volunteers provided for one another and the comfort they found in returning each night to people who spoke English.

Volunteers give the Visions' orientation good reviews. The orientation lasts approximately three-and-a-half-weeks. It consists of two-and-a-half weeks of education on the culture and history of the host country, study of the local language, and the one-week rural home-stay in which volunteers participate in community activities. In Mexico, Visions volunteers told us that the lectures were excellent and that the speakers were animated and knowledgeable. In the first lecture speakers discussed the lives of *campesinos,* the second day the history of Mexico, the third politics, and the fourth issues such as machismo and safety. There were a few hours of Spanish instruction each day. The instruction, however, did not work for all volunteers. Teachers did not provide a review of Spanish grammar and classes were not grouped by Spanish level, and therefore volunteers at advanced levels got less out of the sessions.

Most Visions volunteers felt that Visions gave them an experience that would have been difficult to arrange themselves. Visions helped them find appropriate organizations to work with, housing, and provided them with an orientation to living in the country. For these reasons alone they felt they had received their money's worth. The knowledge that Visions is available to help volunteers with problems gives the parents of volunteers a sense of security they would not have if their children had traveled alone. "If I came here with another organization," said Shonbe Sharp, a Visions volunteer in Zimbabwe, "I could have lived in Zimbabwe for three years and never have had the experience I had during the home-stay in a low-income urban area."

Volunteers we spoke with in Mexico and Africa complained that they had to fight tooth and nail with Visions staff for the expected financial assistance that, after all, comes out of the program fees paid up front. Despite Visions' promise that all apartments would be fully furnished, for example, some volunteers said their apartments were handed over to them lacking the most basic amenities. One volunteer in the state of Oaxaca, Mexico, told us that there was no closet or dresser in her apartment when she moved in. After much discussion, Visions said they would split the cost of a dresser. After further discussion Visions agreed to pay the full cost of the dresser, but when it arrived it was clear Visions had bought the cheapest dresser on the market. Another volunteer told us that it took a long time for Visions to concede to fumigating an infested apartment. Volunteers reportedly wind up paying for most of the items in their apartments, from utensils to furniture. Some volunteers suggested that Visions is not well funded and therefore cannot afford to provide volunteers with the material support they request; others feel that Visions is well funded and wonder what their fees are going toward.

Most of the volunteers we spoke with in Mexico felt as if the Washington, DC, office was worlds away. They felt virtually no support from headquarters staff while in the field. Pre-departure support received mixed reviews. Most of the volunteers we spoke with in Oaxaca were pleased with their in-country staff. Some volunteers in South Africa, however, were not pleased with the level of in-country support. Visions headquarters claims that they have improved both communications with and support for volunteers, especially in Mexico, its newest program.

Visions does not conduct evaluations of volunteers or its host organizations' projects, although volunteers are required to write quarterly reports in which they evaluate themselves and their projects. Some volunteers felt that evaluations of themselves by others would likely be more honest. Some also felt uncomfortable with evaluating their organizations. Volunteers also complained that they had not received any feedback from headquarters concerning their reports. In addition to the quarterly reports, volunteers complete evaluations at the end of their term. They turn these reports in to the very people they evaluate. One volunteer told us that a staff member whom she had given a low score confronted her. We recommend that Visions review and improve its evaluation procedures.

A number of volunteers stay in-country after completing their period with Visions, sometimes with paid jobs at the same organizations in which they volunteered. Some find that the Visions experience gives them a base and a network they can use to find other paid employment. Examples include Polly Dewhirst, who stayed in South Africa as a researcher at the Center for the Study of Violence and Reconciliation, and Dana Starr, who stayed in Burkina Faso as director of the Rural Agricultural Training Center.

Returned Visions volunteers are among the more active we have encountered. Volunteers are asked to do at least one presentation upon returning but are not given much support in preparing this presentation. Some volunteers have taken the initiative to write newspaper articles. Kendall Hunter wrote a book, *Black Taxi*, about her experience in South Africa; Amy Maki made a video titled "Aftermath of Apartheid" about her experience as a volunteer in Johannesburg.

In addition to its overseas programs, Visions hosts the Working for Global Justice

Conference in the Washington, DC, area. The event includes panels, workshops, and presentations with hundreds of returned volunteers and individuals working in various sectors of the international field. The conference is a place for returned volunteers to network and would-be volunteers to learn about their options. The conference features international justice issues like the campaign to ban land mines or the movement for a free Tibet, and also provides students with a chance to build skills for bringing international issues to their campus.

Visions accepts applicants with varying degrees of experience and expertise and provides opportunities to work side by side with local people promoting social justice. While resources are modest and internal management structures often spread thin, Visions does provide meaningful support to some progressive partner organizations overseas while giving volunteers a chance to learn and contribute in the area of their choosing.

Visions is a good choice for people with a commitment to social justice who want some support but can also function well independently. We do not recommend Visions for people who want a consistently high level of support.

Voluntary Service Overseas (VSO)

VSO Canada
151 Slater St., Suite 806
Ottawa, Ontario KIP 5H3
Canada

phone: 613-234-1364
fax: 613-234-1444
e-mail: inquiry@vsocan.com
web: www.vsocanada.org

I wanted a non-denominational organization that was big and well organized. I recommend VSO as a first job in overseas work. VSO makes it very clear what you can expect from it, your work, and from development in general.—Jean Allen, volunteer, Cambodia

Countries where volunteers are placed: Albania, Bangladesh, Belize, Bhutan, Bulgaria, Cameroon, China, Eritrea, Ethiopia, the Gambia, Ghana, Guinea-Bissau, Guyana, India, Indonesia, Kazakhstan, Kenya, Kiribati, Laos, Latvia, Lithuania, Macedonia, Malawi, Maldives, Mongolia, Mozambique, Namibia, Nepal, Nigeria, Pakistan, Papua New Guinea, the Philippines, Romania, Russia, Rwanda, Slovakia, Solomon Islands, South Africa, Sri Lanka, Tanzania, Thailand, Tuvalu, Uganda, Vanuatu, Vietnam, Zambia, and Zimbabwe

Field(s) of work: Accounting, administration, agriculture, business, carpentry/masonry, community development, computer technology, education (English, math/science, primary, special education, teacher training, and art/craft educators), engineering, environmental education, forestry, HIV/AIDS, journalism, livestock management, marketing, medicine, optometry, public health (community nurses, nurse tutors, physiotherapists), social work, and tourism

Requirements or special skills necessary: VSO receives the majority of its funding from the U.K. government but accepts volunteers who are living in the European Union, the United States, Canada, the Philippines, or Kenya. Required qualifications and experience vary with each placement, but volunteers must have work experience in a particular field and be physically and psychologically fit.

Duration and dates: Ninety percent of VSO placements are for two years, although on occasion there are requests from overseas partners for shorter-term placements.

What volunteers pay and what they receive: VSO provides round-trip airfare and visa/permits, a modest living stipend (typically equal to the salary of a local colleague), accommodation, health insurance, pre-departure training courses, language training, and a cultural adaptation course. Applicants pay for transportation to the nearest VSO office for their interview.

Typical volunteer responsibilities: Responsibilities vary widely from placement to placement, but there is an overall emphasis on sharing skills. Tasks may include management and management training, direct service, advocacy, research, or training.

Number of volunteers sent abroad annually: 1,300

Age range: 17–70   **Typical age:** 35

How to apply: Citizens or permanent residents of Canada or the United States should contact VSO Canada for application information. Upon receipt of the completed application, VSO assesses qualifications and decides if an applicant's skills and experience would be an asset to the program. If so, the applicant will be invited to an interview/assessment day at the nearest regional office (located in the Netherlands, Canada, Kenya, and the Philippines, as well as the United Kingdom). If the assessment is successful, the applicant will be sent to the Skills Team responsible for matching volunteers to placements. It takes between four months and a year from the time of application to arrival overseas.

Stated mission: "VSO enables men and women to work alongside people in poorer countries in order to share skills, build capabilities, and promote international understanding and action, in the pursuit of a more equitable world."

History: VSO was created in 1958 and since then has sent more than 27,000 volunteers to Africa, Asia, the Caribbean, Eastern Europe, and the Pacific. VSO is the largest independent volunteer-sending charity in the world.

Observations and commentary: VSO is one of the oldest and most successful volunteer placement organizations in the world. Its emphasis on placing skilled individuals overseas has helped VSO develop a reputation for professionalism. The VSO volunteers we interviewed generally had positive experiences and felt that they were able to share useful skills with organizations abroad.

One important aspect of the VSO program is its responsiveness to requests from local organizations for trained personnel. VSO recruits volunteers for specific positions that have been identified by overseas staff in consultation with local partners. While there are some positions for generalists, most posts require specific work experience and VSO generally succeeds at matching volunteers and hosts. One volunteer we met approached VSO when she first got out of college, but VSO encouraged her to gain some work experience first. After six years working in education she approached VSO again and found a placement in Cambodia where she was able to bring all of this work experience to her host organization. It is not uncommon for VSO volunteers to in turn gain more overseas work experience, staying abroad after completing their volunteer work with VSO. We met several who had finished their assignment with VSO and segued into another professional assignment abroad.

As a government-funded program VSO is able to provide its volunteers with significant support. The six-week orientation, which includes cultural and language training, is reportedly thorough, although volunteers with prior overseas experience may find it a bit rudimentary. We found country-level staff members to be quite experienced. A number of volunteers told us that staff members were responsive to their needs.

Volunteers are primarily British but volunteers from the European Union and North America are becoming more common. VSO has also initiated programs to bring volunteers from overseas to work in England.

VSO has made a concerted effort to recruit volunteers from the outside of North America and Europe. The presence of recruitment offices in Kenya and the Philippines is one example of this commitment. We encourage other volunteer organizations to follow VSO's example and place volunteers from low-income countries in their own or other countries.

The quality of the VSO experience varies greatly, depending on the country and the organization that hosts the volunteer. Volunteers are placed with both governmental and non-governmental organizations overseas. Jean Allen, a nurse, was placed with a local midwives' association. She enjoyed working in a small non-bureaucratic organization. Louisa Norman used her background in marketing to help develop educational videos, radio messages, and print media ads for the Project against Domestic Violence in Cambodia. She found the work to be inherently challenging because of the difficulty in changing attitudes toward violence against women, but felt privileged to work in an NGO with such talented and motivated colleagues.

The stipend reportedly provided for a subsistence lifestyle, but was small enough to create a stressful situation for some volunteers, particularly those living in the bigger cities. Volunteers who wanted to travel, or enjoy things like videos or eating out regularly, had to dip into their savings. However, we counsel against frequent travel and diversions while in the field.

Volunteers are required to comply with rules and regulations, such as wearing helmets on motorbikes, or leaving the country if there is a crisis that is deemed dangerous. While some feel constrained by having to comply with the rules, others argue that the constraints are not significant and they are a worthwhile trade-off for having the support and resources of VSO behind you as a volunteer.

Overseas hosts we spoke with told us that VSO's approach of screening for volunteers with skills and experience benefits the local organizations being served. It also appears to lead to a relatively high level of satisfaction among the volunteers.

We recommend VSO to individuals who want to share their experience with organizations overseas in a long-term placement as well as those who are considering continuing with international work after their volunteer assignment is complete. If you are professionally inexperienced, looking for an intensive group experience, or interested in just getting your feet wet with volunteering overseas, then VSO is probably not for you.

Volunteers for Peace International Workcamps

1034 Tiffany Rd.
Belmont, VT 05730

phone: 802-259-2759
fax: 802-259-2922
e-mail: vfp@vfp.org
web: www.vfp.org

Volunteers for Peace gave me a unique perspective of the culture and people of Ecuador.—Kimberley Colleran, volunteer, Ecuador

Countries where volunteers are placed: Argentina, Armenia, Australia, Austria, Azerbaijan, Bangladesh, Belarus, Belgium, Bolivia, Bosnia, Brazil, Bulgaria, Burkina Faso, Cambodia, Canada, Chile, China, Costa Rica, Croatia, Cuba, Cyprus, Czech Republic, Denmark, Dominica, Ecuador, England, Estonia, Finland, France, Georgia, Germany, Ghana, Greece, Greenland, Guatemala, Haiti, Hungary, India, Ireland, Israel, Italy, Japan, Kenya, Latvia, Lithuania, Mexico, Morocco, Nepal, the Netherlands, Nicaragua, Norway, Palestine, Panama, the Philippines, Poland, Portugal, Romania, Russia, Scotland, Serbia, Slovakia, Slovenia, South Africa, South Korea, Spain, Sweden, Switzerland, Tanzania, Thailand, Togo, Tunisia, Turkey, Uganda, Ukraine, the United States, Vietnam, Wales, and Zimbabwe

Field(s) of work: Construction/renovation, environmental projects and social services

Requirements or special skills necessary: No specific skills are required, and in most camps there is no foreign language requirement (English is generally the workcamp language). Most Volunteers for Peace programs are for volunteers 18 and over. Volunteers for Peace accepts couples, but Kerry Jacox says: "We prefer volunteers to participate individually due to the international make-up of projects. Usually no more than two volunteers from any one country are placed in one program, and couples tend not to integrate as well into the group." Every year Volunteers for Peace offers a small number of 'family' programs in a limited number of locations. There usually are no age restrictions for child participants.

Duration and dates: Workcamps last two to three weeks. It is possible for volunteers to participate in multiple workcamps within the same country or in different countries. Ninety-five percent of camps are held in the months of June, July, August, and September, but there are camps throughout the year.

What volunteers pay and what they receive: A $200 program fee covers food, materials, and accommodations. Volunteers are responsible for their own transportation to and from the volunteer site. Certain programs may have additional fees payable upon arrival.

Typical volunteer responsibilities: Construction and renovation work is focused on low-income housing. Environmental projects include trail building, environmental education, wildlife surveying, park maintenance, and organic farming. Social service projects involve working with children, the elderly, the physically or mentally handicapped, refugees, minority groups, and people in recovery from addictions, and educating people about AIDS.

Number of volunteers sent abroad annually: 1,200 (2000)

Age range: 18+ (some projects are open to younger volunteers)   **Typical age:** 21–25

How to apply: All volunteers must submit a written application. Volunteers who desire to work with children must also submit a letter of recommendation. Prospective volunteers are invited to become members of Volunteers for Peace for $20 and receive the annual International Workcamp Directory featuring over 2,000 projects in seventy countries.

Stated mission: "Volunteers for Peace promotes international voluntary service as an effective means of intercultural education and community service. We provide programs where people from diverse backgrounds can work together to help overcome the need, violence, and environmental decay facing our planet. Workcamps are truly the microcosm of a world where nations join together giving priority to a practical way to both prevent and resolve conflict."

History: Volunteers for Peace has placed over 12,000 volunteers in international workcamps since its founding in 1982.

Observations and commentary: The focus of Volunteers for Peace is organizing workcamps—an international volunteer project where people from different countries live and work together on projects that seek to benefit communities abroad. Typically, Volunteers for Peace workcamps are made up of fifteen volunteers from at least four different countries.

As mentioned in other profiles, one of the main advantages of volunteering on a workcamp is that you can choose from a wide array of projects that present different working and living conditions. In addition to Volunteers for Peace, several other North American organizations place volunteers in workcamps. There are literally hundreds of workcamps worldwide. The majority are located in Europe, North America, and Asia. The number of African workcamps has grown significantly in the past decade, and the network of camps in Latin America is also increasing.

Since there is such a range from workcamp to workcamp it is hard to make general comments about any of the workcamp placement organizations. Potential workcamp volunteers should focus their search by looking for camps in the country of their choosing, then seeking those camps that feature the type of work, languages, and volunteer composition that fits their interests. In order to get firsthand details about a specific camp, we suggest that prospective volunteers contact past volunteers who have worked there. Volunteers may also want to inquire about the likely national origins of other group members; if you want to practice your German, find a camp in Germany or a camp elsewhere with lots of German volunteers.

We met several workcamp volunteers that did not get their first choice of volunteer sites. Our advice is to identify more than one workcamp that interests you and to put in your requests as quickly as you can after the annual International Workcamp Directory is published.

Many people view the decentralized and affordable nature of Volunteers for Peace very positively. By the same token, however, volunteers often receive very little training or preparation before they arrive in-country. The quality of the experience is often dependent on the hosts organizing the camp, the chemistry of the volunteer group, and the skill of the group leader.

Volunteers for Peace, like all workcamp organizations, not only sends volunteers to partners overseas but also hosts incoming volunteers at workcamps in the United States. In 2000, Volunteers for Peace hosted fifteen workcamps in and around its home base in Vermont.

Certainly the highlight of the workcamp experience is getting to know the team of volunteers, most of whom will probably come from Europe. Volunteers for Peace often does not provide the opportunity for full immersion in the local culture, since your primary peer group will be other volunteers. If you are a loner, or if you think you'd like to be the only foreigner on a project, Volunteers for Peace is not for you. If, however, you like working in a group and are looking for an affordable option, Volunteers for Peace may be for you.

Witness for Peace (WFP)

WFP National Office
110 Maryland Ave. NE, Suite 304
Washington, DC 20005

phone: 202-344-0781
fax: 202-544-1187
e-mail: witness@w4peace.org
website: www.w4peace.org

With Witness for Peace I am learning how to work with people. Don't volunteer for this type of work if you get tired being around people. Working with delegations is exhausting but rewarding.—Ellen Sherby, volunteer, Honduras

Countries where volunteers are placed: Colombia, Cuba, Guatemala, Mexico, and Nicaragua

Field(s) of work: Human rights monitoring and reporting, and the planning and facilitation of educational tours or delegations

Requirements and special skills necessary: Volunteers must be U.S. citizens with undergraduate degrees or equivalent experience, good writing skills, physical endurance and strength, and computer literacy. Volunteers must have a willingness to learn about global economics, U.S. foreign policy, and trade and labor issues, and must be conversationally fluent in Spanish (including subjunctive, conditional, and future perfect tenses!). Volunteers need not be associated with any religious group or institution, but they must have a faith commitment and be dedicated to the principles of nonviolence. Experience working with groups and living and traveling abroad, especially in Latin America, is required. Participants in short-term delegations do not need any special skills, but they are asked to commit to documenting and sharing the information they learn through their experience overseas. Young people under the age of 18 can participate in special "teen delegations." WFP accepts couples on delegations but not on two-year programs.

Duration and dates: Volunteers live in the host country for two to three years. Trainings for volunteers are offered at least once a year. Delegations last for one to two weeks.

What volunteers pay and what they receive: Volunteers pay for their own international travel and are expected to raise $1,000 to help WFP provide volunteers with living expenses. If needed, WFP offers consultations on fundraising. WFP covers travel within the host country, room and board, and provides a stipend of $165 a month, health insurance, and an in-country orientation. After one year of service, volunteers are given round-trip airfare to return to their home for one month. Volunteers might be eligible for loan deferrals during the service term, and those who serve at least two years are eligible to receive a post-service stipend of $1,200. Short-term delegations cost approximately $1,000 to $1,300 plus airfare; this fee covers room, board, local transportation, and in-country meetings.

Typical volunteer responsibilities: Volunteers act as hosts for short-term delegations and prepare reports, write articles, and create other educational resources that document the impacts of U.S. economic, military, and diplomatic policy in Central America. While overseas, participants in the delegations, who are not considered volunteers, are involved in documenting human rights issues using eyewitness testimony, interviews, and other research; and they usually volunteer in WFP activities after they return to the United States.

Number of volunteers sent abroad annually: 4–10

Age range: Teens–retirement (short-term delegations)
21–Retirement (long-term volunteers)

Typical age: 25–35 (long-term volunteers)
Varies (short-term delegations)

How to apply: Written applications are usually due by May 15. Interviews are conducted May through June. Candidates are invited to the July training in Washington, DC. Afterwards, candidates attend an in-depth, three-week training in Managua, Nicaragua, which is held in September. After the three-week training, both the volunteer candidate and the current WFP team determine together whether WFP is right for the volunteer.

Stated mission: "Witness for Peace (WFP) is a non-partisan, grassroots organization. We are people committed to nonviolence and led by faith and conscience. Our mission is to support peace, justice, and sustainable economies in the Americas by changing U.S. policies and corporate practices that contribute to poverty and oppression in Latin America and the Caribbean. We stand with people who seek justice."

History: In 1983, WFP began sending delegations of U.S. citizens to Latin America and the Caribbean to bear witness to the human costs of U.S. economic and military policies. Since then, nearly 7,000 U.S. citizens have participated in delegations. To date, approximately 300 people have worked as volunteers with WFP.

Observations and commentary: Witness for Peace provides volunteers with the opportunity to work in the planning and facilitation of delegations of U.S. citizens. The delegations help participants understand the impacts of globalization, corporate practices, and U.S. economic and military policies on the people of Latin American countries. Volunteers interact with delegation participants on both a personal and intellectual level. In preparation for these delegations, volunteers build relationships with local labor organizations, human rights groups, policy analysts, community and church leaders, labor and environmental organizations, and other non-governmental organizations. Volunteers also are responsible for scheduling meetings, facilitating workshops, and organizing logistics. In one delegation, titled "Economic Injustice and Guatemala's Compromised Peace," the delegates "met with sweatshop workers seeking better wages and working conditions, visited a community of relocated Mayan refugees, talked with banana plantation workers about recent attacks on their unions, stayed with Guatemalan families, and experienced firsthand the realities of globalization and free-market reform." Leading delegations is hard work, and given that WFP plans to lead even more delegations in the coming years, volunteers should be enthusiastic about this type of work.

Volunteers also produce grassroots education resources "that bring together well-researched data and personal stories to put a human face on the economic war against the poor." Volunteers produce biweekly updates that are sent out to WFP's grassroots network of fifteen to twenty thousand people throughout the United States, and maintain a website with this documentation.

The WFP orientation has been called a "discernment process" because of its role in helping volunteers decide if WFP is right for them. We were told that the best WFP volunteers "have used the discernment process up until the very last moment to be certain that the program is the best fit for them."

Volunteers in Nicaragua live as a group in the same building as the WFP office. We were told that WFP housing is similar in other countries where WFP works. The living space we visited in Nicaragua was equipped with basic amenities such as electricity, running water, and a functional kitchen. Though volunteers have the option of moving out of the group house after their first year as volunteers, most volunteers stay—a testament to the overall success of the living situation. A few volunteers we spoke with, however, moved out the second year because they did not enjoy living in the same place where they worked. But some of these volunteers felt that the stipend was not adequate to cover the cost of housing elsewhere.

If you meet all of WFP's requirements and have a serious commitment to learning as well as teaching about the effects of global economic trends and U.S. policies on the people of Latin America, then we highly recommend WFP.

World PULSE (Program for Understanding, Leadership, Service, and Exchange)

663 Thirteenth St.
Oakland, CA 94612

phone: 510-451-2995
fax: 510-451-2996
e-mail: info@worldpulse.org
web: www.worldpulse.org

I come from a low-income family so normally I wouldn't be able to afford to volunteer abroad. If not for World PULSE, I would not have had this life-changing experience.
—Tara Harvey, volunteer, Wales

Countries where volunteers are placed: France, Germany, Greece, Mexico, Turkey, the United States, and Wales (U.K.)

Field(s) of work: Environmental conservation, archaeology, renovation of historic sites, construction of community centers and work with children, seniors, or people with disabilities.

Requirements or special skills necessary: Participants must be between the ages of eighteen and twenty-six, San Francisco Bay area residents from low-income families, and have no prior international (solo) travel experience. They must participate in two to three World Pulse weekend or evening activities each month before their departure. Prior local volunteer experience or other civic involvement preferred. Young adults of color encouraged to apply. World Pulse does not accept couples.

Duration and dates: The program runs from November through September. Nine months of weekend/evening activities in the Bay area, beginning in November. Two to four weeks abroad in July or August.

What volunteers pay and what they receive: World PULSE is a scholarship program that covers eighty-five percent of all expenses for the Bay Area and international phases of the program. Participants must contribute fifteen percent ($350 to $500), along with any pocket money for their international experience (room and board are provided during the international volunteer project). World PULSE provides extensive training and support, before, during, and after the international volunteer experience.

Typical volunteer responsibilities: Volunteers must participate in two to three weekend/evening activities a month in the Bay area over the course of nine months, as mentioned above. Volunteers must also write a report after their international volunteer experience and help organize volunteer projects in their home communities. During the international volunteer experience, volunteers are expected to work thirty to forty hours a week in exchange for room and board and to participate in group life on weekends and evenings.

Number of volunteers sent abroad annually: 20

Age range: 18–26   **Typical age:** 22–24

How to apply: For an application, contact the World PULSE office or download it from the website. Applications are available in April. Applicants are required to participate in an in-person interview.

Stated mission: "Through community service, cross-cultural exchange, and educational travel, World PULSE (Program for Understanding, Leadership, Service, and Exchange) involves young people from diverse ethnic backgrounds and low-income communities in promoting respect and understanding between people of different cultures and communities. World PULSE provides the opportunities, tools, and leadership skills for young people to shape their own futures and positively affect their local and global communities."

History: World PULSE was founded in 1996 by family members Jonas Mok, Bettina Mok, and Jennifer Keystone. World Pulse is a not-for-profit project of the Tides Center, its sponsoring agency. To date, all World PULSE programs have been run almost entirely on volunteer efforts. In addition to its cross-cultural leadership and international volunteer program for the San Francisco Bay area youth, World PULSE also invites young volunteers from around the world to participate in U.S.-based volunteer workcamps each summer.

Observations and commentary: World PULSE is one of the few scholarship-based international volunteer programs. It is designed specifically for young adults from low-income families. The emphasis is on giving youth who otherwise would not have the opportunity the chance to travel overseas in a meaningful way by working in community service projects. Due to the small size of the program the application process is competitive.

World PULSE volunteers specifically participate in workcamp projects overseas. These international volunteer projects bring together young people from different countries to live and work together to benefit the communities in which they work. Typically they involve volunteers from several other countries and World PULSE volunteers are often the only volunteers from the United States in the workcamps.

World PULSE provides its volunteers with an accessible and manageable overseas volunteer experience. It also connects this experience to ongoing local volunteer efforts, a connection often missing from international volunteer programs. If you are a young person from a low-income background living in the San Francisco Bay area with an interest in volunteer work both at home and abroad then this is a great option for you.

> *When I traveled abroad I used the knowledge that I gained from World PULSE projects and activities at home to help me get over stereotypes that I might have had. What I wasn't ready for was the amount of time I spent analyzing my culture and especially myself and my values. I recognized more deeply who I was, what people thought of me, and who I represented. I began to get a more clear definition of myself.*
> —Walter Williams, volunteer, Germany

World University Service of Canada (WUSC)

PO Box 3000, Station C
1414 Scott St.
Ottawa, Ontario K1Y 4MB
Canada

phone: 613-798-7477
fax: 613-798-0990
e-mail: wusc@wusc.ca
web: www.wusc.ca

Countries where volunteers are placed: Benin, Botswana, Ghana, Malawi, Peru, Swaziland, Vietnam, and Zimbabwe

Field(s) of work: Capacity building within local organizations working in HIV/AIDS prevention, child protection, environment, community development; also, professional development activities targeting English second language teachers in selected countries

Requirements or skills necessary: Volunteers must be Canadian citizens or permanent residents of Canada. WUSC accepts children accompanied by adults on a case-by-case basis, depending on position and country assignment. Couples are accepted, but unmarried couples "must have resided together for the past 12 months for the partner who is not volunteering to qualify for the dependent allowance."

Duration and dates: Assignments are normally for a two-year period.

What volunteers pay and what they receive: There are no costs to volunteers. WUSC provides the following support: airfare; in-transit allowance, medical and life insurance, and other allowances such as monthly stipends (vary for each country); dependents' allowances if applicable; furnished housing; orientation sessions; annual leave; holidays; and ongoing WUSC in-country support.

Typical volunteer responsibilities: Volunteers are involved in the assessment of needs in their host communities, program development, the training of counterparts, community outreach, and partner support. All WUSC projects support locally driven initiatives in the host country.

Number of volunteers sent abroad annually: 25–35

Age range: 20–65   **Typical age:** 25–40

How to apply: Consult the website for available postings. Qualified applicants should send a statement of interest, resume, and four references—two personal and two employment—to the Recruitment Section at the address above.

Stated mission: "World University Service of Canada (WUSC) is a network of individuals and postsecondary institutions who believe that all peoples are entitled to the knowledge and skills necessary to contribute to a more equitable world. Its mission is to foster human development and global understanding through education and training.

"The goal of the Volunteer Engagement Program is twofold: through the placement of qualified Canadians overseas, to support our country partners in their efforts to improve their standard of living and achieve self-reliance, to work with the postsecondary community in Canada, as we strive to increase Canadian awareness and involvement in development issues and activities."

History: WUSC was founded in the 1920s as the European Student Relief Program.

WorldTeach

Center for International
    Development
Harvard University
79 John F. Kennedy St.
Cambridge, MA 02138

phone: 617-495-5527; 800-4-TEACH-0
fax: 617-495-1599
e-mail: info@worldteach.org
web: www.worldteach.org

WorldTeach was a very well-organized, careful program with a philosophy based on a mission to make an impact on the country without trying to force ideas upon the people but to live and learn as much as we teach.—Matt Budd, volunteer, Costa Rica

Countries where volunteers are placed: China, Costa Rica, Ecuador (Galapagos Islands), Honduras, Mexico, Namibia, and South Africa

Field(s) of work: Teaching English, as well as math, science, and computer skills, and, in select locations, teaching English in an environmental education context through the semester-long Nature Guide Training programs operated in partnership with the RARE Center for Tropical Conservation.

Requirements or special skills necessary: An undergraduate degree is required for six-month and year-long programs. Summer programs are open to current undergraduate students. Applicants should have an interest in teaching and living abroad. Prior experience teaching, tutoring, volunteering, and studying abroad are a plus. Once accepted to the program, volunteers are asked to complete twenty-five hours of teaching English as a foreign language before departure.

Occasionally volunteers bring their children on the program, some as young as three years old. This usually means they pay extra for housing and insurance. People who are thinking about bringing children should call or e-mail WorldTeach for details.

Married couples are welcome but may need to pay extra for housing and insurance. Unmarried couples should call to discuss their specific situation. WorldTeach "believes in equal opportunities for all," but, regarding same-sex couples, "cannot always say the same for the various cultures in which we place volunteers." WorldTeach encourages interested couples to call the office and ask to speak to the Program Director for more information.

Duration and dates: WorldTeach offers eight-week summer programs in China, Costa Rica, Ecuador, and Namibia; six-month programs in Mexico, Honduras, South Africa, and China; and year-long programs in Costa Rica, Ecuador, and Namibia.

What volunteers pay and what they receive: Volunteers pay a program fee, between $3,990 and $5,990, that covers international travel, housing, food, both medical and emergency medical evacuation insurance. Long-term volunteers receive a modest stipend. Volunteers receive pre-departure literature and support from the U.S. staff and support from full-time field coordinators once they arrive overseas. Field coordinators organize a three-to-four week in-country orientation that covers topics such as local language, teaching English as a foreign language, cross-cultural adjustment, and health and safety. Field coordinators also arrange housing, teaching placements, and both an in-service and an end-of-service conference to address classroom teaching issues and taking the experience home.

Typical volunteer responsibilities: Volunteers' primary responsibility is to teach English (or math, science, or computer skills at select locations). Teaching assignments vary but range from teaching in primary and secondary schools to teaching at training institutes, non-governmental organizations, environmental groups, eco-tourism centers, and universities. In addition to classroom teaching, volunteers are encouraged to get involved with local youth or community development work.

Number of volunteers sent abroad annually: 150

Age range: 18–80+   **Typical age:** 23–25

How to apply: The application process involves a written application, two letters of reference, and an in-person interview for long-term volunteers. The written application includes essay questions and a request for a college diploma (for long-term programs) as well as a resume. Applications can be processed as quickly as three weeks but should be submitted three to four months before departure overseas. Applications can be printed from the website or requested from headquarters by phone or e-mail.

Stated mission: "WorldTeach provides opportunities for individuals to make a meaningful contribution to international education by living and working as volunteer teachers in developing countries."

History: Michael Kremer and a small group of Harvard graduate students founded WorldTeach in 1986. WorldTeach was founded based on Michael's realization that Kenyans' desire for volunteer teachers was complemented by the desire of young people in the United States to gain overseas experience. Since its inception, WorldTeach has placed thousands of volunteer educators in communities throughout Africa, Asia, Eastern Europe, and Latin America.

Observations and commentary: WorldTeach consistently receives high marks from both volunteers and the institutions where they teach. The enthusiasm of former volunteers and the number of institutions that renew placements are good indicators of the overall success of the program.

The organization does a good job of supporting their volunteers especially once they arrive in-country. We met a number of volunteers who thought that their field coordinators were outstanding. The fact that the field coordinators work full-time to support the volunteers and handle all of the logistics related to finding volunteers housing and teaching assignments was truly appreciated. In the words of volunteer Carey Spears, "I had fantastic and unforgettable field coordinators who really made the program run smoothly."

As primarily an English teaching program that places volunteers with little or no previous teaching experience, WorldTeach succeeds in getting its volunteers started as teachers. There is some disagreement among volunteers as to whether the requirement to gain experience teaching English as a foreign language in the United States is especially helpful, but most agree that the orientation itself was very useful. As Stacey McCarthy explained, "The orientation was great. We got to study Thai, teach in a team for two weeks, and reflect on how it was to teach. The orientation is what made it worth going on WorldTeach."

There is a wide range of teaching placements available to volunteers. Volunteers may teach in either public or private primary or secondary classrooms. In Ecuador, WorldTeach has many of its volunteers teaching in a quasi-governmental vocational training program. In other placements volunteers may be resource teachers supporting and training other English teachers.

Not unlike participants in other teaching programs, WorldTeach volunteers face many challenges as teachers. Many spoke about the difficulty of developing relationships with local counterparts, who often utilized the presence of the volunteers as a chance to tend to other matters outside of the classroom or school. Volunteers also struggle to work within an unfamiliar curricular framework (or in some cases in the absence of one).

While some WorldTeach volunteers urge potential volunteers not to underestimate the demands of teaching "since you have to plan and that is tiring," others said they had "plenty of free time to hang out with their host family, explore the surrounding area, and get involved in local community work." Lisa Jensen, a volunteer and field director in Ecuador, commented, "Volunteers can do volunteer work as well as their teaching. Volunteers are responsible for at least twenty hours of teaching per week and can do more if they choose. In my case, I really like volunteer work and since I was living in the Galapagos Islands I was really excited about volunteering with the Charles Darwin Center. I volunteered on a fish census project from 7 to 12 in the morning and taught from 4 to 8 in the evening."

For many, the home-stay is the highlight of their experience. Volunteers are asked about their preferred living situation and are matched with an appropriate family. In some instances accommodations are provided by a host institution like a school or a mission and on rare occasions volunteers live independently.

The WorldTeach experience is both an independent and a group experience. While teaching placements and living arrangements are done on an individualized basis and some are placed in isolated areas, volunteers are not alone. As one volunteer commented, "We are out there on our own but we have support and a group of friends." Volunteers placed closer to the in-country staff tend to get more staff support. The support and bonding with the group takes place during the orientation in-country and is continued during the in-service training. We met several volunteers who took long weekends to visit other volunteers as much as eight hours away by bus. Field coordinators travel to visit each volunteer to check on their teaching and living situation.

One attractive aspect of the program is that volunteers in Ecuador, Costa Rica, or Namibia can decide while they are overseas to extend for a second year at little or no cost. Even if volunteers don't decide to extend for a second year, the program can have a lasting impact on volunteers, serving as a stepping stone for many into either continued teaching or continued work overseas. We met several returned volunteers who had decided to pursue teaching as a career, and we also met volunteers who had decided to stay on overseas and work using their language skills, contacts, or teaching experience.

WorldTeach offers several unique programs. In Ecuador there are several volunteer placements amidst the natural wonders of the Galapagos Islands and in Honduras, Mexico, and South Africa volunteers can work in collaboration with RARE Center for Tropical Conservation in a nature guide training program. The guide training gets rave reviews from local fishermen who are eager to improve their English skills so they can participate in the growing eco-tourism industry. As a graduate and volunteer host explained, "The program gave me more opportunities with the tourists, and this is important because the fishing is declining." Cynthia Brown, a former WorldTeach-RARE volunteer and now staff member in Mexico and Honduras, highly recommends the program: "It is incredibly rewarding, but it is a large commitment—seven days a week with a couple of afternoons off. You are tired, but you are really sharing, making these great friendships."

The Shanghai Summer Teaching Program is a worthwhile option for undergraduates wishing to teach in China. Volunteers teach small classes of three to six students from the Shanghai Middle School. The teaching assignment is substantial but not overwhelming, averaging about two hours of teaching and two hours of preparation on weekdays.

We highly recommend WorldTeach for potential volunteers with an interest in teaching. Its reputation as a leading option for volunteer teaching is well deserved. It is an especially good option for someone who desires an independent placement but also wants staff support and connection to a community of volunteers. WorldTeach, while not just for those aspiring to be teachers, does offer a good testing ground for those considering teaching as a profession while providing volunteers with a deep immersion in another culture.

I have no illusions that there are public school children who are fluent because of two years of English teaching by a non-professional teacher. But I feel that on a community level I exposed children to something new and got many of them excited about learning another language.—Ann Lundquist, volunteer, Costa Rica

Overall, I feel that my WorldTeach experience is one of the most extraordinary things I've done.—Marcia Miquelon, volunteer, Namibia

CHAPTER 13

PARTING WORDS

It is our hope that by reading this book you have learned what international volunteering is about, considered the context of international volunteering, and figured out if volunteering abroad is right for you. For those of you who decided that international volunteering matches your interests and aspirations, this book includes plenty of food for thought and concrete suggestions on the best way to select an organization or design your own program, and fundraise and prepare for life overseas. Whether you choose a large organization like the Peace Corps or the smallest volunteer placement organization, we trust that you will take to heart our suggestions for being an effective volunteer and using your experiences overseas as a foundation for continued involvement in working for justice when you return home.

One of the many challenges in compiling this book was balancing the data with the message. We hope that the sheer volume of interviews, facts, and concrete suggestions did not overwhelm the clear messages we have tried to convey about the challenges and opportunities of international volunteering. We hope that if you choose to volunteer overseas, you will embrace these challenges and opportunities, learning and growing from each one.

As volunteers, it is natural to want to see the concrete results of your labor. At times you do get glimpses of the ways in which you touch other lives, but often you don't see immediate results. Change can be slow and is often accompanied by great struggle and effort over generations. Try not to get discouraged when your efforts as a volunteer seem small. As we said at the beginning of the book, we hope that this book helps you write your own stories and embark on your own journey toward creating a more just world. As you volunteer you may realize it is only by weaving together many individual journeys that a vision of change can emerge. Remember that international volunteering can be an important part of transforming the planet over the long haul, but it all depends how you experience being an international volunteer and what you do with this experience in the rest of your life.

We'd like to leave you with some words from the late Archbishop of El Salvador, Oscar Romero. Although he speaks in his own voice as a Roman Catholic priest, his words transcend any particular religion, imploring us to step back and look at our efforts as part of the long road to justice and a better world.

It helps now and then to step back and take the long view. The kingdom is not only beyond our efforts, it is even beyond our vision. We accomplish in our lifetime only a tiny fraction of the magnificent enterprise that is the Lord's work. Nothing we do is complete, which is another way of saying that the kingdom always lies beyond us.

No statement captures all that should be said. No prayer fully expresses our faith. No confession brings perfection. No pastoral visit brings wholeness. No program accomplishes the church's mission. No set of goals and objectives includes everything.

This is what we are about. We plant the seeds that one day will grow. We water seeds already planted, knowing that they hold future promise. We lay foundations that will need further development. We provide the yeast that produces effects far beyond our capabilities.

We cannot do everything and there is a sense of liberation in realizing that. This enables us to do something and do it very well. It may be incomplete, but it is a beginning, a step along the way, an opportunity for the Lord's grace to enter and do the rest.

We may never see the end results, but that is the difference between the master builder and the worker.

We are workers, not master builders; ministers, not messiahs. We are prophets of a future that is not our own.

BONUS SECTION A
ALTERNATIVES TO VOLUNTEERING OVERSEAS

After careful research and introspection, you may decide that volunteering overseas is not for you, or you may just want to explore different options. There are other ways to reap the benefits of international exchange and to make a contribution to the world. In this section, we will focus on four options: study abroad, travel abroad, work abroad, and doing good at home. Remember that, as mentioned in Chapter 2, "Is Volunteering Overseas Right for You?," the line between the different options is fuzzy, and you may be able to find or create a program that has more than one focus.

Before going into detail on these options we want to recommend two outstanding general Internet resources: *Transitions Abroad* (www.TransitionsAbroad.com), an excellent magazine with a wide range of options for study, travel, and work abroad, and the Overseas Opportunities Office (www.umich.edu/~icenter/overseas), a comprehensive site posted by Bill Nolting of the University of Michigan.

Study Abroad

Study programs come in a variety of forms. While university study is still the most common, studying abroad is not just for college students anymore. As you begin your search we suggest that you consult the www.studyabroad.com web page, which includes a searchable database and links to a number of programs. Another useful site, www.worldwide.edu, allows you to look up adult education programs overseas ranging from language schools to university programs.

University Study Abroad

The most well-known international study option is designed for undergraduate students who want to take a semester or a year to study abroad. These programs are offered by domestic colleges and universities in conjunction with institutions of higher learning overseas. A growing number of colleges and universities have programs open not only to their own undergraduates, but also to students of other schools and adults unaffiliated with universities. Advantages of these programs usually include in-depth language training, interesting classes, ability to apply easily for financial aid to cover the costs, affiliation with a university in the host country, and the ability to get a "package deal" that includes room, board, and airfare.

Of course, not all study abroad programs are created equal. Some are merely moneymakers for the university, and others may be well intentioned but disorganized. Disadvantages of study abroad programs can include high expense, lack of rigorous academic courses, lack of opportunity to get to know low-income people in the host country, and an abundance of twenty year olds, which may be fine if you are twenty, but may be a constant source of tension and frustration for older students.

Every program has its own strengths and weaknesses. Be sure to find out the details of the program by e-mailing or talking with past participants.

Programs that accept students from outside their university, have programs in countries throughout Asia, Africa, and Latin America that explore international development issues, and have a generally positive reputation include:

- **World Capitals Program of American University**
  (www.worldcapitals.american.edu, 800-424-2600)

- **Center for Global Education of Augsburg College**
  (www.augsburg.edu/global, 800-299-8889)

- **Study Service Term of Goshen College**
  (www.goshen.edu/sst/sst, 219-535-7000)

Some universities offer entire degree programs linked to study abroad. Programs of this type to consider include:

- **The International Partnership for Service-Learning**
  (www.ipsl.org, 212-986-0989, reviewed in Chapter 12, "Organizational Profiles")

- **Minnesota Studies in International Development** *(www.umabroad.umn/edu, 612-626-9000, reviewed in Chapter 12, "Organizational Profiles")*

- **The School for International Training** *(www.sit.edu/studyabroad)*

Language Schools

There are numerous language schools to choose from, particularly in Latin America. While there are U.S.-based programs that place you in a language school overseas, we suggest passing over (often costly) middlemen and connecting directly with a school. Often former students or nonprofit organizations in the United States represent the schools and help with promotion and signing up new students. Here are a few possibilities for learning Spanish:

- **Amerispan** *(www.amerispan.com, 215-751-1100) coordinates Spanish immersion programs in Mexico, the Caribbean, Central America, South America, and Spain.*

- **Casa de Español Xelaju in Guatemala** *(www.casaxelaju.com, 512-416-6991)*

- **Center for Bilingual Multicultural Studies at Universidad International**
  (www.bilingual-center.com, 800-932-2068)

- **Centro Internacional para la Cultura y la Enseñanza de Lengua (CICE) language school in Cuernavaca** *(www.laneta.apc.org/cice)*
- **Conservation International—Eco-Escuela in Guatemala** *(www.conservation.org/web/fieldact/escuela/, 800-429-5660)*
- **Global Exchange** *(www.globalexchange.org, 415-255-7296, offers a program at the University of Havana)*
- **Institute for Central American Development Studies (ICADS)** *(www.icads.com, profiled in Chapter 12, "Organizational Profiles")*
- **Melinda Anaya Montes Spanish School at the Centro de Intercambio y Solidaridad in El Salvador c/o CISPES** *(www.cispes.org, 212-229-1290)*
- **Nicaragua Spanish Schools** *(http://pages.prodigy.net/nss-pmc, 805-687-9941)*
- **Pop Wuj in Guatemala** *(www.popwuj.org, 707-869-1116)*
- **Universal Language School in Cuernavaca, Mexico** *(www.universal-spanish.com)*

For other languages, contact the area studies or foreign language department of your local university to get recommendations of language schools overseas.

High School Study Programs

There are numerous high school study abroad programs. Programs operate in countries all around the world and have a track record of success include Youth for Understanding (www.yfu.org, 800-TEENAGE) and American Field Service (www.afs.org, 212-807-8686, reviewed in Chapter 12, "Organizational Profiles").

Study Programs for Seniors

A growing number of programs offer international study programs for senior citizens and retired people. The most popular programs for seniors are Elderhostel (www.elderhostel.org, 877-426-8056, reviewed in Chapter 12, "Organizational Profiles") and Interhostel (www.learn.unh.edu/interhostel/programs.html, 800-733-9753 or 603-862-1147).

All Ages Programs

A huge number of short-term study options are open to people of all ages. Topics of study range from history and archaeology to culture and environment. Try a general web search by topic, or find additional resources on study abroad through NAFSA: Association of International Educators (www.nafsa.org, 202-737-3699), Institute of International Education (www.iie.org), or Peterson's guides (www.petersons.com/stdyabrd).

Travel Abroad

Travel is a multibillion dollar a year industry. Forget your image of a tour bus full of ugly Americans whizzing through the European capitals. Tourism now includes a wide range of political tourism (reality tours to meet with Zapatistas in Mexico), eco-tourism (visiting a low-impact lodge in the Costa Rican rain forest), cultural tourism (living with a family in a traditional village in South Africa), and adventure travel (such as camel trips through the desert in Rajasthan).

Independent Travel

One big question in travel is whether to go independently or join a group tour organized by a travel company. With independent travel, you are more likely to have quality interactions with local people and possibly even be invited into their homes. Independent travel also allows you the flexibility to change your itinerary at will. Sometimes, independent travelers can find better deals on airfare and accommodations on their own.

There are hundreds of books and other resources on traveling abroad. Visit your local bookstore or library and check out the travel section. Surf the web for country-specific sites and home pages created by travelers. You might want to start by looking at the websites of popular guidebooks and organizations such as Lonely Planet (www.lonelyplanet.com), Moon Handbooks (www.moon.com), Council on International Educational Exchange (www.ciee.org), or Council Travel (www.counciltravel.com).

Use your network of friends, family, co-workers, and acquaintances to find people who have been where you want to go. Consider joining an organization for travelers, such as Hostelling International (www.iyhf.org) for inexpensive access to international youth hostels, or Servas (www.servas.org) for home-stays in other countries.

Group Travel

With a group tour package, someone else is responsible for all the logistics of meals, lodging, and activities. Tour companies often provide guides who have an intimate knowledge of the area you are visiting. With a package tour, you will be part of a group of people who share at least some of your interests. A tour group also offers a greater sense of security than one has when traveling independently. Sometimes, group travel can actually save you money on airfare and hotels.

When selecting a travel agent or tour operator, consider whether they are sensitive to local customs, support locally owned businesses, and strive to limit the impact of tourism on the environment and culture.

Journeys (www.journeys-intl.com, 800-255-8735) is a good resource for information on international group travel.

Political Tourism, Study Tours, Exposure Trips, and Reality Tours

Exposure trips that focus on a particular sociopolitical issue in a country or a region have become increasingly popular. Also known as reality tours, these trips combine travel and study. They involve participants in learning a different version of reality than what they might read in newspaper headlines, and also encourage people to do something about what they learn. Many volunteer programs operate reality tours as a short-term option, while others are operated by development organizations that have long-term programs in the countries that are visited. For starters, take a look at:

- **Border Links** *(www.borderlinks.org, 520-628-8263)*
- **Global Exchange** *(www.globalexchange.org, 415-255-7296)*
- **Heifer Project International** *(www.heifer.org, 800-422-1311)*
- **Lisle Inc.** *(www.lisle.utoledo.edu, 800-477-1538)*
- **Our Developing World** *(www.magiclink.net/~odw, 408-379-4431)*
- **Third World Opportunities** *(619-449-9381)*
- **Witness for Peace** *(www.witnessforpeace.org, 202-588-1471) (Reviewed in Chapter 12, "Organizational Profiles")*
- **World Neighbors** *(www.wn.org, 800-422-1311)*

Ecotourism

"Ecotourism" has become a buzzword in travel. It is used to describe travel that seeks to benefit both conservation and the local community. Some ecotour operators not only mitigate their impact on the environment but also organize trips that involve vacationers in the protection and/or restoration of ecosystems. Others use ecotourism merely to help market themselves, while they may actually hurt the environment by, for example, dumping trash in local rivers or cutting down trees for campfires. The ecotourism label, therefore, does not guarantee that a tour is environmentally or socially beneficial.

In the effort to protect fragile ecosystems and endangered wildlife, some countries, for example, Costa Rica and Uganda, require that visitors to their national parks have tour guides and/or permits. It is not a bad option, therefore, to pay an honest and responsible ecotour company to arrange all this for you. In addition, many ecotour companies sell ecotours as package vacations.

A few volunteer placement organizations, such as Earthwatch and Amizade (both reviewed in Chapter 12, "Organizational Profiles"), offer ecotours with a volunteer component.

In your search for an eco-friendly travel business, try to find out if the company is locally owned and operated. Does it employ local guides with ecological training and experience? Does it show respect for indigenous peoples and wildlife? Does it seek to conserve energy and resources, such as limiting the use of buses or motorboats to transport tourists? For other questions and advice on selecting tour operators, do an Internet search for "ecotourism."

Several helpful organizations are dedicated to promoting responsible travel:

- **Partners in Responsible Tourism** *(www.pirt.org, 415-675-0420) is a network of individuals and representatives of tourism companies, who are concerned about the impact of tourism on local environments and cultures, particularly those of indigenous peoples.*

- **Rethinking Tourism Project** *(www.planeta.com/ecotravel/resources/rtp/rtp.html, 651-644-9984) is an indigenous people's nonprofit organization dedicated to the preservation and protection of lands and cultures.*

- **Coral Cay** *(www.coralcay.org, 44-0-20-7498-4015) organizes expeditions and preservation tours in coral reef areas.*

- **The International Ecotourism Society** *(TIES) is a membership organization for ecotourism providers (www.ecotourism.org, 802-651-9818).*

Books on ecotourism include:

Ecotourism and Sustainable Development: Who Owns Paradise? Martha Honey. Washington, DC: Island Press, 1999.

The New Key to Costa Rica. Beatrice Blake. Berkeley, CA: Ulysses Press, 2000.

Rethinking Tourism and Ecotravel: The Paving of Paradise and What You Can Do to Stop It. Deborah McLaren. Bloomfield, CT: Kumarian Press, 1997.

Cultural Tourism

Cultural tourism, particularly home-stays, also has grown rapidly over the past several decades. Cultural tourism might range from participating in a Buddhist meditation retreat on an island in Thailand to learning about traditional medicinal practices in the Amazon. It generally includes programs that allow visitors to participate in the routines of daily life. One program to consider is Servas (www.servas.org), which, as we mentioned previously, links independent travelers with host families overseas.

Adventure Tourism

Hundreds of travel companies now offer adventure travel. If the thought of white water rafting in Nepal or trekking in Peru appeals to you, then here are just a few suggestions to get you started in your search for the ultimate adventure: Explorations in Travel (www.exploretravel.com, 802-257-0152), and Where There Be Dragons (www.gorp.com/dragons, 800-982-9203).

Work Abroad

Many of you probably jumped to this section when you realized that volunteering abroad can cost money. We strongly encourage you not to rule out volunteering, as the experience you gain can be well worth the expense. Also, many international jobs require that you already have some international experience. If you absolutely cannot afford to volunteer, or just want to explore other options, the International Career Employment Weekly and International Employment Hotline advertises over 500 current job openings every week (www.internationaljobs.org, 804-985-6444). The International Employment Gazette is a biweekly paper with over 400 current job openings around the world (www.angelfire.com/biz/resumestore, 800-882-9188). Websites www.overseasjobs.com, www.jobsabroad.com, www.teachabroad.com, and www.backdoorjobs.com offer job search options as well as links to other relevant sites, or see the resource page of www.volunteerinternational.org. Transitions Abroad's publications (www.transitionsabroad.com), especially the book *Work Abroad,* are packed with great ideas and advice.

Teaching Opportunities

In every country there are opportunities to get paid to teach English. The demand is especially high for people who have an American accent and some teaching experience. Here are some questions to ask yourself about teaching:

- ***Whom do I want to teach?***

  Opportunities include teaching well-off businesspeople, children of the elite and expatriate communities, low-income urban adults, and poor rural students. The financial compensation of the first two categories will probably be higher, but the latter two may be more rewarding. You may also want to consider if there is a specific age level or type of person you want to teach.

- ***How much do I need to earn?***

  Salaries will range from barely covering room and board to hundreds of dollars a week. If breaking even would be acceptable, you can be much more flexible in the type of assignments you could accept.

- ***Do I need to arrange a job before I leave home?***

  There are many teaching jobs that you will not be able to find unless you are in-country. Do you have the funds, the time, and the chutzpah to get yourself to the country where you want to teach and do your job search there? This option will potentially increase the variety of teaching jobs you could find. Of course there are no guarantees, and networking can be difficult in a foreign land where you have no initial contacts. If you choose this option, do as much research as possible before you go, so that you will have a few ideas about where to look before you get there about where to begin looking.

- ### *What subjects can I teach?*

  If you are able to teach a math or science class, you will be more marketable than if you only can teach English. Also consider any non-academic expertise you may have, such as using computers, playing guitar, or fixing bicycles.

- ### *What training will I need?*

  Being a tutor does not usually require a teaching certificate, but teaching in a prestigious international private school may be impossible if you don't have formal training and/or experience. Even if you don't think you will need a certificate, the more you know about teaching before you go, the better. Consider volunteering at a local school, teaching English to recent immigrants, or investing in an intensive training course (as advertised in Transitions Abroad magazine or on the web at www.transabroad.com).

TIPS ON NON-TEACHING WORK OPPORTUNITIES OVERSEAS

It's a classic catch-22 situation. International jobs that are not teaching-related are particularly hard to come by, particularly if you don't already have international work experience. But besides volunteering, how can you get the experience if you can't get a job? Here are some strategies for increasing your chances.

Tip #1: Consider doing your job search in the host country instead of at home.
Most foreign jobs are difficult to find from outside the country in which you would like to work. If you can scrape up enough money for a plane ticket and one or two months' living expenses and you're good at networking, then you may want to consider this option.

Tip #2: Be willing to do anything.
Be flexible and creative. Consider working overseas as a waiter or waitress, tour guide, translator, computer instructor, researcher, journalist, or musician

Tip #3: Work for room and board.
A hotel, museum, or nonprofit organization may be able to provide living space and meals in exchange for your work.

Tip #4: Network, network, network!
Similar to finding your own volunteer opportunity, finding a paying job usually means spending a lot of time networking. See Chapter 6, "Doing it without a Program," for specific strategies

For more information on teaching opportunities, see www.teachabroad.com, or read one of the following:

Teaching English Abroad: Talk Your Way around the World. Susan Griffith. Oxford, England: Vacation Work Publications, 1999. Includes information on specific regions and countries, as well as first-person reports.

Teaching English Guides, available from Passports Books, 4255 West Touhy Avenue, Lincolnwood, IL 60646, 800-323-4900. Includes separate guides on teaching in Eastern Europe and Southeast Asia.

More Than a Native Speaker: An Introduction for Volunteers Teaching Abroad. Don Snow, Alexandria, VA: TESOL Publications, 1996. Includes classroom survival skills for teaching English, information on lesson plans, and discussions about teaching written and spoken English.

See the "International Careers" section of Chapter 10, "Staying Involved after You Get Back," for more work ideas and resources.

Doing Good at Home

Staying home may have been the last thing on your mind when you picked up this book, but volunteering at home or becoming an international activist working from your own community are valuable and viable alternatives to volunteering abroad.

Full-time Volunteer Opportunities at Home

After looking at the options for overseas volunteering and assessing your own motivations for volunteering you may realize that volunteering abroad is not for you, but volunteering locally sounds more appealing. If that is the case, then one of the first options you may want to consider is a full-time domestic volunteer program.

Americorps is a U.S. government program that provides opportunities for part- and full-time domestic service. Members receive a stipend; full-time members receive $4,500 for tuition or student loans after one year of service. Jobs include environmental preservation, care for seniors, and work with youth programs (202-606-5000 (Eastern), 800-565-7052 (Central); 888-756-2734 (Southeast); 888-629-2029 (Western), www.americorps.org).

Seniorcorps is another U.S. government program that provides opportunities for part- and full-time domestic service. Programs include foster grandparents, retired senior volunteer program, and senior companion program (www.nationalservice.org/senior, 202-606-5000, 800-424-8867).

Teach For America (TFA) places college graduates in underserved school districts. TFA provides training and certification. Members earn salaries equivalent to those of local teachers (www.tfanetwork.org, 800-832-1230, x 225).

Public Allies places volunteers ages 18 to 24 in internships with nonprofit organizations. Members receive extensive training and a stipend (www.publicallies.org, 414-273-0533).

There are also many religious programs focused on serving communities in North

America that provide volunteers with room and board and a small living stipend. The Catholic Network of Volunteer Service (www.cnvs.org, 800-543-5046) is an excellent place to start for information on a wide variety of full-time opportunities to serve with Christian-based programs. A number of organizations that offer international volunteer opportunities also offer domestic volunteer work, including Mennonite Central Committee (www.mcc.org, 717-859-1151), Brethren Volunteer Service (www.brethren volunteerservice.org, 800-323-8039), and Jesuit Volunteer Corps (www.jesuitvolunteers. org, 202-687-1132). All three organizations are reviewed in Chapter 12, "Organizational Profiles").

Part-time Volunteer Opportunities at Home

In addition to full-time programs, there are thousands of part-time opportunities to get involved in service and social change within your community. Contact your local volunteer center. To get information on the volunteer center nearest you, try www.pointsoflight.org, www.servenet.org, www.volunteermatch.org, or www.ysa.org.

The range of volunteer options at home is remarkable. Beyond simply getting involved with social service–oriented volunteer work in your own community, there are meaningful opportunities for you to work for sustainable development right here at home. People in many areas of the United States, for instance, suffer from the same problems people face in the "developing" world: poverty, illiteracy, and lack of political or economic power. There is a growing community of domestic organizations that offer opportunities to get involved in promoting sustainable development here at home.

One way to find out about many of these progressive organizations is to visit the website of Working for Change (www.workingforchange.com), and view the list of outstanding nonprofit organizations that have been awarded annual grants from customers of the Working Assets Long Distance phone company, which gives away millions of dollars each year. You will find links to some inspiring organizations like Greenpeace (www.greenpeaceusa.org, 800-326-0959), Indigenous Environmental Network (www.ienearth.org, 218-751-4967), National Network of Immigrant and Refugee Rights (www.nnirr.org, 510-465-1885), Southern Poverty Law Center (www. splcenter.org, 334-264-0286), Center for Third World Organizing (www.ctwo.org, 510-533-7583), and First Nations Development Institute (www.firstnations.org, 540-371-5615).

Community Supported Agriculture (CSA) has recently come into the forefront of local efforts to promote sustainability. For more information on this movement to connect consumers directly with local organic farms try the Community Alliance for Family Farmers (www.caff.org, 530-756-8518), or the Robyn Van En Center for CSA Resources in the Northeast (www.csacenter.org, 717-261-2880).

Become an International Activist

International solidarity is not an act of charity. It is an act of unity among allies fighting on different terrains toward the same objectives.—Samora Machel, former president of Mozambique

While there is plenty of work to be done with domestically focused organizations, staying at home does not have to mean focusing on local issues. Even if you haven't volunteered overseas, you can still be an advocate and ally to people overseas. Most of the activities and ideas for promoting sustainable development in Chapter 10, "Staying Involved after You Get Back," for example, do not even require you to leave your hometown. Read that chapter as a starting point.

Having an impact overseas often begins with educating yourself about what is going on in other parts of the world. You may want to use a variety of methods to learn about critical development issues abroad. See Chapters 3, 8, and 10 for suggestions of excellent resources. Reading, watching videos, and attending workshops and presentations can give you a solid background in the issues.

Often, getting involved with a group is what makes it possible for individuals to be successful activists and affect change through their actions. There are many excellent organizations and networks focused on international issues. See Chapter 10, "Staying Involved after You Get Back," for more suggestions of groups and networks that you might want to join.

Just because you decide not to work overseas does not necessarily mean you are less interested in international issues. Nor does it make you any less legitimate or effective as an activist. Remember that thousands of people who had never been to Central America provided support to the Nicaraguan people in the 1980s and helped pressure the U.S. Congress to stop funding the Contra war there. Thousands more who had never been to Africa played an essential role in the international campaign against apartheid in South Africa.

You do not need to personally hold and feed a starving baby on another continent to know it is wrong that millions of people on our rich planet go hungry every day. You do not need to visit a war zone to be outraged by the billions of dollars spent by governments around the world on weapons that not only kill, maim, and displace people but also rob them of essentials like housing, health care, and education.

If you feel passionately about working for justice on global issues your immediate reaction may be to get a ticket to the latest hotspot. But take time to consider the proposition that you can be the most effective internationalist by educating yourself, staying at home, and mobilizing your own community to work for change. Sure, it's a different experience than volunteering overseas, but working on international issues in your own community is also a viable option.

There is no one path to becoming a global citizen and making the world a better place. Whether you volunteer overseas, study abroad, travel abroad, work abroad, or get involved in your own community, you can make a concrete contribution to improving people's lives.

BONUS SECTION B
ADDITIONAL VOLUNTEER ORGANIZATIONS
NOT PROFILED

The following list of organizations includes a wide range of overseas opportunities offered by organizations that we did not review in Chapter 12, "Organizational Profiles." Some of these programs are conventional volunteer programs while others are study or travel programs that include some community service. The list includes small, grassroots organizations that only place a few volunteers a year as well as larger, more established organizations that place dozens of volunteers. You may want to start your research by visiting the websites listed below. Note that many of the organizations are based in Canada or Europe; some focus on recruiting citizens of the country where they are based, but many are open to other participants regardless of nationality. As we have counseled throughout the book, as you research a potential volunteer placement, remember to speak with returned volunteers and ask them for honest and critical feedback about the organization you are considering.

Action Against Hunger—USA
875 Avenue of the Americas, Suite 1905
New York, NY 10001

phone: 212-967-7800
fax: 212-967-5480
e-mail: aah@aah-usa.org
web: www.interaction.org/members/aah.html

Adorers of the Blood of Christ
2 Pioneer Lane
Red Bud, IL 62278

phone: 618-282-6229
fax: 618-282-3266
e-mail: ascvol@htc.net
web: www.adorers.org

Africa and Asia Venture
10 Market Place, Devizes
Wilts, SN10 1HT
United Kingdom

phone: 44-1380-729009
fax: 44-1380-720060
e-mail: av@aventure.co.uk
web: www.aventure.co.uk

African Conservation Experience
P. O. Box 9706
Solihull, West Midlands
B91 3FF, United Kingdom

phone: 44-870 241-5816
fax: 44-1626-879-700
e-mail: info@afconservex.com
web: www.afconservex.com/

Agency for Personal Service
Overseas (APSO)^
29–30 Fitzwilliam Square
Dublin 2, Ireland

phone: 353-1-661-4411
fax: 353-1-661-4202
e-mail: recept@apso.ie
web: www.apso.ie

Agua Para La Vida
5464 Shafter
Oakland, CA 94706

phone: 510-528-8318
fax: 510-528-8454
e-mail: aplv@igc.org
web: www-cbe2.ced.berkeley.edu/aplv

Air Serv International
Unit 306
6583 Merchant Place
Warrenton, VA 20186

e-mail: asi@airserv.org
web: www.airserv.org

Alliances Abroad
702 West Ave.
Austin, TX 78701

phone: 888-622-7623
phone: 512-457-8062
fax: 512-457-8132
e-mail: outbound@alliancesabroad.com
web: www.alliancesabroad.com

Amazon-Africa Aid Organization (3AO)*
P.O. Box 7776
Ann Arbor, MI 48107

phone: 734-769-5778
fax: 734-769-5779
e-mail: info@amazonafrica.org
web: www.amazonafrica.org

American Jewish Joint Distribution
Committee
711 Third Avenue
New York, NY 10017

phone: 212-687-6200
e-mail: service@jdcny.org
web: www.jdc.org

American Refugee Committee
ARC International Headquarters USA
430 Oak Grove St., Suite 204
Minneapolis, MN 55403

phone: 612-872-7060
fax: 612-607-6499
e-mail: archq@archq.org
web: www.archq.org

Association for International
Practical Training (AIPT)
10400 Little Patuxent Pkwy., Suite 250
Columbia, MD 21044-3510

phone: 410-997-2200
fax: 410-992-3924
e-mail: aipt@aipt.org
web: www.aipt.org

Associate Missionaries of the Assumption
27 N Bowman Ave
Merion, PA 19066

phone: 610-664-1284
fax: 610-664-7328
e-mail: Fjoseph@sju.edu

Bridges for Education
8912 Garlinghouse Road
Naples, NY 14512

phone: 716-534-9344
email: mdodge@frontiernet.net
web: http://wings.buffalo.edu/bfe/

Bridges to Community
P.O. Box 35, Scarborough
New York, NY 10510

phone: 914-923-2200
fax: 914-923-8396
e-mail: brdgs2comm@aol.com
web: www.bridgestocommunity.org

Border Links
1040 North First Avenue
Tuscon, AZ 85719

phone: 520-628-8263
fax: 520-740-0242
e-mail: program@borderlinks.org
web: www.borderlinks.org

Breakthroughs Abroad*
1160-B Woodstock
Estes Park, CO 80517

phone: 970-577-1908
fax: 970-577-9855
e-mail: info@breakthroughsabroad.org
web: www.breakthroughsabroad.org

BTCV International Conservation Holidays
36 St Mary's Street
Wallingford
Oxon OX10 OEU

phone: 44-491-821-600
fax: 44-491-839-646
email: information@btcv.org.uk
web: www.btcv.org

Canada World Youth
2330 Notre-Dame St. West
Montreal, Quebec H3J 1N4
Canada

phone: 514-931-3526
fax: 514-939-2621
e-mail: cwy-jcm@cwy-jcm.org
web: www.cwy-jcm.org

Canadian-Palestinian Educational Exchange (CEPAL)
323 Chapel Street, 3rd Level
Ottawa, Ontario
Canada K1N 7Z2

phone: 613-236-7825
fax: 613-237-5969
e-mail: volunteer@cepal.ca
web: www.cepal.ca

Canadian Centre for International Studies & Cooperation (CECI)
180 Ste-Catherine East
Montreal Quebec H2X 1K9
Canada

phone: 514-875-9911
fax: 514-875-6469
e-mail: info@ceci.ca
web: www.ceci.ca

Canadian Executive Service Organization^
700 Bay Street
Suite 700, Box 328
Toronto, Ontario ON M5G 1Z6
Canada

phone: 416-961-2376
fax: 416-961-1096
e-mail: toronto@ceso-saco.com
web: www.ceso-saco.com

Capuchin Franciscan Volunteers^
Midwest—4502 Park Heights Ave.
Baltimore, MD 21215

phone: 414-271-0135 x16
fax: 414-271-0637
e-mail: capcorps@junp.com
web: www.capuchinfranciscas.org/
   capcorps.htm

Careforce International
5230 South Service Road
Burlington, ON L7L 5K2
Canada

phone: 905-639-8525
fax: 905-639-8482
e-mail: info@careforceinternational.org
web: www.careforceinternational.org

**Catholic Institute for
International Relations**
International Cooperation for Development
Unit 3 Canonbury Yard
190a New North Road, Islington
London N1 7BJ
United Kingdom

phone: 44-20-7288-8600
fax: 44-20-7359-0017
e-mail: ciir@ciir.org
web: www.ciir.org

Catholic Relief Services (CRS)^
International Development Fellows Program
209 West Fayette Street
Baltimore, MD 21201-3443

phone: 800-235-2772
phone: 410-625-2220
fax: 410-685-1635
e-mail: IDFP@catholicrelief.org
web: www.catholicrelief.org

Center for Exchange and Solidarity (CIS)
Boulevard Universatario, Casa #4
Colonia El Roble
San Salvador, El Salvador

phone: 503-226-2623
fax: 503-226-2623
e-mail: cis@netcomsa.com
web: www.cis-elsalvador.org

**Central and East European Law
Initiative (CEELI)**
740 15th, NW, 8th Floor,
Washington, District of Columbia 20005-1022

phone: 202-662-1950
fax: 202-662-1597
e-mail: ceeli@abanet.org
web: www.abanet.org/ceeli

**Central Rocky Mountain Permaculture
Institute**
P.O. Box 631
Basalt, CO 81621

phone/fax: 970-927-4158
e-mail: jerome@crmpi.org
web: www.crmpi.org

Centro Mexicano de la Tortuga
Apartado Postal #16
Puerto Angel, Oaxaca 70902
Mexico

phone: 958-430-55
fax: 958-430-63
e-mail: cmtvasco@angel.umar.mx
web: http://tomzap.com/turtle.html

Chiapas Media Project
4834 N. Springfield
Chicago, IL 60625
Mexico Office:
Proyecto de Medios de Comunicación
en Chiapas
Calle Josefa Ortiz de Dominguez #7B
Col. Barrio Centro
San Cristobal de las Casas 29230
Chiapas, Mexico

phone: 773-583-7728
fax: 773-583-7738
e-mail: cmp@chiapasmediaproject.org
web: www.chiapasmediaproject.org
phone: 52-967-88396
e-mail: promedia@laneta.apc.org

**Children of God Relief Fund
(Nyumbani Hospice/Orphanage)***
11318 Westbrook Mill Lane #103
Fairfax, VA 22030-5665

phone: 703-934-9698
fax: 703-934-9697
e-mail: info@nyumbani.com
web: www.nyumbani.com

**Choice Humanitarian Outreach
and Inter-cultural Exchange**
phone: 841-474-1937
fax: 841-474-1919

e-mail: nancyk@xmission.com
web: www.choice.humanitarian.org

**CORD: (Christian Outreach Relief
and Development)^**
1 New Street
Leamington Spa
Warwickshire
CV31 1HP
United Kingdom

phone: 44-19-2631-5301
fax: 44-19-2688-5786
e-mail: info@cord.org.uk
web: www.cord.org.uk

Christian Service International^
804 W. McGalliard Rd
Muncie, IN 47303-1764

phone: 800-286-5773
phone: 765-286-0711
fax: 765-286-5773
e-mail: csimail@juno.com
web: http://home.cinci.rr.com/haitihope/
about_CSI.htm

Christian Veterinary Mission
19303 Fremont Avenue North
Seattle, WA 98133

phone: 206-546-7569
e-mail: cvm@crista.org
web: www.vetmission.org

Church World Service
28606 Phillips Street
P.O. Box 968
Elkhart, IN 46515

phone: 800-297-1516
fax: 219-262-0966
e-mail: cws@ncccusa.org
web: www.churchworldservice.org

Comboni Lay Missionary Program
1615 E. 31st St.
LaGrange Park, IL 60526-1377

phone: 708-354-2050
fax: 708-354-2006
e-mail: info@laymission-comboni.org
web: www.laymission-comboni.org

Concern Worldwide, USA
104 East 40th Street, Rm 903
New York, NY 10016

phone: 800-59-CONCERN
phone: 212-557-8000
fax: 212-557-8004
e-mail: info@concern-ny.org
web: www.concernusa.org

Conflict Resolution Catalysts (CRC)
P.O. Box 836
Montpelier, VT 05601

phone: 800-445-1165
phone: 802-229-1165
fax: 802-229-1166
e-mail: crc@sover.net
web: www.crcvt.org

Coral Cay Conservation Ltd
The Tower, 13th Floor
125 High Street, Colliers Wood
London SW19 2JG
United Kingdom

phone: 44-870-750-0668
fax: 44-870-750-0667
e-mail: info@coralcay.org
web: www.coralcay.org

Crudem Foundation
9043 Ladue Rd.
St. Louis, MO 63124-1901

phone: 314-994-7030
phone: 314-994-9638
fax: 314-432-3567
e-mail: joyfulness@earthlink.net
web: www.icon-stl.net/~holc

Dental Health International
847 S. Milledge Ave.
Athens, GA 30605

phone: 706-546-1716
fax: 706-546-1715
e-mail: bsdds@earthlink.net

Dooley Foundation—Intermed
420 Lexington Ave., Suite 2331
New York, NY 10170

phone: 212-687-3620
fax: 212-599-6137
e-mail: intermedinc@aol.com

Doctor to Doctor
1749 Martin Luther King Way
Berkeley, CA 94709

phone: 510-841-8484 ext 104
phone: 510-548-5200
fax: 510-540-1707
email: dolgoff@d2d.org
web: www.d2d.org/d2dcontact.htm

The Experiment in International Living
P.O. Box 676
Brattleboro, Vermont 05302-0676

phone: 800-345-2929
phone: 802-257-7751
fax: 802-258-3428
e-mail: eil@worldlearning.org
web: www.usexperiment.org

EcoLogic Development Fund Internship
P.O. Box 383405
Cambridge, MA 02238

phone: 617-441-6300
fax: 617-441-6307
e-mail: enews@ecologic.org
web: www.ecologic.org

Educate the Children
P.O. Box 414
Ithaca, NY 14851

phone: 607-272-1176
fax: 607-275-0932
e-mail: info@etc-nepal.org
web: www.etc-nepal.org

Educacion Para Todos
182 Hamilton Road
Chapel Hill, NC 27514

phone: 919-969-2998
e-mail: lept@earthlink.net
web: www.fcinet.com/ept

English Language Institute/China^
P.O. Box 265
San Dimas, CA 91773

phone: 888-475-3542, 909-599-6773
fax: 909-592-9906
e-mail: info@elic.org
web: www.elic.org

El Porvenir
2508 42nd Street
Sacramento, CA 95817

phone: 916-736-3663
fax: 916-227-5068
e-mail: info@elporvenir.org
web: www.elporvenir.org

Financial Services Volunteer Corps
10 East 53rd Street, 24 Floor
New York, New York 10022

phone: 212-771-1400
fax: 212-421-2162
e-mail: fsvc@fsvc.org
web: www.fsvc.org

Frontier
50–52 Rivington Street
London, EC2A 3QP
United Kingdom

phone: 44-20-7613-2422
fax: 44-20-7613 2992
e-mail: enquiries@frontier.ac.uk
web: www.frontier.ac.uk

Frontier Internship in Mission
150 Route de Ferney
1211 Geneva 2
Switzerland

phone: 41-22-798-8987
fax: 41-22-788-1434
e-mail: jm@tfim.org
web: http://tfim.org/

Foundation for Sustainable Development*
111 North Highland
Arlington, VA 22201

phone: 703-741-0832
fax: 703-741-0832
e-mail: fsdmail@yahoo.com
web: www.interconnection.org/fsd

Forum SYD^
Box 15407
S 104 65
Stockholm
Sweden

phone: 46-8-506-370-00
fax: 46-8-506-370-99
e-mail: forum.syd@forumsyd.se
web: www.forumsyd.se

GAP Activity Projects (GAP)
GAP House
44 Queens Road, Reading
Berkshire, RG1 4BB
United Kingdom

phone: 44-1189-594-914
fax: 44-1189-576-634
e-mail: volunteer@gap.org.uk
web: www.gap.org.uk

Geekcorps, Inc.*
1121 MASS MoCA Way
North Adams, MA 01247

phone: 413-664-0030
fax: 413-664-0032
e-mail: volunteer@geekcorps.org
web: www.geekcorps.org

Genesis II Cloudforest Preserve & Wildlife Refuge
Apartado 655
7050 Cartago
Costa Rica

phone: 506-381-0739
fax: 506-551-0070
e-mail: info@genesis-two.com
web: www.genesis-two.com

Greenforce
11–15 Betterton St
Covent Garden, London
WC2H 9BP, United Kingdom

phone: 44-20-7470-8888
fax: 44-20-7470-8889
e-mail: greenforce@btinternet.com
web: www.greenforce.org/

Global Vision International
Amwell Farmhouse
Wheathampstead, Herts
AL4 8EJ, United Kingdom

phone: 44-1582 831300
fax: 44-1582 831300
e-mail: GVIenquiries@aol.com
web: http://www.gvi.co.uk

Global Works, Inc.*
RD 2 Box 173A
Huntingdon, PA 16652

phone: 814-667-2411
fax: 814-667-3853
e-mail: info@globalworksinc.com
web: www.globalworksinc.com

The God's Child Project
P.O. Box 1573
Bismarck, ND 58504-1573

phone: 701-255-7956
fax: 701-222-0874
e-mail: godschld@btinet.net
web: www.godschild.org
web: www.ana.org.gt

Good Shepherd Volunteers*
337 East 17th Street
New York, NY 10003

phone: 888-668-6GSV x780
phone: 212-475-4245 x 780
fax: 212-979-8604
e-mail: goodshpvol@aol.com
web: www.goodshepherdvolunteers.com

Handicap International^
14, Avenue Berthelot
Lyon, F-69361, Cedex 07
France
US Office:
P.O. Box 815
Fryeburg, ME 04037

phone: 33-78-69-7979
fax: 33-78-69-7994
e-mail: handicap-international@infonie.fr
web: www.handicap-international.org
phone: 207-935-4217
fax: 207-935-4042
e-mail: sbwhandicap@igc.org

Higher Education Consortium for Urban Affairs (HECUA)
2233 University Ave. W.,
Suite 210
St. Paul, MN 55114-1629

phone: 800-554-1089
phone: 651-646-8831
fax: 651-659-9421
e-mail: info@hecua.org
web: www.hecua.org

Institute for Cultural Ecology
758 Kapahulu #500
Honolulu, Hawaii 96816

phone: 808-739-6123
fax: 808-733-7808
e-mail: info@culturalecology.com
web: www.culturalecology.com

International Association for Exchange of Students for Technical Experience (IAESTE)
c/o Association for International Practical Training (AIPT)
10400 Little Patuxent Pkwy. Suite 250
Columbia, MD 21044-3510

phone: 410-997-3069
fax: 410-997-5186
e-mail: iaeste@aipt.org
web: www.aipt.org

International Christian Youth Exchange
International Office
Grosse Hamburger Str. 30, D - 10115
Berlin, Germany

phone: 49-30-28390550
fax: 49-30-28390552
e-mail: icye@icye.org
web: www.icye.org

**International Communities for
the Renewal of the Earth***
P.O. Box 194
New York, NY 10518

phone: 914-763-5790
fax: 914-763-3715
e-mail: danann0305@aol.com

International Service (UNAIS)
Hunter House
57 Goodramgate, York
YO1 7FX, United Kingdom

phone: 44-1904-647799
fax: 44-1904 652353
e-mail: unais-uk@geo2.poptel.org.uk
web: www.oneworld.org/is

International Voluntary Services, Inc.
1625 K Street, NW Suite 102
Washington, DC 20006

phone: 202-387-5533
fax: 202-387-4291
e-mail: ivs.inc@erols.com
web: www.ivs-inc.org

Islamic American Relief Agency
P.O. Box 7084
Columbia, MO 65205

phone: 800-298-1199
phone: 573-443-0166
fax: 573-443-5975
e-mail: iara@iara-usa.org
web: www.iara-usa.org

International Medical Corps (IMC)
11500 West Olympic Blvd, Ste. 506
Los Angeles, CA 90064-1524

phone: 310-826-7800
fax: 310-442-6622
e-mail: imc@imc-la.org
web: www.imc-la.org

International Volunteer Program*
210 Post St, Ste. 502
San Francisco, CA 94108

phone: 415-477-3667
fax: 415-477-3669
e-mail: rjewell@ivpsf.com
web: www.ivpsf.com

i to i International Projects
One Cottage Road
Headingly, Leeds
U.K., LS6 4DD

phone: 44-870-333-2332
fax: 44-113-274-6923
e-mail: info@i-to-i.com
web: www.i-to-i.com

JustAct: Youth ACTion for Global JUSTice*
333 Valencia St #325
San Francisco, CA 94103

phone: 415-431-4204
fax: 415-431-5953
e-mail: info@justact.org
web: www.justact.org

Lalmba Association
7685 Quartz St.
Arvada, CO 80007

phone: 303-420-1810
fax: 303-467-1232
e-mail: lalmba@aol.com
web: www.lalmba.org

Latin Link^
175 Tower Bridge Road
London SE1 2AB
United Kingdom

phone: 44-20-7939-9000
fax: 44-20-7939-9015
e-mail: ukoffice@latinlink.org
web: www.latinlink.org

Latitudes International*
51 First Avenue
East Haven, CT 06512

phone: 800-398-4960
fax: 203-468-9260
e-mail: info@latitudesint.org
web: www.latitudesint.org

Lay Mission Helpers Association
3424 Wilshire Blvd.
Los Angeles, CA 90010

phone: 213-637-7222
fax: 213-637-6223
e-mail: LMH@la-archdiocese.org
web: http://laymission.la-archdiocese.org

LISLE, Inc.*
900 Country Road 269
Leander, TX 78641

phone: 800-477-1538
fax: 512-259-0392
e-mail: lisle@utnet.utoledo.edu
web: www.lisleinternational.org

Little Children of the World
361 County Road 475
Etowah, TN 37331

phone/fax: 423-263-2303
e-mail: lcotw@tds.net
web: www.littlechildren.org

Madre
121 West 27th St, suite 301
New York, NY 10001

phone: 212-627-0444
fax: 212-675-3704
e-mail: madre@igc.apc.org
web: www.madre.org

Mercy Ships
P.O. Box 2020
Garden Valley, Texas 75771

phone: 800-MERCYSHIPS
phone: 903-882-0887
fax: 903-882-0336
e-mail: info@mercyships.org
web: www.mercyships.org

Michigan Peace Team (MPT)
1516 Jerome St.
Lansing, MI 48912

phone: 517-484-3178
fax: 517-484-4219
e-mail: michpeaceteam@igc.org
web: www.michiganpeaceteam.org

Middle East Children's Alliance
905 Parker St.
Berkeley, CA 94710

phone: 510-548-0542
fax: 510-548-0543
e-mail: meca@mecaforpeace.org
web: www.mecaforpeace.org

Mission Doctors Association
3424 Wilshire Blvd.
Los Angeles, CA 90010

phone: 626-285-8868
fax: 626-309-1716
e-mail: missiondrs@earthlink.net
web: www.missiondoctors.org

Mission of Friendship*
P.O. Box 10397
Erie, PA 16514-0397

phone: 814-824-1230
e-mail: tzoky@eriercd.org
web: www.eriercd.org/missions4asp

Mission Volunteers International
Mission Service Recruitment,
Presbyterian Church
100 Witherspoon Street
Louisville, KY 40202-1396

phone: 888-728-7228, ext. 2530
fax: 502-569-5975
e-mail: msr@ctr.pcusa.org
web: www.pcusa.org/msr/

Musical Bridges
301 Willow Ave. Apt. 1
Hoboken, NJ 07030

e-mail: alina@musicalbridges.org
web: www.musicalbridges.org

New England Biolabs Foundation*
Artcorps
32 Tozer Road
Beverly, MA 01915

phone: 978-927-2404
fax: 978-921-1350
e-mail: cataldo@nebf.org
web: www.nebf.org

Nicaragua Network
1247 E Street SE
Washington, DC 20003

phone: 202-544-9355
fax: 202-544-9359
e-mail: nicanet@afgi.org
web: www.infoshop.org/nicanet

Oceanic Society
Fort Mason Center, Building E
San Francisco, California, 94123

phone: 800-326-7491
phone: 415-441-1106
fax: 415-474-3395
e-mail: Tenofsky@oceanic-society.org
web: www.oceanic-society.org

**Overseas Service Bureau-Australian
Volunteers Abroad^**
P.O. Box 350
Fitaroy, Vic 3065
Australia

phone: 61-03-9279-1788
fax: 61-03-9419-4280
e-mail: avaenq@ozvol.org.au
web: www.osb.org.au

**Partners of the Americas
(Compañeros de las Americas)**
1424 K Street, NW, Suite 700
Washington, D.C. 20005

phone: 202-628-3300
fax: 202-628-3306
e-mail: info@partners.poa.com
web: www.partners.net

**Peace Trees Project
(Earthstewards Network)**
P.O. Box 10697
Bainbridge Island, WA 98110

phone: 206-842-7986
fax: 206-842-8918
e-mail: info@peacetreesvietnam.org
web: www.peacetreesvietnam.org

People to People International
501 E. Armour
Kansas City, MO 64109

phone: 816-531-4701
fax: 816-561-7502
e-mail: internships@ptpi.org
web: www.ptpi.org

**People to People Health Foundation,
Project Hope**
Health Sciences Education Division
Millwood, VA 22646

phone: 800-544-4673
e-mail: recruit@projecthope.org
web: www.projecthope.org

Philanthropy Host Families (GHANA)*
P.O. Box 7781
Santa Rosa, CA 95407

phone: 707-569-8171
fax: 707-253-5144
e-mail: phyllis@inreach.com

Plenty International
P.O. Box 394
Summertown, TN 38483

phone: 931-964-4864
fax: 931-964-4864
e-mail: plenty1@usit.net
web: www.plenty.org

Princeton in Asia^
Princeton University, Room 241
33 First Campus Center
Princeton, NJ 08544-1100

phone: 858-258-3657
fax: 858-258-5300
e-mail: pia@princeton.edu
web: www.princeton.edu/~pia

Project Concern International^
3550 Afton Rd
San Diego, CA 92123

phone: 858-279-9690
fax: 858-694-0294
e-mail: postmaster@projectconcern.org
web: www.projectconcern.org

Public Health International (PHI)
P.O. Box 116
Roseburg, OR 97470

phone: 541-672-0615
e-mail: phi@wanweb.net
web: www.efn.org/~phi

Quaker Overseas Volunteer Ministry
World Ministries, Friends United Meeting
101 Quaker Hill Dr.
Richmond, IN 47374

phone: 317-962-7573
fax: 317-966-1293
e-mail: info@fum.org
web: www.fum.org

Raleigh International
27 Parsons Green Lane
London SW6 4HZ
United Kingdom

phone: 44-20-7371-8585
fax: 44-20-7371-5116
e-mail: international@raleigh.org.uk
web: www.raleighinternational.org

Religious Youth Services
RYS, 4 W 43rd Street
New York, NY 10036

phone: 973-667-0329
email: usa@rys.net
email: jygehring@aol.com
web: www.rys.net

Remote Area Medical Volunteer Corps
1834 Beech Street
Knoxville, TN 37920

phone: 865-579-1530
e-mail: ram@usit.net
web: www.ramusa.org

San Diego Friends of Tibet
4060 Adams Ave.
San Diego, CA 92116

phone: 619-682-7188
fax: 619-543-1211
e-mail: dorykb@san.rr.com
web: www.sdtibet.org

Sports Coaches' OutReach (SCORE)
SCORE—European Office
PO Box 1167
1000 BD, Amsterdam
The Netherlands

phone: 31-229-590208
fax: 31-229-590286
e-mail: willemvriend@planet.nl
web: www.ssisa.com/bodies/score.html

SEVA Foundation
1786 Fifth Street
Berkeley, CA 94710

phone: 510-845-7382
fax: 510-845-7410
e-mail: admin@seva.org
web: www.seva.org

SMA Lay Missionaries
Society of African Missions
256 N. Manor Circle
Takoma Park, MD 20912-4561

phone: 301-891-2037
fax: 301-270-6370
e-mail: smausa-1@smafathers.org
web: www.smafathers.org/SMA2.htm

Student and Youth Travel Organization
2612 Rainbow Way, Suite A
Decatur, Georgia 30034

phone: 404-244-1803
fax: 404-244-1982
e-mail: sytousa@aol.com

Students Partnership Worldwide
17 Dean's Yard
London, SW1P 3PB
United Kingdom

phone: 44-20-7222-0138
fax: 44-20-7233-0008
e-mail: spwuk@gn.apc.org
web: www.spw.org

Study Service Term at Goshen College^
International Education Office
700 S Main St
Goshen, Indiana 46526

phone: 219-535-7346
fax: 219-535-7319
e-mail: wilburjb@goshen.edu
web: www.goshen.edu/sst/sst

Sudan Volunteer Programme
34 Estelle Rd
London
NW3 2JY, United Kingdom

phone/fax: 44-20-7485-8619
e-mail: davidsvp@aol.com
web: www.svp-uk.com

Tahoe-Baikal Institute*
PO Box 13587
South Lake Tahoe, CA 96151-3587

phone: 530-542-5599
fax: 530-542-5567
e-mail: tbi@tahoe.com
web: http://tahoe.ceres.ca.gov/tbi

Tibetan Environmental Network
10 Dunstable Road
Richmond, TW9 1UH
United Kingdom

phone/fax: 44-181-940-3166
e-mail: dalha@aol.com
web: www.aptibet.org/ten.htm

Trekforce Expeditions
34 Buckingham Palace Road
London, SW1W ORE
United Kingdom

phone: 44-20-7828-2275
phone: 44-20-7828-2276
e-mail: info@trekforce.org.uk
web: www.trekforce.org.uk/

United Children's Fund, Inc.*
P.O. Box 20341
Boulder, CO, 80308-3341

phone: 888-343-3199
phone: 303-469-4339
e-mail: unchildren@aol.com
web: www.unchildren.org

Unidas Para Vivir Mejor (UPAVIM)
Calle Principal, Sector D-1
La Esperanza, Zona 12
01012 Guatemala

phone: 502-479-9061
e-mail: upavim@guate.net
web: www.upavim.org/

U.S. Catholic China Bureau*
Seton Hall University
South Orange, NJ 07079

phone: 973-763-1311
fax: 973-763-1543
e-mail: chinabur@shu.edu
web: www.usccb.net

**Vellore Christian Medical College
Board (USA), Inc.**
475 Riverside Dr., Rm. 243
New York, NY 10115

phone: 212-870-2640
fax: 212-870-2173
e-mail: usaboard@vellorecmc.org
web: www.vellorecmc.org

Venceremos Brigade
P.O. Box 7071
Oakland, CA 94601

phone: 415-267-0606 (west)
212-696-7412 (east)
312-409-1486 (mid-west)
e-mail: info@vbrigade.org,
        vbsfbay@latino.com
web: www.vbrigade.org

VentureCo Worldwide
Pleck House, Middletown
Moreton Morrell, Warwickshire
CV35 5AU, United Kingdom

phone: 44-1926-651071
fax: 44-1926-650120
e-mail: mail@ventureco-worldwide.com
web: www.ventureco-worldwide.com/

Veterinarians without Borders
VSF-DZG-Belgium
Rue de Merode 216 B-1060 Bruxelles

phone: 32-02-539-0989
fax: 32-02-539-3490
e-mail: vsf@vsf-belgium.org
web: www.vsf-Belgium.org

Visions
P.O. Box 220
Newport, PA 17074

phone: 717-567-7313
fax: 717-567-7853
e-mail: visions@pa.net
web: www.visionsadventure.com

Voluntarios Solidarios
Fellowship of Reconciliation
Task Force on Latin America
and the Caribbean
2017 Mission Street #305
San Francisco, CA 94110

phone: 415-495-6334
fax: 415-495-5628
e-mail: forlatam@igc.org
web: www.forusa.org

Volunteers in Technical Assistance (VITA)
Suite 710 1600 Wilson Boulevard
Arlington, Virginia 22209

phone: 703-276-1800
e-mail: vita@vita.org
web: www.vita.org

Volunteer Missionary Movement (VMM)

phone: 353-1-837-6565

All Hallows, Senior House,
Grace Park Road, Dublin 9
Ireland

e-mail: vmmeurgo@iol.ie
web: vmm.cjb.net

Volunteer Nepal
P.O. Box 9282
Denver, Colorado 80209

phone: 303-321-8278
e-mail: nepal@goabroad.com
web: www.volunteerabroad.com/nepal

Volunteer Service Abroad (VSA)^
P.O. Box 12-246
Wellington 1, New Zealand

phone: 64-4-472-5759
fax: 64-4-472-5052
e-mail: vsa@vsa.org
web: www.vsa.org.nz

**VOSH International (Volunteer
Optometric Services to Humanity)^**
c/o Charles H. Covington
102 Oak View Cir.
Lake Mary, FL 32746

e-mail: charlescovington@hotmail.com
web: www.vosh.org

Winrock International Volunteer Programs
38 Winrock Drive
Morrilton, Arkansas 72110-9370

phone: 877-857-8040 x234
phone: 501-727-5435
fax: 501-727-5426
e-mail: volunteer-program@winrock.org
web: www.winrock.org/volunteer

World Horizons International, Inc.
P.O. Box 662
Bethlehem, CT 06751

phone: 800-262-5874
phone/fax: 203-266-5874
e-mail: worhorin@wtco.net
web: www.world-horizons.com

**YMCA of Greater New York—
The International Branch**
71 West 23rd Street Suite 1904
New York, NY 10010

phone: 212-727-8800
phone: 888-477-9622
fax: 212-727-8814
web: http://ymcanyc.org/international

YMCA of USA
International Programs (Fellows Program)^
101 N. Wacker Drive
Chicago, IL 60606

phone: 312-977-0031
phone: 800-872-9622
fax: 312-977-0884
web: www.ymca.net/

Youth Challenge International
20 Maud Street, Suite 305
Toronto, Canada
ON M5V 2M5

phone: 416-504-3370
fax: 416-504-3376
e-mail: yci@web.ca
web: www.yci.org

**Youth For Understanding
International Exchange**
YFU International Center
3501 Newark Street, N.W.
Washington, DC 20016-3199

phone: 800-787-8000, 800-TEENAGE
phone: 202-966-6800
fax: 202-895-1104
e-mail: pio@us.yfu.org
web: www.youthforunderstanding.org

Youth International
1121 Downing Street #2
Denver, Colorado 80218

phone: 303-839-5877
fax: 303-839-5887
e-mail: director@youthinternational.org
web: www.youthinternational.org

*=Members of the International Volunteer Programs Association (IVPA)
^=Mentioned in the various chapters of this book

Index of Profiled Organizations

REGION

Note that some organizations frequently change the countries in which they place volunteers. Be sure to check websites or contact the organizations to get the most recent information about the countries where they work.

Organizations Placing Volunteers in Africa

ACDI/VOCA
Adventures in Health, Education, and Agricultural Development (AHEAD, Inc.)
AFS
American Jewish World Service (AJWS)
Amity Institute, Amity Volunteer Teachers Abroad Program
Brethren Volunteer Service (BVS)
BRIDGES Fellowship (Building Responsible International Dialogue
   through Grassroots Exchange)
Canadian Crossroads International (CCI)
Catholic Medical Missions Board (CMMB)
Christian Foundation for Children and the Aging (CFCA)
Concern America
Council on International Educational Exchange (Council)
Cross-Cultural Solutions (CCS)
CUSO
Doctors Without Borders/Médcins Sans Frontières (MSF)
Earthwatch Institute
Elderhostel
Food for the Hungry
Global Citizens Network (GCN)
Global Routes
Global Service Corps (GSC)
Global Volunteers
Habitat for Humanity International
Health Volunteers Overseas (HVO)
Institute for International Cooperation and Development (IICD)
International Executive Service Corps (IESC)
International Foundation for Education and Self-Help (IFESH)

Jesuit Volunteer Corps/Jesuit Volunteers International (JVC/JVI)
Maryknoll Mission Association
Mennonite Central Committee (MCC)
Minnesota Studies in International Development (MSID)
Mobility International (MIUSA)
Operation Crossroads Africa (OCA)
Operation Smile
Peace Corps
Peacework
SCI-IVS USA (Service Civil International-International Voluntary Service)
United Methodists General Board of Global Ministries (GBGM)
United Nations Volunteers (UNV)
University Research Expeditions Program (UREP)
Visions in Action
Voluntary Service Overseas (VSO)
Volunteers for Peace International Workcamps
WorldTeach
World University Service of Canada (WUSC)

Organizations Placing Volunteers in Asia and the Pacific

ACDI/VOCA
AFS
American Jewish World Service (AJWS)
Amity Institute, Amity Volunteer Teachers Abroad Program
Amizade
Brethren Volunteer Service (BVS)
BRIDGES Fellowship (Building Responsible International Dialogue
    through Grassroots Exchange)
Canadian Crossroads International (CCI)
Catholic Medical Missions Board (CMMB)
Child Family Health International (CFHI)
Child Haven International
Christian Foundation for Children and the Aging (CFCA)
Citizens Democracy Corps (CDC)
Council on International Educational Exchange (Council)
Cross-Cultural Solutions (CCS)
Cultural Restoration Tourism Project (CRTP)
CUSO
Doctors Without Borders/ Médecins Sans Frontières (MSF)
Earthwatch Institute
Elderhostel
Food for the Hungry
Global Citizens Network (GCN)
Global Routes
Global Service Corps (GSC)
Global Volunteers
Habitat for Humanity International
Health Volunteers Overseas (HVO)
Himalayan Explorers Club (HEC)

Organizations Placing Volunteers in Latin America and the Caribbean

Doctors Without Borders/ Médecins Sans Frontières (MSF)
Earthwatch Institute
Elderhostel
Esperança
FFA
Flying Doctors
Flying Samaritans
Food for the Hungry
FUNDECI
Global Citizens Network (GCN)
Global Routes
Global Service Corps (GSC)
Global Volunteers
Habitat for Humanity International
Health Volunteers Overseas (HVO)
Institute for Central American Development Studies (ICADS)
Institute for International Cooperation and Development (IICD)
International Executive Service Corps (IESC)
International Partnership for Service-Learning (IPS-L)
International Service for Peace (SIPAZ)
International Volunteer Expeditions (IVEX)
Interplast, Inc.
Jesuit Volunteer Corps/Jesuit Volunteers International (JVC/JVI)
Maryknoll Mission Association
Mennonite Central Committee (MCC)
Minnesota Studies in International Development (MSID)
Mobility International (MIUSA)
New Haven/Leon Sister City Project (NH/LSCP)
NISGUA Guatemala Accompaniment Project
Nuestros Pequeños Hermanos (NPH)
Operation Crossroads Africa (OCA)
Operation Smile
Parroquia San Lucas Toliman
Pastors for Peace/IFCO
Peace Brigades International (PBI)
Peace Corps
Peacework
SCI-IVS USA (Service Civil International-International Voluntary Service)
United Methodists General Board of Global Ministries (GBGM)
United Nations Volunteers (UNV)
University Research Expeditions Program (UREP)
Visions in Action
Voluntary Service Overseas (VSO)
Volunteers for Peace International Workcamps
Witness for Peace (WFP)
World PULSE (Program for Understanding, Leadership, Service, and Exchange)
WorldTeach
World University Service of Canada (WUSC)

Organizations Placing Volunteers in Eastern and Central Europe

AFS
American Jewish World Service (AJWS)
Brethren Volunteer Service (BVS)
Catholic Medical Missions Board (CMMB)
Central European Teaching Program (CETP)
Citizens Democracy Corps (CDC)
Council on International Educational Exchange (Council)
Cross-Cultural Solutions (CCS)
Doctors Without Borders/ Médecins Sans Frontières (MSF)
Earthwatch Institute
Elderhostel
Food for the Hungry
Global Volunteers
Habitat for Humanity International
International Executive Service Corps (IESC)
International Partnership for Service-Learning (IPS-L)
Mennonite Central Committee (MCC)
Mobility International (MIUSA)
Peace Brigades International (PBI)
Peace Corps
Peacework
SCI-IVS USA (Service Civil International-International Voluntary Service)
United Methodists General Board of Global Ministries (GBGM)
United Nations Volunteers (UNV)
Voluntary Service Overseas (VSO)
Volunteers for Peace International Workcamps

Organizations Placing Volunteers in the Middle East

ACDI/VOCA
AFS
American Jewish World Service (AJWS)
Christian Peacemaker Teams (CPT)
Doctors Without Borders/Médecins Sans Frontières (MSF)
Earthwatch Institute
Food for the Hungry
Habitat for Humanity International
International Executive Service Corps (IESC)
International Partnership for Service-Learning (IPS-L)
Interns for Peace (IFP)
Kibbutz Program Center
Mennonite Central Committee (MCC)
Mobility International (MIUSA)
Peace Corps
Project OTZMA
SCI-IVS USA (Service Civil International-International Voluntary Service)
United Methodists General Board of Global Ministries (GBGM)

United Nations Volunteers (UNV)
Volunteers for Peace International Workcamps
World PULSE (Program for Understanding, Leadership, Service, and Exchange)

Organizations Placing Volunteers in the "Global North" (Western Europe, North America, Australia, New Zealand, and Japan)

Note that many of these organizations place volunteers in Native American reservations, low-income neighborhoods, and Aboriginal lands. In addition, many organizations not listed here have administrative volunteer opportunities in their headquarters in the Global North.

AFS
Amizade
Brethren Volunteer Service (BVS)
BRIDGES Fellowship (Building Responsible International Dialogue through Grassroots
    Exchange) (in combination with overseas program)
Christian Peacemaker Teams (CPT)
Council on International Educational Exchange (Council)
Doctors Without Borders/ Médecins Sans Frontières (MSF)
Earthwatch Institute
Elderhostel
FFA
Food for the Hungry
Global Citizens Network (GCN)
Global Routes
Global Volunteers
Habitat for Humanity International
International Executive Service Corps (IESC)
International Partnership for Service-Learning (IPS-L)
Japan-U.S. Community Education and Exchange (JUCEE)
Jesuit Volunteer Corps/Jesuit Volunteers International (JVC/JVI)
Mennonite Central Committee (MCC)
Mobility International (MIUSA)
Operation Smile
Peacework
SCI-IVS USA (Service Civil International-International Voluntary Service)
United Methodists General Board of Global Ministries (GBGM)
United Nations Volunteers (UNV)
University Research Expeditions Program (UREP)
Volunteers for Peace International Workcamps
World PULSE (Program for Understanding, Leadership, Service, and Exchange)

LENGTH OF VOLUNTEER EXPERIENCE

Note that some short- and medium-term programs can be extended; contact organizations for details.

Organizations Offering Short-term Opportunities *(less than 1 month)*

ACDI/VOCA
American Friends Service Committee (AFSC)
Amizade
ARCAS
Catholic Medical Missions Board (CMMB)
Child Family Health International (CFHI)
Citizens Democracy Corps (CDC)
Council on International Educational Exchange (Council)
Christian Peacemaker Teams (CPT)
Cross-Cultural Solutions (CCS)
Cultural Restoration Tourism Project (CRTP)
Earthwatch Institute
Elderhostel
FFA
Flying Doctors
Flying Samaritans
Food for the Hungry
FUNDECI
Global Citizens Network (GCN)
Global Service Corps (GSC)
Global Volunteers
Habitat for Humanity International
Health Volunteers Overseas (HVO)
Institute for Central American Development Studies (ICADS)
International Executive Service Corps (IESC)
International Partnership for Service-Learning (IPS-L)
International Volunteer Expeditions (IVEX)
Interplast, Inc.
Joint Assistance Centre (JAC)
Maryknoll Mission Association
Mobility International (MIUSA)
New Haven/Leon Sister City Project (NH/LSCP)
Operation Smile
Parroquia San Luis Toliman
Pastors for Peace/IFCO
Peacework
SCI-IVS USA (Service Civil International-International Voluntary Service)
United Methodists General Board of Global Ministries (GBGM)
United Nations Volunteers (UNV)
University Research Expeditions Program (UREP)
Volunteers for Peace International Workcamps
Witness for Peace (WFP)

Organizations Offering Medium-Term Opportunities *(1 month to 6 months)*

ACDI/VOCA
Adventures in Health, Education, and Agricultural Development (AHEAD, Inc.)
AFS

American Friends Service Committee (AFSC)
American Jewish World Service (AJWS)
Amigos de las Américas
Amity Institute, Amity Volunteer Teachers Abroad Program
Amizade
ARCAS
BRIDGES Fellowship (Building Responsible International Dialogue through Grassroots Exchange)
Canadian Crossroads International (CCI)
Casa de los Amigos
Catholic Medical Missions Board (CMMB)
Child Family Health International (CFHI)
Child Haven International
Christian Foundation for Children and the Aging (CFCA)
Christian Peacemaker Teams (CPT)
Citizens Democracy Corps (CDC)
Council on International Educational Exchange (Council)
Crispaz
Cross-Cultural Solutions (CCS)
Doctors Without Borders/Médecins Sans Frontières (MSF)
Esperança
FFA
Food for the Hungry
FUNDECI
Global Routes
Global Service Corps (GSC)
Health Volunteers Overseas (HVO)
Himalayan Explorers Club (HEC)
Institute for Central American Development-Studies (ICADS)
International Executive Service Corps (IESC)
International Partnership for Service-Learning (IPS-L)
International Society for Ecology & Culture (ISEC)
International Volunteer Expeditions (IVEX) (for repeat volunteers)
Japan-U.S. Community Education & Exchange (JUCEE)
Joint Assistance Centre (JAC)
Kibbutz Program Center
Mennonite Central Committee (MCC)
Minnesota Studies in International Development (MSID)
Mobility International (MIUSA)
New Haven/Leon Sister City Project (NH/LSCP)
NISGUA Guatemala Accompaniment Project
Nuestros Pequeños Hermanos (NPH)
Operation Crossroads Africa (OCA)
Parroquia San Luis Toliman
Pastors for Peace/IFCO
Peace Corps (Crisis Corps only for former Peace Corps volunteers)
Peacework
United Methodists General Board of Global Ministries (GBGM)
United Nations Volunteers (UNV)
VIA (formerly Volunteers in Asia)

Visions in Action
WorldTeach

Organizations Offering Long-term Opportunities *(more than 6 months)*

Adventures in Health, Education, and Agricultural Development (AHEAD, Inc.)
AFS
American Jewish World Service (AJWS)
Amity Institute, Amity Volunteer Teachers Abroad Program
ARCAS
Brethren Volunteer Services (BVS)
Casa de los Amigos
Catholic Medical Missions Board (CMMB)
Central European Teaching Program (CETP)
Child Family Health International (CFHI)
Christian Foundation for Children and the Aging (CFCA)
Concern America
Crispaz
Cross-Cultural Solutions (CCS)
CUSO
Doctors Without Borders/Médecins Sans Frontières (MSF)
FFA
Food for the Hungry
FUNDECI
Habitat for Humanity International
Health Volunteers Overseas (HVO)
Institute for International Cooperation & Development (IICD)
International Foundation for Education and Self-Help (IFESH)
International Partnership for Service-Learning (IPS-L)
International Service for Peace (SIPAZ)
Interns for Peace (IFP)
Jesuit Volunteer Corps/Jesuit Volunteers International (JVC/JVI)
Maryknoll Mission Association
Mennonite Central Committee (MCC)
Minnesota Studies in International Development (MSID)
Mobility International (MIUSA)
New Haven/Leon Sister City Project (NH/LSCP)
NISGUA Guatemala Accompaniment Project
Parroquia San Luis Toliman
Peace Brigades International (PBI)
Peace Corps
Project OTZMA
United Methodists General Board of Global Ministries (GBGM)
United Nations Volunteers (UNV)
VIA (formerly Volunteers in Asia)
Visions in Action
Voluntary Service Overseas (VSO)
Witness for Peace (WFP)
World PULSE (Program for Understanding, Leadership, Service,
    and Exchange)

WorldTeach
World University Service of Canada (WUSC)

COSTS

Organizations that Cover Most or All Expenses

This list includes only organizations that cover travel expenses and room and board, and have no program fee. There are many additional organizations that have fairly low fees or offer scholarships. Check organizational profiles for details of costs and benefits for other programs. See Chapter 7, "Overcoming Financial Obstacles," for information on how you could afford to volunteer with groups not on this list; don't rule the other organizations out!

ACDI/VOCA
BRIDGES Fellowship (Building Responsible International Dialogue
    through Grassroots Exchange)
Catholic Medical Missions Board (CMMB) (for long-term volunteers)
Citizens Democracy Corps (CDC) (except meals)
Concern America
CUSO
Doctors Without Borders/Médecins Sans Frontières (MSF)
Habitat for Humanity International (International Partners Program)
International Executive Service Corps (IESC)
International Foundation for Education and Self-Help (IFESH)
International Service for Peace (SIPAZ)
Jesuit Volunteer Corps/Jesuit Volunteers International (JVC/JVI)
Maryknoll Mission Association
Mennonite Central Committee (MCC)
Peace Corps
United Methodists General Board of Global Ministries (GMGM)
United Nations Volunteers (UNV)
Voluntary Service Overseas (VSO)
World PULSE (Program for Understanding, Leadership, Service, and Exchange)
World University Service of Canada (WUSC)

TYPE OF WORK

Agriculture/Rural Development

ACDI/VOCA
American Friends Service Committee (AFSC)
American Jewish World Service (AJWS)
Amity Institute, Amity Volunteer Teachers Abroad Program
Brethren Volunteer Service (BVS)
Canadian Crossroads International (CCI)
Concern America
CUSO
FFA
Food for the Hungry

Appropriate Technology

Archaeology/Historical Preservation/Cultural Preservation

Business Development/Fair Trade/Craft Development & Marketing

ACDI/VOCA
American Jewish World Service (AJWS)
Citizens Democracy Corps (CDC)
Global Service Corps (GSC)
Global Volunteers
International Executive Service Corps (IESC)
International Foundation for Education and Self-Help (IFESH)
International Partnership for Service-Learning (IPS-L)
Japan-U.S. Community Education and Exchange (JUCEE)
Maryknoll Mission Association
Mennonite Central Committee (MCC)
Minnesota Studies in International Development (MSID)
Mobility International (MIUSA)
Peace Corps
United Nations Volunteers (UNV)
Visions in Action
Voluntary Service Overseas (VSO)

Computers/Public Relations/Fundraising/Office Work/ Administration/Grant Writing

American Jewish World Service (AJWS)
Canadian Crossroads International (CCI)
Casa de los Amigos
Cross-Cultural Solutions (CCS)
CUSO
Doctors Without Borders/Médecins Sans Frontières (MSF)
Food for the Hungry
FUNDECI
Institute for Central American Development Studies (ICADS)
International Executive Service Corps (IESC)
International Foundation for Education and Self-Help (IFESH)
International Volunteer Expeditions (IVEX)
Mobility International (MIUSA)
Nuestros Pequeños Hermanos (NPH)
United Methodists General Board of Global Ministries (GBGM)
United Nations Volunteers (UNV)
Visions in Action
Voluntary Service Overseas (VSO)
World University Service of Canada (WUSC)

Construction/Housing/Engineering/Architecture/Renovation

Adventures in Health, Education, and Agricultural Development (AHEAD, Inc.)
American Friends Service Committee (AFSC)
American Jewish World Service (AJWS)

Amigos de las Américas
Amizade
Brethren Volunteer Service (BVS)
Concern America
Council on International Educational Exchange (Council)
Crispaz
Cultural Restoration Tourism Project (CRTP)
Elderhostel
Food for the Hungry
FUNDECI
Global Citizens Network (GCN)
Global Service Corps (GSC)
Global Volunteers
Habitat for Humanity International
International Volunteer Expeditions (IVEX)
Joint Assistance Centre (JAC)
Mobility International (MIUSA)
New Haven/Leon Sister City Project (NH/LSCP)
Nuestros Pequeños Hermanos (NPH)
Operation Crossroads Africa (OCA)
Parroquia San Lucas Toliman
Pastors for Peace/IFCO
Peace Corps
Peacework
SCI-IVS USA (Service Civil International-International Voluntary Service)
United Methodists General Board of Global Ministries (GBGM)
United Nations Volunteers (UNV)
Visions in Action
Voluntary Service Overseas (VSO)
Volunteers for Peace International Workcamps
World PULSE (Program for Understanding, Leadership, Service, and Exchange)

Disaster Relief/Refugees/Humanitarian Aid

Catholic Medical Missions Board (CMMB)
Concern America
Crispaz
Food for the Hungry
Joint Assistance Centre (JAC)
Pastors for Peace/IFCO
Peace Corps
United Nations Volunteers (UNV)
Visions in Action

Education/Teaching/Tutoring

Adventures in Health, Education, and Agricultural Development (AHEAD, Inc.)
AFS
American Jewish World Service (AJWS)

Amigos de las Américas
Amity Institute, Amity Volunteer Teachers Abroad Program
Brethren Volunteer Service (BVS)
BRIDGES Fellowship (Building Responsible International Dialogue
    through Grassroots Exchange)
Canadian Crossroads International (CCI)
Central European Teaching Program (CETP)
Child Haven International
Christian Foundation for Children and the Aging (CFCA)
Concern America
Crispaz
Cross-Cultural Solutions (CCS)
CUSO
Elderhostel
Food for the Hungry
FUNDECI
Global Citizens Network (GCN)
Global Routes
Global Service Corps (GSC)
Global Volunteers
Himalayan Explorers Club (HEC)
Institute for Central American Development Studies (ICADS)
Institute for International Cooperation and Development (IICD)
International Foundation for Education and Self-Help (IFESH)
International Partnership for Service-Learning (IPS-L)
International Volunteer Expeditions (IVEX)
Interns for Peace (IFP)
Japan-U.S. Community Education and Exchange (JUCEE)
Jesuit Volunteer Corps/Jesuit Volunteers International (JVC/JVI)
Joint Assistance Centre (JAC)
Maryknoll Mission Association
Mennonite Central Committee (MCC)
Minnesota Studies in International Development (MSID)
Mobility International (MIUSA)
Nuestros Pequeños Hermanos (NPH)
Operation Crossroads Africa (OCA)
Parroquia San Lucas Toliman
Pastors for Peace/IFCO
Peace Corps
United Methodists General Board of Global Ministries (GBGM)
VIA (formerly Volunteers in Asia)
Visions in Action
Voluntary Service Overseas (VSO)
WorldTeach
World University Service of Canada (WUSC)

Environment/Natural Resource Management

ACDI/VOCA
AFS

American Friends Service Committee (AFSC)
American Jewish World Service (AJWS)
Amigos de las Américas
Amizade
ARCAS
Brethren Volunteer Service (BVS)
BRIDGES Fellowship (Building Responsible International Dialogue
    through Grassroots Exchange)
Canadian Crossroads International (CCI)
Casa de los Amigos
Concern America
Council on International Educational Exchange (Council)
CUSO
Earthwatch Institute
Elderhostel
FUNDECI
Global Citizens Network (GCN)
Global Routes
Global Service Corps (GSC)
Institute for Central American Development Studies (ICADS)
Institute for International Cooperation and Development (IICD)
International Foundation for Education and Self-Help (IFESH)
International Volunteer Expeditions (IVEX)
Japan-U.S. Community Education and Exchange (JUCEE)
Jesuit Volunteer Corps/Jesuit Volunteers International (JVC/JVI)
Joint Assistance Centre (JAC)
Minnesota Studies in International Development (MSID)
Mobility International (MIUSA)
Operation Crossroads Africa (OCA)
Peace Corps
Peacework
SCI-IVS USA (Service Civil International-International Voluntary Service)
United Methodists General Board of Global Ministries (GBGM)
University Research Expeditions Program (UREP)
VIA (formerly Volunteers in Asia)
Visions in Action
Voluntary Service Overseas (VSO)
Volunteers for Peace International Workcamps
World PULSE (Program for Understanding, Leadership, Service, and Exchange)
WorldTeach
World University Service of Canada (WUSC)

Health Care/Public Health/Health Education

Adventures in Health, Education, and Agricultural Development (AHEAD, Inc.)
AFS
American Jewish World Service (AJWS)
Amigos de las Américas
Amizade
Brethren Volunteer Service (BVS)

BRIDGES Fellowship (Building Responsible International Dialogue
    through Grassroots Exchange)
Casa de los Amigos
Catholic Medical Missions Board (CMMB)
Child Family Health International (CFHI)
Christian Foundation for Children and the Aging (CFCA)
Concern America
Crispaz
Cross-Cultural Solutions (CCS)
Doctors Without Borders/Médecins Sans Frontières (MSF)
Earthwatch Institute
Elderhostel
Esperança
Flying Doctors
Flying Samaritans
FUNDECI
Global Service Corps (GSC)
Health Volunteers Overseas (HVO)
Institute for Central American Development Studies (ICADS)
Institute for International Cooperation and Development (IICD)
International Foundation for Education and Self-Help (IFESH)
International Volunteer Expeditions (IVEX)
Interplast, Inc.
Japan-U.S. Community Education and Exchange (JUCEE)
Jesuit Volunteer Corps/Jesuit Volunteers International (JVC/JVI)
Joint Assistance Centre (JAC)
Maryknoll Mission Association
Mennonite Central Committee (MCC)
Minnesota Studies in International Development (MSID)
Mobility International (MIUSA)
Operation Crossroads Africa (OCA)
Operation Smile
Parroquia San Lucas Toliman
Pastors for Peace/IFCO
Peace Corps
Peacework
United Methodists General Board of Global Ministries (GBGM)
United Nations Volunteers (UNV)
Visions in Action
Voluntary Service Overseas (VSO)

Human Rights/Democracy/Indigenous Rights/Conflict Resolution and Peacemaking/Legal Aid

Brethren Volunteer Service (BVS)
Casa de los Amigos
Christian Peacemaker Teams (CPT)
CUSO
FUNDECI
International Partnership for Service-Learning (IPS-L)

International Service for Peace (SIPAZ)
Interns for Peace (IFP)
Mennonite Central Committee (MCC)
Mobility International (MIUSA)
NISGUA Guatemala Accompaniment Project
Pastors for Peace/IFCO
Peace Brigades International (PBI)
United Methodists General Board of Global Ministries (GBGM)
United Nations Volunteers (UNV)
Visions in Action
Witness for Peace (WFP)

Social Work/Youth/Elderly/Disabled/Homeless/General Community Development/Community Organizing

AFS
American Friends Service Committee (AFSC)
Amigos de las Américas
Amity Institute, Amity Volunteer Teachers Abroad Program
Brethren Volunteer Service (BVS)
BRIDGES Fellowship (Building Responsible International Dialogue
    through Grassroots Exchange)
Canadian Crossroads International (CCI)
Casa de los Amigos
Child Haven International
Christian Foundation for Children and the Aging (CFCA)
Concern America
Council on International Educational Exchange (Council)
Crispaz
Cross-Cultural Solutions (CCS)
CUSO
Elderhostel
Food for the Hungry
FUNDECI
Global Citizens Network (GCN)
Global Routes
Global Volunteers
Institute for International Cooperation and Development (IICD)
International Foundation for Education and Self-Help (IFESH)
International Partnership for Service-Learning (IPS-L)
Interns for Peace (IFP)
Japan-U.S. Community Education and Exchange (JUCEE)
Jesuit Volunteer Corps/Jesuit Volunteers International (JVC/JVI)
Joint Assistance Centre (JAC)
Kibbutz Program Center
Maryknoll Mission Association
Mennonite Central Committee (MCC)
Minnesota Studies in International Development (MSID)
Mobility International (MIUSA)
Nuestros Pequeños Hermanos (NPH)

Peace Corps
Project OTZMA
SCI-IVS USA (Service Civil International-International Voluntary Service)
United Methodist General Board of Global Ministries (GBGM)
United Nations Volunteers (UNV)
Visions in Action
Voluntary Service Overseas (VSO)
Volunteers for Peace International Workcamps
World PULSE (Program for Understanding, Leadership, Service, and Exchange)
World University Service of Canada (WUSC)

Women's Issues and Organizations

Brethren Volunteer Service (BVS)
Casa de los Amigos
Concern America
Crispaz
FUNDECI
Global Service Corps (GSC)
Institute for Central American Development Studies (ICADS)
International Partnership for Service-Learning (IPS-L)
Japan-U.S. Community Education and Exchange (JUCEE)
Joint Assistance Centre (JAC)
Minnesota Studies in International Development (MSID)
New Haven/Leon Sister City Project (NH/LSCP)
Visions in Action

COUPLES, CHILDREN, AGE, NATIONALITY & DEGREE PROGRAMS

Organizations that Accept Couples *(includes married, unmarried, and same-sex couples unless noted)*

Note that most programs require both individuals in a couple to qualify; check with individual programs. Some programs not listed here *do* accept couples but did not respond to our inquiries for information on their policies.

American Jewish World Service (AJWS)
Amizade
Canadian Crossroads International (CCI)
Casa de los Amigos (warns same sex couples about "cultural impediments")
Catholic Medical Missions Board (CMMB) (married couples and families with children
    welcome, but work not always available for spouse; unmarried couples not accepted)
Central European Teaching Program (CETP)
Child Family Health International (CFHI)
Child Haven International (married couples only)
Christian Foundation for Children and the Aging (CFCA) (no same sex couples)
Christian Peacemaker Teams (CPT)
Concern America ("If we have jobs for both persons")
Crispaz

Cross-Cultural Solutions (CCS)
CUSO (married couples only)
Elderhostel
Esperança (married couples only)
Institute for International Cooperation and Development (IICD)
International Partnership for Service-Learning (IPS-L) (no same-sex couples)
International Society for Ecology and Culture (ISEC) (no same sex couples)
International Volunteer Expeditions (IVEX)
Japan-U.S. Community Education and Exchange
Joint Assistance Centre (JAC) (no same sex couples)
Kibbutz Program Center (married couples only)
Maryknoll Mission Association (married couples only)
Mobility International (MIUSA)
New Haven/Leon Sister City Project (NH/LSCP)
NISGUA Guatemala Accompaniment Project (couples may be required
    to do additional fundraising)
Operation Crossroads Africa (OCA)
Operation Smile
Peace Brigades International (PBI)
Peacework
University Research Expeditions Program (UREP)
VIA (formerly Volunteers in Asia)
Visions in Action
Voluntary Service Overseas (VSO)
Volunteers for Peace International Workcamps
Witness for Peace (WFP)
WorldTeach
World University Service of Canada (WUSC)

Organizations that Accept Children Accompanied by Adult(s)

Age restrictions are noted in parentheses. Some accept accompanied children on a case-by-case basis only.

Amizade (12–18)
Casa de los Amigos ("age is not a restriction" but might reduce opportunities)
Catholic Medical Missions Board (CMMB) (with parents)
Central European Teaching Program (CETP)
Child Haven International
Christian Foundation for Children and the Aging (CFCA)
Concern America
Crispaz
CUSO
Elderhostel (mostly grandparents with grandchildren 9–17, more "learning" than "volunteer
    service" programs)
Global Service Corps (GSC)
International Society for Ecology and Culture (ISEC)
International Volunteer Expeditions (IVEX)
Joint Assistance Centre (JAC)
Maryknoll (under 8)

New Haven/Leon Sister City Project (NH/LSCP)

NISGUA Guatemala Accompaniment Project

Peacework (They make arrangements for pre-existing groups such as college and church groups, not individuals. Check with group organizer for program-specific details)

University Research Expeditions Program (UREP) (16–18)

Voluntary Service Overseas (VSO)

Volunteers for Peace International Workcamps

VIA (formerly known as Volunteers in Asia)

WorldTeach

World University Service of Canada (WUSC)

Organizations that Accept People Age 18 or Younger without Adult Accompaniment

See specific age ranges in parentheses.

AFS (15–29)

American Friends Service Committee (AFSC) (13+ for Joint Service Projects; 18–26 for Summer Projects)

AJWS (IJCC) (18–24)

Amigos (16–24)

Brethren Volunteer Service (BVS) (18+ for domestic program. International volunteers must be 21+)

BRIDGES Fellowship (Building Responsible International Dialogue through Grassroots Exchange) (18+)

Canadian Crossroads International (CCI) (19+)

Casa de los Amigos (18+; youths under 18 would find "few opportunities" but may participate with parental permission)

Council on International Educational Exchange (Council) (18+)

Cross-Cultural Solutions (CCS) (17+)

Earthwatch Institute (16+)

FFA (16–24 for FFA Explorers)

Flying Doctors (18+)

Flying Samaritans (18+)

Global Citizens Network (GCN) ("All ages are welcome")

Global Routes (14–17 for high school program, 18–27 for college program)

Global Volunteers ("All ages" but average age is 50)

Habitat for Humanity International (18+)

Institute for Central American Development Studies (ICADS) (17+)

Institute for International Cooperation and Development (IICD) (18+ by the time you go abroad; may begin training/fundraising at 17)

International Partnership for Service-Learning (IPS-L) (18+)

International Society for Ecology & Culture (ISEC) (18+)

International Volunteer Expeditions (IVEX) (18+)

Joint Assistance Centre (JAC) (18+)

Japan-U.S. Community Education and Exchange (JUCEE) (18+)

Kibbutz Program Center (18–35)

Mennonite Central Committee (MCC) (18+)

Mobility International (MIUSA) (18–24 for youth delegations)

New Haven/Leon Sister City Project (NH/LSCP) (16+)

Nuestros Pequeños Hermanos (NPH) (Under 21 possible "if applicant is mature and has a high school diploma" but over 21 strongly preferred)

Operation Crossroads Africa (OCA) (17–32)

Operation Smile (16+; youth opportunities are in the U.S.)

Parroquia San Lucas Toliman (18+)

Pastors for Peace/IFCO (Under 18 with adult accompaniment and/or parental release form)

Peacework (17+ or as part of a "well supervised youth delegation." Peacework makes arrangements for groups sponsored by established organizations such as schools and civic groups.)

SCI-IVS USA (Service Civil International-International Voluntary Service) (18+)

United Methodists General Board of Global Missions (GBGM) (12+ for mission teams)

University Research Expeditions Program (UREP) (16+, but only 2% of applicants are under 18 and youth are accepted at project leaders' discretion)

VIA (formerly known as Volunteers in Asia) (18+)

Volunteers for Peace International Workcamps (18+; "some projects are open to younger volunteers")

Witness for Peace (WFP) (under 18 on "teen delegations")

World PULSE (Program for Understanding, Leadership, Service, and Exchange) (18–26)

WorldTeach (18+)

Organizations that Specialize in or Regularly Offer Programs Popular with Seniors

The following offer programs with 50 percent or more seniors. Many other groups accept seniors, but seniors will usually be a smaller percentage of volunteers; see individual profiles for age range & typical age.

American Jewish World Service (AJWS)

Amizade

Catholic Medical Missions Board (CMMB)

Citizens Democracy Corps (CDC)

Crispaz

Elderhostel

Flying Doctors

Flying Samaritans

Global Volunteers

International Executive Service Corps (IESC)

Peacework (does not specifically promote a program for seniors, but makes arrangements for organizations that do)

Organizations that Accept Canadian Citizens or Residents Only

Canadian Crossroads International (CCI)

CUSO

World University Service of Canada (WUSC)

Organizations that Offer Formal Academic Program/Degree/Credit

Many other organizations can arrange academic credit on a case-by-case basis.

Institute for Central American Development Studies (ICADS)
International Partnership for Service-Learning (IPS-L)
Minnesota Studies in International Development (MSID)

Survey for Returned and Prospective Overseas Volunteers:
Share Your Story

Future editions of this book will include updated information about volunteering. By sharing your experiences, you can help us make sure that the profiles on volunteer placement organizations stay up to date. In addition, your feedback will help us improve the other chapters of the book, making it more useful for future volunteers.

Please take a moment to answer the following questions and return this form to the address below. The answers can also be e-mailed to survey@volunteeroverseas.org or filled out directly on our website, www.volunteeroverseas.org

Name _____ Today's Date _____

Permanent Address_____

Age_____

City _____ State_____ Zip _____ Country_____

E-mail_____

E-mail #2 _____

Phone _____

Religious Affiliation _____

Ethnicity_____

How you heard about this book:

☐ Web search

☐ Presentation or lecture by_____

☐ Friend

☐ Professor

☐ Other _____

1. **If you have volunteered overseas, what volunteer placement organization did you go with (or did you arrange the experience independently)? If you have not yet volunteered, skip to question 9.**

2. **Where did you volunteer and for how long?**

3. **What were the dates of your volunteer experience?**

4. **What type of work did you do?**

5. **What was the most positive aspect of your volunteer experience?**

6. **What was your biggest challenge or problem?**

7. **If you volunteered with a volunteer placement organization, what should potential volunteers know about that organization (positive and/or negative)?**

8. **If you volunteered independently, do you have any suggestions for improving Chapter 6, "Doing It without a Program?"**

9. **If you have not yet volunteered overseas, why not? Do you plan to volunteer some day? What alternatives to volunteering, if any, will you pursue?**

10. **Additional comments, questions, suggestions for future editions:**

11. **How useful was this book to you?**

NOT USEFUL AT ALL								EXTREMELY USEFUL

1	2	3	4	5	6	7	8	9	10

Please send your responses to: **survey@volunteeroverseas.org,**

or fill the questionnaire out online at : **www.volunteeroverseas.org,**

or mail your responses to: **How to Live Your Dream of Volunteering Overseas, c/o Stefano DeZerega,**

P.O. Box 170063, San Francisco, CA 94117-0063

www.VolunteerOverseas.org

Want updates, links, and connections?

The website for this book includes:

✓ **Links** to most of the organizations listed in the book, and more.

✓ **A calendar** of opportunities to meet the authors and information on how to schedule them to speak at your university, local bookstore, event, or conference.

✓ **Updated information** on volunteering, useful articles, recommended publications, and instructive stories about volunteers.

The website also lets you contact the authors with your feedback about the book, comments about organizations, and suggestions for future editions.

See you online!

ROVE: *Returned Overseas Volunteers*

Are You a Returned Volunteer?

Because most volunteer placement organizations do not provide opportunities for volunteers to share their experiences or stay involved when they return home, we recommend joining Returned Overseas Volunteers (ROVE).

ROVE supports returned volunteers in the re-entry process, assists them in staying involved in international development and global justice work, and provides a forum for sharing experiences, networking, and providing mutual support.

For membership information, upcoming events, job listings, and resources, visit our website at www.returnedvolunteers.org, or e-mail us at info@returnedvolunteers.org.